CLASSICAL COOKING
The Modern Way
Methods and Techniques

CLASSICAL COOKING
The Modern Way

Methods and Techniques

THIRD EDITION

PHILIP PAULI

Translated by
Hannelore Dawson-Holt

WILEY

JOHN WILEY & SONS, INC.

Contents

Translator's Foreword

Translating Philip Pauli's *Lehrbuch der Küche* has been a rewarding experience, a natural extension of both my early culinary training in Europe and my professional career in the United States. My background made the task of translation easier, but, still, there were occasional challenges.

Because European and American terminology for meat cuts is often quite different, for example, reconciling the two was sometimes difficult. I hope I have come as close as possible to bringing the two systems together. My own professional library resolved most such problems. Others were solved by friends in the culinary profession. Thank you all.

My thanks to Melissa Rosati, who originally asked me to undertake the translation and guided me through the first steps of the project. My special thanks to Joan Petrokofsky, who guided the translation to the very end. Thanks also to Brandon Cronin, who read the drafts very carefully and made many helpful suggestions. Gillian Robertson contributed information on United States regulation in Chapter 1. Victoria Cohen copy edited the translation with great care and insight. She removed all traces of my German accent. Thank you very much.

Jerry Holt gave me constant loving support and kindly cheered me on when I was losing my sense of humor.

Preface

My grandfather Ernst Pauli published the first *Lehrbuch der Küche* in 1930 and therein laid the foundation for one of the most important texts in the culinary field. My dear father, Eugen Pauli, assumed my grandfather's responsibilities in 1961 and continued his work with great success. Six new editions were published under his leadership. The books were translated into French, English, Dutch, and Japanese.

With my father's untimely death at the age of fifty-five in 1981, I took over as publisher and author and was responsible for the production of the tenth and eleventh German editions, the second English and French editions, and the first Italian edition. *Unterrichts- und Prüfungsfragen* (a teachers' guide with examination questions) was also made available for the German edition.

My work benefits greatly from the guidance and collaboration of my dear friend Walter Schudel. I not only thank him personally for his untiring commitment and his great professional knowledge, but also express my gratitude in the name of all young cooks and chefs of future generations.

As in previous editions, this book, based on the eleventh German edition, focuses on modern kitchen and preparation techniques based on Auguste Escoffier's classic methods. It has been expanded and revised to incorporate today's preparation methods and current knowledge about nutrition. Because this edition has been completely revised to be the new basic text, the recipes that appeared in previous editions have been published separately, in alphabetical order, for immediate reference.

This book has many uses: as a basic teaching text for cooks and chefs, as a supplementary text for students in hospitality programs, or as an introduction to cooking for the amateur cook. It explores the workings of the professional kitchen in depth, providing an excellent foundation for anyone interested in the culinary arts.

PHILIP PAULI

Introduction

Never has the world experienced such rapid change. Now, at the turn of the millenium, we find ourselves at a critical moment in history. Political systems come and go, new countries are formed, boundaries are redrawn, and new hopes and expectations are raised. Yet, although we experience many changes, we must remember that the future is rooted in the past and its traditions.

Classical Cooking the Modern Way steps into the new century with this edition. Since 1930 ten editions have been published in Europe, two in the United States. This book has been translated into six languages. Its tradition and its great success gave me the energy and courage to produce the current edition. This new edition focuses on the high demand for quality in today's foodservice operations, on modern preparation methods, and on good nutrition.

Generations of cooks, restaurateurs, and hotel managers have relied on earlier editions as standard references. After five years of work, I am pleased to present the completely revised edition in a new format to you.

The goal of the revision was to retain important and fundamental concepts, eliminate what is out-of-date and overdone, and include all that the culinary profession must accomplish and offer in the new century. This book presents the up-to-date, future-oriented, combined knowledge of sixty Swiss culinary experts.

This vast knowledge cannot fail to help the reader. I consider this book a *must* for every personal or professional culinary library. A comprehensive collection of recipes can be found in the companion book, *Recipes*.

I wish this new edition, a book that leads the way into the future, a great success. And once again, I would like to thank heartily all the contributors who have helped so much over the last five years. I hope this book brings great pleasure to all who read it.

CLASSICAL COOKING
The Modern Way
Methods and Techniques

CHAPTER

1

Professional Knowledge

Chapter Contents

1.1 Professional Ethics

Professional ethics can be defined as the rules and standards governing the conduct of the members of a profession and the moral choices made by the individual professional in his or her relationships with others. Every day the professional cook must consider his or her actions at work and take ethical positions that affect such activities as:

- Reducing food and material waste
- Respecting all living creatures
- Conserving energy
- Purchasing local and seasonal products
- Preparing tasty and nutritious meals for all people
- Selecting and using biodegradable cleaning materials
- Recycling

Even in the computer age, the culinary profession can be very creative, multifaceted, and exciting. But such an environment can be achieved only when all members of the organization cooperate and work together. Table 1-1 shows the qualities necessary for teamwork.

Table 1-1. The components and benefits of teamwork.

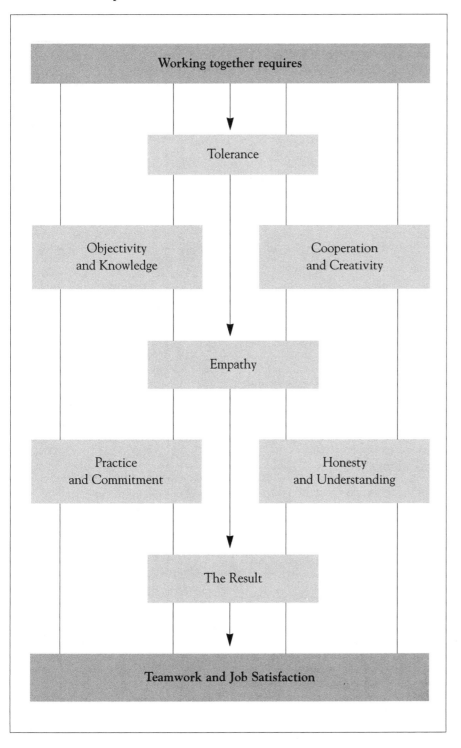

1.2 Government Regulation of the Food Industry

Swiss foods and the food industries are governed by a law called *Lebensmittelgesetz* (LMG). Specific product regulations and ordinances are contained in the *Lebensmittelverordnung* (LMV); meat inspection and production is regulated in a body of laws called *Eidgenössische Fleischschauverordnung* (EFV); additives are governed by regulations called *Zusatzstoffverordnung* (ZuV); and food-processing remains and foreign matter are regulated in a body of laws called *Fremd- und Inhaltsstoffverordnung* (FIV).

Because one's health and well-being are closely linked to the food one eats, food laws are designed:
- To protect consumers from food and household commodities that could threaten their health
- To ensure sanitary handling of food products
- To protect the consumer from fraud in the food industry

Areas Governed by Swiss Food Laws (LMG)

The law regulates:
- The manufacture, treatment, storage, transportation, and delivery of food and household commodities
- The labeling and advertising of foods and household commodities
- The import, transit, and export of food and household commodities
- The agricultural production of food products, from planting and harvesting or raising animals through the delivery of the end product to the consumer

More recent law expands the responsibilities of governing bodies; for example, they are required to:
- Provide information to the public about nutritional developments and warnings about unhealthy food products
- Evaluate substances and set limits and tolerances
- Prohibit future genetic engineering methods that prove harmful to the public health
- Improve border inspections to deter the uncontrolled use of medication in animals
- Institute slaughter weight standards for the livestock trade
- Unify enforcement codes and provide clear definition of agency responsibilities

This law specifically cites the self-governing responsibilities of food producers and manufacturers. The law is future oriented and is in compliance with food laws throughout Europe.

1.2.1 Swiss Regulation of Foods

In addition to the basic food law (LMG), the following detailed regulations govern food and household commodities.

Part A contains general regulations concerning jurisdiction, areas governed by regulations; definitions of food products, spices, household articles, and products; and food sanitation.

Part B contains detailed food product regulations, including exact definitions, detailed specifications, sanitation rules, production regulations, and the like. Culinary apprentices will find this part a valuable source of information for basic and luxury food products.

Part C contains regulations of the materials used in the production and handling of food products, such as legal additives in food and wine production, food coloring, and emulsifiers.

Part D contains the regulations governing household articles and household products, such as dishes, packaging materials, toys, paints, and clothes.

Part E contains penalties and final and temporary regulations.

Swiss food laws are all *positive laws*; that is, anything that is not specifically permitted is illegal.

Areas Covered by Swiss Food Regulations

- Foods: from raw ingredients to finished product
- Food additives: food coloring, preservatives, thickeners, emulsifiers (more in additives regulations)
- Household articles: dishes, containers, pots, pans, utensils, and toys
- Household commodities: packaging material, cosmetic articles, crayons and paints for toys and school products
- Gadgets, equipment, furniture, and space: used in the production, preparation, storage, and sale of foods
- Persons employed in the food industry: hygiene and disease

1.2.2 Swiss Regulation of Meat Inspection

Meat inspection regulations are controlled and governed by the Swiss food laws.

Areas Covered by Meat Inspection Regulations

- All meats and meat products sold for human consumption
- All facilities, equipment, transportation, tools, and ingredients used in the production or sale of meat and meat products
- All personnel involved in the production or sale of meat and meat products

More recent meat inspection laws have revised or reformulated requirements in the following areas:

- Animal requirements: state of health, feeding methods, transportation, and the like.
- Facility regulations: ventilation, lighting, work surfaces, refrigeration, areas where fish, poultry, seafood, and game are sold, and horsemeat production sites.
- Sanitation: all facets of meat production and preparation.
- Butchering: stunning, bleeding, blanching, and chilling; the goal of sanitary butchering is clean, safe meat.
- Meat inspection: Required for horses, cattle, lambs, goats, and pigs. The Swiss legislature has the right to add additional animal types or make exceptions for game. Includes ordinances concerning the inspection of live animals, frequency of inspection, control and inspection of game raised in captivity.
- Butchering facilities: animals can be slaughtered only in approved slaughterhouses. The Swiss legislature regulates the exceptions for fish and game and for home butchering.
- Slaughter weight of animals is prescribed.

1.2.3 Swiss Regulation of Additives

Additives are materials used in the production of foods, such as sodium benzoate (E200), benzoic acid (E236), sodium nitrate (E250), lecithin (E322), and manitol (E421). (The figures in parentheses pertain to the Swiss additives code.) Table 1-2 lists examples of different types of additives. The Swiss Department of the Interior (EDI) controls the Acceptable Daily Intake (ADI) values. The ADI value is the acceptable daily intake of a substance in milligrams per kilogram of body weight; that is, the amount that can be consumed daily for a lifetime without causing physical harm.

Classification of Additives

- Colorings
- Preservatives
- Stabilizers and thickeners
- Alkalines, acids, and minerals
- Flavor enhancers
- Coating materials
- Antioxidants
- Emulsifiers
- Anticaking agents
- Enzymes
- Sweeteners

For a complete listing, the additive regulations should be consulted.

Table 1-2. Examples of additives.

Colors

Name	Origin	Color (U.S. FD&C color)
Turmeric (E100)	Turmeric root	Yellow (Yellow no. 5)
Chlorophyll (E140)	Nettles, grass	Green
Indigo (E132)	Synthetic	Blue (Blue no. 1)
Betaine (E162)	Beets	Red (Red no. 2 or no. 40)
Gold (E175)	Minerals, metal	Gold

Preservatives

Name	Origin	Used For
Sorbic acid (E200)	Synthetic	Deli foods, margarine
Formic acid (E236)	Synthetic	Acidic canned goods, fruit juice products
Sodium nitrate (E249)	Synthetic	Pickled meat and fish

Stabilizers and Thickeners

Agar-agar	(E406)
Pectin	(E440a)
Carob bean gum	(E410)
Alginic acid	(E400)
Carrageenan, or red algae	(E407)

Natural Antioxidants

Lactic acid	(E270)
Lecithin	(E322)
Vitamin E	(E306)
Ascorbic acid	(E300L)
Citric acid	(E330)

Emulsifiers

Lecithin	(E322)
Acetic acid	(E472a)
Lactic acid	(E472b)
Tartaric acid	(E472d)
Sodium potassium compounds	(E470)

Sweeteners

Saccharine No. I
Cyclamate No. II
Aspartame No. III
Acesulfame-K

1.2.4 Swiss Regulation of Food-processing Remains and Impurities

Foreign matter are substances not naturally found in foods (either raw ingredients or partially processed products), but are introduced via a processing method or environmental contamination. Examples of foreign matter are pesticides, sanitizers, mercury, and nitrates. The Swiss Department of the Interior (EDI) controls and regulates foreign matter and sets concentration limits.

Naturally occurring impurities present in foods include solanine and histamine. These naturally occurring substances are also regulated by the EDI, and potentially harmful limits are indicated.

1.2.5 Swiss Federal (Bund) and State (Canton) Roles in Food Law

Generally, writing and administering food laws and regulations are responsibilities of the federal government (Bund) in Switzerland, as are import and export controls. Enforcement and control of laws and regulations are responsibilities of the individual cantons (states). Table 1-3 shows how food-inspection responsibilities are divided. Table 1-4 lists the roles of individual personnel in each area of government.

Table 1-3. Organization of Swiss food controls.

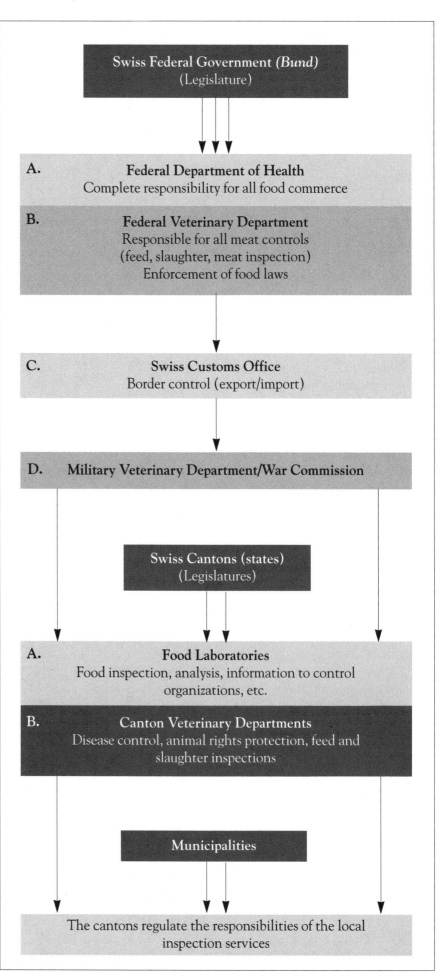

Table 1-4. Enforcement and inspection personnel.

Rank	Personnel	Responsibility
Federal	Customs officials	Border control
	Border veterinarians	Border control
Canton	Canton food chemist	Chief of state food inspections
Top rank	Canton veterinarian	Chief of animal disease control, animal protection, feeding practices, and slaughter of animals for consumption
Middle rank	Health inspectors	On-site inspections; supervision of local inspectors
	Meat inspectors	Inspection and control of all aspects of meat production; supervision of local inspectors
Municipality Front-line defense	Health inspectors, meat inspectors	Inspection of farms, slaughterhouses, storage areas, and stores

1.2.6 Investigation, Penalty, and Protection of Rights

Excerpts of Some Articles in the Swiss Food Law

Article 23
Inspection and test samples
[2] The inspection officials are entitled to take samples and, if necessary, have access to delivery slips, receipts, and other control measures.

[3] As a part of their official inquiry, they can enter grounds, rooms, facilities, and vehicles during regular operation hours.

Article 24
[3] The inspected party can request a written report of the investigation's results.

Article 26
Objection
[1] An objection indicates noncompliance with the law.

Article 27
Control action
[3] Official actions will be taken to protect the public health if safe limits are exceeded.

Article 29
[2] In case of suspected contamination, food products may be confiscated.

Article 47
Violation
[2] If convicted of fraud, the perpetrator will be punished by up to to five years in jail or heavy fines.

Article 48
Transgressions
[1] Imprisonment or fines of up to 20,000 Swiss francs for
(a) Anybody who intentionally violates sanitary food production regulations; list of infractions continues through (m).

Article 53
Appeals procedure
Appeals protesting punitive actions can be filed with the regulatory authorities.

Article 56
Appeal times
An appeal must be filed within five days of the decision.

1.2.7 U.S. Food Laws and Regulatory Agencies

Although the regulation of the food-production and foodservice industries involves government agencies at the municipal, county, state, and federal levels, much of the responsibility for ensuring food safety in the United States falls to two cabinet-level departments in the federal government, the *Department of Health and Human Services* and the *Department of Agriculture*.

The Department of Health and Human Services includes the *U.S. Public Health Service*, which has regulatory authority over the sanitary quality of drinking water, as well as foodservice on interstate and international carriers (planes, ships, trains, and the like).

Within the Public Health Service is one of the most important food-safety agencies in the country, the *Food and Drug Administration*. The FDA administers the Food, Drug, and Cosmetic Act of 1938 and associated laws to ensure that all foods in interstate commerce (except meat and poultry, which are under the Department of Agriculture's control) are pure, wholesome, produced under sanitary conditions, and properly labeled. Factories where such foods are prepared receive periodic inspections covering sanitation, raw materials, adequate processing, and finished product. Some food-processing industries under the FDA's oversight, including fish processors and canned-soup and -vegetable processors, participate in the Hazard Analysis Critical Control Point (HACCP) program, which requires processors to analyze their production methods, identify potential risk points in the production process, and find means of preventing problems from occurring at those points. They must keep careful records to demonstrate to the FDA that quality control is being maintained and any problems have been eliminated.

The FDA is also charged with administering federal/state programs that ensure the safety of milk and seafood.

In addition, the FDA is responsible for monitoring food additives. In 1958, the Delaney clause amended the 1938 act to require manufacturers to prove to the FDA the safety of additives before introducing them into foods. In 1960 another amendment tightened requirements on synthetic or extracted coloring agents used in foods. Both amendments banned the use in foods of substances that cause cancer in animals. The amendments included lists of additives generally recognized as safe (GRAS). Such substances are not legally considered to be food additives and need no safety clearance to be included in foods. The GRAS list today contains thousands of ingredients. The FDA adds and deletes substances every year, based on scientific testing. Examples of GRAS substances include:

- Common spices and natural seasonings and flavorings
- Baking powders, such as sodium bicarbonate and monocalcium phosphate
- Fruit and beverage acids, such as citric acid, malic acid, and phosphoric acid
- Gums, such as agar-agar and gum arabic
- Emulsifiers, such as fatty-acid monoglycerides and diglycerides.

The FDA also enforces the tolerance standards for pesticide residue in food commodities, which are established by the Environmental Protection Agency.

Also part of the Public Health Service are the *Centers for Disease Control*, which investigate outbreaks of food-borne disease, analyze surveillance data, and provide training materials and services concerning sanitation for foodservice personnel.

The Department of Agriculture oversees the distribution, grading, and inspection of meat, poultry, and related products. Its *Agricultural Marketing Service* ensures the safe and efficient movement of products from producer to consumer. The *Animal and Plant Health Inspection Service* safeguards the health and quality of animals and plants and protects the consumer by means of federal and state meat and poultry inspection. The *Food Safety and Inspection Service* provides for federal inspection of poultry, meat, and related products to be sure they are labeled honestly and informatively and that they are safe and wholesome. The *Federal Grain Inspection Service* sets standards and regulates the inspection and weighing of all types of grain.

In addition to mandatory inspections enforced by the FDA and Department of Agriculture, other government agencies administer voluntary inspection services. Examples include:

- *National Marine Fisheries Service*, of the Department of Commerce's *National Oceanic and Atmospheric Administration (NOAA)* for fish, shellfish, and seafood
- *Bureau of Alcohol, Tobacco, and Firearms (ATF)*, of the *Internal Revenue Service (IRS)* for alcoholic beverages
- *National Bureau of Standards (NBS)* for weights and measures
- *Office of Technical Services (OTS)* for packaging and food containers
- *Federal Trade Commission (FTC)* for prevention of unfair and deceptive trade practices

The *Occupational Safety and Health Administration* (OSHA) of the Department of Labor enforces the 1970 Occupational Safety and Health Act, which protects the safety and health of workers throughout the United States. OSHA's Hazard Communication Standard requires employers to inform staff about hazardous chemicals they may be required to use on the job (such as cleaning compounds, fuels, and pesticides). A material safety data sheet (MSDS) must be available for each chemical.

State and Local Regulations

Every state and many municipalities in the United States have their own food laws as well as being subject to federal regulations. State and local health departments provide training for and inspect foodservice establishments.

Other Foodservice Organizations and Associations

The following groups promote professionalism and provide training and educational material to the foodservice industry:

- American Culinary Federation (ACF)
- American Dietetic Association (ADA)
- American Hotel and Motel Association (AHMA)
- American Public Health Association (APHA)
- Association of Food and Drug Officials (AFDO)
- Food Research Institute (FRI)
- Foodservice Consultants Society International (FCSI)
- International Association of Culinary Professionals (IACP)
- International Food Manufacturers Association (IFMA)
- International Association of Milk, Food, and Environmental Sanitarians (IAMFES)
- International Food Service Executives Association (IFSEA)
- National Association of College and University Food Services (NACUFS)
- National Environmental Health Association (NEHA)
- National Institute for the Food Service Industry (NIFI)
- National Restaurant Association (NRA)
- National Sanitation Foundation (NSF)
- Society for the Advancement of Foodservice Research (SAFSR)
- Society for Foodservice Management (SFM)

The FAO and WHO, through their joint *Codex Alimentarius Commission*, set international standards and evaluate food additives and pesticides.

Table 1-5. A selection of international food-related abbreviations.

ADI value	Acceptable Daily Intake limits for humans
EFTA	European Free Trade Association
EC	European Community
FAO	Food and Agriculture Organization (United Nations agency)
GATT	General Agreement on Tariffs and Trade
GMP	Good Manufacturing Practice regulations
WHO	World Health Organization

1.3 Basic Principles of Microbiology

Microorganisms are minute living creatures; they are so small that they can be seen only through a microscope. They consume food, give off waste products, and under the right conditions, can multiply in a very short time.

To understand foodservice sanitation methods, it is essential to have a basic knowledge of microorganisms. Bacteria, molds, and yeast are the most important to consider. These microorganisms can be harmless, beneficial, or very dangerous to human beings. High-quality food products have no or very small amounts of harmful microorganisms.

Microorganisms are *everywhere*. They live in water and air, on furnishings, equipment, appliances, utensils, work and storage surfaces, dish cloths, and cleaning materials. They also live on animals and plants, living and dead. People carry microorganisms on their hands, skin, and hair, in the mouth and nasal passages, and in especially large numbers in the colon (feces) and on uniforms and work shoes.

Helpful and harmful microorganisms live on all food products. During all phases of food production, harmful microorganisms can be transmitted from food to humans or from humans to food. If present in large numbers, they can cause food-borne illnesses. Toxin-producing types can cause an outbreak of food poisoning. Some microorganisms cause food spoilage.

Careful control of food quality and environmental conditions can prevent or reduce the presence and multiplication of harmful microorganisms. Food-borne illnesses and food spoilage are preventable when conditions that allow microorganisms to survive and multiply are eliminated.

1.3.1 Bacteria

Appearance

Bacteria are extremely small (0.001 millimeter in size) single-celled living organisms, which are not usually visible to the human eye. Under the microscope bacteria appear round, rod-shaped, or spiral-shaped.

Growth and Multiplication

Bacteria reproduce by cell division (mitosis). Given enough nourishment, the cell doubles in size, separates in the middle to form two complete cells, then splits apart. Under ideal conditions bacteria multiply explosively. When bacteria multiply, they ingest food and leave waste products. Some types of bacteria can be highly toxic. For bacteria to multiply, they need:

Time: Many bacteria need only twenty to thirty minutes to multiply. Within a few hours, millions of bacteria can be present in food.

Food: Bacteria prefer protein- and carbohydrate-rich foods that are not too salty or too sweet and not acidic. Bacteria prefer a pH of 8.5 to 4.5. Bacteria are not particular and will feed on the best of foods as well as the most disgusting garbage.

Warmth: Most types of bacteria prefer temperatures between 50°F and 120°F (10°C and 50°C). Pathogens, which are disease-producing organisms, thrive at body temperature, 98.6°F (37°C). At temperatures below 32°F (0°C) or above 150°F (65°C), growth practically stops.

Moisture: Bacteria need moisture to multiply. The available moisture content of a food product must be at least 20 percent to host bacteria. A moist food may be safe if its moisture is bound by sugar or salt.

Destruction

Heat destroys bacteria. Most bacteria cannot tolerate temperatures between 150°F and 212°F (65°C and 100°C) and die. Some types of bacteria, such as *Clostridium botulinum*, form spores that can survive such temperatures. Heating foods to 250°F (120°C) for at least twenty minutes kills these spores. However, toxins already present in the food will not be destroyed by normal cooking temperatures.

Beneficial Bacteria

Nature assigns bacteria the job of consuming dead organisms (decomposition). These and other microorganisms therefore multiply in food products, but they have other, beneficial roles as well. Bacteria are essential for the decomposition of dead plants and animals. They help in purifying lakes and streams and in the decomposition of waste in sewage. In the human body, they protect against the multiplication of disease-causing pathogens. They are also required in the production of certain foods, including yogurt, sour cream, cheese, sauerkraut, vinegar, and sausages. They can enhance the flavor of butter, yogurt, and cheese. Bacteria are also used in the production of medicines and drugs.

Harmful Bacteria

Harmful bacteria cause food spoilage and illness. They cause food spoilage by breaking down proteins, sugars, and fats. *E. coli* bacteria are one type that spoils food.

Bacteria can cause sickness either through ingestion of the harmful bacteria themselves or through the toxins they produce as waste.

Staphylococci include pathogens that infect sores, cuts, rashes, and boils. They are also present in the mouth and nasal passages. They contaminate food by direct contact or through sneezing and coughing. Under favorable conditions (warmth), they multiply quickly. As they multiply and die, they leave behind a toxin that is highly heat-resistant. Eating food contaminated with staphylococcus toxin can cause nausea, vomiting, diarrhea, and abdominal cramps within one to seven hours. Serious poisoning can lead to death.

Intestinal bacteria, such as *E. coli*, are present in huge numbers in human feces: 1 gram of feces contains about 1 million *E. coli*. Contamination of food with these bacteria can cause such health problems as nausea, vomiting, and diarrhea; in young children and the infirm or elderly, it can cause death. Hands must be washed thoroughly after using toilets to prevent contamination of foods with *E. coli*.

Salmonella bacteria are a large group of dangerous intestinal bacteria that reproduce rapidly in nonrefrigerated food products. Salmonella-infected food will cause flu-like symptoms from within a few hours to up to two days after consumption. In the case of typhoid, symptoms may not appear for up to twenty-one days. Salmonella infection causes nausea, vomiting, headaches, aching bones, and high fever. A serious infection in very young children and the elderly can lead to death. Salmonella bacteria do not produce toxins in food. Instead, the toxin in salmonella is released during the body's digestive process.

1.3.2 Molds

Appearance

Molds, the largest of the food-borne microorganisms, are composed of many cells. They are usually no more than about $\frac{1}{32}$ to $\frac{1}{16}$ inch (1 to 2 mm) long. However, some molds form colonies that are many inches long. Molds are visible as fuzzy patches of various colors on foods, walls, ceilings, and furnishings.

Growth and Multiplication

Molds are fungi composed of hyphae, which are threadlike. Molds are asexual but do require oxygen to multiply. They reproduce by forming microscopic spores (seeds), which are very lightweight and find their way into foods through the air or via hands, utensils, or other objects that contact food. The spores form a mycelium, which spreads its many threadlike branches into foods and removes valuable nutrients. At the same time, molds change the taste and flavor of foods, leaving a musty taste or odor. Many molds produce very toxic waste products (mycotoxins) and can cause mold poisoning, a rare food-borne illness. To multiply, molds need:

Time: Molds reproduce more slowly than bacteria or yeast do.

Food: Molds prefer to grow on carbohydrate-rich and sour (acidic) foods but can grow on all foods, even on very dry foods, if the pH is between 3 and 7.

Warmth: The preferred temperature of many molds is between 70°F and 75°F (22°C and 25°C), but they can grow in temperatures as low as 10°F (-12°C). Toxin-forming molds prefer temperatures from 85°F to 105°F (30°C to 40°C).

Moisture: Molds can exist in an environment that has as little as 12 percent moisture. They can also remove moisture from the air to survive. It is thus very important to protect foods from mold by storing them in dry rooms.

Destruction

Molds are killed by heat above 140°F (60°C). Mold toxins are heat-stable and will not be destroyed by normal cooking temperatures.

Beneficial Molds

Like bacteria, some molds are beneficial while others are harmful. For example, one mold is intentionally introduced into some cheeses to create special flavors, as is the case for blue cheeses such as Roquefort and some white cheeses, such as Brie and Camembert. Cultured molds are also introduced into the natural casings of some sausages, such as salami, to preserve them and enhance their flavor. In addition, penicillin was originally made from molds; today it is manufactured synthetically.

Harmful Molds

Harmful molds cause food spoilage and food poisoning. Molds are usually detected by their fuzzy growth. Depending on the type, moldy patches can be white, gray, blue-green, black, or yellow. Some molds penetrate the food host deeply and leave behind cancer-causing waste and toxins (such as aflatoxins, which can cause liver malfunction and lead to death). These wastes are not destroyed by cooking or other preparation methods. Scraping mold from food surfaces is not a safe protective measure, because toxins could still remain in the food's interior. Moldy food products are inedible and must be discarded. They should not be fed to people or animals.

1.3.3 Yeasts

Appearance

Yeasts are single-celled organisms that are round, spherical, or oval. Like molds, they are fungi. Yeast cells are ten times larger than bacteria. They are important in fermentation and leavening processes.

Growth and Multiplication

Yeasts multiply by a process called *budding;* rarely do they reproduce through spore formation. When yeast cells bud, they form a bulge that grows quickly into a daughter cell. Some yeast cells separate at this stage, whereas others remain connected. The new cell also buds, forming more cells.

Yeasts need oxygen to grow. In the absence of oxygen, yeast cells grow very slowly. However, their ability to survive with little oxygen is essential in alcoholic fermentation. To multiply, yeasts need:

Time: Yeasts can double in volume in from thirty minutes to two hours.

Food: Yeasts prefer foods high in glucose (pH 3 to 7); they convert the sugar, through fermentation, into alcohol and carbon dioxide.

Warmth: Yeasts multiply rapidly at temperatures between 60°F and 95°F (15°C and 35°C). Many types prefer temperatures from 70°F to 75°F (22°C to 25°C).

Moisture: Like bacteria, yeasts need food that is at least 20 percent moisture.

Destruction

Yeast cells are destroyed at temperatures above 140°F (60°C).

Beneficial Yeasts

Bakers' yeast is grown using pure cultures. Baking yeast multiplies best at temperatures from 75°F to 80°F (25°C to 27°C); the best temperature for fermentation is from 87°F to 95°F (30°C to 35°C). Wine yeast, fruit yeast, and brewers' yeast have been used for centuries in the fermentation of alcoholic beverages. In addition, special strains of yeast are added to some cured sausages to improve color, flavor, and taste. Yeasts are also used in such pharmaceutical products as vitamins and cosmetics and to produce carbonated beverages and dry ice.

Harmful Yeasts

Harmful yeasts cause food spoilage. Especially vulnerable are foods high in both liquid and sugar (for example, fruit juices, compotes, and fruit salads), tomato sauces, and vegetable soups. Typical signs of yeast contamination are the formation of gas bubbles, foam, and cloudiness.

1.3.4 Causes of Food-borne Illness

Food-borne illnesses, food poisoning, and food spoilage result from the rapid reproduction and toxin production of microorganisms in food. Causes include:
- Unclean hands and fingernails, infected wounds, dirt attached to wrist watches, rings, and other jewelry
- Coughing, sneezing, nose picking, seasoning and tasting foods with fingers
- Dirty utensils, dishes, appliances, equipment, cleaning rags, sponges, and brushes
- Contaminated work surfaces (such as cutting boards)
- Touching pets

- Roaches, flies, mice, rats, and insects (germs are present in their saliva, urine, and feces and on their bodies)
- Leaving raw products or prepared dishes for long periods at room temperature
- Defrosting frozen foods incorrectly

Consumption of spoiled foods that contain lethal toxins can cause serious health problems. Aflatoxins present in moldy grain products and nuts can cause liver cancer. Toxins from anaerobic bacteria, such as Clostridium botulinum, which form spores in the absence of oxygen, can cause death. They can grow in sausages, meat products, vacuum-packed meat, and fish. They cause cans to bulge if the contents have been processed improperly and not sterilized completely. Botulism spores are destroyed only at temperatures above 250°F (121°C). In addition, spoiled mushrooms, fish, shellfish, mollusks, and meat may contain not only bacterial toxins but also highly poisonous waste products released during protein decomposition.

1.3.5 Principles for Preventing Food-borne Illness

The two most important principles in preventing food-borne illness are:

1. Start with food products that contain very few harmful microorganisms.

2. Prevent conditions that allow microorganisms to multiply.

One must follow these principles and implement strict professional food sanitation procedures.

1.4 Foodservice Sanitation

1.4.1 Basic Principles

The customer expects healthy and wholesome food, and the law requires it. The goal of foodservice sanitation is to protect public health.

The primary tenet of foodservice sanitation is *absolute cleanliness*. It begins with personal hygiene; the safe handling of foods during preparation; clean utensils, equipment, and appliances; clean storage facilities, kitchens, and dining rooms; and ends with sanitary service to the customer.

For kitchen staff this must be the guiding principle; poor sanitation has serious consequences, not only for public health but also for the financial health of the business.

1.4.2 Personal Hygiene

The most important hygienic measure in the kitchen is *frequent and thorough hand washing*. Germs pass from hand to hand. Clean hands and trimmed fingernails reduce the risk of contamination. Hands must be washed with warm water and liquid soap in hand-washing sinks, which should be equipped with foot pedals. Washing hands in food preparation sinks should be prohibited.

Hands should be washed
- Immediately before starting food preparation
- After taking a break
- After blowing the nose
- After visiting the toilet
- After preparing fresh fruit, potatoes, and raw vegetables
- After handling raw meats, fish, and eggs
- After touching contaminated articles (soiled dishes, packaging, garbage, money, door handles, cigarettes)

Hands should be dried with single-use towels. They should *not* be wiped on aprons or side towels.

Kitchen staff should minimize contact with potentially hazardous foods. They should wear plastic gloves whenever possible, especially when handling foods that will not be heated (such as cold salads, luncheon meats, and desserts).

Food should never be touched by hands that have rashes, open sores, or infected wounds. Even very small cuts or abrasions should be bandaged and covered with waterproof protectors.

The tasting of food with fingers should be prohibited, as should the repeated use of the same spoon for tasting.

Millions of bacteria are present in the mouth and nasal passages. Kitchen personnel should never sneeze or cough unguardedly on or near foods. Nose picking is both disgusting and unsanitary. Tissues should be used for nose blowing, and they should be discarded immediately after use. Hands should then be washed thoroughly. Food handlers with acute respiratory infections or colds should not work with food.

Persons with repeated cases of diarrhea could be carriers of intestinal diseases. They should be treated by a physician before being allowed back at work.

Food handlers should bathe or shower daily. Hair is a breeding ground for bacteria. It must be washed regularly. Hair restraints are not only necessary but should be mandatory.

Smoking and gum chewing should be prohibited in all food-preparation areas.

Soiled clothing carries enormous numbers of germs. Underwear should be changed daily. A clean uniform should be donned at work. Sleeve length should be adjusted to the work situation. Clean and appropriate shoes should be worn in the kitchen, preferably of leather. Absorbent socks should be worn and changed daily. Aprons and side towels should be removed before entering the bathroom. Jewelry (watches and rings) are germ collectors and should not be worn at work.

1.4.3 Food Storage and Sanitation

A sanitary kitchen is most important in a foodservice operation but is very difficult to achieve. Absolute cleanliness during food preparation and correct food storage procedures are essential for all food-handling personnel. These rules should be followed:

Potentially hazardous foods should be kept continuously refrigerated.
- *Below 40°F (4°C):* Milk, heavy cream, cream products, butter, margarine, eggs, creams, stuffing, meats, aspic, mayonnaise, cold roast beef, chicken, turkey, and all other luncheon meats, prepared sandwiches, and all salads that contain meat
- *At 32°F (0°C):* Raw fish and seafood

Frozen products should be stored at 0°F (-18°C) and defrosted only in refrigerators or microwave ovens. Other foods should be protected from cross-contamination by placing defrosting food in pans on the lowest shelf in the refrigerator.

Products should be inspected *daily* for freshness and edibility, especially highly perishable foods.

Raw ground meats and fish should be kept no longer than one day.

Strict time/temperature controls should be observed for prepared food products such as rice, pasta, eggs, mushroom dishes, and sauces, which should not be held for longer than thirty minutes at room temperature. Cold dishes must be held at 40°F (4°C) until service. Hot or warm dishes that are held for any length of time before service must register at an internal temperature of at least 165°F (74°C).

Foods that must be chilled rapidly after cooking, so that they can be included later in other preparations, require special consideration. Stocks, soups, and thin sauces and creams should be placed in a cold-water or ice bath and stirred repeatedly to cool them quickly. They should then be covered (to prevent mold spores from entering) and placed in the refrigerator. Mushroom dishes, fillings, and thick sauces and creams should be spread on sheet pans and placed in the refrigerator or freezer for a quick chill. The chilled product should be removed from the sheet pans (in the refrigerator, not the warm kitchen) and then stored, covered, in the refrigerator until needed.

Deep-frying oils should be filtered and checked daily for usability. Used oil should not be discarded down the drain; it should be collected and recycled via a rendering company.

Prepared dishes should be stored separately from raw products.

Foods should be reheated to a safe internal temperature as rapidly as possible.

Canned goods should be stored in a cool (60°F / 16°C), dry room (to prevent rust). Once a can has been opened, food should be removed from it, or the metal interior will corrode, stain the food, and impart an unpleasant taste. Discard bulging cans, as they may be contaminated with botulism.

Usable leftovers must be sanitary and should be used quickly, ideally within twenty-four hours. Uneaten foods from guests' plates must be discarded.

1.4.4 Sanitation of Utensils, Appliances, Equipment, and Facilities

These guidelines should be enforced:
- Keep utensils (dishes, pots and pans, kitchen tools) and cutting boards clean and in good condition.
- Clean equipment (electric slicers, mixers, etc.) frequently. Sanitize at least once daily **with a chlorine or iodine solution.**
- Thoroughly clean large equipment such as stoves, grills, rotisseries after each service period.
- Clean the kitchen at least once a day. The surfaces of floors, ceilings, and walls must be hard and smooth to facilitate easy cleaning. Wash floors after each service period.
- Keep coolers and refrigerators clean and thoroughly clean them once a week. All refrigerators must have thermometers for monitoring temperature.
- Keep the storage area clean and well ventilated.
- Provide proper water and air controls for lobster and fresh fish tanks and inspect them daily for dead specimens. Clean frequently.
- Change kitchen towels, dish rags, and all other cloths daily. Dirty laundry (such as aprons) should not be stored in the kitchen.
- Keep work tables, butcher blocks, and work counters clean at all times.
- Store garbage in lined, easy-to-clean containers with lids. Whenever possible, containers should be placed in a refrigerated room. In any case garbage should be removed from the kitchen daily. Garbage containers should be washed and sanitized frequently, or they will become breeding grounds for germs.
- Check deliveries, which can bring pests (roaches, bugs, moths) into the kitchen. Dirty containers are breeding grounds for dangerous bacteria and should be kept out of the kitchen and storage areas.
- Control roaches and mice or rats with approved materials. Food must not contact poison. A licensed pest-control company should be regularly employed.

1.4.5 Cleaning and Sanitizing

To clean means to remove dirt and food residue from surfaces or food.

Such things should not remain in the kitchen, as they are food for bacteria. To be most effective, the water temperature should be about 120°F (49°C). In cool water, grease is insoluble and is smeared over, rather than removed from the surface. Boiling hot water creates hard-to-remove deposits on surfaces. Manufacturers' directions should be followed carefully when using cleaning products. After applying cleansers, surfaces should be rinsed with plenty of potable water. Kitchen machines should be disassembled, and their parts washed and sanitized separately. Parts should be placed on a clean, dry surface and allowed to air-dry (or blow dry with high-pressure air).

To sanitize means to destroy microorganisms with chemicals or heat (water above 180°F/82°C, or steam). All equipment used to prepare food must be sanitized regularly. Special care should be given to hard-to-clean items such as automatic whipped-cream dispensers, ice-cream makers, grinders, food processors, and cutting boards. All local health codes should be met or exceeded.

No sanitation procedure will be effective until utensils, equipment, and surfaces have been thoroughly cleaned and all obvious dirt and residue have been removed before sanitizers are applied.

Procedure
1. Remove all dirt and food residue; that is, properly clean all objects that will be sanitized.

2. Rinse in very hot potable water to remove all traces of detergent or food that may interfere with the sanitizing solution.

3. Sanitize by immersing in hot water with a temperature of 180°F to 200°F (82°C to 93°C) or by using chemical disinfectants. The most common are chlorine, iodine, and quaternary ammonia (Quats). These compounds are regulated by the U.S. Environmental Protection Agency (EPA) and have strict

labeling requirements. Always follow directions. The effectiveness of chemical disinfectants depends on acheiving the proper concentration of disinfectant, immersing the object for the proper length of time, and maintaining the proper solution temperature. Since some disinfectants can be dangerous to humans, make sure that they are approved for food-contact surfaces. Store disinfectants separately from food items.

4. Air-dry on a clean surface. Do not wipe dry.

1.5 Safety and First Aid

Almost everyone recognizes dangerous situations at work, but in fact most accidents are caused by carelessness in seemingly harmless settings. The maxim "Prevention is the best cure" still holds. Every foodservice establishment should institute a safety training program and enforce safety procedures.

Prevent Accidents

Accidents do not happen; they are caused. To prevent them, follow these guidelines:
- All equipment, machines, work surfaces and facilities should be kept in good repair and working order.
- Nonslip flooring should be specified when building or remodeling the kitchen and other work areas. Nonskid runners should be used on slippery surfaces in existing facilities.
- Adequate lighting should be installed in work areas, corridors, and near all entrances and exits. Light bulbs should be protected with a metal guard.
- Electric equipment must be properly grounded. Safety circuit breakers must be installed. Electric wires and cords must be properly insulated. Defects should be repaired immediately.
- Fire extinguishers must be installed correctly in appropriate locations and periodically inspected and maintained.
- The building must be equipped with smoke detectors and fire alarms to protect the safety of guests and employees. Exits must be clearly marked and remain unobstructed.
- Emergency numbers for police, ambulance, emergency rooms, fire department, and the poison information center should be posted near telephones.
- Safety glass should be installed in all service doors.
- Coolers and freezer doors must be possible to open from the inside.

Foodservice establishments should have a first-aid kit fully stocked with the following:
- Gauze bandages
- Bandage rolls
- Sterile dressings in sealed envelopes
- Heavy dressings (ABD pads) for heavy bleeding
- Flannel compresses
- Adhesive pads
- Hydrogen peroxide
- Sterile cotton balls
- Elastic bandages
- Triangular bandages with safety pins
- Tweezers and blunt-nose scissors
- Assorted adhesive strips (include flexible fingertips)
- Adhesive tape
- Bandage closures
- Surgical plastic gloves
- Eye cup

Fire Prevention

In addition to the dangers posed to human life by fire, every year many establishments and jobs are lost to careless fires. Many restaurants never reopen. Fire prevention training and fire drills should be held periodically.

To prevent fires from becoming disasters, follow these guidelines:
- If there is a fire, pull the alarm or call fire department *first*. Then save human life and use fire extinguishers.
- Post the fire department number at all telephones.
- Post the location of fire extinguishers, and teach employees how to use them.
- Clearly mark the location of emergency exits. Never lock them during working hours (insert keys in the locks). Keep exits and fire escapes free of obstacles.
- Close fire doors.
- Keep hoods, ventilation equipment, ranges, fryers, griddles, and broilers free from accumulated grease.
- Open and ventilate gas ovens before lighting them.
- Quickly extinguish fires in fryers with a dry-chemical or CO_2 extinguisher.
- Maintain a nonsmoking policy.

Prevention of Burns and Electrical Shocks

- Wear protective gloves while handling hot pans and cooking utensils.
- Stand back when opening doors of pressure steamers and lids of steam-jacketed kettles (long-handled hooks should be used).
- Stir the contents of steam kettles with long-handled paddles or ladles.
- Lift the lids of boiling pots away from oneself to allow steam to escape.

- Keep the handles of pans over the range and away from open flames or hot burners.
- Identify hot pans, lids, or handles of oven-baked dishes to protect others from burns (dust the handle with flour).
- When moving large pots filled with hot foods, seek assistance. Carriers should walk next to each other.
- Alert coworkers of danger using warning shouts of "Attention, hot!"
- Avoid overfilling pans and containers with hot food. Never place them on the floor.
- Wear clean, well-fitting uniforms. Loose sleeves, aprons, and cloths (rags) may catch on equipment or contact a source of heat. To protect against injury from spills of hot foods, wear shoes that have closed toes and heels.
- Avoid splattering liquids in hot fats.
- Never handle electrical equipment with wet hands or while standing in water.
- Report defective wiring immediately. Repairs must be made by qualified electricians.
- Test safety circuit breakers regularly to make sure they function properly.

Prevention of Cuts

- *Important:* Read and understand the directions and operating instructions of all machines before operating the equipment.
- Do not remove safety guards from slicers, grinders, or choppers.
- Secure all machine parts before starting the equipment.

- Keep blades of knives and slicers sharp.
- Store knives in safe holders or racks. Never leave knives in places coworkers will not expect to find them, such as in sinks or hidden under peelings.
- Use the right knife for the intended job.
- Never use knives to open lids, cans, or other containers.
- Hold knives and sharp tools by their handles only.
- Secure cutting boards by placing a damp cloth or sterilized rubber rings beneath them.
- Hold knives correctly.
- Never try to catch a falling knife. Step aside and let it fall.
- When boning meat, cut away from the body. Wear protective aprons and hand guards for extra safety.
- Do not remove foods from a machine until the machine has come to a complete stop.
- Turn equipment switches to "off" when a job is finished.
- Disconnect equipment from the electrical source before cleaning.
- Drain water from a sink before removing broken glass.
- Dispose of chipped and broken glass in separate containers. Do not place it in the garbage or waste containers.
- Sweep up breakage carefully. Use wet paper towels to pick up slivers.

Prevention of Falls

- Use only safe ladders to clean elevated kitchen equipment, lamps, hoods, and the like. Do not use chairs, stools, boxes, or crates.
- Clean and dry wet spots and greasy floors immediately.

- Place "Attention, slippery floor" signs in wet areas.
- Keep stairways and traffic areas free of cleaning equipment, boxes, and other obstructions.
- Stack carts and trolleys below eye level.
- Wear shoes with nonslip soles.

First Aid for Accidents

First aid can mean the difference between life and death for an accident victim. Every member of the staff should be required to know how to administer first aid. In an emergency, follow these guidelines:
- First think, then act.
- Use common sense.
- Keep calm and comfort the victim. Never leave the victim alone unless you must summon help.
- Evaluate the victim's condition.
  - Can the victim speak?
  - Is the victim conscious?
  - Is the victim breathing?
  - Is the victim bleeding?
  - Is there a pulse?

If the victim is not conscious, summon emergency help. Then follow the ABC method to determine the first aid needed: check Airway, Breathing, and Circulation. Certified first-aid training (available through the American Red Cross and the American Heart Association) will enable employees to perform CPR or other emergency measures until trained personnel arrive.

Wounds

Any cut, puncture, or break in the skin requires first aid. Clean small wounds with hydrogen peroxide and

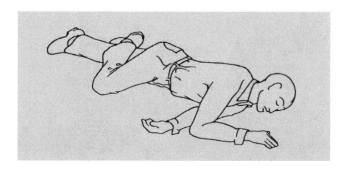

If the accident victim is unconscious, he or she should be placed in the position shown and monitored constantly until medical staff arrives.

cover with a clean bandage. Large wounds should be examined by a physician as soon as possible. Generally wounds that bleed are less likely to get infected.

Burns

Burns are classified by their depth:
- First-degree burns—redness or discoloration
- Second-degree burns—formation of blisters
- Third-degree burns—blackened skin, destruction of cells

Small first-degree burns seldom require medical attention. Such burns should be cooled immediately with ice or cold water. Second- or third-degree burns require the attention of a physician. In the case of large burns, emergency medical personnel should be summoned immediately.

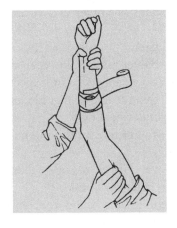

Severe loss of blood can be fatal. The bleeding must be stopped as soon as possible. Position the patient so that the wound is elevated above the heart. Apply pressure with a clean compress. Call for emergency help.

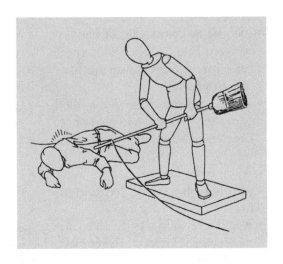

In case of accidents involving electricity, interrupt the circuit immediately. Do not touch the victim, or you could be shocked as well. Use a wooden stick to remove the victim from the electricity source. Wear rubber gloves if available, and administer help only if standing in a dry place.

1.6 Recipe and Menu Book

Personal recipe and menu books are a part of the culinary professional's library and are important tools and valuable resources in a professional career. Culinary apprentices in Switzerland and Germany must keep such books and present them to the head chef upon request.

1.6.1 The Recipe Book and File

Standardized recipes are the basis for excellence in food production. A properly followed recipe guarantees the same quality and quantity at all times. A standardized recipe also serves as a solid basis for cost calculations, because the yield is calculated for an exact quantity and a specific portion size.

Procedure

Develop recipes and record the quantities and production steps. Or type and copy tested recipes from other sources, adapt if necessary, and file.

Recipe Format

A recipe consists of the following:
- Title
- Portion size, yield; pan size and equipment information; time and temperature
- Ingredients
- *Mise en place* (advance preparation steps)
- Method
- Suggestions for service and garnishes (optional)

The ingredients are clearly specified and accurate measurements are given. Ingredients are listed in the order that they are used. Table 1-6 shows a sample recipe.

Recipe Systems

All of the systems that follow depend on an index for quick reference. Group recipes by category and assign each a reference number.

Recipe Book

Use ring binders for recipe books so that additional recipes can be insert-

ed easily. Keep a small notebook handy while developing recipes in the kitchen. Rewrite notes at a more leisurely time.

Advantages: Recipe books are convenient. Recipes can be added without problems. Revised or photocopied versions can be quickly substituted. They also allow for personal creative touches.

Disadvantages: Recipe books are difficult to view. It takes time to find a recipe.

Recipe Card File

File recipe cards in a box alphabetized by heading. Separate the sections with colored cards, with the headings on tabs. Protect the cards: laminate them or place them in plastic sleeves. Cards are very handy for in-house use.

Advantages: Recipe card files are easy to use. Recipes can be quickly located. Recipe cards can be easily corrected, added, or removed. The cards can be used directly in the production area.

Disadvantages: File cards need more space than books. This system is more difficult and expensive to set up.

Computerized Recipe Systems

More and more foodservice operations rely on a computerized recipe system. Choose from many available software programs or customize your own (especially appropriate for large operations and foodservice management companies). Program functions can change and correct recipes, calculate cost or nutrients, evaluate purchasing needs, keep inventory up-to-date, and revise the yield and print recipes for production needs.

Advantages: Computerized systems offer a fast way to correct and change recipes. Recipes are accessible with a couple of keystrokes or mouse clicks and can be instantly printed. Complete computer programs are now available.

Disadvantages: The initial financial outlay is very high. Different computers or software systems may not

Table 1-6. Example of a recipe.

1.4 Soups

Recipe Number: 115

*C*ream of Broccoli Soup
BROCCOLICREMESUPPE
Crème de broccoli

YIELD: 2 QT, 20 OZ (2.5 L)

Ingredients	U.S. Measures	Metric Measure
Broccoli, fresh	2 lb, 10 oz	1.2 kg
Vegetable bouillon (Recipe 27)	2 qt, 20 oz	2.5 L
Onions	3½ oz	100 g
Knob celery (celeriac)	1⅓ oz	40 g
Leeks	3½ oz	100 g
Butter	1⅓ oz	40 g
All-purpose flour	1⅓ oz	40 g
Heavy cream (36%)	6¾ oz	200 ml
Milk	3⅓ oz	100 ml
Seasoning	1 x	1 x

Mise en Place

Clean and trim broccoli.

Select 3½ oz (100 g) broccoli florets for garnish; steam or simmer in vegetable bouillon, reserve liquid.

Dice remaining broccoli.

Dice onions and knob celery.

Wash, trim, and dice leeks.

Method

Sauté onions, knob celery, and leeks in butter. Add diced broccoli, and continue cooking.

Sprinkle with flour; let cool slightly.

Add hot vegetable bouillon. Bring to a simmer, stirring constantly.

Simmer, skimming occasionally, until vegetables are soft.

Puree with immersion blender and pass through a fine-mesh china cap.

Bring to a simmer; add cream and milk.

Season to taste.

Garnish soup with broccoli florets.

be compatible. Sometimes they are useful only in a single facility.

1.6.2 The Menu Book

Recorded and collected menus form a basis for all menu planning. They provide a useful reference for future menu suggestions. They can also be used to document valuable information about problems or successes.

Procedure

Write your own menus or collect and copy others. Organize in a format useful to your operation. Contents might include:
• Daily menus
• Holiday menus
• Banquet menus
• Specialty menus: low-calorie diets, fish, vegetarian, spa (health food)
• Special-event menus: international cuisine, seasonal menus
• Buffets

Menu books can be organized in the same way as recipes are: in ring binders, on file cards, or by computer.

For menu design information, see chapter 5, "Menu Planning."

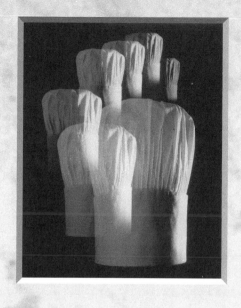

CHAPTER

2

Organization and Equipment

Chapter Contents

In the hospitality industry, the kitchen is one of several departments. A productive and profitable operation requires the team effort of all departments. The employees of the operation form a mutual partnership. Open communication, clear directives and goals, a positive work environment, and personal commitment are essential to success. The organization of a hotel, including the role of the kitchen, is shown in Table 2-1.

In Switzerland most titles would carry the additional designation *Eidg. dipl*, which means "state certified." A very formal apprenticeship and professional advancement system is in place, guided by Swiss law. The professional titles used here reflect the American system.

Table 2-1. Example of a hotel's organizational chart.

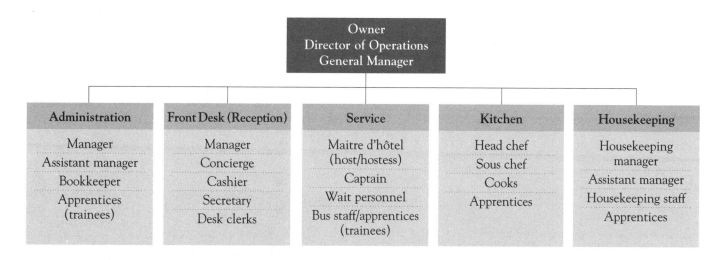

2.1 Kitchen Brigade (Staff)

The kitchen staff is a working team of trained cooks and assistants managed by the head chef. The size of the staff is usually determined by the following factors:

• Type and size of establishment
• Organization of establishment
• Equipment
• Hours of operation
• Menu

Table 2-2 shows the staff used in different-sized kitchens.

The classification of the kitchen staff depends on the type of kitchen organization. It can be organized as:
• Traditional (conventional) kitchen
• Combined production and finishing kitchen
• Separate production and finishing kitchens

• "Open" kitchen
• Fast-food kitchen
• Institutional kitchen

The allocation of duties (rosters and duty schedules) also depends on the type of kitchen organization. Regardless of the type of operation, however, an ideal working environment depends on management with tact and empathy and teamwork.

Table 2-2. Kitchen staff in small, medium, and large kitchens.

Small Kitchen Staff (up to 6 cooks)	Medium-sized Kitchen Staff (7 to 14 cooks)	Large Kitchen Staff (more than 15 cooks)
Head chef—*Chef de cuisine*	Executive chef—*Chef de cuisine*	Executive chef—*Chef de cuisine*
Station cooks—*Cuisiniers de partie*	Station chefs—*Chefs de partie*	Sous chef (second-in-command)—*Sous-chef*
Assistant cooks—*Commis*	Assistant cooks—*Commis*	Station chefs—*Chefs de partie*
Apprentices—*Apprentis*	Apprentices—*Apprentis*	Assistant cooks—*Commis*
		Apprentices—*Apprentis*

2.2   Ranks

In principle, the ranks of those in the profession are the same for both conventional and modern kitchens. Only the duties and functions of the cooks differ. Job responsibilities depend on the cook's rank and position and his or her experience. The duties of each member of the cooking profession are shown in Table 2-3.

In Swiss hospitals, nursing homes, and health spa facilities, dietitians and cooks with training and experience in the preparation of special diets are usually part of the kitchen staff. Their roles are shown in Table 2-4.

2.2.1   Culinary Education

Becoming a cook in Switzerland requires a three-year apprenticeship combined with attendance at a culinary trade school and passing a final exam. To qualify for a position in a setting that requires special diets, an additional year of formal apprenticeship training is required. An advanced professional degree with the title of chef is awarded after further education, with a final exam administered by the Swiss Federation of States. The highest rank is that of the executive chef with a state diploma (master chef). Professional titles are protected by law.

In the United States, culinary education takes place in colleges and universities (foodservice management or hospitality programs) and in special culinary academies, for example, the Culinary Institute of America. Ranks are not indicative of a formal education.

Table 2-3. Duties of kitchen staff members.

Position	Duties
Chef—*Chef de cuisine diplômé* (with culinary degree)	Responsible for all kitchen operations
Chef—*Chef de cuisine*	Responsible for all kitchen operations
Sous chef (second-in-command)—*Sous-chef*	Second-in-command, fills in for chef
Station chefs—*Chefs de partie*	Line cooks, supervising at least one additional person
Station cooks—*Cuisiniers de partie*	Line cook, supervising no one
Independent cook—*Cuisineur seul*	Cook working alone
Assistant cooks—*Commis*	Inexperienced cooks, supervised by station chefs
Apprentices—*Apprentis*	Apprentices training in a kitchen and attending trade school (regulated by law in Switzerland) to become a chef.*

*No uniform formal apprenticeship program exists in the United States.

Table 2-4. Training of staff for special diets.

Position	Training
Hospital or institutional chef—*Cuisinier d'hôtel et d'établissement médicalisé brevet fédéral*	Cook or diet cook, who has passed the Swiss exam for hospital cooks
Dietitian—*Diététicien*	Three years of special training, certified by the Swiss Red Cross
Diet cook—*Cuisinier en diététique*	Trained cook with one year of special training in diet preparation

2.3   Duties

The various kitchen departments have specific duties. These duties should be coordinated with clear and specific directives. Flexibility is essential in today's kitchens; the function of each department and individual duties should at all times meet the needs of the organization. Table 2-5 shows the function of each department in a large kitchen.

Table 2-5. Kitchen departments and their functions.

Position	Duties
Executive chef / Chef—*Chef de cuisine*	• Manages the whole kitchen and supervises kitchen staff • Prepares rosters and assignments • Plans and designs menus • Handles purchasing and controls • Performs cost calculations • Trains apprentices • Responsible for sanitary conditions • Responsible for preparation and presentation • Communicates (visits) with guests
Sous chef—*Sous-chef*	• Takes on the responsibilities of the executive chef when absent • Also responsible for apprentice training • Often also holds a station chef position
Sauce cook—*Saucier*	• Prepares sauces, meat, game, poultry, fish, and warm appetizer dishes
Broiler cook—*Rôtisseur*	• Responsible for the preparation of grilled dishes and roasts and of dishes that are both oven-roasted and deep-fried
A la carte cook—*Restaurateur*	• Only in very large kitchen brigades • Responsible for à la carte preparations
Fish cook—*Poissonnier*	• Only in very large kitchen brigades, to relieve the sauce cook • Prepares fish and seafood dishes
Vegetable cook—*Entremetier*	• Prepares soups, vegetables and potatoes, and pasta, cheese, and egg dishes • Prepares spa cuisine, health-food diets, and vegetarian dishes
Pantry chef—*Garde-manger*	• Monitors all cold-food preparation and controls freezer and refrigeration rooms • Bones and portions meat, game, poultry, and fish • Prepares salads, cold appetizers, sauces, and cold buffets • In large kitchens cold dishes are prepared by an appetizer cook (*hors-d'œuvrier*)
Butcher—*Boucher de cuisine*	• Only in large kitchen to ease the work of the pantry chef • Bones and cuts raw meat
Pastry chef—*Pâtissier*	• Prepares all pastries and desserts; sometimes also warm pasta preparations or hot dishes involving pastries (e.g., beef Wellington)
Swing cook—*Tourant*	• Works as needed in all stations of the kitchen, and replaces station chefs on their days off.
Duty Cook—*Chef de garde*	• Responsible for the kitchen when the staff is not present, during off-peak hours • Prepares dishes ordered during those times and does *mise en place*
Dietitian—*Diététicien*	• Advises guests with special diets and nutritional requirements • Plans and performs cost calculations of special diet menus • Prepares dietary dishes
Staff cook—*Cuisinier pour le personnel*	• Only in very large foodservice operations • Prepares meals for staff

2.4   Mise en Place

Mise en place is "pre-preparation" and is the first step in the preparation of dishes or products. A properly organized kitchen has a correct *mise en place* routinely set up in all departments and at each post. The saying "A good *mise en place* is half the cooking" is as true for small kitchens as it is for large preparation and finishing kitchens. Cleaning and closing a work station, including checking stored products, cleaning equipment and work areas, and performing necessary repairs, are also a part of *mise en place*. The general term *mise en place* encompasses everything from the arrangement of the utensils and ingredients to the presentation of the finished product.

2.4.1   Basic *Mise en Place*

Basic *mise en place* involves assembling the necessary utensils, food in- gredients, and linens needed to perform cooking duties.

2.4.2   Daily and Station *Mise en Place*

Station *mise en place* reflects the daily menu, including any specials offered, banquets, or other special preparation duties. All utensils and ingredients (cleaned and cut as needed) are put into place ready to be used in the day's dishes. Daily *mise en place* includes the control of ingredients. As an example, the *mise en place* of ingredients for the sauce cook would encompass: fats (oil, butter, margarine), flour, corn or potato starch, fresh bread crumbs, white wine, red wine, lemon juice, vinegar, Madeira, Cognac, spices, condiments, herbs, tomato paste, mustard, mirepoix, peeled onions, milk, cream, eggs, grated cheese, diced onions, chopped shallots, chopped parsley, basic stocks, basic sauces, etc.

2.4.3   *Mise en Place* of the Production Kitchen

The *mise en place* of the production kitchen is based on the needs of the daily menu and the station *mise en place*, with an emphasis on food preparation.

2.4.4   *Mise en Place* of the Finishing Kitchen

The *mise en place* of the finishing kitchen is based on the daily menu and the station tasks, with an emphasis on reconstitution and presentation. Most of the foods have been partially or fully prepared in the production kitchen.

2.5   Kitchen Organization

Every establishment must tailor the kitchen organization to its needs. This depends on the type of kitchen, physical facilities, and the technical skills of the kitchen staff.

The goals of a well organized kitchen are:

1. Efficient work flow
2. Effectively planned work areas
3. Correctly placed kitchen equipment and appliances appropriate for the size of the establishment
4. Maximum use of skilled personnel

The organization of the kitchen depends on the following:

- Type of establishment
- Size of establishment
- Organizational management
- Location of establishment
- Kitchen type
- Size of kitchen
- Kitchen staff (brigade)
- Customers' needs
- Menu
- Type of service
- Operating hours

2.5.1   Kitchen Types

The following six kitchen types dictate different organization systems:

1. Conventional kitchen
2. Combined preparation and finishing kitchens
3. Separate preparation and finishing kitchen
4. Open or show kitchen
5. Fast-food kitchen
6. Industrial kitchen

Conventional Kitchen

- Mainly small establishments
- Both preparation and finishing are in the same space
- All stations are grouped together in one block
- Foods are served from one counter

Combined Preparation and Finishing Kitchen

- Mainly medium-size establishments
- Preparation and finishing stations are organized into two blocks

Separate Preparation and Finishing Kitchens

- Generally in large establishments, such as hotels with satellite restaurants, restaurants with banquet rooms, convention centers, or large foodservice cafeterias

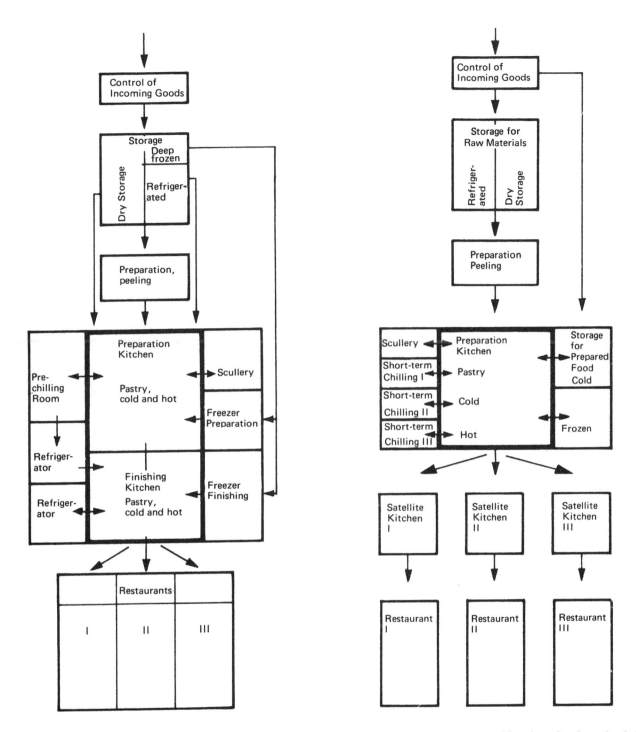

Two kitchen types: combined preparation and finishing kitchen (*left*) and separate preparation and finishing kitchens (*right*).

- Production and finishing blocks (satellite kitchens) are in separate locations
- The finishing kitchen needs reheating equipment, such as microwave ovens and grills

Providing separate spaces for food has these

Advantages
- Work flow is efficient.
- Standardized recipes ensure consistent quality.
- Production is constant.
- Equipment is used efficiently.
- Regular forty-hour work week can be established.
- Sanitation standards can be instituted and controlled.
- Routine tasks can be performed by unskilled labor.
- During peak service hours, production cooks can assist in the finishing kitchen.
- The cooks in the finishing kitchen can concentrate on the constant preparation of orders.
- Work can be more interesting if positions are exchanged.
- Flexible working hours are possible.

Disadvantages
- Separate facilities require more space.
- Initial equipment expenditures are higher.
- Work can be boring if no exchanges take place.

Open Kitchen

- Generally found in new, theme restaurants
- Guests observe food preparation
- Facilitates good communication among guest, server, and cook
- Calm and clean work habits are essential
- Proper attire, friendliness, and good grooming are necessary
- Sometimes supported by a production kitchen

Fast-food Kitchen

- Generally, establishments without a production kitchen

- Purchases are limited to convenience foods
- Efficient production is facilitated by separating the storage area (freezer, cooler) from the cooking area

Industrial Kitchen

- Generally for food-production industries
- Separate test kitchen, production kitchen, and usually a laboratory
- Large storage facilities are essential for large industrial kitchens

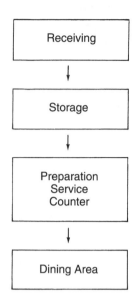

2.6 Data Systems

The incorporation of electronic data systems in the hospitality industry has made the computer a useful tool in the kitchen. A fast and reliable computer can make formerly time-consuming calculations at record speed. Foodservice professionals should understand data-processing systems to make full use of computers in their establishments. Computers can be used for the tasks that follow.

Work Schedules

- To develop vacation, work, and shift plans
- To calculate and record vacation and compensation days

Purchasing

- To list suppliers and purchase arrangements (credit, transportation)
- To access price lists of different suppliers

- To calculate and compare prices
- To purchase goods, with immediate confirmation
- To receive delivery schedules

Cost Calculations

- To determine price and energy costs for recipes or whole menus, with various portion sizes or other modifications
- To compare projected and actual costs
- To calculate overhead costs
- To provide statistical graphs and charts
- To provide planning information for management at short notice

Storage Controls

- To locate food products in several storage areas
- To record inventory turnover
- To flag out-dated products

- To calculate storage costs
- To maintain inventory records

Menus

- To plan menus that can be automatically changed
- To base menu planning on available food products
- To maintain menu records for many occasions that can be quickly adjusted for specific needs
- To translate menus in other languages
- To verify spelling on menus

Recipes

- To update recipe collections and recalculate costs quickly

Correspondence

- To print and alter menus
- To receive and send bids
- To prepare announcements

2.7 Kitchen Design

The organizational structure of an establishment determines its kitchen design. The layout of a kitchen should be planned with the help of a professional foodservice facility designer and experienced cooks. The space should be planned to allow for maximum efficiency of food preparation. To do this, each area in the space must be identified and its

function understood. Table 2-6 lists commonly used kitchen areas and their functions. Local building codes must be followed.

2.7.1 Planning Steps

1. Discuss owner's concept and budget.

2. Document owner's priorities.

3. Identify kitchen organization and kitchen type.

4. Evaluate several building plans.

5. Design space divisions and proper block arrangements for preparation stations.

6. Determine arrangement of kitchen equipment and appliances.

Table 2-6. Kitchen work areas and their functions.

Space	Function
Main kitchen	• Production and service of all warm foods • Integration of the three stations of the sauce cook (*saucier*), broiler cook (*rôtisseur*), and vegetable cook (*entremetier*)
Larder/pantry	• *Mise en place* for fish, seafood, meat, game, and poultry • Production of all cold dishes
Pastry kitchen	• Production of all pastries and desserts
Diet kitchen	• Production of special diets • Generally in spas or hospitals
Staff kitchen	• Production of staff meals • Generally only in very large hotels
Receiving area	• Delivery and control of goods • Scales are essential
Walk-in refrigerators	• Storage of fresh foods (separated by category, e.g., dairy, vegetables, meat, fish)
Deep-freezer	• Storage of frozen foods
Vegetable preparation room	• Cleaning and trimming of vegetables
Pot-washing area	• Cleaning of pots and pans
Dish-washing room	• Cleaning of dishes, glasses, and silverware
Silver-polishing room	• Washing and polishing of silver dishes (silver washer and drier machine) • In large first-class hotels, usually includes a silver burnisher
Storeroom	• Storage for all nonperishable foods
Office	• Work space for administrative duties of the executive and sous chef
Staff dining room	• Dining and lounge space for staff
Locker rooms with shower	• Changing room with individual lockers for staff
Toilets	• Separate staff facilities
Garbage room	• Separate refrigerated room for kitchen garbage • Separate room for flower arrangements • Garbage storage separated for glass, paper, fats, oils, etc.
Utility room	• Storage of cleaning materials and equipment

7. Evaluate production functions and efficient work flow.

8. Resolve details

Explanation of Planning Steps

1. The discussion of the owner's concept should include the establishment's goals, competition, customer base, and finances.

2. In determining the owner's priorities, a detailed description of his or her vision and basic business plan should be considered.

3. The kitchen type and organization must be congruent with goals of the owner.

4. The review of plans should include the evaluation of several bids from architects and kitchen facility designers and a review of their references.

5. The layout of the main kitchen and adjacent areas in blocks should be made according to kitchen type.

6. The types of kitchen equipment and their arrangement should be based on efficient work flow.

7. The layout should be reviewed with regard to function, space utilization, work flow, and conformance to building codes, OSHA standards, and safety.

8. Details include energy connections, water access and drainage, ventilation, lighting, refrigeration, heat recovery systems, garbage removal, and other infrastructure.

2.7.2 Planning Guidelines

• Optimum size ratio among the individual work areas and space arrangements

• Delivery, storage (refrigeration and freezers), preparation, production, and service areas arranged to facilitate a continuous work flow

• Proper positioning with easy access to equipment and appliances, some possibly on wheels

• Good illumination of work surfaces with natural or artificial light

• Optimum ventilation with fresh-air intake; installation of hoods or exhaust fans above equipment to control smoke and steam

• Evaluation of heat recovery system and cost effectiveness

• Conformity of all installations with Gastro-Norm standardized pans (see section 2.12); no thresholds to impede the use of Gastro-Norm food carts from station to station

• Workplace safety design features: nonslip floor materials, fire alarm system, electrical circuit breakers, etc.

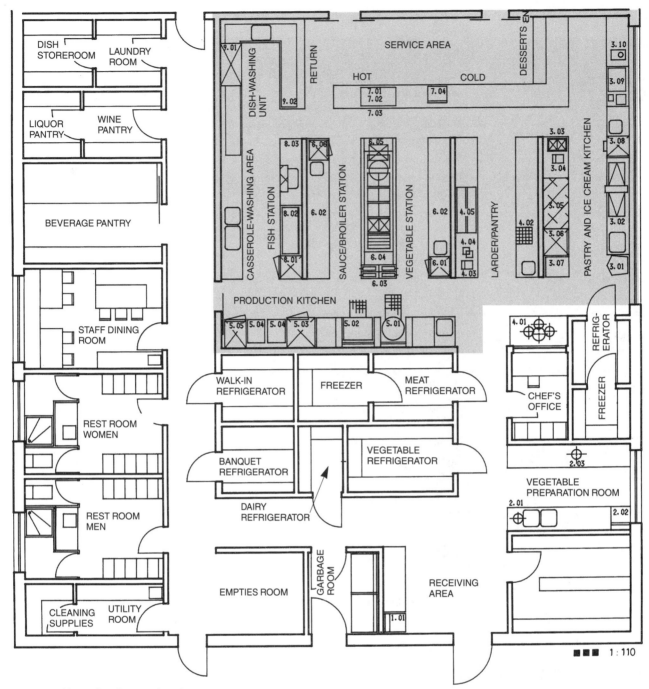

Layout of large kitchen with side rooms

1.   Receiving area
1.01 Floor scale

2.   Vegetable preparation room
2.01 Potato peeler
2.02 Vegetable washer
2.03 Vegetable slicer and cutter (high-speed commercial food processor)

3.   Pastry and ice cream kitchen
3.01 Mixer
3.02 Dough sheeter
3.03 Gas stovetop
3.04 Scales
3.05 Marble-top counter
3.06 Baking ovens
3.07 Cooling rack
3.08 Freezer
3.09 Ice-cream maker
3.10 Whipped-cream mixer

4.   Larder/pantry (garde-manger)
4.01 Universal machine (combination mixer, slicer, grinder, chopper, and blender)
4.02 Chopping block
4.03 Scales
4.04 Meat slicer
4.05 Sandwich-making unit

5.   Production kitchen
5.01 Steam-jacketed kettle
5.02 Tilting frying pan
5.03 Combi stove
5.04 Mobile service carts
5.05 Quick-chill refrigeration (blast freezer)

6.   Vegetable, sauce, and broiler stations
6.01 Steamer

6.02 Refrigerated counter
6.03 Deep-fat fryer
6.04 Stovetop with grill
6.05 Broiler (salamander)
6.06 Combi stove

7.   Service area
7.01 Hot table
7.02 Infrared lamp
7.03 Hot-food warmer cabinet
7.04 Microwave oven

8.   Fish station
8.01 Fish refrigerator
8.02 Fish tank
8.03 Ice maker

9.   Dish-washing unit
9.01 Dishwasher
9.02 Glassware washer

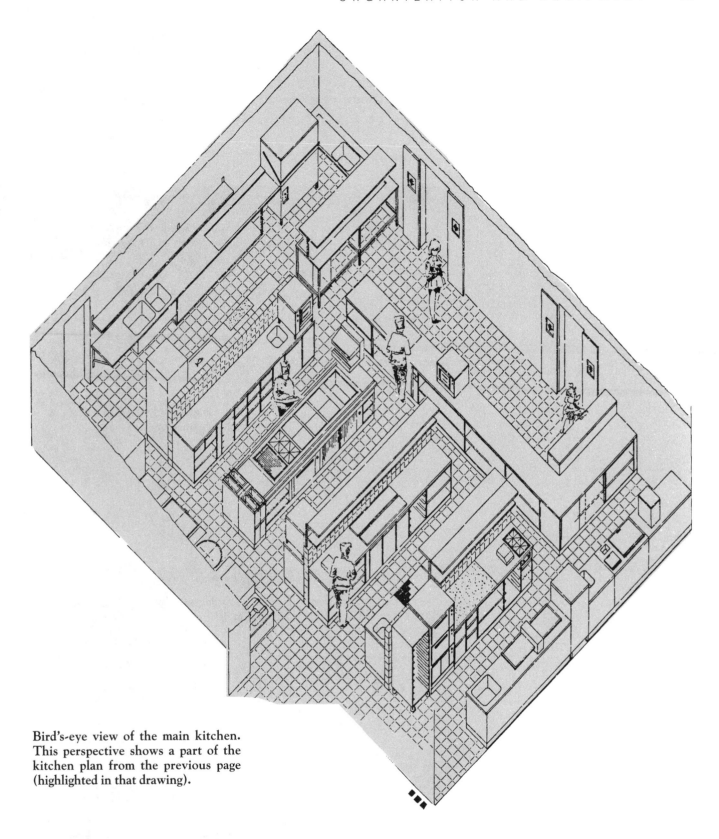

**Bird's-eye view of the main kitchen.
This perspective shows a part of the
kitchen plan from the previous page
(highlighted in that drawing).**

- Washable walls, elimination of grooves and corners to improve sanitation
- Floor drains and catch basins for dish sinks and cooking equipment that tilts
- Adequate access to water and large drainage areas
- Consideration of more than one energy source

- High-voltage outlets
- No equipment installed on walls
- Noise-reducing layout and design, use of sound-absorbing ceilings, rubber mats near dish-washing sinks, separate dish-washing installation
- Adequate refrigeration and freezer space, work and storage surfaces
- Adequate standard-size cabinets, drawers, and shelving

- Separate service and dirty-dish return passes; flexible plans to allow for future task changes.
- Separate refrigerated room for refuse
- Adherence to all laws and regulations

2.8   Heating Methods

To be able to cook, one needs a source of heat. An energy source, such as electricity, gas, oil, or coal, is in turn needed to produce heat. The different types of heat are defined in Table 2-7.

For some preparations, more than one type of heat is used; this is known as combination heating (see Table 2-8).

Table 2-7. Methods of heating.

Heating Method	Energy Source	Equipment	Example of Use
Contact heat	Electricity Gas Fuel oil Charcoal Wood	Electric burner Ceramic stovetop Gas burner Tilting frying pan Grill Griddle	A steak can be cooked in a frying pan, on the grill, griddle, or in a tilting frying pan.
Convection heat	Water Steam Oil Hot air	Convection oven Steamer Combi stove Steam-jacketed kettle Deep-fat fryer Slow-roasting oven	French fries are cooked in oil in a deep-fat fryer
Radiation heat	Infrared Microwaves	Microwave oven Broiler Spit roaster Infrared oven Regeneration oven	An open-face cheese sandwich is melted under the broiler (salamander)

Table 2-8. Combination heating.

Heating Method	Energy Source	Equipment	Example of Use
Combination heating	Electricity Gas Fuel oil Charcoal	Roasting and baking oven Tilting frying pan with high-pressure option Pressure cooker Low and high pressure steam-jacketed kettle	A glazed roast is cooked with contact and convection heat

2.9   Kitchen Equipment

The main function of kitchen equipment is to conduct heat to cook a product. The equipment should complement the kitchen organization. Technical innovations have simplified the control of the cooking process and energy consumption. It is possible to program some cooking processes completely automatically. To use such equipment properly, however, still requires professional knowledge and training. Table 2-9 shows the method of heating employed by commonly used equipment. It is important to understand the effect of each heating method on each food product.

Performance Specifications of Kitchen Equipment

• Easy to work with and control
• Safe
• Good ratio of cost to performance
• Easy cleaning and maintenance
• Requires minimal space, while providing maximum capacity
• Low energy needs, user friendly
• Exact climate controls (temperature, time, and humidity)
• Standard Gastro-Norm pan sizes
• Multiple usage
• Accurate manufacturer's directions and handbooks

Table 2-9. Equipment used for different methods of heating.

Contact Heat	Convection Heat	Radiation Heat	Combination Heat
Ranges	Convection oven	Microwave oven	Roasting and baking oven
Tilting skillet	Steamer	Broiler	Tilting frying pan with high-pressure option
Grill	Combi stove	Roasting spit	Low and high pressure steam-jacketed kettle
Griddle	Steam-jacketed kettle	Infrared oven	
	Deep-fat fryer		
	Slow-roasting oven		

Ranges

Many different range models are available. Those powered by electricity or gas are most common; oil-powered models are rare. Ranges are equipped with a variety of features. Some have separate burners; some, seamless tops. A range may have roasting or baking ovens, warming drawers, a water bath, a water faucet, and/or a wide frame. The restaurant range should have spacing plates to allow for service space. Ranges with temperature regulators help reduce energy costs. Some of the advanced features now available for ranges are listed below.

Conventional Range

- Elements with contact heat
- Temperature regulation in steps
- Heating elements and range frame at the same level
- Seamless cooktop
- Additional options: Incremental temperature regulation, temperature gradation, quick-heating element

Induction Range
- In an induction range, an electronic generator creates a magnetic field; cooking takes place without conducting heat. The range element therefore stays cool because the heat is generated in the bottom of the pot.

Advantages: Saves energy, is immediately ready to use, gives off little heat, has sensitive temperature regulation, and is easy to clean.

Disadvantages: Extremely expensive, high performance is limited, heat conduction occurs only with direct contact of magnetic fields, special pots and pans are necessary, may interfere with heart pacemakers.

Ceramic Cooktops
The elements of a ceramic cooktop are heated with visible infrared radiation.

Advantages: Short preheating time, easy to clean, automatic pan sensors, no special pans necessary (though pans should have flat bottoms).

Disadvantages: Not shatterproof, heat conduction limited to infrared fields, burned sugar can damage ceramic top.

Tilting Frying Pan or Pressure Braising Pan

The tilting frying pan is one of the most versatile pieces of kitchen

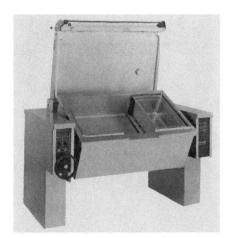

equipment. It can be heated with electricity or gas. Depending on primary use, the pan surface may be steel or stainless steel. A steel surface prevents sticking; a stainless-steel surface prevents oxidization of some foods. The pan can be used to sear, sauté, or braise foods. A pressure-steam option has been developed for the tilting frying pan that allows it to be used to stew, steam, boil, and poach foods as well.

Grill

The surface of a grill is composed of rods, which are heated from beneath. Heating elements may be electric, gas, or charcoal. The lava-stone grill is heated with gas. Use only clean grills and foods with minimal fat to guarantee good flavor and prevent health hazards. Grooved grill rods provide appetizing sear marks.

Griddle

The griddle can be free standing or built in. It has a temperature-regulated surface. Grease is collected in a re-

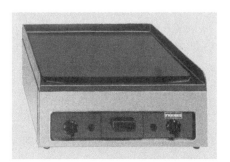

movable catch basin. It can be heated with electricity or gas. The surface top is available in steel, stainless steel, or ceramic. Steel is the most energy efficient. Food residue should be removed frequently to allow continuous cooking with little additional fat and to prevent food from sticking.

Convection Oven

The convection oven operates on the principle of forced hot air in an enclosed space. Fans circulate the hot air evenly over the food. This makes it possible to cook different products on several shelves. The cooking times of the different products should be similar. Several dishes can be prepared in the same unit without flavor transfer if products are placed in separate pans. Foods cook more quickly than in a conventional oven. Convection ovens in Europe feature an automatic water spray that adds humidity to the convected air to prevent food surfaces from drying. Large glass doors, oven lights, thermostats, timers, and comfortable work levels make the convection oven easy to work with and control. The removable racks make the internal oven surfaces easy to clean. Additional options are automatic internal meat temperature control, timed cooking, and adjustable fan speeds.

Advantages include:
• Short preheating time
• Full use of oven space
• Several dishes can be prepared in the same unit without flavor transfer

• Gentle cooking process due to automatic controls
• Food products need not be turned
• Energy efficient compared to conventional ovens

Disadvantages include:
• Upper and lower heat cannot be regulated separately
• Pans with high sides are not suitable

Steamer

Three types of steamers are available: high pressure (15 pounds per square inch or 120°C = 1 bar); low pressure (5 psi or 110°C = ½ bar), and atmospheric (using a convection principle without pressure). Steamers generate their own steam or obtain it from an external source. Steam is injected directly onto the food. The temperature should be evenly regulated. Cooking times are reduced because pressure increases the steam temperature. Steam pressure is affected by higher elevations. Atmospheric steamers can be used for steaming, poaching, and reconstituting prepared foods. Pressure steamers can be used for steaming, blanching, and reconstituting prepared foods.

Advantages include:
• Gentle cooking
• Preservation of flavor, nutritional value, and color
• Excellent in the preparation of dietetic meals
• Multiple use

• Flexible production workload with à la carte menu
• Reduces food, energy, and water costs
• Environmentally friendly
• Easy to clean, minimal use of dishes

Disadvantages include:
• Locked doors under pressure
• Difficult to test doneness

Combi Stove

This equipment, common in European kitchens and in use in many large American production kitchens, is sold under various names such as Combi Stove and Aero-Steamer. It is a valuable innovation that takes the convection oven a step further. Besides hot air, steam or a mixture of the two can be used to cook. The processes can be regulated to be used alone, one after the other, or in combination. A combi stove can be used for roasting, baking, and gratinating; steaming and poaching (140°F–195°F or 60°C–96°C); and reconstituting prepared foods (250°F–285°F or 120°C–140°C).

Low- and High-Pressure Steam-jacketed Kettles

Steam-jacketed kettles are available as round tilting kettles or fixed-base kettles with drains, which are usually square in Europe but round in the United States. They may be powered by electricity, gas, or steam from an external source. The bottom and walls of the kettle can be directly heated, or steam can be generated indirectly by heating water in the jacket of the kettle. Preheating time is reduced, and scorching of food is prevented. Both types of kettle are also available as high-pressure steam units. They operate and cook food under 5 psi (110°C = ½ bar) of pressure.

Fixed Steam-jacketed Kettle

Steam-table pans can be placed in the square kettle, which allows the steaming of several different items at the same time. An automated lift system makes it easy to remove the pans.

Tilting Steam-jacketed Kettle

The jacketed, insulated body of the tilting kettle or pressure kettle saves energy. A large circumference and shallow depth at a proper working level simplifies working with this equipment. Both the fixed and tilted

kettles can be used to blanch, boil, and steam foods (pressure kettles only).

Deep-fat Fryer

Deep-fat fryers can be free standing, table units, or built in. They may be powered by electricity or gas. Accurate temperature settings, large heating elements, and proper frying methods conserve the frying fat. Integrated or external filtration systems make it easy to filter the fat daily to extend its use.

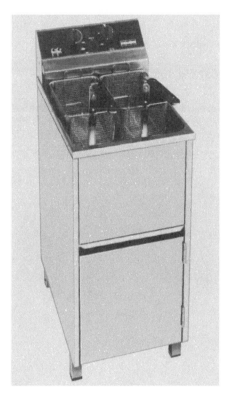

Slow-roasting Oven

This piece of equipment can be used to keep food warm or to slow-roast foods. The oven is heated with electrical elements throughout the whole oven space or with forced hot

air at 140°F to 250°F (60°C to 120°C). The automatic "hold" timer is an important internal temperature control feature. This oven is used mostly to cook very large roasts.

Microwave Oven

The microwave oven generates energy with a *magnetron* that converts electrical energy into short microwaves. The heat develops inside the food itself from an electromagnetic field. This field sets the water molecules in the food in rapid motion, causing heat through friction, which cooks the food in a very short time. The cooking time is dependent on the amount of fat, protein, starch, and water in the food. Metal of all types interferes with the microwaves and will damage the equipment. Escaping microwaves, from defective doors, for example, can cause health problems. The microwave oven is best used for rapid and economical reheating of prepared foods. Combination systems, such as convection heat and broiler units, are generally not useful in professional settings. Microwave ovens with good programming features are easy to operate.

Advantages include:
- Instantly ready to operate
- Rapid reheating of small portions
- Efficient and labor-saving preparation
- Saves dishes and clean up, environmentally friendly
- Defrost option

Disadvantages include:
- Limited dish selection (no gold ornament, no metal)
- Can make foods overly dry

- Only heats foods, does not brown them
- Small capacity

Broiler (Salamander)

The high-temperature heat from above in a broiler is electric or gas fired. The temperature can be regulated. The distance between the food and the broiler elements should be adjustable. A broiler can be used to glaze food, prepare gratinated dishes, and keep food warm.

Roasting Spit

The roasting spit can be a feature of a grill or broiler unit, or it can be a self-contained unit. It may be heated with charcoal, electricity, or gas

(usually with lava rocks). The spit can be automatically adjusted to operate either horizontally or vertically. Meat juices and grease are collected in a removable pan.

Baking and Roasting Oven

The conventional oven is often part of a range. Free-standing models are often stacked in multiple, separately operating units (deck ovens). Ovens at eye level are easier to operate.

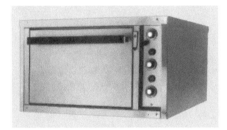

Upper and lower heat temperatures are regulated separately. Disadvantages include the long preheating time and ability to use only one rack at a time. The conventional oven has been replaced in professional kitchens with the more popular convection oven or combi stove. Rotary ovens, rack ovens, and conveyer ovens are also becoming popular in large foodservice operations.

Automated Food Preparation Systems for Industrial Operations

Automated cooking or baking units have been developed for the quantity production of prepared meals and baked goods. They are based on the conveyer principle. These automated cooking units are part of a continuous system that starts with the raw ingredients and ends with the packaged finished product.

Examples include:

Sauté unit	Browns and sautés
Fry unit	Deep-fat fries
Bake unit	Bakes
Cook unit	Boils, blanches
Steam unit	Blanches
Autoclave	Cooks and sterilizes packaged raw foods (canning, bottling)

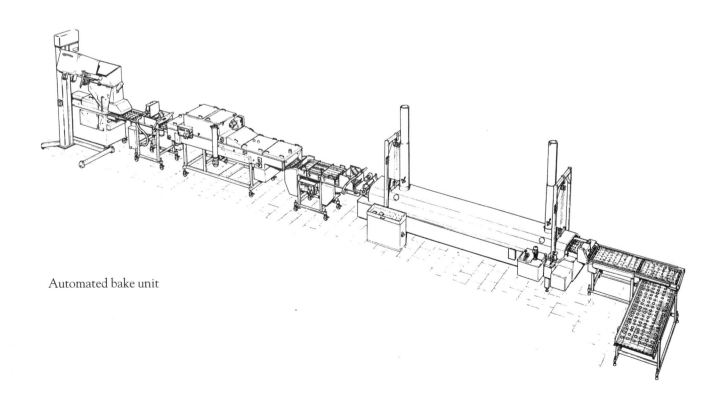

Automated bake unit

2.10 Reheating Equipment and Distribution Systems

The constantly rising expectations of customers for more flexible service times, greater menu variety, more nutritional consciousness, and attractive food presentation require new means of preparing and dispensing foods. A shortage of trained professionals, limited space, and rising costs add to the challenge. Flexible production hours, imaginative presentation, and rapid reheating are all possible solutions to these problems.

Foods that are to be reheated can be cooked in house or purchased partially or fully prepared. The heating system must be carefully considered when selecting prepared foods. Plates or platters can be partially or fully assembled before heating.

2.10.1 Reheating Equipment

Table 2-10 shows equipment commonly used to reheat foods and the dishes used for that equipment.

2.10.2 Delivery Systems

Banquet System

Portable racks are rolled into combination steamers or convection ovens. The racks can hold forty to eighty plates and are covered with insulation wrap. The wrap prevents drying of the cold-plated meals while they are refrigerated and keeps the plates hot for up to twenty min-

Table 2-10. Reheating equipment.

Equipment	Dishes
Combination oven	Plates, platters, Gastro-Norm pans without lids
Convection oven	Plates, platters, Gastro-Norm pans with or without lids
Reheating oven	Plates, platters, Gastro-Norm pans with lids
Microwave ovens	Plates, platters, (nonmetallic), with lids
Steamer	Plates, Gastro-Norm pans

utes after the meal has been reheated.

Advantages include:
- Meals can be prepared ahead of time, without pressure
- Meals can be plated more carefully and attractively ahead of time
- Direct placement of racks in the heating unit simplifies and saves labor
- Ideal for large banquets, ensures quality presentation and proper temperature

Reheating Radiation Oven

This oven is heated by infrared radiation. Heating elements are dispersed throughout the unit. Covered plates or Gastro-Norm pans are rolled on racks into the oven. The food is heated with infrared radiation from below and above.

Reheating Caldomat System

This is a combination chill-and-serve system. The cold-plated foods can be kept refrigerated and later reheated to service temperature in the

same unit. The food is warmed with an inductive heating system. To heat the food, plates with specially coated ceramic bottoms are used. The plates are placed on Gastro-Norm serving trays. Foods to be heated must be covered. Only foods on the ceramic-bottom plates are heated in this system; the rest remains cold.

Banquet Station

A banquet station may be necessary for large affairs where it is impossible to set up a banquet system because of steps, different floor levels, or other obstructions. Foods are kept hot in Gastro-Norm pans for a short time and are plated at the service site.

A banquet station requires the following mobile units:
- A service unit with hot-water bath and food warmers and spacers to plate dishes
- A carving unit with heated cabinet
- Plate and cup warmers

2.11 Kitchen Machines

Kitchen machines reduce labor. Selection depends on the type of kitchen and establishment. All machines should be conveniently placed and in perfect working order. Manufacturers' operating, safety, and maintenance directions should be posted near the equipment and closely followed. The machines

should be thoroughly cleaned after each use and periodically inspected.

Placement of Kitchen Machines

Locating machines using the recommendations in Tables 2-11 and 2-12 will provide optimum use; however, space or technical needs may dictate other locations. Locations in the

tables are keyed with letters, as follows:

A Main kitchen
B Larder/pantry
C Pastry kitchen
D Vegetable preparation room
E Various other areas

Table 2-11. Kitchen machines.

Kitchen Machine	Location	Function
Universal machine	A, B, C, D	Has several attachments for many tasks, including mixing, chopping, puréeing, grating, slicing, whipping, stirring, grinding, and crushing
Food chopper	B	Preparation of forcemeats and farces.
Food mill	A, C	Preparation of soups and purées
Food processor with grater/slicer attachments	A, B, C, D	Grating cheese, bread, nuts, potatoes; cutting and slicing vegetables and potatoes; attachments can be adjusted and exchanged for different tasks
Mixer	A, B, C	Preparation of doughs, fillings, sauces, and creams
Grinder	B	Preparation of ground meat and fillings (farce)
Meat shredder	B	Produces shredded meat, poultry, or game
Roller machine	C	Grinds almond to paste to produce marzipan and almond paste.
Slicer	B	Slices meat, cold cuts, cheese, and vegetables; adjustable blade; operated only with safety guard
Bread slicer	E	Slices breads; adjustable blade
Ice maker	B, C, E	Makes ice cubes of different sizes and shapes
Vegetable washer	D	Washes vegetables, potatoes, and salad greens
Grain mill	E	Cracks and grinds whole grains to be used in spa cuisine and health diets
Potato peeler	D	Peels potatoes and root vegetables; with an additional attachment, can wash and spin-dry salad greens
Butcher bandsaw	B, E	Cuts bones
Vertical cutter/mixer	B, C	Chops, grinds, purées, blends, kneads, and liquefies; used for fillings (farces), doughs, and cold sauces; a high-performance, high-speed self-contained unit
Blender	A, B, C	Purées small amounts of vegetables and fruits, prepares milkshakes, emulsifies and blends soups and sauces in small amounts; has two parts, a motor base and a removable top with blade and lid
Juicer	B, C, E	Presses fruits and vegetables to extract juices
Salad spinner	D	Spin-dries leafy greens, potatoes, and blanched vegetables
Whipped-cream machine	C	Whips and portions heavy cream
Electric immersion blender/turbo blender	A, B, C	Purées directly in large pots; turbo mixer purées large quantities directly in steam-jacketed kettles
Meat tenderizer	B	Mechanically tenderizes steaks and cutlets, helps prevent portions from curling
Dough sheeter	C	Rolls out dough; thickness is adjustable
Vacuum sealer	B, E	Vacuum-packs ingredients, partially or fully prepared dishes; add nitrogen when vacuum-packing very soft products; in the United States, approval from health authorities is necessary before a vaccum sealer can be installed
Scales	A, B, C, E	Essential to control portions; mechanical or electronic models available

Table 2-12. Cleaning equipment.

Equipment	Location	Function
Garbage compactor	E	Compacts packaging material
Dishwasher	E	Cleans and dries dishes, silverware, and glasses; available in several models, from cabinet to conveyer units
Pot scrubber	E	Cleans pots and pans
Floor and carpet cleaner	E	Used to clean the various rooms; many different models available, e.g., high-pressure cleaner, wax and polisher, water suction, etc.
Silver polishing machine	E	Deoxidizes and polishes hotel silverware

2.12 Gastro-Norm

Gastro-Norm is a foodservice standard measure for containers used by all foodservice operations in Europe. The Gastro-Norm size is the same as the standard American foodservice pan size. The Gastro-Norm system established uniform sizing standards throughout the foodservice industry. All containers in various combinations fit all the standard carts, racks, and equipment, which saves labor and ensures efficient work flow.

The basic pan size, GN 1/1, is 20¾ inches by 12¾ inches (530 mm by 325 mm). The inserts are available in various depths.

Applications
Gastro-Norm standards are used for:
• Ovens and steamers
• Steam table and self-service units
• Refrigerators and freezers
• Built-in drawers and cabinets
• Work counters
• Buffet lines and cabinets
• Transport racks, food carts, and storage equipment
• Elevators and dumbwaiters

Advantages
• Speeds preparation

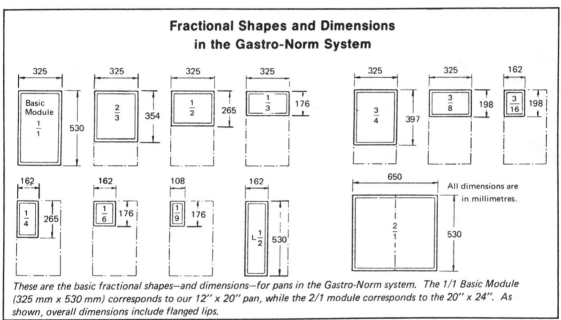

Fractional Shapes and Dimensions in the Gastro-Norm System

These are the basic fractional shapes—and dimensions—for pans in the Gastro-Norm system. The 1/1 Basic Module (325 mm x 530 mm) corresponds to our 12″ x 20″ pan, while the 2/1 module corresponds to the 20″ x 24″. As shown, overall dimensions include flanged lips.

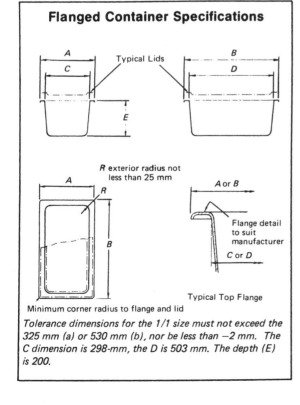

Flanged Container Specifications

Typical Lids

R exterior radius not less than 25 mm

Flange detail to suit manufacturer

Typical Top Flange

Minimum corner radius to flange and lid

Tolerance dimensions for the 1/1 size must not exceed the 325 mm (a) or 530 mm (b), nor be less than −2 mm. The C dimension is 298-mm, the D is 503 mm. The depth (E) is 200.

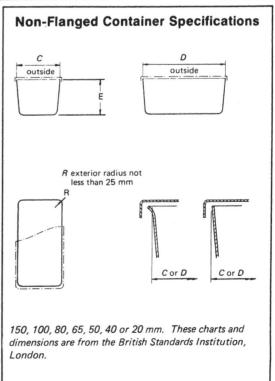

Non-Flanged Container Specifications

outside

outside

R exterior radius not less than 25 mm

150, 100, 80, 65, 50, 40 or 20 mm. These charts and dimensions are from the British Standards Institution, London.

- Improves work-flow efficiency
- Stacking volume increases limited storage space
- Allows optimum use of available space
- Various depths allow great flexibility

- Shortens walking distances at work
- Allows use of same unit for transportation and preparation
- Streamlines in-house transport
- Saves labor
- Enables interchangeable use of standard pan sizes

Materials

Inserts are made of stainless steel, aluminum, glass, porcelain, or plastic. Some inserts have perforated bottoms.

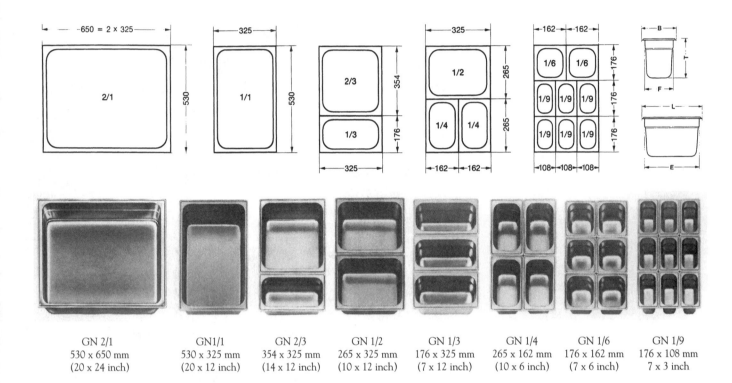

GN 2/1	GN1/1	GN 2/3	GN 1/2	GN 1/3	GN 1/4	GN 1/6	GN 1/9
530 x 650 mm	530 x 325 mm	354 x 325 mm	265 x 325 mm	176 x 325 mm	265 x 162 mm	176 x 162 mm	176 x 108 mm
(20 x 24 inch)	(20 x 12 inch)	(14 x 12 inch)	(10 x 12 inch)	(7 x 12 inch)	(10 x 6 inch)	(7 x 6 inch)	7 x 3 inch

2.13 Materials for the Manufacture of Kitchenware

Various materials are used in the manufacture of dishes and kitchen tools. Each material has advantages and disadvantages. In choosing kitchenware, select materials based on intended use, to guarantee the best application, versatility, cost, and durability.

Classification

Metals
Made from a single metal, such as aluminum, copper, steel (sheet steel, cast iron).

Alloys
Composed of two or more metals that have been alloyed, such as stainless steel, silver plate.

Breakable
Glass, ceramic (porcelain), and the like.

Unbreakable
Plastic, wood, and the like.

Aluminum

- Aluminum is extracted from the raw material bauxite.
- Aluminum is a soft metal and is often used as an alloy with other metals.
- Aluminum is hardened and made more resistant to chemical corrosion through electrolytic oxidation (anodized aluminum).
- Handles of aluminum cooking utensils should be welded.

Usage
- Various, for pots, pans and storage containers, utensils, cans, tubes, and foil
- Nonstick surfaces added by coating with polytetrafluoroethylene

(trade names include Teflon, Silverstone)

Care
- It is easy and quick to clean.
- Strong metal cleaners and metal scratch pads should not be used.

Advantages
- Uniform heat conduction
- Lightweight
- Ideal for all types of burners

Disadvantages
- Soft, easily deformed
- Reacts with acids and alkalines, which causes discoloring and a metallic taste
- Wears away when rubbed against hard metals (such as metal spatulas, forks, whisks)
- Riveted handles do not hold very well in soft aluminum

Copper

- Basic material is copper sulfate, which is extracted from copper ore
- Interiors of copper pots and pans must be lined with tin, nickel, stainless steel, or silver; eggwhite bowls and sugar-boiling pans can remain unlined.

Usage

- Pots and pans and decorative serving pieces
- Can be used on most types of burners
- Serving and decorative pieces cannot be used for heating; bottoms will buckle

Care

- Copper requires extensive care and polishing.
- Special copper cleaners are required.
- Tinned copper must frequently be relined.

Advantages

- Excellent heat conduction
- Minimal danger of scorching
- Very durable (little corrosion), long life cycle
- Beautiful presentation with correct care

Disadvantages

- High purchase costs, expensive to maintain
- Corroded lining will cause loss of vitamin C in foods; copper acetate (green color) is poisonous

Steel and Cast Iron

- Cast iron is extracted from iron ore; steel is an alloy of iron and carbon.
- Several types of steel are used in the kitchen: mild carbon steel, sheet steel, cast iron, black or blue steel, and the well-known stainless-steel alloys

Usage

- Lyoner frying pans are made from sheet steel.
- Cast iron is heavy and is used in the production of grill pans and oven tops.

Care

- New cast-iron pans must be seasoned to seal the porous surface before use.
- A warm pan is cleaned with a cloth and dried well; any hard-to-remove particles should be rubbed with salt.
- Cast iron should be dried well and oiled lightly to prevent rust.

Advantages

- Long life span; retains heat well
- Ideal for high-heat browning
- Uniform heat conduction (if properly cared for)

Disadvantages

- Heavy
- Rusts if not cared for correctly; may discolor and give food a metallic taste
- Thin sheet steel buckles at high heat (sheet pans, rotisseries)

Stainless Steel

- Steel alloys with chrome, nickel, or molybdenum are considered stainless steel
- More than fifty varieties available
- The most common stainless steel alloys in the kitchen are:
  - Chrome-nickel-steel INOX 18/10 (18% chrome, 10% nickel)
  - Chrome-nickel-molybdenum-steel 18/10/2 (18% chrome, 10% nickel, 2% molybdenum)

Usage

- Stainless steel is the most commonly used metal in kitchens. It is ideal for pots, pans, equipment, utensils, storage shelves, and more.
- Heat conduction in pots and pans is much improved with an aluminum- or copper-cored disk bottom.

Care

- Easy and simple
- Calcium deposits easily removed with vinegar or lemon juice

Advantages

- Durable; universally available
- Resists moisture, odor, color, taste, heat, cold, and alkalis
- Easy care; sanitary
- Has cooking and service applications

Disadvantages

- High purchase costs
- Scorches easily
- Poor heat conductor without copper or aluminum core
- Partially dissolved salt crystals attack the alloyed metal, leading to corrosion (pitting)

Silver Plate

- Sterling silver is soft and bends easily; therefore, only silver-plated cutlery is used in hospitality service.
- An alloy of copper, zinc, and nickel is referred to as Alpaka in German and hotel silver in English.
- The amount of silver plating is recorded in grams. An impression of 90g means that 12 large spoons and forks were plated with 90 grams of sterling silver.

Usage

- Serving dishes and table silver
- Decorative service items, place settings, covers, candlesticks, and more

Care

- Requires extensive care and polishing
- Cleaning options: special silver polishes, tarnish soaks, silver-polishing machine

Advantages

- Durable; very decorative
- Excellent heat conductor
- High inventory value

Disadvantages

- Labor-intensive care
- Heavy, easily scratched
- Oxidizes when in contact with foods containing sulfur
- Very high purchase costs

Glass

- Depending on its final use, glass can be a combination of quartz sand, soda, and calcium; for clarity, very small amounts of dolomite and mica are added.

- Large amounts of recycled glass are used today; green glass is usually completely recycled.
- Glass can be blown, pressed, or rolled.
- Wide varieties of glass are available in different combinations and forms.
- *Enamel* is glass powder and color that is bonded by immersion or a spray method to various metals as a protective coating.

Usage
- Glass is used for cooking in heat-proof pots and pans, and as attractive service dishes.
- Glass is especially useful for gratinating dishes and in the microwave oven.

Care
- Glass must be washed at high temperatures and dried with grease-free towels.

Advantages
- Many uses
- Nonreactive, clear, and sanitary
- Stylish and decorative

Disadvantages
- Breaks when handled carelessly
- Conducts heat poorly; scorches easily

Ceramics

- Ceramics are made from clay, kaolin, and similar materials.
- The most precious ceramic product is porcelain.

Usage
- Ceramics with a fired glaze can be used as heat-resistant cookware, as decorative serving ware, and as crockery.

Care
- Ceramic dishes must be cleaned at high temperatures.
- They should be periodically cleaned with specially designed cleansers.
- Sharp utensils must not be used with ceramics.

Advantages
- Ceramic dishes are beautiful and decorative.
- They maintain temperature well and are nonreactive.

Disadvantages
- Breaks and scratches easily
- Poor heat conductor
- Chips cause problems with appearance and sanitation

Plastics

- Plastics are made from natural resins or by causing a reaction in petroleum resin that produces plastic.
- Of the many available types of plastic, only two are of importance in the kitchen: soft plastic, or thermoplastic resin, and hard plastic, or thermoset resin.

Usage
- Many uses, especially for disposables, busing, and storage

Care
- No harsh cleaning materials

Advantages
- Lightweight, inexpensive, low noise
- Resistant to acids, and easy to clean

Disadvantages
- Poor shape retention, not heat resistant
- Easily cut and scratched
- Absorbs strong odors, which are difficult to remove

Wood

- Wooden cabinets, counters, and utensils are rarely used in professional kitchens.

Usage
- For special kitchen utensils, such as a butcher block, rolling pins, wooden ladles, and knife handles

Care
- To maintain hygiene, surfaces and utensils must be smooth, without nicks or cuts.
- Carving boards should be thoroughly washed, sanitized, and air-dried.

Advantages
- Natural, long-lasting material
- Decorative, rustic look for service

Disadvantages
- Moisture causes warping
- Burns and scorches easily
- Absorbs odors

2.14 Cookware

Pots and pans are available in different shapes and sizes for specific uses (see Table 2-13). The most common materials for pots and pans are steel, stainless steel, cast iron, aluminum, and copper. Heavy-duty pans are more expensive but are much more durable. Most pots have *solid-core* or *sandwiched* bottoms made from heat-conductive materials. Maintenance depends on the material from which the pan was made.

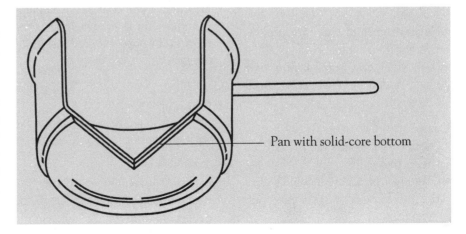

Pan with solid-core bottom

Pans should be handled carefully during use, cleaning, and storage. Well-maintained pans save energy, shorten cooking time, and produce better product. A gleaming variety of perfect pots and pans is the pride of every kitchen.

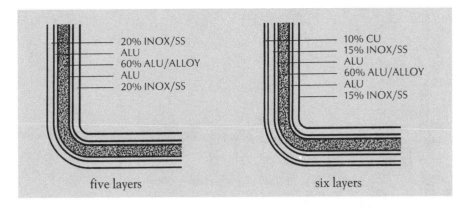

20% INOX/SS	10% CU
ALU	15% INOX/SS
60% ALU/ALLOY	ALU
ALU	60% ALU/ALLOY
20% INOX/SS	ALU
	15% INOX/SS
five layers	six layers

Section of pan with sandwiched bottom

Table 2-13. Cookware.

Name	Illustration	Special Features and Applications
Fry pan *Poêle lyonnaise*		• Generally made from steel or cast iron • Sauté, brown, and fry
Nonstick frying pan (Teflon) *Poêle au Teflon*		• Cannot withstand high heat, not scratch resistant • Sauté with little or no fat
Crêpe pan *Poêle à crêpes*		• Small pan with low sides • Special, to prepare thin pancakes (crêpes) and blinis
Griddle pan *Poêle à griller*		• Round or square pan, usually cast iron • Thick bottom requires longer preheating • Grill
Paella pan *Poêle à paëlla*		• Steel pan with two handles and lid • Used as a cooking pan and serving dish • Prepare and serve the Spanish specialty paella
Sauté pan *Sauteuse*		• Shallow skillet with sloping sides • Glaze, stew, and sauté
Saucepan *Sautoir*		• Small, shallow pan • Poach, sauté, boil, stew, and braise small portions
Saucepan (high-sided) *Casserole à manche*		• Pan with long, spot-welded handle • Multiple uses • Blanch, boil, poach, stew, braise, and butter-roast

Name	Illustration	Special Features and Applications
Pressure cooker *Marmite à pression*		• Safety valve and rubber ring must be in good condition • Includes steamer basket • Pressure-steam small portions
Braising pot *Rondeau*		• Shallow pan with loop handles • Poach, stew, braise, roast, butter-roast
Low sauce pot *Marmite basse*		• Pot with loop handles • Blanch, boil, poach, stew, butter-roast, braise
Tall stock pot *Marmite haute*		• Tall pot with loop handles • Blanch, boil
Roasting pan *Rôtissoire*		• Usually black steel or stainless steel • Rectangular pan with rounded corners • Roast, poach in water bath
Braising pan with lid *Braisière*		• Higher sides than roasting pan • Always with lid • Pan and lid have folding handles • Braise, butter-roast
Fish poachers *Poissonnière*		• Includes a steamer with handles and a lid • Used as a cooking and serving pan • Poach in fish stock, stew or braise whole fish

2.15 Kitchen Utensils

Kitchen utensils are tools used daily in commercial kitchens. They must be scrupulously clean and in excellent working order. They should be cleaned immediately after each use and returned to their proper place. They are grouped as follows:

• Knives
• Kitchen utensils
• Kitchenware
• Serving ware

2.15.1 Knives

Knives are expensive, delicate tools. They are available in many sizes, for many uses. The blade should be made of high-grade, rust-free steel.

The handles should be made of plastic or hardwood (for example, rosewood). Careless handling damages the edge and increases the danger of accidents. Sharpening knives regularly with a steel is an integral part of good knife maintenance. The cleaning and proper storage of the knife is the user's duty.

1. Chef's knife (large)
2. Chef's knife (regular size)
3. Butcher knife
4. Bread knife (serrated)

5. Meat slicer
6. Smoked-salmon slicer
7. Fileting knife
8. Boning knife

9. Cheese slicer
10. Turning knife (bird's beak)
11. Paring knife
12. Peeler

2.15.2 Kitchen Utensils

A variety of small tools are used for everyday tasks as well as for very specialized work. The variety of sizes and shapes are infinite. The proper use of hand tools requires professional and product knowledge. Many of these tools belong in the professional cook's tool kit.

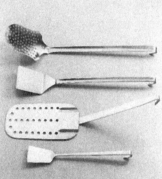
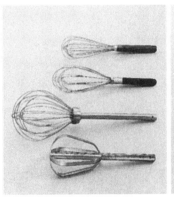

Ladles
Wire skimmer/spider
Sauce ladle
Perforated skimmer
Soup ladle

Lifters
Roasting spatula
Stir-fry spatula
Fish lifter
Rösti spatula

Whips
Wire whisk
Balloon whisk
Machine whisk
Banded whisk

Wooden Spoons
Wooden spoon
Slotted wooden spoon
Stirrer
Spatula for Teflon

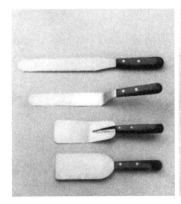
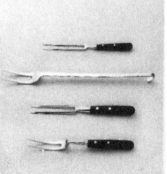
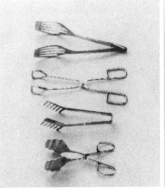

Spatulas
Palette knife
(flexible metal spatula)
Offset spatula
Rounded-tip turner
Square-tip turner

Forks
Delicatessen fork
Pot fork
Bayonet meat fork
Carving fork

Tongs
Universal tongs
Grill tongs
Spaghetti tongs
Asparagus tongs

Presses
Potato ricer
Garlic press
Vermicelli press
Lemon juicer

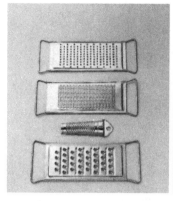

Graters
Bircher grater
Cheese grater
Nutmeg grater
Rösti grater

Slicers
Vegetable slicer
Cheese slicer
Truffle slicer
Mandoline

Cutters
Hors d'oeuvre cutters
Confection cutters
Puff-pastry cutter
Cookie cutters
(plain, fluted)

Pastry Tubes
Filling tube
Decorating tubes
Plain tubes
Star tubes

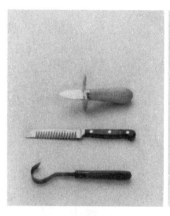

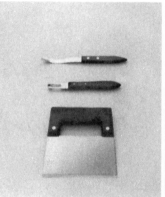

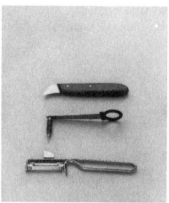

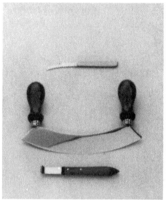

Specialty Knives
Oyster knife
Demidov knife
Butter curler

Grapefruit knife
Decorating knife
Cheese knife

Chestnut knife
Radish cutter
Swivel-bladed peeler

Dough switchblade
Mezzaluna
Citrus zester

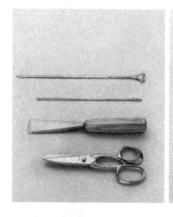

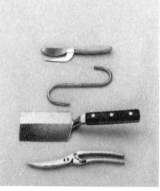

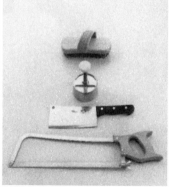

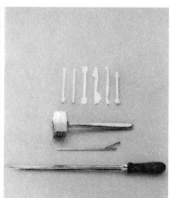

Tools for the Garde-manger
Ornamental skewer
Trussing needle
Ice chisel
Fish scissors

Fish scaler
Meat hook
Meat mallet
Poultry shears

Butcher-block brush
Hamburger press
Meat cleaver
Rip-toothed bone saw

Modeling dowels
Meat tenderizer
Larding needle
Larding knife

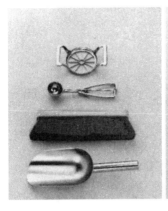

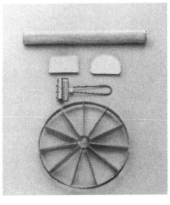
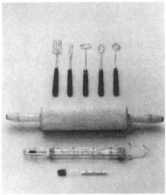

Bakery Tools

Apple corer/slicer
Ice-cream scoop
Flour brush
Flour scoop

Stencil
Sugar sifter /sprinkler
Pastry crimper
Pastry wheel

French-style rolling pin
Dough scrapers
Roller docker
Cake divider

Chocolate dipping forks
Two-handled rolling pin
Candy thermometer
Density meter

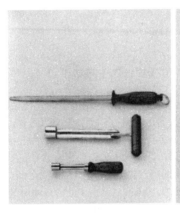

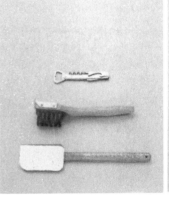

Miscellaneous Tools

Sharpening steel
Pineapple corer
Apple corer

Pastry bag
Can opener
Egg slicer

Bottle opener
Grill brush
Rubber spatula

Melon baller
  (parisienne spoon)
Olive pitter
Pastry brush

2.15.3 Kitchenware

Kitchenware includes utensils used daily to prepare, store, and transport foods. Materials and finishes vary and so do costs, accordingly. Proper handling and good maintenance are essential.

Sheet Pans	Pans and Bowls	Sieves
Baking sheet	Clearing bowl	Drum sieve (tamis)
Gastro-Norm sheet pan	Gastro-Norm insert	*Knöpfli* mill (batter)
Jelly roll pan	Pastry bowl	Flour sifter
Roasting pan	Mixing bowl	Colander
Cookie sheet	Copper kettle for	*Spätzle* mill
	beating egg whites	Cone sieve, china cap,
Perforated pan	Bread bowls	*chinois*

Baking Pans and Molds	Miscellaneous	
Brioche pan	Draining rack or icing	Cake-cooling rack
	grate	
Cake pan	Cake frames	Cake ring
Loaf pan	Twine dispenser	Carving board
Ladyfinger mold	Meat thermometer	Covered pail
Ice-cream bombe molds	Foil dispenser	Funnel
Gugelhupf pan	Spice box	Storage canister
Tube pan	Measuring cups	
Rectangular mold	Food mill	
Pudding mold	Cheesecloth	
Savarin pan	Ravioli board	
Spring pan	Cutting board	
Timbale	Ice-cream storage containers	

2.15.4 Serving Ware

Serving dishes are used primarily to present food, although some are suitable for food preparation as well. Only sparkling clean dishes and highly polished platters should be used. Suitable are dishes made from copper, stainless steel, silver plate, glass, ceramic, porcelain, and wood.

Platters, Plates, Bowls	Cook-and-serve Dishes	Miscellaneous
Ornate platter	Soufflé dish	Chafing dish
Fish platter	Melted butter pan	Buffet mirror
Meat platter	Egg plate	Parfait glasses
Gratin dish	Fish kettle	Ornate carving board
Hors d'oeuvre platter	Flambé pan	Fruit basket
Cake stand	Fondue pot (Caquelon)	Cheese board
	Paella pan	Smoked-salmon board
Bread plate	Snail plate	Sauce boat
Dessert bowl/plate	Terrine mold	Toast basket
Flat plate		Plate cover (domes)
Specialty plate		
Soup plate/soup bowl		
Vegetable dish		
Salad bowl		
Glass bowl		
Ceramic pot		
Soup terrine		

2.16 Refrigeration

Every foodservice operation needs various types of refrigeration. A refrigeration system can lower temperatures in specific rooms and areas. Refrigeration controls the growth of microorganisms and prevents spoilage and fermentation of foods, keeping them fresh longer.

Advantages
- Cost-effective purchasing
- Longer storage of perishable foods
- Greater menu variety
- Greater profits

Disadvantages
- High energy cost if heat cannot be recaptured
- Environmental pollution and expensive maintenance

2.16.1 Refrigeration

Cold is produced by removing heat from the air.

The Process

Refrigeration occurs when a coolant is evaporated, removing heat from the air. The coolant is liquid until it reaches the evaporator. When the coolant changes to gas, it uses heat from the air. The heated gas moves through the system to a condenser, where it is chilled with water or air and again becomes liquid and ready to use more heat energy from the air. The movement of the coolant through the closed system is driven by a compressor.

Coolants
The most common coolants are fluorochlorocarbons.

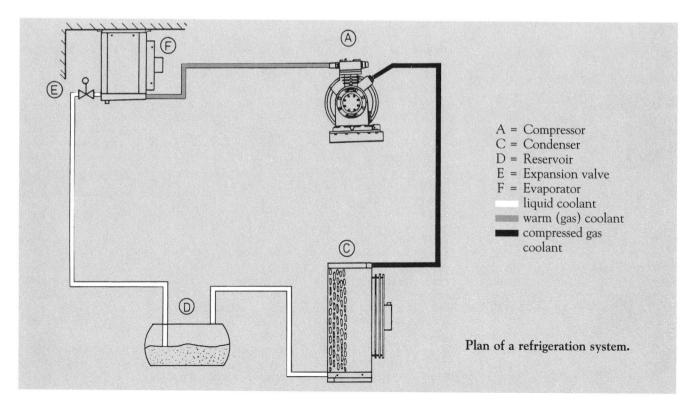

A = Compressor
C = Condenser
D = Reservoir
E = Expansion valve
F = Evaporator
□ liquid coolant
■ warm (gas) coolant
■ compressed gas coolant

Plan of a refrigeration system.

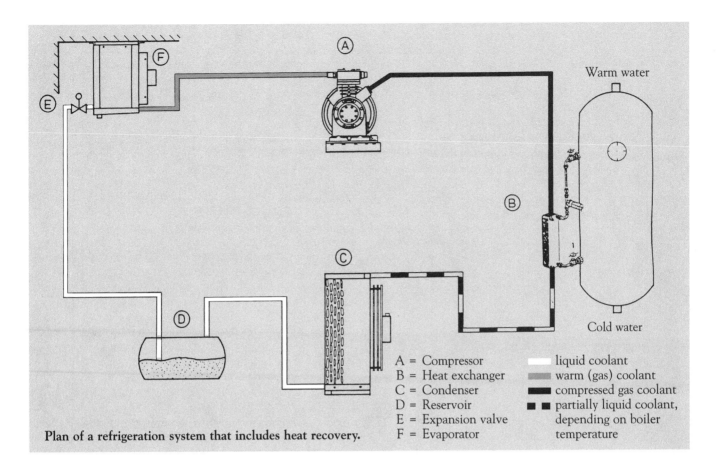

A = Compressor
B = Heat exchanger
C = Condenser
D = Reservoir
E = Expansion valve
F = Evaporator

▭ liquid coolant
▬ warm (gas) coolant
▬ compressed gas coolant
▪ ▪ partially liquid coolant, depending on boiler temperature

Plan of a refrigeration system that includes heat recovery.

2.16.2 Heat Recovery

The heat from refrigeration units can be recovered with special equipment and used, for example, to heat rooms or water. Doing so saves large amounts of energy, thus justifying the initial construction cost of a heat recovery system.

2.16.3 Cooling Temperatures and Relative Humidity

Temperature is regulated with a *thermostat* and read with a *thermometer*. *Relative humidity* is regulated with a *hygrostat* and read with a *hygrometer*. Table 2-14 lists common refrigerated products and the appropriate storage temperature and relative humidity for each.

2.16.4 Refrigerator and Freezer Rooms

Size, configuration, and use of refrigeration units depend on the foodservice organization.

Basic Guidelines

- Insulation thickness according to local code
- Large doors with low threshold to facilitate use of carts and racks with wheels (possibly pallets)
- Self-closing, well-sealed doors
- Floors and walls with hard, smooth, washable surfaces
- Sanitary, easy-to-clean shelves, drawers, and the like, depending on local code
- Shelving affixed to walls to allow for easy floor washing
- Waterproof floor with rounded corners
- Floor drain
- Drip drain for expansion valve
- Humidifier or dehumidifier, as needed
- Thermometer at eye level and easy to read
- Cold-resistant lighting, protected from water spray

Table 2-14. Storage temperature and relative humidity of commonly refrigerated foods.

Products	Storage Temperature	Relative Humidity
Meats and sausages	32°F–35°F (0°C–+2°C)	85–90%
Fish	30°F–33°F (–1°C–+1°C)	90–95%
Dairy products and eggs	32°F–40°F (+2°C–+4°C)	75–80%
Desserts (pastry)	40°F–42°F (+4°C–+5°C)	75–80%
Fruits and vegetables	40°F–44°F (+4°C–+6°C)	85–90%
Potatoes	45°F–49°F (+7°C–+9°C)	85–90%
White and red wines	47°F–50°F (+8°C–+10°C)	85–90%
Frozen foods	0°F–-6°F (–18°C–-22°C)	—
Walk-in refrigerator	40°F–50°F (+4°C–+6°C)	85–90%
Deep-freezer	0°F–-6°F (–18°C–-22°C)	—

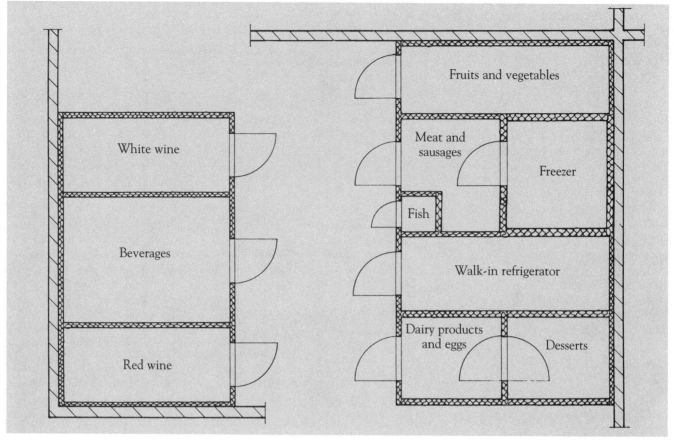

Configuration of Refrigerator Units

- Light switch with control light
- Appropriate temperatures for each product
- Coolers near daily work areas
- Professional installation, maintenance, and repairs

Additional Guidelines for Freezer Rooms

- Alarm systems for people and for temperature control
- Door opens from inside, latch has reflective markings

2.16.5 Prefabricated Refrigerator and Freezer Spaces

If a refrigerator or freezer room is full, cooling space can be increased by adding prefabricated refrigerator or freezer spaces.

Advantages
- Minimal construction
- Immediate installation and readiness
- Removal and reinstallation option
- Needs neither masonry nor painting

Disadvantages
- Level installation space is needed
- Not as durable as built-in units

2.16.6 Refrigerators and Freezers

Refrigerators, freezers, and sandwich-making units fit into the cooling system of commercial kitchens especially well because they accommodate Gastro-Norm pans. Their cooling systems are very efficient and cool products quickly. They can be easily moved and require only an appropriate electrical outlet. However, they are more costly to operate, because the frequent opening of doors or lids allows much warm air to enter.

2.16.7 Freezer Systems

The following freezer systems are generally used in industrial-size kitchens.

Freezing with Cold Air
- Freezer tunnel
- Conveyer freezer tunnel
- Conveyer blast-freezer tunnel

Freezing with Chilled Contact Plates
- Contact freezer system

Freezing with Liquid Gases
- Nitrogen tunnel

2.16.8 Specialty Refrigeration and Freezer Units

These practical units are used in many ways in the foodservice industry:
- Crushed-ice maker
- Ice-cube maker
- Blast freezer
- Quick chiller
- Ice cream displays and carts
- Hors d'oeuvre and sandwich making units
- Pastry displays
- Salad bars and carts

2.16.9 Ice-Cream Makers

Various models of ice-cream freezers are available. All must have high freezing power to guarantee smooth ice cream. They should also be easy to clean and sanitize.

Types
- Crank freezers
- Soft ice-cream machines

Guidelines

Crank Freezers
- Floor model with vertical freezer cylinder
- Table model with horizontal freezer cylinder
- Stainless-steel cylinder and paddle
- Preferred: floor models that blend, pasteurize, and freeze in the same cylinder
- Desirable: speed-control regulation

- Built-in automatic cleaning and sanitizing

Soft Ice-Cream Machines
- Equipped with special mixer or stirrer
- Firmness of product can be individually selected
- Very quick freezing process

Sanitation
- Ice-cream units should be cleaned according to strict sanitation codes.
- During each phase of ice-cream production, strict sanitation standards must be followed.

- Equipment and tools should be in excellent condition.

2.16.10 Cooling Chain

The cooling chain is a linked series of steps, from production to service, that maintains the quality of frozen foods. From the time the food is prepared, through its transport, storage, and service or use, the temperature of the product must be kept at a constant maximum of 0°F (−18°C).

2.17 Culinary Terms

French culinary terms are used in many professional kitchens. Knowing the most common words facilitates communication among culinary professionals.

In addition to the terms listed in Tables 2-15, 2-16, and 2-17, it is advisable to be familiar with the French terms for job positions and ranks; kitchenware and utensils; menu terms; basic cuts and dimensions for vegetables, potatoes, meat, fish, and poultry; and cooking stages and preparation methods.

Table 2.15. French terms for food preparations and activities.

annoncer	to call out an order
arroser	to baste roasting foods
barder	to bard or cover game or poultry with back fat before roasting
beurrer	to coat with butter
brider	to truss poultry, meat, or game
chemiser	to coat a form with gelatin or coat an ice-cream bombe
ciseler	to make small incisions (especially in fish)
clarifier	to clarify liquids
déglacer	to deglaze particles from the bottom of a pan, using liquid
dégorger	to soak food in cold running water
dégraisser	to remove fat from liquid
démouler	to unmold
désosser	to debone
égoutter	to drain
émincer	to cut into thin slices, shred
farcir	to stuff meat, poultry, or vegetables with filling
fouetter	to fold in with a wire whisk
fumer	to smoke
garnir	to arrange food attractively on a plate
goûter	to taste
larder	to bard meat with back fat using a larding needle
lier	to bind soups and sauces (liasion)
mariner	to marinate
mêler	to mix
monter	to whip egg whites or to improve a sauce by incorporating cold butter over low heat
napper	to coat evenly with sauce or gelatin
parer	to trim to the proper shape
passer	to strain through a cloth or sieve
piquer	to bard
réchauffer	to reheat
réduire	to reduce liquid to a certain amount
rissoler	to fry golden in fat
tamiser	to push through a fine-mesh sieve
tourner	to turn, a special cutting technique for vegetables and potatoes
tremper	to dip, soak

Table 2-16. French terms for foods and dishes.

abattis	poultry wings, gizzard, liver, heart, neck, and fat
appareil	finished mixture
beurre manié	equal amounts of kneaded butter and flour
caramel	caramelized sugar
carcasse	poultry or crustacean carcass
coulis	thick, concentrated sauce without flour
court-bouillon	fish-poaching stock
croûtons	toasted bread cubes or slices in various shapes
farce	filling
fleuron	puff-pastry crescent
fond	basic stock
friture	fat for deep-frying
fruits de mer	all types of fish and seafood
fumet	concentrated stock
garniture	garnish
galettes	small cakes
infusion	infusion of aromatics
jus	roasted meat juices
liaison	thickener (e.g., egg yolk and cream)
pie	dough-covered farce, pie
pulpe	fruit concentrate or purée
roux	cooked mixture of fat and flour
salpicon	meat, vegetables, or fruit cut into small dice
suprême	small chicken breast or fish fillet
tartelette	small pastry (tartlet)
zeste	zest or thinly sliced peel of citrus fruits

Table 2-17. French terms for kitchen equipment and utensils.

bain-marie	hot-water bath or steam table
barquette	boat-shaped pastry form (small)
bordure	ring mold
canneleur	decorating knife
cassolette	oven-proof casserole
chinois	conical sieve, china cap
cloche	plate cover (dome)
cocotte	casserole in which food is cooked and served
couteau	knife
cuillère	spoon
dariole	porcelain cup molds
écumoire	skimmer
égouttoir	colander
étamine	cheesecloth
fourchette	fork
lardoire	larding needle
légumer	vegetable serving dish
louche	ladle
passoire	sieve
plateau	service tray
ravier	service bowl for cold appetizers
saucière	sauceboat
spatule	spatula
sorbetière	ice-cream storage container
tamis	drum sieve, flour sieve
tranchelard	slicer, carving knife

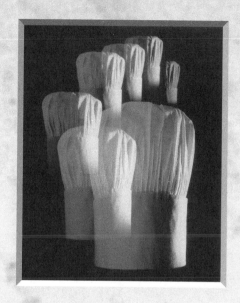

3

Nutrition

Chapter Contents

A diet lacking in variety and nutrients or containing too many rich foods can cause illness and disease. A cook or chef must understand nutritional principles and exercise the responsibility to keep customers healthy. It is not enough to present a guest with a filling and satisfying dish: the meal should also be nutritionally well balanced. Most guests are concerned about their figures and their health and expect a chef to understand and apply nutritional principles. Therefore, a good education in nutrition is essential for the culinary professional.

3.1   The Human Cell

Like all living creatures, the human body is composed of billions of tiny cells. Each cell contains everything needed to sustain life. Although all living cells are similar in composition, there are marked differences among cells within an individual species as well as among cells of different species, depending on a cell's function. For example, unlike animal cells, plant cells contain an additional protective, form-giving cell wall made of cellulose.

The body is composed of the same nutrients contained in the foods we eat (Table 3-1). Complicated chemical processes convert them into building blocks for the body.

Table 3-1. Composition of the human body.

1% carbohydrates	in liver, blood, and muscles
4–6% minerals	in bones and teeth
10–15% fat	beneath the skin
15–20% protein	in all cells
60–70% water	in all cells

3.2   Nutrients

A proper diet is not determined by the foods we eat but by the nutrients these foods contain. Most foods contain a variety of nutrients, but very few contain all the necessary nutrients in optimal amounts. A varied and balanced diet contains all essential nutrients for good health (Table 3-2). Lack of certain nutrients for long periods of time can cause nutritional diseases. Conversely, too much food can cause obesity and related diseases.

Functions of Nutrients

Nutrients are substances found in foods. They are necessary to promote growth and maintenance of the human body and to supply energy (Table 3-3).

Table 3-2. Food components.

Provide Energy	Essential, but No Energy	Other
Carbohydrates	Water	Fiber
Fats	Minerals	Flavorings
Proteins	Vitamins	Aromatic oils
		Colorings
		Harmful substances

Table 3-3. The roles of nutrients in the body.

Function	Nutrients
Promote growth and maintenance	Proteins, minerals, water
Provide energy	Carbohydrates, fats, proteins
Regulate body processes	Vitamins
Transport nutrients	Water

3.3   Energy

All living creatures need energy to fuel their activities. Greater activity requires more energy. The human body gets its energy from food.

The *joule* (J) is the international unit for energy, effort, and heat; 1,000 joules equals 1 kilojoule (kJ). One joule is the amount of energy required to lift 102 grams 1 meter. One kilojoule is the amount of heat required to heat ¼ liter of water 1 degree Celsius. An older unit, the calorie (cal), is still commonly used in many places. The standard in the United States, called a calorie, is actually a kilocalorie (kcal). It is the amount of heat necessary to raise the temperature of 1 kilogram (1 liter) of water 1 degree Celsius. To convert, 1 kcal equals 4.2 kJ and 1kJ equals 0.24 kcal. Hereafter, *calorie* is used for kilocalorie.

Basal metabolism: The number of calories the body needs to sustain life for twenty-four hours, even if completely at rest, is referred to as basal metabolism. Basal processes are heartbeat, digestion, brain function, cell activity, maintenance of body temperature, and respiration. The rate at which the body uses energy just to exist is called the *basal metabolic rate* (BMR). The basal metabolic rate is influenced by age, gender, weight, health, and stress. The rule of thumb for calculating the BMR in kilojoules for twenty-four hours is:

Body weight times 100

To calculate the calories needed to sustain basal metabolism:

1. Convert your weight from pounds to kilograms: divide by 2.2.
2. Multiply kilograms by 1 for men and 0.9 for women.
3. Multiply by 24.

For example:

Male, 190 lb.:
$$86.4 \text{ kg} \times 1.0 = 86.4$$
$$\times 24 = 2{,}074 \text{ calories}$$

Female, 142 lb.:
$$64.5 \text{ kg} \times 0.9 = 58.1$$
$$\times 24 = 1{,}394 \text{ calories}$$

To calculate total daily caloric needs, determine the amount of calories used in twenty-four hours, based on your level of activity (See Table 3-4; rest equals 0). Add that to your basal metabolic rate. The total is the number of calories you need to consume to fuel your activities daily.

Different nutrients have different caloric values:

1 gram fat	9 cal (39 kJ)
1 gram protein	4 cal (17 kJ)
1 gram carbohydrates	4 cal (17 kJ)
1 gram alcohol	7 cal (30 kJ)

A person with average physical activity should get needed calories from the three basic nutrients in these proportions:

Proteins	12–15%
Fats	23–30%
Carbohydrates	55–60%

The body can burn calories for energy from all three nutrients interchangeably. However, it cannot use fats and carbohydrates to rebuild or maintain body cells because they do not contain *nitrogen*.

If energy output equals energy intake in the diet, a person's weight stays constant. If diet intake is higher, weight increases; if diet intake is lower, weight decreases. For every 3,500 calories (14,700 kJ) eaten in excess of energy output, the body stores 1 pound of fat.

Table 3-4. Calories used for different levels of activity (per hour).

Job	Male	Female
Light physical work	below 75 cal (315kJ)	below 60 cal (250kJ)
Moderate physical work	75–150 cal (315–630 kJ)	60–120 cal (250–500 kJ)
Heavy physical work	150–200 cal (630–840 kJ)	above 120 cal (500 kJ)
Very strenuous work	above 200 cal (840 kJ)	—

3.4 Carbohydrates, or Saccharides

Carbohydrates are the major components of plants. They are the earth's most abundant organic substance. Even though all carbohydrates are composed of the same chemical elements, their different structures determine taste and form.

Composition and Classification

Chemical Elements
- Carbon (C)
- Hydrogen (H)
- Oxygen (O)

Simple Carbohydrates, or Monosaccharides
The name is derived from the Greek word *monos*, which means "one." Monosaccharides are the building blocks of all carbohydrates.

- *Glucose*, also called *dextrose*, is found in fruits and honey.
- *Fructose*, the sweetest natural sugar, is found in fruits and honey.
- *Galactose* occurs only in the presence of lactose.

Double Sugars, or Disaccharides
The name is derived from the Greek word *di*, which means "two." Disaccharides are composed of two linked monosaccharides.

- *Sugar*, or *sucrose*, is the chemical name for cane sugar, beet sugar, and granulated sugar. It is found in fruits, sugar cane, and sugar beets.
- *Milk sugar*, or *lactose*, is found in milk and uncured cheeses (cottage cheese).

- *Malt sugar,* or *maltose,* is found in germinating grains and is produced in the beer-brewing process.

Complex Carbohydrates, or Polysaccharides

The name is derived from the Greek word *poly,* which means "many." Complex carbohydrates are composed of many monosaccharides (several hundred or thousand) linked together in long chains.

- *Starch* is found in grains, starchy vegetables (potatoes), and legumes.
- *Dextrin,* a shortened starch chain, is a product of digestion in the mouth or the application of heat to starch, for example in toast, roux, and the crusts of bread and baked goods.
- *Glycogen* is the only animal polysaccharide. The body stores glucose in the form of glycogen in the liver and muscles. Only glycogen from the liver can be converted to glucose and enter the bloodstream.
- *Fiber* is found only in plant foods and is not digestible.

Other polysaccharides are pectin, hemicellulose, chitin, and lignin.

Importance of Carbohydrates

Most people in the world rely on carbohydrates for the greatest proportion of their diet. Although the body can produce some carbohydrates, they must be included in the diet.

Functions: Important source of energy, 1 gram carbohydrates provides 4 cal (17 kJ); helps build cell membranes.

Contribution to energy needs: Carbohydrates should supply more than half of the body's energy (about 55 to 60 percent).

Daily requirement: The minimum amount should be 50 grams, or 2 ounces, the amount needed to supply the brain with glucose. Depending on activity level, the body needs 300 to 500 grams (4 to 6 grams per kilogram of body weight).

Deficiency: Can lead to metabolic disorders, especially ketosis, if the body must burn protein for fuel in the absence of carbohydrates.

Excess: The body stores extra carbohydrates in the liver and muscles in the form of glycogen (up to 400 grams, which provides glucose to the brain and energy to the muscles for about twelve to eighteen hours). Unused carbohydrates are converted to fat and stored in the body.

Recommended carbohydrate sources: From starchy foods, select whole-grain products, potatoes, winter squash, yams, and legumes. From sugar-containing foods, select fruits, vegetables, and fresh, uncured cheeses. Besides providing the body with fuel for energy, these foods provide valuable vitamins, minerals, and fiber.

Poor carbohydrate sources: Avoid such sugar-containing foods as sweets, chocolates, syrup, and soft drinks. Refined starchy foods such as white refined flour and white rice are nutritionally less desirable.

Metabolism of Carbohydrates

To use most carbohydrates, the body must disassemble them into simple building blocks, or monosaccharides. Only in this form can carbohydrates be absorbed and transported in the blood to perform their functions.

Digestion of Carbohydrates

Mouth: Starch is broken down through enzymes in saliva into dextrin and eventually into maltose.

Stomach: Enzymes from the saliva continue to act for a short time.

Small intestine: In the duodenum, polysaccharides are reduced to disaccharides and partially to monosaccharides with the assistance of enzymes from the pancreas. Digestion continues in the small intestine, where more enzymes break down carbohydrates into monosaccharides, which are absorbed by and

circulated through the bloodstream.

Dietary Fiber

Fiber is not digestible; however, its capacity to expand increases the volume of the digestive mass.

Function and Characteristics

- Dietary fiber stimulates peristaltic action of the digestive organs.
- It neutralizes excessive stomach acid.
- Fiber slows absorption of nutrients, causing a more constant blood sugar level and a sense of satiety, as foods remain longer in the stomach.
- Dietary fiber moves the chyme rapidly in the small intestine, thus preventing the formation of disease-causing by-products.
- It provides few calories even in large amounts of food.
- Undesirable by-products (harmful substances) and metabolic by-products such as bile and cholesterol are bound and eliminated.
- Dietary fiber (roughage) helps prevent constipation.

Recommended daily intake: 30 to 50 grams (1 to 2 ounces) of dietary fiber.

Good sources of dietary fiber: Cellulose and hemicellulose, found in plants, and pectin, found in the peels and seeds of fruits.

Food products with high fiber content: Whole-grain foods, vegetables, legumes, fruits, and potatoes.

Food products with low fiber content: Meat and meat products, fats and oils, refined flour products, white rice, and sugar.

Possible problems caused by a low fiber diet: Constipation, diseases of the digestive tract, metabolic disorders and circulation problems.

3.5   Lipids, or Fats

Plants manufacture lipids from carbohydrates. Animals and humans consume lipids (fats) in foods and convert excess calories to lipids to be stored in the body.

Structure of Lipids

Chemical Elements
- Carbon (C)
- Hydrogen (H)
- Oxygen (O)

Basic building blocks: Glycerol and fatty acids.

Classification of fatty acids: Fatty acids are classified by their degree of saturation. The degree of saturation is determined by how the carbon and hydrogen are bonded in the fat molecule. Those molecules without any double or triple bonds between elements are *saturated;* those with a single double or triple bond are *monounsaturated;* those with many double or triple bonds are polyunsaturated. Polyunsaturated and monounsaturated fatty acids help lower cholesterol in the bloodstream.

The human body can manufacture all fatty acids but two from fats, proteins, or carbohydrates. The exceptions are *linoleic acid* and *linolenic acid,* which must be provided in the diet and are therefore classified as *essential fatty acids.* Oils with large amounts of linoleic fatty acids are safflower oil, grape seed oil, sunflower seed oil, soybean oil, corn oil, canola oil, and wheat germ oil.

Composition of fats/lipids: Most lipids in foods are in the chemical form of triglycerides. Triglycerides form when one glycerol molecule bonds with three fatty acid molecules (usually different ones). During this process water is eliminated.

Glycerol is a constant in all lipids. It is the composition of the fatty acids that determines the characteristics of a fat or oil. Fatty acids differ in the length of their carbon chains and their saturation. Fats with shorter carbon chains and larger amounts of polyunsaturated fatty acids:

- have a lower melting point
- are more easily digested
- spoil rapidly if not protected from heat, oxygen, light, moisture, and microorganisms

Fats with long carbon chains and largre amounts of saturated fatty acids:

- have a higher melting point
- are more difficult to digest
- are more stable when exposed to heat, oxygen, light, moisture, and microorganisms

Importance of Lipids

Functions: In the body, lipids perform a number of functions:

- Energy source: 1 gram fat provides 9 cal (39 kJ). Energy storage: the body stores lipids beneath the skin, which can lead to obesity.
- Protection against injuries and cold temperatures.
- Transport medium for fat-soluble vitamins A, D, E, K, and beta carotene.
- Transport medium of linoleic acid, which is essential for cell formation and hormonal functions.
- Transport medium for flavor substances that stimulate digestion. They increase the taste of foods, many are fat-soluble substances.
- High satiety effect. Fat stays longest in the stomach (carbohydrates and proteins are digested first), causing a longer-lasting sense of fullness.

Contribution to energy needs: Fats should supply 25 to 30 percent of the daily calorie intake.

Daily requirement: 50 to 70 grams, or 1¾ to 2½ ounces, depending on level of physical activity.

Problems caused by a diet too high in fats: obesity, high blood cholesterol, high blood pressure, heart infarction, diseases of the joints, and lower back problems.

Lower fat consumption can be achieved by removing visible fat from meats and poultry, using small amounts of spreads (butter and margarine), choosing low-fat food preparation methods, and limiting the consumption of fatty foods (cold cuts, cream and high-fat cheeses, nuts, cream and butter sauces, mayonnaise, chocolates, cakes, and whipped-cream desserts).

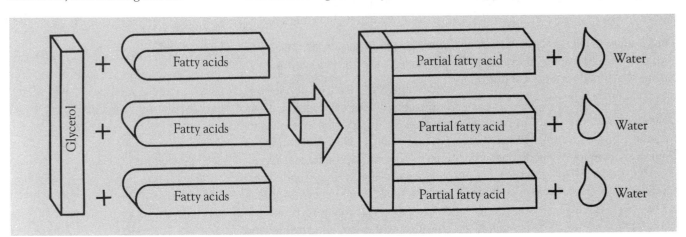

Formation of triglycerides

Table 3-5. Foods containing the Recommended Daily Allowance (300 mg) of cholesterol.

⅓ oz. (10 g) calf's brain	4¼ oz. (120 g) butter	10½ oz. (300 g) lard
⅔ oz. (17 g) egg yolk	4½ oz. (130 g) sweet breads	12¼ oz. (350 g) veal, pork, lamb
2¼ oz. (64 g) whole egg	5¼ oz. (150 g) lobster or oysters	or fish
2⅔ oz. (75 g) calf's liver	7 oz. (200 g) mussels	17½ oz. (500 g) poultry
3½ oz. (100 g) caviar	7¼ oz. (207 g) Emmentaler cheese	4.4 lb. (2 kg) cottage cheese
4 oz. (115 g) mayonnaise	8½ oz. (240 g) shrimp or beef	68 fl. oz. (2 liter) whole milk

Metabolism of Lipids

A phenomenon of fat digestion is the incomplete separation of the fatty acids from the glycerol. After digestion, besides the basic building blocks—glycerol and fatty acids—partial fats, such as mono- and diglycerides, are also left. Sometimes the pancreatic enzymes leave the middle fatty acid attached to the glycerol to form mono- and diglycerides that are not digested.

Digestion of Fats/Lipids

Mouth: No digestion of lipids.

Stomach: Some enzyme activity on emulsified lipids such as fats found in milk and eggs.

Small intestine: In the duodenum, bile salts from the gall bladder emulsify lipids into minute fat globules so that enzymes from the pancreas can break down the triglycerides into glycerol, fatty acids, and mono- and diglycerides. Enzyme activity of the small intestine further breaks down the fat globules. The free glycerol and short-chain fatty acids are water-soluble and readily absorbed. Fatty acids and some monoglycerides are covered with chylomicron, a type of lipoprotein, to make them water-soluble for transport via the portal vein in the blood and lymph.

Fatlike Substances, or Phospholipids

Phospholipids are a part of cell membranes and play a role in the movement of lipids in and out of the cell structure. They do not provide energy.

Cholesterol

Sources: Cholesterol is found in all animal fats. It is in the blood because lipoproteins are a part of the body's transportation system. Two types of cholesterol are found in the bloodstream, low-density lipoproteins (LDL) and high-density lipoproteins (HDL). HDL are believed to return unused cholesterol to the liver for disposal. LDL seem to be implicated in the deposit of unused cholesterol on the inner walls of blood vessels.

Function: Participates in cell formation (especially brain and nerve cells), is a part of bile acids, and forms sex hormones.

Daily intake limit: 300 milligrams; however, average daily consumption is closer to 600 milligrams. Cholesterol can be manufactured by the body. Table 3-5 indicates the quantity of common foods that provides 300 milligrams of cholesterol.

Problems resulting from too much LDL cholesterol in the blood: Increased risk of heart and circulatory diseases.

To influence blood cholesterol levels through diet:

- Maintain ideal body weight
- Reduce fat consumption (ideally, one third animal fats and two thirds vegetable fats)
- Consume mostly polyunsaturated fatty acids to lower blood cholesterol
- Eat high-fiber diets, which lowers blood cholesterol

Lecithin

Lecithin is found naturally in many foods. In addition, it is an ingredient in many commercially prepared foods. Lecithin is also manufactured by the human body.

Sources: Egg yolk, brain, bone marrow, fish roe, milk, soy beans, and rape-seed oil.

Functions: Assists in the building of cell membranes, nerves, bone marrow, and blood cells. It is sometimes presribed as a restorative. Because lecithin has fat- and water-soluble properties, it functions as an emulsifier in mayonnaise, hollandaise, chocolates, margarine, and baked goods.

Other fatlike substances are the pro-vitamins *carotene* and *ergosterol* and *volatile oils.*

3.6 Protein, or Amino Acids

Plants are capable of manufacturing protein from nonorganic materials; humans and animals must obtain proteins from foods. Protein is an essential nutrient.

Structure of protein

Chemical elements
- Carbon (C)
- Hydrogen (H)
- Oxygen (O)
- Nitrogen (N)

- frequently also sulfur (S) and phosphorus (P)

The basic building blocks of all proteins are the amino acids. Twenty kinds of amino acids have been identified in foods. Eight amino acids are essential for adults, and ten for children, because the body cannot synthesize these amino acids. Long strands of amino acids bond chemically to form protein. During this process the amino acids release hydrogen and oxygen, which form water. Some proteins can form strands that contain a thousand amino acids.

Importance of Proteins

Proteins are the most valuable of the nutrients because only they contain nitrogen; they cannot be replaced by any other nutrient. No life can exist without protein.

Sources: Proteins are in all naturally occurring foods in varying amounts. Animal proteins are plentiful in meats and meat products, while plant proteins are present in greater amounts in legumes, nuts, and whole grains.

When animal and plant proteins are correctly combined in the diet, they complement each other and provide better nourishment. The quality of protein is determined by the number of essential amino acids they contain. Proteins that contain all eight essential amino acids are called *complete proteins*. All animal proteins are complete. Most plant proteins are incomplete (soybeans are an exception) and must be eaten either with an animal protein or a complementary plant protein that supplies the missing amino acids.

Functions: Proteins are vital for growing children to build new tissue. Proteins are essential to all life and are present in all cells. They form enzymes, hormones, and even antibodies that fight illness. They participate in brain function, and they determine hereditary factors in the cell. Proteins are also needed to help repair and replace injured or worn-out cells. Because cells have only a limited life span, the body constantly breaks down, rebuilds, and re-forms protein to produce new cells. Consequently, the body needs adequate daily amounts of protein.

Daily requirement: 50 to 70 grams (approximately 0.8 grams per kilogram or 0.36 grams per pound of body weight), depending on age, size, height, and type of protein.

Contribution to energy needs: Proteins should constitute 12 to 15 percent of the daily caloric intake. Proteins can contribute energy: 1 gram of protein provides 4 calories (17 kJ) of energy.

Deficiency: Can lead to metabolic disorders, reduce performance (physical and mental), cause weight loss, and weaken the immune system and thus increase susceptibility to disease. In industrial countries protein is not in short supply.

Excess: The body does not store proteins. Daily excess is converted to glucose and burned for energy or stored as fat.

Metabolism of Protein

Proteins can be metabolized only in their basic form, as amino acids.

Digestion of Protein

Mouth: No digestion of proteins.

Stomach: Strong stomach acid expands and denatures the protein. The stomach enzymes then break the protein down into large pieces (peptides).

Small intestine: In the duodenum, enzymes from the pancreas complete the breakdown of the peptides to smaller amino acid strands. Enzymes in the lining of the small intestine continue to break down proteins into small fragments and then into free amino acids. These then cross the capillary walls of the intestine and enter the bloodstream.

3.7 Water

Water is the foundation of all life. For the body to function properly, the water level in the body must remain constant. If the water level drops, the sensation of thirst reminds us to drink. The body stores only small amounts of water. Deprived of water, the body can generally function for only three days. Loss of 10 percent of the body's normal water content is life threatening; loss of 20 percent is fatal. All metabolic processes occur in the presence of water. Water is an essential nutrient.

Composition: Water molecules consist of two hydrogen atoms and one oxygen atom: H_2O.

Daily Requirement: About 3 quarts (2.5 liter), depending on age, climate, body mass, physical activity, and salt content of the diet (each gram of salt binds about 1 deciliter water). Tables 3-6 and 3-7 show how the body obtains and releases water.

Table 3-6. Sources of water.

Beverages	40 fl. oz. (1.2 liter) per day
Foods containing water	34 fl. oz. (1.0 liter) per day
Water from oxidation	10 fl. oz. (0.3 liter) per day
	84 fl. oz. (2.5 liter) per day

Table 3-7. Excretion.

Urine (kidneys)	47 fl. oz. (1.4 liter) per day
Breath (lungs)	17 fl. oz. (0.5 liter) per day
Sweat (skin)	17 fl. oz. (0.5 liter) per day
Feces (colon)	3 fl. oz. (0.1 liter) per day
	84 fl. oz. (2.5 liter) per day

Function

Building material: About 50 to 70 percent of the body's weight is water. Blood is 90 percent water. Cells both contain water and are surrounded by water. Fluids are constantly exchanged between the interior and exterior of cells to maintain water balance; this exchange is accomplished with the help of minerals.

Solvent: Water dissolves nutrients, liquefies the blood, lubricates the joints, and dissolves waste materials.

Transport medium: Water transports nutrients to the digestive tracts; dissolved nutrients, hormones, and antibodies to the cells; and wastes to the kidneys, bladder, and colon.

Temperature regulation: Water emerges as sweat through the pores of the skin, which evaporates and cools the body's surface. Salts make up about 0.1 to 1.35 percent of sweat. Hence, sweating reduces not only the amount of water but also the amount of salts in the body. The body recovers these salts through a balanced, lightly salted diet. Only under unusual conditions is it necessary to replenish salts with salty liquids.

3.8 Catalysts and Biological Agents

If left unregulated, the processes of a cell could run down in seconds or minutes. They must be regulated and slowed, or life would end after a few hours. These processes are regulated with the help of catalysts (micronutrients) and biological agents. They activate, regulate, and precisely calibrate the cell's processes.

Inorganic Catalysts

Minerals must be ingested from foods and water.

Organic Catalysts

Vitamins must be ingested from foods.

Enzymes are manufactured by the body.

Hormones are manufactured by the body.

3.8.1 Minerals

Source: Minerals are vitally important inorganic substances found in foods, and they are essential nutrients for humans. They are found in soil and water and are absorbed by plants. The body gets its minerals either directly from plant foods or indirectly through the meat and milk of animals.

Classification: Minerals present in the body in large quantities are called *major minerals or elements.* The essential major minerals are calcium, phosphorus, sodium, chloride, potassium, magnesium, and sulfate.

Minerals present in minute quantities are called *trace minerals or elements.* Knowledge about trace minerals is constantly evolving. The essential trace minerals are iron, iodine, fluorine, zinc, copper, cobalt, chromium, silicon, vanadium, nickel, and tin.

Functions: The body needs minerals as building components. When dissolved in body fluids, they function as *catalysts.* They act:

- as part of the body's structure
- as components of hormones and enzymes
- to regulate metabolic activities
- to assist in nerve functions
- to maintain water balance
- to maintain pH balance

Problems: Either deficiency or excess can cause such problems as kidney disease, fever, vomiting, diarrhea, cramps, fatigue, blood-clotting problems, bone and joint diseases, water imbalance, and disturbances in metabolism.

Daily Requirement: 7 to 10 grams of all minerals combined (see individual listings of each mineral for recommended daily allowance of each). During illness or pregnancy, the body requires greater amounts of minerals. Women need to include enough iron in their diets to compensate for that lost during menstruation. Sweat and excretion constantly reduce minerals in the body. Therefore, it is necessary to replenish them daily. It is the *proper balance* of all minerals that is important, not the quantity of an individual mineral. A varied, balanced diet ensures the body's mineral needs are supplied.

Excellent mineral sources: Fruit, potatoes, vegetables, milk, dairy products, whole-grain products, eggs, fish, organ meats, meats, fruit and vegetable juices, and mineral water.

Foods with little or no mineral content: Sugar, pure fats, cornstarch, and refined flour products and white rice that have not been enriched with iron during processing.

Characteristic property: Water-soluble.

Preventive measures: To reduce mineral losses during food preparation:

- Do not permit foods to soak in water for long periods of time.
- Wash fruit and vegetables briefly before cutting them.
- Cover prepped vegetables with plastic wrap, not with water.
- Dip peeled potatoes in ascorbic acid solution instead of soaking them in water.
- Blanch only if necessary; for example, to prevent color loss in cut green vegetables or to remove bitterness.
- Choose mineral-sparing preparation methods, such as braising, steaming, and glazing.
- Use the cooking liquids of vegetables in other preparations.
- Peel fruits and vegetable very thinly or not at all. Many minerals are located just beneath the skin.

Calcium (Ca)

A variety of illnesses, such as rickets, osteomalacia (adult rickets), osteoporosis (bone thinning), and periodontal disease are associated with deficiencies of calcium. Milk and milk products are the richest sources of calcium. Certain other foods make contributions to the daily diet: leafy green vegetables, fruit, eggs, canned fish, and shellfish. Drinking water also contains some calcium, but this varies with the water supply. The allowance of 800 milligrams per day ensures an adequate supply of calcium in the diet for adult men and women. Additional dietary calcium should be consumed during pregnancy and lactation.

Iron (Fe)

Iron-deficiency anemia is fundamentally a dietary disease. This is probably the most widespread form of malnutrition in the United States. In iron-deficiency anemia, lack of iron produces defective red blood cells and results in faulty body functioning. Good to excellent sources of iron are liver and other organ meats, lean meat, egg yolk, leafy green vegetables, dried fruit, whole-grain and enriched cereal products, legumes, shellfish, and molasses. Adult males have an allowance of 10 milligrams of iron per day. The allowance for adult females during lactation is 18 milligrams; during pregnancy the allowance exceeds 18 milligrams.

Iodine (I)

Iodine is necessary for the proper functioning of the thyroid gland and regulation of basal metabolism. Lack of iodine results in enlargement of the thyroid glands and a condition known as a simple goiter. Cretinism, caused by an iodine deficiency at birth or during infancy, is characterized by physical and mental retardation. An increased incidence of thyroid cancer is associated with iodine deficiency. Food and water sources of iodine are variable depending upon the soil content and composition of animal feed. Soil in coastal regions is generally richer in iodine than soil in inland areas. Seafood is the only excellent, consistent source of the mineral. Therefore, the regular use of iodized salt in food preparation and at the table is a better safeguard to assure nutrient adequacy. The daily requirement for adults is 50 to 75 micrograms. Growing children, as well as pregnant and lactating women, need more. Iodine may be restricted if certain skin conditions, such as acne, exist.

Phosphorus (P)

A phosphorus deficiency does not result in the failure of vital functions. Nevertheless, phosphorus assumes many widely varying roles, giving rigidity to the bones and teeth; serving as an essential component in many metabolic processes, including brain and nerve metabolism, particularly in regulatory processes; and being a constituent of substances that control heredity. Phosphorus is present in many foods, especially high-protein foods. Good to excellent sources are meat, milk and milk products, eggs, legumes, nuts, and whole-grain bread and cereal products. The recommended dietary allowance of 800 milligrams for adults has been established. Higher levels are set for pregnancy and lactation.

Magnesium (Mg)

Magnesium deficiency is likely to occur in association with a number of diseases or stressful conditions when food intake and/or absorption is altered. Since magnesium is necessary for regulatory functions, such as transmission of nerve impulses and muscle contractions, a deficiency state produces neuromuscular dysfunction. Major food sources of magnesium are dairy products, whole-grain breads and cereals, dry beans and peas, soybeans, nuts, and green leafy vegetables. Adults have an allowance of 300 to 350 milligrams magnesium per day. Allowances are higher for pregnancy and lactation.

Sodium (Na)

Sodium deficiency in humans is rare, but excessive retention or excretion usually related to disease or extreme environmental conditions leads to sodium imbalance. The principal source of sodium is table salt, sodium chloride, and many sodium compounds are used in food processing and preparation. Animal foods, specifically milk, eggs, meat, poultry, and fish, are natural sources.

Potassium (K)

Potassium regulates osmotic pressure in the body cells, activates enzymes, and plays a role in the transmission of nerve impulses. Potassium is also necessary for muscle functions. It is available from vegetables and fruits, especially peaches, apricots, and oranges, as well as from meat. A balanced diet supplies the daily requirement of 400 milligrams.

Fluorine (F)

Fluoride, a compound that contains fluorine, is necessary for healthy bones and teeth and for the prevention of cavities. The recommended daily allowance is 1 to 2 milligrams. Fluoride is frequently added to the water supply in the United States. Fluoride supplement tablets are also available.

3.8.2 Vitamins

Vitamins are essential organic compounds that must be included in the diet because the body produces them in insufficient quantities or not at all.

Functions: Like minerals, vitamins are catalysts that work in conjunction with enzymes and hormones. Each vitamin performs specific functions and cannot be replaced by another. Vitamins promote and maintain health and vitality. They:

- are involved in metabolic processes
- are involved in growth and reproduction
- increase immunity to diseases.

Daily Requirement: Daily vitamin requirements vary (approximately 100 mg of all vitamins combined are generally recommended). Vitamin requirements are higher for children, the elderly, pregnant and lactating women, world-class athletes, smokers, alcoholics, and those doing heavy labor, as well as during illness. Vitamins are medicinal in character and should be treated as such (consume only the recommended dosage).

Major vitamin sources: Fruits, vegetables, whole-grain foods, potatoes, milk, dairy products, fish, eggs, organ meats and meat.

Vitamin deficiencies: Can be caused by a limited diet, incorrect storage of foods, preparation methods that destroy vitamins in foods, loss during the refining of foods such as flour, rice, and sugar, absorption difficulties (diseases of the stomach, duodenum, liver, or gall bladder), and use of medications that inhibit the absorption of vitamins. The consequences of vitamin deficiencies are poor health, low performance, loss of concentration and appetite, and susceptibility to infectious diseases. Certain specific diseases are the direct consequence of a deficiency of a particular vitamin. These are mentioned in the discussion of individual vitamins that follows. A varied, balanced diet should provide enough vitamins for human needs.

Classification: Vitamins are classified by their solubility:

- *Water-soluble vitamins,* which cannot be stored by the body, are the B-complex vitamins—B$_1$ (thiamine), B$_2$ (riboflavin), B$_6$ (pyridoxine), B$_{12}$ (cobalamin)—nicotinic acid, pantothenic acid, biotin, folacin (folic acid), and vitamin C (ascorbic acid).
- *Fat-soluble vitamins,* which can be stored by the body, are vitamins A, D, E, and K.

Provitamins: Some compounds in foods are precursors to vitamins. They are changed by the body into active vitamins. The provitamins include:

- *Carotene:* becomes Vitamin A. A-carotenoid, orange-yellow in color, is present in large quantities in carrots, deep orange fruits, and dark green vegetables.
- *Ergosterol:* becomes Vitamin D.
- *Cholesterol:* becomes Vitamin D.

The body stores fatlike ergosterol and cholesterol just under the skin and converts them, with the help of the sun's ultraviolet rays, into vitamin D.

Vitamins can be destroyed by water, heat, oxygen, light, ultraviolet rays, copper, iron, and alkalis. Therefore:

- Do not store foods in water for long periods.
- Wash foods briefly before cutting.
- Blanch only when absolutely necessary.
- Incorporate vegetable cooking liquids into food products.
- Prepare foods with little or no water.
- Cook foods (especially vegetables) only until done.
- Keep potatoes, vegetables, and vegetable soup hot only for short periods (bain-marie).
- Immediately chill fruits and vegetables prepped for *mise en place*.
- Improve reheated vegetables nutritionally with the addition of fresh herbs.
- Offer fresh produce (fruits, salads, juices) on the menu.
- Do not leave chopped and minced vegetables at room temperatures for long periods.
- Cover foods with a lid, and stir them rarely during cooking.
- Store foods in dark, cool places for short periods.
- Avoid contact with copper and iron.
- Do not add bicarbonate of soda to cooking water.

Vitamin A

Vitamin A deficiency results initially in night blindness or diminished vision in dim light, and later, in eye diseases, skin changes, reduced rate of growth, and a lowering of resistance to infection. Vitamin A is fat soluble and fairly heat stable but is sensitive to light and air. It is found only in animal foods, mainly fish liver oils, milk, whole milk cheese, fortified margarine, butter, liver, and egg yolks. However, in many vegetable products there is a provitamin, carotene, which easily converts into vitamin A in the liver. Therefore, plant foods with carotene are considered vitamin A sources. All leafy green vegetables, green stem vegetables (asparagus and broccoli), yellow vegetables (carrots, sweet potatoes, pumpkin, and winter squash), tomatoes, and yellow fruits (apricots, peaches, and cantaloupe) are rich in vitamin A. White and red cabbage, celery ribs, and white root and bulb vegetables have a low vitamin A content. The daily recommended allowance for adults is 5,000 International Units.

Vitamin D

Infants, growing children, adolescents, pregnant and lactating women, and persons who have limited exposure to sunlight are most susceptible to some form of vitamin D deficiency. It is characterized by such problems as insufficient or delayed calcification of the bones and teeth (rickets), slow rate of growth, predisposition to dental caries, and muscle twitchings and cramps.

Vitamin D is fat soluble and resistant to heat. In the human skin, a substance is present that is converted into vitamin D by the action of the ultraviolet light of sunshine. For this reason, it is not absolutely necessary for the total vitamin D allowance to be contained in the food consumed. Practically the only natural vitamin D sources are milk, cream, fatty fish, fish liver oils, liver, and egg yolk.

The recommended daily allowance of vitamin D for infants, children, adolescents, and pregnant and lactating women is 400 International

Units. Although no recommended allowance is indicated for adults, a dietary intake of 400 International Units for healthy adults of all ages will not produce risk.

Thiamine (Vitamin B1)

Chronic deficiency of thiamine leads to serious disorders and damage to the nervous system and heart—beriberi disease, which is prevalent in the Orient. A mild deficiency is characterized by such symptoms as loss of appetite, nausea, apathy, fatigue, dizziness, and numbness. Thiamine-deficiency states are found in the alcoholic. Thiamine is water soluble and therefore is often lost in food processing, preparation, and cooking. Preparation and cooking losses depend upon preparation methods, such as soaking, amount of water used in cooking and retained after cooking, length of cooking period, and amount of surface area exposed. Thiamine is extremely sensitive in an alkaline medium. The addition of baking soda or bicarbonate to a food very quickly destroys the vitamin. Thiamine is comparatively heat-resistant in dry form and in solution in an acid medium. Little loss occurs in cooking procedures such as baking bread and cooking breakfast cereal, because the water used in preparation is absorbed.

Thiamine is naturally present in an exceptionally wide range of foods, such as whole-grain and enriched bread, cereal, and flour products; lean meat, especially pork, organ meats, and sausage; eggs; green leafy vegetables and legumes; and nuts. A daily allowance for adults of 0.5 milligrams per 1,000 calories is recommended. Older persons should maintain an intake of 1 milligram per day, even if the intake is less than 2,000 calories daily. Requirements increase during pregnancy and lactation.

Riboflavin (Vitamin B2)

A severe riboflavin deficiency disease in human beings has not been identified. However, lack of riboflavin does produce symptoms involving the skin and mucous membranes, especially the mouth and eyes. Typical eye changes include inflamed eyelids, itching and watering, inability to focus properly, sensitivity to light, and rapid tiring.

Like thiamine, riboflavin is water soluble and reasonably heat resistant for short periods, but it is very susceptible to light. Small losses may occur in food processing and preparation. In general, when cooked in liquid form, precautions taken to conserve thiamine will protect riboflavin. Riboflavin is found in significant quantities in organ meats, such as liver and kidney, lean meat, milk, cheese, eggs, whole-grain bread and cereal products, and leafy green vegetables.

Riboflavin allowances are computed as 0.6 milligrams per 1,000 calories for people of all ages. Recommended levels increase during pregnancy and lactation.

Niacin

Pellagra, the deficiency disease caused by lack of niacin, is characterized by changes in the skin and mucous membranes, diarrhea, and mental disturbances. Pellagra is practically nonexistent today in the United States. However, incidence of the disease has been reported among chronic alcoholics and is secondary to other illnesses.

Niacin is the most stable of the vitamin B group, but because it is water soluble, some may be lost in cooking water and meat drippings. Both animal and plant foods are good sources of both niacin and the dietary factor tryptophan that converts to niacin. The chief sources are liver, lean meat, poultry, fish, milk, eggs, whole-grain and enriched bread and cereal products, legumes, and nuts.

The niacin allowance recommended for adults is 6.6 milligrams per 1,000 calories, with a minimum of 13 milligrams regardless of caloric intake. Increases are recommended for pregnancy and lactation.

Vitamin B12

Lack of vitamin B_{12} is seldom seen in the United States because of the high protein diet consumed. However, individuals on borderline diets, such as food fad diets, and vegetarians may show signs of lack of this vitamin. Nervous disorders and changes in mucous membranes may result. An absorption defect in some persons may cause pernicious anemia, a blood disease. Other illness may decrease vitamin B_{12} absorption and produce vitamin deficiency.

Vitamin B_{12} is water soluble and could be washed out of food that is soaked too long. It is not especially sensitive to heat or air, but does lose its potency on exposure to light, strong acids, and alkali.

Vitamin B_{12} is present in large quantities in liver and kidneys. Meat, fish, eggs, milk, and cheese also supply good amounts. There is very little, if any, of the vitamin in vegetable foods. The recommended daily dietary allowance for this vitamin is 3 micrograms for adolescents and normal adults. Four micrograms per day is the recommended allowance for pregnant and lactating women.

Ascorbic Acid (Vitamin C)

The classic illness that results from deficiency of vitamin C is scurvy. Lack of ascorbic acid results in abnormalities in the supporting or intercellular tissues, which could result in hemorrhage, bleeding gums, malformed and weak bones, degeneration of muscle fibers, and anemia. Ascorbic-acid deficiency is a factor involved in reduced resistance to infection and retarded wound healing. Mild deficiency produces vague symptoms, such as weakness, irritability, weight loss, and pain in muscles or joints. Ascorbic acid is water soluble and chemically unstable. Therefore, undue exposure to oxygen, alkali, copper and iron (copper utensils and carbon-steel knives), and prolonged cooking at high temperatures accelerate the rate of vitamin loss. If vegetables are finely cut up or chopped, ascorbic acid is very quickly destroyed by exposure to oxygen (oxidation) and light. If potatoes are cooked after being peeled, more ascorbic acid and B vitamins are lost than when cooked in the jackets. Baking soda also reduces the ascorbic-acid level if added to green vegetables. Proper preparation and cooking methods, such as short soaking and cooking times, moderate heat exposure, and minimum holding periods, will reduce losses of all water-soluble vitamins. Consumption of raw fruits and vegetables helps ensure adequate daily vitamin intake.

Ascorbic acid is present in fair to good quantities in potatoes, vegetables, and fruits. The largest amounts are found in citrus fruits, cantaloupe, guavas, pineapple, rose hips, strawberries, broccoli, Brussels sprouts, cabbage, green peppers, kale, spinach, tomatoes, and turnips. In nearly all cases, dried products contain no ascorbic acid. Milk and meat are practically devoid of the vitamin.

An allowance of 45 milligrams per day is recommended as an adequate supply for health in normal adults. An increased intake is recommended during pregnancy and lactation and may be appropriate during periods of continued stress or drug therapy.

3.8.3 Enzymes

Enzymes are catalysts that interact with other substances and make metabolism possible. They control the construction and destruction of various substances in the body. Enzymes are complex proteins that speed up chemical changes without being changed themselves. They are particularly important in the digestion of food.

Functions: Over two thousand different enzymes have been identified in the human body. Such large numbers are necessary to regulate the body's complex metabolic processes. Each enzyme performs only one specific function. A catalytic reaction occurs when the enzyme bonds with another substance, such as a hormone, mineral, or vitamin.

Origin: Enzymes are not only essential for human metabolism, but they are also necessary to regulate the life processes of animals, plants, and microorganisms. Enzymes are present in all unprocessed foods. They continue to function outside the living cell.

Conditions for enzyme activity: To function properly, enzymes need:

- *Warmth:* from 50°F to 120°F (10°C to 50°C). At lower temperatures, enzyme activity slows down. Above 140°F (60°C), enzyme activity stops, because the protein in the enzymes becomes denatured.
- *Moisture:* free, available water.
- A specific *pH value*.

Regulating enzyme activity: Enzyme activity constantly changes food. Enzyme activity can be encouraged to advantage by:

- providing appropriate temperatures (warmth)
- providing enough moisture (for example, in the production of yeast dough, wine fermentation, and the ripening of cheeses and fruits)

Enzyme activity can also be stopped to advantage by:

- Lowering temperatures (storage in refrigerators and freezers).
- Removing moisture (drying, sun-drying, and freeze-drying).

- Destroying with heat (blanching before freezing, or cooking fresh pineapple and kiwi fruit before adding to gelatin).
- Adding acids (adding lemon juice or ascorbic acid to freshly peeled artichoke bottoms, salsify, celeriac, white mushrooms, apples, and potatoes).
- Reducing freely available water. Some substances (salt, sugar, fat, milk proteins) bind available moisture in foods to which they have been added (for example, a yeast dough high in fat will not rise well; a yeast dough without salt will ferment rapidly, causing large uneven holes in the baked product).

3.8.4 Hormones

Hormones are biological agents with many different chemical configurations. They act as chemical messengers and specifically regulate growth, metabolism, and reproduction.

Origin and function: Hormones, which are produced by different glands in the body, are released into the bloodstream to reach specific organs, where they regulate the organ's functions. The brain is the largest and most influential gland. Hormones and enzymes work closely together.

An example of a hormone is insulin. Insulin, which is produced by the pancreas, helps regulate the level of glucose in the blood. If too much insulin is produced, a person has hypoglycemia, which causes the level of glucose in the blood to drop and can result in cramps and fatigue. If too little insulin is produced, the blood glucose level rises; this is diabetes, which has numerous associated symptoms and complications.

3.9   Flavor Substances and Taste Agents (Stimulants)

Source: These compounds are found in almost all foods. Mixtures of various substances (volatile oils, acids, bitters, tannins), they are found in minute quantities in foods, herbs, spices, and seasonings. They are also produced by various preparation methods (grilling, deep-frying, baking, roasting, gratinating).

Function: Flavor substances and taste agents have no nutritive value, but they are extremely important to a healthy diet. They stimulate the appetite, the digestive glands, and consequently, the metabolic process. A flavorful, tasty dish not only pleases the diner but also assists in digestion and causes a sense of well-being. A bland, tasteless meal will depress the appetite, be eaten with reluctance, and cause distress to the digestive system.

3.10   Metabolism

Metabolism is the sum total of all chemical reactions that occur in a living cell. Without metabolic activity, life is not possible. Metabolic activity encompasses:

- Ingestion of oxygen, food, and water
- Digestion
- Intermediary metabolism, which changes and converts nutrients in the cell into components the body can use (to promote growth and replace dead cells) and to produce energy (to maintain body functions and provide strength to work)
- Elimination and excretion of undigestible food (feces) and waste products produced by the intermediary metabolism (water, carbon dioxide, and urine)

3.10.1   The Digestive System

Digestion is the process by which food is broken down in the gastrointestinal tract. Nutrients are absorbed into the bloodstream, and waste matter is eliminated or excreted. Digestive functions physically break down food into smaller particles and chemically make them soluble, so that they can be absorbed in the small intestine and reach the lymph or blood. Digestive glands produce approximately 2 gallons (8 liters) of digestive juices daily.

The Digestive Organs and Their Functions

The Senses

Although the senses are not digestive organs, they do affect digestion. They perceive and react to foods and, through the nervous system, stimulate the digestive juices.

Vision: "We eat with our eyes." The mere appearance of a dish can stimulate the appetite and causes one to be hungry.

Taste: Located mostly on the tongue, taste buds sense food flavors. Distinct taste sensations are sweet, sour, salty, and bitter. Taste buds also help sense hot and cold.

Smell: Nerves in the lining of the nose signal their impressions to the brain. Pleasant aromas stimulate the digestive glands to produce digestive juices; nasty smells cause them to tighten. Smell also influences taste.

Mouth
- The teeth mechanically break down food and grind it into small pieces.
- The tongue, with the help of saliva, mixes it further.
- Carbohydrate digestion starts.

Esophagus
- Through swallowing, the mixture moves down this tube to the stomach.

Stomach
- Hydrochloric acid in the stomach denatures proteins and kills most bacteria.

- Enzymes and hydrochloric acid break apart the complex protein molecules and start the digestion of protein.
- Partial digestion of fats in milk and eggs begins.
- The pylorus (pyloric sphincter), a circular muscle at the lower end of the stomach, ejects very small amounts of the food mixture into the small intestine.

Small Intestine

This organ is about 20 feet long but is smaller in diameter than the colon. Most digestion and absorption occurs here.

- *Duodenum: Bile*, stored in the gallbladder, is dispatched as needed to the small intestine. Bile emulsifies the fats present and activates enzymes to break down the fats into fatty acids. The *pancreas* secretes its enzymes, which help break down the three major nutrients. In addition, the pancreas sends bicarbonate to change the acidic chyme into an alkaline mixture.
- *Rest of small intestine:* Pancreatic and intestinal enzymes complete the breakdown of fats, carbohydrates, and proteins. The components of these nutrients are absorbed through the intestinal villi into the lymph system and bloodstream. The blood delivers all newly digested nutrients to the liver. The liver processes, controls, and detoxifies all materials in the circulatory system.

Colon

- The colon reabsorbs and recycles water, causing the contents of the intestine to become a paste.
- The chyme decomposes with the help of beneficial intestinal bacteria.
- Feces are stored in the rectum before elimination from the bowel.

The contents of the intestinal tract are moved by muscular contraction in the wall of the intestines. This muscular contraction is called peristalsis. Dietary fiber plays an important role in assisting peristaltic action.

3.10.2 Intermediary Metabolism

All the changes and conversions that nutrients undergo in the body's cells are referred to as intermediary metabolism. These chemical processes are activated and regulated with the help of hormones and enzymes. Metabolism consists of two processes: building substances (*anabolism*) and breaking them down for energy (*catabolism*).

Anabolism, or Constructive Metabolism

All body substances must be renewed over time. The most important building blocks are the proteins, more precisely the amino acids. Amino acids are absorbed by the blood and transported to the liver, where they are synthesized into the different amino acids the body needs. The body can store only very limited amounts and delivers them via the blood to the cells. A cell converts them into necessary proteins to rebuild itself according to instructions in its genetic code.

Catabolism, or Destructive Metabolism

Glucose is absorbed into the bloodstream and delivered to the tissues or the liver. The blood sugar level is normally 70 to 100 milligrams per 100 milliliters of blood. Insulin, a hormone from the pancreas, converts glucose to glycogen, a polysaccharide, which can be stored in the liver and the muscles.

When quick energy is needed, the hormone adrenaline (also called epinephrine) causes immediate release of large amounts of glucose into the bloodstream to be used by all body cells.

In the cell, the glucose molecules are split in half and release energy. At this point the split halves can rejoin as glucose; however, if further broken apart with the help of oxygen (oxidized), the resulting small fragments can never become glucose. The oxygen combines with the carbon and hydrogen of the glucose to form carbon dioxide and water. During oxidation more energy is released, to be used or stored.

Fats and proteins can also be converted to provide energy. The process is similar to that for glucose. Carbon dioxide and water are the by-products. Proteins also release ammonia, which must be removed with the help of the liver and eliminated by the kidneys in the urine.

3.11 Harmful Substances in Foods

Unfortunately, humans ingest not only essential nutrients with foods but also harmful substances. These can be introduced in the following ways:

- Some toxins occur naturally, for example, nitrate, oxalic acid, solanine, and arsenic.
- Some preparation methods cause harmful substances to form, for example, benzine pyrense, nitrites, nitrosamines, epoxides, and peroxides.
- Long and incorrect storage allows toxic substances to form.
- Spoilage causes toxic substances to form, for example, aflatoxins.
- Harmful substances can be absorbed by animals and plants while they are alive, such as fertilizers, insecticides, hormones, antibiotics, and heavy metals, which are ingested when the animal or plant is eaten.
- Harmful additives are introduced during food processing, for example, carcinogenic preservatives and food colorings.

3.12 Principles for a Nutritious Diet

A good diet is a healthy diet, with foods that are nutritionally balanced, well prepared, and tasty.

Eat Regular, Balanced Meals

- Consume only the number of calories the body needs to function.
- Balance foods according to dietary guidelines (12 to 15 percent protein, 25 to 30 percent fats, and 55 to 60 percent carbohydrates).
- Drink plenty of liquids.

Eat a Variety of Foods

Include a large variety of foods to ensure that all essential nutrients are consumed for optimal physical wellness.

- Select half the protein foods from plant sources and the other half from animal sources.
- Choose complex carbohydrates, especially whole-grain products, potatoes, and legumes.

Eat Whole-grain Products and Fresh Fruits and Vegetables Daily

These foods are exceptionally high in vitamins, minerals, and dietary fiber. Fresh, uncooked fruit and vegetable salads or juices should be offered on the menu.

Eat Small, Frequent Meals

Eating three meals a day stresses the digestive organs, causes fluctuating blood sugar levels, and can cause hunger pains, loss of concentration, and lower productivity. Five or six small meals spaced throughout the day keeps blood sugar levels even, causes a general sense of well-being, prevents fatigue, and reduces the chance of storing excess fat.

Use Salt Sparingly

Consuming large amounts of salt causes excessive water retention, contributes to high blood pressure, increases the risk of cardiovascular diseases, and causes unnatural thirstiness. Too much salt stresses the kidneys.

Use Fats in Moderation

Fat is a concentrated energy source. The body stores it for emergency use and for strong physical feats. Fat will be stored in the fat cells if it is not needed for energy. This leads to excess weight, which is a contributing factor to many illnesses associated with obesity and a sedentary lifestyle. Therefore:
• Use fats sparingly.
• Select low-fat preparation methods.
• Eliminate foods high in fat.
• Choose plant fats over animal fats if cholesterol is a concern.

Avoid Sugar and Sweets

A diet high in sugar can cause:
• excess weight
• imbalance in blood sugar levels
• caries and tooth decay

Drink Alcohol in Moderation

Alcohol should constitute only a small percentage of the calories in one's daily diet. Long-term alcohol abuse can lead to high blood pressure and can damage the brain, heart, liver, kidneys, and the digestive tract.

Prepare Foods to Retain Nutrients

• Wash fruits and vegetables well, but briefly.
• Cut after they have been washed and as close to final preparation time as possible.
• Cook foods with small amounts of fat and/or water.
• Keep cooking times for fruit and vegetables at a minimum.
• Avoid holding foods in warmers for long periods of time.
• Chill prepared foods for *mise en place* quickly.

Enjoy Dining

Choosing and preparing food correctly for good health are essential, but so is one's state of mind. Enjoy unhurried meals in a relaxed atmosphere.

3.13 Special Diets

3.13.1 Whole-Foods Diet

The goals of a whole-foods diet are
• to provide the body with all essential nutrients
• to promote good health and protection from disease
• to encourage optimum physical and mental development
• to reduce the cost of health care
• to promote ecologically sound preparation methods

Foundations of the Diet

The whole-foods diet is based on using fewer animal proteins and more plant proteins. Plant proteins are always eaten in complementary combinations or with animal proteins to ensure all essential amino acids are part of the diet. Examples of foods with complementary proteins are potatoes and eggs, grains and legumes, or wheat and milk.

Grains and Grain Products

Preferred are whole grains and products made from whole grains, such as whole-grain breads, rye crackers, whole-grain pasta, brown rice, and dishes made with corn, unmilled barley, millet, buckwheat flour, and oats. All refined food products, especially foods made with refined white flour such as white bread, rolls, noodles, and polished rice, are avoided.

Vegetables, Legumes, and Fruit

The recommended diet consists of 60 percent raw foods (fruits, salads, grated vegetables), of which 20 percent are vegetables, 10 percent fruit, and the rest uncooked grains (muesli), milk, and nuts.

Vegetables contain the most minerals and vitamins and are low in calories. Potatoes are important because of their high content of essential amino acids, vitamin A, B_1, B_2, C, and niacin, plus large amounts of minerals.

Among plant foods, legumes contain the most protein, especially soybeans. Because they contain large amounts of high-quality protein, soybeans are the basis for many food products, including tofu, soy protein, soy milk, soy flour, soy sausage and Yasoya (a product made from soybeans and milk protein).

Vegetables and fruits have been part of the human diet for thousands of years. They therefore have had a dominant influence on the structure and function of the human digestive system.

Fats and Oils

Recommended are oils that have been cold-pressed and are unrefined. Butter, of course in moderation, is also recommended because of its favorable composition of milk fats (provided the butter has not been heated to a high temperature). Refined oils have fewer beneficial fat properties, but they also have fewer harmful substances, which are removed during the refining process.

Animal Foods and Foods of Animal Origin

Animal foods are not recommended in the whole-foods diet, though they can be included in moderation. No more than one or two meat meals and one fish meal a week, plus one or two eggs, are recommended; this was the custom about a hundred years ago. Milk and milk products are, however, to be consumed on a daily basis.

Principles of the Whole-Foods Diet

- Seasonal, organically grown foods
- Freshly prepared foods (no packaged or frozen foods)
- Primarily lacto-ovo (milk and egg) foods and vegetables
- Natural fats and cold-pressed oils
- Only whole-grain products
- Plenty of raw foods
- Avoidance of refined foods, such as sugar, white flour, refined fats, delicatessen, sweets, and alcohol
- Less protein and fat and more fiber
- Nutrient-retaining preparation methods

Cooking meals in this manner demands more of the cook than the more common meals do. The preparation of whole-wheat noodles and whole-grain side dishes, for example, is a little more difficult and requires experience.

The whole-foods diet is not a medical diet per se but a life-long commitment to healthy eating. It is as good for a healthy person as it is for those under medical care.

3.13.2 Vegetarian Diets

An increasing number of people are choosing diets devoid of meats. The reasons for choosing a vegetarian diet differ. People elect to be vegetarians because of religious, health, ecological, and ethical considerations. Choosing a vegetarian diet for a lifetime requires a thorough understanding of nutrition, with special care given to the diet's composition, to ensure all nutrients are included (protein in particular). Vegetarian diets fall into three categories.

Strict Vegan Diet

In the vegan diet, only foods from plants (fruits, vegetables, legumes, grains, and mushrooms) are allowed. Not allowed are foods from animals of any type (meat, game, poultry, fish, and seafood) nor any foods of animal origin (egg and dairy products).

The vegan diet can be dangerous if nutrient intake is inadequate. Of special concern are the essential amino acids and Vitamin B_{12} (which exists only in foods from animal sources). Extreme vegan diets, such as a macrobiotic diet or a diet based only on raw fruits and vegetables, can lead to nutritional deficiencies.

Lacto-vegetarian Diet

The lacto-vegetarian diet includes milk and dairy products, as well as food from plants. Not allowed are any foods from animal sources, nor any eggs.

Lacto-ovo Vegetarian Diet

Included in the lacto-ovo vegetarian diet are milk, dairy products, and eggs, as well as food from plants. Not allowed are foods from animals (meat, fish, seafood, and poultry).

3.14 Nutrition and Health

Nutrition and health are closely related. A healthy body functions well when dietary needs are met and all essential nutrients are included in a varied diet. A healthy body is capable of digesting food, absorbing nutrients, and transporting these nutrients, via blood and lymph, to organs and tissue where they are needed. Intermediary metabolism changes nutrients to substances the body needs to build, repair, and fuel itself; residual products are detoxified and excreted. The body regulates this process through many functions to keep body weight and the composition of blood and body fluids reasonably constant.

Various types and quantities of food can be metabolized without great difficulty or unhealthy effects as long as all essential nutrients are included. The principles of a healthy diet are based on the need for growth, function, and performance of the body.

A well-balanced, nutritious diet is composed of:

- 12 to 15 percent protein
- 25 to 30 percent fat
- 55 to 60 percent carbohydrates
- enough vitamins, minerals, water, and dietary fiber

Meals should provide the correct amount of nutrients in the appropriate proportions for maximum value. The number of calories consumed should match the body's energy needs. Unfortunately, this is often not the case. People of most industrialized countries suffer from diseases exacerbated by overeating.

Though genetics may play a role in the occurrence of these diseases, poor dietary practices can hasten their onset. Statistical evidence shows a correlation between overweight or obesity and diabetes, heart diseases, liver diseases, and gout in 70 to 90 percent of all cases. A longer, healthier life is possible when one eats a nutritious, calorie-conscious diet.

Major dietary mistakes include overeating; eating too much fat, too much sugar, and too much salt in the diet; not including enough variety in the diet, not eating enough fiber, and eating meals that are too large (only three meals a day).

Health problems caused by these mistakes include overweight, high blood pressure, high blood cholesterol

(LDL), heart infarction, diabetes, gout, lower back and joint pains, liver and gallbladder diseases, metabolic disorders, stomach and digestive tract ailments, and tooth caries.

Dietary allowances and recommendations to prevent disease and keep people healthy vary from country to country. The above recommendations are Swiss; the United States issues its own recommendations. The recommendations of the United Nations' World Health Organization (WHO) are also widely used. The *Recommended Dietary Allowances* (RDA) in the United States are published by the government. They are based on available scientific evidence and are changed from time to time. They include a range of recommendations for different groups of healthy people. Individual needs may differ. The RDAs included on all packaged foods are the standard recommendations for adults. They indicate the percentage of the daily allowances that one serving of the food provides.

3.15 Therapeutic Diets

Modified diets are usually prescribed by physicians as a preventive measure or to combat certain disorders. For long-term diets, it is especially important to include as much variety as possible in the menu while still following a physician's recommendations.

Many illnesses lead to disturbances in the metabolism and thus are harmful to the body; on the other hand, certain illnesses may be controlled or cured by altering the metabolic process. The regulation of the food consumed by the patient is important under these circumstances. The choice of food and mode of preparation depends upon the type of illness and general condition of the patient.

Dietetics is the name given to the application of the science and art of human nutrition in helping people select and obtain food for the primary purpose of nourishing their bodies in health or disease throughout the life cycle.

The term *modified diet* refers to the choice of food as a preventive, supportive, or key therapeutic measure to meet the patient's nutritional, psychological, and aesthetic needs. In this way, the diet can be considered as part of, or the principal, medical treatment. The physician and dietitian determine the patient's dietary needs and prescribe the diet modification. The dietitian translates the diet order into palatable menus, directs the mode of preparation, evaluates the patient's response to the diet, and counsels the patient and family. The kitchen chef prepares the special dietary food according to specifications established by the dietitian and receives feedback concerning patient acceptance of the diet.

The normal menu serves as the basis for planning daily modified diets. The main principles of special dietary cooking are the same as those for preparation of the normal diet. The difference lies in the selection of food and ingredients most appropriate for the individually planned modified diet. Strict sanitation must be practiced in every respect. Only a few types of food are specially prepared for dietary purposes, such as salt-free foods. The physician and dietitian determine the type and quantity of food. The diet of each patient is dependent upon the type and stage of illness, the patient's condition, and food preferences. Therefore, the diet selected for patients all suffering from the same illness can vary considerably. Nevertheless, there are certain basic medical principles that form the basis for planning diets for some of the main types of illnesses.

3.15.1 Diets for Gastrointestinal Conditions

Many special dietary recommendations are made for the management of a number of digestive tract disorders. Although the recommendations that follow, which aim to reduce stress on the system, are useful, a physician's advice should be followed for any individual condition.

Basic Guidelines

- Select foods that are easy to digest.
- Meals should be small and offered five times a day (three small main meals and two snacks).
- Allow plenty of time to eat; chew meals carefully and thoroughly.
- Include plenty of dietary fiber to encourage peristalsis in the small intestine. Include many fresh fruits and vegetables in the diet, and at least one salad a day.
- Drink plenty of fluids.

Guidelines for Foodservice Establishments

Every cook should be able to plan a menu that allows a guest on a modified diet to select easily digested foods from the basic menu.

- Choose simple preparation methods: steaming, braising, and poaching. Roast or sauté foods only lightly, or cook them in aluminum foil.
- Do not include gratinated and breaded pan-fried dishes. Do not brown meat (frying or high-temperature roasting).
- Avoid strong spices, such as curry, hot pepper sauce, paprika, and horseradish; use fresh herbs instead.
- Salt dishes normally.
- Use minimum amounts of fresh butter or plant fats (margarine) and oils (polyunsaturated, high in essential fatty acids). Use heavy cream sparingly.
- Salads are an important part of the modified diet. Modify fat content of dressings by using yogurt, lemon

juice, cottage cheese, and low-fat sour cream instead of vinegar, oils, and mayonnaise.

Dishes for the Modified Diet

Soups: Consommé, low-fat broth, vegetable, potato, and cream soups. No cabbage, lentil, or pea and bean soups.

Meats: Lean cuts of meat, such as lamb, veal, rabbit, and game. Filet of pork and trimmed pork loin are acceptable. Poultry without skin, fat-free cooked ham, and tongue can be served.

Fish: All low-fat types.

Eggs: Scrambled, poached, and boiled eggs.

Cheeses: Mild, semisoft cheeses, such as Tilsit and Fontina; soft cheeses such as Brie, Tomme, and Camembert; fresh cheeses such as cottage cheese, Quark, Gala, and Gervais. No baked cheese dishes.

Vegetables: Young, tender vegetables, such as carrots, cauliflower, broccoli, peas, fennel, spinach, salsify, celery, asparagus, green beans, and kohlrabi. They should be steamed or served in a salad. A garnish of mushrooms is permissible. Exclude all flatulence-inducing vegetables, such as legumes, cabbages, onions, leeks, raw bell peppers, and cucumbers.

Potatoes: All forms except french fries and hash browns.

Pasta: Serve with small amounts of olive oil, butter, or grated cheese; no gratinated dishes.

Rice: Steamed or boiled, risotto with low-fat stock only.

Semolina: Semolina dumplings. But no cornmeal dishes.

Bread: White and whole-wheat bread, toast, zwieback, hardtack, and rolls; no freshly baked breads.

Baked goods: Ladyfingers, low-fat *génoise*, and angel-food cake.

Desserts: Quark and yogurt creams, light puddings with fresh berries, caramel, custard, rice, and semolina puddings, light vanilla puddings with

fruit sauces; avoid rich Bavarian creams, ice creams, and cakes.

Fruits: Only fully ripe fruits: berries, apples, pears, citrus fruits, grapes, kiwi, mango, and papaya; fresh fruit salads, juices, and compotes. No stone fruits.

Beverages: Water, noncarbonated mineral water, milk, tea, fruit and vegetable juices. Avoid coffee and carbonated beverages. Alcohol only with a doctor's permission.

3.15.2 Diet for Diabetics

The hormon insulin, secreted by the pancreas, makes the conversion from glucose to energy possible. The disease diabetes mellitus causes metabolic irregularity with a high blood sugar level and excessive amounts of glucose in the urine. Diabetes is a disorder of blood sugar regulation because of the body's inability to produce sufficient or effective insulin. Cells can convert little or no glucose to glycogen, causing high blood sugar. The body tries to compensate by signalling for more fluids to flush the sugar from the blood.

The first symptoms of diabetes are increased urination, excessive thirst, fatigue, and low energy. As the disease progresses, other, more serious problems arise, including difficulty with fat and protein metabolism, frequent infections, electrolyte imbalance, bruising of the skin, narrowing of the arteries to the heart, kidney failure, and circulatory problems. Because diabetics often have difficulty regulating their glucose levels, they may experience *hypoglycemia* when the blood sugar level is too low, or *hyperglycemia* when the blood sugar level is too high. Both are serious and can lead to coma and death unless emergency medical assistance is obtained.

Diabetes is classified in one of two categories. *Type I*, once known as juvenile onset diabetes, occurs when the body does not produce enough insulin. Type I diabetes is usually ge-

netic in origin and appears during childhood. Such diabetics are insulin dependent. Type II diabetes, sometimes called adult onset diabetes, occurs when the insulin produced by the body somehow can no longer facilitate the entrance of blood sugar into the cells. The causes of Type II diabetes are not yet fully understood, but it seems to be related to obesity and aging. Such diabetics may need insulin injections to control their diabetes, but for many, dietary management can correct the problem.

Rules for a Diabetic Diet

Diet prescriptions regulate not only what a diabetic can eat but how much of the permitted foods and how frequently (especially important with Type I diabetes) they can be eaten. The basic rules are:

- Consume no sugar of any kind.
- Divide the daily food intake into six meals.
- Measure all carbohydrates (doctor prescribes amounts).
- Eat only small amounts of fat.
- Increase consumption of foods high in protein.

Avoid:

- Sauces made with flour or starch.
- Breaded dishes.
- Alcohol (only with a doctor's permission)
- Fatty meats, poultry, fish, and sauces

3.15.3 Weight-loss Diets

Excess weight is usually a result of overeating and lack of exercise. Weight loss can only be acheived by limiting daily food intake and by increasing the energy expenditure of the body. Long-term success can only occur with a long-term change in eating behavior and life-style.

Principles of Weight-loss Diets

- Reduce calories (fewer fats and carbohydrates)
- Eat adequate amounts of protein, minerals, and vitamins.

Eliminate the following from the diet:
- Foods high in fat
- Foods high in salt
- Sweets
- Alcohol

To succeed, it is neccessary to:
- Have will power
- Control food intake (scales and calorie counter)
- Practice daily weight control
- Have patience (fat gained over many years cannot be reduced overnight).

3.15.4 Diets for Heart and Circulatory Diseases

Causes

- High blood pressure
- High cholesterol count

These illnesses are often the result of
- Overweight
- Poor diet
- High sodium consumption
- Stress
- Lack of exercise (sedentary lifestyle)
- Smoking
- Alcohol abuse
- Diabetes

Basic Dietary Rules for Heart and Circulatory Diseases

- Tailor caloric intake to need (overweight requires weight reduction).
- Restrict cholesterol.
- Avoid foods high in fat.
- If fats must be used, choose those high in polyunsaturated fatty acids.
- Balance animal and plant proteins.

- Curtail consumption of sugar, alcohol, and coffee.
- Eat a high-fiber diet.
- Eat a low-sodium diet.

Further Action

- Increased exercise
- Daily relaxation and leisure time
- No smoking

CHAPTER

4

Foods

Chapter Contents

1. Pacific Ocean	7. Norwegian Sea	13. Black Sea
2. Caribbean Sea	8. Skagerrak	14. Azovskoye Sea
3. Western Atlantic Ocean	9. Kattegat	15. Caspian Sea
4. Eastern Atlantic Ocean	10. Baltic Sea	16. Indian Ocean
5. English Channel	11. Mediterranean Sea	
6. North Sea	12. White Sea	

Knowledge of the purchase and handling of raw ingredients is essential to correctly preparing foods.

Purchasing Basics
• Correctly identify raw materials.

• Know where foods are from.
• Know when foods are in season.
• Set standards with quality specifications.
• Know federal food laws and local regulations.

Usage
• Store foods correctly.
• Apply appropriate preservation methods.

4.1   Purchasing and Controls

Purchasing

Purchasing involves obtaining the necessary foods in the right quantity, of the best quality, at the right time, in the right place, for the most economical price. The best purchaser considers price, supply and demand, transportation, and storage costs before placing an order.

Controls

Strict procedure should be followed when foods are received. When a delivery is made, it should be checked for both quality and quantity. Also of major importance is constant control of storage. Proper purchasing controls are outlined in Table 4-1.

Classifications

The foods in this chapter are classified into these categories:

• Animal foods (seafood, meat, and poultry)
• Foods of animal origin (dairy products and eggs)
• Edible fats and oils
• Plant foods (grains, vegetables, fruits, herbs, and spices)
• Sugars
• Food additives
• Salts
• Coffee and Tea
• Cocoa and Chocolate

Table 4-1. Proper purchasing controls.

Competitive buying (bids)
The lowest price is not always the best.

↓

Optimum purchasing
Depends on price, need, transportation, and storage cost.

↓

Ordering
All orders should be carefully considered. Purchase orders should contain the following information:

• item/brand name   • delivery date/time
• unit price   • mode of transportation
• quantity   • special terms
• quality/specs   • payment terms

↓

Delivery
Delivered goods should be checked against the purchase order. Count foods, record shortages, check weights, inspect cases, reject unacceptable quality, and obtain credit slips.

↓

Invoice control
Invoices must be checked against delivery forms.

↓

Storage control
Maintain:
• beginning inventory
• kitchen requisitions
• ending inventory

No food should leave the storeroom without a signed requisition. Perpetual and physical inventories should be kept. The perpetual inventory is a record of foods in stock. The physical inventory involves counting every item in storage at least once a month (storeroom, freezer, refrigerator).

↓

Food-cost control
Calculate total food use; evaluate percentages.

4.2   Animal Foods

Animal foods have been an important part of the human diet from the beginning of recorded time. With the discovery of fire, fish and meats became more digestible and tastier.

Today fish, poultry, and meat are enjoyed for their good taste and high nutritional value. A diet based solely on meat, however, is neither practical nor healthy; a balanced diet consists of plenty of grains, vegetables, and fruits, with moderate amounts of meat, poultry, and fish.

Fish, poultry, and meat are highly perishable foods, requiring the kitchen staff to exercise great care and have extensive professional knowledge in their storage and preparation.

Classification of Animal Foods

- Fish
- Shellfish (crustaceans, mollusks)
- Meat
- Sausages and meat products
- Poultry
- Game

4.2.1 Fish — FISCHE — *Poissons*

Classification of Fish

Fish can be grouped in various ways. Technical terminology is defined in Table 4-2.

Zoological Classification

Cartilaginous (nonbony) fish: The cartilaginous fish comprise about 500 species, including the sharks and rays.

Bony fish: The bony fish group has about 20,000 species. The largest of these are tuna, which can grow up to 6 feet long and weigh up to 700 pounds.

Classification by Origin

- *Freshwater fish*
- *Saltwater fish*

Fish that spend some of their lives in both fresh and saltwater — for example, salmon — are classified as freshwater fish.

Classification by Fat Content

Nutritional considerations determine the classification of these fish.

- *Oily fish* have large amounts of oil embedded in their flesh; examples are eel, herring, and salmon.
- *Lean fish* contain little or no oil in their flesh; fatty deposits are generally in the gut, which is removed. Examples are cod and haddock.

Classification by Quality

The method of preparation and price play important roles in whether a species is considered to be high, medium, or low quality. Price, in turn, depends on supply (many species are scarce) and preference. Firm-fleshed fish with few bones are in heavy demand. Seasonal catches and farm-raised fish also influence pricing. Fish that are abundantly available and of average quality command reasonable prices, for example, herring, perch, and cod. High-quality fish in high demand command high prices, such as sole, turbot, and wild salmon.

Classification by Skeletal Types

- *Round fish* have a backbone at the top, with two fillets on each side.
- *Flatfish* have a backbone that runs through the center of the fish, with two upper and two lower fillets. Flatfish start out as round fish but, to adapt to their environment and feeding needs, turn on their sides and become flatfish, with both eyes on top.

Nonbony fish (shark, skate, monkfish) are generally grouped with round fish.

Nutritional Value of Fish

Nutritional value differs greatly among different types of fish:

- *Protein* content ranges from 17 to 20 percent.
- *Fat* content of lean fish is about 0.8 to 2 percent; of oily fish, about 4.5 to 12 percent. Eel has an extremely high fat content, approximately 25 percent.
- *Carbohydrate* content is below 1 percent.
- *Water* content is about 75 percent.
- *Mineral* content is 1 to 1.5 percent, mostly sodium, calcium and phosphorus. Saltwater fish also contain iodine.
- *Vitamins* in fish include vitamin A, thiamin (B_1), riboflavin (B_2), and niacin.
- *Caloric* content depends on the amount of oil in the flesh.

Importance in the Diet

Compared to meat, most fish is low in fat. Fish flesh has little connective tissue and a loose cell structure, which allow the human digestive enzymes to break down the flesh quickly. Fish, therefore, is more easily digestible than red meat but produces a relatively low satiety.

Freshness and Quality

Fresh fish must be transported rapidly, chilled continuously from boat to consumer, and should never be frozen or preserved in any way. Large fish, such as cod, monkfish, or ray, have their heads removed before shipping to save transportation costs. Fresh fish is shipped on ice in disposable containers (Styrofoam). Check for the following signs of freshness upon delivery:

- *Skin* should be shiny and of good natural color, not faded; it should be undamaged and moist to the touch. Slime on the skin should be clear.
- *Scales* should be firmly attached.
- *Gills* should be bright red and not sticky.
- *Eyes* should be bulging, shiny, and clear.
- *Flesh* should be firm and resilient; it should spring back when poked with a finger.
- *Smell* should be **fresh!** A fishy odor indicates long or poor storage.
- *Belly* should be cleanly gutted and fresh smelling; any blood residue should be bright red.
- *Guts* in whole fish should be well rounded; a fish that has been dead

for a while has flat guts that have lost their obvious contours.

Storage

Fresh fish should be kept on ice under refrigeration. Melting ice water should be drained: a standard-size stainless-steel Gastro-Norm (hotel-cafeteria) pan with a perforated insert works well for this task. Iced fish must be checked daily and, if necessary, repackaged in fresh ice and clean containers. Large pieces of fish can be vacuum-packed and stored at 30°F to 32°F(-1°C to +1°C). Live fish in tanks should have clean water and sufficient air. The water temperature should be about 48°F to 53°F (9°C to 12°C). The fish tank should be cleaned once a week.

Preservation Methods

Freezing

Most fish can be frozen. Safe storage time is approximately six months. Fish should be vacuum-packed and well sealed to prevent freezer burn, caused by evaporation. Oily fish do not freeze as well as lean fish do because enzyme activity breaks down the fat. Some fish are *glazed*: whole fish are repeatedly sprayed with water and frozen, until the entire fish is coated with several layers of ice.

Smoking

Cold-smoked fish are prepared in smoking chambers in which the temperature reaches only 72°F to 77°F (22°C to 25°C). The amount of time in the chamber depends on the type and thickness of fish; it can be from one to six days. Color and flavor are affected by the type of wood used. Cold-smoked fish will keep approximately fourteen days refrigerated and two to three weeks if vacuumed-packed and chilled. Fish suitable for cold-smoking are salmon, sea and lake trout, whitefish (Great Lakes), and sable fish (Pacific Northwest).

Hot-smoked fish require a short-term soaking (about one hour) in a salt solution, followed by thirty minutes to three hours of smoking, depending on the type and size of the fish. The fish is smoked at temperatures of about 160°F to 195°F (70°C to 90°C), which gives it a beautiful color and an excellent flavor. The special smoky flavor is created near the end of the smoking process. The vents in the chamber are closed, and the fire is doused with damp wood chips to produce a dense, smoldering smoke. Fish smoked under these conditions can be stored for about three to four days, or three to four weeks if vacuum-packed. Fish suitable for hot-smoking are brook and rainbow trout, whitefish, eel, herring, sprats, mackerel, halibut, *Schillerlocken* (dogfish belly flaps), and sturgeon. Kippered salmon American style (fillet or steak) is brined and hot-smoked. Lox is a brine-cured and cold-smoked salmon.

Drying

Cod, pollock, and haddock are the most commonly dried fish; in northern Europe lumb (a type of cod) and leng are also dried. The best-known products are stockfish (whole fish, gutted, with the head removed, air-dried) and salted cod (filleted, brined, and dried).

Salting

Salt removes water from fish. After a certain amount of salt has been absorbed, the fish protein is denatured. Natural enzymes present in various types of fish are responsible for specific aromatic flavors that develop during the brining process. An example of salted fish is matjes herring, a favorite in Europe, which are caught before the spawning season and then mildly salted and cured for about eight weeks.

Marinating or Pickling

The pickling process begins by marinating raw fish fillets in a vinegar and salt mixture, which denatures the protein and makes the raw fish edible. After marinating, the fillets are placed in a highly spiced, hot liquid. Well-known products are pickled herring, rollmops (a rolled-up pickled herring fillet with a piece of pickle and sliced onions inside, secured with a toothpick), Bismark herring (herring fillets marinated in vinegar and spices), and herring bits in sour cream.

Marinated fish are only partially preserved and so must be kept refrigerated. They can be stored only for a limited amount of time (check the label for the expiration date).

Canning

Canned fish is fully preserved and can be stored at room temperature. High-pressure canning brings the temperature of the fish above 212°F (100°C) and kills all harmful microorganisms and spores. Canned fish such as sardines and anchovies have a storage life of about one year; tuna in oil can be stored for more than two years.

Surimi

This washed fish paste has been produced in Japan for centuries and is now marketed extensively as a substitute for crabmeat. Flesh, without skin or bones, is washed frequently and kneaded into a smooth white mass. Starch and flavorings are added, and the result is either baked or cooked. The frozen-food industry has adapted the traditional method, producing a modern surimi, a white substance without odor or taste that can be flavored to simulate particular fish or shellfish products.

Health Hazards

Fish spoil rapidly, and incorrect storage and preparation can cause food poisoning. Raw or partially cooked fish or shellfish can cause parasitic infections and hepatitis. Clams or mussels harvested from "red tide"–infested waters will carry a toxin affecting the nervous system. The toxin is not destroyed by heat. Only shellfish with an FDA-approved shellfish tag should be accepted. U.S. law requires foodservice establishments to keep shellfish tags on file for ninety days.

Cooking Techniques

Fish can be prepared in many ways. The method to be used depends on the size, oil content, and market form of the fish. For example, small, whole, firm-fleshed fish and steaks from large fish are suitable for grilling. For more detailed information, see section 7.11.

Aquaculture

Aquaculture, a growing industry all over the world, is becoming more and more important. Fish hatcheries are primarily concerned with raising small fish from eggs in a protective environment and releasing the young fish into freshwater ponds and streams for sport fishing. Fish farms raise fish to market size for the food industry.

Fish Farming in Ponds

Most freshwater fish are raised in ponds. *Extensive farming* relies on naturally available foods to nourish the fish. *Intensive farming* provides additional fish food especially formulated for the type of fish being raised. The most common farm-raised freshwater fish are rainbow trout, char, catfish, eel, and carp. To increase yield, large natural bodies of water are sometimes covered with netting to protect the fish from predators.

Fish Farming in Weirs

Use of netting makes it possible to farm fish in "open" waters of large lakes, rivers, and bays. The weirs are protected from bird predators with netting. Freshwater fish farmed in lake weirs are trout and carp. Saltwater fish farmed in bay weirs are salmon, sea trout, and halibut. Turbot farming is still in the experimental stage.

Fish Farming in Oceans

Fish can be farmed in bays, fjords, and lagoons. Barriers prevent the fish from escaping into the open sea. Salmon, sea trout, and halibut are raised in Norwegian fjords, salmon and sea trout in North Pacific bays, and the lagoons of the Adriatic sea are used to raise mullet and bream.

1. Saltwater Fish

Most of the many thousands of fish species live in the ocean, and most fish that are eaten are saltwater fish. Ninety percent of all fish that are caught live near the coast and the continental shelf in waters less than 600 feet (200 m) deep. Deep-sea fishing and large catches are only profitable in waters up to about 2,400 feet (800 m) deep.

Many different species of fish are often misnamed or are sold under various local names that are difficult to differentiate. This section discusses well-known, globally available species and North American fish from the Atlantic and the Pacific coasts. The illustrations should make identification easier. Fish are discussed in alphabetical order within subgroups.

Common Saltwater Fish

Nonbony Fish

Sharks

Dogfish—DORNHAI—*aiguillat/chien de mer*

Leopard shark (small spotted)—KLEINGEFLECKTER KATZENHAI—*petite rousette*

Leopard shark (large spotted)—GROSSGEFLECKTER KATZENHAI—*grande rousette*

Mako shark—HERINGSHAI—*requin taupe/veau de mer*

Skate

Smooth skate—GLATTROCHEN—*raie cendrée/pocheteau*

Stingray—NAGELROCHE/KEULENROCHE—*raie bouclée*

Bony Fish

Cod Family

Atlantic cod—DORSCH/KABELJAU—*morue fraîche, cabillaud*

Black cod (sablefish)—KÖHLER/DUNKLER SEELACHS—*lieu noir*

Cusk—LUMB—*brosme*

French cod—FRANZOSEN DORSCH—*tacaud*

Haddock—SCHELLFISH—*églefion/égrefin/aigrefin/aiglefin*

Hake—MEERHECHT/SEEHECHT—*colin/merlu*

Ling—LENG—*lingue*

Ling, blue—BLAULENG—*lingue bleue*

Pollock—POLLACK/HELLER SEELACHS—*lieu jaune*

Whiting—WITTLING/WEISSLING—*merlan*

Herring Family

Anchovy—SARDELLE—*anchois*

Herring—HERING—*hareng*

Sardine/pilchard—SARDINE—*sardine*

Sprat—SPROTTE—*esprot*

Mackerel Family

Atlantic mackerel—ATLANTISCHE MAKRELE—*maquereau de l'Atlantique*

Table 4-2 Technical Terms

Aquaculture	Growing fish in ponds, ocean farms, weirs, etc.; for example, salmon, trout.
Barbel	Threadlike, sometimes ragged, attachments of various sizes on the jaws of some fish, for example carp, catfish.
Stocking	The release of fish bred in hatcheries into streams or lakes; for example, char, brook trout, pikes, and pike perch.
Adipose fin	A small, fleshy fin located between the dorsal and caudal fins.
Anadromous	Fish that leave salt water to spawn in freshwater; for example, salmon.
Catadromous	Fish that leave freshwater to spawn in salt water; for example, river eels.
Stationary	Fish that stay in the same waters.
Parasite	An organism that lives inside another, feeding off it without killing it, and sometimes depositing harmful waste.
Population	The numbers and types of fish present in a particular body of water.

Bonito—ECHTER BONITO—*bonite*

Spanish mackerel/Pacific mackerel—MITTELMEER MAKRELE—*maquereau espagnol*

Swordfish—SCHWERTFISCH—*espadon*

Tuna, albacore—WEISSER THUNFISCH—*thon blanc/germon*

Tuna, bluefin—GROSSER ROTER THUNFISCH—*thon rouge*

Flatfish

Brill—GLATTBUTT—*barbue*

Dover sole—SEEZUNGE—*sole*

Flounder—FLUNDER—*flet*

Halibut, white—WEISSER HEILBUTT—*flétan*

Halibut, black—SCHWARZER HEILBUTT—*flétan noir*

Lemon sole—ECHTE ROTZUNGE—*limande sole*

Plaice/dab—SCHOLLE/GOLDBUTT—*plie/ carrelet*

Sole—SEEZUNGE—*sole*

Turbot—STEINBUTT—*turbot*

European Mullet

These are not the same fish as American Gulf Coast mullet.

Large-headed mullet—GROSSKÖPFIGE MEERÄSCHE—*mulet à grosse tête/muge à grosse tête*

Leaping mullet—SPRINGMEERÄSCHE—*mulet sauteur/muge sauteur*

Thin-lipped mullet—DÜNNLIPPIGE MEERÄSCHE—*mulet porc/muge porc*

Bream (American Porgy)

Bag bream—SACKBRASSE—*pagre*

Gilt-headed seabream—GOLDBRASSE—*dorade royale/daurade*

Red bream—ROTBRASSE—*pageot*

Mullet/Barbel

Red mullet (barbel)—ROTE MEERBARBE—*rouget-barbet/rouget de vase/rouget-barbet de vase*

Striped mullet (barbel)—STREIFENBARBE—*rouget de roche/rouget-barbet de roche/surmulet*

Ocean Perch Family

Greater weever—GROSSES PETERMÄNCHEN/DRACHENFISCH—*grande vive*

Ocean perch—ROTBARSCH/GOLDBARSCH—*rascasse du nord/grand sébaste*

Sea bass—WOLFBARSCH/MEERBARSCH—*bar/loup de mer*

Spotted sea bass—GEFLECKTER MEERBARSCH—*bar rayé*

Eels

Conger eel—MEERAAL—*congre*

Wolffish

Atlantic or striped wolffish/ocean catfish—GESTREIFTER SEEWOLF/KATFISCH/STEINBEISSER—*loup de l'Atlantique/loup du nord/loup marin*

Spotted wolffish—GEFLECKTER SEEWOLF—*loup tacheté*

Monkfish

Monkfish—ATLANTISCHER SEETEUFEL—*baudroie/lotte de mer*

John Dory

John Dory—PETERSFISCH/HERINGSKÖNIG—*saint-pierre*

Scorpion Fish

Scarlet rascasse—GROSSER ROTER DRACHENKOPF—*rascasse rouge*

Drums/Gurnards

Gray drum/gurnard—GRAUER KNURRHAHN—*grondin gris*

Red drum/gurnard—ROTER KNURRHAHN—*grondin perlon*

Sea robin—SEEKUCKUCK—*grondin rouge*

Snappers

Red emperor snapper—KAISER SCHNAPPER—*vivaneau bourgeoise*

Red snapper—ROTER SCHNAPPER—*vivaneau rouge*

Nonbony Fish

Sharks—HAI—*requins*

Of the approximately 250 different types of sharks, only a few are desirable as food. Commonly available are mako, dogfish, blue, leopard, yellow-tip, and blackfin shark. The flesh is sweet and firm. In some countries dried shark fins, used in soup, are of economic importance.

Dogfish — DORNHAI — *aiguillat*

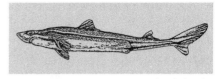

Description: Long, stretched body, with a short, sharp mouth.

Origin and occurrence: Dogfish is a bottom fish and loves cooler waters. They live in schools of up to one thousand fish, which often wander close to the coast. They feed on herring, cod, crabs, and mollusks.

Quality characteristics: Dogfish has great economic importance as a common table fish. The flesh is very tasty and is excellent when smoked. It is served fresh under the names "king" or "sea eel." The smoked belly flaps are sold as *Schillerlocken*.

Leopard shark—KATZENHAI—*rousette*

Origin and occurrence: East Atlantic and Mediterranean Sea.

Species and description: Spotted leopard sharks may be small or large. Leopard sharks have a long, stretched body, with a short, round mouth. The back is covered with many spots.

Quality characteristics: This fish is known as *saumonette* in France and is sold skinned, without the head and tail. The flesh is firm and tasty, similar to dogfish.

Mako shark—HERINGSHAI—*requin taupe/veau de mer*

Description: A fast swimmer, mako feeds on mackerel and squid. It is about 9 feet long and rarely grows longer then 12 feet. Its color, dark gray, and shape are similar to tuna.

Origin and occurrence: Temperate parts of the Atlantic Ocean. Shortfin mako, a close relative, lives in the South Pacific.

Quality characteristics: Mako flesh is firm and similar in taste to veal. The flesh of the side muscle contains dark red spots (blood nets) that must be removed, since they can cause allergic reactions in some people.

Usage: Shark meat is often soaked in milk or acidulated water before cooking. Shark is usually offered as steak and can be grilled, broiled, poached, or sautéed. It is excellent in chowders and fish stews. It can also be cubed for kabobs.

Smooth skate – GLATTROCHEN – *cendrée/pocheteau*

Stingray – NAGEL or KEULENROCHEN – *raie bouclée*

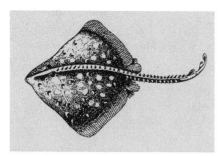

Description: The large breast fins (wings) are merged with the head and body. The mouth is located on the underside of the disk-shaped body, and the eyes are located on top. The entire body of the stingray is covered with little thorny spines. The smooth skate has few spines and a long, pointed jaw. The Atlantic barndoor skate and the Pacific big skate can grow up to 8 feet long. In the American marketplace, California skate is most common. The stingray can grow to about 50 inches (125 cm); the smooth skate to about 95 inches (240 cm).

Origin and occurrence: Skate live near the bottom of coastal waters and in the open sea. They are caught along the coast. In Europe they are found in the northeast Atlantic, the North Sea, the Baltic Sea, and the Mediterranean Sea.

Quality characteristics: With a fat content of less then 0.2 percent, skate is a lean fish. The delicious flesh is firm, white, and has a rodlike texture. Only the wings are used for

culinary purposes. Fresh skate is usually sautéed. In Europe skate is also available smoked.

Bony Fish

In Europe, the Atlantic Ocean, North Sea and the Mediterranean Sea supply most of the saltwater fish. In the United States, the Atlantic and the Pacific coastal waters and the Gulf of Mexico are the major sources of saltwater fish.

Codfish

Ten families and about two hundred different types of cod are grouped together. Most live in the waters of the northern hemisphere. Of culinary importance are:

Atlantic cod – DORSCH/KABELJAU – *morue fraîche, cabillaud*

Black cod (sablefish) – KÖHLER/ DUNKLER SEELACHS – *lieu noir*

Cusk – LUMB – *brosme*

French cod – FRANZOSEN DORSCH – *tacaud*

Haddock – SCHELLFISH – *églefin/égrefin/aigrefin/aiglefin*

Hake – MEERHECHT/SEEHECHT – *colin/merlu*

Ling – LENG – *lingue*

Ling, blue – BLAULENG – *lingue bleue*

Pollock – POLLACK/HELLER SEELACHS – *lieu jaune*

Whiting – WITTLING/WEISSLING – *merlan*

The misnamed ling cod, found from Mexico to Alaska, is not a cod at all; it belongs to the greenling family.

Cod – DORSCH/KABELJAU – *morue fraîche/cabillaud*

Description: The cod has a long body with closely spaced, rounded fins. The cod has a strong, stubby head with a protruding upper jaw and long barbels. The light lateral line along its sides curves slightly until

the third fin and runs straight after that. Cod can reach a length of 5 feet (200 cm) and weigh up to 45 pounds (20 kg).

Origin and occurrence: Cod are caught in Europe in the North Atlantic from Spain to Iceland and in the Mediterranean and Baltic seas. In the United States, cod can be found in the Atlantic waters from Virginia to the Arctic but are most abundant along the continental shelf from the Grand Banks of Newfoundland to the George's Bank and off Block Island. Pacific cod are caught from the coast of Oregon to Alaska. Cod feeds on bottom dwellers and mollusks and, when older, also eats small fish. Commercially, cod is of major importance. It is the most commonly consumed fish in Europe.

Quality characteristics: Its flaky, grayish white flesh is rather fragile. It flakes easily when cooked. Cod is an excellent chowder fish.

Usage: Cod is sold whole, without the head, and as steaks or fillets. It is available fresh or frozen. Almost all fishsticks and processed fish products are made from cod. Cod cheeks and tongues are eaten as a delicacy. *Scrod* or *schrod* is the name for young cod (or haddock) weighing less then 2½ pounds. As *stockfish*, cod is gutted, the head is removed, and the body is air-dried. As *salted cod*, the backbone is removed, the fish is salted, and it is dried only after it is properly salt-cured. This method is also applied to black haddock, haddock, "leng," and cusk. Producers are Sweden, Norway, Spain, Portugal, and Italy. A brine-packed cod from Alaska and Puget Sound is available in the U.S. market. Cod can be poached, steamed, baked, sautéed, fried, or smoked. Dried or salted cod is soaked before it is cooked.

Black cod/sablefish – KÖHLER/ DUNKLER SEELACHS – *lieu noir*
Description: A long, narrow body, with clearly separated first and second dorsal fins. Older fish have a pro-

truding jaw. A light straight line runs along the entire length of the fish.

Origin and occurrence: North Atlantic (Europe and North America), North Sea, Skagerrak and Kattegat. Young fish eat crabs and fish larvae; older fish attack schools of fish.

Quality characteristics: An important table fish, with a tasty but somewhat gray flesh.

Usage: Can be roasted, grilled, and fried.

Cusk – LUMB – *brosme*

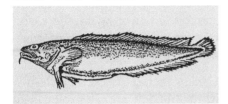

Description: A long, narrow body, with one continuous dorsal fin. Remarkable is the black fringe edging the fins. The skin is thick and covered with scales. The mouth has strong barbels.

Origin and occurrence: North Atlantic above rocky grounds in waters about 325 feet (1000 m) deep. It feeds on crabs, mollusks, and small fish. Average length on the market is about 24 to 35 inches (60 to 90 cm).

Quality characteristics: The firm white flesh, with a lobsterlike flavor, is a bit oilier than cod. Usually sold as filets.

Usage: Same as cod.

French cod – FRANZOSEN DORSCH – *tacaud*

Description: The French cod can be identified by its high back and a dark spot near the pectoral fin.

Origin and occurrence: Along the Atlantic coast of Europe and in the western Mediterranean. Average market length is 5 to 14 inches (12 to 35 cm).

Quality characteristics: Not of great economic importance, but has a very delicate taste and a tendency to spoil quickly.

Usage: Same as cod.

Haddock – SCHELLFISCH – *églefin/ égrefin/aigrefin/aiglefin*

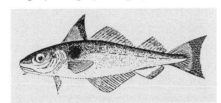

Description: Haddock has a long body with two distinctly separate fins. The back is grayish brown, and the belly is white. Above the pectoral fin is a black dot, and the line down the length of both sides is black. Look for these identifying marks to distinguish haddock from cod.

Origin and occurrence: Haddock is caught in the North Atlantic, the North Sea, Skagerrak and Kattegat. It prefers deeper water then cod. It feeds on fish eggs, bottom dwellers, and small fish.

Quality characteristics: The flesh is white, tender, and firm, with a mild flavor. Haddock is a low-fat fish.

Usage: Haddock is available fresh or frozen. It is available whole and as steaks or fillets. Finnan haddie is a salted, smoked, partially boned piece of haddock. It is sold under the English name haddock in Europe. It is produced in New England for the U.S. market. Haddock can be broiled, poached, baked, stewed, or fried.

Hake – MEERHECHT/SEEHECHT/ HECHTDORSCH – *colin or merlu*

Description: Hake is a long, thin fish with a pointed head. It has a wide mouth with strong teeth. The back is gray-black with black spots. The sides are silvery white and have a thin black line running the length of the fish. Hake are plentiful and have gained in commercial importance since the advent of flash freezing. The size on the market is usually between 1½ and 2 feet.

Origin and occurrence: Hake, a member of the cod family, is caught in the

Mediterranean Sea, on both sides of the Atlantic, along the Pacific Northwest coast, and in the colder waters of the southern hemisphere. Hake feeds on mackerel, herring, and sardine.

Quality characteristics: The flesh is fine, white, and low in fat.

Usage: Hake can be used in any recipe that calls for haddock or cod. It is a little less expensive than haddock or cod. It is available whole and as steaks and fillets. The preferred method is to sauté thin slices of hake or to braise it with bell peppers and tomatoes.

Ling – LENG – *lingue*
Blue ling – BLAULENG – *lingue bleue*

Description: Both of these fish are just beginning to appear on the Swiss market and are increasing in sales. Ling has a slim, eel-like body, with large eyes. The market size of ling is 26 to 63 inches (65 to 160 cm) and that of blue ling is 23 to 47 inches (60 to 120 cm).

Origin and occurrence: They are found from northern Norway and southern Iceland to the southwestern coast of Ireland.

Quality characteristics: The flesh of the blue ling is white and firm, with only 0.6 percent fat content. Its taste is a little more delicate than that of the ling. It is sold only as fillets.

Pollock, pollack – POLLACK/LYR/ HELLER SEELACHS – *lieu jaune*

Description: A long body with clearly separated fins. Its lower jaw protrudes slightly and has no barbels. Pollock has a brown-green line that curves above the pectoral fin and runs straight along the sides. Pollock can grow up to 4 feet.

Origin and occurrence: Pollock is caught in the North Atlantic, North Sea, Sea of Juteland (Skagerrak), and Kattegat. It feeds on crabs and small fish.

Quality characteristics: In contrast to black cod, the flesh of Atlantic pollock is white and firm but somewhat dry. It is rarely available whole; in the United States, it is available fresh as fillets, but is sold mostly frozen. Fresh pollock tastes best in the summer season. Pacific pollock is plentiful, but the flesh is softer and does not have the large flakes of the Atlantic pollock. Pacific pollock is used in the preparation of imitation crabmeat.

Usage: Pollock is available fresh, frozen, and smoked. A good chowder fish, pollock can also be baked, broiled, fried, steamed, or poached.

Whiting – WITTLING/WEISSLING – *merlan*

Description: A small gray body with three dorsal and two anal fins. The large mouth has a protruding upper jaw and no barbels. There is a dark spot near the pectoral fin and a silvery line along the body. Its market length is 10 to 20 inches (25 to 50 cm).

Origin and occurrence: The whiting, also called silver hake, is found in the North Atlantic and in the northern and western Baltic Sea. It is abundant on the continental shelf from Newfoundland to Cape Hatteras. In the Pacific Northwest, whiting is also called walleye pollock. Whiting feeds on plankton and crustaceans.

Quality characteristics: Whiting has white, firm-textured, delicately flavored flesh. It is sensitive to pressure and spoils quickly.

Usage: Whiting is marketed fresh or frozen, whole or in fillets. It can be poached, baked, pan-fried, or broiled. Whiting is also available smoked.

Herring Family

Members of the herring family are saltwater fish with slim bodies covered with thin, silvery scales. The head has no scales. Herring have only one dorsal fin and a forked tail. They travel long distances to spawn; some spawn in rivers. Like cod, the herring family is another large group of commercially very important fish, especially in northern Europe. Herring have an average fat content of 11 percent, which classifies them as oily fish. Their high nutritional content makes herring an important food in the diet of northern European countries. Members of the herring family include:

Anchovy – SARDELLE – *anchois*

Herring – HERING – *hareng*

Sardine/pilchard – SARDINE – *sardine*

Sprat – SPROTTE – *esprot*

Anchovy – SARDELLE – *anchois*

Description: An anchovy has a very slim body with a dark back and silvery belly. It is usually about 3 to 5 inches (10 to 15 cm) long and does not grow longer than 8 inches (20 cm).

Origin and occurrence: Anchovies are abundant in the northern Atlantic from Norway to West Africa and in the Mediterranean and Black seas. In North America, they range from the Delaware Bay to the West Indies and are found as far north as Nova Scotia. Five species are found on the Pacific coast.

Quality characteristics: Very strong flavored flesh.

Usage: Anchovies are salted or packed in oil in cans, usually as fillets. Anchovy is also marketed as paste or sauce for flavoring. Export countries are Portugal, Spain, and Italy.

Herring – HERING – *hareng*

Description: A long body with a ventral fin. The back is greenish blue, and the sides and belly are shiny silver. The herring has a protruding jaw. The dorsal fin is centered on the back. The average length is 10 inches (25 cm).

Origin and occurrence: The Atlantic herring is found in the Baltic Sea and on both sides of the North Atlantic from Greenland to North Carolina and from the Arctic Ocean to the Straits of Gibraltar. The Pacific herring is found from northwestern Alaska to San Diego. Herring travel in large schools. They stay on the bottom during the day and rise to the top in the night. Herring feed on plankton, small shrimp, and fish eggs.

Quality characteristics: The flesh is white and delicate. Herring caught in the fall are lean and more flavorful than spring herring. Young herring that are not sexually mature are marketed as *matjes herring.* Adult herring are caught before spawning with the milt or roe full.

Usage: Green (fresh) herring are sautéed and grilled. Other market forms are smoked (kippers), pickled (rollmops), and marinated in wine or sour cream sauces (herring bits). *Matjes* are usually skinned and filleted and cured in a sugar-vinegar brine.

Sardine/pilchard – SARDINE – *sardine*

Description: Sardines and pilchard are slim and elongated. The back is bluish green, and the belly, silvery white. The scales are fairly large. Immature fish are called sardines, probably originating from the fact that they were first caught near the island of Sardinia. Sardines should be no longer than 5 to 6 inches. The mature fish is called a pilchard and can grow to a length of 12 inches.

Origin and occurrence: Atlantic sardines are caught from the northeastern Atlantic to the Canary Islands and in the northern Mediterranean.

The Maine sardine is an Atlantic herring. The Pacific sardine is found from southwestern Alaska to the Gulf of California. The young migrate to the coast and move offshore after they have reached a length of about 7 inches. Sardines move in large schools and feed on plankton, fish eggs, and larvae.

Quality characteristics: The flesh is tender and high in fat. Sardines are rich in protein, iron, calcium, and phosphorus.

Usage: Fresh sardines are available in Portugal and the Mediterranean. In the United States, fresh sardines are available during the summer months near the coast. Sardines are otherwise salted or canned and packed in oil. Maine sardines are packed in a variety of sauces, for example, mustard or tomato.

Sprat – SPROTTE – *esprot*

Description: The sprat has a slim, oval body with a distinguishing belly fin. The eyes have small, fatty lids, and the lower jaw protrudes. It is typically 6 inches long.

Origin and occurrence: The most important fishing grounds are off the Norwegian coast and in the Baltic and North seas. They are also found in the Mediterranean and the Black Sea.

Quality characteristics: Sprat flesh is very oily, and they taste best when caught during the months of November and December.

Usage: In Europe they are prepared fresh; they are also salted in the south and smoked in the north. In Germany smoked sprats are known as *Kieler Sprotten*, a much prized delicacy. Fresh sprats are also marinated with salt, sugar, spices, and herbs. After they have been cured in this fashion, they are packed in jars or barrels. They must be kept refrigerated and used within a short period of time.

Shad

Description: Shad, a fish popular in North America, belongs to the herring family. Shad has a notched mouth and, unlike the herring, no teeth. It has one back fin and large scales. It typically weighs 3 to 5 pounds.

Origin and occurrence: The shad is one of the largest fish in the herring family. They spawn in rivers off the Atlantic coast from Florida to Canada from December to May, which is when they are caught. Atlantic shad has been introduced to the Pacific coast, and they thrive there as well. Shad spawning runs start in California in January and continue till May in the Northwest.

Quality characteristics: Shad has sweet, moderately oily, white flesh, unfortunately with many small bones. Fresh shad roe is a delicacy. Both are featured on restaurant menus during shad runs.

Usage: After boning, shad is usually cut into four fillets, which can be broiled or sautéed. Traditionally shad is pan-fried with bacon and served with the sautéed roe.

Mackerel Family

Mackerels are fast-swimming deep-sea fish. They swim near the top and travel in large schools. They have long, streamlined bodies, with separated back fins and five to seven short finlets near the tail. The tail is forked symmetrically. Varieties include:

Atlantic mackerel – ATLANTISCHE MAKRELE – *maquereau de l'Atlantique*

Bonito – ECHTER BONITO – *bonite*

Spanish mackerel/Pacific mackerel MITTELMEER MAKRELE – *maquereau espagnol*

Swordfish – SCHWERTFISCH – *espadon*

Tuna, albacore – WEISSER THUNFISCH – *thon blanc/germon*

Tuna, bluefin – GROSSER ROTER THUNFISCH – *thon rouge*

Mackerel – MAKRELE – *maquereau*

Description: The mackerel has a torpedo-shaped body, covered with small scales. It has a very pointed, wide mouth. It is greenish blue in color, with dark blue zebralike stripes on the back and along the sides. The belly is silvery. The mackerel can reach a length of 20 inches, but the average market size is 10 to 14 inches (25 to 35 cm).

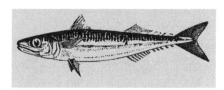

Origin and occurrence: The Atlantic mackerel is found on both sides of the Atlantic. It averages about 1 to 2 pounds. Chub mackerel, a smaller species, is found on the Pacific coast and along the Atlantic coast of North America. The Spanish mackerel is caught off the Florida coast from October to March and off the Atlantic coast as far north as Narraganset Bay in the summer. Spanish mackerel weighs about 3 to 4 pounds. The king mackerel, which can grow to 5 feet and weigh 100 pounds, is caught in the tropical Atlantic and as far north as the Carolinas in summer. Mackerel swim in large schools and feed on small fish, crabs, and herring.

Quality characteristics: Fresh mackerel should be firm and not bend easily. Mackerel is oily and has firm-textured, reddish flesh. Spanish mackerel is the best of the mackerel family to eat.

Usage: Mackerel is available fresh (usually whole), or smoked, salted, or marinated, and canned. Fresh mackerel can be broiled, grilled, sautéed, baked, or barbecued. The flesh flakes easily when cooked. Because of its high fat content, an acid sauce or marinade complements the fish. It is often smoked and canned with tomato sauce, hot chilies, or in oil.

Swordfish – SCHWERTFISCH – *espadon*
Description: The swordfish has a torpedolike body. A long, flat sword extends from its upper jaw (about one third of its total body length); the lower jaw is much shorter. It is otherwise similar to the tuna in body

shape. The colors range from bronze brown to gray. The average commercial weight is about 200 pounds.

Origin and occurrence: Swordfish live in deep (2,500 feet/800 m) temperate waters worldwide. They feed on schools of small fish.

Quality characteristics: Muscular but tender, very tasty flesh, with a unique flavor. Swordfish is unlike most other fish in texture.

Usage: Fresh swordfish is available from spring to late summer; otherwise it is sold frozen. It is usually sold as steaks or in chunks. Swordfish can be baked, grilled, broiled, or poached. Thin slices can be sautéed. The most popular swordfish preparation method is grilled and drizzled with lemon juice and olive oil.

Tuna – THUNFISCH – *thon*
Description: All tuna have torpedo-like bodies. Scales cover the upper part of the body but only to the first dorsal fin. The back is dark blue, and the sides are gray with silvery spots. They have a well-developed blood vessel system. Tuna are found in all oceans. In the summer they move nearer to the coast to spawn, where many of them are caught. Tuna travel long distances to feed, generally in the company of other tuna. The winter months are spent in deep waters.

Bluefin is the largest of the tunas. It is caught in nets. Yellowfin is similar to the bluefin. It is smaller in size (about 150 pounds/68 kg) and has bright yellow fins. Tuna can grow to about 10 feet (3 m) and weigh one thousand pounds. Four types of tuna are commercially important: albacore, bluefin, yellowfin, and bonito.

Tuna, albacore – WEISSER THUNFISCH – *thon blanc/germon*
Description: Albacore tuna has the longest pectoral fin of all tuna. Its color is similar to the bluefin, but it is smaller, only about 4 feet (1.45 m) long, and weighs up to 300 pounds (136 kg).

Origin and occurrence: Albacore are found worldwide in warm and temperate waters, they migrate long distances in schools but stay in open waters far from the coast. Albacore feed on squid, shrimp, and small fish.

Quality characteristics: Light (almost white with a pinkish cast), firm flesh, with a delicious flavor. Albacore is the most important tuna in the worldwide economy.

Usage: Albacore is prized for its light meat. It is usually canned and rarely available fresh. Albacore is the top grade in canned tuna. It is primarily used cold in salads; occasionally it is an ingredient in a hot dish.

Tuna, bluefin – GROSSER ROTER THUNFISCH – *thon rouge*

Origin and occurrence: Bluefin tuna is found in temperate waters in the eastern Atlantic, Mediterranean, and Pacific. It feeds on mackerel, herring, hake, and squid.

Quality characteristics: Young bluefins have a light-colored flesh that turns dark red in the mature tuna. The flesh is firm and has a flavor similar to veal.

Usage: Bluefin tuna is sold as fillets, chunks, and steaks. The dark streak of meat running along the fillet must be removed, as it is very oily and strong tasting. Fresh tuna can be roasted, broiled, grilled, barbecued, sautéed, or baked. Commercially, it is most important canned in oil or water. American grades are solid, fancy, chunk, and grated. Like albacore, canned bluefin is used primarily in cold salads.

Bonito – ECHTER BONITO – *bonite*

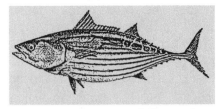

Description: Bonito is different from other tuna. It has four to seven dark stripes running along its belly. It is quite small, about 31 inches (80 cm) long, and usually weighs no more than 25 pounds.

Origin and occurrence: Bonito is caught worldwide in warm and temperate waters but is most abundant near the North American Atlantic and Pacific coasts. Bonito is commercially very important in the United States and Japan.

Quality characteristics: Bonito has tasty, tender flesh, the darkest among tuna, and is moderately oily.

Usage: It is available fresh, canned, or dried. Many Japanese dishes use dried bonito flakes; the best known is *dashi*, a soup stock.

Flatfish
The most distinctive characteristic of flatfish is their flat, wide bodies. As larvae, flatfish start out with a body like a round fish. When they are about 1 inch long, one of the eyes wanders from the side of the body to the top. This is also the side that takes on color, whereas the "blind" side is generally light and colorless. Flatfish are disk shaped. The fins form a fringe all along the body, and the fish have a distinct tail. There are right- and left-eye species among the flatfish. They have great commercial value since they live in large numbers in shallow water. Flatfish species are the most popular edible fish. Varieties include:

Brill – GLATTBUTT – *barbue*

Dover sole – SEEZUNGE – *sole*

Flounder – FLUNDER – *flet*

Halibut, white – WEISSER HEILBUTT – *flétan*

Halibut, black – SCHWARZER HEILBUTT – *flétan noir*

Lemon sole—ECHTE ROTZUNGE—
    limande sole

Plaice/dab—SCHOLLE/GOLDBUTT—
    plie/carrelet

Sole—SEEZUNGE—*sole*

Turbot—STEINBUTT—turbot

Brill—GLATTBUTT—*barbue*

Description: The brill's elliptical body is covered with tiny smooth scales. Its upper body is grayish brown with orange spots. It typically grows to a length of 12 to 20 inches (30 to 50 cm) and is never more than 39 inches (100 cm).

Origin and occurrence: Brill live in about 200-foot-deep (70-m) waters above sandy bottoms along the Atlantic coast from Norway to the Mediterranean. It feeds on small crabs and bottom fish. The Pacific petrale sole is also called brill.

Quality characteristics: The tasty white flesh is rather fragile, but its taste pales in comparison to that of its cousin, turbot.

Usage: Brill is best sautéed, poached, or deep-fried. It cannot be grilled.

Dover sole—SEEZUNGE—*sole*

Description: Dover sole is the best known and most prized flatfish. Dover sole has an elongated, tongue-shaped body, with a rounded head. It is right-eyed. Dover sole is thicker than other flatfish. The upper body is brown, with small scales, and covered with slime. It typically grows to about 12 to 16 inches (30 to 40 cm) in length, never more than 24 inches (60 cm). Dover sole is sold sized. The smallest size is called *solette* and weighs less than 7 ounces (200 g).

Origin and occurrence: Dover sole lives in the coastal waters of Europe, in the western Baltic and the Mediterranean. It feeds on sea worms, mussels, small crabs, and fish. The fish that most closely resemble Dover sole in American waters are the Atlantic winter flounder and the Pacific petrale sole.

Quality characteristics: The best sole comes from the English Channel and is also called Ostend sole. These fish have a great deal of flesh, which is very white, firm, and delicate in taste. Channel sole is preferred over the darker sole from the North Sea and Italian waters. The fish sold as sole on the American market is usually flounder.

Usage: Dover sole can be prepared in many ways. It can be poached, baked, broiled, sautéed, or deep-fried. It is often combined with other seafood and sauces.

Flounder—FLUNDER—*flet*

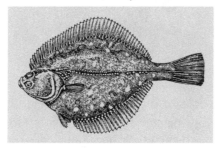

Description: Flounder has an oval body. The upper skin is brown with red and yellow spots. The belly is yellowish white, and along the side line it has small, thorny warts. It is a very thin flatfish.

Origin and occurrence: Flounder is caught in the North, Baltic, and western Mediterranean seas. It is also found along the Atlantic coast, from the Gulf of Saint Lawrence to New Jersey, and in the Pacific from California to Alaska. Flounder feed on small shrimp, crabs, and small fish.

Quality characteristics: Firm, white, and very tasty flesh.

Usage: Fresh flounder is available whole or in fillets. Very small flounders are usually smoked in Europe. When used whole, it can be broiled, baked, or pan-fried. Fillets can be prepared in the same way as sole and can be substituted in any recipe calling for sole.

Halibut, white—WEISSER HEILBUTT—*flétan*

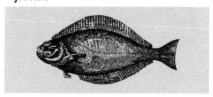

Description: This long, thick fish, the largest flatfish, can weigh up to about 625 pounds (300 kg). The head is pointed, the upper side is colored gray-brown, and the belly is white.

Origin and occurrence: Halibut is found in the Atlantic and Pacific oceans.

Quality characteristics: The flesh is white, rich in protein, and low in fat. Halibut freezes well.

Usage: Halibut is available on the market from 4 to 90 pounds (2 to 40 kg); larger fish are no longer commercially available. Halibut is available fresh most of the year, but especially from March to September. Halibut is sometimes cut into fillets but more often into steaks. It is suitable for all types of preparation but is best when poached or baked.

Halibut, black—SCHWARZER HEILBUTT—*flétan noir*

Description: Black halibut is less asymmetric than other flatfish. The left eye is located on the edge of the head. The upper body is very dark, almost sooty black, with a dark underside.

Origin and occurrence: The black halibut lives in Arctic waters, as deep as 6,000 feet (2,000 m), from Norway to Iceland and from Greenland to Newfoundland. It grows only to about 47 inches (120 cm) and weighs about 110 pounds (50 kg). It feeds on cod, small bass, and shrimp.

Quality characteristics: A commercially very important fish. Black halibut, in contrast to white, has a 9 percent fat content. The flavorful flesh can be prepared in many ways. It is not suitable for grilling. It is excellent smoked.

Lemon sole – ECHTE ROTZUNGE – *limande*

Description: Lemon sole, a type of flounder, has a wide, oval body, with a small head and a tiny mouth opening. The skin is slimy. The upper body is reddish brown with marble-like markings; the bottom is white.

Origin and occurrence: It is found from the Bay of Biscay (Spain) to the English Channel and from the North Sea to the White Sea. Lemon sole lives on both side of the Atlantic in northern waters and is abundant off the New England coast. In the Pacific it is found from southern California to Alaska.

Quality characteristics: The flesh is white, lean, and has an excellent taste but is difficult to fillet and to skin.

Usage: Lemon sole is available whole or as fillets, fresh or frozen. The whole sole can be deep- or pan-fried or dredged in flour and sautéed. Fillets are fragile but can be sautéed, baked (in sauce), or poached. It is not suitable for grilling.

Plaice/dab – SCHOLLE/GOLDBUTT – *plie/carrelet*

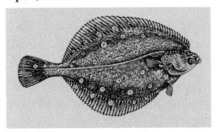

Description: Plaice has a wide, oval body covered with small gray scales. It has a small mouth. A small row of warts runs from the eyes to the beginning of the side line. The upper body color is grayish brown, with round red or orange dots; the bottom is white. It can grow 35 inches (90 cm) long and weigh up to 15 pounds (7 kg). Market size is about 16 to 20 inches (40 to 50 cm) long and from 11 to 14 ounces (300 to 400 g).

Origin and occurrence: Plaice, a member of the flounder family, is caught from the Bay of Biscay (Spain) to the White Sea, but not in the English Channel nor in the southern North Sea. Plaice (sand dab) is also abundant off the North American coast. The Pacific sand dab is caught from Baja to the northern coast of Alaska. The Pacific sand dab is light colored with thin scales and a straight lateral line.

Quality characteristics: The flesh is white, mild, soft-textured, and sweet in flavor. Plaice is low in fat.

Usage: Plaice is available fresh or frozen, whole or filleted. It is suitable for most preparation methods.

Turbot – STEINBUTT – *turbot*

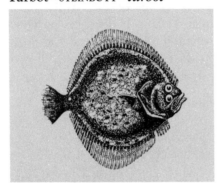

Description: Turbot is a large flatfish with a disk-shaped body. Stonelike bony patches on the top account for its characteristic appearance. Turbot is left-eyed. The coloration depends on its environment, but a variegated brown with light specks is common. The belly is white.

Origin and occurence: Turbot lives in the Atlantic and is found from Iceland to the Mediterranean and in the Baltic Sea. It feeds on small crabs, mussels, and bottom fish. Small turbots are called *turbotin*.

Quality characteristics: White, firm flesh that has good keeping qualities and a delicious mild flavor. In Europe turbot is considered the finest Atlantic sea fish and it is therefore overpriced. It is best between April and September. The light-colored turbot from the Atlantic, known as Boulogne turbot, is more highly prized than the darker variety from the North Sea and the Baltic.

Usage: Turbot can be grilled, poached, or stuffed and baked.

European Mullet
Not the same fish as American Gulf coast mullet, European mullet include the following:

Large-headed mullet – GROSSKÖPFIGE MEERÄSCHE – *mulet à grosse tête/ muge à grosse tête*

Leaping mullet – SPRINGMEER-ÄSCHE – *mulet sauteur/muge sauteur*

Thin-lipped mullet – DÜNNLIPPIGE MEERÄSCHE – *mulet porc/muge porc*

Description: Long body with large, round scales. The mouth is wide and blunt. Very fine teeth line the edges of the jaws.

Origin and occurrence: European mullet are found in the tidal waters of the eastern Atlantic; the exception is the leaping mullet, which lives in Mediterranean waters. The fish are extraordinarily adaptable and can swim up streams or live in muddy water. They grow to a length of 24 to 47 inches (60 to 120 cm) and can weigh from 11 to 20 pounds (5 to 9 kg).

Quality characteristics: Firm, slightly oily, white flesh with excellent flavor.

Usage: Poaching, grilling, sautéing, baking, and deep-frying.

Bream (American Porgy)
About 200 types of ocean bream can be found in temperate and tropical waters (the Mediterranean Sea alone is home to 20 species). Common varieties include:

Bag bream – SACKBRASSE – *pagre*

Gilt-headed sea bream – GOLDBRASSE – *dorade royale/daurade*

Red bream – ROTBRASSE – *pageot*

Gilt-headed sea bream – GOLDBRASSE – *dorade royale/ (vraie) daurade*

Description: The body is oval, slightly flattened at the sides, with a large head and a high forehead. The snout is very small with thick lips. A distinguishing mark is a wide golden band between the eyes, which fades slowly after death. There is also a dark spot at the beginning of the side line. Market size ranges from 8 to 20 inches (20 to 50 cm) long, with none more than 27 inches (70 cm); the fish weighs no more than 15 pounds (7 kg).

Origin and occurrence: Gilt-headed sea bream can be found in the east Atlantic from the northwestern African coast to the northern Bay of Biscay, near the Azores, and the Mediterranean. It lives in depths of about 95 feet (30 m), above rocky formations and beds of seaweed. It feeds on crabs and mollusks.

Quality characteristics: Firm, white, tasty flesh, with few bones. It is best when caught from July to October.

Usage: Bream can be baked whole, grilled, or fried. *American red porgy* is a good substitute for this European fish.

Mullet/Barbel

Mullets (barbel) are bottom fish and live in temperate and tropical waters. From autumn to spring, they live in small schools in deep water; in the summer, they move near the coast, even into tidal pools. Varieties include:

Red mullet (barbel) – ROTE MEERBARBE – *rouget-barbet/ rouget de vase/rouget-barbet de vase*

Striped mullet (barbel) – STREIFENBARBE – *rouget de roche/ rouget-barbet de roche/surmulet*

American mullet

Description: A long body with a sharp head profile. The large eyes are located near the edge of the upper head. Two long, pronged barbels that are attached at the chin help the fish hunt for food. It has two distinctly separate dorsal fins. The color is silver gray with a red tone. The tail is slightly forked.

Red mullet (barbel) – ROTE MEERBARBE – *rouget-barbet*

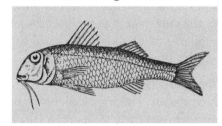

Description: The basic color is silver-gray with a red cast. Average market size is 6 to 8 inches (15 to 20 cm). It feeds on crabs and mollusks. It is not available in the United States.

Origin and occurrence: This fish is found along the Mediterranean and the Black Sea.

Striped mullet (Barbel) – STREIFENBARBE – *rouget de roche/rouget-barbet de roche, surmulet*

Description: The coloring varies with the seasons, but the fish always has identifying dark red and yellow stripes that run from the eye to the tail fin. The market size is 6 to 14 inches (15 to 35 cm).

Origin and occurrence: The striped mullet lives on both sides of the Atlantic and in the Mediterranean. It feeds on crabs and mollusks that it finds on the ocean floor with the help of its long barbels.

Quality characteristics: The flesh is white and delicate, with few bones.

Usage: Usually sautéed or grilled, it is often prepared with its guts, since it has no bitter gall bladder, and it is referred to as the snipe of the sea. The roe of the mullet is salted to make *tarama*. Tarama is used to make the Greek specialty *taramasalata*, a creamy spread made from tarama, lemon juice, olive oil, and milk-soaked bread.

American Mullet

In the United States, mullets are most abundant off the Florida Keys, where whole or gutted fish are reasonably priced. They are moderately fatty fish with a firm, white flesh. They can be pan-fried, baked, or broiled. The striped mullet is caught of the North American Atlantic and Pacific coasts.

Bass-type Fish (Ocean Perch)

Among spiny-finned fish (Latin name *acanthopterygians*), bass-type fish are the most numerous and varied in European waters. Most live in the deep ocean, some in tidal waters, a few in freshwater. Types include:

Greater weever – GROSSES PETERMÄNNCHEN/DRACHENFISCH – *grande vive*

Ocean perch – ROTBARSCH/ GOLDBARSCH – *rascasse du nord/ grand sébaste*

Sea bass – WOLFSBARSCH/MEERBARSCH – *bar/loup de mer*

Spotted sea bass – GEFLECKTER MEERBARSCH – *bar rayé*

Greater weever – GROSSES PETERMÄNNCHEN/ DRACHENFISCH – *grande vive*

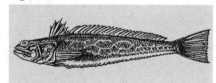

Description: A bottom fish with a long, slim body and slightly flattened sides. The gill covers are studded with poisonous spikes; the five to seven dorsal fin rays are spiky and poisonous and are usually removed before the fish comes to market. The rays contain a nerve-attacking poison, which is destroyed by heat. A puncture wound should immediately be treated with very hot water. Market size about 8 to 12 inches (20 to 30 cm).

Origin and occurrence: Lives in the northeast Atlantic. Buried in sand, the fish preys on shrimp and small fish.

Usage: A popular fish used in making classic *bouillabaisse*.

Ocean perch (red rockfish) –
ROTBARSCH/GOLDBARSCH – *rascasse du nord/grand sébaste*

Description: Large body with big eyes and a wide mouth. The gill covers have sharp spikes pointing backward. It grows to 11 to 31 inches (30 to 80 cm), with a maximum size of 39 inches (100 cm), and to 5½ pounds (2.5 kg).

Origin and occurrence: It is caught in the North Atlantic from Scotland to Norway and from Iceland to the White Sea. Ocean perch feed on plankton and herring. In the United States, a West Coast rockfish caught from southern California to Washington is similar and sold as ocean perch.

Quality characteristics: Firm, slightly oily, pinkish white flesh. Because ocean perch has very hard scales and sharp spikes, it is usually filleted for the market.

Usage: The fillets can be poached, baked, sautéed, or deep-fried.

Sea bass – WOLFSBARSCH/SEEBARSCH – *loup de mer*

Description: Long, elegant, silvery body, gray on top with a light belly. It has two dorsal fins; the first is spiny. It is available on the market in lengths from 16 to 24 inches (40 to 60 cm), weighing about 1.3 to 3.3 pounds (0.6 to 1.5 kg).

Origin and occurrence: Found in the eastern Atlantic from Senegal to Norway, in the southern North Sea, the Baltic, and the Mediterranean.

Quality characteristics: Very lean, firm, delicious flesh. It is highly valued in *haute cuisine* and is quite ex-

pensive. Sea bass farming is in the experimental stages.

Usage: Excellent poached, baked, sautéed, grilled, or served in sauce.

Spotted sea bass – GEFLECKTER MEER-BARSCH – *bar rayé*
Description: Distinguishable from the common sea bass by a dark spot on the gills and by the dark irregularly placed spots on the back and sides. The spotted sea bass is found in the same places as the sea bass, of similar quality and can be used instead of sea bass in recipes.

American Bass
Description: Two types of bass are available on the U.S. market. Black sea bass is brownish black or dark green, with sharp dorsal fins and a thick body weighing about 3 to 5 pounds (1.4 to 2.3 kg). Striped bass is olive green, with a silvery shine, and six to eight longitudinal stripes. The market size ranges from 4 to 12 pounds (1.8 to 5.5 kg). Striped bass are called stripers in New England; from the Chesapeake south, they are called "rockfish," not to be confused with the rockfish species.

Origin and occurrence: Both types are abundant in coastal waters from Maine to Florida. The striped bass was introduced to the Pacific coast, where it can be found from Oregon to south of San Francisco.

Quality characteristics: Moderately fat with firm, white, flaky flesh.

Usage: Available whole, filleted, or as steaks. They are excellent broiled, grilled, baked (stuffed), fried, poached, or barbecued.

Eels
Conger eel – MEERAAL – *congre*

Description: A conger eel has no scales. The back fin runs the length

of the entire body, starting above the pectoral fin. The usual market size is about 2 to 6 feet (60 to 200 cm). However, it can grow to about 10 feet (300 cm) and weigh about 143 pounds (65 kg).

Origin and occurrence: Eel lives in coastal waters in the Atlantic, Baltic, and the Mediterranean. A solitary fish, it hides during the day in its cave. It hunts at night and feeds on crabs, fish, and octopus.

Quality characteristics: Coarse, firm flesh, low in fat but with many bones.

Usage: Conger eel is used in simple *bouillabaisse* and can be smoked.

Wolffish/Ocean Catfish
Atlantic or striped wolffish/ocean catfish – GESTREIFTER SEEWOLF/ KATFISCH/STEINBEISSER – *loup de l'Atlantique/ loup du nord/ loup marin*

Spotted wolffish – GEFLECKTER SEEWOLF – *loup tacheté*

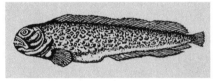

Description: The long, slim body has no scales. The dorsal fin is spiky. The big head has a wide mouth with sharp, caninelike teeth. The whole body is covered with slime. It can grow to a length of about 48 inches (120 cm) and weigh 40 pounds (18 kg).

Origin and occurrence: The cold waters of the North Atlantic from Iceland and Greenland to the White Sea and in the North Pacific to the Bering Strait. Wolffish is also caught in the Gulf of Maine and George's Bank. It feeds on hard-shelled crabs and mollusks.

Quality characteristics: Tasty, firm white flesh.

Usage: Wolffish is available whole, skinned and without head, or as fillets on the market. The skin of the spotted wolffish is made into leather. A very popular table fish in Scandinavia and Spain, it can be baked, poached, fried, or broiled. It is used in fish stews and soups. Wolffish is now being farmed in Norway. Though available, it is hard to find in American markets.

Monkfish
Monkfish – SEETEUFEL – *baudroie/ lotte de mer*

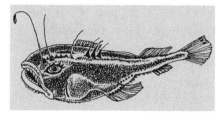

Description: The body of the monkfish is wide, with a narrow tail. The gigantic flat head has small eyes on top and an enormous snout with a protruding lower jaw and two rows of sharp, strong, pointed teeth. The pectoral fins are enlarged; monkfish use them to "walk" along the ocean floor.

Origin and occurrence: Monkfish for the European market are caught in the northeastern Atlantic, North Sea, and western Baltic Sea. In North America they are found from Newfoundland to North Carolina. Buried in the sand, they bait fish with the fluttering fishing spine attached to their head and catch it with the huge mouth.

Quality characteristics: Firm, white flesh, with a flavor similar to crustaceans (lobster or crab).

Usage: Only the tail is marketed, generally without skin. Totally free of bones, monkfish has always been prized in Europe. Considered a trash fish in the United States only a few years ago, monkfish has been elevated to an expensive restaurant fish in this country as well.

John Dory
John Dory – PETERSFISCH/ HERINGSKÖNIG – *saint pierre*
Description: A disk-shaped body with sharply flattened sides and spiny fins. The mouth points upward. The gray body is spotted, with a large round black spot on each side. The first dorsal fin has long, flaglike fin extensions that can fold back to reach the tail. It is a very

odd-looking fish.

Origin and occurrence: John Dory is found in the eastern Atlantic, the Mediterranean, and the Black Sea.

Quality characteristics: The flesh is white, firm, and delicious.

Usage: Grilled, poached, or sautéed.

Scorpion Fish
Scarlet rascasse – GROSSER ROTER DRACHENKOPF – *rascasse rouge*
Description: Large body with a large spiny head. At the base of the spiky dorsal fin are poison-producing glands, which can cause dangerous injuries. Scarlet rascasse is a slow-moving bottom fish that sheds its skin regularly.

Origin and occurrence: It is found in the Mediterranean and the Atlantic Ocean. This fish is not found in American waters. Red perch can be substituted.

Quality characteristics: White, firm flesh.

Usage: Much prized for *bouillabaisse*.

Drums (Gurnards)
Varieties include:

Gray drum – GRAUER KNURRHAHN – *grondin gris*

Red drum – ROTER KNURRHAHN – *grondin perlon*

Sea robin – SEEKUCKUCK – *grondin rouge*

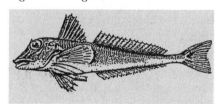

Description: The drum has a large head with a ducklike mouth and large pectoral fins. Two or three spines of the pectoral fin are free moving. The drum uses these spines to "walk" on the ocean floor to sense its food. It feeds on small crabs and fish. Drums get their name from the loud drumming noise they produce with their air bladder.

Origin and occurrence: Drums are found in the Atlantic, North Sea, Baltic, Mediterranean, and Black

Sea. They can grow to a length of about 28 inches (70 cm) and weigh about 13 pounds (6 kg). The market size is about 10 to 12 inches (25 to 30 cm).

Quality characteristics: Firm white tasty flesh. The carcass waste is high, about 60 percent.

Usage: Popular *bouillabaisse* fish.

Snappers
Varieties include:

Red emperor snapper – KAISER SCHNAPPER – *vivaneau bourgeoise*

Red snapper – ROTER SCHNAPPER – *vivaneau rouge*

Description: There are many varieties of snapper, which can be found in tropical waters all over the globe. Economically, the red emperor snapper is most important. This fish is similar in shape and taste to the red snapper but can reach a size of about 39 inches (1 m). Average weight of red snappers is 4½ to 6½ pounds (2 to 3 kg). Snappers are bright red, with an oval-shaped body. The large head has big eyes and a large mouth.

Origin and occurrence: Red snapper is caught from North Carolina to Florida and in the Gulf of Mexico.

Quality characteristics: Most of the snappers are of excellent quality and are prized by restaurants and gourmets. Red snapper flesh is white, lean and moist, with few bones.

Usage: Snapper is sold whole or filleted. It can be broiled, baked, steamed, or poached.

Other Saltwater Fish on the American Market

Dolphin Fish/Mahi-Mahi
Mahi-mahi is the Hawaiian name for the dolphin fish. It is not related to the mammal dolphins.

Description: Mahi-mahi are fast swimmers. The body is long and slender, with a dorsal fin running the length of the back to the forked tail. It is turquoise blue with orange pectoral fins. It ranges in weight from 5 to 65 pounds (2.2 to 29.5 kg); market size is usually 25 pounds (11.4 kg).

Origin and occurrence: It is found in warm waters worldwide and caught on the Pacific coast from Baja to Oregon.

Quality characteristics: Mahi-mahi is firm and moderately oily, with a meatlike texture.

Usage: Mahi-mahi is marketed as steaks or fillets; rarely whole. Any dark meat must be removed because of its strong oily flavor. The skin is tough and inedible. Mahi-mahi can be prepared by all cooking methods but is best grilled or broiled.

Grouper

Groupers are part of the sea bass family. Fifty different types are found off the Florida coast. The most commonly available is red grouper.

Description: Groupers are brown, gray, red, or black patterned fish, with big heads and large mouths.

Origin and occurrence: They are found from the Carolinas to the Florida Keys, off the Bahamas, and in the Caribbean.

Quality characteristics: Grouper has lean, firm, white, moist flesh. It is very similar to bass in flavor and texture.

Usage: The skin is removed before cooking. Small fish can be cooked whole or filleted. Large grouper is sold in chunks or as steaks. It can be prepared in all possible ways. It is excellent broiled or cooked with sauces.

Pompano Fish

Description: Small, slender body, with a silvery bluish green back and silvery sides. Pompano weigh about 1 to 4 pounds (0.5 to 1.8 kg).

Origin and occurrence: A member of the jack family, pompano are found from Chesapeake Bay to the Caribbean. They are most abundant in the Gulf of Mexico. The Pacific pompano is a member of the butter-fish family.

Quality characteristics: Considered the finest of America's saltwater eating fish, pompano flesh is white, slightly fatty, moist, and fine textured.

Usage: Whole or filleted, it is often broiled or baked in parchment paper, *en papillote*.

Tilefish

Description: Tilefish are large, green-ish gray fish with yellow spots. The anal fin and tail are pink to purple in tone. The body is very stout and can weigh up to 50 pound (22.7 kg).

Origin and occurrence: Tilefish is found along the continental shelf from Nova Scotia to southern Florida. It is also caught in the Gulf of Mexico. As a bottom fish, it likes water temperatures of 45°F to 53°F (112°C to 127°C). Tilefish feed on crabs, mollusk, and sea cucumber.

Quality characteristics: Tilefish flesh is low in fat, tender but firm, and white with a pink hue. Its taste is described as being similar to lobster.

Usage: Tilefish is available fresh or frozen, as steaks or fillets. Atlantic tilefish is reasonably priced. The fish can be prepared in many ways. It is excellent in chowders and grilled.

Miscellaneous Saltwater Fish

Butterfish, a small, fatty fish, is usually sold whole and is excellent smoked. *Cobia*, a fast swimmer, is caught off the south Florida coast and in the Gulf of Mexico. Its white flesh is very firm, moist, and delicious and can be sautéed, baked, broiled, or braised. Two types of *sheepshead* are available, one from south of Chesapeake Bay and the other from the southern California coast. Although they are of different species, they taste similar. Their flesh is white, firm, and mild. *Triggerfish* is a warm-water fish that lives near reefs and feeds on crustaceans and mollusks. Its flesh is sweet and firm and can be prepared in many ways; it is excellent grilled.

2. Freshwater Fish

Approximately fifty different fish species live in Switzerland's lakes and rivers. Many fish cannot be sustained in their natural habitats because their spawning grounds have been polluted or destroyed. Fish-breeding stations and farms are helpful in increasing the number of fish in Swiss waters.

Consistently enforced waste-water controls will improve water quality and protect the natural habitats of lakes and rivers to restore the native fish population. The major source of pollution in inland lakes is runoff from agricultural fertilizers. Fertilizer causes algae and other water plants to flourish and take over the lakes. In these waters, whitefish can survive only under fish-farming conditions.

About five hundred Swiss fishermen catch 3,500 tons of fish annually: on the average, 900 tons of whitefish, 350 tons of trout, 800 tons of perch, 25 tons of char (saibling), and 12.5 tons of carp. Fishermen help maintain the ecological balance by regulating the size of the various fish populations. To protect preferred market fish, they may curtail the carp population, for example, which would otherwise decimate eggs in spawning grounds and tiny young fish.

Freshwater fish live in streams and lakes. Included in this category are anadromous fish, which are born in freshwater, migrate to the oceans, and return to freshwater to spawn. Although access to many rivers is restricted by dams, fish ladders have been installed to assist the spawning fish. *Stocking* has also widely increased the natural range of many freshwater fish in European as well as American waters.

Common Freshwater Fish

The most common and most often prepared freshwater fish are listed and then briefly described below. Color descriptions have been deliberately omitted, since many fish change their color with age or adapt coloring to their environment.

Eels
Freshwater eel—FLUSSAAL—*anguille*
American river eel—AMERIKANISCHER FLUSSAAL

European river eel—EUROPÄISCHER FLUSSAAL

Perch Family
European Perch—FLUSSBARSCH/EGLI-*perche*

Pike perch—ZANDER/SCHILL/HECHTBARSCH-*sandre*

Tilapia—BUNTBARSCH/TILAPIA-BARSCH-*perche tilapia*

Yellow perch—KANADISCHES EGLI-*perche canadienne*

Pike
Pike—HECHT-*brochet*

Grayling
Grayling—ÄSCHE-*ombre*

Whitefish
Whitefish—FELCHEN/RENKE-*féra*

Swiss types are: Sandfelchen, Blaufelchen, Gangfisch, Aalbock, Albeli/Brienzling, palée, bondelle.

Salmon Family
Char—SAIBLING/RÖTEL—*omble/salmerin*
Brook char—BACHSAIBLING-*omble de fontaine*

Canadian char—KANADISCHER SEESAIBLING

Lake char—SEESAIBLING-*omble chevalier*

Salmon—LACHS—*saumon*
Atlantic salmon/wild salmon—WILD-LACHS (*salmon salar*)—*saumon*

Chinook/king salmon—KÖNIGSLACHS-*saumon royale*

Coho salmon—SILBERLACHS/COHO-LACHS-*saumon argenté*

Danube salmon—HUCHEN/DONAU-LACHS-*huch/saumon du Danube*

Pacific salmon—PAZIFISCHER LACHS (*Oncorhynchus*)-*saumon du Pacifique*

Pink (humpback)—BUCKELLACHS-*saumon rose*

Siberian salmon—KETA LACHS-*saumon Kéta*

Sockeye salmon—ROTLACHS-*saumon rouge*

Trout—FORELLE—*truite*
Brook trout—BACHFORELLE-*truite de rivière*

Lake trout—SEEFORELLE-*truite du lac*

Rainbow trout—REGENBOGENFORELLE-*truite arc-en-ciel*

Sea trout—MEERFORELLE-*truite de mer*

Cod-type Fish
Burbot—TRÜSCHE/AALRUTTE-*lotte de rivière*

Sturgeon
Beluga—HAUSEN/BELUGA-STÖR—*grand esturgeon*

Sevruga—STERNHAUSEN/SEVRUGA-*sévruga*

Lake sturgeon—STERLET-*sterlet*

Osetra—WAXDICK/OSIETRA-STÖR-*oscètre*

Sturgeon—STÖR-*esturgeon*

Carp
Barbel—BARBE-*barbeau*

Bream carp—BRACHSE-*brème*

Chub sucker—SCHLEIE-*tanche*

Leather carp—LEDERKARPFEN-*carpe à cuir*

Mirror carp—SPIEGELKARPFEN-*carpe miroir*

Roach—ROTAUGE/PLÖTZE-*vangeron/vengeron*

Wild carp—SCHUPPENKARPEN/WILDKARPFEN-*carpe*

Sheatfish
Catfish—ZWERGWELS-*poisson chat*

Sheatfish (wels)—WELS/WALLER-*silure/glanis*

Eel Family
Freshwater Eel—FLUSSAAL—*anguille*
Two types are of culinary importance: the European river eel and the American river eel. A related species is the Moray eel.

Description: The body is snakelike, with a thick, slimy skin covered with tiny oval scales. The dorsal fin is continuous and connects with the tail.

Origin and occurrence: The young eel leaves the sea and migrates to rivers and lakes, where it lives for four to ten years before returning to the ocean to spawn. The European river eel heads for the Sargasso Sea, a journey of approximately 3,500 nautical miles. The migration can take about a year and a half. Eels die after spawning.

Carried by the Gulf Stream, the spawn drift east for three years toward the European coast. When they have reached a length of 4 to 6 inches (10 to 15 cm), the eel enter river deltas and start moving upstream. Males often stay in the brackish waters at the mouth of the river.

Even though many rivers have dams, the tiny eels are almost everywhere because they have been seeded into them. Eels are very tenacious and very adaptable and can even "wander" across land to reach other waters, as long as the weather conditions are damp. They eat worms, insect larvae, small crabs, and frogs.

Quality characteristics: Eels are oily (25 percent) and rather hard to digest. Eels from ponds often have an unpleasant taste and should be kept in a fish tank with flowing fresh water for several days. Eels are skinned before cooking. They are sold on the market live or smoked.

Perch Family
European perch—FLUSSBARSCH/EGLI-*perche*

Pike perch—ZANDER/SCHILL/HECHTBARSCH-*sandre*

Tilapia—BUNTBARSCH/TILAPIABARSCH-*perche tilapia*

Yellow perch—GELBBARSCH/KANADISCHES EGLI-*perche canadienne*

In the United States the name *perch* is used for a variety of fresh- and saltwater fish. The perch described here are European. They are closely related to the North American yellow perch.

European perch – FLUSSBARSCH/EGLI – *perche*

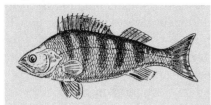

Description: Perch have a somewhat high-backed body, a blunt head with a wide mouth, and pointed gill covers. The dorsal fins have large, spiny rays.

Origin and occurrence: European perch live in still and moving waters at elevations of up to 3,000 feet. They feed on spawn and small fish. River perch usually grow 5 to 6 inches (12 to 15 cm) long, never longer than 15 inches (40 cm), with a maximum weight of 2.2 pounds (1 kg).

Quality characteristics: Perch is one of the best-tasting freshwater fish, with firm, white flesh that is very lean.

Pike perch – ZANDER/SCHILL/ HECHTBARSCH – *sandre*

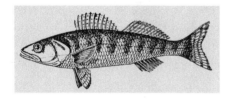

Description: Pike perch have a long, pikelike body with a small, pointed head and wide mouth. The gill cover has a sharp barb. This fish is known in Hungary and Austria as *fogosch*. They average 16 inches (40 cm) in length, but do not grow beyond 27 inches (70 cm); the average weight is 2¼ to 3¼ pounds (1 to 1.5 kg).

Origin and occurrence: Pike perch are found in central and eastern Europe. They prefer large rivers, huge dams, and lakes with gravel bottoms. Stocking has increased the number of pike perch in northern Europe. They eat small fish.

Quality characteristics: White, tender flesh with an excellent taste, similar to pike.

Tilapia perch – BUNTBARSCH/TILAPIA-BARSCH – *perche tilapia*

Description: Tilapias have laterally flat bodies that range from 4 to 12 inches (10 to 30 cm) in length.

Origin and occurrence: Native to Africa, tilapias have become more available on menus around the world as a result of aquaculture. They have become important commercial fish in Israel, Southeast Asia, and South America, where they are cultivated on fish farms and exported. They feed on insect larvae, crustaceans, young fish, and worms.

Quality characteristics: Available fresh or smoked, tilapias have a very tasty flesh.

Yellow perch – GELBBARSCH/ KANADISCHES EGLI – *perche canadienne*

Description: The yellow perch is similar to the European perch, but somewhat smaller. The average market size is 6 inches (15 cm); weight, about 7.5 oz (220 g), although they can grow to 4.5 pounds (2 kg).

Origin and occurrence: The yellow perch is native to North American rivers and streams east of the Rocky Mountains. It feeds on a variety of insects, invertebrates, and small fish.

Quality characteristics: A favorite among anglers because of its delicious flavor, yellow perch has firm, white flesh that is low in fat.

Pike

Pike – HECHT – *brochet*

Description: The most identifiable feature of the pike is its duck-billed head. The short dorsal and anal fins are set far down on the back. One-year-old pikes are light green and are called grass pike in Europe. The average length of a pike is 16 to 28 inches (40 to 70 cm). It can reach a maximum length of 59 inches (150 cm). The preferred weight is 2.2 to

6½ pounds (1 to 3 kg), though it can grow as large as 77 pounds (35 kg).

Origin and occurrence: Pike live in lakes and rivers in milder regions of Europe, Asia, and North America. Pike can be found in mountain waters up to 4,500 feet (1,500 m). It does not leave its territory and prefers clear waters with gravelly bottoms. It feeds on small fish, even its own kind.

Quality characteristics: The firm, lean, white flesh is very tasty flesh but full of bones. It is, however, excellent in fish farces (forcemeats) and deep-fried.

Grayling

Grayling – ÄSCHE – *ombre*

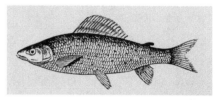

Description: The body is somewhat stretched, with a noticeably high dorsal fin and an adipose fin. The grayling has a small head with large eyes and a small mouth.

Origin and occurrence: Grayling live in quick-moving, clear waters. They are plentiful in the Rhine before it enters Lake Constance, and in the rivers Aare, Reuss, Limmat, and Doubs. Grayling is a sport fish in the United States and is found in the upper Mississippi basin, Montana, and Alaska.

Quality characteristics: The firm, lean, white flesh has an aroma and taste resembling thyme; hence its Latin name *Thymallus*. They can be pan-fried, steamed, poached, and grilled.

Whitefish

Whitefish – FELCHEN/RENKE – *féra*

Listing the different types of whitefish is extraordinarily difficult, because so many regional varieties have evolved. Generally two distinctions are made, between the floaters (deep, open-water fish) and bottom dwellers. In Switzerland they are categorized by size into large, medium, small, and midget whitefish. In the United States, lake whitefish, mountain whitefish, and round whitefish are caught.

Description: Some whitefish are anadromous (migrate to the ocean), whereas others are nonmigratory fish. Whitefish are slim, silver fish with slightly flattened sides. The scales are larger than those of char or trout. They have an adipose fin and deeply notched caudal fin (tail). Market size is 8 to 24 inches (20 to 60 cm).

Origin and occurrence: All lakes in central Europe contain whitefish, but they can also be found in lower mountain lakes. They feed primarily on tiny crustaceans and aquatic insects.

Quality characteristics: The white, tasty, but slightly dry flesh has a tendency to fall apart during cooking. Whitefish should be consumed as fresh as possible. It does not freeze well.

Salmon Family
To the salmon family belong salmon, trout, char, grayling, whitefish, and Danube salmon (called *Huche* in German). All have elongated bodies with flattened sides covered with many small scales. The wide mouth is studded with sharp teeth. Members of the salmon family always have a small adipose fin between the dorsal fin and the caudal fin. All fish in this family prefer cold, oxygen-rich waters and spawn in the spring, fall, or winter, depending on climate. The migrating types live for long periods in the ocean but spawn in freshwater. The others never leave their rivers and lakes and are nonmigratory. All members of the salmon family have great economic value because of the superior quality of their flesh.

Char – SAIBLING/RÖTEL – *omble/salmerin*
Arctic char – KANADISCHER SEESAIBLING

Brook char – BACHSAIBLING – *omble de fontaine*

Lake char – SEESAIBLING – *omble chevalier*

There are many different types of chars in Swiss lakes. Those caught in Zuger Lake, Thuner Lake, and Vierwaldstätter Lake are called *Rötel*. The Zuger Rötel (Zugersee) is very small, weighing only about 5 ounces (150 g). Chars from Lake Tessin are called *salmerino,* and chars from Lake Geneva are called *omble chevalier.* Char was introduced into European waters from North America at the end of the nineteenth century. Char has various colors. The migrating types have many sub- and miniature species, and some variation exists in the stationary lake populations. Chars are often farm-raised in mountain lakes. They lives in cold, oxygen-rich waters. They can grow to a length of about 24 inches (60 cm) and weigh about 6½ pounds (3 kg). Char has very tasty, tender, salmon-pink flesh.

Brook char – BACHSAIBLING – *omble de fontaine*
Brook char, a native of the cold waters of North America, is now at home in many European rivers as well. Char must have clean, clear water to survive. Offspring from mating char and trout are called *tigerfish.* The less habitat-sensitive, more prolific rainbow trout is pushing brook char out of many waters; this is one reason why much char is a result of aquaculture.

Salmon – LACHS/SALM — *saumon*
Atlantic wild salmon/wild salmon – WILDLACHS– *saumon*

Atlantic salmon (farm-raised)

Pacific salmon – PAZIFISCHER LACHS (*Oncorhynchus*) – *saumon du Pacifique*

Atlantic salmon/wild salmon – WILDLACHS – *saumon*
Description: Salmon have long, slim bodies covered with small scales and have small heads with pointed mouths. Immature wild salmon have dark round spots on the head and silvery sides.

Under normal conditions salmon swim far upriver to spawn. There, their skin thickens and becomes tough, with red and black spots. The color of the male's underbelly turns red, and a sharp barbel forms on the lower jaw, which shrivels after spawning. Spawning occurs from November to February. After one to five years (depending on location) in freshwater, the young salmon migrate to the ocean and feed on fish and crustaceans. Their flavor and pink color are attributable to the diet of crustaceans. Salmon gain weight very rapidly in the ocean. Their average weight is 6¼ to 8½ pounds (3 to 4 kg). But fish 5 feet (1.5 m) in length weighing about 77 pounds (35 kg) have been caught.

Origin and occurrence: Wild salmon are found in the waters off Iceland, Norway, Sweden, Denmark (Bornholm), Scotland, and Ireland. In North America salmon are still present in large numbers. Pollution and the obstruction of spawning grounds has greatly reduced the population of wild European salmon, in some areas, for example the Rhine, eliminating it completely.

Quality characteristics: The flesh of the Bornholm salmon is light pink, almost white, whereas the flesh of the other types is almost red. The flesh is firm and very tasty, with a fat content of 11 percent.

Atlantic farm-raised salmon

Description: The key to success in farm-raising Atlantic salmon is to recognize their natural tendency to remain in freshwater from two to four years before moving into a salt-water environment, which has more food available and thus causes the salmon to grow quickly. It is therefore extremely important in farm-raising salmon to shorten the stay in freshwater and hasten the transfer of the young salmon to the saltwater environment. This is accomplished by increasing the light intensity, the length of daylight, and water temperature, which artificially shortens the seasons. In this way is it possible to farm-raise salmon for the market in just one or two years.

Origin and occurrence: The major producers of farm-raised salmon are Norway, Scotland, Ireland, and Canada.

Quality characteristics: Farm-raised salmon is fed mostly with prepared feed made from fish and shrimp meal with natural plant materials. These modern feeding methods allow the flavor, color, and fat content to be predictably controlled, producing salmon of reliable quality and constant availability. The flesh of farm-raised salmon is softer and has a higher fat content than wild salmon. Farm-raised salmon is available on the market freshly killed, graded, and packed on ice in Styrofoam packing and as fillets, smoked or marinated (*gravlax*), which may be whole or presliced.

Pacific salmon – PACIFISCHER LACHS (*Oncorhynchus*) – *saumon du Pacifique*

Description: Pacific salmon are larger than Atlantic salmon, with much larger anal fins. Pacific salmon migrate up rivers that flow into the northern Pacific and the Arctic oceans. Varieties of Pacific salmon include:

Chinook or king salmon – *saumon royale:* The Chinook salmon is the largest and tastiest of the Pacific salmon.

Coho or silver salmon – *saumon argenté:* From a culinary point of view, the Coho is the second-best Pacific salmon. Approximately 30 million Coho salmon are farm-raised yearly. Coho is pond-raised in Europe.

Humpback salmon – *saumon rose:* This is the smallest Pacific salmon, with an average weight of 4¼ pounds (2 kg).

Siberian salmon – *saumon Kéta:* The roe of this salmon is the source of *keta caviar.*

Red or sockeye salmon – *saumon rouge:* This variety is usually canned or exported frozen to Japan for sushi.

Trout – FORELLE – *truite*

Brook trout – BACHFORELLE – *truite de rivière*

Lake trout – SEEFORELLE – *truite du lac*

Rainbow trout – REGENBOGENFORELLE – *truite arc-en-ciel*

Sea trout – MEERFORELLE – *truite de mer*

Trout differ from salmon in that they have rounder bodies and blunter heads. Trout are the most commonly served freshwater fish because of intensive fish farming and because of their excellent quality. Despite their ubiquity, they remain a popular menu item. They are available fresh or frozen. All trout varieties have firm, basically tasty flesh. They taste best when they are prepared freshly killed.

Brook trout – BACHFORELLE – *truite de rivière/truite de ruisseau*

Description: This nonmigratory trout is a smaller version of the lake trout and is much prized by sport fishermen.

Origin and occurrence: Brook trout prefer to live in cool, oxygen-rich running waters with plentiful hiding places. They feed on insect eggs, crayfish, and flying insects (jumping

to catch them). Older trout will also feed on small fish. They reach a length of 16 inches (40 cm) and can weigh close to 6¼ pounds (3 kg). The average size is 10 inches (25 cm), and the average weight is 11 ounces (300 g).

Quality characteristics: The flesh is white to salmon-pink.

Lake trout – SEEFORELLE – *truite du lac*

Description: Lake trout is a migrating fish that lives in the large deep lakes of middle and northern Europe. Spawning takes place in tributary rivers and in gravel pits of the lakes themselves. It is a fish of only regional culinary importance (e.g., "*Rheinlake*").

Rainbow trout – REGENBOGEN-FORELLE – *truite arc-en-ciel*

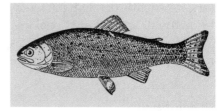

Description: Rainbow trout have long, slim bodies with slightly flattened sides. The head is blunt, and the dorsal, adipose, and tail fins are covered with small black dots. They feed on insects and small fish. Rainbows can grow up to 28 inches (70 cm) long and weigh 15 pounds (7 kg). An especially beautifully colored rainbow trout is the golden trout from North America.

Origin and occurrence: Since 1880, when they were introduced to Europe from North America, two types of rainbow trout have populated European waters: the migrating rainbow, which lives in coastal waters, and the nonmigratory type, which stays in freshwater streams. In rivers and brooks, it unfortunately often displaces the less robust char.

Quality characteristics: The rainbow is well suited to fish farming, since it is a voracious feeder and resistant to disease. The composition of feed can positively influence the taste of the flesh. Farm-raised rainbow trout is often served whole.

The **salmon trout**—LACHSFORELLE—*truite saumonée* on the market is actually a rainbow trout, and should not be confused with the true sea trout or steelhead (salmon) trout. To produce farm-raised salmon trout, rainbow trout are fed shrimp and carotene, which cause the flesh to change from white to salmon pink within 14 days. These rainbow trout are sold as salmon trout.

Sea trout—MEERFORELLE—
truite de mer

Description: Sea trout is a migrating trout that can be found from the White Sea to the coast of northern Spain. Along the Atlantic coast of North America, sea trout is known as silver or spotted trout. Sea trout spawn from December to March. The young fish stay in freshwater up to five years, when they have reached a length of 6 to 10 inches (15 to 25 cm). Sea trout is farm-raised in Norway.

Cod Family
Burbot—TRÜSCHE/AALRUTTE—
lotte de rivière

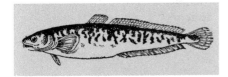

Description: The burbot is the only member of the cod family that lives in freshwater. The long, tubular body is somewhat pinched near the tail and has tiny scales. The wide, long head has three barbels. The second dorsal fin and the pectoral fin are very long, similar to those of an eel, which is why it is called *Aalrutte* in German. They grow about 50 inches long and weigh about 1 pound.

Origin and occurrence: Burbot are found in cool running waters; in mountain regions, they can be found at elevations of up to 3,500 feet

(1,200 m). They are also found in deep lakes in North America. They feed on bottom feeders, fish eggs, and small fish.

Quality characteristics: White, very tender, and flavorful flesh. The burbot has few scales but has tough skin, and so is usually skinned. The extra-large liver is considered a delicacy, but caution should be exercised, since the liver is often full of parasites.

Sturgeon
Sturgeon—STÖR—*esturgeon*

Description: Sturgeon are anadromous and are found only in the northern hemisphere. The body is shaped like a shark's and is covered with five rows of bony scutes. The caudal fin has a larger top flap. The small toothless mouth with four anterior barbels can be extended, snoutlike. Sturgeon leave the ocean and swim upstream to spawn in rivers. After two years, the young fish return to the ocean. Varieties include:

Beluga—*grand esturgeon:* length 80 to 100 inches (200 to 250 cm)

Sturgeon—*esturgeon:* length 40 to 60 inches (100 to 150 cm)

Sevruga—*sévruga:* length 52 to 56 inches (130 to 140 cm)

Lake sturgeon (nonmigratory)—*sterlet:* length up to 40 inches (100 cm)

Osetra—*oscètre:* length 56 to 64 inches (140 to 160 cm)

Origin and occurrence: Sturgeon are found in the Black and Caspian seas and in the Sea of Azov. The lake sturgeon can be found only in large river deltas near the ocean and in large lakes. In the United States, sturgeon are caught in the Pacific Northwest and along the southern Atlantic coast. Sturgeon are of great economic importance because of their very tasty flesh. In Russia sturgeon are stocked in large dams and are farm-raised.

Quality characteristics: The flesh of smaller sturgeons is very tasty and the market demand cannot be met. Smoked sturgeon is much appreciated. The air bladder (isinglass) of the beluga sturgeon is used to clarify wine. The roe of sturgeons is the *true* caviar.

Caviar—KAVIAR—*caviar*
Description: Caviar is the prepared and salted roe of sturgeon. *True* caviar is extracted from four types of sturgeon. The only two countries that produce caviar are Russia and Iran. Good caviar must be taken from living females. In order to extract the roe, the fish is killed with a gill slash and bled. The roe is gently pushed by hand through a hemp sieve to remove any extraneous cells and then is salted lightly. About ten minutes elapse from the removal of the roe to its packaging. The ideal packaging for fresh caviar is still a lined can with an inverted lid, which contains about 4 pounds (1.8 kg). The lid is used to extract excessive brine. The can is vacuum-sealed and tied with a wide rubber ring. The unopened can preserves the caviar at top quality for up to one year. From this large can, smaller amounts are repackaged.

Caviar is a highly sensitive product and should be stored at a constant temperature of 28°F to 32°F (-2°C to 0°C). If stored at even 25°F (-4°C) the taste and consistency change dramatically. Modern refrigeration and transportation methods make it possible to have fresh caviar available anywhere in the world. The world export center for caviar is the freight airport Zürich-Embraport.

Quality characteristics: **Beluga** is the best and most expensive caviar; with large eggs (3.5 mm), it is also the coarsest caviar. The color is dark gray. Extraction yields 37 to 44 pounds (17 to 20 kg) per fish.

Osetra is the favorite among caviar lovers. The eggs are smaller, with a stronger membrane, and are less perishable. The taste is nutty and very distinctly different from other caviars. The color is yellowish to light brown. Extraction yields 6½ to 15 pounds (3 to 7 kg) per fish.

Sevruga comes from the smallest of sturgeons. The eggs are tender and very perishable, with a distinct spicy aroma. The color is medium to steel gray. Extraction yields about 2 to 6½ pounds (1 to 3 kg) per fish.

Sterlet, a small golden caviar, is rarely available.

Malossol, a term used to describe Russian caviar, means "little salt" in Russian, about 3 to 4 percent. The eggs of any caviar should by clear, dry, full, and of the same size, shape, and color. Their taste should be mild, without salty or bitter flavors.

Storage: When possible, fresh caviar should be stored on ice at 28°F to 32°F (-2°C to 0°C); keep pasteurized caviar refrigerated.

Usage: The value of caviar is relative to the price and is better defined by its symbolic value. The nutritional value of caviar is secondary to its pure enjoyment value.

Caviar should not come in contact with silver or stainless-steel utensils, as oxidation of the silver causes caviar to have a fishy taste. Neutral materials such as bone, mother-of-pearl, tortoiseshell, and wood, should be used. Caviar is always served chilled, whenever possible on a block of ice. Chopped onion and too much lemon juice can spoil the delicate flavor.

In addition to true caviar, a few good-quality substitutes are available:

Keta caviar (salmon or red caviar) is prepared from the roe of chum salmon (Siberian salmon) from the northern Pacific. The eggs are large and naturally salmon pink in color.

Trout caviar, the prepared roe from large trout, is of the same quality as salmon roe. The best tasting is fresh and only lightly salted.

Lumpfish caviar is the lowest-priced substitute caviar extracted from lumpfish. It is dyed red or black and is very salty.

In the United States, domestic caviar is available from farm-raised sturgeon.

Carp Family

The fish belonging to the carp family are probably the most varied of all fish types. They are very bony fish. Two fish in this family are served in restaurants, the carp and chub sucker (tench). However, the flesh of all fish belonging to the carp family is very tasty and could find a place in family restaurants.

Barbel – BARBE – *barbeau*
Description: Barbel can be identified by the elongated mouth with four barbels on the upper lip. It grows to about 32 inches (80 cm) and weighs up to 17 pounds (8 kg).

Origin and occurrence: This slim fish lives in large schools in clear running waters with gravelly bottoms. It feeds on small bottom dwellers and spawn.

Quality characteristics: Gourmets value barbel as a delicious table fish. Caution is necessary during spawning times, as the roe can be poisonous.

Bream carp – BRACHSE – *bréme*
Description: This carp has a very high back but flattened sides.

Origin and occurrence: Bream carp prefer lakes rich in food with very slow-moving waters. Bream carp feed on small bottom dwellers.

Quality characteristics: The flesh has many bones, some quite large. It is best cut into strips and deep-fried.

Carp – KARPFEN – *carpe*
Mirror carp – SPIEGELKARPFEN – *carpe miroir*
Leather carp – LEDERKARPFEN – *carpe à cuir*
Wild carp – SCHUPPENKARPFEN/ WILDKARPFEN – *carpe*
Description: Carp originated in Asia. The ancient Chinese cultivated them in ponds. The Romans brought the carp to Italy, and from the thirteenth to the fifteenth centuries, carp was raised in ponds all over Europe. It was introduced to North America from Europe.

Carp can be identified by the two barbels, one short, one long, on each side of its mouth. The varieties are identified by their distinctive scales. Wild carp (carpe) has even scales. Mirror carp has few, irregularly placed, large, mirrorlike scales. Leather carp has no or very few scales but a tough, leatherlike skin.

Origin and occurrence: Carp are found in warm, slowly moving or still waters with muddy bottoms and plenty of aquatic plants. They feed on small bottom creatures and plants. A carp in the wild can live to forty years of age, grow to about 39 inches (1 m) in length, and weigh 89 pounds (40 kg).

Quality characteristics: The tasty, oily flesh has many bones. Carp taste best in winter. To remove a possible muddy taste, carp are often kept in moving freshwater for several days before they are killed. For culinary purposes, farm-raised three-year-old carp that are about 12 inches (30 cm) long and weigh about 2.5 to 4 pounds (1 to 2 kg) are the tastiest.

Chub sucker/tench – SCHLEIE – *tanche*

Description: With a strong body, small eyes, a small mouth, and slimy skin, the chub sucker is similar to the carp. The fish prefers the dark and swims alone. They grow to about 24 inches (60 cm) in length and can weigh up to 15 pounds (7 kg). Market size is about 10 to 12 inches (25 to 30 cm) and 1¼ to almost 2 pounds (600 to 800 g).

Origin and occurrence: Chub suckers live in still or very slow-moving waters with many plants and a muddy bottom in which they bury themselves during the winter. Chub suckers can be farm-raised. They feed on small bottom dwellers and plankton.

Quality characteristics: Tasty, soft, and somewhat fatty flesh. Before killing chub suckers, it is best to keep them in clear running water for a few days.

Roach – ROTAUGE/PLÖTZE – *vangeron/vengeron*

Description: The body usually has a high back and flattened sides, a small mouth, and large red eyes. Some roach types migrate; others stay put.

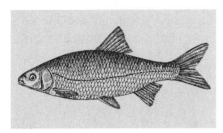

Origin and occurrence: The roach lives in still and moving waters and feeds on small animals and plants. It grows 12 inches (30 cm) long and weighs about 9 ounces (250 g).

Quality characteristics: The flesh contains many very fine bones and should be filleted and slashed several times to cut the remaining bones into small pieces. Marinating the fish will soften the bones and make the fish more enjoyable to eat.

Sheatfish
Catfish – ZWERGFELS – *poisson chat*
Description: The catfish has a slim body free of scales, with the sides slightly tapered near the tail. It has a wide head with eight barbels: two very long ones on the upper jaw, four shorter ones on the lower jaw, and two short ones anterior to the nose. It also has an adipose fin like the salmon's.

Origin and occurrence: Catfish, now at home in Europe, are originally from North America. They are very successfully farmed in the United States. They are very robust and are

now also farmed in Europe. However, their population often overwhelms other table fish in a body of water.

Sheatfish – WELS/WALLER – *silure/glanis*

Description: This European catfish has a tubular body with slightly flattened sides and a wide head. There are two barbels on the upper jaw and four barbels on the lower jaw. Color changes with age and location. Sheatfish can grow to a length of 10 feet (3 m) and weigh as much as 330 pounds (150 kg).

Origin and occurrence: Sheatfish are found in large, warm middle European rivers and lakes with muddy bottoms. They feed on all kinds of fish and frogs and even attack water birds. Sheatfish are very destructive to other popular table fish. They stop eating during winter.

Quality characteristics: Only young sheatfish weighing about 6½ pounds (3 kg) are used as table fish. Sheatfish have no scales and are skinned. The almost boneless flesh is white and somewhat fatty (11 percent).

4.2.2 Crustaceans, Mollusks, Cephalopods, and Echinoderms

1. Crustaceans – KRUSTENTIERE – *crustacés*

In European markets crustaceans are often sold under their English names.

Crabs
Crab – TASCHENKREBS – *tourteau*

King crab – KÖNIGSKRABBE – *crabe royal*

Spider crab – SEESPINNE – *araignée de mer*

Crayfish
Freshwater crayfish – FLUSSKREBS – *écrevisse*

Norway lobster/Dublin Bay prawn – NORWEGISCHER HUMMER/KAISER-GRANAT/SCAMPO – *langoustine*

Slipper lobster – BÄRENKREBS – *cigale mer*

Lobster
Lobster – HUMMER – *homard*

Spiny lobster – LANGUSTE – *langouste*

Shrimp
Shrimp – KREVETTE/GARNELE – *crevette/grise*

King prawn – RIESENKREVETTE – *crevette rose*

Crustaceans are spineless animals covered with horny shells. The various body parts are connected by soft joints. Because the hard shell cannot stretch, the animal must regularly molt to accommodate growth. The shell color depends on the presence of various pigments. Red pigmentation is immune to heat but dissolves in fat.

Crustaceans are killed by plunging them head first into boiling court bouillon. Dead crustaceans should not be cooked, since the flesh develops toxins after death. *A dead or dying crustacean can be easily identified: it will have a straight and very flexible tail when manupulated.*

All crustaceans have five pairs of legs; the front pair usually terminate in claws. Also typical are long antennae (crabs are an exception). The tastiness of the meat and high protein content is somewhat flawed by the high cholesterol content (150 mg per 100 g).

Live crustaceans are packed in porous containers, placed on damp wood shavings or seaweed, and are shipped via express mail. They cannot be shipped on ice because of animal rights laws. The ideal storage space is a saltwater tank (*vivier*).

Crustaceans are used in cold and hot appetizers, for buffets, in soups, as entrees, and as a garnish for fish dishes.

Crabs
Crab – TASCHENKREBS – *tourteau*
Description: The crab looks like its body is wedged between two flat bowls. The two front legs have large claws. The back is reddish brown, and the bottom shell is yellowish.

Origin and occurrence: Crabs stay in the same locale throughout their life and inhabit sandy or gravelly ocean bottoms in water from 3 to 165 feet (1 to 50 m) deep. In Europe crabs are harvested in Scotland, Spain, and Brittany. In the United States, Dungeness crabs along the Pacific coast, stone crabs in Florida, and blue crabs along the Atlantic coast and Chesapeake and Delaware bays are of great commercial importance. The soft-shell crab is a molting blue crab. Crabs feed on mussels and ocean-bottom dwellers. They are harvested when they are about 4 to 15 inches (10 to 40 cm) long.

Quality characteristics: The large body contains very little meat; most of the meat is picked from the claws and the breast. Crab meat is expensive. Crabmeat in the United States is sold in several grades; in order of cost, they are backfin, lump, flake, and claw.

King crab – KÖNIGSKRABBE – *crabe royal*
Description: The shell is covered with long spikes. Only males, which are much larger than the females, are caught. The legs, shell, and claws are reddish pink. They are up to 3 feet (1 m) long and weigh from 6 to 22 pounds (3 to 10 kg).

Origin and occurrence: The king crab lives in Arctic and Antarctic waters on rocky ocean floors at a depth of about 1,500 to 1,800 feet (500 to 600 m). The king crab loves cold temperatures of 38°F to 50°F (3°C to 10°C) King crab is harvested in Alaska, Chile, and Antarctica.

Quality characteristics: King crabs contain large amounts of meat. Almost all meat (claws, legs, and tail) is edible. Most popular is the meat from the legs. The frozen meat, packaged under the name "fancy king," contains about 40 percent leg meat and 60 percent body meat. The preferred canned king crab is from Russia and is called *chatka*.

Spider crab – SEESPINNE – *araignée de mer*
Description: This crab resembles a spider, with its high rounded body and long legs. The front of the shell sports prickly spines; the top shell is reddish brown. They grow to an average length of 3 to 6 inches (10 to 20 cm) but no more than 10 inches (25 cm).

Origin and occurrence: Spider crabs prefer to live on algae-covered sandy ocean floors or algae-covered rocky outcroppings in depths below 60 feet (20 m). They live along the coast of the Mediterranean to the English Channel, along the European Atlantic coast, and along coastal north Africa. They feed on plants.

Quality characteristics: The spider crab has very tasty meat, but yields very small amounts. Leg and body meat are used.

Freshwater crayfish – FLUSSKREBS – *écrevisse*

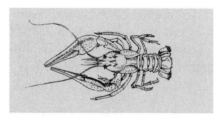

Description: The wide, hard, somewhat rough breast shell is of the same length as the tail. The color varies depending on habitat, from olive green to gray-black or gray-green. Varieties include the European river crayfish ("noble" crayfish), the American freshwater crayfish, and the pond or marsh crayfish (Galician crayfish). It grows 3 to 5 inches (10 to 15 cm) long, and weighs from 3 to 5 ounces (80 to 140 g).

Origin and occurrence: The noble crayfish lives in shallow, clean, lime-rich streams, ponds, and lakes. Water pollution and disease have decimated the European river crayfish. In Switzerland crayfish are imported from Turkey, Spain, and the United States, especially from Mississippi and the eastern states. Freshwater crayfish is farm-raised in the United States, and is available year-round.

Quality characteristics: The taste and quality of crayfish meat depends on the purity of the waters they inhabit and the food they eat. The meat is juicy, tender, and slightly sweet.

Norway lobster/Dublin Bay prawn – NORWEGISCHER HUMMER/ KAISERGRANAT/SCAMPO – *langoustine/scampo*
Description: These saltwater crayfish are called *scampi* in Italian. They have slim bodies, noticeably thin claws, and a smooth, salmon-colored shell. When cooked, their color, in contrast to other crustaceans, barely changes. They grow to a length of about 4 to 10 inches (10 to 25 cm).

Origin and occurrence: Scampi live in water depths of 150 to 750 feet (50 to 250 m) on soft ocean floors, in which they can bury themselves during the day. They are nocturnal creatures that grow very slowly. Scampi are harvested in South Africa, Iceland, Norway, Ireland, and Scotland.

Quality characteristics: The colder the water, the tastier the scampi. Because the claws are of no culinary importance, only the tails are sold. The size of scampi tails is given in number of tails per pound. For example, 9/12 means that nine to twelve tails weigh approximately 1 pound, so that each weighs about 1¼ to 1¾ ounces (35 to 50 g).

Lobster – HUMMER – *homard*
Description: Lobsters have smooth shells and two claws; the left claw is for cutting, and the right claw is for crushing. The claws are banded while the lobster is transported to prevent the lobsters from attacking each other. The coloring of the top shell varies from strong bluish to blue-green or purplish black, de-

pending on the color of the ocean floor. American and Canadian lobsters can be identified by their orange-colored bellies. They range from 10 to 28 inches (20 to 70 cm) in length, rarely growing beyond 30 inches (75 cm).

Origin and occurrence: Lobsters live near algae-covered rocky ledges, in depths of 60 to 120 feet (20 to 40 m). Lobsters are solitary nocturnal creatures that love cold waters. Lobsters refuse to feed at temperatures of less then 42°F (5°C), and they die if the water temperature rises to 70°F (20°C). American lobster is harvested in Canada and the United States; European lobster comes from Norway, Ireland, and Greenland. Live lobster is kept in large holding tanks along the North American coast. Lobsters feed on mussels, dead fish, and their own kind.

Quality characteristics: Lobsters are sold live. The tail should be curled and elastic. A much-prized part of the lobster is the coral (ovaries). The most popular market weight for lobster is 11 ounces to 2 pounds (330 to 900 g). In the United States, 1½-pound lobsters are most commonly served in restaurants. Hard-shell lobsters have the most meat for their size.

Spiny lobster/rock lobster –
LANGUSTE–*langouste*

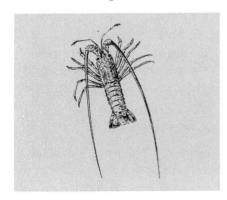

Description: The spiny lobster has very long antennae and a spiky top shell but no claws. The coloring depends on its habitat. They grow from 10 to 22 inches (25 to 60 cm) long, with a maximum length of 30 inches. Spiny lobsters weighing 1 to 2 pounds (400 to 800g) are preferred.

Origin and occurrence: Spiny lobsters live on rocky ocean ledges in depths of 150 to 450 feet (50 to 150 m). They are solitary creatures that prefer moderate temperatures. Major sources are Ireland, South Africa, Australia, Cuba, Portugal, the Caribbean countries, and countries that border the Indian Ocean. They feed primarily on mollusks.

Quality characteristics: Spiny lobsters are sold live and frozen (tails only). The large tail must be curled, whether live or cooked. The meat is very tasty but a little drier than lobster meat.

Slipper lobster – BÄRENKREBS–
cigale mer
Description: Slipper lobsters have flat bodies with broad breast shells that have notched edges. In contrast to the spiny lobster with its long antennae, slipper lobsters have only very short, broad feelers. They are about 4 to 18 inches (10 to 45 cm) long and can weigh up to 4 pounds (2 kg).

Origin and occurrence: Slipper lobsters live in coastal waters with sandy or rocky bottoms. They can also be found near coral reefs in tropical waters. Major suppliers include Australia, Singapore, and countries near the Indian Ocean.

Quality characteristics: Slipper lobsters are tasty, similar to spiny lobsters in flavor. They are sold frozen—whole or as tails. Their market name is *slippers*.

Shrimp
Shrimp are classified by size.
Small: Shrimp–
KREVETTE/GARNELE– *crevette grise*
Large: King prawn–
RIESENKREVETTE–*crevette rose*

In the United States, size categories of shrimp are: *colossal* (10 per pound),

jumbo (11 to 15 per pound), *extra large* (16 to 20 per pound), *large* (21 to 30 per pound), *medium* (31 to 35 per pound), *small* (36 to 45 per pound), and *miniature* (100 per pound).

Shrimp – KREVETTE/GARNELE–
crevette grise

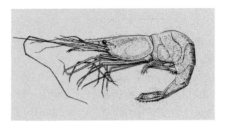

Description: Shrimp have small, slightly curved bodies, with a tapered tail end and very long antennae. Many varieties appear opaque. Their coloring varies, depending on their environment. They grow to about 1¼ to 2 inches (3 to 5 cm) in length, no longer than 2½ inches (6 cm).

Origin and occurrence: Shrimp are categorized as saltwater, freshwater, or tidewater. Saltwater shrimp live near sandy coasts in depths of up to 600 feet. Freshwater and tidewater shrimp are usually farm-raised in rice paddies or tidewater plains. Major exporters include Greenland, Norway, Denmark, Sweden, Turkey, Senegal, Chile, and India.

Quality characteristics: Cold-water shrimp are of better quality. Europeans prefer deep-water shrimp from northern countries. The meat is very tasty, but very perishable, and is therefore immediately cooked and frozen aboard fishing vessels. Top-quality shrimp are juicy, clean, peeled, and deveined.

Prawn – RIESENKREVETTE–
crevette rose
Description: Prawns have small, slightly curved bodies, with a tapered tail end and very long antennae. The color varies, depending on the place of origin. They grow to a length of about 2¼ to 3 inches (6 to 10 cm), with a maximum length of 6 inches (15 cm).

Origin and occurrence: Prawns are found in salt water, tidal waters, and freshwater. Saltwater prawns live in water 60 to 300 feet deep with a sandy or muddy bottom. Freshwater prawns are farm-raised in large quantities in rice paddies. They are imported from China, Indonesia, Taiwan, Thailand, Bangladesh, and India. In the United States, colossal and jumbo shrimp are often referred to as prawns.

Quality characteristics: Prawns are equally good from fresh or salt waters. The flesh is very tasty but perishable. Top-quality prawns are juicy, plump, sweet, and deveined. They are sold whole or as tails, frozen and sorted by size.

2. Mollusks – WEICHTIERE – *mollusques*

Shellfish – MUSCHELN – *coquillages*
Clams – MUSCHELN – *polourdes*

Comb scallop – KAMMUSCHEL – *pétoncle*

Mussels – MIESMUSCHEL/ PFAHLMUSCHEL – *moule*

Oysters – AUSTERN – *huître*

Pilgrims scallop – PILGERMUSCHEL – *grande peigne*

Razor clam – SCHWERTMUSCHEL – *couteau*

Scallop – JACOBSMUSCHEL – *coquille Saint-Jacques*

Snails – SCHNECKEN – *escargots*
Abalone – SEEOHR – *oreille de mer*

Land snails – LANDSCHNECKEN – *escargot de Bourgogne*

Periwinkles – MEERESSCHNECKEN – *bigourneau*

Squid – TINTENFISCH – *calmar/encornet*
Cuttlefish – GEMEINER TINTENFISCH – *seiche*

Miniature octopus – ZWERGSEPIA – *sépiole*

Octopus – KRAKE/OKTOPUS – *pieuvre/poulpe*

Squid – GEMEINER KALMAR – *calmar/encornet*

Clams – VENUSMUSCHELN – *palourdes or praires*
Description: Europeans prefer mussels to clams; there, some mussels are called "Venusmuscheln" and are marketed as clams. In the United States, clams are much more common and frequently used. Eastern clams are the soft-shell clam and the quahog. Very small quahogs are called littleneck clams; the next larger size is cherrystone, and quahogs larger than 3 inches are called chowder clams. Quahogs are oval and hard-shelled, with a purple border on the inside of the shell.

Origin and occurrence: Soft-shell clams and quahogs are found along the Atlantic coast and vary in size, depending on habitat. Razor clams are found on both coasts. Other West Coast clams include the Pacific littleneck and butter clams. European clams, known as carpet shells, grow in Atlantic and Mediterranean waters.

Quality characteristics: Clams must be gathered from safe, unpolluted environments, and in the United States they must be approved by the health department (shellfish tag). Clams are sold live, shucked, or smoked. Clam liquor is bottled as clam juice or broth.

Razor clams – SCHWERTMUSCHELN – *couteau*
Description: The shells of the razor clam are small, narrow, and razor-shaped. Their thin shells are fragile, making these clams difficult to dig.

Origin and occurrence: Razor clams are found all over the world, except in very cold waters. They prefer sandy soft ocean floors, in which they bury themselves quickly, as far down as 3 feet (1 m).

Quality characteristics: These clams can be eaten raw but are not too tasty. They must be cleaned very well, because they are very sandy.

Other types of European clams
Venus clam – STRAHLIGE VENUSMUSCHEL – *clovisse, petite praire*

Vongola (Italian) – *palourde*

Cross vongola (Italian) – KREUZMUSTER/TEPPICHMUSCHEL – *palourde crisée*

Edible heart clams – ESSBARE HERZMUSCHEL – *coque bucarde*

Common heart clam – GEMEINE HERZMUSCHEL – *bigon/rigadot*

Coarse venus clam – RAUHE VENUSMUSCHEL – *coque rayée*

Velvet clam – SAMTMUSCHEL – *amande de mer*

Large sandpaper clam – GROSSE SANDKLAFFMUSCHEL – *mye/clanque*

Sand clam – SANDMOUSCHEL/ STRANDAUSTER – *bec-de-jar*

Mussels – MIESMUSCHELN/ PFAHLMUSCHELN – *moules*
Description: Mussels have long, oval-shaped shells that are blue black to dark violet in color; the interior of the shell is whitish blue with a slight mother-of-pearl sheen.

Origin and occurrence: Mussels grow naturally in about 30 feet (10 m) of water on rocks, pilings, and other natural outcroppings along the European and American coasts. Mussels are cultivated along every European coast and along the coast of Maine in the United States. Mussels are farmed and exported from Spain, France, Denmark, and Holland.

Quality characteristics: Top-quality mussels have tightly closed shells and smell fresh and briny. They are cleaned and sold in baskets or bags. The tasty flesh is very nutritious.

Oysters – AUSTERN – *huître*

Flat oysters: Atlantic oyster – *huître platte*

Round-bellied oysters: Portuguese oyster/rock oyster – *huître creuse/huître portugaise*

Pacific oyster/Japanese oyster – *huître creuse de Pacifique/ huître japonaise*

Description: The oyster's upper shell is rather flat and flaky looking; the lower shell is round and deeper.

Origin and occurrence: Oysters are found in all temperate coastal zones with a salinity of 2 to 3 percent. They have been cultivated since Greek and Roman times. Oysters are farmed in artificially created barriers; farming is quite labor intensive. Major oyster producers are France, Holland, Denmark, England, Ireland, the United States, Canada, Japan, China, and New Zealand.

Flat oysters are farmed along the Atlantic and the North Sea coasts in many countries. They are generally marketed under the name of regional beds from which they are harvested, as the following list exemplifies.

France: Belons, Marennes, Gravettes d'Arcachon.

Holland: Impériales

Belgium: Ostendes

Ireland: Rossmore, Redbank, and Galway

Denmark: Limfjords

England: Colchester, Helford, Pyefleet, Whitestable, and Native

In aquaculture, the Portuguese oyster has lost on ground ever since the sixties and has been replaced by the Pacific rock oyster, which is much more resistant and has moved into a dominant position among farmed oysters. These oysters are marketed under the name of the farming method used, for example, *huîtres de parc, fines de claire, spéciales de claires;* sometimes they are identified by origin: *creuses de Zélande, Marennes-Oléron.*

In the United States, eastern oysters are considered superior to Pacific oysters. Bluepoint, Cape Cod, Wellfleet, Indian River, Chincoteague, and Malpeque are Atlantic oysters. Olympia (very small) and Japanese (very large) are Pacific oysters.

Quality characteristics: Raw oysters must be eaten live. Top-quality oysters are tightly closed, full-bodied, and briny. They should fill the whole shell, which should contain a small amount of ocean water. They

are sold by size. Classification varies depending on variety and country.

Scallop – JAKOBSMUSCHEL – *coquille Saint-Jacques*

Description: The almost white shell of the scallop can reach a diameter of 4 to 5 inches (10 to 13 cm). The unevenly closing lower and upper shell are sharply grooved. In Europe the whole shell is sold; in the United States, generally only the adductor muscle is available. The comb scallop (*pétoncle*) is similar to the scallop in shape and flavor.

Origin and occurrence: Scallops prefer sand or coral ocean floors. Large numbers are found in the Mediterranean Sea. In the United States, three types of scallops are available: large sea scallops, the smaller bay scallops, and the calico scallop; found near the coast of Florida and the Gulf of Mexico.

Quality characteristics: Edible are the white muscle and the salmon colored coral (roe). Top-quality scallops are whole, plump, and light colored. Scallops are sold live in the shell or as muscle only, fresh and frozen.

Pilgrims scallop – PILGERMUSCHEL – *grande peigne*
Description: The pilgrims scallop can be distinguished from the scallop by its uneven reddish brown shell, which has ribbed grooves that are rounded.

Origin and occurrence: This scallop usually lives in shallow coastal waters that have sandy bottoms but can be found in depths up to 600 feet (200 m). Pilgrims scallops are harvested in the Atlantic ocean, near Norway and the British Isles, never in the Mediterranean.

Quality characteristics: The edible part is the adductor muscle and the coral. The best quality is plump and light colored.

Snails – SCHNECKEN – *escargots*
Among mollusks snails are the most numerous in variety. They are found everywhere, on land and in rivers, lakes, and the sea. Of culinary importance are only one type of land snail and some sea snails.

Description: Most snails have a spiral-shaped shell. There are a few types that have a shell that resembles the shape of a clam. Snails have a visible head with "feelers," their sensing organ.

Storage: Land snails are offered prepared, frozen, or canned. Sea snails are generally offered fresh and for immediate consumption.

Land Snails
Edible snail – WEINBERGSCHNECKE – *escargot de Bourgogne*

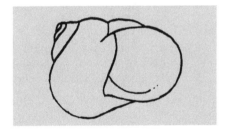

Description: Snails have now become a delicacy, but they used to be a common food. Because demand can no longer be met with free-ranging snails, they are now raised commercially in so-called snail gardens.

Origin and occurrence: Snails can be found in all temperate climate zones in Europe. Snails caused enormous devastation in vineyards by devouring young shoots. Although this problem has been eradicated, edible snails are still called vineyard snails in Europe. They are now found in gardens, parks, and the outskirts of forests. Snails are imported from Turkey, France, Poland, and Hungary.

Quality characteristics: Large, meaty snails are preferred. They are marketed frozen or canned. In addition, a tropical snail is imported to Europe from Thailand, Taiwan, and Vietnam.

Ocean Snails

Abalone – SEEOHR – *oreille de mer*

Description: The abalone has a strong adductor muscle – a broad foot that fills the entire opening of the shell. The abalone uses this foot to cling tightly to rocks, which makes it difficult to remove. The shell is plain, with small holes along the rim. The interior of the shell is covered with mother-of-pearl.

Origin and occurrence: Abalone is found in the surf to a depth of 24 feet (8 m). Europe imports mostly canned abalone from Japan, the United States, and Australia.

Quality characteristics: Abalone is a culinary delicacy, used especially in Japanese and Chinese cuisine. The muscle meat is tough and must be tenderized by pounding or by simmering for an extended time. In the United States, abalone is also available fresh, dried, or salted. To be tender, fresh abalone should be pounded and sautéed very briefly.

Edible Periwinkles – *bigorneaux*

Description: Periwinkles have a conical spiral shell with a pointed end. They are gray-green with reddish brown bands. Along the French Atlantic coast, periwinkles are commercially raised in so-called snail-parks.

Origin and occurrence: The most common sea snail is found along the entire Atlantic coast in Europe and North America.

Quality characteristics: Periwinkles are boiled in salted water. The flesh is removed with a small pick and is very much appreciated by connoisseurs.

Other European Sea Snails

Mediterranean snail – MITTELMEER-
  SCHNECKE/HERKULUSKEULE –
  murex massue

Common periwinkle – GEMEINE
  STRANDSCHNECKE – *bigorneau*

Shore snail – UFERSCHNECKE – *vigneau*

Cornucopia snail – WELLHORNSCH-
  NECKE – *buccin/ondé/bulot*

Cephalopods

Cephalopods are the most evolved of the mollusks. They live only in salt water. Some varieties are among the fastest-moving sea inhabitants. Squid have ten arms, and octopus have eight. Though both are cephalopods, they belong to different families and are not closely related.

The tentacles, which are attached to the head (squid and cuttlefish) or body (octopus), are covered with suction discs that serve as sensors and feeders. Edible are the body and head, with beak, eyes, and viscera removed. Some have a sac that contains brown-black liquid (ink).

Fresh cephalopods spoil rapidly and must be used immediately. They are sold fresh or frozen — whole, bodies only, or sliced into rings.

Cuttlefish – GEMEINER TINTENFISCH – *seiche*

Description: The body is round to oval, with undulating large fins along the sides. Characteristic are the stripes on the back that resemble pedestrian crosswalks. The cuttlefish has ten tentacles; two are used to catch prey. In contrast to squid, it has a calcified internal shell.

A smaller variety (*Zwergsepia* — *sépiole*) has almost no internal shell and reaches a length of 1 to 2 inches (3 to 6 cm). It is found in the coastal waters of the Mediterranean. Best quality is white and tender.

Origin and occurrence: The cuttlefish is a bottom dweller of sandy ocean floors. With the help of its fins, it can bury itself in the sand. It can be found in all oceans. It is imported from countries near the Mediterranean Sea and the Atlantic Ocean.

Quality characteristics: Top-quality cuttlefish have white meat and are about 12 inches (30 cm) long. The liquid from the ink sac of fresh cuttlefish is often used to color pasta, risotto, and sauces.

Octopus – KRAKE/OKTOPUS – *pieuvre/poulpe*

Description: The head with its long tentacles sits atop its soft, short body. The octopus has eight arms and no internal shell. Its color is a reddish brown.

Origin and occurrence: During the day the octopus hides in rock crevasses and grottos. It is at home in all oceans of the world. Imports are from Morocco and the Canary Islands.

Quality characteristics: Young octopus meat is tender; older animals must be simmered for a long time to be tender. The tentacles are used after they have been peeled.

Squid – GEMEINER KALMAR – *calmar*

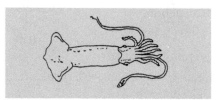

Description: The squid has a slender, torpedo-like body with ten tentacles and broad triangular caudal fin. The coloring ranges from light beige to violet. Squid has an opaque internal cartilage. Commercial specimens weigh from 3½ to 28 ounces. (100 to 800 g).

Origin and occurrence: Squid is found near the coast of the Mediterranean and the Atlantic Ocean, and a prolific supply exists off the California coast. Squid lives in schools and travels long distances, depending on the seasons. It feeds on mussels, clams, crabs, and small fish.

Quality characteristics: Best-quality squid are white, tender, and meaty. In Europe they are offered by size under their Italian names: large ones are *calmares* or *calamari*, and small ones are *calamaretti*.

3. Echinoderms – STACHELHÄUTER – *échinodermes*

The best-known edible echinoderms are the sea urchin and the sea cucumber, which is especially popular in Asia. Echinoderms have leathery smooth or prickly skin. The edible portion is extremely small. They are usually consumed where they are caught. Sea urchins are sold live and must be used immediately. Sea cucumbers are always sold dried and can be stored for a long time.

Sea Urchin – SEEIGEL – *oursin*

Description: Edible sea urchins range in color from bluish white to violet to reddish green. They are pried open with a sharp knife, starting at the mouth, and cut with scissors all around. Gloves should be worn, since the prickly spines can cause infection if embedded in the skin.

Origin and occurrence: Sea urchins live on algae-covered rocky ocean floors in the tidal zone, in waters as deep as 120 feet (40 m). Sea urchins feed on seaweed and algae. A few are carnivores, and some eat dead seafood and bait. Sea urchins are imported from North Atlantic regions in Iceland, Norway, and Portugal. The United States exports sea urchins to Japan for use in sushi.

Quality characteristics: The edible portion of the sea urchin is limited to the orange-colored roe, which is arranged star-shaped in the shell and is best removed with a small spoon. The roe is usually eaten raw after a brief poaching.

Sea Cucumber – SEEGURKE – *bêche de mer*

Description: Also known as sea slug, the sea cucumber gets its name from its cucumber-like shape.

Origin and occurrence: Sea cucumbers are found in water up to 120 feet (40 m) deep with sandy or muddy bottoms near Polynesia, New Guinea, Indonesia, and the Malaysian archipelago.

Quality characteristics: After being caught, sea cucumbers are boiled. The much shrunken sea cucumber is then sun-dried, intermittently steamed two or three times, and finally smoked for several months. Dried sea cucumbers are sold as *trepang* (Malaysian). They are mostly used in Asian fare, especially *trepang* soup.

4.2.3 Meat

European meat cuts differ from American meat cuts. United States Department of Agriculture (USDA) inspection, yield, and grade stamps are included herein where appropriate.

In Switzerland meat is supplied primarily from locally raised animals. Imports are limited to specialty cuts such as beef sirloin (sirloin strip, filet) and rack and leg of lamb.

Meat is composed of muscle fibers, which vary in texture and strength and can be thick or thin, short or long.

Terminology

Meat

The term *meat*, as defined by Swiss government regulations, signifies *fresh* meat only—all animals or parts of animals used as food for human consumption. This includes muscles with the attached tissues, fat, variety meats (organs), and fresh blood (prohibited in the United States). With the exception of chilling, these meats have not been prepared, processed, or preserved, nor have they undergone any other type of treatment (tripe, which is blanched, is an exception).

Frozen Meat

Frozen meat is all meat that is solidly frozen, including meat that has been previously frozen and then thawed for sale. Frozen meat is usually packaged in small portions and stored at 0°F (-18°C).

Processed Meats

Processed meats are foods that contain meat that has been preserved through such processes as salting, smoking, drying, roasting, cooking, or canning. Sausages, canned meats, meat marinades, meat pies, meat pâtés, hams, and bacon are a few examples. All food products derived from meat are subject to government regulation.

Meat in the Diet

Meat is a valuable source of protein,

minerals (iron), and vitamins (B and A). Meat protein is of high nutritional value: very small portions satisfy human protein needs. The protein content of most meats is about 15 to 22 percent.

With the exception of liver, meat contains few carbohydrates, between 1 and 5 percent.

The fat content of meat depends not so much on the type of animal as it does on the cut of the meat. Lean meat cuts contain about 1 to 6 percent fat; marbled meat cuts, from 15 to 25 percent fat. The type of animal, grade, meat cut, and the preparation method all determine the amount of fat in the dish.

Undesirable substances in meat can include heavy metals and pesticides. Drug residue, used in growth hormone therapy or disease control, can present a problem if the animals have been treated illegally.

The most easily digested meats are tender cuts from young animals.

Meat Inspection

The purpose of meat inspection is to guarantee healthy meat and to protect consumers from unsanitary processing and diseased carcasses. Continuous controlled inspections include periodic inspection of pharmacological materials to prevent misuse and abuse.

In the United States, meat is inspected in the processing plant and the packinghouse. The Department of Agriculture maintains permanent inspectors on-site who enforce sanitary standards. All meat must have an inspection stamp that indicates its fitness for consumption before it can be sold. Federally inspected meat is marked with a round stamp that reads "US Insp'd and P'S'D."

Grading of meat, however, is voluntary. Grading indicates whether the carcass has met the standards of a certain category of meat. It is used primarily for price and quality comparisons. The Federal Grading Service, part of the USDA, determines

Department of Agriculture inspection and grade stamps

the grade, which is identified by a shield, and stamped with a roller across the whole length of the carcass.

Meat Storage

Meat spoils quickly and must be handled with care. Maintaining quality during storage depends on the personal hygiene of the meat handler and the sanitary conditions of the operation. Optimum storage times for meat are shown in Table 4-3.

Meat and meat products must be kept refrigerated at all times. The meat cooler should be kept at a temperature of 32° to 35°F (0° to 2°C), with a relative humidity of about 82

Table 4-3. Storage Times, from Slaughter to Preparation

Veal	
Short order cuts	2–3 weeks
Cooked roasts, glazed	6–8 days
Beef	
Short order cuts	3–5 weeks
Braised roasts/boiled beef	4 days +
Pork	
Short order cuts	7–10 days
Cooked roasts, glazed	4–8 days
Lamb	
Depending on use	1–3 weeks

to 85 percent. If the air is too dry, the meat will shrink; if the air is too moist, slime will cover the meat and spoilage will occur.

Meat should be hung, separated by type, or placed on sheet pans. To prevent loss from leakage, meat should not be stacked.

Because it has a high moisture content, all meat will shrink, even under ideal storage conditions. For this reason, meat is quickly portioned and vacuum-packed (Cryovac) until needed. This method has proven successful for veal and beef but has not significantly extended the shelf life of pork. Vacuum packaging must be combined with refrigeration to protect meat from spoiling. All packages should be dated. Vacuum packaging is recommended when freezing meat, as it helps prevent freezer burn.

Aging of Meat

Aging causes the muscle fiber of meat to become more tender; the meat is therefore more easily digestible and has more flavor. Proper breeding and raising of animals is a prerequisite for good meat quality. If the animals are slaughtered when stressed or have a raised temperature, proper aging of meat will be affected and may even be impossible.

Enzyme activity starts as soon as the animal has been slaughtered. Enzymes break down glycogen to sim-

ple sugars and convert them to lactic acid. Lactic acid enhances flavor in meat and reduces bacterial growth. Meat that will be cooked for a long time can be prepared a few days after slaughter. Meat that is to be sautéed or otherwise briefly cooked must be aged, or it will be tough. Depending on the cut, optimal aging time can vary from 1 to 4 weeks.

Aging and spoilage are closely related. Meat that has been aged too long can show signs of spoilage (protein decomposition). In such cases affected parts must be generously trimmed and discarded.

Handling of Meat

- Refrigeration should be constant to safeguard meat.
- Meat should be handled as little as possible with the bare hands, and never with wet hands, which causes slime to form on the meat's surface.
- Vacuum-packed meats should be dried with toweling when removed from the packaging. The meat should be allowed to rest, uncovered, in the refrigerator for about 30 minutes. Its coloring will then become fresh and bright red.
- It is not advisable to vacuum-pack small cuts for use *à la minute*, as the quality suffers; moreover, the excessive use of plastic is not ecologically sound.
- Poor handling practices, which result in spoiled meat, cause more food-borne illnesses than the transmission of illnesses from a sick animal to humans.

Meat Quality

To judge the quality of a piece of meat correctly requires consideration of various meat properties. Only by evaluating several criteria, including the age of the animal, its nutritional status, meatiness, and fat content, can the meat's quality be accurately assessed.

Nutritional status provides the basis for the meat's usability.

Age influences foremost the use of

and preparation method for a piece of meat. All animals have fine and coarse muscle fibers. Young animals have mostly fine-grained muscle tissue. For *à la minute* presentations, meat from young animals is preferable. But all animals provide tough and tender meat cuts.

Meatiness defines the proportion of muscle tissue to bone. Meat cuts with large amounts of bone and little meat can be expensive relative to yield.

Fat, in the correct amount, is essential for excellent meat. The proper amount of fat guarantees juiciness, tenderness, and flavor during preparation. *Surface fat*, for example, as seen in the bacon side of a pig, indicates proper feeding. The visible fat deposits around muscle parts is called *finish*. Finish determines the meat grade in the United States, especially the fat streaking in the ribs. The small fat particles inside the muscle are called *marbling*. Marbling is the fine network of almost invisible fat in the muscle fiber. It is most important for the flavor of meat.

Meat coloring is another factor in meat quality but should be carefully weighed in combination with all other factors. Marbled meat is always lighter in color than meat cuts with little fat in the muscle fiber. Cut meat surfaces discolor quickly through contact with oxygen (oxidization). Light-colored veal should not be confused with the flesh of anemic animals. Fat is basically creamy white; a yellow tone can be the result of feed. (Yellow fat is caused by vitamin A, often from green pasturage, and can be an indicator for meat from aged dairy cows.)

Intended *usage* is an important consideration in evaluating meat quality. Selecting the best-quality cut of meat for a particular preparation method will produce first-class results.

Meat Prices

Meat can be expensive. High prices are often the result of high demand for specific cuts and the difficulty of marketing the less popular cuts successfully. A balance must be found, with fewer top cuts and many lesser cuts. Beef cattle, for example, produce twenty times as much braising, stew, and ground beef as filet. Price value in meat purchasing depends on planned purchasing, based on choosing the best quality for the preparation method being used. Selecting meat only by price may result in high shrinkage, which can be costly and can ultimately cause the meat to be expensive.

Meat Categories

Beef
Veal – KALB – *veau*

Bullock – JUNGER OCHSE – *bœuf*

Heifer – JUNGE KUH – *génisse*

Bull – OCHSE – *bœuf*

Steer – STIER – *taureau*

Cow – KUH – *vache*

In the United States, another category is the stag, a mature male that has had its hormone glands removed.

Pork
Suckling pig – SPANFERKEL – *porcelet de lait, cochon de lait*

Young pig (immature) – FERKEL – *porcelet*

Pig – SCHWEIN – *porc*

Lamb
Spring lamb – MILCHLAMM – *agneau de lait*

Lamb – LAMM – *agneau*

Yearling mutton – SCHAF – *mouton*

Ewe – MUTTERSCHAF – *brebis*

Ram – HAMMEL – *mouton*

Goat
Kid – ZICKLEIN/GITZI – *chevreau/cabri*

Goat – ZIEGE – *chèvre*

Horse
Horse – PFERD – *cheval*

Rabbit (Domesticated)
Rabbit – KANINCHEN – *lapin*

Veal

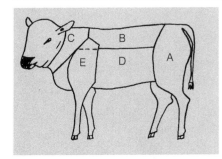

A Leg – STOTZEN – *cuisseau*
B Saddle – KARREE – *carrè*
C Neck – HALS – *cou*
D Breast – BRUST – *poitrine*
E Shoulder – SCHULTER – *épaule*

Table 4-4. Veal Cuts and Their Uses

Leg – STOTZEN – *cuisseau*	Roasted whole
The most expensive cuts from the leg are top round, bottom round, rump.	
Top round/butt – ECKSTÜCK – *noix*	*À la minute* dishes
Bottom round – NUSS – *noix pâtissière*	*À la minute* dishes, glazed roasts (basted in their own juices)
Rump – HUFT – *quasi*	*À la minute* dishes
Bottom round/silverside – UNTERSPÄLTE – *longe*	*À la minute* dishes, roasts
Eye round – RUNDER MOCKEN – *pièce ronde*	*À la minute* dishes, roasts
Bottom round – ROSENSTÜCK – *faux jarret*	Glazed roasts, centerpiece for stew, and the rest for shredded veal
Shank – HAXE – *jarret*	Glazed roasts, *osso buco*

Veal calves are butchered when they are three to four months old. Veal that is darker pink has a better flavor and shrinks less during cooking.

Swiss domestic veal producers can handle demand, and veal is rarely imported. Swiss veal grades are first and second quality. In the United States, milk-fed calves are called vealers. U.S. veal grades are USDA Prime, USDA Choice, USDA Good, USDA Standard, and USDA Utility.

In contrast to beef, veal is cut into halves, not quarters. The various cuts of veal and their uses are listed in Table 4-4.

First Quality

Meat quality: Thick flesh, slightly marbled. Light color, firm texture; *à la minute* cuts are very tender.

Fat content: Thinly covered with fat, which is firm, dry, and white.

Second Quality

Meat quality: Thin flesh; texture of lean is watery. Color is bright red.

Fat content: Poorly covered with fat or too much fat. Fat texture is spongy.

Other characteristics: Animal is too light or too heavy, portioning is difficult.

Table 4-4. Veal Cuts and Their Uses - continued

Saddle-back – RÜCKEN – *selle*	Roasted whole
Filet – FILET – *filet mignon*	Tenderloin steaks, filet mignons, roasts
Boneless loin – NIERSTÜCK – *filet*	Steaks, veal-kidney roast, roasts
Rack – KOTELETTSTÜCK – *côtes*	Chops, roasts
Shoulder – SCHULTER – *épaule*	
Chuck arm roast – DICKE SCHULTER – *épais d'épaule*	Glazed roasts
Shoulder clod – SCHULTERSPITZ – *palette*	Glazed roasts
Shoulder eye roast – SCHULTERFILET – *filet d'épaule*	Stews, ragouts
Brisket – BUG – *gras d'épaule*	Stews, ragouts
Shoulder blade – SCHULTERDECKEL – *couvert d'épaule*	Stews, ragouts
Shank – HAXE – *jarret*	Osso buco
Neck – HALS – *cou*	Rolled roasts, stews
Breast – BRUST – *poitrine*	Rolled roasts, glazed roasts, stuffed breast, stews, breast slices

Beef

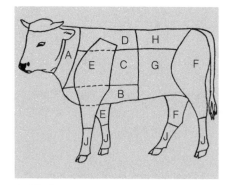

A Neck – HALS – *cou*
B Breast – BRUST – *poitrine*
C Rib – FEDERSTÜCK – *côte plate*
D Short loin – RÜCKEN – *train de côtes*
E Shoulder/chuck – SCHULTER – *épaule*
F Leg/round – STOTZEN – *cuisse*
G Flank – LEMPEN – *flanc*
H Sirloin – NIERSTÜCK – *aloyau*

Table 4-5. Beef Cuts and Their Uses

Hind Quarters	
Leg/round – STOTZEN – *cuisse*	
Beef shank – SCHENKEL – *jarret*	Stew, goulash, boiled beef, braised roast (bone-in)
Bottom round/silverside – UNTERSPÄLTE – *tranche carrée*	Larded pot roasts, braised steaks
Eye round – RUNDER MOCKEN – *pièce ronde*	Larded pot roasts, braised steaks
Top round – VORSCHLAG – *noix pâtissière/ fausse tranche*	First-quality (USDA Prime), properly aged: *à la minute* dishes, steak tartare; second-quality (USDA Choice): braised steaks, larded roast
Top round – ECKSTÜCK – *coin*	First-quality (USDA Prime), properly aged: *à la minute* dishes, steak tartare; second-quality (USDA Choice): braised steaks, larded roasts
Bottom round – ROSENSTÜCK – *faux jarret*	Stews

J Shank–FÜSSE–*pieds*

The best-quality beef are young, grain-raised animals about eighteen months old.

Muscles vary in tenderness. Tender meat is located in the less exercised muscles; working muscles are tougher, for example, those of the leg. Cuts of beef and their uses are listed in Table 4-5.

In Switzerland specialty cuts, such as filets and sirloins, are mostly imported.

Beef can be vacuum-packed or frozen.

First Quality (USDA Prime)

Meat quality: Very high ratio of meat to bone. The lean meat is well marbled. The meat has a bright red color with a tender texture and firm flesh.

Fat: The meat is evenly covered with fat but is not too fat. The fat texture is soft, and the meat is light in color.

Other characteristics: Young animals have white, soft cartilage.

Second Quality (USDA Choice)

Meat quality: Ratio of meat to bone is no longer very high; little marbling or too much (fatty). Firm, good consistency; *à la minute* pieces are only medium tender.

Fat: Either little or too much fat cover; fat is hard and brittle.

Other characteristics: Almost no cartilage, because cartilage has matured into bone.

Table 4-5. Beef Cuts and Their Uses - continued

Sirloin–NIERSTÜCK–*aloyau*	
Quality characteristics: The sirloin should not have more than four to five ribs, and should not have any flank meat. Cartilage should be white and soft, and the meat should be covered evenly with fat.	
Sirloin with bone and filet–NIERSTÜCK–*aloyau*	Porterhouse steak, T-bone steak, club steak (no filet), rib roast (*côte de bœuf*)
Filet–FILET–*filet*	Chateaubriand, tenderloin steaks, tournedos, filets mignons, filet goulash, whole tenderloin
Rib roast–ROASTBEEF–*faux-filet/ contre-filet*	Rib roast, *entrecôte, entrecôte double, entrecôte château* (for 3 or more people)
Sirloin–HUFT–*culotte*	Club steak, roast beef, *à-la-minute* dishes, tartare
Sirloin butt–HUFTDECKEL–*aiguillette*	First-quality (USDA Prime), properly aged: roast beef (whole); second-quality (USDA Choice): pot roast, boiled beef

Flank–LEMPEN–*flanc*	
Flank–LEMPEN–*flanc*	Boiled beef; generally very fatty

Front Quarters
Front quarter (without shoulder)–SCHILT–*quartier de devant sans épaule*

Short loin–RÜCKEN–*train de côtes*	
Prime rib–HOHRÜCKEN–*côte couverte*	First-quality (USDA Prime): roast beef, steak (rib-eye); second-quality (USDAChoice): boiled beef, pot roast
Cross-rib pot roast–ABGEDECKTER RÜCKEN–*basse côte*	Boiled beef, pot roasts

Short Plate–FEDERSTÜCK–*côte plate*	
Short plate–ABGEDECKTES FEDERSTÜCK–*côteplate découverte*	Boiled meat

Brisket –BRUST–*poitrine*	
Clod tip–BRUSTSPITZ–*pointe de grumeau*	Boiled meat
Clod/lower brisket–BRUSTKERN –*grumeau*	Boiled meat
Short ribs–NACHBRUST–*os blanc*	Boiled meat
Neck–HALS–*cou*	Ground beef, stew, and boiled meat

Shoulder/chuck–SCHULTER–*épaule*	
Foreshank–SCHENKEL–*jarret*	Stews, meat for clarification
Chuck roast–DICKE SCHULTER–*épais d'épaule*	Pot roasts, stews
Shoulder filet/mock tender–SCHULTER FILET–*filet d'épaule*	Pot roasts, stews
Shoulder clod/chuck–SCHULTERSPITZ–*palette*	Pot roasts, boiled meat
Brisket–BUG–*gras d'épaule*	Stews, ground beef
Shoulder blade–-SCHULTERDECKEI–*couvert d'épaule*	Stews, ground beef

Pork

Pigs are raised for the market in 5½ to 6 months. They are much leaner now than in the past.

Storage time for pork cannot be extended because it is not suitable for vacuum packaging. Pork can be frozen only for a maximum of 3 months.

Suckling pigs are very young animals with a weight of about 27 pounds (12 kg). The pig skin is so tender

that the piglet is roasted whole, not skinned. Cuts of pork and their uses are shown in Table 4-6.

First Quality (USDA Prime)

Meat quality: Very high ratio of meat to bone. The lean meat is well marbled. The meat has a bright red color with a tender texture and firm flesh.

Fat: The meat has an even fat covering but is not too fat. The fat texture is soft, with a light color.

Other characteristics: Young animals have white, soft cartilage.

Second Quality (USDA Choice)

Meat quality: Very high ratio of meat to bone, the lean meat is well marbled, the meat has a bright red color with a tender texture and firm flesh.

Fat: The meat has an even fat cover but not too fat, and the fat texture is soft and the color is light.

Other characteristics: Young animals have white, soft cartilage.

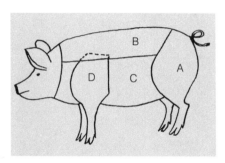

A Leg—SCHINKEN—*jambon*
B Loin—KARREE—*carré*
C Side—BRUST—*poitrine*
D Shoulder—SCHULTER—*épaule*

Table 4-6. Pork Cuts and Their Uses

Leg—SCHINKEN—*jambon*	
Fresh ham, inside—ECKSTÜCK—*noix*	À *la minute* dishes, roasts
Boneless fresh ham—NUSS—*noix pâtissière*	À *la minute* dishes, roasts
Fresh ham, outside—UNTERSPÄLTE—*longe*	Roasts, à *la minute* dishes
Eye round—RUNDER MOCKEN—*pièce ronde*	À *la minute* dishes
Fresh ham, shank end—ROSENSTÜCK—*faux jarret*	Stews
Hocks—HAXE—*jarret*	Braised; salted or smoked ham hocks
Loin—KARREE—*carré*	
Tenderloin—FILET—*filet mignon*	Mignons, whole tenderloin
Boneless loin—NIERSTÜCK—*filet*	Cutlets, à *la minute* dishes, roasts
Center rib—KOTTELETSTÜCK—*côtes*	Chops, roasts
Butt—HUFT—*quasi*	À *la minute* dishes
Neck—HALS—*cou*	Roasts, cutlets, stews, *coppa* (a northern Italian specialty; brined and air-dried neck
Shoulder—SCHULTER—*épaule*	Roasts, stews
Side—Brust—*poitrine*	Spare ribs, roasts, bacon

Lamb

Full-grown lambs are butchered at six to eight months. Spring lambs are milk-fed (MILCHLAMM—*agneau de lait*) and slaughtered at about three months. Easter lambs, when sold in Europe, can be younger than that. *Mutton* is the term for meat from lambs older than 12 months.

In Switzerland lamb is domestically produced and imported. French lamb (*agneau pré-salé*) is not of great importance in the Swiss market; major imports come from New

Zealand, Scotland, and England. More and more in demand are fresh lamb parts, such as rack, kidney chops, and loin. Cuts of lamb and their uses are shown in Table 4-7.

Only lean lamb meat is suitable for freezing.

First Quality (USDA Prime)

Meat characteristics: Good yield; evenly marbled; firm, with a light red color.

Fat: Even, thin fat covering; firm, brittle, and white.

Second Quality (USDA Choice)

Meat characteristics: Poor yield, little marbling, dark red flesh.

Fat: Overall, too fatty.

In the United States, the USDA quality standards for lamb are based on conformation, color, and firmness of lean and fat, and on the texture of the flesh. Yield Grade No. 1 represents the highest yield of retail cuts; Grade No. 5, the lowest yield. The quality grades for lamb are US Prime, US Choice, US Good, US Utility, and US Cull.

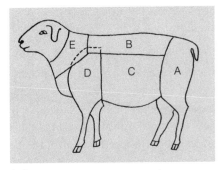

A Leg—SCHLEGEL (GIGOT)—*gigot*
B Rack—KARREE—*carré*
C Breast—BRUST—*poitrine*
D Shoulder—SCHULTER—*épaule*
E Neck—HALS—*cou*

Table 4-7. Lamb Cuts and Their Uses

Leg—GIGOT—*gigot*	First-quality (USDA Prime): rare roasts, lamb steak, boneless leg for *à la minute* dishes; second-quality (USDA Choice): stews or braised lamb
Saddle, Rack—RÜCKEN—*selle*	Rare roasts
Loin—NIERSTÜCK—*filet*	*À la minute* dishes (chops), rare roasts
Rib—KOTELETTSTÜCK—*côtes*	*À la minute* dishes (rib chops), rare roasts
Tenderloin—FILET—*filet mignon*	*À la minute* dishes, rare roasts
Shoulder—SCHULTER—*épaule*	Roasts and stews
Breast—BRUST—*poitrine*	Stews. *ebigramme* (grilled or pan-fried specialty)
Neck—HALS—*cou*	Stews

Goat (Kid)—GITZI / ZICKLEIN

Young goats are butchered as a specialty for Easter. Imported meat must fill the demand in Switzerland. The carcass weight is about 11 to 18 pounds (5 to 8 kg).

Goat meat is generally cut into large pieces, roasted, and then sliced.

First Quality
Meat characteristics: High yield and pink flesh.

Rabbit

Males and females are slaughtered at about 12 weeks of age. Carcass weight is generally about 3¼ pounds (1.5 kg). In Switzerland domestic production and imports meet demand.

Stewed rabbit legs, usually boneless, are most often prepared. However, the back and loins are good roasted or sautéed.

First Quality
Meat characteristics: Very meaty, light pink flesh; little white, firm fat.

Variety Meats

Organs and extremeties vary in popularity. Most organs are tender and should be used as soon as possible, since they tend to spoil quickly. Organs that contain a lot of blood, for example, brains and sweetbreads, are soaked in water to prevent blood spots from marring the finished product. The most commonly prepared variety meats are listed in Table 4-8.

Table 4-8. Commonly Prepared Variety Meats

Variety Meats	Veal	Pork	Beef
Liver—LEBER—*foie*	• *à la minute*	• *à la minute*	• dumplings
Brain—HIRN—*cervelle*	• deep-fried, poached	—	—
Kidneys—NIEREN—*rognons*	• *à la minute*	—	—
Sweetbreads—MILKEN—*ris*	• *à la minute*	—	—
Tongue—ZUNGE—*langue*	• fresh boiled	• cured, boiled	• cured, boiled • smoked, boiled
Tripe—KUTTELN—*tripes*	—	—	• braised
Ruffle/pluck—GEKRÖSE—*fraise*	• braised	—	—
Feet—FÜSSE—*pieds*	• stocks, sauces • aspic	—	—
Head—KOPF—*tête*	• boiled	• cured	—
Snout—MAUL—*museau*	—	• cured, boiled	• salad
Tail—SCHWANZ—*queue*	—	—	• oxtail soup, stew

4.2.4 Cured Meats

In the past, curing was an essential means of protecting meats from spoilage. Today curing is more prized for the variety it provides than as a means of preservation. Curing removes moisture from the meat, which helps preserve it. The pickling salts also stabilize the red color in the muscle. Butchers in the United States refer to this process as *rubefacient*.

In *dry curing*, the meat is rubbed with a mixture of dry salt and spices. A natural brine forms after a short time.

In *brine curing*, salt and spices are dissolved in liquid, and the meat is submerged in the solution.

In *quick curing*, a brine made with salt and spices is injected into the meat or veins. Some hams are massaged after the injections to distribute the brine evenly in the muscles. The protein dissolves, holds the parts of formed hams together when cooked, and keeps the slices from breaking.

Many products are not only salted but also smoked to improve preservation further. In *cold smoking*, temperatures should not exceed 76°F (25°C), for example, bacon. In *hot smoking*, temperatures should be about 160° to 175°F (70° to 80°C), for example, cooked sausages.

A number or cured and smoked products are listed in Tables 4-9 and 4-10.

Table 4-9. Raw Cured Products

Product	Meat Ingredients	Preparation
Bündner ham	Pork leg Fresh ham without hock	Dry-cured, air-dried in the Bündnerland (Switzerland)
Parma ham	Whole pork leg Fresh ham without hock	Dry-cured and very slowly air-dried in Italy
Coppa	Pork neck	Dry-cured, air-dried
Bacon – BAUERNSPECK	Pork breast	Dry-cured, cold-smoked
Walliser bacon	Pork breast	Dry-salted, air-dried in the Valais
Pancetta	Rolled pork breast	Dry-cured, air-dried
Smoked loin – LACHSSCHINKEN	Boneless loin without fat	Dry-cured, lightly smoked
Black Forest ham	Pork shoulder	Dry-cured, cold-smoked, and air-dried, Black Forest, Germany
BINDENFLEISCH	Beef, hind quarter, bottom round	Dry-cured, very slowly air-dried
BÜNDNER FLEISCH	Beef, hind-quarter cuts, e.g., bottom round, top round	Dry-cured, very slowly air-dried in Bündnerland, Switzerland
WALLISER	Beef, hind-quarter cuts, e.g., bottom round, top round	Dry-cured, very slowly air-dried in Valais, Switzerland
MOSTBRÖCKLI	Beef, hind-quarter cuts	Dry-cured, cold-smoked, air-dried

Table 4-10. Cooked Cured Products

Product	Meat Ingredients	Preparation
Molded hams – MODELSCHINKEN	Pork leg pieces	Injection-cured, pressed, poached, and possibly smoked
Shoulder ham – VORDERSCHINKEN	Pork shoulder	Injection-cured, pressed, poached, and possibly smoked
Smoked loin – NUSS-SCHINKEN	Pork loin	Brine- or injection-cured, smoked, and poached
Ham – BEINSCHINKEN	Whole hind leg	Brine- or injection-cured, smoked, and poached
Farm ham – BAUERNSCHINKEN	Rolled pieces from hind leg	Brine- or injection-cured, smoked, and poached
Shoulder ham with blade – SCHÜFELI (Swiss)	Pork shoulder with blade	Brine- or injection-cured, smoked, and cooked
Rolled ham – ROLLSCHINKLI (Swiss)	Boneless pieces from pork hind leg	Brine- or injection-cured, smoked, and poached
Smoked spare ribs – RIPPLI (Swiss)	Pork loin	Brine- or injection-cured, smoked, and poached
Lean bacon – MAGERSPECK	Pork breast	Brine- or injection-cured, smoked with rind; cook or fry
Breakfast bacon – FRÜHSTÜCKSPECK	Pork breast	Brine- or injection-cured, smoked, without rind or cartilage; fry
Backfat – SALZSPECK/GRÜNER SPECK	Pork breast	Brine-cured; cook
Ham hocks – WÄDLI (Swiss)	Pork hocks	Brine-cured; cook

4.2.5 Sausages

Sausages are divided into three groups: fully cooked, partially cooked, and raw. Most spoil easily, with the exception of some cured sausages. It is absolutely essential to keep them refrigerated at all times.

The surface of cut sausage discolors quickly. Seal the cut with plastic wrap.

Most sausages have a relatively high fat and salt content.

Fully Cooked Sausages

Sausages can be made from beef, pork, and/or veal, with the addition of back fat, rinds, ice, salt, pickling salts, and spices. The meats are ground, mixed well, forced into casings, and portioned. Most fully cooked sausages are smoked, and practically all are cooked before they are sold. They are chilled in cold water to prevent shrinkage. All fully cooked sausages should be refrigerated at about 45°F (6° to 8 °C).

Smoked fully cooked sausages include cervelat, Vienna sausages, frankfurters, and others. Vacuum packed, they keep for about ten days. Packaged to be frozen, they can be stored for eight weeks.

Unsmoked sausages include veal bratwurst, chipolatas, and Weisswurst. Because they spoil more rapidly than smoked sausages, they can be kept no longer than five days refrigerated, up to eight weeks frozen.

Raw sausages include links, green sausages, Appenzeller, and raw bratwurst. They are highly perishable because they have been neither cooked nor smoked. They should be cooked within two days. They should be poached before they are frozen.

Aufschnitt is a type of specialty sausage that is not stuffed into casings but is poached or baked in forms. It must be refrigerated and used as quickly as unsmoked sausage.

Raw Sausages

To make raw sausages, beef or pork is ground with back fat to the desired consistency; then pickling salt and spices are added and mixed well. In contrast to poached sausages, no ice is added.

These sausages must be dried to be palatable; some are also smoked to hasten the process. The drying process can take several weeks, during which the sausage generally loses about one-third of its weight. This type of sausage should never be frozen.

Smoked or dry sausages (DAUERWÜRSTE), for example, salami, pepperoni, and beef jerky, can be kept unrefrigerated for a few weeks but should be stored at 50° to 55°F (10° to 12°C).

Cured sausage spreads, for example, Mettwurst and Teewurst, contain large amounts of fat and must be kept refrigerated at all times.

Cooked Sausages

Many cooked sausages are very similar to terrines. Some ingredients may be either cooked or sautéed before being mixed with other ingredients. Variety meats are often used for this type of sausage, for example pork liver for liverwurst. The mixture is usually ground very finely and is placed into a natural (intestinal) casing or into a dish and poached.

Head cheese and similar products are made from cooked meats and mixed with aspic, placed into an artificial casing, and chilled.

Black (blood) sausage, liverwurst, head cheeses, terrines, and other aspic specialties are all categorized as cooked sausages.

All cooked sausages are highly perishable and must be kept refrigerated at about 33° to 34°F (1° to 2°C). They should be used immediately.

4.2.6 Poultry

The word *poultry* refers to commercially available domestically raised white- and dark-meat fowl. Chicken, turkey, duck, goose, guinea hen, and Rock Cornish game hen are the types commonly available on the market. Pigeon (squab) is also available. The market forms of poultry are listed in Table 4-11.

Importance in the Diet

Poultry meat, especially the white meat of young birds, is easy to digest. Generally, poultry meat is low in fat (duck, goose, and boiling fowl are exceptions). The skin is high in fat. Poultry meat is high in protein, minerals (iron, phosphorus, potassium, and calcium), and vitamin A and vitamin B-complex.

Table 4-11. Market Forms of Poultry Parts (Fresh and Frozen)

Chicken	Turkey	Duck	Goose	Guinea fowl
Whole legs	Drumsticks	Legs	Legs	Legs
Drumsticks	Thighs	Breasts (*magret*)	Breasts (*magret*)	Boneless, skinless breasts
Thighs	Breasts	Smoked breasts	Smoked breasts	
Breasts	Smoked breasts	Liver	Liver	
Boneless breasts	Boneless breasts			
Breast cutlets	Breast cutlets			
Tenders	Ragout meat			
Ragout meat	Stir-fry meat			
Stir-fry meat	Rolled roasts			
Wings	Turkey ham			
Liver	Liver			

Classification by Meat Color

- *White-meat poultry:* chicken, Rock Cornish game hen, and turkey
- *Dark-meat poultry:* guinea fowl, duck, goose, and pigeon

The difference between white- and dark-meat poultry is a result of the blood content and the coloring of the meat. Coloring changes with age (younger birds have lighter meat than older ones), as well as cut (legs have darker meat than breasts). Table 4-12 lists common varieties of white-meat poultry; Table 4-13, of dark-meat poultry.

Quality Characteristics

Young poultry has less connective tissue and a finer texture than that from older animals. Good-quality poultry should be plump and fleshy, with a broad breast, and a small amount of evenly distributed fat.

Poultry meat and livers should be fully cooked to avoid the danger of salmonella contamination.

Storage

Refrigerate fresh poultry at 34° to 37°F (1° to 3°C), at a relative humidity of 70 to 75 percent. Under such conditions, poultry can be stored for up to seven days. Poultry must be immediately drawn when killed.

Table 4-12. White-meat Poultry

Type	Description	Source for Swiss Market	Average Weight (pan ready)
Broiler—HÄHNCHEN—*poussin*	Called *Mistkratzerli* on the Swiss menu and *coquelet* in France. A very small young chicken may be called a *poussin* in the U.S.	Switzerland, France	14–24 oz. (400–700 g)
Fryer—MAST HÄHNCHEN—*poulet/poulet reine*	Hens or cocks, sometimes called *Griller* on Swiss menus	Switzerland, France	28–50 oz. (800 g–1.3 kg)
Roaster—MASTHUHN—*poularde*	Specially raised hens; well known is the Bresse hen, a very meaty, fine-boned chicken with blue feet	Switzerland, France	50–64 oz. (1.3 to 1.8 kg)
Capon—MASTHAHN—*chapon*	A specially fed castrated cockerel, known commonly as a roaster in the U.S.	France	4 lb., 7 oz.–6 lb., 10 oz. (2–3 kg)
Fowl	A fully grown hen, usually butchered after she has laid her first eggs	Switzerland	2 lb., 10 oz.–4 lb. (1.2–1.8 kg)
Young turkey—JUNGER TRUTHAHN—*dindonneau* Turkey hen—TRUTHENNE—*dinde* Tom turkey—TRUTHAHN—*dindon*	Leg tendons should be removed before preparation. In Switzerland, in contrast to the U.S., large turkeys are cut into pieces before cooking.	Originally from the U.S., major sources France and Hungary	5–7 lb. (2–3 kg) 7–14 lb. (3–6 kg) 11–28 lb. (5–12 kg)

Table 4-13. Dark-meat Poultry

Type	Description	Source for Swiss Market	Average Weight (pan ready)
Guinea fowl—PERLHUHN—*pintade*	Poultry with a lot of flavor	France	24–50 oz. (900 g–1.3 kg)
Duckling—JUNGE ENTE—*caneton* Duck—ENTE—*canard*	Very tasty meat; duck liver (foie gras) is a delicacy.	France: Nantes, Bresse and Barbary ducks; Germany: "Bölts"; Poland, Hungary; U.S. varieties are Moulard, a hybrid, Muscovy (Barbary), Pekin (Long Island), and Mallard.	50–60 oz. (1.3–1.7 kg) 4–5 lb., 12 oz. (1.8–2.6 kg)
Young goose—JUNGE GANS—*oison* Goose—GANS—*oie*	Only the meat of young geese is tasty; goose liver is a delicacy	France, Poland, Hungary	9–14 lb. (4–6 kg)
Pigeon (squab)—TAUBE—*pigeon*	Young birds have white meat.	France, specialty, Bresse pigeons Italy (Tuscany), Meleta pigeons	10–21 oz. (300–600 g) 1 lb (450 g)

Store frozen poultry at 0° to -6°F (-18° to -22°C). Thaw frozen poultry in the refrigerator on racks with drip pans beneath. Drip liquid should be discarded carefully, to prevent salmonella contamination. Refrigeration should never be interrupted when storing poultry.

Production Countries

Fresh poultry is produced in Switzerland, France, Holland, Germany, Hungary, Poland, and the Czech and Slovak republics. In the United States, major producers are Delaware, Arkansas, Texas, and California.

4.2.7 Game

Game is the term used to classify animals that live in the wild and are hunted for consumption. However, much game is now raised in captivity.

Furred Game – HAARWILD – *gibier à poil*

Roe deer – REH – *chevreuil*

Venison – ROTHIRSCH – *cerf*

Fallow doe/fallow buck (farm-raised deer) – DAMWILD – *daim*

Alpine deer – GEMSE – *chamois*

Ibex – STEINBOCK – *capricorne*

Hare – HASE – *lièvre*

Wild rabbit – WILDKANINCHEN – *lapin de garenne*

Wild boar – WILDSCHWEIN – *sanglier*

Bear – BÄR – *ours*

Reindeer – REN/RENTIER – *renne*

Elk – ELCH – *élan*

Springbok – SPRINGBOCK – *springbock*

The meat of all wild animals is called game (*Wildbrett* in German, *venaison* in French). About one-quarter of demand in Switzerland is supplied locally; the rest must be imported. Because game is offered now in a large variety of dressed cuts, with or without legs, it is no longer advantageous to buy the whole animal (with fur). It is also more sanitary to buy dressed game.

It is very important to identify game accurately on the menu. At this point in time, there is no game inspection law in Switzerland, other than inspection of bear and wild boar for trichinosis. In the United States, game is subject to inspection; trichinosis testing is not required. Imported vacuum-packed cuts of New Zealand game are becoming popular in the United States.

Nutritional Value

Game meat is low in fat and is fine grained. It is an important part of today's health-conscious diet and consumption should be increased.

Storage

- Refrigerated, at 32° to 35°F (0° to 2°C), securely wrapped or vacuum-packed; whole animals with fur in a separate cooler
- Frozen, at -5°F (-18°C)
- In a marinade in the cooler
- Prepared and packaged game should be dated

Sanitation

- Strict kitchen and staff sanitation are extremely important when working with game.
- Work with clean tools and cutting boards and sanitize after use.
- Keep game chilled, 40°F (4°C).
- Game should not be allowed to sit in its own juices (i.e., frozen game that has been thawed).

Roe Deer – REH – *chevreil*

Buck (REHBOCK): male with antlers

Doe (REHGEISS): female

Fawn (REHKITZ): young animal

Fawn (GEISSKITZ): immature female

Description: Lives alone during the summer, in herds during the winter. Prefers mixed woods with lots of underbrush, fields, and meadows. A fully grown deer (about three years old) weighs, dressed, with fur but without head, 29 to 39 pounds (13 to 18 kg). Fresh meat is available during the summer and fall hunting seasons. In the United States, hunted wild deer cannot be sold to the public.

Major exporters: Switzerland, Germany, Austria, eastern European countries, Italy.

Market forms: Whole deer from Swiss hunts. Dressed meat carcasses with bone: hind-leg quarter, saddle (with ten ribs), haunch, and shoulder. Cuts without bone are tenderloin, meat for cutlets (butt, loin tips, bottom round, top round), and shoulder.

Venison – ROTHIRSCH – *cerf*

Buck (HIRSCH): male with antlers

Doe (HIRSCHKUH): female

Fawn (HIRSCHKALB): young animal

Description: Prefers living in herds in dense forest in alpine regions. It has a highly developed sense of smell. Venison meat is dark red; only the meat of young animals is light in color. The meat from young animals (three years old) is tender and tasty . Meat from older animals is often braised and marinated before roasting. During the mating season, the meat may develop an off-flavor.

Major exporters: New Zealand, eastern European countries, Austria, Germany, and Switzerland.

Market forms: About 50 percent of venison is farm-raised and 50 percent is wild. Venison quarters with and without bones are the norm in the marketplace. Venison with bone: saddle, haunch, and shoulder. Venison without bone: tenderloin, loin, shoulder, cutlet meat (butt, loin tips, top round), thin strips (shredded veal), air-dried venison (bottom round). Venison stew meat (jugged venison) is classified as A (neck) and B (breast).

Fallow Doe/Fallow Buck – DAMWILD/DAMHIRSCH – *daim*

Description: Fallow wild deer is native to eastern Mediterranean countries. It is the most common farm-raised deer. Fallow deer are identified by their palmed antlers. The meat is very similar to venison, and meat cuts are marketed with the same names as venison.

Alpine Deer – GEMSE – *chamois*

Description: The alpine deer has curved horns; the males and females have the same names as roe deer. They live in herds in alpine regions and have a highly developed sense of smell and hearing. Their fur is beige-brown in the summer and brown-black in the winter. The winter fur of the male is called beard (GAMSBART) and is used as a hat decoration for native costumes. The meat of the male during mating season has a peculiar taste, and the fat of old animals has a very strong, unpleasant taste.

Major exporters: Switzerland, Germany, and Austria.

Market forms: Saddle, haunch, shoulder, meat strips, and stew meat.

Ibex – STEINBOCK – *capricorne*

Description: Ibex live above the treeline. They are hunted in the wild but have little culinary importance, as only about five hundred are shot each year.

Hare – HASE – *lièvre*

Buck (RAMMLER): male

Doe (HÄSIN): female

Bunny (JUNGHASE): immature young

Description: Two types of wild hare are available on the Swiss market: the field hare and the snow hare. The top fur of the field hare is a rusty beige color, the belly and throat are white, and the tips of the ears are black. The fur of the snow hare is white in winter and gray-beige in summer, and the tips of the ears are black; it lives in the high mountains, above 3,600 feet (1,200 m). Hare eat seeds, cabbage, root vegetables, herbs, and buds. The best-quality hare are no older than eight months and are caught in the fall.

Major exporters: Switzerland, Austria, Italy, and Argentina.

Market forms: Whole with pelt, saddle, loin; leg meat, neck, and shoulder are made into the well-known ragout *Hasenpfeffer* (jugged hare).

Wild Rabbit – WILDKANINCHEN – *lapin de garenne*; Young Wild Rabbit – JUNGES WILDKANINCHEN – *lapereau*

Description: Wild rabbits are smaller than field hare and should not be confused with them. Rabbits dig hollows underground, whereas hare

build nests and the young leave the nest. The top fur is brownish gray, the belly is grayish white, and the ears are solid brown-gray without black tips.

Major exporters: France, England, and Australia; very rare in Switzerland, found near Basel and on the island of St. Peter in Lake Bienne.

Market forms: Same as hare.

Wild Boar – WILDSCHWEIN – *sanglier*

Tusker (KEILER): male

Wild sow (BACHE): female

Young wild boar (FRISCHLING, *marcassin*): two-year-old

Description: Lives in large mixed woodlands and eats everything. The fur is light gray and short in summer, dark black and long in winter. The fur of the young has light stripes until they reach six months of age. Wild boar meat is of good quality till the animal is three to four years of age.

Major exporters: Poland (mainly), Hungary, the former Yugoslavia, Austria, and Germany.

Market forms: Whole carcasses, saddle, haunch, and shoulder. A feral form of domesticated pig is imported from Australia, but it lacks the quality of wild boar.

Bear – BÄR – *ours*

Bear is rarely prepared in culinary establishments. It is generally farm-raised when available. Market forms are saddle, ribs, haunch, and paws.

Reindeer – REN/RENTIER – *renne*

Reindeer live in extreme northern Europe, Asia, and North America. Lapps, Finns, and Siberian Russians have domesticated and now farm reindeer. Fully mature bucks can weigh as much as 260 to 330 pounds (120 to 150 kg). Market forms are saddle, haunch, shoulder, stew meat, and steaks.

Elk – ELCH – *élan*

Elk is the largest member of the venison family. Average weight is 660 to 880 pounds (300 to 400 kg). One- and two-year-old elk provide excellent, tender meat. Market forms are saddle, cutlet meat, stew meat, and steaks. A specialty is smoked elk tongue.

Springbok – SPRINGBOCK – *springbock*

Springbok is the most important game antelope in South Africa. Springboks are raised on farms or kept in fenced reservations. They live in large herds (five hundred head). The meat is similar to deer meat but must be identified on the menu as springbok. Major exports are from South Africa, Namibia, and New Zealand. Market forms are saddle, haunch, and shoulder.

Game Birds – FEDERWILD – *gibier à plume*

Game birds are lean, with little fat, with one exception – wild duck. The meat has a distinct gamy flavor. On the market, whole birds are no longer the norm; the trend is toward packaged game bird parts, especially breasts and legs from pheasant and wild duck. Refuse is processed into animal feed. Only young game birds are tender.

Storage

- Vacuum-packed, dated
- Frozen at 0°F (-18°C)
- Hung in an airy place before plucking (except waterfowl), a practice called *gaming*.

Characteristics of Age

Young birds have soft breastbones and eiderdown under the feathers.

Wild Duck – WILDENTE – *canard sauvage*

Description: Wild duck is a waterfowl. There are many species. The two basic types are swimmers and divers. Swimmers float high in the water and search for food in the shallows without diving. The teal duck is the largest and the most common. The male has a green head with a white collar and rust-colored belly. The female is uniformly brown. The divers search for their food on the bottom. They lie low in the water, with their tail feathers resting on the water. Wild ducks should be drawn and chilled immediately, as they tend to spoil quickly.

Major exporters: Belgium, eastern European countries, France.

Market forms: Whole with feathers; whole, plucked with giblets; or pan-ready breasts and legs. All are available fresh or frozen.

Pheasant – FASAN – *faisan*
Description: Originated in Asia but now found almost everywhere. Today's hunted pheasant is a crossbreed. Pheasant love an environment that includes forest, water, and meadows. Many are bred on farms and released in the wild for hunting. Young male pheasants can be identified by their blunt spur. Male birds have a brightly colored plumage; females are a dull gray-brown. Both male and female have very long tail feathers.

Major exporters: Belgium (breed farms), England, Scotland, Poland, Hungary, Romania, the Czech Republic, Slovakia, France, and Austria.

Market forms: Whole with feathers; whole, plucked; and pan-ready breasts and legs. All are available fresh or frozen.

Quail – WACHTEL – *caille*
Description: This very small migratory bird can be identified by the cream-colored stripe on the head. Males also have a black throat. Quail are on the protected species list and cannot be hunted in many countries. American quail are not of the same species as European quail. The best-known American quail is the bobwhite. Its meat is white and mild.

Major exporters: Switzerland, France, Italy, and eastern European countries (farms only).

Market forms: Pan-ready, boneless, whole; fresh and frozen breasts.

Partridge – REBHUHN – *perdrix grise*
Description: After pheasant and duck, partridge are the most common game birds in Europe but are now rare in Switzerland. Partridge have a rust-colored head and tail.

Major exporters: Holland, Belgium (breed farms), and eastern European countries.

Market forms: Whole with feathers; whole, plucked; and pan-ready breasts. All are available fresh or frozen.

Grouse – SCHOTTISCHES MOORHUHN – *grouse*
Description: Found in Scotland and England, this very desirable game bird is dark brown.

Major exporters: Scotland, England.

Market forms: Whole with feathers, frozen.

Alpine Partridge – ALPENSCHNEE-HUHN – *perdrix blanch/ perdrix de neige*
Description: Alpine partridge are the only birds that have white winter plumage. They live in the northern tundra and in the high mountains above the treeline. They are rarely served.

Snipe/Woodcock – WALDSCHNEPFE – *bécasse*
Description: Earth-colored plumage, with a long, pointed beak. Found only in a few places in Switzerland. Woodcock is common in the United States, where its tender meat and gamy taste are appreciated.

Major exporters: Northern Italy.

Market forms: Whole with feathers.

Moor Hen – BIRKHUHN – *petit coq de bruyère*
Description: The moor hen has an almost black plumage with white wing tips and bowed tail feathers. It can be found in moors and heath in the lowlands and in the high mountains up to the treeline. It is rarely available on the market.

Wild Pigeon – WILDTAUBE – *pigeon sauvage*
Description: Wild house pigeons are everywhere. They can be hunted all year long. These descendants of cliff pigeons nest in city houses. Their coloring varies from almost black to white, rust colored, and gray-blue. The ring dove is a large pigeon variety, with a white neck, spots on the wings, and a long tail. It can be found in the fields in winter, especially in fields of brussels sprouts. It nests in deciduous trees and conifers. The common pigeon can be identified by the black band around its neck and its dusty brown top coat. It has adapted to humans and nests in trees in parks and gardens. Originally at home in the former Yugoslavia, it has now spread all over central Europe.

Major exporters: Italy.

Market forms: Whole with feathers; whole, plucked; and pan-ready breasts. All are available fresh or frozen.

4.3 Foods of Animal Origin

4.3.1 Milk

Goats and sheep provided the first milk for humans. As agriculture developed, cows also became milk suppliers. Today, in all western countries, consumer milk is from cows. Milk from goats and sheep must be identified as such and is rarely available.

Importance of Milk in the Modern Diet

The nutritional importance of milk is recognized throughout the world. Milk plays an important role in the modern diet. Like bread, it is an inexpensive source of nutrients. However, milk is the only low-priced product that provides almost all essential nutrients. Milk promotes proper body functions and assists the body in fighting such diseases as metabolic malfunctions, caries, bone deformation, arteriosclerosis, and heart attacks. It is not only a great thirst quencher and a nourishing food, but it also helps prevent gastrointestinal illnesses, stress, and nervous disorders and increases energy, immunity, and vitality.

Composition of Milk

Milk contains ninety different elements. What makes milk especially valuable in the human diet is the natural balance of these nutrients. On average, 3½ fluid ounces (100 g) of milk contains:

- **3.2 g protein:** Milk protein is highly nutritious. It contains all the essential amino acids in sufficient quantity to built and repair cells in the body.
- **4.9 g carbohydrates (lactose):** Lactose in milk is composed of glucose and galactose. Lactose has a positive effect on intestinal bacteria.
- **3.7 g fat:** The melting point of milk fat is between 85° and 90°F (28° and 32°C). Hence, milk fat is liquid at body temperature, which makes it easily digestible. Milk fat contains the fat-soluble vitamins A and D.
- **0.8 g vitamins, minerals, and trace minerals:** Milk is a major source of calcium and phosphorus, which are essential for healthy teeth and strong bones. Milk also contains good amounts of magnesium and potassium. Milk's vitamin content is high and balanced: it contains large amounts of vitamin A, the B vitamins, and vitamins D and E.

- **87.4 g water:** Milk contains large amounts of water, making it a good thirst quencher.

Calories in Milk

1 cup (244 g) whole milk (3.5 percent fat) provides 160 calories.

Swiss Laws Governing Milk

Milk (whole milk) is the unadulterated product of properly fed cows, which are milked at regular intervals until their udders are empty, to be consumed or used in milk products.

Partially defatted milk or milk from other animals must be properly identified as such. Milk production, storage, preparation, and sales must be strictly sanitary. Milk containers must be sanitized (with hot water and no toweling) and be kept in good condition. Milk should not be stored in unlined copper or brass vessels. Milk should be stored at 40°F (4°C) and protected from light and odors. Unhomogenized milk must be stirred before resale, or it is considered substandard, since the fat content is not uniform.

American Laws Governing Milk

All states and most municipalities regulate and set their own standards. All are based on the Pasteurized Milk Ordinance of the U.S. Public Health Service. Overseen are herd testing, sanitation in milking parlors and of personnel on farms, pasteurization, and laboratory testing of milk to check fat content and protect against unwanted additives.

Preservation of Milk

Raw milk, if not thoroughly chilled after milking, will spoil quickly. Naturally present bacteria will multiply rapidly in warm milk and cause spoilage.

Pasteurization

Swiss regulations allow for three means of pasteurization. In the United States, the second and third methods are in use, with short-time pasteurization being most prevalent.

High-temperature pasteurization: Milk is heated to 178° to 193°F (80° to 90°C) and held for 4 to 15 seconds at that temperature.

Short-time pasteurization: Milk is heated to 161° to 167°F (72° to 75°C) and held for 15 to 30 seconds at that temperature.

Long-time pasteurization: Milk is heated to 147°F (65°C) and held at that temperature for at least 30 minutes.

Regardless of the method used, after heating, all milk must be immediately cooled to 45°F (5°C).

Pasteurized milk can be sold only in sealed containers, except restaurant sales by the glass. Metal milk cans must be affixed with a lead seal.

The shelf life of pasteurized milk is limited. Swiss law prescribes that packages must be printed with the instruction "Store at 37°–42°F (3°–5°C) protected from light" and must include a sell-by date. In Switzerland this is the fourth day after pasteurization. Milk stored correctly will, however, keep perfectly for one to two days after that date.

Ultra-Heat-Treated (UHT) Milk

In ultra-heat treatment, milk is directly or indirectly (through steam injection) heated very quickly to 265° to 300°F (130° to 150°C) and, after two seconds, quickly chilled. This process sterilizes the milk, but does not destroy nutrients. UHT milk is sold in sterilized containers that are impermeable to bacteria, gases, and light. UHT milk can be stored at room temperature for a *maximum of 11 weeks* after the UHT process. This milk is basically a canned product and useful for emergencies and in remote restaurant/resort locations.

Evaporated and Condensed Milk

Evaporated and condensed milks are produced by extracting water from the milk (3:1), using a heated vacuum method. Evaporated milk is sterilized. Sugar is added to condensed milk, and because sugar is a preservative the milk needs only to be pasteurized or to undergo ultra-heat treatment. Evaporated milk can be stored for one year; condensed milk about 2 years. Both are good emergency products for coffee and tea.

Dry Milk

Dry milk powder is usually produced through one of two methods. In *drum drying*, a thin layer of steamed evaporated milk is sprayed onto a hot rotating drum. After a half turn, the dried layer is scraped off and made into a fine powder. In *spray drying*, concentrated milk droplets are sprayed into a chamber with hot circulating air and are dried. Dry milk powder can be made from whole, low-fat, or nonfat milk. Dry milk can be used in baking and cooking. It is water soluble and has a storage time of one year. In the United States, nonfat dry milk and instant dry milk powder are available.

Homogenization

The fat particles in raw milk float to the top and create a layer of cream. Homogenization prevents this separation by breaking the fat molecules into tiny parts that remain in suspension. Milk is homogenized by forcing slightly warmed milk (60° to 80°C) through a very fine nozzle, which mechanically breaks down the fat molecules. Homogenization is usually combined with pasteurization or UHT processing of milk.

Milk Categorized by Fat Content

Whole Milk – VOLLMILCH – *lait entier*

Milk that contains at least 36 grams of milk fat per 1 kilogram of milk. (U.S., 3.25 percent milk fat).

Reduced-Fat Milk – TEILENTRAHMTE MILCH – *lait partiellement écrémé*

Milk that contains less than 36 grams of milk fat but not less than 18 grams per 1 kilogram of milk. (U.S., 2 percent milk fat).

Low-Fat Milk 1% – HALBEN-TRAHMTE MILCH – *lait demi-écrémé*

Milk that contains 18 grams of milk fat per 1 kilogram of milk. (U.S., 1 percent milk fat).

Skim Milk – MAGERMILCH – *lait écrémé*

Milk with less than 5 grams of milk fat per 1 kilogram of milk (U.S., 0.1 percent milk fat).

Approved Milk

In Switzerland, milk to be consumed in restaurants, group homes, schools, and at sporting events or other activities or used in milkshakes must be approved milk. Approved milk products are:

- boiled milk
- pasteurized milk
- UHT milk
- certified milk, i.e., approved raw milk with a low bacterial content

Other Milk Products

Acidulated Milk – SAUERMILCH – *lait acidulé*

Pasteurized skim milk is heated and treated with the bacterium *Lactobacillus acidophilus*, which enhances bacterial cultures. The consistency varies from liquid to almost solid. Acidophilus milk is easily digestible and used to increases bacterial flora in the intestinal tract. Cream is added to "Nordic acidophilus milk," which contains about 6 to 12 percent milk fat.

Buttermilk – BUTTERMILCH – *babeurre*

Buttermilk is a milk by-product that results when cream is churned to butter. Buttermilk contains little milk fat (0.5 percent) and large amounts of milk solids (8 percent). The large quantity of milk solids increases the nutritional value, as they are especially high in lactic acids and phospholipids. Buttermilk is a refreshing, thirst-quenching drink, which is available plain or flavored.

In the U.S., buttermilk is generally a cultured product made by adding *Streptococcus lactic* to milk, which is incubated at 68° to 72°F (20° to 22°C).

Mixed Milk Drinks – MILCHMISCH-GETRÄNKE – *boissons mélangées à base de lait*

A flavored milk drink is made of pasteurized and homogenized whole, low-fat, or skim milk to which flavorings have been added. Common additions are chocolate, malt, and fruit syrup.

4.3.2 Dairy Products

Milk is a basic food product, used in the preparation of many other products. The same essential nutrients are present in all milk-containing products, regardless of the preparation method. Food laws explicitly specify the composition and preparation of dairy products. The most important dairy products are:

Fresh Products
- Yogurt – JOGHURT
- Liquid yogurt – TRINKJOGHURT
- Kefir/kumiss – KEFIR
- Bifidus

Cream
- Specialty heavy cream – DOPPELRAHM
- Heavy whipping cream – VOLLRAHM/SCHLAGRAHM
- Cream for sauces (not available in U.S.) – SAUCENRAHM
- Whipping cream – SCHLAGBARER HALBRAHM
- Light cream – HALBRAHM
- Coffee cream – KAFFEERAHM
- Sour cream – SAUERRAHM
- Light sour cream – SAURER HALBRAHM

Butter
- Best-quality butter (U.S. Grade AA/U.S. 93 Score)
- Sour-cream butter (U.S. Grade B/U.S. 90 Score)
- Sweet-cream butter (U.S. Grade A/U.S. 92 Score)
- Sweet-cream butter, salted or unsalted
- Dairy butter
- Cheese dairy butter
- Cooking butter
- Refined butter (frying butter)
- Composed butters (e.g., herb butters)
- Light butter

Cottage Cheese (Quark)

Unlike cottage cheese, quark has no curds. It is fine-textured, like farmer cheese. Cottage cheese should be sieved for recipes using quark.
- Creamy cottage cheese – RAHMQUARK
- Low-fat cottage cheese – HALBFETTQUARK
- Farmer cheese – MAGERQUARK
- Cottage cheese with herbs – KRÄUTERQUARK
- Cottage cheese with fruit – QUARK MIT FRÜCHTEN
- Cottage cheese with artificial sweetener – DIÄTQUARK

Cheese
- Grating cheese – EXTRAHARTKÄSE
- Hard cheese – HARTKÄSE
- Semisoft cheese – HALBHARTKÄSE
- Soft cheese – WEICHKÄSE
- Fresh cheese – FRISCHKÄSE

Table 4-14. Types of Cream

Type	Processing	Characteristics	Storage/Usage
Heavy cream (45%), a foodservice specialty cream—DOPPELRAHM—*double-crème*	Separation (centrifugal force), pasteurization	Thick specialty cream with a fat content of at least 45%. In Switzerland it is sold in plastic cups; in the U.S., in cartons. Crème de la Gruyère is sold in 2-dl cups or in 1-L cartons. 50 grams (1 dl) = 426 kcal (1,790 kJ).	Unopened, will keep at least 2–3 days beyond imprinted date. Does not need whipping, since it is thick and creamy. Served with fresh berries or fruit salads.
Heavy whipping cream (36%)—VOLLRAHM/ SCHLAGRAHM—*crème entière/crème à fouetter*	Separation (centrifugal force), pasteurization or ultra-pasteurization	Fat content of at least 35%. Pure smell and taste. Excellent whipping capacity. Volume increase is 80–100%. Sold in plastic cups and cartons in 1-,8-, 2-, 2.5-, 5-dl, and 1-L volumes. 50 grams (1 dl) = 338 kcal (1,420 kJ).	Ultra-pasteurized whipping cream can be stored for up to 2 months without loss of quality. Opened cartons must be used within 1–2 days. Ideal temperature for whipping cream is 42°F (5°C). Foam does not form properly at 48°F (8°C) and may lead to the formation of butter granules.
Sauce cream—SAUCENRAHM (unavailable in U.S.)	Starch added	Specialty cream with at least 35% fat content.	Suitable for all cream sauces. Heat-stable and will not separate, even when lemon juice, white wine, or vinegar is added. Thickens sauces without the addition of flour or cornstarch.
Specialty light cream—HALBRAHM—*demi-crème*	Separation (centrifugal force), ultra-pasteurization	At least 25% fat content, with binding agents. Can be whipped but is not heat-stable. 50 grams (1 dl) = 250 kcal (1,050 kJ).	Whip chilled and use for Bavarian creams, mousses, and frozen desserts.
Coffee cream—KAFFEERAHM—*crème à café*	Separation (centrifugal force), ultra-pasteurization, homogenization for bottles/cartons and sterilization for single-service containers. Homogenized coffee cream lightens coffee better.	Fat content at least 15%. Very sensitive to light; is sold in light-resistant packaging. Special regulations for the hospitality industry are outlined in Swiss food laws (LMV). 50 grams (1 dl) = 164 kcal (690 kJ).	Coffee cream can be kept unopened in the refrigerator for about 2 months. It cannot be whipped. It is used for coffee and to improve cold sauces.
Sour cream—SAUERRAHM—*crème acidulée*	Heavy cream inoculated with lactic acid cultures, packaged, and incubated in a warm room at 68°–72°F (20°–22°C) for 24 hours, then rapidly cooled to about 41°F (5°C) when incubation is complete.	Soured cream with a fat content of at least 35%. Sold in plastic cups. 50 grams (1 dl) = 338 kcal (1,420 kJ). In U.S., sold in 8- and 16-ounce cups plus institutional sizes.	Sour cream can be kept in the refrigerator for 2–3 days beyond the printed date. Excellent with game, game stews, and sauces.
Light sour cream—SAURER HALBRAHM—*demi-crème acidulée*	Same as sour cream	Fat content at least 15%. Smooth and creamy texture, heat-stable with a pleasant sour taste. Sold in plastic cups. 50 grams (1 dl) = 172 kcal (723 kJ).	Use like sour cream. Low in calories. Used for sauces of all kinds, meats, salads, asparagus, baked potatoes, in mueslis (Bircher), and in fruit crèmes.

- Sheep- or goats'-milk cheese – KÄSE (SCHAF- ODER ZIEGENMILCH)
- Pasteurized processed cheese – SCHMELZKÄSE

Fresh Products

Yogurt – JOGHURT – *yogourt*
Yogurt is produced from pasteurized milk that has been fermented, which causes it to thicken like custard and produces a distinctive sour aroma and pleasant taste. To make yogurt, pasteurized milk is cooled and inoculated with heat-loving bacterial cultures (for example, *Streptococcus thermophilus, Bacterium bulgaricum*) and fermented at 107° to 110°F (42° to 43°C). The fermentation is complete after two to three hours. The yogurt is then chilled quickly to 40° to 42°F (4° to 5°C) to stop the fermentation process.

Yogurt is very nutritious and is somewhat useful in special diets, as it is easily digestible.

In today's cuisine, plain yogurt is used to produce fine sauces, salad dressings, and a variety of desserts.

Unopened yogurt, properly refrigerated, can be stored for up to a month.

Liquid Yogurt – TRINKJOGHURT
Low-fat yogurt is flavored with fruits and fruit extracts. It has the same nutritional properties as regular yogurt. Liquid yogurt is sold in Europe in 2.5- or 5-deciliter bottles.

Kefir/Kumiss – KEFIR
Kefir is a creamy, fermented, slightly effervescent milk product. Pasteurized milk is fermented by adding lactic acid to it, which promotes the growth of organisms and yeast *(Kefir kernels)*. Kefir contains milk protein and all minerals contained in milk. It also contains a small amount of alcohol. It was originally made from camels' milk.

Kefir is sold in 5-ounce (140-gram) cups, plain or with fruit flavoring.

Bifidus – BIFIDUS – *bifidus*
Bifidus is considered a health food and is occasionally found in Ameri-

can health-food stores. The bacteria added to cause fermentation is thought to prevent the growth of unhealthy bacteria in the intestinal tract. About 90 percent of the lactic acid in bifidus is metabolized by the body. A 100-gram serving of plain bifidus contains only 33 calories. Bifidus is used in salad dressings, sauces and dips, fresh fruit salads, and tropical fruit combinations. It is an ideal addition to a healthy breakfast of whole grains and fresh fruit.

Cream – RAHM – *crème*
Cream contains the fatty particles of milk. It is produced by letting the cream rise to the top or through centrifugal force. Depending on the fat content, it is sold as heavy, whipping, or light cream or half-and-half. Cream is sold pasteurized, ultra-pasteurized, or sterilized, and as sour cream. The various types are listed in Table 4-14.

Butter – BUTTER – *beurre*
Butter has always been of major importance in cooking. It is used in almost all classical recipes. Cooks and gourmets both cannot envision a kitchen without butter. The typical aromatic butter taste improves the taste of many dishes without overpowering them.

Butter is made from pure cream without chemical additives or artificial manipulation, and therefore contains all valuable nutrients in their natural state. Table 4-15 lists the components of Swiss butter.

Butter should be protected from light and air. It should be stored at about 33° to 37°F (1° to 3°C), at 75 percent relative humidity. Butter can be preserved longer by freezing

Table 4-15. Average Composition of Swiss Butter

Butterfat, minimal	83.0%
Protein (approximately)	0.5%
Lactose (approximately)	0.5%
Minerals (approximately)	0.2%
Water	15.8%

(about five months). Federal regulations governing the production, storage, and use of butter must be strictly followed.

It is essential to understand the various types of butter to be able to use them effectively in the kitchen. Table 4-16 lists the types of butter commonly available in Switzerland, along with information about each.

The yellow coloring in butter is caused by the presence of carotene (vitamin A). Butter also contains the vitamins D and E and linoleic acid.

In the United States, butter must by law be at least 80 percent butterfat. The USDA grades butter and prints the grade in a shield and a numerical score on each package. The best grade is AA 93, followed by A 92, B 90, and C 89.

Production
Butter is made by churning pasteurized cream until the butter solids separate from the buttermilk. The buttermilk is drained off, and the butter is washed in icy water. It is then kneaded by machine, formed, and packaged.

In Switzerland two different-flavored butter types are: *sour cream butter* (FLORALP), which is made from pasteurized cream to which a lactic acid starter has been added; and *sweet cream butter* (ROSALP), which is made from pasteurized sweet cream without a starter. The production of both sweet and sour cream butter is illustrated in Table 4-17.

Cottage Cheese – QUARK – *fromage blanc*
Quark, unlike cottage cheese, has no curds. It is fine textured, like farmer cheese. Cottage cheese should be sieved or puréed in a blender before using it in recipes specifying quark. The types of quark on the Swiss market are listed in Table 4-18.

Cottage cheese is a fresh cheese. Lactic acid starter or rennet and heat are used to coagulate the casein (milk protein). Fresh cheese is not ripened.

Table 4-16. Types of Butter

Type	Production Method	Storage and Usage
Sour cream butter—SAUERRAHM-BUTTER (FLORALP)—*beurre de choix/beurre de crème ensemencée*	Made with pasteurized cream with sour cream starter; 83% butter fat.	Can be stored under refrigeration for about 1 week longer than the printed date. Use opened packages as soon as possible. Can be frozen for 2–5 months. Used as a spread for bread, for composed butters, and to flavor and enrich foods.
Sweet cream butter—SÜSSRAHMBUTTER (ROSALP)—*beurre de choix/beurre de crème fraîche*	Made with pasteurized cream without sour cream starter; 83% butter fat.	Protect from light, or it will discolor. Used as a spread for breads and butter frostings.
Light butter—BUTTER LIGHT—*beurre allégé*	Butter fat content must be at least 50%; "Linea butter light" has a butter fat content of 40%.	As a spread for breads for those concerned about weight. Cannot be used in cooking.
Salted butter—GESALZENE BUTTER—*beurre salé*	Made with lightly salted cream (0.7% to no more than 2% salt); 83% butter fat.	Especially good with potatoes boiled in their skins (GSCHWELLTI), on toast, and to flavor dishes.
Dairy butter—MOLKEREIBUTTER—*beurre de laiterie*	Made with pasteurized cream separated from fresh milk; 83% butter fat.	For hot and cold food preparation.
Cheese dairy butter—KÄSEREIBUTTER—*beurre de fromagerie*	Made from a mixture of sweet cream and creamy whey in local cheese dairies; 83% butter fat.	As a bread spread and in sautéing vegetables.
Cooking butter—KOCHBUTTER—*beurre de cuisine*	A mixture of several butter types; minimum 82% butter fat.	Ideal for cooking and baking. Especially useful in recipes that should have a distinct buttery flavor.
Refined butter—EINGESOTTENE BUTTER—*beurre fondu*	Water is evaporated, and the resulting butter is packaged in 450-g cans and 1.8- and 5-kg buckets. *Ghee*, a similar product, is available in specialty stores in the U.S. However, it is browned, which gives it a nutlike flavor.	Packed in closed cans or buckets, protected from light, can be stored for about 6 months. Useful in butter sauces and especially for frying and for browning meat since the almost pure butterfat can be heated to 320°F (160°C).
Clarified butter—KLARIFIZIERTE BUTTER—*beurre clarifié*	Made in restaurant kitchens: heat butter until it looks like clear oil, remove from heat, and set aside until the butter milk sinks to the bottom; pour butter off carefully. Clarified butter should be clear.	For frying and butter sauces

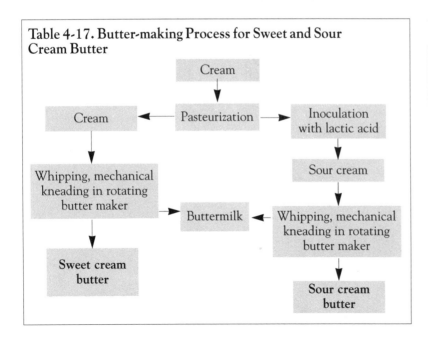

Table 4-17. Butter-making Process for Sweet and Sour Cream Butter

Table 4-18. Cottage Cheese in Switzerland

Name	Minimum % Fat in Dry Matter
Creamed cottage cheese—RAHMQUARK	50
Whole-milk cottage cheese—VOLLMILCHQUARK	40
Low-fat cottage cheese—MAGERQUARK/SPEISEQUARK	below 15

In the United States, cottage cheese is sold as small-, medium-, and large-curd, and in creamed (extra cream added), whole milk, 2 percent fat, and 1 percent fat versions. Farmer cheese is a dry, firm, slightly granular cheese that has been drained.

Cottage cheese is popular for breakfast and lunch, as a spread for bread, and for desserts, salad dressings, puddings, soufflés, baked goods, and low-fat diet dishes. Low-fat cottage cheese (SPEISEQUARK) is low in calories (100 g = 60 cal or 250 kJ) and is an ideal food in a weight reduction diet.

Cheese – KÄSE – *fromage*

Cheese is the oldest and most natural milk concentrate. From the time people started keeping milking animals, cheese in one form or another has been made. Preserving milk by making milk products has been an important way of using milk animals to their full abilities. Food laws strictly regulate the milking process and the handling and making of milk products. The laws are strictly enforced.

Nutritional Content
Table 4-19 lists the composition of Swiss Emmentaler cheese.

Fat: Fat is distributed throughout the cheese in minute globules. Improper storage can cause the fat to melt out of the cheese. It is customary to list the fat content as a percentage of the dry weight of the solids.

Protein: Cheese is especially high in proteins and amino acids, such as casein and albumin.

Water: The water content of cheese defines its consistency, storage stability, appearance, and, indirectly, taste.

Minerals: Cheese is rich in calcium, sodium, potassium, chlorides, iron, phosphate, fluoride, copper, and other trace minerals.

Vitamins: Cheese contains several water-soluble vitamins from the B-complex group and is especially high in fat-soluble vitamins A, D, E, and K, plus carotene, which also gives butter its natural yellow tone.

Table 4-19. Nutritional Compositon of Cheese (100g Swiss Emmentaler)

31%	milk fat
29%	protein
36%	water
4%	minerals and vitamins

Carbohydrates: Ripened cheese contains no carbohydrates; fresh cheese has very small amounts. Milk sugar (lactose) changes to lactic acid during the curing process.

The Process for Making Swiss Emmentaler
Raw ingredient, milk: It takes 265 gallons (1,000 L) of milk to produce one wheel of Emmentaler weighing 176 pounds (80 kg), which is the average daily milk production of eighty cows.

Coagulation: Milk is heated in a sterile kettle to 90°F (32°C). Rennet (produced from the fourth stomach membrane of veal calves; today produced synthetically) and bacteria such as *Lactococcus* and *Lactobacillus* (also important later in the ripening process) are added. The rennet curdles the milk, and it slowly becomes a coagulated mass.

Curdling: As soon as the mass reaches the desired firmness, a cheese harp (a wire-strung cheese-making tool) is used to cut the mass into grain-size cheese particles. The watery liquid called *whey* separates at this stage from the curd.

Scalding : The cheese is heated further to 128°F (53°C) while being stirred constantly for about thirty minutes. This gives the cheese particles the necessary firmness.

Draining: Approximately two hours after the rennet has been added to the milk, the cheese is drained by being lifted with a cloth from the kettle or by using the modern method, in which the whey is pumped off.

Pressing: The cheese mass is then placed into a mold, and the whey is pressed out. The mold is turned several times a day.

Salt bath/salt cellar: The next day, the cheese wheel is placed in a salt-water bath for about two days. During this process the cheese loses additional liquid and absorbs salt. This process also encourages the formation of the rind and preserves and flavors the cheese. The cheese is then placed on racks in a cool, 50° to 57°F (10° to 14°C), so-called salt cellar for about fourteen days. The cheese is turned daily.

Fermentation cellar: The cheese is then transferred to a warm, 68° to 73°F (20° to 23°C) cellar, to ferment for an additional six to eight weeks. During this process, the carbon dioxide that causes the characteristic holes and aroma in Swiss cheese forms.

Storage cellar: The wheels are then stored for four to five months in a cool, 50° to 57°F (10° to 14°C) ripening cellar. The maturation of the cheese occurs from the inside out. The cheese becomes more digestible and develops its typical flavor. During this time the cheese must be continuously turned, and any mold must be cleaned off. Emmentaler cheese can be consumed after five months and is fully mature at about ten months.

One Basic Ingredient, Many Different Cheeses
Some of the factors that make it possible for one basic ingredient to produce so many varieties of cheeses include:

• Geographical location, climate, soil, agricultural methods, and feeding practices influence the milk's composition and its fermentation ability.

• Milk can be from different animals, for example, cow's milk, sheep's milk, or goat's milk.

• Milk can have different fat contents. There are double cream, cream, full-fat, three-quarter-fat, half-fat, quarter-fat, and whey (low-fat) cheeses.

• Different coagulation methods can be used, such as rennet or lactobacillus starters.

- Diverse strains of helpful bacteria and molds can be introduced.
- Cheese can contain different amounts of water.
- The type of ripening and attention provided in the ripening cellar affect the cheese. All, other than fresh cheeses, are cured.
- The length of the ripening process varies, depending on water content and the size of the cheese.
- The addition of natural flavorings, for example, caraway seeds and herbs, affects flavors.

Table 4-20 provides information about the most commonly used cheeses in Switzerland. The most common American cheeses are American processed cheese, Cheddar, Colby, Monterey Jack, cottage cheese, and cream cheese. Most foreign cheeses can be imported, and many are available. Some are also produced in the United States; "Swiss" cheese is one example.

What Does "Fett I. T." mean?

This important fat content marking is common for European cheeses. This abbreviation means that the fat content of cheese is measured as a percentage of the dry weight of the solids. During the ripening process, water evaporates from cheese, which is why the fat content is listed in percentages of the dry weight— whole weight minus water content. The percentage figure indicates only the richness of the cheese, not the absolute fat content of the cheese. For example, a double-cream fresh cheese with a 65 percent fat content of dry weight solids contains no more fat than the full-fat cheese Sbrinz with 48 percent fat content of dry weight solids; 100 grams of each cheese has about 33 grams of fat. Table 4-21 lists the Swiss classifications of cheese according to their fat content by dry-weight solids.

Classification by Firmness

The firmness of cheese depends on its water content: the softer the cheese, the more water it contains. The amount of water left in a cheese depends on how much the cheese was heated, milled, pressed, and

Table 4-20. Types of Cheese

Cheese Classification	Fat Content	Country of Origin
Grating cheese, extra hard		
Hobelkäse	full fat	Switzerland
Sbrinz	full fat	Switzerland
Parmesan	three-quarters fat	Italy
Hard cheese		
Emmentaler	full fat	Switzerland
Gruyère	full fat	Switzerland
Comté	full fat	France
Alpkäse	full fat	Swizerland
Bergkäse	full fat to low fat (whey cheese)	Switzerland, Austria, Germany
Semisoft cheese		
Appenzeller	full fat	Switzerland
Tilsit	full fat	Switzerland
Tête de Moine	full fat	Switzerland
Edam	three-quarters fat	Netherlands
Fontina	full fat	Italy
Glarner Kräuterkäse (Sapsago)	low fat (whey cheese)	Switzerland
Raclette-cheese	full fat	Switzerland, France
Cheddar	full fat	Great Britain
Freiburger Vacharin	full fat	Switzerland
St. Paulin	full fat	Switzerland, France
Bel Paese	full fat	Italy
Soft cheese, white mold		
Camembert	full fat	France, Switzerland, Germany
Brie	full fat	France, Switzerland
Soft cheese, milk mold		
Tomme	full fat	Switzerland
Soft cheese, bifidus bacteria		
Bifidus-cheese	low fat	Switzerland
Soft cheese, red mold cheese		
Vacherin Mont d'Or	full fat	Switzerland
Reblochon	full fat	France, Switzerland
Münster	full fat	France, Switzerland, Germany
Blue-veined cheese		
Gorgonzola	full fat	Italy
Roquefort (sheep's milk)	full fat	France
Danish blue cheese	full fat	Denmark
Stilton	full fat	Great Britain
Soured milk (no cream)		
Mainzer Käse	low fat	Germany
Harzer Käse	low fat	Germany
Fresh cheese		
Mozzarella	quarter fat	Italy
Various fresh cheeses*	low fat to creamy	France, Switzerland, Germany
Hüttenkäse	quarter fat	Switzerland
Cottage cheese (quark)	Double cream to low fat	Switzerland
Mascarpone	Double cream	Italy

ripened. Breaking the curd into smaller particles, heating, and pressing it longer makes the cheese firmer by reducing its water content. During storage and ripening, additional water is lost through evaporation. Cheeses with a low water content are hard cheeses and can be stored longer. Table 4-22 lists the classifications of cheeses by water content and their storage times.

Processed Cheeses

Processed cheeses, processed cream cheese, and flavored processed cream cheeses are produced by shredding natural cheeses, pasteurizing them alone or with flavor ingredients, and adding emulsifiers for smoothness. The packaged product must be stored dry and cold.

Cheese Purchasing

Purchasing cheese requires professional knowledge. Before choosing a product, these factors should be considered:

- ripening stage
- texture
- aroma
- clean, smooth rind

Storage and Handling of Cheese

Whole cheeses: The storage of large quantities requires a special cheese cellar. The ideal storage temperature for cheese is 50° to 58°F (10° to 15°C), at a relative humidity at 90 to 95 percent. For sanitary reasons, cheese should not be covered with kitchen toweling. Surface-ripened rind cheeses, such as raclette cheese or Appenzeller, must be immediately unpacked if they are are wrapped in plastic.

Cheeses in waxy rind and vacuum packages: These cheeses do not need special handling other than cool and dry storage.

Cut cheeses: Cut surfaces must be covered with plastic wrap to prevent discoloration and drying. Separate shelf space in the milk cooler is desirable.

Soft cheese: Soft cheeses are kept in their original packaging. The ripening process can be slowed or has-tened depending on the storage temperature. Lightly applying finger pressure to the center of the cheese helps to measure ripeness. Never store soft cheeses below 40°F (4° C).

Fresh cheese: Fresh cheeses that are not packaged in oil have a limited shelf life. The imprinted date must be noted. Fresh cheeses should be stored below 38°F (3°C). Table 4-23 lists the fat content of various fresh cheeses.

Cooking with Cheese

Only fully ripened cheeses should be used so they will melt properly. Fat-reduced and fat-free cheeses will not melt and should be used only for cold dishes.

Proper Use of the Most Important Cheeses

Breakfast: Milder cheeses should be selected, such as Emmentaler, Tilsit, Camembert, fresh cheeses, and regional specialty cheeses.

Cheeses for glazing and gratinating: Gruyère or Emmentaler, Tilsit (extra mild), raclette cheese, and Appenzeller for a strong-flavored gratin.

Cheese mixtures for savory tarts: The classic mixture to produce the most flavor is Gruyère and Sbrinz; regular mixture, Gruyère, Emmentaler, and Sbrinz; mild mixture, Emmentaler and Sbrinz.

Grating cheeses: Strong-flavored cheeses that will not be stringy are Sbrinz and Parmesan.

Fondue: The most common cheese mixture is Gruyère and Freiburger Vacherin or Emmentaler.

Raclette: Raclette cheese from Switzerland or the Valais Alps.

Table 4-21. Cheeses by Fat Content of Dry-weight Solids

Double cream cheese	65% minimum fat content
Full cream cheese	55% minimum fat content
Full-fat cheese	45% minimum fat content
Three-quarter-fat cheese	35% minimum fat content
Half-fat cheese	25% minimum fat content
Quarter-fat cheese	15% minimum fat content
Low-fat cheese	below 15% fat content

Table 4-22. Cheeses by Water Content

Classification	Water Content (wff)*	Storage Time
Grating cheese, extra hard	up to 50%	up to 3 years
Hard cheese	up to 54%	several months to 1 year
Semisoft cheese	up to 63%	several weeks to a few months
Soft cheese	up to 73%	a few weeks
Fresh cheese, 45% fat (i.T)	up to 87%	several days
Fresh cheese below 45% fat (i.T)	up to 84%	several days

*The abbreviation *wff* is a Swiss indicator of the firmness of the cheese. The percentage is the measurement of water in the cheese minus the amount of fat (*wff* stands for *Wassergehalt im fettfreien Käse*).

Table 4-23. Fresh Cheeses

Double cream	minimum 65% fat
Cream	minimum 55% fat
Full fat	minimum 45% fat
Hüttenkäse	minimum 15% fat
Quark with cream	minimum 55% fat
Quark (farmer's cheese)	less than 15% fat

Cheese salads: A variety of cheeses can be combined.

Appetizers: Sbrinz shaved or cut with a special Sbrinz knife into small pieces.

Cheese platter and individual plates: Emmentaler, Gruyère, Tilsit, Appenzeller, Freiburger Vacherin, Tête de Moine, Camembert, Brie, double-cream soft cheeses, Tomme, Vacherin Mont d'Or, Romadur, Reblochon, Roquefort, Gorgonzola, goat's cheese, and fresh cheese. When composing a plate, consideration must be given to creating balanced tastes, with hard and soft, sharp and mild, and so on.

Important Pointers for Cheese Service

- The age of the cheese is important. Young cheese is mild; mature cheese has more flavor.

- Ripening stops as soon as a wheel has been cut into wedges or blocks.

- White-mold cheeses are generally served when the center has become slightly runny. The white mold is an important part of the flavor and also improves digestibility.

- The rind of red mold cheese, which tends to be sticky, is usually well scraped before service, but not removed.

- It is important to portion white and red mold cheeses with separate knives.

- The higher the fat content of a cheese, the greater its flavor and texture will be.

- Only fresh cheese is served chilled; all others are served at room temperature, 60° to 65°F (16° to 18°C).

- For presentation purposes, a neat display of holes in cheese is attractive.

- "Salt stones" is the name of the small white granules that form in the cheese and holes of Emmentaler and Gruyère.

- "Saltwater drops (tears)" is the name for the small droplets that form in the holes of well-aged Emmentaler and Gruyère.

4.3.3 Eggs

The term *eggs* signifies eggs from chickens; any other type of egg must be further identified, for example, quail eggs, sea-gull eggs, duck eggs.

Quality Regulations

In Switzerland, consumer eggs are classified as follows:

Class Extra: These are packaged and dated no later than five days after the egg has been laid and must be sold within twelve days; never older than seventeen days.

Class A: Refrigerated eggs must be packaged and dated no later than eight weeks after the egg was laid and sold no later than eighteen days after the packaging date; maximum age, seventy-four days.

Class B: Class B is not sold in the shell. It is shelled, beaten, pasteurized, and vacuum-packed. Beaten eggs are used in the foodservice industry.

In the United States, eggs are graded based on the interior quality of the egg and the condition of the shell. Grading is a U.S.D.A. service but is not mandatory. Grade is determined by candling the egg. The best-quality grade is based on the condition of the yolk (centered), the white (thick and firm), and the size of the air cell (small). Three consumer grades are available:

- U.S. Grade AA (or Fresh Fancy)
- U.S. Grade A
- U.S. Grade B

Wholesale grades are:

- U.S. Special
- U.S. Extra

Nutritional Value

Eggs are a highly nutritious food. Eggs contain a large amount of complete protein and all essential amino acids. They also contain almost all essential vitamins (except vitamin C) and large amounts of minerals, especially potassium, sodium, magnesium, iron, and lecithin (which contains phosphorus) in the yolk. One egg contains about 270 grams of cholesterol, which is the total daily requirement. Eggs have a high food value and are easily digested. Table 4-24 lists the calorie content of eggs, egg yolks, and egg whites. Table 4-25 lists their nutritional composition. Soft-cooked eggs are no longer recommended because of the increasing incidence of salmonella bacteria in eggs.

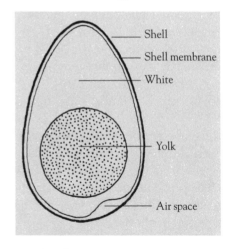

Egg Freshness

A number of means can be used to determine how old an egg is. These include:

- *Visual* (cracked-egg method): The yolk should be round and firm. It should be surrounded by a ring of firm egg white that is clearly distinguishable from the more liquid white that supports it. The yolks of old eggs are flat, and the white is thin and runny.

- *Water method* (swim test): 3½ ounces (100 g) of salt is dissolved in 1 quart (1 L) of water, and the eggs are placed in the solution. Fresh eggs sink to the bottom, old eggs float.
- *Candling:* All eggs are placed in front of a light. Fresh eggs have a very small air cell (6 mm), and the yolk is centered. Bad or rotten eggs show dark spots. Eggs with blood spots are also sorted out.
- *Shaking:* Fresh eggs make no sound.
- *Odor test* (cracked-egg method): Fresh eggs smell fresh and clean; old eggs have a slightly sulphuric odor.

Weight Classes

In Switzerland, eggs are sold by size. The classifications are:

Large eggs: above 2¼ ounces (65 g), one egg

Regular eggs: 1¾ to 2¼ ounces (50 to 65 g), one egg

Small eggs: all eggs below 1¾ ounces (50 g)

In the United States, eggs are also sold by size, based on the minimum weight of one dozen eggs:

Jumbo: 30 ounces

Extra large: 27 ounces

Large: 24 ounces

Medium: 21 ounces

Small: 18 ounces

Peewee: 15 ounces

Additional Information

This information can be used on cartons or in advertising for Class Extra (U.S. Grade AA) or Class A (U.S. Grade A) eggs.

Free range eggs: Eggs from hens with outdoor access.

Mass-produced eggs: Eggs from caged hens. Label misrepresentation is punishable.

Imported eggs: Individual eggs must be marked with a letter identifying the source country or with the abbreviation "imp."

Measures

In quantity food production, eggs are measured in liters; in bakeries, in grams. In the United States, eggs are measured by weight. The number of eggs required to produce a particular volume or weight is listed in Table 4-26.

Tips for Cooking with Eggs

- Egg white coagulates at temperatures from 145° to 148°F (63° to 65°C).
- Egg whites from very fresh eggs (less than twenty-four hours old) cannot be whipped to a stiff stage.
- Egg white causes baked items to be light but also dry.
- Egg yolk gives baked items a better texture and keeps them moist.
- Pasteurized eggs should be substituted for fresh eggs in products that are not heated to above 148°F (65°C) to avoid the possibility of salmonella contamination.

Preservation Methods

Cool Storage

Eggs should be stored refrigerated, from 32° to 34°F (0° to 1°C), at a relative humidity of 85 to 90 percent. Such storage will preserve eggs for six to eight months. The storage time can further be increased if gas, such as ozone, carbon dioxide, or both, is added to the air.

Frozen Eggs

Eggs are flash frozen at -35°F (-45°C) and stored at -10°F (-25°C). Frozen mixed whole eggs, frozen egg yolks, and frozen egg whites are available. All three products must be pasteurized. Egg yolks will not be liquid when they are thawed. In the United States, sugar or glycerin is added to prevent the eggs from toughening. They are sold in institutional-size 30-pound cans.

Table 4-24. Energy Provided by Eggs

3½ oz (100 g) whole egg	(about 2 eggs)	158 cal (664 kJ)
3½ oz (100 g) egg yolk	(about 6 yolks)	354 cal (1487 kJ)
3½ oz (100 g) egg white	(about 3 whites)	49 cal (206 kJ)

Table 4-25. Nutritional Composition for 3½-oz. (100-g) Portion (in grams)

	Whole Egg	Egg Yolk	Egg White
Protein	12.8	16.1	10.9
Fat	11.5	31.9	0.2
Carbohydrates	0.7	0.6	0.8
Water	74.0	50.0	87.6
Cholesterol	0.42	1.31	—
Minerals	1.1	1.1	0.6
Vitamins	A, B_1, B_2, E, K, niacin, carotene, pantothenic acid	A, E, B_1, B_2	B_1, B_2

Table 4-26. Eggs by Volume and Weight

1 L (1.06 quarts) whole eggs	approx. 24 eggs
1 L (1.06 quarts) egg white	approx. 34 egg whites
1 L (1.06 quarts) egg yolk	approx. 44 egg yolks
100 g (3½ oz.) whole egg	approx. 2 eggs
100 g (3½ oz.) egg white	approx. 3 egg whites
100 g (3½ oz.) egg yolk	approx. 6 egg yolks

Dried Eggs

Dried eggs are produced through a spray or heated-roller process. Whole eggs, yolks, and whites are processed this way. In the United States, freeze-dried eggs are also available. Dried eggs can be kept for up to one year when properly stored. They should be protected from light and air and should be stored cool and dry. One egg = approx. 2 ounces (55 g) = ⅓ to ½ ounce (10 to 15 g) dried egg.

Pasteurized Eggs

Unsorted eggs, not older than four weeks, are used for pasteurization. Pasteurized eggs are produced in the Netherlands and Germany. The fully automated process and packaging guarantee low bacterial contamination. The eggs are pasteurized for approximately six minutes at 148°F (65°C), immediately chilled, and then are packed in opaque plastic bags (2- or 10-L size), equipped with clear plastic pouring spouts. The product can be whole eggs, egg yolks, or egg whites. When refrigerated at 35°F (2°C), they will keep unopened for about ten days. They should be kept refrigerated *at all times*; after opening, they should be used within two days.

All frozen, dried, or pasteurized eggs are processed and packed under continuous federal inspection.

Preparation Possibilities

If properly prepared, egg dishes are easily digested. They are useful in diets for sick people, for example, boiled eggs, scrambled eggs, and omelets.

Egg white is used to clarify broth and meat jellies. Beaten egg whites leaven soufflés and batters. Egg yolk will emulsify soups, sauces, and cream puddings. Whole eggs are leavening agents for a large variety of doughs and farces.

<hr/>

4.4　Edible Fats and Oils

Fats are found in milk, in the pulp or seeds of plants, and in the fatty tissues of animals. Table 4-27 illustrates the types of fats produced by animals and plants. Like other nutrients, fats are essential for a healthy human body. They provide the body with energy and essential fatty acids, and they serve as a medium for fat-soluble vitamins. Fatty acids are a fundamental part of human cell membranes.

Importance of Fats

Fats provide the following important benefits in food preparation:

- *Fats enhance ingredients and add flavor:* Many dishes taste balanced only when they contain a certain amount of fat, for example, farces, sauces, doughs, and batters.
- *Fats conduct heat:* Fats improve the transfer of heat from the pan to the food. Only after temperatures have reached 250° to 320°F (120° to 160°C) do nutrients contribute to flavor. For example, sugar becomes caramel, starch becomes dextrose, and protein releases roast aromatics.
- *Fats act as a buffer:* Fats prevent food from sticking to pots, pans, and baking tins. They also separate food layers, for example, fat and dough layers in puff pastries.

- *Fats enhance texture:* Foods with enough fat are spreadable (liverwurst), moist (sausages, terrines, pâtés), and creamy (sauces and soups).
- *Fats act as a preservative:* Baked goods do not dry out as quickly.

Storage

Fats should be stored in cool, dry spaces, protected from light.

Fat Breakdown and Spoilage

Fats and oils can be heated to very high temperatures and are therefore suitable for frying (sautéing) and deep-fat frying. Fats should not be overheated, however, or disease-causing by-products may develop. When fat comes in contact with very hot surfaces (such as charcoal), cancer-causing compounds may form. When fat is heated to a particular temperature (which varies depending on the fat), it breaks down. The temperature at which a fat breaks down is called its *smoke point*.

Exposure to warm temperatures, oxygen, light, ultraviolet rays, or some metals (especially copper), can cause fats to spoil. So can the presence of microorganisms and enzymes

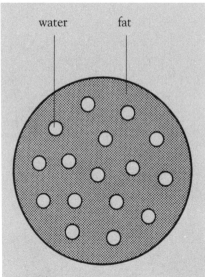

Liquid/fat emulsion
(e.g., butter, margarine, light margarine)

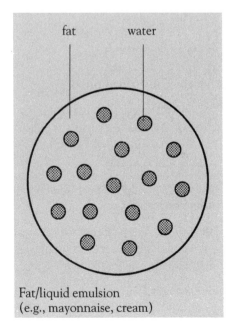

Fat/liquid emulsion
(e.g., mayonnaise, cream)

(only in the presence of water). Especially vulnerable are fats high in polyunsaturated fatty acids and fat emulsions. Fats absorb odors easily and thus should be stored in non-penetrable packaging, separate from strong-smelling foods.

Fat Emulsions

An emulsion is a more or less stable mixture of liquids. If water is dispersed evenly in fat, the result is called a liquid/fat emulsion. Butter and margarine are liquid/fat emulsions. If fat is evenly dispersed in water, the mixture is a fat/liquid emulsion. Mayonnaise and cream are fat/liquid emulsions. Completely stable emulsions must have emulsifiers added. Natural emulsifiers are proteins and lecithins.

Classification by Consistency

The standard for evaluating the consistency of fats is their liquidity, or state, at 68°F (20°C). Table 4-28 shows different classifications based on consistency. *Vegetable oils* are combinations of different plant oils. *Cooking fats* are combinations of different fats (animal or plant).

Production of Fats

Various methods are used to produce fats:

Separating by centrifugal force: Cream and olive oil

Rendering with heat: Body fats

Pressing: Seed oils and fruit oils

Extracting: Seed oils and fruit oils

4.4.1 Animal Fats

In the kitchen the most frequently used animal fat is butter. It is the cook's responsibility to choose the right fat for the right purpose. Table 4-29 lists various types of animal fat and their uses. Most fat products on the market are refined and hydrogenated.

4.4.2 Plant Fats

Production of Fats from Plants

Clean oil-containing fruits and seeds are chopped or crushed, and the fats and oils are pressed or chemically extracted. The chemical hexane (a solvent) is used to dissolve the oil in plants. After the extraction, the hexane is recaptured through the process of distillation.

Heat Pressing

The oil-containing seeds or fruits are first cleaned and sometimes hulled. They are then pressed at around 212°F (100°C) in a cylindrical grinder. The ground pulp still contains large amounts of oil, which is extracted with the help of the solvent hexane. The protein-rich

Table 4-27. Classification of Fats by Origin

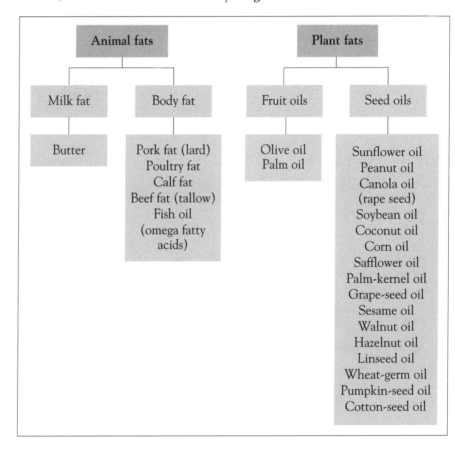

Table 4-28. Consistency of Fats

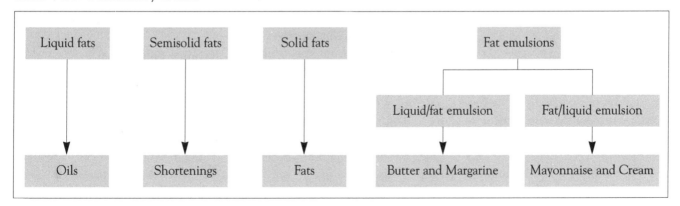

Table 4-29. Animal Fats and Their Uses

Fat Type	Usage	Notes
Butter – BUTTER – *beurre*	Used as a spread, to braise and sauté, to improve the texture and flavor of sauces and soups, and in the production of doughs and farces.	The most often consumed animal fat.
Lard – SCHWEINEFETT – *graisse de porc*	Lard – SCHMALZ – *saindoux*, for pie dough, for hearty and filling dishes, and for the Swiss potato specialty *Rösti*. Back fat for larding and barding and in sausage making.	Limit use: pork fat is high in saturated fatty acids.
Poultry fat – GEFLÜGELFETT – *graisse devolaille*	Body fat is used to braise cabbage vegetables, to cover poultry terrines, and in the preparation of risotto. Rendered poultry fat is used as a spread for breads (duck and goose).	The white (in the U.S., usually yellow, due to feed) body cavity fat is used. The rendered fat of geese is needed in the preparation of *confit*, duck roasted in a fat bath.
Veal fat – KALBSFETT – *graisse de veau*	Veal kidney fat is used to braise white vegetables and is added to fat mixtures. Marrow (*amourettes*) is used in filling for puff pastries and specialty dishes.	Not used very often in today's kitchens.
Beef fat – RINDSFETT – *graisse de bœuf*	Beef kidney fat (suet) is used in the preparation of Yorkshire pudding and in English desserts, e.g., plum pudding. Marrow is sliced and added to soups and is used in the preparation of risotto and dumplings (*quenelles*).	Difficult to digest; composed mostly of saturated fatty acids.

Oil production by pressing

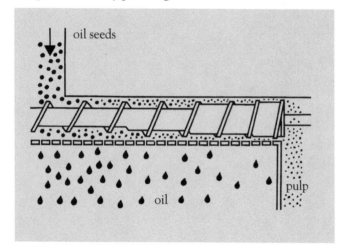

Oil production by extraction

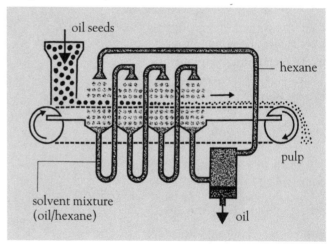

residue is fed to livestock in the form of pellets (oil cake). The oil is then further processed to create a neutral-tasting, shelf-stable oil.

Cold Pressing (Natural or Cold-pressed Oils)

Natural or cold-pressed oils are produced with gentle mechanical or physical processes. The pressing temperature never exceeds 122°F (50°C). Cold-pressed oils are never refined; they may, however, be washed, filtered, centrifuged, and cleared of sediment through settling. Cold-pressed oils are increasingly popular. They are usually more expensive because a smaller amount of oil is extracted from the fruits or seeds. They have a stronger taste and intense color and are generally used only in cold-food preparation. Cold-pressed oils may contain traces of pesticide and heavy metals. They are much more perishable than warm-pressed oils. These oils are used primarily for their excellent flavor. All olive oils are cold-pressed. The oil from the first pressing is sold as fine virgin (*huille vierge*) or extra virgin (*huille extra vierge*) olive oil.

Refining Oils

Unrefined or crude oils contain plant particles, substances that cause cloudiness, and free fatty acids. Crude oil must therefore be refined, through several chemical or mechanical processes. Refined oil is clear, light, and has a neutral taste and aroma. The valuable polyunsaturated fatty acids are not affected by the refining process. Refining processes include:

- *Clarification:* Proteins and carbohydrates are removed with water and sodium chloride.
- *Neutralization:* A caustic soda solution neutralizes acidity; glycerin and fatty free acids are also removed.
- *Bleaching:* Unwanted color is bleached out.
- *Filtering:* Plant particles are removed by this process.
- *Deodorizing:* Pressure-steaming eliminates any unwanted odor or taste.

Table 4-30 illustrates how the refining process works.

Hydrogenation

Natural fats such as coconut fat or animal fats are solid at room temperature. The melting point of liquid oils must be raised to harden fats and make them semisolid. The hardening is achieved by attaching hydrogen to the double bonds of the unsaturated fatty acids in liquid oils, a process called hydrogenation.

Specialty Deep-fat Frying Fats and Oils

For deep-fat frying, ideal oils are plant-fat combinations that are heat stable, neutral in taste and odor, and have a very high smoke point. All fats will break down when heated repeatedly to high temperatures and thus should be completely replaced frequently. The used oil is sold for soap production. Solid or semisolid fats used for deep-fat frying are called *shortenings*.

Important Oil-producing Plants

Table 4-31 lists the most common plant oils and their uses. The plants from which they are produced are:

- Soybeans
- African palms
- Sunflower
- Rape
- Coconut palms
- Olive trees
- Corn
- Safflower (saffron thistle)
- Sesame plant

4.4.3 Margarine

Margarine is a liquid/fat emulsion of water and milk with plant or animal fats or oils, sometimes with the addition of milk fats. The emulsion con-

Table 4-30. Refinement of Raw Oils

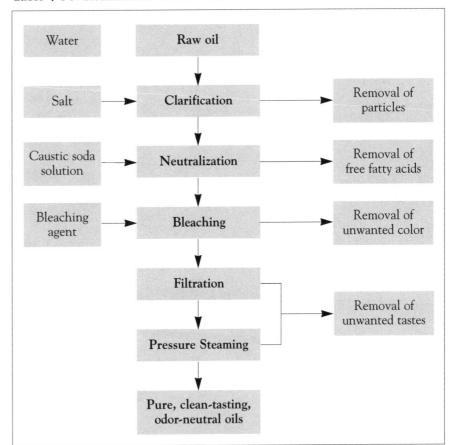

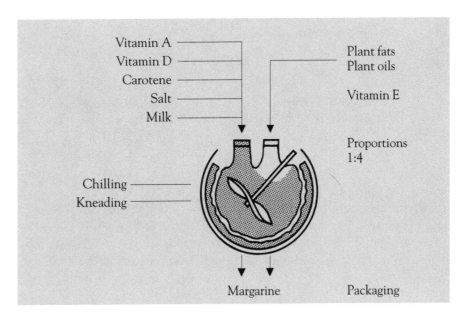

sists of about 83 percent oils or fats and 17 percent milk or water.

History

The invention of margarine is credited to the French emperor Napoleón III, who commisioned a search for a cheap, less perishable butter substitute for his soldiers. In 1869 the chemist Hippolyte Mège-Mouriès produced a cheap, stable

Table 4-31. Important Plant Fats and Their Uses

Fat/Oil	Origin	Source	Usage and Notes
Sunflower oil – SONNENBLUMENÖL – *huile de tournesol*	Sunflower seeds	Russia, U.S., Europe, India, Argentina, South Africa	Versatile oil for preparation of warm foods and especially cold foods; used to produce margarine. Sunflower seed oil is high in essential fatty acids.
Peanut oil – ERDNUSSÖL – *huile d'arachide*	Raw peanuts	China, U.S., India, west Africa, South America	Versatile oil for hot and cold food preparation, excellent for deep-fat frying.
Canola oil – RAPSÖL – *huile de colza*	Rape seeds	Europe (Switzerland), China, Russia, Canada, India	Excellent oil for cold-food preparation, used in the manufacture of margarine and shortening.
Soybean oil – SOJAÖL – *huile de soja*	Soybeans	U.S., Europe, Brazil, Russia, Argentina, China, Japan	Versatile golden-yellow oil used mostly in the cold pantry and in the manufacture of margarine.
Coconut oil – KOKOSFETT/ÖL – *graisse de coco/huile de coco*	Dried coconut meat, called *copra*	Philippines, Indonesia, India, Mexico, Sri Lanka	Used to manufacture shortening and margarines. Especially good for deep-fat frying of pastries. Limited storage time due to rapid saponification (soapy taste).
Corn oil – MAISKEIMÖL – *huile de germes de mais*	Endosperm of corn kernel	U.S., western Europe, Brazil, Japan, South Africa	Valued for its high vitamin content, corn oil is used primarily in cold-food preparation. Used in the manufacture of margarine.
Safflower oil – DISTELÖL/SAFLORÖL – *huile de carthame*	Safflower seeds (saffron thistle)	U.S., Mexico, north Africa, India	Valued for its high concentration of essential fatty acids, safflower oil is used in cold-food production. It is used in the manufacture of diet margarine.
Olive oil – OLIVENÖL – *huile d'olive*	Fruit of olive trees	Mediterranean countries, U.S., Argentina	Cold-pressed olive oil for salads and cold-food preparation. Refined olive oil is used in the preparation of Mediterranean specialties.
Palm oil – PALMÖL – *huile de palmier*	Fruit pulp of African palm tree	Malaysia, Indonesia, west Africa, Latin and South America	This distinctive-flavored oil has a reddish color with a high carotene content. Used in the manufacture of margarine.

spread from beef tallow and skim milk. The procedure was patented, and the product was called *margarine* (from the Greek *margaron*, "pearl").

Manufacture

Margarine is manufactured by first producing a mixture of fats from oils and solids. At this stage, the *solids phase*, fat-soluble vitamins, the pro-vitamin coloring agent *carotene*, and the emulsifier *lecithin* are added. In the next step, the *liquid phase*, skim milk, water, and salt are added. The production of margarine depends on the thorough mixing (amalgamation) of these two phases and simul-

taneous cooling (solidification) to achieve the proper consistency. The processing of margarine is today highly automated, providing sanitary processing, portioning, and packaging.

Margarine is used to meet nutritional dietary needs, as an ingredient in baked goods (puff pastry), and in quantity-production kitchens. To meet the requirements of these varied uses, different margarines of varied composition are produced.

Usage

Margarine is used as a bread spread, in the preparation of doughs and batters, to braise vegetables, and to

sauté meat, fish, potatoes, and other foods.

Light Margarine (Minarine)

Light margarine is a liquid/fat emulsion with a fat and oil content of 39 to 41 percent. As a spread, it is 50 percent lower in calories than regular margarine and offers consumers a product conducive to weight reduction. Due to its high water content, it can be used only in cold-food preparation.

Table 4-31. *(continued)*

Fat/Oil	Origin	Source	Usage and Notes
Palm-kernel oil – PALMKERNÖL – *huile de palmiste*	Kernel or nut of palm trees	Malaysia, Indonesia, west Africa, Latin and South America	Palm-kernel oil is similar in taste and color to coconut oil. Perishable due to rapid saponification. Used in the manufacture of margarine and in processed and prepared foods.
Grapeseed oil TRAUBENKERNÖL *huile de pépins de raisin*	Seeds of grapes	Europe, USA	Valuable, taste-neutral oil with a high smokepoint is useful in cold and hot food preparations. Used in the manufacture of margarine.
Sesame oil – SESAMÖL – *huile de sésame*	Sesame seeds	Africa, East Indies	Light yellow, taste-neutral oil, unless toasted, which it is when used in Oriental cuisine to flavor dishes.
Walnut oil – BAUMNUSSÖL – *huile de noix*	Walnuts	France, Italy	Versatile light oil with a lovely nutty taste. It is highly perishable and must be used quickly.
Hazelnut oil – HASELNUSSÖL – *huile de noisette*	Hazelnuts (filberts)	France, Italy	Can be used in salads, cold sauces, and fish dishes. It has a very strong flavor and must be used sparingly. It turns rancid quickly and should be used as soon as possible after opening.
Linseed oil – LEINSAMÖL – *huile de lin*	Flax seeds	U.S., Asia	It is used in special diets and for cold dishes and has a high concentration of essential fatty acids.
Wheat-germ oil – WEIZENKEIMÖL – *huile de germes de blé*	Wheat germ	Western Europe, U.S.	Used in the preparation of cold foods. Valued for its high concentration of essential fatty acids and large amounts of vitamin E.
Pumpkin-seed oil – KÜRBISKERNÖL – *huile de citrouille/huile de courge*	Pumpkin seeds	Austria, Romania, Russia	A thick green oil with a very intense flavor. Does not heat well and is used exclusively for cold-food preparation.
Cotton-seed oil – BAUMWOLLSAMENÖL – *huile de grains de cotonnier*	Cotton plant seeds	U.S., west Africa	A refined oil that is used in institutional foodservice and in the manufacture of shortening and margarine.

4.5 Plant Foods

Edible plants, parts of plants, and plant products constitute the largest group of foods we eat. Most are high in carbohydrates and fiber. Due to their relatively high amounts of vitamins and minerals, they form the basis for a healthy diet.

4.5.1 Cereals

Wild grasses are the ancestors of most of our grains. The first cultivated cereal was probably oats, which were known in ancient Mesopotamia in about 5000 B.C. Wheat has been cultivated, and its various forms de-

Cereal grain composition and nutrient content

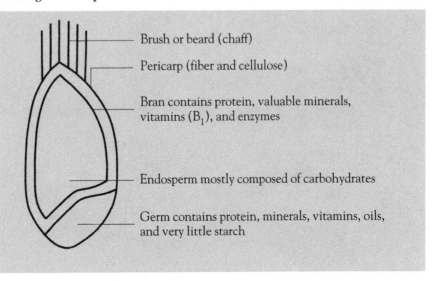

Brush or beard (chaff)

Pericarp (fiber and cellulose)

Bran contains protein, valuable minerals, vitamins (B_1), and enzymes

Endosperm mostly composed of carbohydrates

Germ contains protein, minerals, vitamins, oils, and very little starch

veloped, for thousands of years. Rice and corn have been planted for about five thousand years, first in tropical Southeast Asia, Latin America, and South America. In the tropical and subtropical areas of Asia and Africa, two old grains are prevalent: millet and sorghum. Sorghum is cultivated worldwide.

The cereals most important for the human diet are:

Bread cereals: Wheat, rye, and spelt (German wheat)

Other grains: Barley, oats, millet, corn, rice

Fagopyrum *fruit:* Buckwheat

Table 4-32 lists the nutient content of these grains.

Storage of Grains

All grains should be stored, protected from pests, in dry, dark areas in bags or in silos. Depending on the type of processing they have undergone, they can be stored up to two years.

Bread Cereals

Wheat – WEIZEN – *froment*

Hard Wheat
Cultivation: Grown in moderate climates with short, hot summers.

Major producers: Argentina, Canada, and the United States.

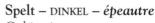

Products: Semolina, dunst, farina, flour, starch.

Usage: Semolina is used in soups, gnocchi, desserts, and more. *Dunst* is a finely milled flour used to make pasta. *Farina* is used in puddings. *Hard-wheat flour* is added to all-purpose flour for baking. *Starch* is used in fine pastry production and as a thickening agent.

Note: About 10 percent of the worldwide wheat production is hard wheat.

Soft Wheat
Cultivation: Grown in moderate climates with warm summers.

Major producers: France, Italy, Switzerland.

Products: Flour, flakes, starch, wheat-germ oil.

Usage: Flour is used to thicken sauces and soups and in bread and baked goods. *Flakes* are used for muesli and other health foods. *Starch* is used in ladyfingers and other specialty pastry products. *Wheat-germ oil* is used to dress salads.

Note: Soft wheat has a larger percentage of starch in the endosperm than hard wheat. Most starch is therefore produced from soft wheat.

Rye – ROGGEN – *seigle*
Cultivation: Moderate climates, at elevations up to 5,000 feet (1,700 m).

Major producers: Russia, Poland, Germany.

Products: Rye berries, groats, coarse meal, flakes, flour.

Usage: Rye berries are used for sprouts in salads. Soaked whole berries and *coarse meal* are mixed to produce pumpernickel bread. *Flakes* are used in health-food products. *Rye flour,* in contrast to wheat flour, is gray and is mainly used in specialty breads.

Spelt – DINKEL – *épeautre*
Cultivation: Grown in moderate climates with poor soil.

Major producers: Germany, Switzerland.

Products: Whole grain, groats, semolina, flour, and flakes.

Composition of the grain kernel and distribution of nutrients

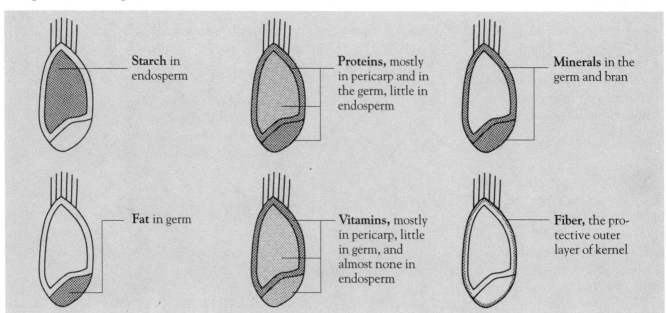

Starch in endosperm

Proteins, mostly in pericarp and in the germ, little in endosperm

Minerals in the germ and bran

Fat in germ

Vitamins, mostly in pericarp, little in germ, and almost none in endosperm

Fiber, the protective outer layer of kernel

Table 4-32. Nutrient Content of Different Grains (per 100 g)

	Carbohydrates (g)	Protein (g)	Fat (g)	Thiamin (mg)	Riboflavin (mg)	Iron (mg)	Fiber (g)	Energy (kcal)
Wheat	59.4	11.5	2	0.5	0.1	3.3	10.6	309
Spelt	62.4	11.6	2.7	0.5	0.1	4.2	8.8	327
Rye	53.5	8.6	1.7	0.35	0.17	4.6	13.1	269
Barley	57.7	10.6	2.1	0.43	0.18	2.8	9.8	299
Oats	61.2	12.6	7.1	0.52	0.17	5.8	5.6	368
Millet	59.6	10.6	3.9	0.26	0.14	9	3.8	323
Rice	74.6	7.4	2.2	0.41	0.09	2.6	4	353
Corn	65.2	9.2	3.8	0.36	0.2	1.5	9.2	338

Usage: Polished *whole grains* are cooked like rice pilaf. *Groats* are used in porridge and soups. *Flour* is used in cream soups, baked goods, and breads. *Flakes* are used in muesli and granolas.

Note: The immature spelt kernel is dried and made into green spelt flour and groats. Spelt is an ancient, rarely planted wheat variety.

Other Grains

Barley – GERSTE – *orge*
Cultivation: Moderate climate. Barley reaches maturity more quickly than all other grains.

Major producers: Russia, Canada, United States, France.

Products: Pearl barley, whole hulled barley, flakes, malt, flour, and coarse meal.

Usage: Pearl barley and *whole hulled barley* are used in soups and vegetarian dishes. *Flakes* are used in health-food products. *Malt* is sprouted and kiln-dried barley that is used as a nutritious additive to foods and in the brewing of beer. *Flour* is used for diet and cream soups and breads. *Coarse meal* is used in multigrain breads.

Note: Barley is also used in the production of some types of whiskey.

Buckwheat – BUCHWEIZEN – *sarrasin*
Cultivation: Moderate climate with cool summers and poor, sandy soil.

Major producers: Russia, China.

Products: Groats, toasted groats (kasha), flakes, flour, and coarse meal.

Usage: Groats and *kasha* are available whole, coarse, and in medium or fine grinds and are used in ethnic and vegetarian dishes. *Flakes* are used in breakfast cereals. *Flour* is used to prepare blinis, pancakes, the regional specialty *pizokel,* noodles, and waffles. *Coarse meal* is used in a European specialty cookie (a dried fruit cookie bar).

Note: Buckwheat is not a grain. It is an herb belonging to the *Fagopyrum* genus. The seeds have been prepared like grains for centuries. Buckwheat dishes have a strong specific taste. Buckwheat flour is not a good thickener and is always combined with other flours when used in baking.

Corn – MAIS – *maïs*
Cultivation: Moderate climate, in areas with hot summers.

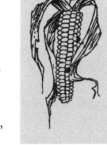

Major producers: United States, China, Brazil, Mexico, Europe, and Africa.

Products: Cobs, kernels, flakes, meal, flour, starch, grits, and oil.

Usage: Fresh *cobs* are cooked or roasted; small, unripe cobs are canned or pickled in vinegar. Whole *kernels* are frozen or canned for use as a vegetable side dish and in soups and salads. *Flakes* are used in breakfast cereals (corn flakes). *Cornmeal* is used in polenta, gnocchi, soups, and baked products. *Flour* is used in breads and flat breads (tortillas).

Cornstarch is used to thicken sauces, soups, puddings, and pastries. *Grits* are a popular breakfast food in the southern United States. *Oil* is used in cooking and for salads.

Note: Dextrose, also known as corn sugar or grape sugar, is extracted from corn.

Millet – HIRSE – *millet*
Cultivation: All climates of the northern and southern hemispheres.

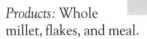

Major producers: United States, India, Argentina, China, and north Africa.

Products: Whole millet, flakes, and meal.

Usage: Hulled millet is cooked like risotto and featured in vegetarian dishes. *Flakes* are used in hot and cold breakfast cereals. *Flour* is added to commercially prepared infant foods.

Note: Millet is high in minerals.

Oats – HAFER – *avoine*
Cultivation: Northern climates.

Major producers: Russia, United States, Canada, Poland, Switzerland.

Products: Whole-grain, steel-cut oats ("Irish"), rolled oats, quick oats, and instant oats.

Usage: Whole-grain oats, steamed, are used in specialty breads. *Steel-cut oats* (dried and roughly sliced) are used for breads, cookies, and hot cereal. *Rolled oats* ("old-fashioned") are steamed, rolled into flakes, and dried; they are used for muesli, porridge, and soups. *Quick* and *instant oats* are sliced more finely and are rolled into flakes over a heat source that partially cooks them; they are used for hot breakfast cereals.

Note: Oats have the highest fat content of all grains and are rich in protein. Before the potato was imported to Europe, oats were the staple of the European diet.

Rice – REIS – *riz*

Cultivation: Tropical and subtropical climates of Asia, Australia, America, and Europe (the Po and the Rhône deltas, and Spain).

Major producers: China, India, Indonesia, Thailand, United States, Latin America, Italy.

Products: Brown rice, polished rice, rice flour, starch, and flakes.

Usage: Whole grains are used for rice dishes. *Rice flour* is used in soups. *Starch* thickens Oriental dishes. *Flakes* are used for breakfast cereals. Rice is also used to produce brandy (arrak), rice wine (sake), and rice vinegar.

Round or short-grain rice is less than ¼ inch (4 to 5 mm) long, only one-and-a-half to two-and-a-half times as long as it is thick. This rice is produced in Italy, for example, Originario and Camolino. The major production areas are in the Far East.

Medium-grain rice is about ¼ inch (5 to 7 mm) long, two to three times as long as it is thick. It is produced mostly in Italy, the United States, and Argentina; for example, vialone, arborio and gamoli.

Long-grain rice is a bit more than ¼ inch (6 to 8 mm) long, four to five times longer than it is thick. It is produced primarily in the United States and Asia; for example, Carolina, Siam-Patna, Basmati and Jasmine rice.

Information about the varieties of rice can be found in Table 4-33.

Rice Processing

Harvested rice is called *raw rice*. In its original form, the rice kernel is surrounded by a hard husk (chaff), which is rich in silicic acid.

In the first step of processing, this husk is removed, usually in the country of origin. At this stage the rice is still unpolished and is called *brown rice*.

The hull covering the rice contains vitamins, minerals, proteins, and fat. Since the fat could decompose during long storage and change the taste of rice, the hull is removed through polishing. The fat-containing germ is also removed. These steps are generally performed in the rice mills of the production countries. This is the basic *white rice* available for sale.

Converted Rice

At the beginning of World War II, research commissioned by the American army developed a rice processing method that restored the vitamins and minerals lost during the removal of the kernel's husk. This particular method, which produces converted rice, was based on a centuries-old preservation method used in India.

To produce conveted rice, the washed raw rice is first soaked in hot water. This dissolves the vitamins and minerals contained in the hull and germ. Under very high hydraulic pressure, these minerals and vitamins are forced into the kernel's heart, which is then sealed with steam. The rice is dried in a vacuum, which also hardens its surface. After this process, the rice is finished in the usual manner.

Converted rice has a yellow sheen. Cooked converted rice becomes white and stays firm. This rice contains more vitamins and minerals than regular white rice and is much prized in the household as well as in quantity production kitchens because its kernels remain separate after cooking. The rising preference for converted rice has led to further improved production methods in the United States and Italy.

Red Rice – ROTER REIS – *riz rouge*

Cultivation: Southern France.

Description: Red rice was developed from a wild rice plant and must be cultivated. Its reddish brown color gives this rice its name. It is also known as Camargue rice (*camargue sauvage*), so named after the area of its origin. It has an aromatic taste and complements highly flavored dishes. This rice has a longer cooking time, and its cooking water will have a reddish tinge.

Wild Rice – WILDREIS – *riz sauvage*

Cultivation: Moderate climates with hot summers.

Major producers: Canada, United States (in the rivers and near the shores of the Great Lakes region

Table 4-33. Rice Varieties

Type	Cooking Qualities	Usage
Carolina, Uncle Ben's brown rice, Siam-Patna	Separate kernels, fluffy, not sticky	Plain rice, pilaf, rice salads, stuffings
Basmati, Texmati, red rice	Separate kernels, fluffy, a little sticky, long cooking time	Plain rice, Indian and Indonesian ethnic dishes
Arborio, vialone, paddy rice, raw rice, natural rice	Increases greatly in volume, sticky, gelatinous	Risotto, pilaf, sticky rice, rice salads, vegetarian fare
Camolino, Originario	Increases significantly in volume, porridge-like	Soups, rice pudding, and rice desserts

Table 4-34. Grains and Milled Products

Product	Features	Type of Grain	Usage
Whole grain	Cleaned and sometimes processed unmilled grain	Spelt, rye, rice, corn, millet, barley	Spelt, rye, rice, corn, millet, and barley dishes
Meal	Coarse to fine	Wheat, rye, barley, oats	Whole-grain breads and pumpernickel
Gruel	Bran removed, coarse to fine milling	Oats, barley, buckwheat	Soups and porridges
Groats	Polished round grains	Barley: rolled, coarse, medium, fine	Soups
Puffed grains	With steam, under pressure, grain size is enlarged 10 to 15 times	Wheat, oats, corn, millet, rice	Breakfast cereals and snacks
Flakes	Bran removed, cut, processed, rolled	Wheat, rye, barley, millet, oats, corn, rice	Soups, porridges, cereals, baby foods, health foods, and diets
Semolina	Milled (rough grade)	Wheat, corn, millet	Soups, porridges, pastry, gnocchi, puddings, dumplings, pasta
Dunst	Milled to a grade between semolina and flour	Wheat, rice, corn	Pasta, pastries, porridges, and soups
Flour	Fine powder	All types	Soups, sauces, dough, farinaceous products

near the Canadian border), Amazon delta.

Products: Kernel with the chaff removed.

Usage: As a side dish for meat, poultry, and fish, in stuffings and salads. It is often mixed with white long-grain rice.

Note: Wild rice shares only its name with regular rice; botanically, it belongs to the grasses. Even today, it grows mostly wild. It is quite rare. Wild rice is rich in fiber, minerals, and vitamins.

4.5.2 Cereals and Milled Products

Milling

The process of milling grain begins after the grain is harvested. First, the grain is sifted. A quality sample is then taken, and the water content of the grain is determined. The harvest is then stored in silos. The grain is cleaned through a dry sorting process, in which straw, dust, metal bits, and stones are removed with special equipment. It is then prepared for milling. To regulate water content and facilitate the milling process, the grain is sprayed with water. Specially designed machines use brushes to remove the beard and

Table 4-35. Milling Fineness

Meal – SCHROT – *blé égrugé*	coarsely crushed kernels
Semolina – GRIESS – *semoule*	coarse to medium kernels
Fine semolina – DUNST – *cendrée*	fine
Flour – MEHL – *farine*	very fine

Table 4-36. Milling Grades of Some Flours

Whole-wheat flour – *farine complète*	Milling grade 98%
Degermed flour – *farine bise*	Milling grade 80%
Light whole-wheat flour – *farine mi-blanche*	Milling grade 72%
White flour – *farine fleur*	Milling grade 60%

the bran. For all-purpose flours, hard and soft wheats are mixed in specified amounts. The grain is then milled to the desired degree of fineness by using rollers, sifters, and purifiers. Table 4-34 lists various types of milled products, with information about each. Table 4-35 lists the degrees of fineness to which grains are milled.

Milling Grade
The milling grade indicates the percentage of the whole grain left in the milled flour. Flour types are classified by milling grade, as indicated in Table 4-36.

White flour – WEISSMEHL – *farine fleur*
White flour is milled from soft wheat. It contains mostly starch (carbohydrates) and very little gluten (protein). White flour is lacking in natural vitamins and minerals, which are contained in the bran and germ and so are lost during milling. The wheat germ is high in fat and can deteriorate rapidly, which is why it is removed during milling. White flour is easier to work with than whole-wheat flour.

All-purpose flour is the common white flour in the United States. It is composed of soft and hard wheats. Other flours are *cake* or *pastry flour* (made from soft wheat that is low in gluten and high in starch), *self-rising flour* (an all-purpose flour with baking powder and salt added), and *bread flour* (high-gluten hard-wheat flour).

Enriched white flour has had vitamins and minerals that were removed during the milling process partially restored. Enriched (especially with B-complex vitamins) white flour is almost as nutritious as flour that has had only the germ removed. This, of course, is also true for baked goods made with enriched flour. Various types of flour are listed in Table 4-37.

Flour should be stored in a dry, dark space at low humidity. Its shelf life is three to six months. It is vulnerable to pest infestation, particularly by flour moths, flour mites, and flour weevils.

4.5.3 Starches

Starch is the most common naturally occurring carbohydrate (polysaccharide). It is obtained from grains, legumes, tubers, and roots through milling or extraction. Starch is white and odorless. It is insoluble in cold water. Starch gelatinizes at approximately 170°F (75°C). Starches

must be suspended in cold liquids and stirred into almost boiling liquids to cook properly. The various starches are listed in Table 4-38.

4.5.4 Bread

The basic definition of bread is a baked product produced from whole wheat, degermed, partially white, and white flour or other grains, combined with water, yeast, and salt.

Swiss Laws Governing Bread Production

Bread types must contain the prescribed amount and type of flour. Breads made from corn, five grains, or other special mixes must be identified as such. Mixtures and percentages must be listed. Additions such as fruits, sprouts, and the like must contain at least 5 percent of the product relative to the weight of the flour.

With the exception of small breads below 0.5 kilograms and specialty loaves, all standard breads must weigh 0.5, 1.0, 1.5, or 2.0 kilograms. Some states (Kantone) can regulate even the weights of small loaves.

Bread should not taste flat or sour.

Bread that is stringy or moldy is considered spoiled.

Nutrient Content of Bread

Bread is a major source of carbohydrates and contributes appreciably to daily protein needs as well. Plant protein, of course, is not a complete protein, but animal proteins, in the form of milk and dairy products, eggs, fish, and meat that are eaten in a sandwich will complement and complete the bread protein. Other important nutrients include the vitamins thiamin (B_1) and riboflavin (B_2), minerals (iron), and dietary

Table 4-37. Types of Flour

Baking Flours	Soup Flours
Wheat flour – WEIZENMEHL – *farine de froment*	Oat flour – HAFERMEHL – *farine d'avoine*
Rye flour – ROGGENMEHL – *farine de seigle*	Barley flour – GERSTENMEHL – *farine d'orge*
Spelt flour – DINKELMEHL – *farine d'épeautre*	Green spelt – GRÜNKERNMEHL – *farine de blé vert*
Buckwheat flour – BUCHWEIZENMEHL – *farine de sarrasin*	Rice flour – REISMEHL – *farine de riz*
Soy flour – *farine de soya*	Bean flour – BOHNENMEHL – *farine de haricots*
	Pea flour – ERBSENMEHL – *farine de petits pois*

Table 4-38. Starch Products

Starch	Origin	Characteristics	Usage
Arrowroot – *arrow-root*	Tropical tuber of the West Indies	Fine white powder	Pastries and cookies and as a binder
Cornstarch – *fécule*	Corn kernels; starch content 65–75%	Velvety squeak, white with yellow tones	Soups, sauces, fondue, fine pastries, puddings and crèmes
Potato starch – *fécule*	Potatoes; starch content 17–24%	Coarse starch, pure white, strong squeak	Binder for brown sauces
Rice starch – *poudre de riz*	Rice kernels, broken rice	Finest starch, pure white	Oriental dishes, soups, sauces, and desserts
Sago – *sagou*	True sago, from the stem of the sago palm; imitation sago, from potato starch	Pearly with a shiny surface, white to slightly yellow	Soups and puddings
Tapioca – *tapioca*	From tropical tubers (cassava root); starch content 28–32%	Hard, white, sharp-edged grains or as pearl tapioca	Soups, English puddings and fruit desserts
Wheat starch – *poudre de blé/amidon de blé*	Wheat kernels; starch content 60–70%	Velvety squeak, pure white	Puddings, crèmes, fine pastries, desserts

fiber. Table 4-39 lists common bread products and their nutrient contents.

Bread Production

Example: In a mixer bowl, 25 to 50 grams of yeast and 30 to 40 grams of salt are dissolved in 1 liter of water. Depending on the gluten content, 1.5 to 2.0 kilograms of flour is added in batches, until a workable dough is formed.

Fermentation

The time required for fermentation depends on the amount of yeast used and the temperature of the room and the dough. It can take from one to two hours. The yeast develops carbon dioxide during this stage, which makes the dough rise.

When fermentation has reached its peak, the dough is formed into loaves and allowed to rise once more before baking.

Baking

Baking temperatures and times, as well as the injection of steam into the oven, depend on the size and type of bread and the type of oven. A loaf will shrink by about 10 to 20 percent during baking. Table 4-40 lists guidelines for baking assorted yeast breads and pastries.

Storage

Breads can be stored for one day in a cool, dry, well-ventilated room. They should be placed on latticed racks without touching. Cut loaves should be placed cut side down on breadboards, or the cut side should be covered with plastic wrap to prevent drying.

Deep-freezing

If bread must be stored for long periods of time, it should be frozen. Freezing is suitable for all types of bread. Fresh, cooled bread should be wrapped with moisture-resistant packaging and quickly frozen at -20°F (-28°C) and stored at -3°F (-2°C). Storage time depends on the fat content of the baked goods. Several kinds of equipment are available to reconstitute bread or

Table 4-39. Nutritional Value of Some Breads (100 g)

Bread/Rolls	Protein	Carbohydrates	Fat	cal (kJ)
Whole-grain bread	9.5	47.6	2.1	231 (971)
Dark-wheat bread	8.2	51.0	1.7	245 (1,028)
Light whole-wheat bread	7.6	52.8	1.0	249 (1,047)
Toast bread	8.8	52.0	6.8	319 (1,339)
Rolls	8.3	54.5	2.6	281 (1,180)
Sweet rolls	9.2	54.0	7.6	389 (1,423)
Croissant	8.3	46.5	20.6	417 (1,753)

Table 4-40. Approximate Baking Temperatures and Time

Large yeast pastries	375°–425°F (190°–220°C)	35–45 min.
Small yeast pastries	410°–465°F (210°–240°C)	15–25 min.
Large breads	465°–500°F (240°–260°C)	up to 60 min.

pastry. Directions for proper defrosting should be followed.

4.5.5 Pasta

Pastas are all noodle-dough products that can be kept in dry storage. Most of these products are commercially produced.

Swiss Food Laws

Egg pastas must contain at least 5⅓ ounces (150 g) of whole eggs (fresh or frozen) or 1⅓ ounces (40 g) of dried egg per 2.2 pounds (1 kg) of flour or fine semolina. Pastas that include vegetables, soy flour, or other grain flours in their ingredients must clearly identify their inclusion on the package.

Nutrient Content

Pasta is high in carbohydrates. It consists of approximately 70 percent carbohydrates, 12 to 14.5 percent protein, 2.9 percent fat (egg noodles), 1 percent minerals, and 0.5 percent fiber. Nutrient values vary depending on the use of specific ingredients. According to government regulations, egg noodles must contain 5.3 percent egg in the finished product.

Basic Ingredients

Hard-wheat (durum) and soft-wheat dunst, eggs, water, and salt are the primary ingredients in pasta.

Production

Flour (dunst or semolina) is *mixed* with water, salt, and possibly eggs. The proportion of flour to liquid is 10:3. The mixture is allowed to *expand*. The dough is then *kneaded* in a vacuum to create a dense, elastic dough.

To *form* the various pasta shapes, the dough is pressed through a spiral cylinder with 150 to 200 bar (psi) and cut. Some noodle types are rolled and cut or spindled, such as vermicelli. Dough strands (such as spaghetti) are partially *dried* until they no longer stick to one another and then dried in steps at 100° to 140°F (40° to 60°C) to reduce the water content to 20 to 24 percent. The process is halted to allow equalization of the water content in the outer and inner layers, to prevent cracking. The drying process then continues until a water content of 11 to 13 percent is achieved.

Packaging for retail sales is usually in 12-ounce or 1-pound boxes or cellophane bags; for foodservice sales, pasta is usually packed loose in 20-pound cartons or paper sacks.

Quality Characteristics

All pastas should have a smooth, even surface and an opaque structure. They should be brittle and snap sharply. They should be elastic when cooked. Pasta should have a clean, fresh wheat taste, which will not be quite so pronounced in egg noodles. Cooked pasta will increase to three times in size over its dry form; egg pasta can swell to three and a half to four times in size when cooked.

Pasta Products

- Fresh egg pasta
- Egg noodles
- Durum semolina pasta (Tipo Napoli)
- Premium pasta
- Vegetable-flavored pasta
- Soy noodles
- Whole-wheat pasta
- Buckwheat noodles
- Special-diet pastas

Storage

When stored in cool, dry, well-ven- tilated rooms, pasta has a shelf life of one year.

Usage

Cooking times vary, depending on thickness, quality, and type of pasta. Pasta is a low-cost, stable grain prod- uct, which can be useful as an emer- gency reserve. Pasta can be used as a side dish or with other ingredients in a main dish.

Table 4-41. Swiss Bread Varieties

Classification/Name	Shape	Appearance/Texture
Large breads		
Basler bread	Long, oval	No slashes, floury crust, coarse, irregular crumb
Berner bread	Round, oval	Shiny crust
St. Galler bread	Formed, round	Shiny crust, dense crumb
Zürcher bread	Long loaf	3 to 5 cross cuts, flat ends, shiny or floury crust
Specialty breads, whole-grain		
Graham bread	Long oval or pan-shaped rectangle	Made from whole grain, 93% wheat and 7% rye, fine, coarse, or medium crumb
Steinmetz bread	Long oval or pan-shaped rectangle	Made from whole grain, 75% wheat and 25% rye, with fiber removed
Five-grain bread	Long oval or pan-shaped rectangle	Made from a flour mixture, 60% wheat, 20% rye, 7% oats, 7% barley, 6% millet; usually yeast, rarely baking powder
Walliser rye bread	Round, flat	Made from fine- or coarse-milled rye flour, sourdough, often with walnuts
Specialty breads, white flour		
Milk bread	Rectangle or round	Center slash, shiny crust, must contain 50% whole milk
English bread, toast bread, sandwich bread	Square, rectangle, round, and long	Dull crust; regular, fine, tender crumb; milk dough; and 100–200 g added fat per liter liquid
Parisette	Long	2–3 diagonal slashes; pale, shiny crust; irregular crumb
Tessiner bread	5–6 attached pieces	Long slashes, light color
Diet breads		
Bread for diabetics	Rectangle	Made from low-carbohydrate flours
Low-salt breads	Rectangle or round	Low-sodium salts or spices are used
Gluten-free breads	Rectangle	Made from gluten-free specialty flours
Soy bread	Long, oval	For diabetics, high protein content, ⅓ less carbohydrates
Rolls, water dough		
Semmel	Round	Large cut, split, and crisp crust
Schlumberger roll	Round	Rosette-like splits, floury top, but crisp
Bürli	Round, connected pieces	Made from white and whole-wheat flours
Graham rolls	Long, oval or round	Made from graham flour, no cut
Rolls, milk-and-butter dough		
Weggli	Round, oval	Pressed into deep two-piece division, thin tender crust
Sandwich roll (Schinkenbrötli)	Long, oval	Quickly baked; thin, tender crust
Cornetti	Crosslike twist	Two separately rolled pieces; dough contains oil; tender, crisp, airy crumb
Small rolls, sweet pastry dough		
Brioches	Round, ribbed	Topped with a dough ball, high egg and butter content
Nut croissants (Nussgipfel)	Crescent or straight	With filbert (hazelnut) or almond filling
Croissant (Pariser Gipfel)	Crescent	Yeast dough with butter rolled in; tender, light, and flaky
Danish snails (Schnecken)	Round	Dough rectangle with a nut or raisin filling, rolled up and sliced

Table 4-42. Legumes

Market Forms	Appearance	Usage
Beans – BOHNEN – *haricots*		
Borlotti beans – *haricots Borlotti*	Light brown, speckled	Soups and salads
Bretonne beans – *haricots bretonne*	Light, round, and white	Soups, vegetables, purées, salads
Cannellini beans – *haricots cannellini*	Creamy white	Italian dishes, salads
Flageolet beans – *flageolets*	Elongated, light green	Soups, vegetables (lamb dishes)
Kidney beans – *haricots rouges*	Kidney-shaped, dark red	American dishes, salads
Mung beans — *haricots mungo*	Small, round, and green	Oriental dishes, bean sprouts
Black bean – *haricots noirs*	Kidney-shaped, black	South American dishes
Lima beans – *haricots soissons*	Large, white	Soups, vegetables, stews, salads
Navy beans – *haricots blancs*	Round, white	Soups, vegetables, cassoulet
Peas – ERBSEN – *pois*		
Yellow split peas – *pois jaunes*	Round, yellow	Soups, purées
Green split peas – *pois verts*	Round, green	Soups, purées
Chickpeas/garbanzo – *pois chiches*	Round, pointed, beige	Soups, vegetables, stews
Lentils – LINSEN – *lentilles*		
Green lentils – *lentilles vertes*	Flat, olive green	Soups, vegetables
Brown lentils – *lentilles brunes*	Round, light brown	Soups, vegetables, salads
Red lentils – *lentilles rouges*	Flat, orange red	Soups, purées

4.5.6 Legumes

Legumes are the dried seeds of plants that form pods. The pod splits when it is ripe and yields the seeds. The unripe tender green seeds and pods are prepared as vegetables; the ripe seed is used whole or peeled and split and served as legumes. Table 4-42 lists various legumes and their uses.

Nutritional Value

Legumes contain more protein than any other vegetable. Legumes are the basic food in many countries and often the only available protein source. They also contain large amounts of carbohydrates and vitamins B_1, B_2, and B_6, as well as minerals such as calcium, iron, and phosphate. They are also higher in fiber than all other vegetables. Table 4-43 lists their nutrient values.

Sources

Legumes are grown in all climates worldwide. Major producers include India, China, Russia, Brazil, Mexico, the United States, and Europe.

Products

Legume products include whole beans, bean flours, bean sprouts, whole peas, split peas, pea flours, and lentils.

Usage

Legumes can be served as a vegetable or an entrée or in salads, soups, and regional and ethnic dishes.

Quality Characteristics

Legumes should be full and shiny. Dull, wrinkled-looking legumes indicate long storage: they will float in water and barely soften.

Storage

When stored under dry, airy, cool conditions, protected from moths and other pests, legumes can be kept for about two years.

Table 4-43. Nutrient Values for Dry Legumes (100 g)

(Nutrient)	Dry Soybeans	Dry Peas
Protein	34.1	24.2
Carbohydrates	29.6	61.5
Water	10.0	9.3
Fat	17.7	2.2
Minerals	2.9	1.6
Fiber	4.9	1.2
Vitamins	B-complex	A, B

Tofu

Origin

Tofu, also known as *bean curd* or *soybean curd*, has been eaten in Asia (China, Japan) for over two thousand years. Since 1970, tofu has become more and more important as a food in the United States and Europe.

Production

Soaked and ground soybeans are cooked, and the resulting liquid is extracted as soy milk. The fiber residue is called *okara*. The next production steps are similar to cheese production: the soy milk is curdled with the addition of *nigari* (a magnesium chloride that is also contained in sea salt). The curdled soy mass is pressed and drained, and the resulting cake is tofu. The drained liquid is used in animal feed.

Composition

100 grams of plain tofu contains:

12.0 g protein (high in amino acids)

7.0 g fat (no cholesterol)

2.5 g carbohydrate (no milk sugar)

0.5 g minerals (low in sodium)

78.0 g water

lecithin, vitamins

120 cal

Market Forms

Tofu is sold plain or spiced. Some available products combine soy and milk proteins.

Shelf Life

Pasteurized and chilled, tofu can be stored for seven weeks. Fresh tofu can be kept for a week; the water in which it is stored should be renewed daily. Fresh tofu cakes cannot be frozen, as freezing affects texture and color. Prepared tofu dishes, however, can be frozen.

Usage

Plain tofu has no specific taste. It is a basic ingredient that must be part of a dish. The smooth exterior of tofu does not absorb spices and marinades very well, therefore it is best to cut it into smaller pieces. Tofu can be sautéed, grilled, fried, steamed, and baked. If tofu is served in a hot sauce, it can simply be warmed in the sauce without further preparation. It can be used in:

Cold appetizers: Terrines, pâtés, canapés, composed salads with different sauces

Warm appetizers: Pizzas, mushroom-tofu toast, lasagna, ravioli, turnovers, vegetable-tofu tarts.

Main courses: Tofu with sauces, for example, curry, saffron, caper, mustard, tomato, herb, or green peppercorn

Desserts: Small pastries, cakes, and tarts.

4.5.7 Vegetables

Vegetables are plants or parts of plants that, either raw or cooked, are part of the human diet. Not considered to be vegetables are herbs and spices, fruits, and grains.

Preserved Vegetables

To store over time, one can purchase canned, dried, or deep-frozen vegetables, and vegetables that are pickled and preserved with salt and vinegar.

Fresh Vegetables

Fresh vegetables are raised in a number of ways. In *conventional cultivation*, they are raised with approved fertilizers and pesticides to produce the largest possible yield. In *organic cultivation*, vegetables are grown without chemical fertilizers or pesticides, in areas of low pollution. *Aquaculture (hors-sol method)* is vegetable cultivation without soil. *I.P.* is integrated production of vegetables.

Importance

Vegetables have always played an important role in the human diet. Prehistoric gatherers searched for wild herbs and edible roots. As humans started to settle during the early Stone Age, they farmed animals, cultivated the land, and planted wild plants in their gardens. Over time, plants changed, sometimes unintentionally, but more often through selection of higher-producing strains. Many of today's common vegetables were already known to the Greeks and Romans. It was the Romans who brought many vegetables to northern Europe. The intermingling of native plants with imported species created more variety, and gardeners constantly upgraded the original wild plants.

We owe gratitude to the monks of the Middle Ages for our knowledge about vegetables grown during their time. Not only did they cultivate herbs in their gardens, but they also documented the healing properties of these plants. Many of today's common vegetables are mentioned in these works. Even then, without knowledge of vitamins and calories, vegetables were valued for their healthy contribution to the diet.

Today, thanks to nutritional research, vegetables are rightfully prominent in the modern diet. Local vegetable production is an important factor in securing the food supply in Switzerland.

Nutritional Value

Vegetables contain large quantities of water, about 65 to 95 percent. The water is of high quality, since it contains a variety of valuable minerals, vitamins, volatile oils, and enzymes, which are all of major importance in the regulation of body functions. Vegetables usually have few fats, proteins, or carbohydrates but are very high in fiber.

Fresh vegetables are not only healthy but can be prepared in a variety of ways. Each vegetable has a very specific taste that positively stimulates the appetite. It is very important to prepare all green vegetables and salads as soon as possible after harvest to retain most of their nutrients.

Usage

Vegetables are at their best in their proper season, when they are fully ripe and readily available at a low price. Table 4-44 lists the most common vegetables and their peak seasons. Depending on the type, vegetables can be consumed raw or cooked. In the kitchen some minerals and vitamins will be lost during preparation and cooking. To keep these losses at a minimum, vegetables should be washed only very briefly and should be kept whole when possible. Soaking cut vegetables in water can lead to nutrient losses of from 2 to 30 percent after only fifteen minutes.

Basic preparation methods include blanching (pre-prep), boiling/simmering, steaming, braising, glazing, gratinating, sautéing, grilling, deep-frying, and roasting in the oven.

Purchase

Purchase only the quantity of vegetables that will be used immediately (as a rule, purchase for daily use

Table 4-44. Seasonal Availability of Swiss-grown Vegetables

Main season ▨   **Storage time** ■

Legend: M = Main season (light), S = Storage time (dark)

	Jan.	Feb.	March	April	May	June	July	August	Sept.	Oct.	Nov.	Dec.
Artichoke*								M	M	M		
Asparagus, green & white				M	M							
Beans, green*												
Beets	S	S	S						M	M	M	S
Broccoli					M	M		M	M	M		
Brussels sprouts	M	M	M						M	M	M	M
Cabbage, Chinese*	S	S							M	M	M	S
Cabbage, green*	S	S	S	S							S	S
Cabbage, red	S	S	S						M	M	M	S
Cabbage, Savoy	S	S	S						M	M	M	S
Cardoon	M										S	S
Carrots*	S	S	S	M	M	M	M	M	M	M	M	M
Catalonia								M	M	M		
Cauliflower*						M	M	M	M	M		
Celeriac*	S	S	S	S	S	S			M	M	M	S
Celery*	M						M	M	M	M	M	M
Chicory, curly					M	M	M	M	M	M		
Chinese artichoke	M	M	M									
Corn							M	M	M			
Corn salad*	M	M	M	M					M	M	M	M
Cress*	M	M	M	M	M	M	M	M	M	M	M	M
Cucumber*					M	M	M	M	M	M		
Eggplant*						M	M	M	M			
Endive, Belgian*	M	M	M					M	M	M	M	M
Escarole	M	M	M					M	M	M	M	M
Fennel*					M	M	M	M	M	M		
Garlic*							M	M	M	M		
Jerusalem artichoke	M	M	M								M	M
Kohlrabi				M	M	M	M	M	M	M		
Leeks, green*	M	M	M					M	M	M	M	M
Leeks, white							M	M	M	M	M	M
Lettuce, Boston*				M	M	M	M	M	M	M		
Lettuce, iceberg				M	M	M	M	M	M	M		
Lettuce, loose-leaf				M	M	M	M	M	M	M		
Melon*							M	M	M			
Onion*	S	S	S				M	M	M	M	M	M
Peas						M	M					
Peas, snow						M	M					
Peppers*							M	M	M	M		
Purslane, winter	M	M	M	M	M							
Radicchio								M	M	M	M	
Radish, red*				M	M	M	M	M	M	M		
Radish, white				M	M	M	M	M	M	M		
Rhubarb				M	M	M						
Romaine (cos)*				M	M	M	M	M	M	M		
Salsify	M	M	M						M	M	M	M
Shallots*	S	S	S				M	M	M	S		
Spinach				M	M	M	M	M	M	M		
Squash, pattypan							M	M	M	M		
Swiss chard				M	M	M	M	M	M	M		
Tomato*						M	M	M	M	M		
Turnips, white	S				M	M			M	M	M	S
Zucchini					M	M	M	M	M	M		
Zuckerhut (winter salad)									M	M	M	S

*available all year

only). Vegetables that will not be prepared immediately should be refrigerated promptly and covered or stored in perforated plastic bags to reduce loss of moisture. Cut and prepared vegetables will wilt and oxidize rapidly. Protect vegetables from warmth, light, frost, and odors.

Storage

Fresh vegetables have the most nutrients when they are harvested. During transport and storage, vegetables are subject to deterioration. Valuable nutrients are lost. Microorganisms speed ripening and aging, which can lead quickly to spoilage. Fresh vegetables are living organisms. Therefore, refrigeration is most important. A temperature from 32° to 40°F (0° to 5°C) slows down ripening and retards spoilage-causing agents.

Fresh vegetables can be stored for short periods of time under refrigeration. Cool cellars with high humidity can also be used. For long storage of fresh vegetables, it is necessary to have refrigerated and controlled-atmosphere (CA) storage units available. In such mechanically refrigerated storage coolers, the temperature and the humidity can be controlled, making them superior to naturally cooled storage cellars. In controlled-atmosphere storage, vegetables are kept in hermetically sealed coolers. In addition to temperature and humidity, the amount of available oxygen and carbon dioxide in these coolers can also be regulated, which slows the ripening process by about 50 percent. Such control enables some fresh vegetables to be stored until spring, or even

close to the time of the next harvest. Quality can be preserved by this method, but some deterioration will always occur. The degree of loss during storage, of vitamins, for example, depends on the storage conditions but increases with the length of storage.

Preservation

Vegetables are preserved by deep-freezing, heat sterilization, and drying, all of which deactivate and destroy the microorganisms responsible for ripening and spoilage.

Deep-freezing causes the smallest nutrient loss of the preservation methods. Losses occur during preparation, prior to freezing (washing, paring, cutting, and blanching). Vitamins are most likely to be destroyed. The losses vary greatly, depending on the type of vegetable and vitamins. The vegetable-processing industry strives to incorporate production methods that are product specific to keep nutrient losses small.

Quality Characteristics

Fresh vegetables should be fresh, clean, and sorted by type. They should be ripe, having been harvested at their peak. They should have good color, should not be overly wet, and should show no signs of frost or weather damage. Washed product should be well drained. Quality specifications in Switzerland are based on European Union (EU) standards, as listed in Table 4-45. United States grades are U.S. Fancy, U.S. Choice, U.S. No. 1., U.S. No. 2.

Artichoke – ARTISCHOKE – *artichaut*

Description: The artichoke is an Oriental thistle plant of great nutritional value. Artichokes are a culinary delicacy that stimulate the appetite and are therefore often served as a first course. Artichokes are also the basis of a number of apéritifs.

Quality: Healthy green plants that are heavy for their size, with tight leaves that show no sign of drying. Sorted by size. Peak season in the United States is from March through May.

Cultivation: Mediterranean countries and California. Artichokes are grown in fields and are very sensitive to cold weather.

Varieties: In the United States, the Green Globe artichoke is most common and is offered in grades 1 and 2. In Europe two types are prevalent. The round variety with very tight leaves is the French Prince de Bretagne, and the more elongated type with pointed loose leaves from Italy or Spain is the Violette de Palermo.

Storage: Keep cool and protected from air to prevent drying or spotting. Best used the same day.

Preservation: Artichoke hearts and bottoms are marinated in oil or canned.

Usage: Whole artichokes, hearts, or bottoms are served as appetizers, in soups, and in salads. They are simmered, steamed, gratinated, or deep-fried.

Table 4-45. European Union (EU) Standards

Class	Quality	Characteristics	Usage
Extra	Premium	Select, damage-free product of same size and type.	Vegetable platters
I	First choice	Perfect, fresh product, with minor shape or color blemishes.	Salads and steamed vegetables
II	Second choice	Minor blemishes in color, shape, or surface. Taste and storage quality only slightly impaired.	Stewed vegetables and vegetable soups
III	Third choice	Same quality characteristics as in class II; blemishes more pronounced and numerous.	Same as class II

Asparagus – SPARGEL – *asperge*

Description: Green asparagus is most common in the United States. It grows *above* ground. White and purple asparagus, common in Europe, grow under the ground, in very sandy soil. White asparagus cultivation is very labor intensive; asparagus cannot be harvested until the plant is three years old, making it expensive. Hills covered with plastic produce an earlier harvest. Fresh white asparagus is usually imported. Green asparagus is exported from the United States to Europe.

Quality: White apparatus should be fresh, straight, and without blemishes. It should be clean and should not be woody, hollow, or cracked. No. 1 quality asparagus stems should be between ½ and ¾ inch (16 mm) in diameter and sorted by color. Thinner stems are sold as No. 2 quality and are cheaper. Asparagus is sold loose (in the United States, in pyramid crates) or in bundles. Green asparagus should be bright green, firm with closed tips, and free of rust.

Cultivation: Major suppliers of fresh white asparagus are France (Cavaillon, Loire, Drôme, Alsace-Lorraine), Spain, Italy, Hungary, Holland, Belgium, and Germany. White asparagus season is from May to July; out of season, Europe imports American asparagus. Fresh green asparagus is cultivated commercially in the states of California and Washington. Canned white asparagus is available from Taiwan; canned green and white asparagus, from California.

Varieties: White, violet, and green asparagus. In the United States, the most common variety is Martha Washington.

Usage: White and green asparagus are served as appetizers, side dishes, and in soups and salads. They are usually steamed. White asparagus is offered as a specialty dish with Westphalian ham.

Storage: Refrigerate, covered with moist toweling.

Bean, green – BOHNE – *haricot*

Description: The name refers to the seed as well as the pod. This vegetable originated in South America.

Quality: Tender, healthy, meaty, same-size pods that snap easily. Beans should not be stringy or have rust spots.

Cultivation: Switzerland, Italy, Spain, France, the United States.

Varieties: Bush beans, pole beans, and dry beans. Tender *bush beans* are used as salad beans and, when medium-size, as vegetable side dishes. Stringless types in Europe are Bobby beans, Cornetti, and Kenia. *Pole beans* come in several varieties. A dry bean variety is the Borlotti bean, with speckled red or purple pods. Fava beans have broad flat green pods with very broad seeds. *Princess beans* have short, green, tender pods. *Wax beans* are yellow and tender. For dry bean varieties, see the discussion of legumes, earlier in this chapter.

Storage: Keep fresh beans refrigerated but unwashed to prevent rust spots from forming. Because beans are very high in protein, they will release heat and spoil if stored in large baskets at room temperature.

Preservation: Freezing, canning, and drying.

Usage: Salads, soups, vegetable side dishes, and stews. Beans can be blanched, boiled, steamed, braised, and sautéed.

Beets – RANDE/ROTE RÜBE/ROTE BETE – *betterave rouge*

Description: Beets are a round or elongated barrel-shaped root vegetable with deep red flesh. In the United States, in addition to the root, beet greens are also popular.

Quality: Clean, washed, firm, without blemishes, with deep red flesh. Should have a diameter of 2 to 4 inches (5 to 10 cm). Large beets are stringy. Clip-top beets are also sold, usually in 50-pound units, for the restaurant industry.

Cultivation: Switzerland, Italy, Germany, Holland, and United States.

Storage: Keep cool.

Usage: Salads (raw or cooked), as juice, in soups, hot (as a sweet-and-sour vegetable), and pickled. Beets are also used as a coloring agent.

Broccoli – BROCCOLI/SPARGELKOHL – *brocoli*

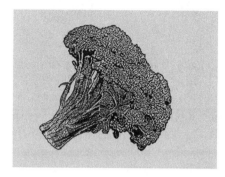

Description: Broccoli is a cauliflower-type vegetable, with dark green flowered heads. It is an excellent vegetable.

Quality: Broccoli should be fresh and bright green, with tight heads that have no yellow blossoms. The stems should be tender, about 5 to 6 inches (12 to 15 cm) long. *Brocoletti di rape* (broccoli rabe) has smaller buds and thinner stems.

Cultivation: Switzerland, Italy, Spain, other Mediterranean countries; in the United States, California, Texas, Oregon, and Arizona.

Varieties: Italy produces more than thirty varieties; important are head broccoli and broccoli rabe.

Storage: Broccoli must be refrigerated. It is sensitive to light, warmth, and pressure. It should be used as quickly as possible, as it can only be held for a few days.

Preservation: Deep-freezing.

Usage: Same as cauliflower: broccoli can be prepared gratinated, boiled, steamed, and deep-fried.

Brussels Sprouts – ROSENKOHL – *choux de Bruxelles*

Description: Small, compact, tightly closed sprouts, which grow in clusters on the stalks of the plant. Brussels sprouts can withstand cold and are an ideal winter vegetable. Cold weather improves their flavor and digestibility.

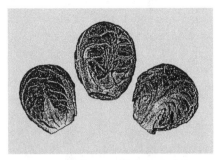

Quality: The sprouts must be fresh, healthy, green, and tightly closed. No. 1 quality sprouts have a diameter of ¾ to 1¼ inches (1.5 to 3.5 cm). No. 2 quality sprouts are not tightly closed and are larger than 1¼ inches (3.5 cm) in diameter.

Cultivation: Switzerland and all of Europe, especially Holland and Belgium; Mexico, Canada; in the United States, California and Long Island, New York.

Storage: Cool storage, with high humidity or the sprouts will turn yellow and wilt.

Usage: Served as a vegetable side dish. Can be blanched, sautéed, steamed, and boiled.

Cabbage, Chinese – CHINAKOHL – *chou chinois*

Description: Chinese cabbage is oval and about 12 inches (30 cm) long. It has a firm head with white, yellow, or light green ribbed leaves.

Quality: Tightly closed heads, cleanly trimmed, with light, crisp leaves.

Cultivation: Switzerland and all Europe, eastern Asia, and the United States.

Varieties: Many, especially in Asia; they differ in the shape of the head. A squat, compact version popular in the United States is napa cabbage.

Storage: Cool storage, protected from light.

Usage: In salads or soups and as a vegetable side dish or in Oriental dishes. Chinese cabbage can be braised, boiled, stewed, or stir-fried.

Cabbage, Green – WEISSKOHL/ WEISSKABIS – *chou blanc*

Description: Very firm, heavy heads with tight, fine-ribbed, light green leaves.

Quality: Fresh, healthy heads with clean outer leaves, without bruises. Should not weigh more than 5½ pounds (2.5 kg).

Cultivation: Switzerland and all of central Europe, especially Germany; Canada; in the United States, Florida, Texas, California, New Jersey, and New York.

Varieties: A spring variety with a pointed head and looser leaf is called *Spitzkohl. Summer cabbage* has round green heads and *winter cabbage* has round white heads. *Sauerkraut* is produced from large winter cabbage that weighs up to 10 pounds (4 kg). To make sauerkraut, finely cut and salted cabbage is placed in a vacuum, where natural lactic acids form and cause fermentation. Sauerkraut is ready to eat in four to six weeks.

Storage: Cool storage. Handle with care, as bruises cause cabbage to rot quickly.

Usage: Salads, soups, vegetable side dishes, and stews. Sauerkraut is best braised.

Cabbage, Red – ROTKABIS/ROTKOHL/ BLAUKRAUT – *chou rouge*

Description: The heads are very firm and heavy. The leaves have fine ribs and are purplish red in color. The typical red color comes from the plant pigment anthocyanin.

Quality: Crisp, firm heads with leaves that cover the head. The stem should be cut short. Heads should weigh at least 1 pound but not more than 4 pounds (0.5 to 2 kg).

Cultivation: Switzerland (major imports from Holland) and all of Europe and North America.

Varieties: Early and late varieties; later cabbage is darker in color and more popular.

Storage: Can be kept in cool storage all winter but must be protected from bruising or cracks, which will cause spoilage.

Usage: Raw and cooked as a vegetable, mostly braised.

Cabbage, Savoy – WIRZKOHL/ WIRSING – *chou frisé léger/ chou frisé lourd*

Description: Savoy cabbage is the third most common cabbage, after green and red. In contrast to green cabbage, the leaves of Savoy cabbage are curly and green-yellow.

Quality: The heads and leaves should look fresh and healthy.

Cultivation: Switzerland, Germany, Austria, France; in the United States, Florida, Texas, California, New Jersey, and New York.

Varieties: The heads of spring and summer varieties are loose-leaved; winter varieties are heavier and have tighter heads, which can be stored longer.

Storage: Loose-leaf heads must be used quickly; tight heads can be stored in a cool, dark space.

Usage: Savoy cabbage is served as a vegetable side dish and in soups; the spring and summer varieties can be used in salads. It is blanched, sautéed, boiled, and braised.

Cardoon – KARDY – *cardon*

Description: A true French vegetable, the cardoon is related to the artichoke but looks like a bunch of spiny celery. It grows to a height of 4½ feet (1.4 m) and consists of a bundle of veined, prickly leaves. The inner leaves are very tender. Cardoons are in season in the fall and are hilled toward the end of their growing season. Cut cardoons turn black and must be placed in a *blanc de légumes* (water with lemon juice and flour) immediately.

Quality: Firm, without spots.

Cultivation: In Switzerland only near Geneva, Spain, the south of France, Italy; in the United States, California.

Varieties: In Europe the preferred variety is called *Cardy de Tours;* it has meaty leaf-stems without the thorny leaves.

Storage: Wrapped, to protect it from light, in cool storage.

Usage: Cooked in water with vinegar and salt, cardoons are served like asparagus or are gratinated.

Carrot – KAROTTE/RÜBLI/MÖHRE – *carotte*

Description: Carrots are an important vegetable all over the world. Many colorful varieties have been developed, which are planted everywhere in the world. Carrots contain about 4 to 5 percent sugar, which accounts for their high nutritional value. They are also the best available source for beta carotene.

Quality: Carrot bunches should have fresh healthy tops and washed, ten-

der carrots; available usually in spring and summer. *Paris carrots* are small, round, washed, and offered in bunches in spring and summer. They are also mass-produced for canning. *Summer carrots* are sold without tops; they should be washed, tender, and completely edible. *Storage carrots* should be healthy, washed, and have few green ends.

Cultivation: Switzerland, Italy, and France; in the United States, California, Texas, Arizona, Michigan, and Florida.

Varieties: Storage types in Europe are Nantaise, Flakeer, and Pfälzer. In the United States, the farther west the carrot grows, the sweeter it is; Canada and the Northeast produce carrots with less sugar and a tougher flesh (woody).

Storage: 50°F (10°C), with high humidity.

Usage: Vegetable side dish and salads. Can be raw, steamed, stewed, and glazed.

Catalonia – CATALONIA – *catalogne*

Description: Catalonia is a vegetable similar to dandelion greens, with long dark green leaves.

Quality: Tight leafy bundles with a tender inner heart, up to 23 inches (60 cm) long. The leaves have a characteristic bitter taste.

Cultivation: Rarely in Switzerland, mostly in Italy.

Storage: Cool storage, remains good for only a short time.

Usage: Usually in salads; also as a vegetable. It can be blanched, boiled, and stewed.

Caulibroc – ROMANESCO/GRÜNER BLUMENKOHL – *romanesco*

Description: Knobby green florets that look like castle turrets. An attractive vegetable that botanically belongs to the broccoli family but is sold commercially as cauliflower.

Quality: Caulibroc is tastier and retains a more attractive color after

cooking than regular cauliflower. It is abundantly available in October and November. The average weight of a head is about 14 to 20 ounces (400 to 600 g).

Cultivation: Switzerland, Italy, Holland; in the United States, California and Florida.

Preservation: Freezing.

Usage: Can be prepared whole or in florets and used in cauliflower recipes. Caulibroc will keep its shape and does not fall apart after cooking.

Cauliflower – BLUMENKOHL – *chou fleur*

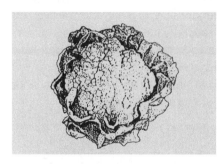

Description: Cauliflower is a head of very tightly packed florets, surrounded by large leaves. Because of its tender cell structure, it is one of the finer vegetables.

Quality: White, firm heads, free of damage, spots, and pests. The leaves should be trimmed around the head and the stalk cut close to the head. The leaves and stalk should constitute less than 20 percent of total weight. Heads that are smaller than 4 inches (11 cm) or larger than 9 inches (23 cm) in diameter are not of first quality.

Cultivation: Switzerland, Italy, France, Holland, Canada; in the United States, California, Texas, Oregon, New York, and Florida.

Varieties: Many varieties: the head can be white, slightly yellow, or violet (Sicilian cauliflower).

Storage: Cool storage, refrigeration. Cauliflower can be kept for only a short time.

Usage: Cauliflower is served whole or as florets. It can be served as a side dish or main course, prepared in many ways, with different sauces. Cauliflower can be served cooked or raw in salads. It is usually boiled, steamed, deep-fried, or served gratinated.

Celeriac/Knob Celery – SELLERIE/ KNOLLENSELLERIE – *céleri-rave/ céleri-pomme*

Description: Knob celery is used all over Europe, where it is a favorite fall and winter vegetable.

Quality: Leaf celeriac (spring) has no root but fresh, tender, highly aromatic leaves, which are used as a seasoning. *Soup celeriac* (spring and summer) has a small root and usable tender leaves. *Knob celery with leaves* (late fall) has a medium-size root, no cracks, and healthy, tender, usable leaves. *Knob celery without leaves* (all year) has a large root, no cracks or side roots, and no leaves.

Cultivation: Switzerland and central and southern Europe; unusual in the United States but beginning to be grown as a vegetable. Available in Europe all year except June and July.

Storage: Leaf and soup celery can be stored for a few days under refrigeration. Knob celery has a very long shelf life.

Usage: Raw as salad, cooked as salad or vegetable. Cleaned peelings should be used in stocks or sauces. Knob celery can be boiled, glazed, stewed, or deep-fried.

Celery – STANGENSELLERI/BLEICH- SELLERIE – *céleri en branches*

Description: Originally an English vegetable, celery is a stem vegetable consisting of a small root with light green, fleshy stems. Grown as a bunch, the center or heart is especially tender.

Quality: Each bunch should have stalks about 12 inches (30 cm) long, with light green leafy tops. The ribs should not be broken, stringy, bruised, or split.

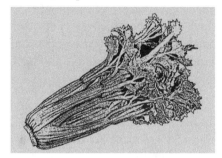

Cultivation: Small amounts in Switzerland; in the United States, California, Florida, New York, Michigan, and Ohio.

Varieties: Pascal and Golden.

Storage: Cool, dry, refrigerated.

Usage: Appetizers, salads, and as a vegetable side dish. Celery can be blanched, braised, and served gratinated.

Chicory, Curly/Curly Endive – ENDIVE, GEKRAUST – *chicorée frisée*

Description: Curly chicory, as the name indicates, has very curly, fine, ragged-edged leaves. The outer leaves are green, with the heart light green to yellow. Curly chicory tastes slightly bitter and spicy.

Quality: Fresh, healthy heads, with light centers, free of rot, with trimmed short stems.

Cultivation: Switzerland, Italy, Spain, France, and the United States.

Varieties: In the spring, the very fine curly *très fine maraîchère;* in the summer, the larger *d'été à cœur jaune;* in the fall, the strong flavored *grosse pommant seule;* in the late fall, the medium curly, dark-green, large *Walloune.*

Storage: Dry, cool storage.

Usage: Salads and garnish.

Chinese Artichoke (Chorogi) – STACHYS/KNOLLENZIEST – *crosne (du Japon)*

Description: This very rare vegetable is a native of Japan and is also known as Japanese artichoke or knotroot. The tubers are edible, weigh about 2 grams, and are about ½ inch (1 cm) in diameter and about 1 inch long (2 to 4 cm). They are pearl white and spiral shaped and taste like a mixture of salsify and artichoke. This gourmet vegetable is harvested by hand in October; the work is labor intensive and so the vegetable is very expensive. Harvest depends on demand.

Quality: Firm, white, clean rhizomes.

Cultivation: Japan, England, and France.

Storage: When in contact with air, Chinese artichokes turn dry and brown. Store for a short period, wrapped in moist cloth.

Usage: Served as a vegetable. Chinese artichokes can be used as is, but sometimes their strings and ends must be trimmed, and they must be blanched and rubbed in salt to be cleaned completely. They must be rinsed before they can be used. Cook fully but carefully, or they will turn to mush. Blanch, boil, stew, and sauté.

Corn – ZUCKERMAIS/SÜSSMAIS – *épi de maïs/grains de maïs*

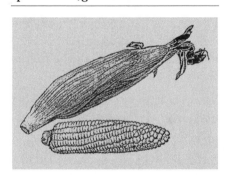

Description: The sugar in sweet corn changes slowly to starch during the ripening process. Only carefully selected, perfect cobs with not fully ripe kernels are good to eat. To protect the corn, keep it in the husk during storage.

Quality: The corn cob should be fully formed, with white to yellow, milky, healthy kernels, which should not be tough.

Cultivation: Switzerland, Spain, Israel, Canada, and the United States.

Varieties: Types are differentiated as sweet and super-sweet.

Storage: Protect from light and keep cool to prevent further ripening. Use as quickly as possible.

Preservation: Canning and freezing.

Usage: As a vegetable, in salads, and as a garnish. Boil, grill, and sauté.

Corn Salad – NÜSSLISALAT/FELDSALAT/RAPUNZEL – *mâche*

Description: Corn salad is also known as field salad and lamb's lettuce. It has narrow, rounded leaves with a nutlike flavor. It can be grown in the field or cultivated in greenhouses or in plastic tunnels. It is very resistant to cold. The dark green, small, bunched variety is most popular.

Quality: The tender variety grown in greenhouses and plastic tunnels is sold washed and cleaned and can be used completely. The stronger-flavored field variety should be washed, cleaned, and eaten without roots.

Cultivation: Switzerland, southern Germany, Holland.

Storage: Cool and moist.

Usage: Usually in salads, but it can be braised.

Cress – KRESSE – *cresson*

Description: In the wild, *watercress* grows in damp ditches and along creeks, but the commercial variety is cultivated. Watercress has a sharp radish bite and slightly bitter flavor. *Garden cress* is similar but milder. The first sprout with its three leaves is usually harvested.

Quality: Both types should be green. Garden cress should be loose, dry, tender, and aromatic. In the United States, garden cress is sold uncut in a grow pack. Watercress should be crisp and fresh. The leaves must be clean and free of weeds.

Cultivation: Switzerland, France, Germany, and the United States.

Varieties: Watercress: *cresson de fontaine;* garden cress: *cresson de jardin* and *cresson d'Inde.*

Storage: Cut garden cress must be used within twenty-four hours; watercress, within a couple of days.

Usage: Both types are excellent in salads or as a garnish with grilled main courses. Dress cress in salads at the very last moment, as they wilt very quickly. Watercress can be chopped and used like parsley or cooked and puréed for soups.

Cucumber – GURKE – *concombre/cornichon*

Description: Cucumbers are categorized both by the method of cultivation, as field or greenhouse cucumbers, and by the way they are used, as salad or pickle cucumbers. They contain lots of water and have few calories. Pickled cucumbers are preserved with vinegar, spices, salt, and sugar. Depending on their size and the spices used, they are marketed as gherkins, delicatessen pickles, mustard pickles, dill pickles, or sweet pickles.

Quality: Cucumbers should be dark green, without blemishes, clean, not bitter, and should have small seeds.

Cultivation: Field cultivation worldwide; greenhouse cultivation in Holland and the Balkan countries.

Storage: Cucumbers have a limited storage time; bruising leads to quick spoilage. Discard yellow cucumbers.

Usage: As salad or as a vegetable. Cucumbers can be blanched, stewed, or glazed.

Eggplant – EIERFRUCHT – *aubergine*

Description: Eggplants, with their bright purple color and round oval shape, are a fruit vegetable of high nutritional value. Eggplant contains large amounts of vitamins A, B, and C, potassium, and phosphorus. The fruit is 4 to 8 inches (10 to 20 cm) long, 2 to 3 inches (5 to 7 cm) thick, and contains large amounts of water.

Quality: Smooth, firm, plump fruits, with a ½-inch (2-cm) attached stem. The fruit should have a high gloss and be without spots; dull eggplant is overripe and tastes bitter.

Cultivation: Eggplant originated in India and thrives in warm weather. In Switzerland it is grown in Tessin and near Geneva. Italy and other Mediterranean countries are major producers. Holland grows them in greenhouses. In the United States, major areas of cultivation are Florida, the Carolinas, and California. Mexico ships eggplant to the United States in winter.

Varieties: Long and slightly bowed or round and egg-shaped are two types. Small Italian, white, and Japanese eggplant are also available in the United States.

Storage: Eggplant should be stored above 42°F (5°C), with 95 percent humidity. It is sensitive to water, pressure, and sunlight.

Usage: Eggplant can be mixed with other vegetables, stuffed, or served as a vegetarian entrée. It can be grilled, deep-fried, baked, braised, or sautéed.

Endive, Belgian – CHICOREÉ – *endive/witloof/chicon*

Description: The root of the plant is cultivated in the summer (witloof) and year-round in underground tunnels and greenhouses. The roots are forced to produce endive. The tender white cone is formed with the help of heat and humidity but without light.

Quality: First-quality are sprouts, from about 3 to 8 inches (10 to 20 cm), about 1 inch (2.5 cm) in diameter. They should be clean, firm, pale, and without damage. They should not have green tips. Second quality is at least ¾ inch (1.8 cm) in diameter, 2 to 7 inches (5 to 18 cm), with small blemishes.

Cultivation: Mainly Belgium and Holland.

Varieties: Besides the pale white, a red type, called Dark Red Treviso, is cultivated.

Storage: Protected from light, it can be stored without a problem for several days.

Usage: Prepared as a salad, Belgian endive has hardly any waste. It is also excellent braised. Any bitterness can be eliminated by removing the core from the bottom of the endive. Endive can be stewed, braised, and sautéed.

Escarole – ENDIVIE/GLATT – *chicorée/scarole*

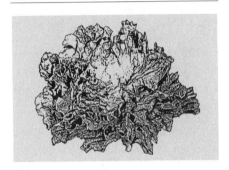

Description: Loose heads with smooth dark green outer leaves and tender yellow inner leaves. The light, bitter taste stimulates the appetite.

Quality: Large heads with big yellow centers.

Cultivation: Europe, North America.

Storage: Healthy, dry plants can be stored refrigerated for quite some time.

Usage: As a bitter green in salads and soups or braised and sautéed with garlic and olive oil as a vegetable.

Fennel – FENCHEL/KNOLLENFENCHEL – *fenouil*

Description: Fennel, which grows in temperate southern climates, is a tightly closed leafy bulb that has a characteristic anise aroma. Fennel is also referred to as giant anise. Depending on type, the bulb is ei-

ther short and squat or thin and long. The color ranges from light green to white. It must be washed carefully, as sand tends to get trapped in the layers.

Quality: White or light green bulbs with trimmed tops.

Cultivation: Switzerland, Italy, France; in the United States, California and New Jersey. It is generally available in fall and winter, as it does not grow in hot weather.

Varieties: Summer and fall fennel.

Storage: The bulb is sensitive to pressure, which will cause brown spots that can be trimmed. Store in a cool, airy place.

Usage: As a vegetable and in salads. Fennel can be braised, steamed, boiled, and served gratinated.

Garlic – KNOBLAUCH – *ail*

Description: Originally from central Asia, garlic has been in use for a long time, in Europe since the Middle Ages. Garlic grows in the soil as bulbs formed by about ten curved cloves enclosed by a dry white skin. During the spring fresh garlic with green shoots is also available in European markets.

Quality: Firm, healthy bulbs with dry white skins.

Cultivation: Italy, France, and the United States.

Varieties: Two types are available: the purple colored *rose-rouge d'Albi* and the very shelf-stable pearl-white garlic called *blanc du tarn.*

Storage: In dry storage, garlic keeps for several weeks.

Preservation: Stored in oil, or dried and pulverized.

Usage: Especially used to flavor warm foods and salad dressings; garlic should not be fried.

Jerusalem Artichoke/Sun Chokes – TOPINAMBUR/ERDBIRNE – *topinambour*

Description: A knotty tuber with wartlike potrusions, about the size of

a medium potato. The Jerusalem artichoke has a high water content. It has an earthy taste combined with a turniplike flavor. Jerusalem artichokes are not a substitute for potatoes, however; they are a fruit vegetable, similar to melons and tomatoes. They are considered gourmet and specialty diet vegetables. Native to North America, they are often called sun chokes in the marketplace.

Quality: Firm, fresh white, yellow, red, or purple tubers.

Cultivation: France, Germany, Switzerland, and California.

Storage: Refrigerate; they dry, shrink, and spoil quickly after harvest.

Usage: Must always be peeled and placed in water to prevent oxidation. They can be served raw in salads or cooked as a vegetable.

Kohlrabi – KOHLRABI – *chou rave/ chou pomme*

Description: The bulblike stem grows aboveground. Green or purple kohlrabi is available; both have the same characteristics.

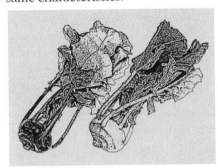

Quality: The leaves on the bulbs should not be wilted. Leafy bulbs are sold in bundles. Cut bulbs are sold by weight. The fresh, firm bulbs should have no tears, crisp, nonwoody flesh, and fresh green tops. Avoid large bulbs.

Cultivation: Switzerland and all of Europe, with winter production in Sicily; North America, with limited winter cultivation in Florida and California.

Varieties: Greenhouse varieties are more tender, but the field-grown kohlrabi has better flavor.

Storage: Cool, with high humidity.

Usage: Prepared as vegetable or salad. Kohlrabi can be boiled, sautéed, or steamed.

Leek – LAUCH – *poireau*

Description: Leeks have a bulbous root end with a long cylindrical white stalk and loose dark green leaves. A very common vegetable in Europe, leeks are becoming more reasonably priced and available in the United States.

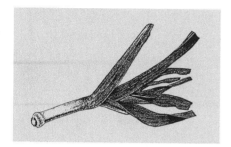

Quality: Crisp and healthy, with typical coloring for specific types. Blanched leeks must be all light colored (see varieties).

Cultivation: Switzerland and all of Europe, North America.

Varieties: Soup leeks are immature leeks. Summer leeks are tender and light green. Winter leeks are stronger flavored and have dark green leaves. Blanched leeks are grown protected from light.

Storage: Store cool. Soup leeks must be used quickly; summer and winter leeks can be stored for long periods of time. Blanched leeks are perishable and will turn green if exposed to daylight.

Usage: In soups, vegetables, or salads. Leeks can be sautéed, steamed, and gratinated.

Lettuce, Boston – KOPFSALAT – *laitue pommée*

Description: Among the many lettuce varieties, butterhead or Boston lettuce is a favorite. It is the most consumed lettuce in Europe. Years of cultivation have produced today's superior product. Its good qualities are freshness, simple preparation, and easy digestibility. The fresh taste

results from its high ascorbic acid content. To prevent vitamin loss and wilting, it should be dressed just prior to service.

Quality: Healthy, fresh, clean heads of similar size. Boxes contain usually twelve, eighteen, or twenty-four heads.

Cultivation: Switzerland, France, Italy, Spain, Holland, and Belgium; in cool climates in the United States and in California and Florida during winter months.

Varieties: Boston lettuce that is cultivated in plastic tunnels and through aquaculture tends to be more tender; field-cultivated heads are heavier and not quite as tender. In the United States, *bibb lettuce*, or limestone lettuce, is a smaller variety with tiny heads and darker green leaves.

Storage: Refrigerate, covered with plastic; use as soon as possible—very perishable.

Lettuce, Iceberg – EISBERGSALAT/ KRACHSALT – *salade iceberg/ laitue d'hiver*

Description: Iceberg lettuce has tightly layered, firm, curled, shiny, light green leaves. It is crisp, fresh, and has a nutty taste.

Quality: Firm, tight, round, big heads that are about 6 to 8 inches (15 to 20 cm) in diameter. The leaves have thick ribs.

Cultivation: United States (California), Italy, Holland, Israel, Spain, and northern Germany. Iceberg lettuce is grown in greenhouses, under plastic tents, and in the open field.

Storage: Refrigerated, it has a long storage time.

Usage: It is served quartered or cut, with a variety of salad dressings.

Lettuce, Loose-leaf – LOLLO/ SCHNITTSALAD – *lattughino*

Description: Loose-leaf lettuce is a collective name for many lettuce varieties in the marketplace. The

plants are usually 8 inches (20 cm) tall with loose heads and curly green, yellow, rust, or reddish leaves that have a mild flavor.

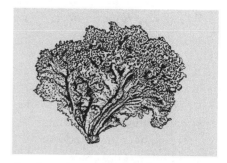

Quality: Crisp, healthy leaves, free of spoilage.

Cultivation: Worldwide.

Varieties: Red leaf: compact bunch of curly leaves with dark red edges. *Green leaf:* compact bunch with light green curly leaves. *Salad Bowl:* light green oakleaf lettuce. *Red Salad Bowl:* red oakleaf lettuce. *Grand Rapids:* light green lettuce with very curly edges. *Rubin:* reddish brown, very curly leaf edges.

Storage: Refrigerate.

Melon – MELONE – *melon*

Description: Melons are vegetable fruits. They are very popular during the warmer months. The two main types are watermelons and sugar melons, each with subgroups.

Quality: Healthy, ripe, clean fruits, true to type, without tears or bruises. They should not be soft.

Cultivation: Few in Switzerland; mostly France, Spain, Italy, Israel. In North America most melons are grown in Florida, California, Texas, and Mexico.

Varieties: Watermelon: round or barrel shaped with green, yellow, or speckled skin. The flesh is red, pink, yellow, or white, with black seeds. Neither the color of the flesh nor the skin indicate ripeness. Watermelons grow very large and very heavy. *Cantaloupe (charentais and net melon):* fruits are small, oval, and sometimes lightly segmented, with a rough, netlike covering. The salmon-colored flesh is sweet and flavorful. It is the most popular melon. *Honeydew melon*: round, smooth, yellow or light green fruits with a long storage capacity. Major producer in Europe is Spain. They often seem very hard and unripe, but their flesh is honey sweet. *Ogen (Santa Claus) melon*: this winter specialty comes from Israel. Round, with light segmentation, the skin is yellow with green stripes. It is very sweet and aromatic when fully ripe. *Crenshaw*: called "Wintermelon" in Switzerland, it is imported from the United States. It has a smooth light-colored skin with a pale but sweet flesh. Crenshaws will continue to ripen at room temperature.

Storage: Depending on type and ripeness, store at room temperature or refrigerate. All melons should be served chilled.

Okra – LADYFINGER – *gombo*

Description: Okra is a pod vegetable. The skin is ridged and green, with a flavor similar to young green beans. The pods grow about 1 to 2 inches (3 to 5 cm) long.

Quality: Pods should be fresh, meaty, and large. Canned product is poor. In the United States, okra is available frozen.

Cultivation: Greece, Turkey, and subtropical countries; in the United States, okra is grown in Florida, Texas, and Georgia and imported during winter from Mexico.

Storage: Very perishable; remove any pods with signs of spoilage.

Usage: Prepared like beans or in salads. When cooked, okra gives off a viscous substance; rinse and drain before serving. (The viscosity of okra is desirable when making gumbo).

Onion – ZWIEBEL – *oignon*

Description: The many onion varieties are diferentiated by shape, size, color, flavor, and storage ability. The common cooking onion is medium-sized, brown- or yellow-skinned, with white, mild, juicy flesh.

Quality: Firm, fully ripe, true to type in shape and color, with dry skin,

free of blemishes and unsprouted. Average size is 1½ to 3 inches (3.5 to 7.5 cm).

Cultivation: All of Europe, Egypt, and North America.

Varieties: Spring onions: white in bunches, available only in the spring. *Scallions or green onions*: young onions, harvested before full bulb forms; both green tops and trimmed tiny bulb are used. They are available in the United States year-round. *Summer onions (Bermuda onions)*: yellow or white skins, medium size, with green tops attached. *Red onions*: fresh, very sweet, flavorful; available fresh in summer or dried for fall storage. *Yellow onions*: flat or oval, medium size, dried for storage. *Spanish onions*: Large onions, bigger than 3 inches (7.5 cm). *Boiling and pearl onions*: small white, usually not larger than 1 inch (2 to 3 cm) in diameter. *Shallots*: purplish, small, garlic shaped, about ½ to 1 inch (2 to 3 cm) large. *Wild onion*: sold unwashed, the size of walnuts; served as a vegetable.

Storage: Cool, dry, and airy.

Usage: Raw or cooked as a flavoring for salads, sauces, soups, and as a garnish. Regional onion specialty dishes are very popular. Onions can be sautéed, glazed, fried, and prepared gratinated.

Pea – ERBSE – *petit pois*

Description: Peas are the unripe seeds in the pea pod. Peas are usually available frozen or canned.

Quality: Well filled pods, evenly green with tender, juicy, round seeds.

Cultivation: Italy, Spain, France; in the United States, in local markets

in summer, from California and Mexico in winter.

Varieties: Eighty different pea varieties are available. Four types are important: the *English pea*, the most common, with round seeds that must be shelled. The seed will continue to ripen and become mealy. The European *mark pea*, which is only used when very young, has a slightly green seed. The *snow pea* has a flat edible pod and tiny seeds. *Sugar snap peas* have round edible pods; in the United States, they are available year-round.

Storage: Cool and airy; limited storage time, as they yellow and spoil quickly. Preserved frozen and canned.

Usage: Prepared as a vegetable and in salads. Peas can be blanched, sautéed, and braised.

Peppers – PEPERONE/GEMÜSEPAPRIKA/ CHILI – *piment doux/poivron/ piment*

Description: Peppers grow in all colors and shapes (green, yellow, red, purple). Smaller varieties, called chilies, can range from mild to very hot. Peppers are constantly being crossbred, with new varieties appearing regularly on the market, so that today almost any color, in any size, can be found.

Quality: Glossy, firm fruits without spots or tears. True-to-type color and shape.

Cultivation: Southern countries are the major producers, with some hothouse products from Holland; in winter they are imported from the United States.

Varieties: Green bell peppers are most common. These firm, crisp, large fruits are the most reasonably priced. Most green peppers will turn another color in the fall. *Large yellow and red peppers* are much more expensive and are more perishable. *Pimientos* are shaped like tomatoes; they are sweet, mild, dark red, and flavorful. *Hungarian yellow peppers* are long, pointed, mild-flavored peppers, produced mostly in the Balkan countries. *Cubanelles or Italianelles* are long, green frying peppers; they also turn yellow or red in color as they ripen. *Peperoncini (chilies)* are small, narrow peppers in all colors, with various degrees of hotness. *Cayenne pepper,* small and green (similar to the Serrano), is very hot and should be used only as a spice.

Storage: Refrigerate; because they are riper, yellow and red peppers will spoil faster than green peppers.

Usage: Peperoncini and cayenne, mostly as spice. All other peppers can be used in salads or sauces and as a vegetable. They can be stuffed, braised, sautéed, and steamed.

Radicchio – CICORINO/ZICHORIEN-SALAT – *chicorée amère/chicorée de Trévise*

Description: Radicchio can be red (*Cicorino rosso*) or green (*Cicorino verde*). Red is available all year; green is of importance only in the spring. Radicchio has a slightly bitter taste.

Quality: Fresh, crisp, red-violet leaves with white ribs, without signs of bruising or rot. The root stem should be washed.

Cultivation: Switzerland, Italy, and the United States.

Varieties: Head radicchio, called *palla rossa,* has dark red, firm, fist-size large heads with white ribs. The rosette radicchio *Grumolo* has pretty red-and-white loose leaves, *Treviso* has cylindrical loose-leafed heads, and *Castelfranco* is red-green with white stripes. The cut-leaf radicchio has tender yellow-green oval leaves.

Storage: Remove blemished leaves and keep cool.

Usage: As a colorful addition to salads or as a garnish.

Radish – RADIESCHEN – *radis rose*

Description: The most common variety of radish is a small, round, tender root with a brilliant red skin. The flesh is white, crisp, and juicy. A member of the mustard family, radishes have a sharp flavor. Another radish variety is long and slender and is used and handled the same as the round radish.

Quality: Young, clean, tender, with fresh green tops; no cracks and not hollow.

Cultivation: Europe and North America.

Varieties: Spring varieties from greenhouses are milder and juicier. Field-grown radishes tend to be sharper in flavor. Two-color and long white radishes are also available.

Storage: Cool and moist; use immediately.

Rhubarb – RHABARBER – *rhubarbe*

Description: Rhubarb is a perennial leafy plant with thick, large roots that can survive frost. The red or green stems are edible and grow about 24 inches (60 cm) long. The leaves are poisonous.

Quality: The stems should be meaty and light to dark red. The leaves should be neatly trimmed, just above the stem.

Cultivation: All of Europe, with hothouse product from Holland. In North America rhubarb is field-grown in New England, the Midwest, and the Mid-Atlantic states. Hothouse rhubarb is grown in California, Michigan, and Oregon.

Storage: Refrigerate; prevent contact with metal, as rhubarb contains large amounts of oxalic acid.

Preservation: Jam, canned, and frozen.

Usage: Used in compotes, sorbets, cakes, and pies.

Romaine/Cos – LATTICH – *laitue romaine*

Description: Romaine is an ancient cultivated plant. It has elongated heads. The sturdy leaves with the prominent center ribs are crisp and mostly dark green. The heads of most varieties are medium firm and tight. Light green and red varieties tend to form looser heads.

Quality: The head should be medium to dark green with tender light green center leaves. It should show no sign of bolting. The bottom should be neatly trimmed.

Cultivation: Switzerland, Spain, France, Italy, Germany, and North America.

Storage: Refrigerate and store like other head lettuces. Romaine lasts longer and is sturdier.

Usage: Raw in salads, cooked as a vegetable side dish. It can be blanched, steamed, and braised.

Rutabaga – BODENKOHLRABI – *chou rave*

Description: Rutabaga is a round-oval root vegetable with yellow flesh and a thick, rough rind. In the United States, it is also called yellow turnip or Swede.

Quality: Round, solid roots, 3 to 4 inches (8 to 12 cm) in diameter.

Cultivation: All of Europe, Canada, and the United States.

Varieties: Rutabaga is a cross between kohlrabi and a large white field turnip used to feed cattle.

Storage: Cool, dry storage. To preserve taste, use quickly. In the United States, rutabaga is often waxed for longer storage.

Usage: As a vegetable side dish or included in stews. Rutabaga can be boiled and braised.

Salsify/Oyster Plant – SCHWARZ-WURZEL – *scorsoné/salsifis noir*

Description: Salsify has a black skin and milky white flesh. It grows underground. The leafy tops are removed at harvest time. Raw, peeled salsify oxidizes rapidly and should be immediately immersed in a *blanc de légumes* (water, flour, and lemon juice solution).

Quality: Firm, smooth, straight roots, with no blemishes or side shoots.

Cultivation: Switzerland (Bern), Belgium, Germany; in the United States, grown in home gardens, rarely available commercially.

Storage: When kept in a cool, dark space, salsify will keep for a couple of months. It is preserved by canning or deep-freezing.

Usage: As a vegetable, salsify can be boiled, deep-fried, and served gratinated.

Shallot – SCHALOTTE – *échalote*

Description: Shallots are small, elongated, white-purplish onions with dry reddish brown skins. The bulbs have additional small side clusters.

Quality: Firm, copper-colored, small, pear-shaped onions. Elongated varieties are available from the Loire valley and the Bretagne.

Cultivation: All of Europe, especially Mediterranean countries.

Storage: Stored cool and dry, they will last for a very long time.

Usage: As a flavoring for sauces and farces, or whole as a garnish. They can be sautéed and glazed.

Spinach – SPINAT – *épinards*

Description: Spinach is a popular leafy vegetable with tender dark green leaves. It supposedly found its way via Arabia and Iran to Italy and Spain. The New Zealand bush variety is supposed to have been brought to Europe by eighteenth-century navigators. Spinach is high in iron and vitamins A, B, and C and has good amounts of calcium and some protein.

Quality: Spinach leaves should be washed, fresh, and unbruised, with short stems and no flowers or buds.

Cultivation: Switzerland, Italy, Germany, France, and North America.

Varieties: Spring varieties have small, tender leaves. Winter spinach has large, tough, sturdy, stronger-flavored leaves. Leaf spinach is cut above the root; bunch spinach has the roots attached. Much of the spinach on the market is washed, dried, and packaged in plastic bags.

Storage: Cool and airy.

Usage: Spinach is prepared as soup, salad or a vegetable side dish. It can be blanched and sautéed.

Swiss Chard – KRAUTSTIEL – *côte de blette*

Description: In Switzerland chard is sold with leaves or as stems only. The stems are white, with strong white ribs in the dark green leaves. A broad-stemmed variety, called *Stielmangold,* is popular in Switzerland.

Quality: The leaves must be fresh and crisp. Stems are bundled or sold by the pound, with the leaves neatly trimmed.

Cultivation: Switzerland and all of Europe, North America.

Storage: Refrigerated, with high humidity; chard has a short storage life.

Usage: Prepared as a vegetable side dish, including leaves. The leaves can be stuffed; very tender leaves can be added to salads. Chard can be blanched, boiled, sautéed, steamed, or served gratinated.

Tomato – TOMATE – *tomate*

Description: Tomatoes hold first place in produce sales because they are available year-round. The tomato is a fruit vegetable and has many uses, especially in today's diet. Tomatoes come in all shapes and sizes and many different flavors. New varieties are introduced constantly. They are cultivated in fields and, more and more, in hothouses.

Quality: Top quality in Europe must be absolutely without blemishes, sorted by size, with a green stem and free from pesticide residue. These are generally hothouse tomatoes. No. 1 quality must be ripe, even in size and shape, with no pesticide residue. They must be 1¾ inches (45 mm) in diameter and firm when sliced. No. 2 quality is similar to no. 1 but uneven in color and shape; they can be smaller in size.

Cultivation: In Switzerland early field tomatoes are grown in large quantities in Ticino and Valais and as a hothouse product everywhere. Major hothouse producers are Holland and the Balkans. Field tomatoes are exported from Spain, Italy, Morocco, and France. In winter tomatoes are exported from the Canary Islands, Egypt, and Israel. In the United States, major producers are California and Florida; in the winter they are imported from Mexico.

Varieties: Tomatoes are differentiated by the number of seed lobes: small round have two to three lobes; medium flat round tomatoes have four to five lobes; others are the multilobed beefsteak; the oval Italian plum tomato (Marzano or Peretti); and the tiny cherry tomato. Most tomatoes are light or dark red; the yellow varieties have not been a commercial success.

Storage: Store in a cool place but do not refrigerate. To prevent the spread of rot, discard tomatoes with signs of spoilage.

Usage: In vegetarian diets, salads, soups, sauces, as a vegetable side dish, and a garnish. Tomatoes can be eaten raw, blanched, sautéed, grilled, and served gratinated.

Turnip, White – WEISSRÜBE – *navet*

Description: Round roots with flattened tops, smooth skin, and green leaves, turnips belong to the cabbage family. In the Middle Ages, before the discovery of the potato, turnips played a major role in the human diet.

Quality: Young, firm, tender, unblemished roots.

Cultivation: Switzerland (especially the western cantons), France, Germany, Italy; in the United States, turnips are grown both for the root and, especially in the South, for the turnip greens.

Varieties: In Europe two additional varieties are cultivated: the more elongated Parisian white turnips and the best variety, called *navets de tel-tow,* which was originally grown only in the town of Teltow, near Berlin, Germany.

Storage: Cool.

Usage: Turnips are used in soups, stews, and as a vegetable side dish. They can be boiled and glazed.

Zucchini – ZUCCHETTO/ZUCCHINO – *courgette*

Description: Zucchini is a vegetable squash, shaped like a cucumber but hectagonal when sliced. Zucchini is edible even when immature. The average size is between 6 and 8 inches (15 and 20 cm). Most popular are the speckled varieties. Yellow varieties are also available.

Quality: Crisp, young, and not spongy. First-quality zucchini should not weigh more than 5 ounces (150 g) each.

Cultivation: Switzerland, Italy, France, Spain, and the United States.

Storage: Refrigerate; discard rotten fruit.

Usage: Prepared as a vegetable side dish and in salads. Zucchini can be eaten raw, braised, sautéed, glazed, and fried. Squash blossoms can be deep-fried in batter or stuffed.

ZUCKERHUT (Sugar cone) – *pain de sucre*

Description: This lettuce is light green with a firm, cone-shaped head, similar to romaine. A winter lettuce, it got its name from its shape. It belongs to the same lettuce variety as radicchio. It is crisp and has a nutty flavor.

Quality: Clean, tight heads, without waste.

Cultivation: Switzerland, France, Italy.

Storage: Store in a cool area. In contrast to other lettuces, it has a very long storage life.

Usage: Salad.

4.5.8 Potatoes

Botanically speaking, the potato is neither a fruit nor a vegetable. The potato tuber is an enlarged part of an underground stem.

Origin

As long as four thousand years ago, the Incas of South America cultivated potatoes in different climate zones. The first potatoes were probably grown in the Andes, near today's border between Bolivia and Peru. Spanish seafaring explorers brought the first potatoes to Spain in the year 1573. The introduction of the potato to other European countries depended on the intelligence and understanding of its political ruler. It took a committed leader in each country to insist that potatoes be cultivated as a basic foodstuff for the general population before they were accepted.

In the eighteenth century, the South American potato was introduced to North America by Irish settlers.

Cultivation

Potatoes are cultivated all over the globe. Switzerland grows potatoes only for inland sales. The earliest (new) potatoes, available beginning in May and June, are grown in the area around Lake Geneva and the Tessin. In the United States, major producers are the states of Maine, Idaho, California, Florida, Minnesota, and the Dakotas.

Europe gets early "new" potatoes starting in January from Egypt and Israel; in February from Algeria, Morocco, and Italy; in March from Spain; and in April from France. In the United States, new potatoes are grown in Florida, California, Texas, and Arizona and are sold beginning in February.

Nutritional Value

Potatoes have 18 percent fewer carbohydrates than grains and therefore have fewer calories. Potatoes contain important proteins, large amounts of vitamin C, good amounts of potassium, and some calcium.

Varieties

In Switzerland the potato crop is regulated by the Department of Alcohol. Potatoes must be sold according to type, clean and free of dirt. Varieties must be clearly identified on all bags and boxes. Potatoes from cool storage must be identified and are usually labeled *Frigo*. Early or new potatoes can be sold as such only until July 31. After that date only identification by type is permissible. New potatoes cannot be larger than 1¼ inch (30 mm), the permissible size for regular potatoes cannot exceed 2¾ inches (70 mm).

The U.S. Department of Agriculture provides a voluntary grading service as a guide to the purchase of quality potatoes. U.S. Extra No. 1, the premium grade, allows for few defects. The types of potatoes generally found on the United States market are classified by their shape and skin color. Potatoes are long or round, and white, red, or russet. The principal varieties of each of these types are the long russet Burbank, the long white rose, the round white Katahdin, and the round red Pontiac. Red bliss potatoes are a winter potato, not a "new" potato. Norgold long russet and Norland round red potatoes are also available, as well as the Idaho potato. Gourmet blue potatoes are a highly prized novelty.

Quality

Potatoes must be firm, well shaped, and free of defects such as cuts, bruises, sprouts, gnaw marks, and decay. They should have the specified size of their type.

Potatoes are sorted by size or use on the market. They are classified as boiling, frying, raclette (a Swiss specialty), and baking potatoes. Potatoes are offered in 50-pound bags for quantity foodservice operations.

Storage

New potatoes should be refrigerated. All other potatoes should be stored in a dark and cool space, above 48°F (8°C), on racks (in bags or crates for about two months), with a humidity of 85 to 95 percent. Washed potatoes cannot be stored.

As soon as potatoes come into contact with daylight, they turn green and start to sprout. A poison, solanin, which is harmful to humans and animals, forms. Potatoes that are stored below 40°F (4°C) will convert starch to sugar, causing an unpleasant sweet taste. The sugar will also cause potatoes to brown too quickly when they are fried.

Classification

Potatoes are also classified by their use. Depending on their cooking characteristics, they are categorized as type A, B, or C. If classified between categories, as B-C for example, the potato will have characteristics predominantly of the B type. Varieties of Swiss potatoes, their classifications, and their uses are shown in Table 4-46.

Type A: Firm potatoes for salads. They will not fall apart when cooked and keep their shape. The potato is moist, fine grained, and not mealy, with a low starch content. (In the United States, these are new potatoes.)

Type B: Reasonably firm potatoes, can be used for all purposes. The potatoes will show some signs of bursting and falling apart; they are somewhat mealy and have a medium starch content. (In the United States, these are general-purpose potatoes.)

Type C: Mealy potatoes. These potatoes burst during boiling; they are mealy, quite dry, grainy, and have a high starch content. (In the United States, these are baking potatoes.)

Table 4-46. Swiss Potato Varieties

Variety	Shape, Characteristics	Cooking Type	Usage
Early varieties			
Charlotte June–April	Long oval, flat eyes, deep yellow flesh	B-A	For salads, boiled and jacketed potatoes, pan-fried potatoes
Christa May–October	Long and short oval, flat eyes, deep yellow flesh	B-C	All preparation methods
Ostara May–November	Short oval, almost flat eyes, light yellow flesh	B	All preparation methods
Sirtema May–October	Round to short oval, medium-deep eyes, light yellow flesh	B	Especially good salad and boiled potato
Fall varieties			
Bintje November–July	Oval to long oval, flat eyes, light yellow flesh	B-C	All preparation methods
Desirée November–April	Short to long oval, red, irregular peel, flat large eyes, light yellow flesh	B-C	All preparation methods
Granola November–June	Round, few eyes, yellow to deep yellow flesh	B	All preparation methods
Nicola November–February	Long to long oval, flat eyes, deep yellow flesh	A	Jacketed and boiled potatoes, salads
Palma September–December	Short to long oval, medium deep eyes, yellow flesh	B	All preparation methods
Stella August–September	Round but tapered, flat eyes, yellow to light yellow flesh	A	Especially good for salads
Urgenta September–April	Red peel, long to long-oval, medium-deep eyes, light yellow to almost white flesh	B	All preparation methods, especially good for *rösti* (Swiss potato cake)

Preparation Methods

Potatoes can be steamed, boiled, baked in the oven, prepared au gratin, deep-fried, sautéed, and roasted.

Potato Products

Raw, peeled, or cut potatoes are available vacuum-packed. Prepared potato salad is available commercially. Dry potato products include potato flakes, instant mashed potatoes, and potato starch. A large assortment of French fries and prepared potato dishes are available deep-frozen.

The Potato's Sweet Relatives

Sweet Potatoes – SÜSSKARTOFFEL – *batate/patate*

Origin: The sweet potato originates from Brazil and was introduced to Europe in about 1519.

Cultivation: All subtropical countries; major producers are China, Vietnam, Indonesia, India, Japan, Brazil, many parts of Africa, Spain, and Portugal. Sweet potatoes are produced in all the southern states of the United States; Louisiana, North Carolina, and California are major producers.

Description: Sweet potatoes are cultivated in the same way as regular potatoes; they do, however, require a warm to tropical climate. The tubers grow underground, are round or elongated, and range in color from white-yellow to deep orange red. They are mealy and sweet in taste. Sweet potatoes are also mistakenly called yams (a different botanical genus). Sweet potatoes are not as prolific as potatoes but are often a staple food in producer countries. World production is about one-third that of potatoes.

Sweet potatoes have a higher carbohydrate content than potatoes, about 27 percent; cassava roots, about 32 percent; and true yams, about 24 percent.

Season: Depends on producer country. In the United States, fresh sweet potatoes are best from August to September. The rest of the year, cured sweet potatoes that have been kiln-dried are available. '

Usage: Prepare like potatoes. Can be used in baked goods and breads.

Tapioca is made from cassava root, and in Brazil another sweet root is used to make arrowroot powder.

Note: In Europe these roots are available from the major consolidated produce markets.

4.5.9 Mushrooms

Mushrooms have a special place in nature. In contrast to other plants, they lack chlorophyll and can grow without sunshine. They will grow in total darkness and live off organic matter. They can grow as destructive fungus on rotting plants or as parasites on living organisms. Mushrooms, in their many different forms, grow all over the globe. It is estimated that approximately twenty thousand mushroom varieties have been identified, but more are constantly discovered.

Origins

Each mushroom requires a specific environment. Mushrooms need moisture to flourish. Edible mushrooms are the fleshy, aboveground reproductive portions of higher forms of fungus. The real plant actually consists of an underground network of fine filaments called a *mycelium*. Mushrooms reproduce via spores. Most edible mushrooms grow in forests, depending on a high-humus soil produced by leafy trees or evergreens.

The white and brown mushrooms and the oyster mushroom are cultivated on mushroom farms. Shiitake, porcini, and portobello mushrooms are now also cultivated in limited quantities. Other highly valued varieties have not yet been successfully farmed.

White (button) mushrooms, grown on manure beds, are one of the best edible mushrooms. They are raised in complete darkness in windowless buildings or in mountain caves on specially prepared beds of horse manure or a mixture of peat moss and straw.

Quality

Mushrooms must be dry and crisp when pulled apart and show no evidence of worms. The cap should be clean, fresh, and free of bruises.

Mushrooms spoil quickly and must be prepared as soon as possible. Mushrooms that have become old and slimy may no longer be digestible.

Mushrooms are classified as edible, nonedible, and poisonous. It takes thorough knowledge and long experience to identify wild edible mushrooms from poisonous ones. There is no foolproof system to test mushrooms other than knowledge. All types of folklore suggestions should be ignored, as they could cost lives.

Mushroom Certification

In Europe all wild mushrooms must be accompanied by a certificate when offered for sale. The certificate states the type, weight, date, and time when the mushrooms were checked by a certified mycologist. The goal is to protect the consumer from eating poisonous mushrooms and prevent health hazards. During the wild-mushroom season, most larger communities have an official mushroom control office. The expert mycologist takes responsibility for inspecting fresh mushrooms, canned mushrooms, and freeze-dried products. All wild-growing mushrooms must pass the official mushroom inspection. Cultivated mushrooms need not be inspected.

Nutritional Value

Mushrooms are similar to vegetables in their composition. They consist of approximately 90 percent water, 2 to 3 percent protein, 3 to 5 percent carbohydrates, 1 to 4 percent fat, minerals, and micronutrients, vitamins A, B, B_1, B_2, C, and D. In addition, mushrooms can contain color pigments, aromas, fermenting gases, and hallucinogenic and pharmacological substances.

Digestibility

Even though mushrooms consist of 90 percent water, they are considered difficult to digest. The protein of mushrooms is coated with chitin, a substance the human body has difficulty breaking down. It is very important that most mushrooms be thoroughly cooked. Very few mushrooms can be eaten raw. White and black truffles, for example, can be enjoyed raw in small quantities. In the United States cultivated white mushrooms, cleaned well, are often added raw to salads.

Preservation

Drying

Thinly sliced (⅛ inch, or 2 to 3 mm) mushrooms can be strung on threads and hung to dry, or they can be arranged on screens that are placed in dry, airy spaces. The mushrooms on screens must be turned occasionally. Mushrooms can be dried in an oven at very low temperature with the door ajar. Best, of course, is a specially designed fruit and vegetable dryer. Dried mushrooms must be stored in airtight containers. To reconstitute such mushrooms, they should be placed for two to four hours in lukewarm water; any sand residue should be discarded.

Freezing

Cleaned mushrooms can be frozen sliced or whole. Some varieties, chanterelles, for example, must be blanched, chilled, and drained before freezing. Vacuum-packed mushrooms should be frozen at -15°F (-25°C). Boletes (cèpes), whole or sliced, can be frozen without blanching and packaged. Frozen mushrooms can be stored for six to eight months.

Marinating (Hot)

Cleaned and sliced mushrooms can be cooked in a marinade with oil for about 5 minutes. They can then be hermetically sealed in a pressure canner. In the United States, it is not permitted to serve home-canned products in foodservice establishments.

Canning

Mushrooms are canned commercially and are available whole, sliced, in pieces, or in an oil marinade.

Usage

Mushrooms are served as a main course or as a side dish. They are also used as a garnish, in fillings, and as a flavoring.

Commonly Used Mushrooms in Restaurant Kitchens

Cultivated white (button) mushroom—ZUCHT CHAMPIGNON/ TAFELPILZ—*champignon de couche/ champignon de Paris*

Chanterelle—EIERSCHWAMM/ECHTER PFIFFERLING—*chanterelle*

Field mushroom—FELD/WIESEN CHAMPIGNON—*psalliote champêtre*

Common morel—SPEISEMORCHEL— *morille ronde*

Conical morel—SPITZMORCHEL— *morille conique*

Cèpe (bolete)—STEINPILZ— *bolet/cèpe*

Black trumpet—TOTENTROMPETE/ HERBSTTROMPETE—*corne d'abondance*

Black truffle—SCHWARZE TRÜFFEL— *truffe du Périgord*

White truffle—WEISSE TRÜFFEL—*truffe blanche*

Summer truffle—SOMMER TRÜFFEL— *truffe d'été*

Oyster mushroom—AUSTERNSEITLING —*pleurote*

In addition, the following mushrooms are commonly sold and served in the United States: cremini (Italian brown), enoki, shiitake (golden oak), and portobello.

Cultivated White (Button) Mushroom—ZUCHT CHAMPIGNON/ TAFELPILZ—*champignon de couche/ champignon de Paris*

Description: This mushroom has a short, thick stem. The cap is 2 to 4 inches (5 to 10 cm) in diameter, domed, with small scales. The color varies from white to light brown. The meat changes in color from white to slightly red. It has a faint, nutlike, pleasant aroma.

Origin: Originally cultivated in France, this mushroom is now commercially grown in many European, American, and Asian countries. The cultivated mushroom is grown in dark places. For a quality spawn, a constant temperature of between 57° and 64°F (15° and 18°C) is essential. Most important, however, are cleanliness, sanitation, and frequent soil tests to prevent infestation by insects and vermin.

Usage: Mushrooms are prepared whole, quartered, or sliced. They can be prepared sautéed in butter, with herbs, in a cream sauce, or cooked Provençal style. They can be made into soups or a duxelle and added to sauces. They are served cold for hors d'œuvres, Greek style, with cocktail sauce, as salad or fluted as a garnish.

Chanterelle—EIERSCHWAMM/ECHTER PFIFFERLING—*chanterelle*

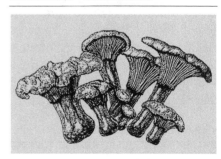

Description: The cap of the chanterelle grows to a width of 1 to 3 inches (3 to 10 cm). It starts out with a flat cap that becomes funnel-shaped. The edge of the cap is ragged and wavy. The color is that of egg yolk, either strong or pale, depending on where it grows. The stem, the same color as the cap, is about 1 to 2 inches (3 to 8 cm) long and tapers toward the base of the cap. The yellow meat has a mild, pleasant, peppery taste. This mushroom rarely carries vermin.

Origin: The chanterelle is found from June to September in mixed-growth forest, mostly under pine and spruce among moss and wild low-bush blueberries. Most chanterelles on the American market are imported from Europe, but some grow in the Pacific Northwest and in the Northeast.

Usage: Chanterelles are offered as a main course, either sautéed in butter with herbs or in a cream sauce. They are also pickled in wine or vinegar and are served as a salad or Greek style. In Europe they are most often served with wild game.

Field Mushroom – FELD/WIESEN CHAMPIGNON – *psalliote champêtre*

Description: The meaty cap is almost dome shaped, with a flat center. The cap flattens and spreads with age, growing in diameter from 1 to 6 inches (5 to 15 cm). The color varies from white to light brown, with a silky smooth surface with sometimes fibrous scales in the center. The gills of the young mushroom are pink (*never* white). They soon turn to a brown-reddish color and ultimately a dark chocolate brown. The white stem tapers toward the cap's base and is about 1 to 2 inches (3 to 5 cm) long. The stem is hollow and ringed with a small white frill. The meat is white and turns slightly red when cut. The aroma and taste are faintly reminiscent of anise.

This variety can be easily confused with the fool's mushroom or carbolic champignon, both of which are very poisonous. The fool's mushroom always has white gills, and the flesh from the base of the stalk of carbolic champignon turns intensely yellow. Both have a double frill and smell of carbolic acid or ink.

Origin: The field champignon grows from summer to fall in circles or groups on naturally fertilized soils. It grows especially well in dry years, since heavy dew is adequate to form the fungi.

Usage: Same as cultivated mushrooms. Especially used in farces and in mixed wild mushroom dishes. They can be sautéed or braised.

Common Morel – SPEISEMORCHEL – *morille ronde*

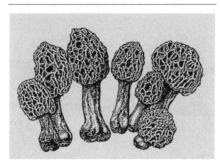

Description: The common morel exists in many variations. The honeycombed cap can be yellow to dark brown, round or conical. The honeycomb pattern of the common morel, in contrast to the conical one, is irregular and not arranged in even long rows. The mushroom surface resembles that of a sponge. The stem, seamlessly attached to the cap, is white-gray to light yellow. The stem is hollow, thinly fleshed, and grooved with a bulbous wide base. The stem barely has a mushroomlike aroma.

Origin: The common morel is harvested from March to May, definitely a spring mushroom. This morel is found on sandy, brushy riverbanks, in gardens and parks, on recovering burned grounds, and in airy deciduous forests. They are constant and reappear in the same areas.

Usage: Morels are sautéed with fresh herbs or served creamed on toast. They are added to light and dark sauces. Large morels can also be stuffed. Morels are excellent dried.

Note: Old morels should not be harvested, as they tend to have maggots and also can cause digestive difficulties. *All morels are poisonous when raw or undercooked.* The poisonous

substances contained in morels dissipate when cooked or when dried. They are an excellent mushroom when fully cooked.

Conical Morel – SPITZMORCHEL – *morille conique*

Description: The cap is always pointed and miter-shaped. The honeycombed surface is marked by regular longitudinal lines. The cap is reddish brown to chestnut brown, sometimes with olive green tones. There is an indentation between the stem and cap. The stem is not cylindrical but conical, narrowing toward the base (just the opposite of the common morel). The stem and the cap are hollow, yellow to rust colored, thin-walled, and usually smooth. The stem has little aroma or flavor.

Origin: The conical morel loves coniferous forests at higher elevations, from 1,968 to 4,921 feet (600 to 1,500 meters). It grows especially well under hawthorn bushes. The conical morel can be harvested until June. They usually grow in large numbers in one location.

Usage: Same as the common morel.

Porcini/Cèpe (Bolete) STEINPILZ – *cèpe*

Boletes are also marketed as *cèpes* (French) and *porcini* (Italian) in the United States.

Description: The cap is round when young and grows pillow-shaped to about 4 to 8 inches (10 to 20 cm), occasionally to 12 inches (30 cm). This giant mushroom can weigh over 2 pounds (1 kg). The surface is smooth and shiny and slimy when exposed to damp weather. The color varies depending on type, age, and locality, from dark reddish brown to sometimes almost black and from light brown to ochre. The rim of the cap is bent under and straightens with age. The pores of the cap are white when young and become yellow to green with age. They are easily removed from the flesh of the cap. The firm flesh softens with age. The flesh color is brown to purplish red. The cap cannot be skinned. Porcinis have a strong, fat stem, almost round when young and cylindrical and stout when fully grown. The color is lighter than the cap. At the upper end, the stem is covered with dense white netting. The taste is nutty.

Origin: Porcinis grow from summer to fall, June to November, depending on the weather, in forests, near the outskirts of forests, and on slopes. They like acidic soil and are found often under groups of mountain spruce, rarely under deciduous trees. A brownish black–capped porcini is found in southern climates in sparse oak and beech forests.

Usage: Porcinis are used in soups, warm appetizers, side dishes, sautéed with fresh herbs, and braised with heavy cream. Porcinis are excellent dried, which intensifies their wonderful aroma. Porcinis are also frequently prepared in a variety of marinades. They can be frozen whole or sliced without problem.

Black Trumpet – TOTENTROMPETE/ HERBSTTROMPETE – *corne d'abondance/trompette de mort*

Description: The cap and stem form a tube that expands, trumpetlike. The edges are thin and irregularly crinkled, wavy and slightly leathery. The black trumpet is dark brown to black. When dried it becomes even darker. The ash-gray stem is thinner at its base. Full-grown mushrooms can reach a size of 1½ to 4 inches (4 to 10 cm). They have a pleasant aroma and taste.

Origin: Grows from July to the end of November in large quantities in coniferous forests. They are especially plentiful in the dead leaves of beech forests.

Usage: Black trumpets, considered seasoning mushrooms, are used primarily to flavor mushroom sauces and mixed mushroom dishes. They are often used for dramatic effect in stuffings and as a garnish. Most black trumpets are dried.

Black Truffle – SCHWARZE TRÜFFEL – *truffe du Périgord/truffe noire*

Description: Black truffles are ½ to 3 inches (1 to 8 cm) wide and covered with small warts. The color varies from black to brownish red to purplish black. The black — sometimes purplish black — flesh is marbled with light veins. Truffles have a pungent, unmistakable aroma.

Origin: Truffles grow underground in lime-rich soil under deciduous trees in warm climates. They are found primarily in France in the areas of Vaucluse, Lot et Garonne, and Périgord from November to the end of February. They are also found in Italy in the regions of Piedmont and Tuscany and in the area of Aragón in Spain. Truffles thrive beneath the soil at depths not greater than 12 inches (30 cm). The tuber-shaped truffle grows in symbiotic relationship with the root systems of oaks, chestnuts, beeches, and hazelnuts. To find truffles, it is necessary to use trained pigs or dogs. Some experienced hunters can find hidden truffles by watching diving flies.

Usage: Truffles are used raw or cooked. They are added to elegant stuffings, soups, or sauces and can serve as a garnish for many cold and warm presentations. Truffles are very expensive.

Summer Truffle – SOMMER TRÜFFEL – *truffe d'été*

Description: This truffle is tuber shaped, brown, and covered with striped, bumpy warts. The flesh varies from grayish white to yellowish brown, with light colored veins. It is similar to the black truffle but has only a faint aroma.

Origin: The summer truffle grows widely in many areas of Europe. It is found in France, Italy, southern Germany, and some parts of Switzerland. Truffles are harvested from April to August. Truffles grow underground, covered by 1 to 2 inches (3 to 5 cm) of humus in deciduous woods.

Usage: Summer truffles are used in complete mushroom dishes or in other dishes. They are added raw to salads or braised with fresh herbs as a side dish.

Note: Summer truffles are often dyed black. In France they cannot be sold as truffles.

White Truffle – WEISSE TRÜFFEL – *truffe blanche*

Description: This irregularly tuber-shaped whitish yellow mushroom is the size of a duck's egg, about 1½ to 5 inches (4 to 12 cm) in diameter, and weighs a little bit more than a pound (500 g). The skin is leathery and smooth, without warts but occasionally with cracks; sometimes it is spotted like marble. White truffles are very fragrant.

Origin: The white truffle grows primarily in the Piedmont region of Italy but is also found in central Europe. It grows in deciduous and coniferous forests just below the surface. It can be harvested from July to October.

Usage: White truffles are used raw in salads and appetizers and added, finely shaved, to risotto and pasta dishes. Cooked, they are prepared sautéed, added to mixed wild mushroom dishes, or used to flavor other dishes. They are the most expensive edible mushroom.

Oyster Mushroom – AUSTERN-SEITLING – *pleurote*

Description: The cap reaches a diameter of 2 to 6 inches (5 to 15 cm). The color can vary from gray, gray brown, dark gray, blue gray, olive gray, or light beige to almost white. The cap is round or scalloped and smooth; the flesh is thick and soft. The cap's edges are often torn or split.

Origin: The oyster mushroom grows on the tree trunks of deciduous trees. Oyster mushrooms are usually cultivated today, on birch trunks. In the wild, they grow on live and dead tree trunks and can be found from late fall to the beginning of winter. They form overlapping colonies, resembling shingles.

Usage: Oyster mushrooms can be braised and served as entrées or sautéed in butter mixed with other mushrooms or used as a garnish for meat dishes.

Other Edible Swiss Mushrooms

These edible mushrooms are rarely offered in restaurants and are here listed only by their German names: Perlpilz, Riesenschirmling, Edelreizker, Maronenröhrling, Butterpilz, Semmelstoppelpilz, and Schweinsohr.

4.5.10 Fruit

In the culinary world, fruit is the collective term for all edible fruits of cultivated or wild-growing perennial plants and certain kinds of seeds, such as almonds and other nuts.

Fruit in the Diet

Fruit is very juicy and tasty and is easily digested. It is low in calories because of its high water content (nuts are an exception because of their high fat content). Fruits contain vitamins, minerals, fructose and maltose, pectin and acids, aromatic oils, and fiber, making them nutritionally valuable additions to the human diet.

Classification

In the marketplace fruits are categorized into the following groups:

Berries: Blackberry, blueberry, cranberry, currant, gooseberry, grape, raspberry, strawberry

Citrus fruits: Grapefruit, kumquat, lemon, lime, mandarin oranges (clementine, tangelo, temple orange), orange, ugli fruit

Deciduous fruits (includes both stone and seed fruits):
• *Seed fruits:* Apple, pear, quince
• *Stone fruits:* Apricot, cherry, nectarine, peach, plum

Hard-shelled fruits (nuts): Almond, Brazil nut, cashew, chestnut, filbert (hazelnut), macadamia nut, pecan, walnut

Tropical and subtropical fruits: Avocado, banana, carambola, cherimoya, coconut, date, fig, grenadine, guava, kiwi, kiwano, loquat, lungan, lychee, mango, mangosteen, medlar, olive, papaya, passion fruit, peanut, persimmon, pineapple, pinenut, pistachio, pomegranate, prickly pear, yellow passion fruit

Quality Characteristics

In Europe all fruits, native and imported, are placed in two categories: those that are served fresh as table fruits and those that are served cooked. *Table fruits* are of first quality and are offered in class extra, I, and II. They should be fully ripe and free of blemishes and conform in color and size to type. *Cooking fruits* are ripe, clean fruits that are suitable for cooking, drying, or canning.

In the United States, fruits are priced and classified according to their quality and size. U.S. grade standards may be either Fancy or U.S. No. 1 for fresh fruits and U.S. Grade B or C for canned fruits. Both B and C grades are good quality, but C may contain broken or uneven pieces. Fruits are also classified by size, with different numerals assigned for class sizes based on the count per weight.

Purchasing and Storage

Fresh fruits should be purchased only for a specific use, in the quantity needed. Berries especially are highly perishable and can be stored for only to two days. Store all fruit at 38° to 42°F (3° to 6°C), at humidity levels of 80 to 90 percent.

Preservation

Fresh fruit is best in season. Table 4-47 shows the seasonal availability of the most popular fruits. However, the season can be extended using fruit that has been dried, canned, frozen, cured, or candied.

Almond – MANDEL – *amande*

Description: Almonds are classified as sweet, bitter, or shell. *Malaga almonds* are large and sweet. *Bitter almonds* are indistinguishable in form from sweet almonds. Sweet-almond products must not contain more than 1 percent bitter almonds. Since bitter almonds contain prussic acid (a strong poison), they are allowed to be used only in very small quantities. The sale of bitter almonds is illegal in the United States. *Almond extract* is made from bitter almonds. *Shell almonds* have brittle shells. *Paper-shell almonds* are easy to break.

Quality: Excellent almonds are large, smooth, and light brown. The nut meat is white and firm.

Cultivation: Italy, Spain, north Africa, California, France, and east Asia.

Storage: Store in a cool, dry space protected from light, tightly sealed to prevent odor absorption.

Usage: Whole, peeled sweet almonds are used in *Lebkuchen* (a gingerbread specialty), confections, and as decoration. Split, sliced, slivered, and ground almonds are used in many dishes and desserts. Almond paste and marzipan are used in baked goods and confections. Roasted, salted, and sometimes smoked almonds are offered with cocktails.

Apple – APFEL – *pomme*

Description: Apples are the most frequently consumed fruit. Because controlled-atmosphere storage is now available, it is possible to store some

4-47. Seasonal Availability of Fruits and Nuts

	Jan.	Feb.	March	April	May	June	July	Aug.	Sept.	Oct.	Nov.	Dec.
Almond	■	■	■	■	■	■	■	■	■	■	■	■
Apple*	■	■	■	■	■	■	■	■	■	■	■	■
Apricot						■	■	■				
Avocado	■	■	■	■	■	■	■	■	■	■	■	■
Banana	■	■	■	■	■	■	■	■	■	■	■	■
Blackberry							■	■	■			
Blueberry							■	■	■			
Brazil nut	■	■	■									■
Cherimoya	■	■	■	■					■	■	■	■
Cherry						■	■					
Chestnut	■									■	■	■
Clementine	■	■	■									
Coconut	■									■	■	■
Cranberry										■	■	■
Currant						■	■	■				
Date	■											■
Fig								■	■	■		
Gooseberry						■	■	■				
Grapefruit*	■	■	■	■	■	■						■
Grapes*								■	■	■	■	■
Hazelnut	■	■	■	■	■	■	■	■	■	■	■	■
Kiwi	■	■	■	■	■					■	■	■
Kumquat	■	■	■								■	■
Lemon	■	■	■	■	■	■	■	■	■	■	■	■
Lime	■	■	■	■	■	■	■	■	■	■	■	■
Lychee	■	■									■	■
Mandarin	■									■	■	■
Mango	■	■	■	■	■	■	■	■	■	■	■	■
Nectarine						■	■	■	■			
Olive							■	■	■	■		
Orange	■	■	■	■	■							■
Papaya	■	■	■	■	■	■	■	■	■	■	■	■
Passion fruit	■	■	■	■	■	■	■	■	■	■	■	■
Peach						■	■	■	■			
Peanut									■	■	■	■
Pear*	■	■	■					■	■	■	■	■
Persimmon										■	■	■
Pineapple	■	■	■						■	■	■	■
Plum							■	■	■			
Plum, Italian								■	■	■		
Pomegranate									■	■	■	■
Prickly pear	■	■	■									
Quince									■	■	■	
Raspberry						■	■	■	■	■		
Strawberry				■	■	■	■					
Walnut	■	■								■	■	■

*Further information about seasonal availability can be found in the tables accompanying the individual discussions of these fruits.

varieties for up to eight months without significant loss of quality. About 90 percent of Switzerland's apple demand is covered by its own production. Swiss apples are on the market from August to June (see Table 4-48).

During the other months, and to add variety during the season, apples are imported. In the United States, the most popular apples are the Red Delicious, Golden Delicious, McIntosh, and Granny Smith.

Quality: In Switzerland the quality of apples is controlled by the Swiss Fruit Growers Association and is guided by the food laws. Apples should be crisp and not fully ripe. A ripe apple is mealy and soft.

Cultivation: Switzerland, Italy, France, Germany, Asia, Africa, North America (the northern part of the United States and Canada).

Storage: Cool, airy, and not too dry.

Usage: For cold and warm garnishes, cakes and pastries, cold and warm desserts, compotes, and juice. Peeled apples must immediately be blanched or dropped into an acidulated solution (lemon juice) or they will oxidize (turn brown).

Apricot – APRIKOSE – *abricot*

Description: The orange or dark yellowish apricot is a freestone fruit, originally from China. Ripe apricots are juicy, sweet, and very aromatic, with a loose stone. Only a fully ripe fruit has full flavor.

Quality: Swiss qualities are Class I with red tag, II with green tag, and III with blue tag (for jam production). In the United States, they are graded as U.S. Grade No. 1, U.S. Grade No. 2, in size counts 84, 96, 108.

Cultivation: Switzerland (Valais), Mediterranean countries, United States (California), China, and South Africa.

Storage: Store ripe fruit in a cool space; fully ripe fruit spoils rapidly.

Usage: As a table fruit, for cakes, jams, compotes, sauces, creams, fruit salads, ice cream, liqueurs, and brandy.

Avocado – AVOCADO – *avocat*

Description: Avocados are oval or pear-shaped, with a large, brown, free stone. The leathery skin is dark green to brownish. The light green flesh of ripe avocados is very buttery, with a nutty taste. Cut avocados blacken rapidly. Avocados are high in fat and therefore high in calories (Florida avocados, or alligator pears, have about half the fat of California avocados).

Quality: First-class fruits should weigh about 7 to 10 ounces (200 to 300 g) and should be ripe and free of bruises.

Cultivation: Central America, United States, Israel, Africa.

Storage: Avocados are sensitive to cold and pressure. Hard fruits will ripen at warm temperatures. Refrigerate only fully ripe fruit for a few days.

Usage: As an appetizer (avocado cocktail), for soups and salads, and as an addition to sauces.

Banana – BANANE – *banane*

Description: Bananas ripen in specialized storage areas after they are harvested. They are high in vitamins and potassium and contain large amounts of fructose, which accounts for their relatively high number of calories. Plantains, relatives of bananas, are not as sweet and are higher in starch. Plantains are always served cooked.

Quality: Ripe bananas are golden yellow. Brown spots on the skin indicate overripe bananas. Avoid those with a grayish hue as these were chilled and will not ripen fully.

Cultivation: Bananas grow in hot, tropical climates: Latin America (major producer, Ecuador), the Caribbean islands, India, Malaysia, Africa, Thailand, Hawaii, Canary Islands.

Varieties: Various types are cultivated in different areas. In addition to the common yellow banana, there are red bananas and a miniature called lady fingers, as well as plantains.

Storage: Bananas must never be stored below 50°F (10°C). They are also very sensitive to pressure.

Usage: Bananas are used as fresh table fruits, in cold, warm, or frozen desserts, as garnishes, and in baked desserts. They can also be dried and are often used in specialty fruit breads.

Blackberry – BROMBEERE – *mûre/meuron/mûron*

Description: Blackberries grow on brambles in shady woods and sunny groves and hedges. Wild blackberries are sold from August to September in Europe. Cultivated varieties are usually available from May to October.

Quality: Berries should be purplish black, fresh, dry, and free of mold.

Table 4-48. European Apples

Variety	Season
Klarapfel	July–August
Gravensteiner	August–September
Canadian–Reinette	October–January
Golden Delicious	October–July
Jonathan	October–June
Cox' Orangen-Reinette	September–December
Red Delicious, Starking, Starkrimson	October–February
Boskoop	December–April
Idared	November–May
Maigold	December–June
Glockenapfel	December–July
Primerouge	September–October
Kidd's Orange	October–December
Spartan	October–January
Jonagold	October–May
Gloster	October–May

Cultivation: All of Europe; in the United States, major producers are the Northwestern states, Michigan, and New Jersey.

Varieties: Cultivated varieties differ in size, sweetness, and aroma. Thornless blackberries are also available. Loganberries, boysenberries, and youngberries are hybrid blackberry varieties that are larger and sweeter.

Storage: Harvested blackberries are highly perishable and must be protected from sunlight. They should be stored in shallow containers, kept refrigerated at all times, and used immediately.

Preservation: Blackberries can be frozen, canned, marinated in alcohol, or made into jam and jelly.

Usage: Blackberries are served fresh and are used in compotes, jams, jellies, ice cream, sauces, syrups, yogurts, cold desserts, and baked goods.

Blueberry — HEIDELBEERE/BLAUBEERE — *myrtille*

Description: The blueberry bush, common throughout Europe and the United States, bears round, pea-sized berries, which are first green, then red, and then ripen to a blue-black color. They are juicy and contain minuscule seeds. Wild blueberries have been replaced on the market by cultivated ones, also called high-bush, which are much larger than the small wild berry.

Quality: The best blueberries have a powdery blue color; a waxy natural coating called bloom. This fades with age; a shiny dark berry has been stored for a while. Blueberries should be dry and firm.

Cultivation: Europe, Asia, North America; in the United States, early cultivated berries are available in May from Florida and Georgia, in June from New Jersey, and until September from Massachusetts, Michigan, and Washington, as well as from Canada. Wild blueberries are a major crop in Maine.

Storage: Fresh berries have a short storage life: refrigerate and use quickly. Blueberries are flash-frozen in large quantities.

Usage: Fresh, in yogurt, as compotes and sauces, and in tarts and cakes.

Brazil Nut — PARANUSS — *noix du Brésil, châtaigne du Brésil*

Description: The round fruit, which grows on trees, weighs about 4 to 6 pounds (2 to 3 kg). Wedged inside the fruit are clusters of twenty-four to forty three-cornered nuts. The nuts are prized for their white meat and good flavor. They are called Para nuts in Europe, for the Brazilian harbor city from which they are exported.

Quality: The cracked nuts should be dry and covered completely with a papery brown seed skin.

Cultivation: South America, especially Brazil.

Storage: In a cool, dry space, protected from light. They turn rancid very rapidly.

Usage: Raw with cheese; roasted with cocktails; ground and chopped in baked goods and desserts.

Carambola/Starfruit — KARAMBOLE/STERNFRUCHT — *carambole/pomme de Goa*

Description: This five-pointed, longish, yellow, watery fruit has a refreshing sweet-tart flavor.

Quality: Shiny yellow fruit (green are unripe), well formed, without brown spots or blemishes.

Cultivation: The carambola grows in many tropical countries on low bushy trees. In Switzerland, the fruit is imported year-round from Brazil, Israel, and Thailand. In the United States, Florida supplies most of the market.

Storage: Keep unripe green fruit at room temperature; refrigerate ripe yellow fruits.

Usage: Unpeeled carambola is used for compotes and chutneys, is added to salads and appetizer cocktails, and is used as a garnish. In Switzerland carambola is most often used to decorate food.

Cherimoya — ZIMTAPFEL/RAHMAPFEL — *chérimole*

Description: The fruit looks somewhat like a pine cone, with a grayish green skin. The flesh of a ripe cherimoya is white to bluish, with large, black, inedible seeds. The flavor is sweet-sour, like a mixture of pear, mango, and cinnamon. The fruit is easily digested and high in a variety of vitamins, notably vitamin C.

Quality: The fruit can be harvested unripe and will ripen at room temperature. It is ripe when the skin begins to blacken.

Cultivation: Originally from Peru, cherimoyas are now cultivated on trellises in warm, tropical, elevated areas. Producers are Peru, Israel, Spain, Thailand, and Vietnam. It is also cultivated in Puerto Rico, Florida, and California.

Storage: Very perishable, cherimoya will keep two or three days at room temperature. Do not refrigerate. It bruises easily.

Usage: Served as a table fruit and used in creams, ice cream, sorbets, and milk shakes.

Cherry — KIRSCHE — *cerise*

Description: A beloved stone fruit, cherries are light red to almost dark purple-blue in color, depending on the variety.

Quality: Cherries should be plump, firm, large, and dark in color. Cherries for the table are always first-quality grade.

Cultivation: Native to the Middle East, cherries are now cultivated all over the world in temperate climates. In the United States, the biggest producer and exporter of cherries, they are grown commercially in the Northwest and California (sweet cherries), and in Michigan and New York (sour cherries). In Switzerland cherries are cultivated in the north (Basel and

Aargau), east (Thurgau), and central (Zug and Schwyz) parts of the country and are in season from the middle of June to the end of July. Imports come mostly from Italy and France and are available from the end of May to the middle of June.

Varieties: Cherries are classified as *table cherries* (heart shaped to round; black, dark red, yellow-red and light red), *canning cherries,* and *distillate cherries* (for brandy). Or they are simply divided into *sweet* and *sour* cherries. In Switzerland, common varieties of sour cherries are Morello and Weichsel; of sweet cherries, Bigarreaux, Schumacher, and Fricktaler. American varieties of sweet cherries are Bing (the best), Burlatt, Lambert, and Royal Anne.

Storage: Cherries will keep, refrigerated, for two to six days.

Usage: Taste and color determine usage. For table fruit, cherries that are juicy and sweet and dark in color are selected; the rest are made into jams and used for cooked or baked desserts. Cherries without pits can be canned or frozen.

Cherry Plum – MIRABELLE – *mirabelle*

Description: The mirabelle is similar in shape, size, and stone to the cherry, which is why it is called a cherry plum in England. However, the skin is bright yellow. This plum is native to the Middle East. The ripe fruit is juicy and very sweet, with a delicious, subtle tang.

Cultivation: Southern Europe and southeast Asia; available in August and September.

Storage: Ripe cherry plums have a very short storage life and are more often sold marinated or canned.

Usage: For table use, made into juices, jams, compotes, rumpot (preserved in rum with other fruits), and liqueurs.

Chestnut – EDELKASTANIE/MARRONE – *châtaigne/marron*

Description: Shiny chestnuts are especially suitable for cooking purposes, because they are easy to peel. The skin of the gray-flocked chestnut is more difficult to remove. Shiny chestnuts are macerated for cooking purposes.

Quality: Firm, plump, whole nuts with undamaged shells. Chestnuts are low in fat and high in carbohydrates.

Cultivation: Switzerland (Tessin), Italy, Spain, France, north Africa, Portugal, and the Far East. The United States, once a major producer, lost most of its chestnut trees to a blight and thus must import chestnuts. Fresh chestnuts are available from September to January.

Varieties: Cultivated chestnuts are *châtaignes;* wild chestnuts, *marrons d'Inde.*

Preservation: Frozen and dried chestnuts can be stored for a long time. The dried product must be soaked before cooking. Also available are canned chestnuts, whole in water or in syrup, and unsweetened or sweetened purée.

Storage: Store chestnuts in cool, dry place; shelled chestnuts should be refrigerated.

Usage: Glazed chestnuts are served with red cabbage, brussels sprouts, and game. They can also be roasted; the shell must be cut before roasting. Chestnuts are also used in stuffing (turkey and goose) and are puréed for desserts.

Clementine – KLEMENTINE – *clémentine*

Description: The clementine is a seedless mandarin orange. Clementines are very sweet, small, and round, with a thin, bright orange peel.

Quality: Clementines should be firm, juicy, and free of bruises. They are on the market from October to March.

Cultivation: Spain, north Africa, Greece, Israel, Italy, and the United States.

Storage: Clementines should be stored in a cool, dry space.

Usage: Used primarily as a table fruit and for some desserts and ice cream. Canned mandarins are used in pastry production.

Coconut – KOKOSNUSS – *noix de coco*

Description: Coconuts are the fruits of the 100-foot-tall (30-m) coconut palm. The round fruit—almost as big as a human head—is double-shelled. The green outer shell, which is difficult to remove, has been stripped from the fruit by the time it reaches the marketplace, so that only the inner shell, covered with hairy brown fibers, remains. This hard shell contains a lining of coconut meat; the hollow center of the fruit is filled with coconut milk. The three small, round depressions, called eyes, must be punctured to extract the milk before the nut can be split open to extract the meat.

Quality: Fresh coconuts should be heavy and contain lots of milk.

Cultivation: Indonesia, Sri Lanka, India, Philippines, Brazil, west Africa; in the United States, most coconuts come from Puerto Rico and Central America.

Storage: Coconuts will keep at room temperature for a long time, although the milk will eventually dry up.

Usage: In desserts and as a condiment for Far Eastern specialty dishes. Coconut is also sold dry, shredded, sweetened, and toasted; canned sweet coconut cream or milk is also available.

Cranberry – PREISSELBEERE – *airelle rouge*

Description: The European cranberry is a smaller relative of the American cranberry. The fruit grows on a low evergreen bush. The American variety is cultivated in bogs. The taste is astringently sour; cranberries develop a pleasant flavor only after cooking.

Cultivation: Scandinavian countries, Canada, and the United States.

Storage: Fresh berries keep well refrigerated or frozen.

Usage: Served cooked as a side dish for game and poultry, as a fruit dessert, as juice, and in baked goods.

Currant – JOHANNISBEERE – groseille (à grappe)

Description: Three types of currants are available: red currants (*groseilles rouges*), black currants (*cassis*), and white currants (*groseilles blanches*).

Quality: The best currants are dry, stemmed fruit clusters with plump berries without blemishes.

Cultivation: The various types of currants are usually locally produced. They are in season from June to August.

Storage: Currants freeze very well.

Usage: In desserts, jellies, jams, yogurt, and Swiss muesli. Black currants are used primarily for cassis juice and liqueur.

Date – DATTEL – datte

Description: The date is the fruit of the date palm, which can grow as tall as 97 feet (30 m). The harvest from each palm is between 110 and 220 pounds (50 and 100 kg).

Quality: Fresh dates should be oval and firm outside, with soft flesh inside.

Cultivation: Israel, Iraq, north Africa, and California.

Storage: Dry, cool, airy.

Usage: Fresh or dried dates are used in desserts and baked goods. Fresh date purée is used as a sweetener.

Fig – FEIGE – figue

Description: The fig looks like a large drop. It is covered with a thin green or blue skin, which can easily be removed when the fruit is ripe. The flesh is sweet, soft, and white, with edible pink seeds in light-colored figs and dark red seeds in purple figs.

Quality: Figs are highly perishable and are difficult to ship and handle. Fresh, ripe figs are expensive. Most figs on the market are dried.

Cultivation: The fig tree or bush is cultivated in the Mediterranean and Middle Eastern countries. Fresh figs are cultivated in Italy and Greece in Europe and in California (Mission figs) in the United States.

Storage: Protected from pressure, fresh figs can be stored for only a very brief time. Dried figs should be stored cool and dry.

Usage: Fresh figs are served as a table fruit, marinated, in salads, baked, as compotes, and in ice cream.

Gooseberry – STACHELBEERE – groseille à maquereau

Description: About five hundred varieties of gooseberry are known. Gooseberry varieties are classified by color, as red, yellow, green, and white.

Quality: Firm, clean berries.

Cultivation: Europe, north Africa, and the western part of Asia. Fresh

gooseberries are rarely available in the United States.

Storage: Gooseberries will keep in a cool, dry space for a few days. They freeze well.

Usage: Served as fresh fruit, in baked desserts, compotes, gelatins, and as jams and juice.

Granadilla/Yellow Passion Fruit – GRENADILLE – barbadine/ pomme liane

Description: The granadilla has an elongated oval shape with a smooth, leatherlike, yellow or orange skin. The flesh is gelatinous and sweet-sour, with green seeds and a raspberry-like flavor. Granadillas are a variety of passion fruit. Two types are available, one with white flesh and the other with yellow flesh.

Cultivation: Central America, Colombia, Caribbean islands, Hawaii.

Storage: Granadillas can be stored cool for about a week but must not be refrigerated.

Usage: Fresh as table fruit, in desserts, as juice, and as garnish.

Grapefruit – PAMPELMUSE – pamplemousse

Description: Each branch of the grapefruit tree carries several fruit in grapelike clusters, hence the English name. Only tree-ripened fruit will achieve full flavor.

Varieties: Many types and subspecies are available (see Table 4-49). Grapefruits are generally classified by the yellow or pink color of their skin and flesh, sometimes by the quantity of fructose, aroma, or bitter flavor. The *pomelo* is the most noticeably different subspecies: much

Table 4-49. Important Grapefruit Varieties

Area of Cultivation/Variety	Availability	Characteristics
Israel: *Jaffa*	December–May	White flesh, very juicy, sour-bitter flavor, thin skin, seedless
U.S.: California	April–September	White and pink flesh
Florida	September–January	White and pink flesh, juicy, skin has "rust" marks
South Africa: *Outspan*	July–August	White and pink flesh, juicy

Table 4-50. European Table Grapes

Variety	Approximate Harvest	Area of Cultivation	Characteristics
Panse (white)	July–August	Italy	Fairly large grape, greenish yellow, early harvest, very sour
Regina dei Vigneti (white)	Mid-August	Italy	Yellow skin with a musky flavor, large grape
Chasselas (white)	Late August–September	Spain, Italy, France	Medium-size grape, light yellow skin, sweet, very perishable
Uva Italia (blue)	September–October	Italy	Large grape, golden yellow skin, musky flavor
Regina (white)	September–October	Italy	*Major white variety*; crisp, large, elongated, golden yellow skin, sweet
Grosverts (white)	September–October	France	Green-yellow to golden yellow, large, tough thin skin
Lavallée (purple)	September–October	France	*Major purple variety*; round, big, dark blue, sweet, first quality
Americana or Concord (purple)	September–October	Italy, Tessin	Black-blue, peculiar earthy taste, harvest easily

larger and with a thicker peel, it is significantly sweeter than a regular grapefruit.

Cultivation: Countries with tropical or subtropical climates are major producers: Israel, United States (California, Florida), South Africa, Malaysia, Jamaica, India, China, and Japan.

Storage: Grapefruits kept in cold storage can be held for quite some time.

Usage: Cut in half, grapefruit is offered at breakfast or as an appetizer. It is used in cocktails, desserts, and as a garnish and can be prepared as jam. Grapefruit juice is an excellent source of vitamin C.

Grape – WEIN- und TAFELTRAUBE – *raisin*

Description: The fruit clusters of the grapevine are called grapes.

Varieties: Grapes are separated into two types: table grapes for eating and grapes for wine production. The most important European table grapes are listed in Table 4-50. The most common table grapes in the United States are Emperor, Thompson seedless, Tokay, and Ribier. Grape juice and jelly are made from Concord grapes.

Cultivation: Europe, Asia, Africa, Australia, and North and South America.

Guava – GUAVE – *goyave*

Description: This apple- or pear-shaped fruit with yellow-green skin contains hard seeds in its light green or pink flesh. Guava tastes like a combination of pear, fig, and quince and is quite sweet.

Quality: Fruit should be yellow, fragrant, and soft to the touch. It will ripen at room temperature.

Cultivation: A native of the American tropics, it is cultivated in the Caribbean islands, Mexico, the United States (Hawaii, Florida, and California), South Africa, and Israel. Harvest depends on the climate. It is usually available in the spring and summer. In the United States, guavas are available from December to March.

Storage: At room temperature until ripe.

Usage: As fresh table fruit and in desserts, juices, compotes, jams, and jellies.

Hazelnut/Filbert – HASELNUSS – *noisette*

Description: Hazelnuts, also known as filberts, grow on shrubs in temperate climates. The nuts have light brown, smooth, hard shells. The nut meat should be white to ivory in color. Hazelnuts are available year-round whole, shelled, roasted,

chopped, ground fine, or mixed with sugar as hazelnut paste.

Quality: Hazelnuts should be even in size.

Cultivation: In Switzerland small amounts grow wild. They are found wild in large quantities in the coastal areas of the Black Sea and the Mediterranean Sea. Italy, Spain, Turkey, and Greece are the major producers. Oregon and Washington produce most of the hazelnuts sold in the United States.

Storage: Because hazelnuts are high in fat, they must be stored in a cool, dry, dark place to prevent rancidity. They can be stored in the freezer.

Usage: Hazelnuts are used in the preparation of desserts, cakes, confections, candy, dessert creams, and ice cream and are served roasted with an apéritif. Large quantities are used to produce hazelnut oil.

Italian Plum (Prune Plum) – ZWETSCHGE – *prune/quetsche*

Description: Italian plums are medium-sized oval fruits. Their skin is a dusky violet color. The fruit inside is yellowish green, very aromatic, and slightly sour. These plums are frequently dried and sold as prunes.

Quality: Plums are traded in first quality only. The Swiss grower association regulates size and quality. U.S. grades are U.S. Fancy, U.S.

No. 1, U.S. No. 2, and Combination. Sizes are large, medium, small, and extra small.

Cultivation: The Italian plum is a native of Europe. Middle and southern European countries produce enough for the Swiss market. They are also cultivated in Asia and near the Black Sea. In the United States, Washington is the major producer, followed by Oregon, California, Michigan, and New York. They are in season from July to August. Dried with and without stones, they are available year-round.

Storage: Firm fruit can be kept refrigerated for a few days.

Usage: Fresh as a table fruit and in jams, compotes, and cold and warm desserts. In France and the former Yugoslavia, these plums are distilled into an excellent liqueur.

Kiwano – HORNMELONE – *kiwano*

Description: Kiwano is oval with a yellow-orange skin that has wartlike points. The flesh is bright green, sour, and full of seeds. The taste is faintly reminiscent of banana.

Cultivation: Available year-round from Kenya and New Zealand.

Usage: Eaten fresh or used in cocktails, fruit salads, and ice cream.

Kiwi – CHINESISCHE STACHELBEERE – *kiwi*

Description: Kiwis are the fruit of a Chinese climbing vine, which is now cultivated in many temperate zones. They have a rough brown skin and light green, sour, very aromatic flesh with a white center and very small, black, edible seeds.

Quality: Fruit should be plump and slightly soft. It will ripen at room temperature.

Cultivation: France, Italy, Israel, Switzerland (West Switzerland and Tessin). In the United States, kiwi fruit is grown in California and is exported from New Zealand, the first country to export and rename the fruit (it was formerly known as Chinese gooseberry). Kiwi can be kept in commercial cold storage for ten months before going to market.

Storage: Keep at room temperature until soft, and chill.

Usage: Eaten fresh as a table fruit and used in desserts, cold appetizers, and as a garnish.

Kumquat – KUMQUAT/GOLDORANGE/ ZWERGORANGE – *kumquat*

Description: The fruit is golden yellow, oval, and the size of a nut. It grows on thorny bushes. The fruit, which usually has two pits, an edible thin peel, and five slightly sour-tasting flesh segments, can be eaten raw.

Cultivation: Kumquats are native to southeastern China. They are cultivated in Africa and the United States, as well as in most countries that grow citrus fruits.

Varieties: Light and darker varieties have been cross-bred with other citrus fruits; there are limequats, citranquats, and orangequats.

Storage: Kumquats will keep for a few days at room temperature or for two weeks refrigerated.

Usage: Fresh as a table fruit; seeded, in jams, desserts, as garnish, cocktail fruit, and in Chinese sauces and other Oriental dishes.

Lemon – ZITRONE – *citron*

Description: Lemons are oval and usually have a nipple at the blossom end. Their yellow tone varies, depending on origin. Thin-skinned varieties are preferred. The pale to light green flesh is very juicy and contains several seeds. Fruits are picked green and ripened in storage houses. Blemish-free fruits are sorted according to size. A variety called zitronat-lemon grows to about

2 pounds (1 kg) in size.

Quality: U.S. grades are U.S. No. 1, U.S. Export No. 1, U.S. Combination, and U.S. No. 2.

Cultivation: Originally from southern Asia, lemons are cultivated in all Mediterranean countries and in California and Florida. They are in season from August to May and available year-round.

Storage: Store cool.

Usage: As a garnish for fish and meat entrées. They are primarily made into juice, which adds flavor to cold and warm sauces. Finely grated rind (*zest*) is used in desserts.

Lime – LIMETTE/LIMONE – *citron vert/lime/limette*

Description: The thin skin of limes is green and turns yellow when fully ripe. The flesh is green and has few or no seeds. The juice is very aromatic.

Quality: Lime grades in the United States are U.S. No. 1, Combination, and U.S. No. 2; they are sized by count.

Cultivation: All citrus-growing countries; available year-round.

Storage: Store cool.

Usage: Used in marinades, salad dressings, desserts, and beverages.

Lychee – LITSCHI – *litchi/lichee*

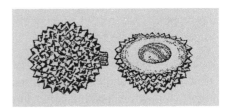

Description: These almost round fruits grow on trees in clusters of about thirty. The scaly skin is deep pink and turns reddish brown when the fruit dries. The juicy flesh is opaque white, firm, and very sweet, with a taste reminiscent of sour cherries, nutmeg, and ginger. The large seed is dark brown and shiny. Lychees are related to longans.

Quality: The fresher the fruit, the redder the skin. The best quality is heavy and has the stem attached.

Cultivation: Lychees are native to China, but are cultivated all over Asia and in South Africa and Madagascar. Fresh lychees are air-freighted and available all year.

Storage: Unpeeled and refrigerated, they will keep for two to three weeks.

Usage: Fresh as table fruit and used in compotes, ice cream, Chinese dishes, fruit salads, and as a garnish.

Longan – LONGANE – *longane/ litchi ponceau*

Description: Longans grow like grapes in clusters on trees. The yellow-green, almost round fruits turn brown-beige when ripe. The flesh is bluish white with a seed and is not as sweet as lychees.

Quality: Longans should be heavy when fully ripe; overripe fruit cracks.

Cultivation: Native to China, longans grow in the tropical areas of Indochina and India. They are in season from July to September. In the United States, they are grown in Florida and can be found in Oriental markets.

Storage: They can be stored refrigerated for several weeks. Longans freeze well.

Usage: Eaten fresh or used in compotes and mixed drinks; also available canned.

Loquat – NESPOLA/JAPANISCHE MISPEL/ WOLLMISPEL – *nèfle*

Description: About the size of a plum, these apricot-colored fruits have a shallow blossom end. The skin is thin but tough. The firm, juicy fruit contains three to six pits.

Cultivation: Of Chinese origin, this fruit is much loved in Italy and Asia. Loquats are grown all around the Mediterranean, in Central and South America, and in California, Florida, and Hawaii. Fresh loquats

are on the market from April to May.

Storage: Loquats are very perishable; use immediately.

Usage: Only fully ripe fruit is eaten uncooked. Peeled and seeded, they are used in fruit salads and compotes. Juice and jelly and canned loquats are also available.

Mandarin Orange – MANDARINE – *mandarine*

Description: Mandarins are slightly flat citrus fruit with very loose, easily peeled skin. The juice of mandarins is very sweet; the flesh, tender and delicious. Another mandarin type is the tangerine, a Chinese native. Tangerines are very small, seedless, and also easily peeled. Tangerine peel is the basis for the production of the liqueur Curaçao. They are eaten fresh or as canned segments.

Quality: Healthy-looking deep-orange fruit with blemish-free skin, round, with juicy flesh. Mandarins with stems and a few leaves add a decorative touch to a fruit basket.

Cultivation: Italy, Spain, north Africa; Satsumas, the earliest mandarin on the European market, come from Spain; the Paterno, from Sicily. In the United States, they are cultivated in Florida and California. California varieties are Satsumas and Kinnows; Florida grows the most common variety, the tangerine. The tangelo is a hybrid cross of the tangerine with other citrus fruits. The late Florida variety is called Mineola.

Storage: Store at room temperature or refrigerated for up to two weeks.

Usage: As a table fruit, in cold, warm, and frozen desserts, candied, or as a liqueur.

Mango – MANGO – *mangue*

Description: Mangos are a tropical fruit. Round-oval or kidney-shaped, they have a very flavorful, aromatic flesh with a taste reminiscent of apricots and pineapple. The thin leathery skin is yellow-green with a

red blush. The pit is attached to the fruit and difficult to remove.

Quality: Ripe fruits should yield slightly to pressure. Since they are shipped unripe, they should be allowed to ripen at room temperature. Totally green fruit will not ripen.

Cultivation: All tropical zones; major producers are India, Mexico, South Africa, Kenya, Israel, and Brazil.

Storage: Careful handling is essential. Keep unripe fruit at *cool* room temperature; refrigerate ripe fruit for three to four days.

Usage: Mangos taste best fresh. Mangos are cut in half, the pit is removed, and they can be spooned directly from the shell; they are often served sliced or cubed. They are used in milk shakes, ice creams, cakes, and fruit salads and are made into jams and chutneys.

Mangosteen – MANGOSTANE/ BREIAPFEL – *mangoustan (du Malabar)*

Description: Mangosteens grow on tall trees. They are about the size of a medium apple but are flatter on the top and bottom. The skin is reddish brown and leathery. Four or five creamy white fruit segments contain light green, edible seeds. They are considered the most fragrant and delicious of the tropical fruits.

Cultivation: A native of the tropics, mangosteens are exported from Brazil and Indonesia from June to November.

Storage: Should be eaten within a few days.

Usage: Fresh as table fruit, and in cold desserts.

Medlar – MISPEL – *nèfle*

Description: Walnut-size, rusty brown, and hard, this fruit must undergo a fermentation process for about fourteen days to break down the tannic acid it contains (exposure to freezing temperatures also will work). Two varieties exist: the short-stem apple medlar and the long-stem pear medlar.

Cultivation: Native to the Middle East, medlars are cultivated in southern and western Europe, even in England. Only Italy exports medlars, from May to October.

Usage: For compotes, marinated in wine or syrup, as juices and jellies.

Olive – OLIVE – *olive*

Description: Olive trees can live for about two thousand years. Olives are small, green, oval fruits. *Green olives* are harvested unripe, often sold stuffed or with pits. *Black olives* are harvested when ripe. Olives contain 22 percent oil; even the seed has a good amount of oil.

Cultivation: Mediterranean countries, California, South America, and the countries bordering the Black Sea. Fresh olives are available from July to November.

Preservation: Canned, marinated, brined, and dried in oil. Depending on the preservation method, the olives should be plump and smooth and should not be bitter.

Usage: Most often used as a garnish with cold and warm fish and meat dishes, served with apéritifs and Greek salads. Olive oil is used in cold and warm food preparation.

Orange – ORANGE/APFELSINE – *orange*

Description: Pale oranges have yellow flesh, half blood oranges have reddish flesh, and blood oranges have blood-red flesh. The peel of blood oranges shows some red pigmentation.

Quality: Good oranges should be firm and heavy. All varieties have minimum size regulations. In the United States, grades differ for the four states that grow oranges, but the top grade, U.S. Fancy, is the same in Texas, Arizona, California, and Florida.

Cultivation: Orange trees have been cultivated in China for centuries. Major producers are Italy, Spain, Algeria, Morocco, South Africa, Brazil, and the United States. Oranges from North and South America are usually larger and have thicker skins and firm, juicy flesh. Oranges from other countries tend to have thinner skins, are medium size, and are almost always seedless.

Varieties: Pale orange varieties in the European market are Navels, Shaouti, Jaffa, and Valencia. *Half blood oranges* are Tarocco dal Muso and Sanguigno ovale. *Blood orange* varieties are Moro, Tarocco, and Sanguinello. The sour orange (Seville) is a bitter orange used to make marmalade and candied oranges. American varieties are Hamlin (seedless but pulpy), Navel (excellent for eating), Valencia (most widely grown, good eating and excellent for juice), Pineapple (very juicy with many seeds), and blood oranges.

Storage: Oranges should be stored cool, with high relative humidity to prevent drying.

Usage: For table use, in cold, warm, and frozen desserts, and in marmalade and liqueurs. Orange juice is an excellent source of vitamin C.

Papaya – PAPAYA/BAUMMELONE – *papaya/melon tropique*

Description: Papaya fruit has light green to yellow skin and pale yellow to salmon-pink flesh, which is sweet and smooth when ripe. Red-flesh papayas have more flavor than the yellow ones do. The flavor is a mixture of raspberry and woodruff. When the fruit is sprinkled with lime or lemon juice, its aroma intensifies. The center is filled with a large number of small gray-black seeds. The seeds are edible and have a slight peppery quality. Ground, they can be used as a seasoning; specialty papaya seed salad dressings are on the market.

Quality: Papayas can weigh as much as 13 pounds (6 kg). The fruits on the market usually weigh about 2 pounds (1 kg) and are available all year. The Hawaiian papayas on the American market are smaller and weigh about 8 to 10 ounces (300 g) each.

Cultivation: Originally from Mexico, papayas are now cultivated in Central and South America, India, Thailand, South Africa, and Hawaii.

Storage: Store unripe papaya at room temperature. Ripe papaya, when refrigerated, will keep for up to a week but is best if used within two days.

Usage: Eaten fresh as a table fruit, papaya is also used in salads, sorbets, desserts, cocktails, and drinks. The juice of the papaya is a natural meat tenderizer, as it contains the enzyme papain.

Passion Fruit – PASSIONSFRUCHT – *fruit de la Passion*

Description: The size and shape of a large plum, passion fruit has a crinkly, brittle, wine-colored or almost purple rind with brown dots. The juicy, yellow, gelatinous flesh tastes of raspberries, strawberries, or peaches, depending on its place of cultivation. The many flat little seeds are edible. Gold-colored passion fruit juice is slightly sour and cloudy. The fruit is sensitive to pressure.

Cultivation: Native to Brazil, the fruit is cultivated in many tropical countries. Imports for the European market come from Brazil, Kenya, South Africa, Taiwan, and the United States (Hawaii, Florida, and California). Fruit concentrate is imported from Australia.

Storage: If the skin is smooth, keep at room temperature until it is crinkled, then refrigerate for a few days.

Usage: Used as a table fruit and in desserts.

Peach – PFIRSICH – *pêche*

Description: Peaches are round fruits that are classified into white- and yellow-fleshed varieties and as cling-stone or freestone.

Quality: Peaches in Europe are marketed according to size: A and AA are large, B is medium, and C and D are small fruits that are generally canned or made into jam. The fruit should be firm and nicely juicy. American grades for peaches are U.S. Fancy, U.S. Extra No. 1, U.S. No. 1, and U.S. No. 2; a minimum diameter must be listed on the container.

Cultivation: As is the case with oranges and apricots, the peach also is a native of China, where peaches have been cultivated lovingly for over four thousand years. Few peaches are produced commercially in Switzerland. Italy, which is called the "peach orchard of Europe," is the major producer, followed by the United States, France, Spain, Greece, Argentina, South Africa, and Australia. The peach season runs from June to September, but they are also offered from December to May when they are exported from Australia, New Zealand, and South America.

Storage: Ripe peaches have a short shelf life and should be refrigerated.

Usage: For table use and in warm, cold, and frozen desserts and the refreshing peach wine punch. Peach stones are the basis for persipan, a marzipan substitute, used in the commercial food industry.

Peanut – ERDNUSS – *cacahuète arachide*

Description: The peanut plant is about 27 inches (70 cm) tall and belongs to the legume family. After the plant has bloomed, the blossom stem grows downward and pushes the fruit into the ground, where the pod ripens.

Quality: Dried peanuts should have firm, crunchy kernels and should not be rancid. Roasted peanuts are available all year. The main season runs from October to February.

Cultivation: Major producers are the United States, Argentina, Chile, Indonesia, Africa, India, Mexico, and Israel.

Storage: Store nuts in the shell in a dry, cool space for short periods. Shelled nuts are generally vacuum-packed and are very stable.

Usage: Fresh peanuts are roasted and served salted or plain with cocktails. They are used in Oriental and African specialty dishes. Peanut butter is used as a spread (92 percent of American children eat peanut butter twice a week). Peanuts are also used to produce oil.

Pear – BIRNE – *poire*

Description: After apples, pears are the most frequently eaten table fruit. Only ripe pears are juicy and achieve their full flavor. Pears are available in many varieties; Table 4-51 lists the most important European varieties. American varieties are Anjou, Bartlett, Bosc, Comice, and Seckel.

Quality: American standards for pears are, for *summer and fall pears*, U.S. No. 1, U.S. Combination, and U.S. No. 2, and for *winter pears*, also U.S. Extra No.1. Sizing is by count.

Cultivation: All of Europe, United States, Africa, Japan, and China.

Storage: Allow pears to ripen at room temperature. Refrigerate when ripe.

Preservation: Canning, heat-drying, air-drying, and distilled into liqueur (Williams pear brandy).

Usage: For table use, in desserts, such as compotes, cakes, pear bread (Swiss specialty Birnenbrot). Used as a garnish for cold and warm dishes (game), and made into juices, ciders, liqueurs, and brandy.

Pecan – PECAN-NUSS – *noix de pacane/pacane*

Description: Native to North America, pecans are a species of hickory. On the tree pecans are covered by a hairy, oval outer shell. The nut shell itself is smooth, shiny, and thin. The pecan, similar to the walnut, was not separately named until this century. Pecans do not turn rancid as quickly as other nuts because they have less fat.

Quality: Best quality are large nuts with smooth, shiny, brown shells, with full kernels and good flavor.

Cultivation: United States, Canada, north Africa, Spain, and Israel. Pecans are in season during the winter months.

Storage: Cool and dry.

Usage: Offered shelled with cheese and used in pastries and desserts.

Table 4-51. European Pears

Variety	Season
*Coscia	July
*Early Trévoux (import only)	July–August
*Dr. Jules Guyot	July–August
*Williams-Christ	August–October
*Gellert and Hardys Butter	September–November
Gute Luise	September–January
**Conférence	October–March
**Bosc (Kaiser Alexander)	October–March
**Passe-Crassane	December–April

*Short storage time
**These varieties are available from Swiss producers until December or January; after that they are imported from other European producers and from countries in the southern hemisphere.

Pineapple – ANANAS – *ananas*

Description: Pineapple plants are perennials with conelike fruit. The green shell of the fruit turns yellow tinged with red when ripe. The flesh is yellow. Only ripe fruits develop the substance that gives the pineapple its flavor and sweet-sour taste. Size varies with the source country.

Quality: Fruit will not ripen further, so it is essential to start with quality ripe fruit.

Cultivation: Tropical and subtropical countries. Hawaii is the major producer for the American market; some pineapples are also imported from Mexico.

Storage: Pineapples are sensitive to cold and should be stored at 58° to 68°F (15° to 20°C).

Usage: Fresh and canned pineapple is used in the preparation of many desserts, punches, and fruit, vegetable, and protein salads. Pineapple can be used as a garnish or side dish for many dishes. It is also candied and used to decorate fine pastries.

Pine Nut – PINIENKERN – *pignon*

Description: Pine nuts are the fat- and protein-rich seeds of the cones of various pine nut trees in many parts of the world. They vary from the small Italian *pignoli* to that which is about 2 inches (5 cm) in size from South American trees.

Cultivation: Southern France, Italy, Spain, Portugal, Turkey, United States, Mexico, and South America.

Usage: Lightly toasted, they are added to vegetables and salads. They are used in baked goods, as a garnish, and to make pesto.

Pistachio – PISTAZIE – *pistache*

Description: The evergreen pistachio tree prefers volcanic soil. The nut meat is light green and creamy, with a very high oil content.

Quality: Unshelled nuts should show a crack, which is a sign of maturity. Shelled nuts should be plump and show no signs of mold. Pistachio nuts must be blanched to remove their maroon skins.

Cultivation: Italy, Spain, United States (California), China, Russia, and Asia Minor.

Storage: Cool and dry; shelled nuts freeze well.

Usage: Used in small pastries, desserts, ice cream, stuffing, pâtés, galantines, and sausage (*mortadella*).

Plum – PFLAUME – *prune*

Description: Plums are round and ripen earlier than the Italian plum. The juicy flesh is golden yellow to green-yellow (some red-fleshed varieties are on the American market). Plums are sweet and slightly sour in taste.

Quality: Practically all plums on the market are first quality; the Swiss fruit growers' association regulates size and quality. U.S. grades are U.S. Fancy, U.S. No. 1, U.S. Combination, and U.S. No. 2.

Cultivation: California, Italy, Germany, and France, the countries that were formerly Yugoslavia. Swiss production is minor. Plum season is from July to August. Pitted and dried plums are available all year.

Storage: Firm ripe fruit can be kept in cool storage for about one day.

Usage: As a table fruit, in cold, warm, and frozen desserts. In France and Yugoslavia, plums are made into excellent liqueurs and brandies.

Pomegranate – GRANATAPFEL – *grenade*

Description: Although it is the size of an orange, the pomegranate is a berry. The leathery smooth yellow or reddish skin protects the inside from drying out. The red pulp, with many edible seeds, is sweet, tangy, and very refreshing.

Cultivation: Spain, Italy, and Israel. Harvest time is from June to October. California also produces pomegranates; they are in season from October to January.

Storage: Cool, dry place, for about one month.

Usage: Used as a table fruit, added to salads, as a garnish, in desserts, and made into grenadine syrup.

Prickly Pear – KAKTUSFEIGE/KAKTUS-BIRNE – *figue de Barbarie*

Description: Depending on the variety, prickly pears can be green, reddish, yellow, salmon-colored, or brown. The flesh is reddish yellow with a sweet taste similar to pear, with many small, flat seeds. Because the peel is studded with sharp barbs, hands should be protected when handling prickly pears. (In the United States, the barbs are removed before they reach the market).

Cultivation: In the sixteenth century, the prickly pear was brought to Europe by Spanish sailors. Prickly pears are now common in the Mediterranean. Sicily exports to most markets in Europe starting in July. In the United States, prickly pears are grown in southern California.

Storage: Ripen at room temperature; refrigerate ripe fruit.

Usage: Fresh as a table fruit, for cold appetizers and desserts, and in jams.

Quince – QUITTE – *coing*

Description: Yellow fruit with a greenish fuzz. The fruit has a sharp sour taste. Fruit harvested after the first frost has the best flavor.

Cultivation: Switzerland for the home market, but quinces are grown all over the world.

Storage: Because quinces exude a strong aroma, they should be stored separately from other fruits. They keep best at about 32°F (0°C), at a relative humidity of 90 to 100 percent.

Usage: Quinces are used to make jam, jelly, desserts, liqueur, and as a garnish for game.

Rambutan – RAMBUTANE – *ramboutan*

Description: These berries grow on long stems in bunches on trees in Malaysia. They are about the size of chestnuts, with an orange-red wooly cover. The yellow-green sweet-sour flesh is translucent and clings to the small pit.

Cultivation: Rambutans are grown in all of southeast Asia. They are available fresh from June to October.

Storage: Fruit must be used immediately.

Usage: Fresh as a table fruit, as compote, in salads, fruit sauces, or mixed drinks.

Raspberry – HIMBEERE – *framboise*

Description: Many raspberry varieties grow wild or cultivated in moist, partially shady areas. Wild raspberries have more flavor than cultivated ones.

Quality: Dry berries in flat containers, with no signs of mold.

Cultivation: Switzerland, central to northern Europe, Asia, north Africa, and North America.

Storage: Raspberries spoil quickly and should be used immediately.

Usage: Fresh with cream for dessert, in tarts and tartlets, ice cream confections, compotes, jams, juices, syrups, and jellies.

Strawberry – ERDBEERE – *fraise*

Description: The tasty strawberry is grown worldwide. Wild strawberries are called wood berries and are at home in Switzerland. The small ever-bearing (monthly) and the large cultivated garden strawberry

were promulgated from the wild berry. Many varieties of different sizes, shapes, colors, and flavors are available.

Quality: Good-quality berries are dry and fully red with fresh green stems.

Cultivation: Switzerland (Tessin, Valais, Thurgau, and western Switzerland), southern and central Europe, Israel, South Africa, and the United States. Strawberries are grown in all fifty states and are available from California all year long.

Storage: After harvesting, strawberries must be protected from sun and heat. They should be refrigerated immediately, because they spoil rapidly.

Usage: Strawberries are dessert fruits and are used in a variety of sweet desserts and tarts. They are also made into jams and purées.

Walnut – BAUMNUSS/WALNUSS – *noix*

Description: Walnuts consist of an outer green shell, an inner wooden shell, and the nut kernel. Varieties are listed in Table 4-52.

Quality: Large, whole, dry nuts are of the best quality.

Cultivation: All of Europe and the United States.

Storage: Walnuts can be stored only for a brief period because of their high fat content. To prevent rancidity, they must be stored cool and dry. After harvest, nuts must be dried thoroughly to prevent mold.

Usage: Walnuts are used whole or ground for desserts, as a garnish for cold dishes, in salads, with cheese, in muesli, and to produce walnut oil, which is used exclusively in salads.

4.5.11 Fruit Products

Fruit Pulp – FRUCHTMARK – *pulpe de fruits*

Fresh fruit are mashed to a purée.

Usage: In ice cream and fruit sauces.

Fruit Drinks – FRUCHTNEKTAR – *nectar de fruits*

Drinks made from fruit juice, fruit concentrate, or fruit purée combined with water, carbonated water, sugar, and/or honey.

Usage: Beverage

Fruit Juice – FRUCHTSÄFTE – *jus de fruits*

Fruit juices are pressed from fresh juice for immediate consumption or additional processing. They are pasteurized or frozen to prevent spoilage. Products labeled as juice must be 100 percent fruit juice.

Fruit juice in bottles or cans must be refrigerated after opening and can be kept for a few days only.

Usage: Orange, apple, grape, and berry juices for mixed drinks.

Candied Fruits – KANDIERTE (KONFIERTE) FRÜCHTE – *fruits confits*

To candy fruits, the fruit is immersed in a sugar syrup, which enters the fruit and replaces its water. The process begins with a thin syrup and progresses to a more and more concentrated solution, in which the fruit is held for a longer time, causing the fruit to to become candied. Both fruits and their peels can be candied (citron, orange, angelica).

Usage: To decorate cakes; added to cakes and desserts for flavor and texture.

Table 4-52. Walnut Varieties

Producer Country	Variety	Harvest	Characteristics
Italy	Sorrento	October	Small, medium quality
U.S.	California	October	Thin-shelled, good quality, price value
France	Grenobler	November	Top quality

Jam – MARMELADE – *marmelade*

Jam is a mixture of puréed fruits, sugar, pectin, and corn syrup that are boiled and cooled to form a spread.

Usage: Mainly as a spread for breads at breakfast, as a filling for pastries, or as a glaze for tarts.

Preserves (Pure Jam) – KONFITÜRE – *confiture*

Preserves are made from crushed and whole pieces of fruit to which only sugar is added. The mixture is boiled until it reaches the desired consistency.

Usage: Mainly as a spread for breads at breakfast and as a filling for omelets, pancakes, and layer cakes (tortes).

Fruit Jelly – OBSTGELEE – *gelée de fruits*

Jelly is made by boiling fruit juices with sugar and pectin. Fruit jelly should be translucent and firm.

Usage: Mainly as a spread for breads at breakfast and in the bakery to glaze cakes, small pastries, and fruit tarts.

Canned Fruits – OBSTKONSERVEN – *conserves de fruits*

Canned fruits are processed without or with sugar, sterilized, and vacuum-sealed. Canned fruit pieces, purées, mustard fruits, and marinated fruits are the four types available.

Usage: Canned fruit can be served in place of fresh fruit or fruit compotes.

Fruit Purée – OBSTMUS – *purée de fruits*

Puréed cooked fruit, sometimes concentrated, is canned. It is generally eaten in this form, for example, applesauce, jellied cranberry sauce, and plum and strawberry purée.

Usage: Eaten plain or served with pork dishes, game, poultry, blood and liver sausages, and dessert.

Mustard Fruits – SENFFRÜCHTE – *fruits à la moutarde*

Fruits are poached in sugar and mustard solution and then canned.

Usage: Served with boiled meat and *pot-au-feu*, with some Asian dishes, and as a garnish for cold-food presentations.

Dried Fruit – TROCKENFRÜCHTE – *fruits sèchés*

Fruits are air-dried, sun-dried, or placed in drying ovens, to extract about 15 to 20 percent of their water content.

Usage: In stuffing for meats, served with cheese, and added to breads and cakes.

4.5.12 Sugar

Importance

Sugar is both an important food and a treat. It is an important source of energy. Whether from sugar beets or sugar cane, it has the same chemical properties. Sugar is important as a sweetener and preservative and as an energy reserve.

Negative Consequences of High Sugar Consumption

Too much sugar can be harmful. Excess sugar that is not needed for energy will be converted to fat by the body, possibly resulting in obesity. Sugar does not cause diabetes, but it can make its symptoms worse.

White refined sugar is considered an empty calorie source, as it is void of other nutrients (minerals, vitamins).

Excessive sugar consumption is frequently the principal cause of poor teeth (cavities). In the mouth, bacteria convert sugar on the teeth to acid, which degrades the tooth enamel.

Raw Product

The *sugar cane* is a reedy plant that reaches a height of about 19 feet (6 m). It is cultivated in tropical climates. The sugar (18 to 20 percent) is contained in the marrow of the stalk.

Sugar beets are 2- to 4-pound (1- to 2-kg) heavy roots with a sugar content of 14 to 17 percent. They are cultivated primarily in Europe.

The transformation of the raw product into sugar is shown in Table 4-53.

Types of Sugar

Glucose (Corn Syrup) – TRAUBENZUCKER

Glucose is found in most sweet fruits and in honey. This sugar is extracted from potato starch and cornstarch. It has only about half the sweetening strength of cane and beet sugars.

Fructose – FRUCHTZUCKER

Fructose is also found in sweet fruits and in honey. It is the sweetest of all sugars.

Lactose – MILCHZUCKER

Lactose is found in milk and fresh cheese. It is extracted through evaporation of whey.

Malt Sugar (Maltose) – MALZZUCKER

Malt sugar is extracted from germinated grains (barley, corn, and rice). Available as sugar or syrup, it is used in bread baking.

Invert Sugar – INVERTZUCKER

When sucrose is hydrolyzed (inverted), equal parts of glucose and fructose are formed. It is used in the production of imitation honey, syrup, candy, and liqueur.

Molasses – MELASSE

Molasses is a by-product of the manufacture of sugar. The molasses remaining after sugar has been extracted from the sugar beet is inedible and is used in animal feed and alcohol production. Sugar-cane molasses, called sulfured molasses, is used as a syrup and in the production of imitation honey and yeast cakes.

Vanilla Sugar

Vanilla sugar is sugar that has been flavored with 1 percent vanilla powder. Vanillin sugar is flavored with a synthetic vanilla. Vanilla sugar is not available in the United States. Adding a vanilla bean to a sealed container of sugar will, however, produce a flavorful vanilla sugar.

Caramelized Sugar – ZUCKERCOULEUR

This type of sugar is diluted caramel. The dark brown liquid is used to color and flavor foods and candies.

Sugar cane

Piece of cane   Sugar beet

Table 4-53. Sugar Extraction and Processing

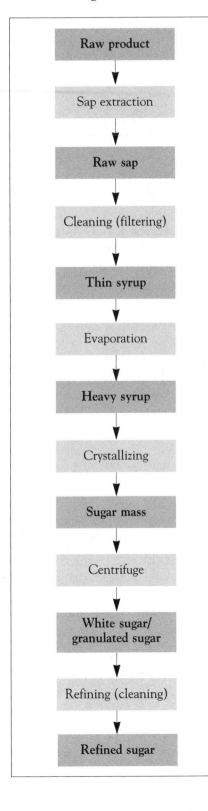

Raw product

↓

Sap extraction

↓

Raw sap

↓

Cleaning (filtering)

↓

Thin syrup

↓

Evaporation

↓

Heavy syrup

↓

Crystallizing

↓

Sugar mass

↓

Centrifuge

↓

White sugar/ granulated sugar

↓

Refining (cleaning)

↓

Refined sugar

Sugar Forms

Turbinado Sugar from Sugar Cane – ROHZUCKER – *sucre brut*

This raw sugar is not fully refined. It contains small amounts of molasses.

Granulated Sugar – KRISTALLZUCKER – *sucre cristallisé*

The most common household sugar, granulated sugar is available in coarse, fine, and extra-fine granules.

Sugar Cubes – WÜRFELZUCKER – *sucre en morceaux*

Damp sugar is pressed into cubes and dried. Cubes allow for better individual portioning.

Superfine Sugar (Castor Sugar) – GRIESSZUCKER – *sucre semoule*

This sugar is ground and sifted. It dissolves quickly and is more expensive than granulated sugar.

Confectioners' Sugar – PUDERZUCKER/STAUBZUCKER – *sucre en poudre/sucre glace*

Confectioners' sugar is finely ground granulated sugar. In the United States, about 3 percent cornstarch is added to prevent lumps from forming.

Rock Candy – KANDISZUCKER – *sucre candi*

Pure white sugar is crystallized into chunks; it is often colored light brown.

Decorating Sugar – HAGELZUCKER – *sucre grèle*

This white, very coarse sugar is composed of many small sugar crystals bunched together.

Storage

Sugar can be stored indefinitely when kept dry.

4.5.13 Herbs and Spices

Herbs and spices are natural parts of plants, such as roots, rinds, leaves, blossoms, fruits, and seeds, that contain aromatic substances called etheric oils.

Storage

Proper storage of herbs and spices is essential, as etheric oils are very volatile at room temperature.

Fresh herbs: Use immediately. Fresh herbs can be kept in perforated plastic bags in the refrigerator for a very short time.

Dried herbs and ground spices: When kept dry and sealed tightly, they can be stored for up to nine months.

Frozen herbs: Loosely packed in sealed plastic bags, frozen herbs will keep for about six months at 0°F (-18°C).

Herbs preserved in vinegar: Unopened bottles can be kept for several months.

Importance

Spices and herbs are used to enhance the flavor of foods and to stimulate the gastric juices. Synthetically produced aromatics are more and more prevalent in the food industry. These chemical substances smell and taste very much like the natural flavoring, but they have no digestive significance.

Origins

Spices and herbs grow all over the world. They were the most valued discovery of the early seafaring explorers. The spices from southern Asia, Madagascar, and Latin America in particular enriched European cuisine. In cloister gardens local herbs and spices were cultivated and tended, and their flavoring and/or healing properties were recorded. Switzerland grows large quantities of spices and herbs, even saffron in Valais. A large variety of fresh herbs is available from March to November. In the United States, fresh herbs are readily available all year.

Allspice – PIMENT – *poivre de Jamaïque*

Allspice is produced from the berries of a small tropical evergreen tree that grows in Jamaica. It is also cultivated in Mexico, the Antilles Islands, and South America. The red or dark brown to yellowish berries are about ¼ inch (6 mm) in diameter and contain dark brown seeds. The flavor and aroma are reminiscent of cloves, nutmeg, and cinnamon.

Usage: Allspice is used in the preparation of sausages, fish, pickles, relishes, and desserts.

Anise – ANIS – *anis*

The spice anise consists of the seeds from an annual plant belonging to the parsley (Umbelliferae) family. Anise must be protected from light and stored in tightly closed containers. This spice should not be confused with star anise, used in Asian dishes, which is an entirely different plant from the magnolia family.

Usage: Anise is used in dessert creams, cakes, breads, and cookies. It is one of the pickling spices and is also used to flavor mushroom and fish dishes.

Basil – BASILIKUM – *basilic*

Depending on the variety, silky soft basil leaves can be light green, dark green, or purple in color. The flavor of fresh leaves is reminiscent of cloves and nutmeg. The basil leaves

are the plant part that is primarily used, but blossoms and roots can also be used in food preparation.

Usage: Basil is used in salads, sauces, flavored butters, and soups, and in mushroom, fish, meat, egg, and cheese dishes. It is most often used in Italian cuisine.

Bay Leaf – LORBEERBLATT – *feuille de laurier*

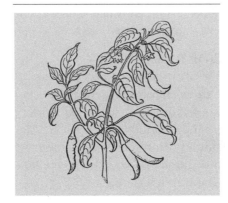

The long oval leaves of the bay laurel are dark green and shiny on top, with a dull underside. Dried leaves of good quality are without spots, elastic, and light green.

Usage: Used in *mirepoix*, *bouquets garni*, marinades, soups, stock, and braised meat, game, and vegetable dishes.

Borage – BORRETSCH – *bourrache*

Borage grows about 24 inches (60 cm) tall and looks somewhat like a

nettle. The leaves are covered with a prickly fuzz. It is also referred to as the cucumber herb because of its cool cucumber flavor. The plant also has edible blue or pink flowers.

Usage: Borage is always finely chopped and can be added to salads (cucumber, tomato, and leaf lettuce), vegetable dishes, sauces, and sautéed or grilled meat and fish.

Caraway – KÜMMEL – *carvi/cumin*

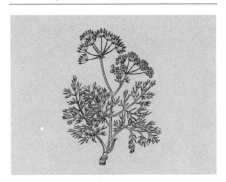

The dried light and dark brown seeds of the caraway plant, which belongs to the parsley family, are used as a spice. Caraway seeds have a sharp, pungent, but pleasant distinctive taste.

Usage: Caraway seeds are used primarily in German and Austrian cuisine. They are excellent in sauerkraut, red and green cabbage, potato dishes, vegetable stews, tripe, goulash, pork roast, mutton, cheese, and savory cookies. They are also used to flavor rye breads.

Cardamom – KARDAMOM – *cardamome*

The cardamom plant is a bush about 6 to 12 feet (2 to 4 m) tall belonging to the ginger family. The beige pods, about the size of hazelnuts, contain tiny black-brown seeds that are used as a spice. The seeds have a spicy, fiery taste and should be used sparingly.

Usage: Cardamom is added to gingerbread (*Lebkuchen*), baked goods, sausages, pâtés, and curry dishes.

Chervil – KERBEL – *cerfeuil*

Chervil grows about 20 to 23 inches (50 to 60 cm) tall, with fine parsley-like leaves. The strong flavor has a sweet anise note, which is strongest when the plant starts to bloom.

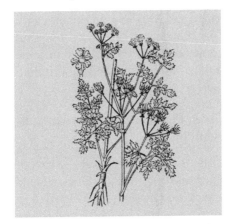

Usage: Just before service, chervil is added to soups, sauces, salads, and fish, poultry, egg, and vegetable dishes. Chervil should not be cooked, or it will lose its flavor and high vitamin C content.

Chili Pepper – CHILI – *chile*

Hot chili peppers are native to Central America. Of the many varieties, the most common are the very hot, tiny ½-inch-long (1-cm) orange to dark red chilis. Sold fresh are the pico peppers (chili pequins) and, as dried pods or ground, cayenne peppers. Chili peppers are not related to the plants from which the table seasoning pepper and the assorted peppercorns come.

Usage: Fresh or dried, only very small amounts of chilis are added to marinades, South American fish, meat, poultry, and mussel dishes, and spicy sauces. Chilis are one of the pickling spices and are used in curry powder.

Chive – SCHNITTLAUCH – *ciboulette/civette*

Chives belong to the allium family and have pink to violet flowers,

which are edible. The hollow stems have a sharp, spicy taste and are rich in vitamin C. Chives should be cut before flowering, as they will lose most of their flavor at that time.

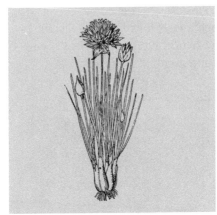

Usage: Snipped chives are added to herbed cottage cheese (quark), cream cheese, soups, sauces, salads, salad dressings, fish, and egg dishes. In the United States baked potatoes are topped with sour cream and chives.

Cinnamon – ZIMT – *canelle*

The true Ceylon cinnamon tree (cinnamomum zeylanicum) grows about 30 feet (10 m) tall and belongs to the evergreen laurel family. This variety is preferred in Europe. Stick cinnamon is produced from the yellow to reddish inner bark of the trunk and branches. The peeled bark is dried, which causes it to curl tightly. The sweet, spicy, mild, flowery-smelling cinnamon is also available ground. In North America a darker, bittersweet, and more pungent cinnamon (cinnamomum cassia) is used.

Usage: Cinnamon is added to meat and curry dishes but is used primarily in desserts, baked goods, compotes, rice pudding, ice cream, and parfaits.

Clove – GEWÜRZNELKE – *clou de girofle*

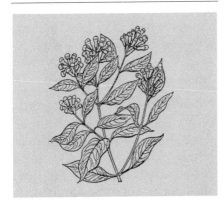

Cloves are the dried, unopened flower buds of the tropical clove tree, which can grow 35 to 40 feet (10 to 12 m) tall. Cloves are available whole or ground.

Usage: Cloves are pressed into onions and added to sachet bags and *bouquets garnis* in the preparation of stocks and basic sauces. Cloves are used to flavor ragouts, game stews, and game dishes.

Coriander/Cilantro – KORIANDER – *coriandre*

Coriander is a member of the parsley family. It has white blossoms and grows about 8 to 24 inches (20 to 60 cm) tall. The small, round, dried seeds, known as coriander, are about the size of peppercorns and have a sweet aniselike flavor. The fresh green leaves, known as cilantro, are also used.

Usage: The dry seeds are used whole or ground in sausages (salami), in gingerbread (*Lebkuchen*), in the manufacture of mustard, in the pickling of sauerkraut, beets, and red cabbage, and in marinades for smoked ham, game, poultry, and lamb. The green leaves, or cilantro (also known as Chinese parsley or fresh coriander), are a prized herb for many Mexican and Asian dishes.

Cumin – KREUZKÜMMEL – *cumin*

Cumin is distinctly different in flavor from caraway, though both are members of the parsley family. In Germany they are both called *Kümmel*; in France they are both called *cumin*, but in Spain, cumin is *comino* and caraway is called *carvi*. The common form is beige to light brown in color; a black variety is sold in Asian markets.

Usage: Cumin is a part of chili and curry powders. It is a favorite spice in Indian, Moroccan, and Mexican cuisine. Whole or ground cumin is used commercially in the preparation of cold cuts, pickles, cheese, meats, and breads.

Curry Leaf – CURRYBLATT – *feuille de curry*

Curry leaf looks like a bay leaf but is harvested from the murraya bush, a native of southern Asia. It has a pungent spicy flavor. Curry leaf gives Madras curry its special aroma.

Usage: Curry leaf is used mostly in the vegetarian cuisine of east India, in curries, and in some chutneys. In the United States, curry leaf can be purchased fresh in Indian markets.

Curry – CURRYPULVER – *poudre de curry*

Curry powder is a mixture of ten to twenty different spices. The major components are turmeric, pepper, cinnamon, cloves, chili, ginger, coriander, cardamom, cumin, nutmeg,

and mace. Because curry powder loses its flavor quickly, the spices are freshly ground in authentic Indian cuisine.

Usage: Curry is used to spice salads, soups, sauces, poultry, meat, fish, egg, rice, and vegetable dishes. It is a major component of bottled condiments.

Dill – DILL – *aneth*

Dill, which can grow over 3 feet (1 m) tall, has delicate feathery fronds and yellow flowering heads with lentil-shaped two-part seeds. Dill weed has a somewhat sweet flavor reminiscent of fennel. The seeds are slightly bitter and taste faintly like caraway seeds.

Usage: Dill weed is used mostly to flavor fish dishes, cucumber, egg, and bean salads, sauces, and potato dishes. Dill seed is used in the pickling of cucumbers.

Fennel Seed – FENCHELSAMEN – *fenouil*

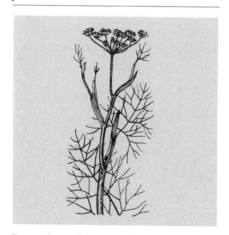

Fennel seeds come from the dried fruit of the common fennel plant, which grows about 4 to 6 feet (1 to 2 m) tall. The seeds resemble caraway seeds. Depending on the growing area, fennel can differ in size, color,

and shape. The aniselike flavor may vary from sweet to slightly bitter.

Usage: Fennel seed is used in breads, baked goods, salads, marinades, with crustaceans, and in some rice and potato dishes. It is also used in some Italian pasta sauces and fresh Italian sausage.

Green Plantain – GEWÜRZWEGERICH – *plantain*

This is an Asian herb (*Plantago lanceolata*), with small lance-shaped leaves held by their grooved stem to form a rosette of leaves close to the ground.

Usage: The young leaves can be added to herb soups, green salads, and exotic rice and vegetable dishes. They can be minced and used to flavor egg dishes. In China they are made into a tea to treat diarrhea.

Ginger – INGWER – *gingembre*

The 8-inch-long (20-cm) root of this reedy plant is used as a spice. Ginger root should be plump, not wrinkled, and not too stringy. Fresh ginger has a fruity, sweet, spicy taste. Ginger is also sold dry, whole or ground.

Usage: Ginger complements fish, poultry, and meat dishes. It is also used in soups, sauces, baked goods, and desserts.

Juniper Berry – WACHOLDER – *genièvre*

Juniper berries are the two- to three-year-old berries of the juniper bush. The berries have a bittersweet taste with a piney flavor.

Usage: Juniper berries are used in the preparation of game and poultry dishes, sauerkraut, sauerbraten, pork roast, and fish stock and marinades.

Lemon Balm – ZITRONENMELISSE – *citronelle*

Lemon balm leaves have pointy edges and are slightly fuzzy. They smell and taste refreshingly of lemon. The plant grows about 32 inches (80 cm) tall.

Usage: Lemon balm is added to salads, soups, sauces, yogurt, and fish, poultry, rice, and mushroom dishes. It is also used as a bright green garnish for desserts.

Lovage – LIEBSTÖCKEL – *livèche*

Lovage is a perennial member of the parsley family. Both leaf and root are used in the kitchen. They have a strong celery flavor and should be used sparingly.

Usage: The root is used to flavor sauces and soups. The leaves are added to soups, sauces, stews, roasts, salads, and stuffing for lamb and pork roasts.

Marjoram – MAJORAN – *marjolaine*

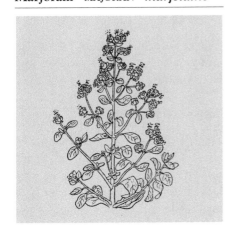

Marjoram has hairy stems, small oval leaves, and tiny white, pink, or pale violet blossoms. It grows about 20 inches (50 cm) tall. The small spicy leaves taste somewhat like thyme and are used fresh or dried.

Usage: Marjoram is used in the preparation of potato and legume soups, added to ground meat and to blood and liver sausages, and can flavor roast pork, lamb, goose, and tomato and mushroom dishes.

Mint – PFEFFERMINZE – *menthe*

Mint, a perennial herb of many varieties, grows about 35 inches (90 cm) tall. The reddish stem carries the oval, ribbed, dark green leaves and pink flower spikes. The leaves are strongly scented and taste of menthol.

Usage: Mint is used to flavor lamb, mutton, and poultry roasts. Mint is especially good with vegetables, such as potatoes, peas, leeks, tomatoes, and carrots. Mint is used to decorate desserts and drinks and can be brewed into tea.

Mugwort – BEIFUSS – *armoise*

This plant is closely related to the wormwood plant. It belongs to the composite, or daisy, family. The feathery, tender, young leaves, which have a feltlike underside, have a pleasant spicy, slightly bitter taste.

Usage: Mugwort is used for very fatty dishes, such as duck, goose, and pork roast. It is always cooked or braised with the meat.

Mustard Seeds – SENF(KÖRNER) – *grains de moutarde*

Three different kinds of mustard seeds are available. *Brown* mustard seeds are small, dark brown, and very spicy. *White* or *yellow* mustard seeds are larger, light beige to yellow, and not as spicy. *Serepta*, an Indian mustard seed, is smaller and gray; it is seldom found on the market.

Usage: All three types can be used whole or ground and are the basis for prepared mustard. Prepared mustard is versatile and is used to flavor marinades, grilled meats, sausages, smoked ham, and beef or veal birds (*paupiettes*). Prepared mustard is excellent in cold and warm sauces, salad dressings, stuffing, and egg dishes. Mustard seeds are added to marinades, mustard fruit, cold cuts, sauerkraut, and pickles.

Nutmeg – MUSKAT – *noix de muscade*

Although its name suggests that this spice is a nut, the nutmeg is the seed kernel of the apricot-like fruit of the 35- to 40-foot-tall (10- to 12-m) nutmeg tree. The ripe fruit is picked and split to release the nutmeg seed. The nutmeg is covered by a membrane, which is dried and sold as the spice *mace*.

Usage: Nutmeg is used sparingly to flavor soups, sauces, meat and cheese dishes, sausages, pâtés, vegetables, mushrooms, rice, noodles, egg dishes, and Christmas cookies. Mace is used in spice cakes, cookies, and blueberry desserts.

Oregano – ORIGANO – *origan*

Oregano, a relative of marjoram, grows to about 24 inches (60 cm) tall. It has small pointed leaves with a slightly bitter, marjoram-like taste. The best-quality oregano is harvested in southern Italy, where it grows wild.

Usage: Oregano can be used fresh, dried, crushed, or ground to flavor tomato and eggplant dishes, roasts, salads, potato and legume soups, and pizza.

Paprika – PAPRIKA – *paprika*

Paprika is a spice made from mature bright red bell peppers that are dried and ground. The many paprika types and quality grades depend on the ripeness and the manufacturing process. For mild paprika (*Delikatess/Edelsüss*), only the dried fruit flesh is ground, and for hot paprika (*Rosenparika*) the whole pod with seeds is ground. In the United States, the best-flavored paprika is Hungarian sweet and hot.

Usage: Paprika is added to meat, fish, and poultry dishes. It is blended into cheese and butter mixtures and can flavor soups, sauces, eggs, and mushrooms. Because the sugar contained in paprika will burn and turn bitter, paprika should never be dry-roasted.

Parsley – PETERSILIE – *persil*

Two types of parsley are used in the kitchen: flat-leaf (Italian) parsley, which has more flavor; and curly parsley, which is excellent as a garnish. The sweet-flavored roots and stems are as much valued as the leaves.

Usage: Parsley leaves, finely chopped, are added shortly before service to flavor salads, soups, vegetables, fish, and meat dishes, and they are added to herb butter. The roots and stems are cooked in stocks, soups, and vegetable and meat casseroles.

Pepper – PFEFFER – *poivre*

Peppercorns are the fruits of a tropical climbing plant that forms its fruit on long hanging spikes. Four types of pepper are available. *Green pepper* is picked immature. *Black pepper* is picked unripe and dried. *Red pepper* is picked ripe. *White pepper* is picked ripe, fermented (to remove the red skin), and dried. Green and red peppercorns are generally sold in brine; black and white peppercorns are sold whole or ground. These peppers are unrelated to the capsicum peppers, which include bell and chili peppers.

Usage: For almost all meat, fish, vegetable, and egg dishes, salads, soups, and sauces.

Rosemary – ROSMARIN – *romarin*

Rosemary is a tall, bushy shrub. The pinelike leaves are slightly curled at the edge, dark green on top and gray-white on the underside. Rosemary has a camphorlike aroma. A whole twig is often added to a dish.

Usage: Rosemary is used to flavor poultry, rabbit, lamb, game, pork, and veal dishes. Ground rosemary is usually added to soups and sauces.

Saffron – SAFRAN – *safran*

Saffron is made from tiny dried and usually ground stigmas of the autumn crocus, a member of the iris family. It is the most expensive spice sold today. To produce 2.2 pounds (1 kg) of saffron eighty to one hundred stigmas are needed. Its gentle, bitter, spicy taste, bright yellow color, and wonderful aroma have made saffron one of the most loved spices. Saffron is very sensitive to light and must be stored tightly sealed, away from light.

Usage: Saffron is used to flavor fish and rice dishes, soups, sauces, and baked goods.

Sage – SALBEI – *sauge*

Sage is a garden plant that grows about 12 to 28 inches (30 to 70 cm) tall. It has grayish green, velvety leaves with a slightly bitter but pleasantly spicy flavor. Sage has the best flavor just before it blooms.

Usage: Sage is used to flavor fish, poultry, lamb, veal, and liver dishes. Sage is added to tomato and egg dishes. Whole sage leaves, dipped in batter and deep-fried, are served with an apéritif.

Salad Burnet – PIMPERNELL/ PIMPINELLE – *petite pimprenelle*

Salad burnet grows about 20 inches (50 cm) tall and has light green, oval, lightly feathered, pointed leaves. The leaves have a refreshing taste similar to cucumber.

Usage: Salad burnet is added to salads, sauces, herb butter, cottage cheese (quark), and vegetable dishes.

Savory – BOHNENKRAUT – *sarriette*

Savory is a plant, about 12 inches (30 cm) tall, with small, slender leaves and tiny white to violet flow-

ers. It has a spicy, peppery flavor and is also called pepperweed (*Pfefferkraut*) in German.

Usage: The small, tender leaves are added to salads (beans, cucumber, zucchini). Whole twigs are cooked in soups, sauces, and potato, legume, and bean dishes.

Sorrel – SAUERAMPFER – *oseille*

Sorrel looks like spinach. The leaves taste sour and slightly bitter. Sorrel should not come in contact with iron utensils or it will discolor.

Usage: Sorrel is used fresh in salads, sauces, soups, and egg and fish dishes. It should be cooked very briefly.

Tamarind – TAMARINDE – *tamarin*

Tamarind grows on 65-foot (20-m) tropical tamarind trees. The pulp of the 8-inch-long (20-cm) dark brown tamarind pod is used as a spice. It is available as a juice or dried. Tamarind is very acidic and can be stored for a long time.

Usage: Tamarind is used to marinate meat and fish, to give acidity to curries, and is made into sorbets.

Tarragon – ESTRAGON – *estragon*

Tarragon, a bushy garden plant that grows to almost 5 feet (1.5 m) tall, has light to dark green long, slender leaves. Only the fragrant fresh or dried leaves are used as a flavoring.

Usage: Tarragon is added to soups, sauces, and poultry, fish and seafood dishes. It is used to produce tarragon vinegar and mustard and is an important flavoring in the pickling of cucumbers.

Thyme – THYMIAN – *thym*

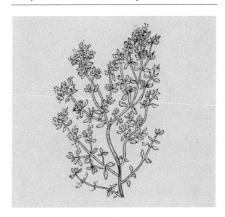

Two varieties of thyme are grown. The tall *garden thyme* grows about 4 to 15 inches (10 to 40 cm) tall and has a strong, spicy marjoram-like flavor. To this variety belong French and English thyme. *Wild thyme* grows in low, thick patches. It has a similar flavor but broader leaves. Lemon thyme belongs to this variety.

Usage: Thyme is a component of dry herb mixtures in Italian, French, and Greek cuisine. It is used to flavor lamb and pork dishes, vegetable soups, mushrooms, pâtés, cold cuts, and liver dumplings.

Turmeric – KURKUMA – *curcuma*

Turmeric is prepared from the root and ¾- to 2¼-inch-long (2- to 6-cm) side shoots of this gingerlike plant. Peeled, dried, and ground, the spice powder is bright yellow; hence, it is also called yellow root (*Gelbwurz*) in German. Turmeric has an aromatic, gingery smell and a peculiar spicy, slightly bitter taste.

Usage: Turmeric is the major component in curry powder. It is also used to color desserts and in the production of mustard and Worcestershire sauce.

Vanilla – VANILLE – *vanille*

The vanilla plant is a climbing orchid with white-yellow blossoms. The large blossoms open for only one day and produce long, thin 12-inch (30-cm) pods, which are harvested just before they are mature. The pods are specially fermented to give them their characteristic aroma and the black color. The best quality Bourbon vanilla is grown on the island of Réunion in the Indian Ocean, where the plants are hand-pollinated because the necessary insect does not live on the island.

Usage: Vanilla is used to improve and flavor crèmes, ice creams, chocolate, compotes, and baked goods. To produce the full flavor from vanilla beans, they should be split and scraped; the granules are then added to dishes. The beans themselves should be cooked briefly.

4.5.14 Condiments

Vinegar – ESSIG – *vinaigre*

Vinegar is a dilute solution of acetic acid, which is extracted from alcoholic liquids or fermented fruits or grains through various processes. The alcohol of grape or fruit wine or other alcoholic liquids is oxidized by an aerobic bacterium, *acetobacter,* or by synthetic means, into acetic acid.

Characteristics: Vinegar assists with other processes in the preservation of vegetables, fish, and meats. Vinegar inhibits the growth of microorganisms in salads and marinades. Because vinegar toughens cellulose, it is added only after food is fully cooked. Vinegar enhances the flavor

of many foods. It reduces the bitterness in some salad greens and makes them more palatable. Vinegar helps dissolve calcium from calcified pans.

Production: In the *surface process* of oxidation, acetobacteria are placed on loosely heaped beech tree shavings. The alcohol is drizzled over them from above, and air is pumped in from below. This method causes the acetobacteria to feed more rapidly on the alcohol, producing vinegar after a few repeated sprinklings. The automated process, using a Frings acetator, produces vinegar within twenty-four hours. In the *slow method* (New Orleans method) the alcoholic liquid is inoculated with a vinegar mother. At temperatures from about 70° to 90°F (20° to 30°C), the alcohol is oxidized into acetic acid in about six to ten weeks. A wine with 7 percent alcohol content produces a vinegar with a 7 percent acidity. This type of vinegar can be produced in barrels or large bottles.

Essence of vinegar (ESSENZESSIG) is distilled from petrochemicals and wood. This chemically pure acetic acid is diluted with water to an acidity of 60 to 80 percent. This very strong acid solution is then further diluted with water to produce an essence vinegar of about 14 percent acidity.

Swiss food laws stipulate: Fermented vinegar is the product of alcohol fermented with acetators, for example:

Fruit vinegars (OBSTESSIG): From fruit wine or fermented fruit juice concentrate

Whey vinegar (MOLKENESSIG): From concentrated whey

Spirit vinegar (ALKOHOLESSIG): From liqueurs obtained from vegetables

Wine vinegar (WEINESSIG): From fermented red or white wine

Beer, honey, or malt vinegar (BIER-, HONIG-, MALZESSIG): From fermented beer, honey, or malt

Table vinegar (SPEISE/TAFELESSIG): A mixture of different vinegars, which do not have to be identified, with a

minimum acidity of 4.5 percent, not exceeding 9 percent

Distilled vinegar (ESSENZESSIG): Diluted to a maximum of 14 percent acidity; must be labeled as essence for table use; illegal to mix distilled vinegar with fermented vinegar

Lemon vinegar: A mixture of one part lemon juice or lemon juice concentrate to two parts vinegar variety

Flavored vinegars: Flavored vinegars have products added to create a specific aroma or flavor, for example, herbs, spice essence, honey, fruits, or fruit juices. They must be clearly identified. The following labeling is authorized:

- Wine vinegar with herbs
- Fruit vinegar with honey
- Distilled vinegar with spices or herbs
- Spice vinegar

Specialty vinegars: Aceto balsamico, aceto di Modena, and *balsamic vinegar* are all names for vinegars from the Italian province of Modena, which are specially produced. Wine from local grapes is barrel-fermented into vinegar and stored for at least six to twenty years. During the storage time, additional amounts of sweet grape juice are added, which gives balsamic vinegar its sweet-sour taste. *Sherry vinegar* is produced from fermented four- to five-year-old sherry. It is flavored by the wooden sherry barrels.

Usage: Vinegar is used for salads, salad dressings, cornichons, pickles, miniature corn cobs, mixed pickles, cocktail onions, marinades, mushrooms, various vegetables, pickled peppers, herbs and pumpkins, mustard, chutney, ketchup, Tabasco sauce, reductions, capers, relishes, cold and condiment sauces, and sweet-sour prunes.

Note: Distilled vinegar is not often used in Swiss kitchens; it is more often used in the canning industry.

Herb vinegar contains approximately 4 percent salt, which should be taken into consideration in food preparation.

Monosodium Glutamate (MSG) – GLUTAMAT – *glutemate*

Monosodium glutamate is a white crystal powder that is extracted from wheat gluten or sugar beet by-products. It is a nonessential amino acid. Monosodium glutamate, which has a salty-sweet taste, is most important as a flavor enhancer, in that it amplifies the natural flavors of food.

Usage: It is used in low-sodium diets to enhance food with little flavor. It is also used instead of salt in Chinese and Japanese cuisine. MSG is used primarily in the commercial food industry for frozen and dried foods and canned fish and meat.

Market forms: Monosodium glutamate is available in pure crystalline form or as one ingredient in flavor enhancers.

Notes: Pure MSG is difficult to measure, as only 0.1 to 0.35 percent is enough to enhance a finished dish. When used as part of a flavoring powder, it is often mixed 50 percent with salt, which must be considered when it is added to foods.

Mustard – SENF – *moutarde*

Table mustard is usually a mixture of ground mustard seeds, vinegar, and wine or water, with the addition of salt, sugar, and other spices.

Swiss food laws stipulate: By dry weight, only 10 percent rice starch or cornstarch can be added to prepared mustard. Turmeric and other food colors may be added, but the mustard must be labeled accordingly.

Preparation: White, brown, or black mustard seeds are ground, milled, or crushed. Vinegar, wine, or water is added to let the powder expand. Salt, sugar, and other flavorings (for example, horseradish), and coloring agents are added. The whole mixture is amalgamated into a spreadable paste.

Market forms: Mustard is sold in glasses, tubes, cans, vacuum-packed aluminum pouches, and pails.

Varieties: English mustard is produced mainly from ground white mustard seed that is colored with turmeric, to which a little water and vinegar are added.

German mustard is made from light-colored mustard seed, with horseradish added for sharpness.

French mustard: Moutarde de Dijon is made from white, brown, and black mustard seeds, either ground, milled, or crushed. *Verjus*, a freshly fermented grape juice, is added instead of vinegar. This mustard is rather loose. In *Moutarde de Bordeaux*, the mustard seeds can be ground finely or coarsely, and unfermented grape juice is added for acidity. *Moutarde de Meaux* is a mustard made from coarsely milled seeds, which is sold in sealed ceramic pots.

Italian mustard: Senape di Cremona has candied chopped fruit added.

Austrian mustard: This mustard can be coarse or fine and is made from milled brown mustard seeds, powdered dill weed, and sugar. It is very mild, has little acidity, and is an excellent accompaniment to *Weisswurst*.

Usage: Mustard is used to flavor sauces, relishes, piccalilli sauce, and marinades. It is excellent with cold roasts, cold cuts, boiled meats, and roasts.

Notes: Mustard contains salt. If a marinade contains mustard, the marinating time should be short.

Flavoring Sauces – WÜRZSAUCEN/TAFELSAUCEN – *sauces aux condiments*

These condiments are sauces, pastes, or preserves composed of spices, vinegar, salt, sugar, fruits, or vegetables; some are mixed with oil. They enhance the flavor of specific dishes.

Anchovy Sauce
Composed primarily of salted anchovies, it has a brown-reddish color.

Usage: Added to meat dishes.

Barbecue Sauce
Barbecue sauce is composed of a large amount of tomato paste, onions, garlic, salt, vinegar, Worcestershire sauce, and smoke flavoring.

Usage: Meat dishes from the grill.

Chili Sauce
Two types of chili sauce are available. Chinese chili sauce is very hot, similar to Tabasco, but with the consistency of a paste. The milder variety contains tomato paste, chili powder, sugar, vinegar, salt, and onions.

Usage: To flavor a variety of dishes.

Ketchup
Ketchup is composed of tomato paste, salt, sugar, vinegar, powdered ginger, cloves, pepper, nutmeg, cinnamon, cayenne, garlic, and lemon juice.

Usage: Served with cold and warm dishes.

Lime Pickle
A paste made from limes, salt, ginger, mustard seeds, hot chili peppers, and coriander.

Usage: It is offered with dishes from Sri Lanka and India.

Mango Chutney
Prepared from mango fruit, sugar, vinegar, curry powder, pepper, tamarind, ginger, and currants.

Usage: Offered with curry dishes.

Piccadilly Sauce
A sauce flavored with heavy cream and chopped fennel weed.

Usage: Served with cold meats.

Piccalilli Sauce
Creamy English mustard pickles flavored with curry powder.

Usage: Served with cold meats.

Relishes
A variety of mixtures usually containing cucumbers, onions, herbs, mustard seeds, and mustard.

Usage: Offered with cold meat dishes and fast foods.

Sambal
A large variety of hot spicy sauces used in Indian and Indonesian cuisine. They are generally based on hot pepper powders.

Usage: Added to flavor Indian and Indonesian dishes.

Soup Flavoring

A flavoring similar to soy sauce that is derived from plant proteins.

Usage: Used to flavor cold and hot dishes.

Soy Sauce

A fermented product made from soybeans. The pleasant flavor is pro-duced when the soy protein breaks down into amino acids. Soy sauce has been used in China for thousands of years.

Usage: To flavor Oriental dishes.

Tabasco Sauce

A trademark name for hot pepper sauce, prepared from hot chili peppers with vinegar and salt.

Usage: To flavor cold and warm dishes.

Worcestershire Sauce

An English sauce that has been produced for more than 250 years. The major ingredients are meat extract, tamarind pulp, vinegar, rum, molasses, soy, anchovies, tomato paste, shallots, sherry, and other spices.

Usage: Added to or served with cold and warm dishes.

4.6   Salt

Table salt, or sodium chloride, is produced through various processes. It is not a spice but a seasoning that enhances the natural flavor of foods.

Adults require about 3 to 6 grams of salt per day, which a balanced diet of mildly salted foods should easily provide. Too much salt masks the natural flavor of foods and creates unnatural thirst. Moreover, 1 gram of salt retains 100 milliliters of water in the body, adding 100 grams (3½ ounces) body weight.

Too much salt in the diet may lead to metabolic problems. Only if a person has experienced prolonged sweating is it necessary to ingest salt puposely, in the form of a lightly salted broth, for example.

Today's diet tends to contain more salt than may be good for the well-being of the body.

Composition

Table salt is composed of sodium chloride (NaCl), no more than 3 percent water, 2.5 percent other minerals (such as magnesium, calcium chloride, and calcium sulfate), and some trace elements.

Characteristics

Salt is water-soluble and is absorbed by foods. It adds flavor and enhances the taste of foods. Highly concentrated salt acts as a preservative of foods. Salt is hygroscopic, which means it attracts water. Foods that will lose moisture should not be salted in advance.

Storage areas for salt should be dry; the relative humidity should be below 70 percent, or the salt will not pour properly.

Salt Deposits in Switzerland

Salt is mined in the salt mines of Le Bouillet in Bex (Vaud), only for the canton Vaud. Brine salt is produced in the Swiss Rheinsalinen in Schweizerhalle/Pratteln BL and Rheinfelden/Riburg AG for all other cantons but Vaud. Sea salt must be imported into Switzerland. Large sea salt beds (gardens) are farmed in the Rhône delta of France and in Italy and Spain.

Extraction

Mine salt is extracted from salt mines in the earth. The large salt chunks are cracked, ground, and sifted to remove unwanted minerals and dirt.

Brine salt is made by evaporating brine solution found in naturally occurring underground salt wells. The brine solution contains a minimum of 4 grams of salt per liter. The evaporation process is done at about 230°F (110°C) under vacuum pressure. The resulting mass is centrifuged, and the excess water is removed. The salt is then dried and ground to market specifications.

Sea salt is extracted from sea water that has been piped into large flat beds. The water is left to evaporate, with the help of the sun and wind. This slow process causes large crystals to form. The coarse salt kernels are washed, dried, sifted, and, depending on intended use, ground finely or coarsely.

Food Laws

Swiss food laws specify the permissible salt content in specified foods. In the laws governing meat preparation, the amount of saltpeter, or sodium nitrate, allowed in pickling salt is strictly controlled.

Market Forms

In Switzerland, table salt with a blue label is a granulated salt without iodine. Table salt with a red label is a granulated salt with iodine or potassium iodide. In the United States, the word *iodized* must appear on the label. Iodine prevents goiter and other diseases of the thyroid. Swiss table salt with a green label is a granulated salt with iodine and fluoride. Fluoride, or more specifically sodium fluoride or potassium fluoride, is known to strengthen tooth enamel and protect against caries. Another Swiss table salt sold in blue packaging is called Gresil. It is ground extra fine and has tricalcium phosphate added to prevent caking; it also contains iodine.

Specialty Salts

In *diet salt*, part of the chloride in sodium chloride compound has been exchanged for potassium, calcium, magnesium, glutamate, and various acids (succinic, carbonic, lactic, hydrochloric, tartaric, and citric acid).

Diet salt is used in the preparation of low sodium diets.

Garlic, celery, onion, and similar salts have the flavoring substances added in powdered form.

Curing salt with nitrite (in the United States, known as TCM, tinted curing mix) is composed of table salt and sodium nitrite (0.5 to 0.6 per-

cent) with or without sodium nitrate (0.9 to 1.0 percent). To differentiate it from other salts, food coloring or paprika is added.

Curing salt with saltpeter is a mixture of table salt with 35 percent saltpeter.

Saltpeter, or potassium nitrate, has a strong odor. It is mined in Chile. It gives a red color to cured meat. In

slow curing, it protects against botulism, but it is a suspected carcinogen.

Notes

Curing salts retain the red coloring of animal blood and make it heat stable. Rock salt, industrial salts, decalcifying salts, and feed salts are not permitted for human consumption.

4.7 Additives

Additives is the collective name for products that are added to foods to enhance flavor or color or to stabilize them.

Storage

Store additives in a dry, cool space, tightly sealed and protected from light.

4.7.1 Aromatics/Essences

Aromatics are volatile compounds available as liquids, pastes, or powders. They affect the smell and taste senses and stimulate the digestive system.

Classification

Natural aromatics are produced by the pressing, evaporation, extraction, or distillation of plant or animal materials. Examples include fruit paste, fruit juice, etheric oils, and extracts.

Synthetic aromatics are made through chemical processes and are not found in nature. An example is pineapple with an essence of rose.

Usage

Aromatics add flavor or enhance aromas in commercial products such as pudding powders, vanillin sugar (artificial), ice creams, baked goods, fillings, soups, and sauces.

Notes

Regardless of the type, all aromatics should be used judiciously.

4.7.2 Food Coloring

The natural colors of plants are extracted by physical or chemical methods. They can also be produced synthetically. Swiss food laws specify which colors are permitted in the production of foods. In the United States, the FDA (Food and Drug Adminstration) regulates the use of food coloring. The FDA issues a list of permissible food colorings.

Classification

Yellow: From turmeric and saffron, is used to color mustard, pudding powders, and confections. The synthetic yellow color is Yellow No. 5 (tartrazine).

Orange: Carotene from carrots is used to color pudding powders, fats, yogurt, and beverages.

Red: From beet root, is used to color milk shakes, yogurt, preserves, and jams. The synthetic red color is Red No. 3 (erythrosine).

Blue: From blueberries, used for the inspection stamp on meats, and in beverages and liqueurs. The synthetic blue color is Blue No. 2 (indigotine).

Green: The chlorophyll from green leaves (such as spinach), used to color gelatins, liqueurs, and confections.

Notes

Even a very small amount of coloring will be intensely vivid. With color, a little less is better than too much.

4.7.3 Gelatin

Gelatins are thickening agents that will firm cold liquids and masses. The gelatinizers are composed of proteins or polysaccharides and are made from animal or plant products.

Animal Products

Aspic
Aspic can be made from flavored and colored aspic powder or through the process of boiling and concentrating the broth of veal hocks and pig skins.

Usage: For cold meat platters, cold cuts, and garnishes.

Gelatin
Gelatin is derived from boiling defatted bones, pig skins, and tendons. Gelatin is composed primarily of proteins and is available in leaf or powdered form.

Preparation: Gelatin leaves are softened in cold water for about 5 minutes, squeezed well and heated in a hot-water bath. Gelatin powder is softened in cold water (eight parts water to one part gelatin powder) and heated in a hot-water bath. Instant gelatin is a concentrated dried and ground gelatin mixture that can be used immediately. All gelatins form a firm gel when chilled.

Usage: One leaf of gelatin weighs about 1 gram. Gelatin is used to stabilize crèmes and whipped cream. It takes 5 to 6 grams of gelatin to gel 1 liter of liquid. If the crème dessert is to be served free-standing and is to be sliced, the gelatin content must be raised to 10 to 30 grams per liter of liquid.

Notes: Fresh pineapple, papaya, and kiwi contain enzymes that will digest the gelatin proteins. To produce a firm dessert, these fruits must be cooked or eliminated.

Vesiga

Vesiga (*wjasiga* in Russian) is the dried spinal cord from the back of the sturgeon.

Preparation: Vesiga is softened for about twenty-four hours and cooked in broth.

Usage: Vesiga is used in the preparation of *coulibiacs* and *piroshki* and to clarify expensive wines.

Plant Products

Seaweed Powder – ALGINATE

Seaweed powder is made from dark algae. The powder can be dissolved in cold or warm liquid.

Usage: Seaweed powder is used to gel, stabilize, and thicken crèmes, ice creams, fillings, puddings, sauces, and salad dressings.

Agar-Agar

Agar-agar is a product derived from red algae, which has been boiled and dried. The powder is colorless and has no taste or smell. It is dissolved in hot water. The thickening power is eight times greater than that of leaf gelatin. Agar-agar expands in cold water, is dissolved at temperatures from 178° to 192°F (80° to 90°C), and when chilled gels at 89° to 103°F (30° to 40°C).

Usage: Agar-agar is used to glaze fruit tarts.

Carrageen – CARRAGEN

Carrageen is made from a reddish purple seaweed variety; it is also called Irish moss.

Usage: It is used like agar-agar and also as a thickener for puddings, ice creams, and soups.

Carob Bean Gum – CARUBIN

Carob bean gum is made by grinding the seeds of the carob bean tree, which grows in Mediterranean countries and the Middle East.

Usage: It is used to thicken desserts and to increase the water absorption of wheat flour. It is also used as a preservative.

Guar Gum – GUARKERNMEHL

Guar gum is produced by milling the seed of the guar plant.

Usage: Guar gum is used to thicken sauces, soups, ice cream, and milk products. It is very useful in the preparation of special diets.

Gum Arabic – GUMMI ARABICUM

Gum arabic is the dried plant juice from the acacia tree, a rubber tree variety that grows in Africa and India. The dried juice is ground into coarse pellets.

Preparation: Dissolve one part gum arabic in five parts water and let expand. Before use, it must be heated in a water bath and passed through a sieve.

Usage: Added to cottage cheese (quark), gingerbread, and confections.

Pectin – PEKTIN

Pectin is found in most plants. Commercially available pectin is made from the apple pulp left in the cider press or from the peel of citrus fruits. It is available in liquid or powder form. Many product mixtures have pectin already added.

Preparation: Pectin powder is mixed with fruit juice and a small amount of tartaric acid. The acid helps to thicken the liquid.

Usage: Used to gel jellies and preserves, it is also used to glaze fruit tarts and small pastries and is added to stabilize egg white and butter creams.

Notes: An added benefit of pectin is its ability to absorb poisonous substances in the intestines.

Tragacanth Gum – TRAGANT

Tragacanth gum is a white to brown plant gum derived from the juice of the astragalus plant in Greece, Iran, Syria, and Turkey.

Preparation: Tragacanth gum must be allowed to expand in cold water for about forty-eight hours. It may be necessary to add more water. It is passed through a sieve and is mixed with enough confectioners' sugar to form a soft dough.

Usage: It is used as a thickener in ice cream and cake garnishes and to stabilize candies and sugar confections.

4.7.4 Commercial Bakery Products

Almond Paste

Fresh peeled or unpeeled almonds are softened, ground, and mixed with equal amounts of sugar and made into a paste.

Almond or Hazelnut Substitute – BACKMASSE

Soy products, sesame seeds, starch, and thickeners are combined to produce a paste that is totally or partially substituted for almonds and hazelnuts.

Apricot Glaze – APRIKOSEN-GEL – *abricoture*

Produced from fruit paste, concentrated fruit juices, or fruit essence, with sugar, pectin, and approved food coloring, this fruit glaze is a firm, heat-stable product that can be sliced. It is used primarily for fillings and toppings in commercial baked goods.

Confectionery Coating – FETTGLASUR

Confectionery coating is a chocolate-like mixture in which the cocoa butter has been replaced with other plant fats. In contrast to *couverture*, this glaze does not need to be tempered, which makes it much easier to use. Swiss food laws allow confectionery coating to be used only in the production of cakes, tarts, and small pastries. Chocolate candy and specialty products cannot be made with this coating.

Crumb Toppings – STREUMATERIAL

These commercially prepared toppings consist of chopped, caramelized, or toasted almonds and hazelnuts and dried, ground sponge cake or other cake crumbs. They are used in bakeries. They should always be sifted, for a clean, neat presentation.

Fondant

Fondant is a sticky, pliable mixture of sugar, glucose, and tartaric acid.

Usage: Fondant is used to ice cakes and to produce sugar decorations.

Gianduja

To produce gianduja, one part roasted almonds or hazelnuts is ground with one part confectioners' sugar into an oily paste and then mixed with one part melted *couverture*.

Usage: Used for decoration, chocolate candy, and to cover cakes and small pastries.

Macaroon Mixture – MAKRONENMASSE

This mixture is a finely ground paste of almonds, hazelnuts, sugar, and egg white.

Usage: Used to prepare almond confections, macaroons, and specialty decorations.

Marzipan

To produce marzipan, ground almonds and bitter almonds are mixed with sugar syrup that has been boiled to the soft-ball stage (95° to 100° Réaumur). In the United States, it is sold canned or in logs.

Usage: Marzipan is used to make confections to coat cakes and small pastries; it is molded into all kinds of shapes (fruits are popular).

Nougat

Nougat is a mixture of finely ground roasted almonds or hazelnuts, honey, sugar, and sometimes cocoa powder.

Usage: Used to make nougat eggs and candy confections, for decorations and showpieces.

Persipan

An imitation marzipan, persipan is made from apricot and peach kernels from which the bitterness has been extracted. It is prepared like marzipan.

Usage: Used like marzipan.

Pineapple Ether – ANASÄTHER

Pineapple ether is a synthetically produced substance that is used mostly in the aromatic extract industry. Pineapple ether contains various forms of butyric acid. Fruit ethers are added to alcohol solutions and called fruit extracts.

Praline Brittle – PRALINEMASSE

To make praline brittle, equal parts toasted hazelnuts and almonds, with and without skins, are heated with sugar until the sugar crystallizes and melts. This mixture is poured on marble slabs or sheet pans and left to cool. Depending on further use, it is broken into bits, crushed, ground, or pulverized.

Usage: Used in crèmes, fillings, and ice creams, or made into candy confections.

Candied Fruits

Angelica
Angelica, also called angel root, is an herb that belongs to the carrot family. The hollow stalks are candied.

Usage: As green decoration for cakes and desserts.

Candied Cherries
Royal Ann cherries, with or without stones, are preserved in a red-colored sugar solution.

Candied Lemon Peel – ZITRONAT
This is the candied peel of lemons (Zedrat lemon).

Usage: Alone or mixed with candied orange peel, it is added to cakes, stollen, and English puddings.

Candied Orange Peel
The peels of bitter Seville oranges are candied.

Usage: Alone or mixed with candied lemon peel, it is added to cakes, stollen, or English puddings.

Dried Grapes

A variety of dried grapes is used in baked goods, muesli, raw vegetable salads, "natural" food products, desserts, and trail mixes.

Raisins – ROSINEN
Raisin is the collective name for a variety of medium-size dried grapes with seeds. In the United States, no distinction is made between seedless or seeded raisins. The most common raisin is made from Thompson Seedless grapes.

Currants – KORINTHEN
Unrelated to the fruit of the same name, dried currants are dark blue, small, seedless raisins from a Greek grape variety, the Zante grape.

Golden Raisins – SULTANINEN
Golden raisins are produced from a seedless large grape hybrid of the Sultana grape. On the market are bleached light-colored raisins. In Europe, brown *Sultaninen* are also available.

Weinbeeren
Large brown raisins with seeds from specially selected large grapes.

4.7.5 Sugar Substitutes and Artificial Sweeteners

Sugar Substitutes

Sugar substitutes can take the place of cane or beet sugar. They are manufactured from elements found in abundance in nature and are sugar alcohols. The nutritional value approximates that of sugar. Sugar substitutes are stable when used in cooking and baking.

Sorbitol
Found in many fruits, especially in the berries of the mountain ash. Basic raw materials are cornstarch and potato starch.

Mannitol
Found in the ash tree. Raw materials for mannitol are invert sugar and fructose.

Xylitol

It is found in most fruits, vegetables, and mushrooms. Xylitol does not attack tooth enamel and thereby prevents tooth decay. It has the same sweetening power as sugar.

Artificial Sweeteners

Chemically produced, artificial sweeteners are much sweeter than sugar but have no nutritional value. Not all artificial sweeteners can be used in cooking or baking; special recipes are required. Stored in a dry place, they can last for years. They are available in cubes or pills and as liquids or powders. Artificial sweeteners used in large amounts may be hazardous to one's health.

Saccharin

Chemically pure saccharin is about 550 times sweeter than sugar; the pills on the market, about 110 times sweeter. It has no nutritional value. Saccharin gives foods a bitter aftertaste if too much is used.

Brand name: Hermesetas; in the United States, for example, Sweet and Low.

Cyclamates

Cyclamates have a mild sweetness and no nutritional value. When mixed with saccharin, sweetness is improved without producing an aftertaste. Cyclamates are illegal in the United States, as they are a suspected carcinogen.

Brand names: Assugrin, Sucrosin, Zucrinet.

Assucro

A combination of cyclamates, saccharin, and cornstarch. It has about 10 percent the nutritional value of sugar.

Aspartame – ASPARTAM

A naturally occurring protein that is sweeter than saccharin, aspartame has a minute nutritional value. It has no metallic or bitter aftertaste. Aspartame is used to flavor beverages.

Brand names: Canderel; in the United States, Nutra-Sweet.

4.7.6 Honey

Honey, a special product of nature, was known as a sweetener long before sugar was developed.

Production

Bees carry minute drops of nectar and other sweet plant secretions to their hives and store it, with some of their own body secretions, in the honeycombs. The water evaporates, and the thick, sweet juice ripens to honey.

Extraction

Honey is removed by centrifugal force from the combs.

Composition and Nutritional Value

70% invert sugar

5% sucrose

10–20% water (food laws allow no more than 20%)

traces of aromatic substances, acids, minerals, and enzymes

Quality and Labeling

Swiss honey must be labled *kontrolliert* (controlled), which means it has been certified for purity, quality, and maturity. Imported honey must be labeled as such. In the United States, extracted honey grades are Grade A (81.4% soluble solids and no defects), Grade B (81.4% soluble solids and few defects), Grade C (80% soluble solids and some defects).

Honey Varieties

The type and flavor of honey is determined by the nectar-producing plants. Blossom honey is generally light and superior in quality to the tree or forest honeys, which are darker in color and stronger in flavor.

Storage and Stability

Honey can be kept for years if properly sealed. If honey comes in contact with air, it will absorb moisture, which can cause it to ferment and spoil. Honey should be stored in a dry place, at room temperature.

Characteristics

Honey may form sugar crystals, which do not impair its quality. Crystallized honey can be liquefied in a warm-water bath. It should not be heated above 102° to 112°F (40° to 45°C), or some of the trace elements, especially the valuable enzymes, will be destroyed.

4.7.7 Convenience Foods

The term *convenience food* originated in the United States but is now a familiar term worldwide. The term indicates that raw materials have been partially or fully processed and are sold and marketed as a labor-saving product. The term *ready foods* is applied generally to fully prepared dishes or complete ready-to-eat menus.

Standards

The following conditions should generally be met by convenience foods:

- Sanitary and safe production
- Good reliable quality and a natural-looking product
- Minor loss of nutrients
- No waste and weight loss
- Long-term storage without problem
- Fast, simple preparation
- Little labor and material cost
- Reduced overhead and accurate cost calculations

Usage

The use of convenience foods is unlimited. They can be served practically anywhere, for example:

- in households
- in restaurants
- in cafeterias
- in group homes and spas
- in hospitals
- in airplanes and dining cars
- in the armed forces
- during staff shortages
- in establishments with insuffient preparation areas
- during unexpected peak periods
- when time is short

Degree of Preparation

Convenience foods are classified as follows:

- partially processed product
- ready-to-cook, fully prepared product
- ready-to-heat fully cooked product
- ready-to-serve product

Reconstitution

The following methods can be used to reheat (reconstitute) fully prepared convenience foods:

- poach or simmer in stock or water
- with convection steam or with steam pressure
- with convection heat and steam
- with convection heat
- with infrared heat or microwaves
- in the oven
- in the deep-fat fryer
- with contact heat (frying pan or grill)

Product Types

- Pasteurized, ultra-pasteurized, and sterilized products in cardboard pack-ages, vacuum bags, glasses or cans
- Air- and heat-dried or freeze-dried products
- Frozen products
- Ready-to-serve meals wrapped in heat-tolerant foils, bowls, portioned on plates
- Vacuum-packaged, fully cooked dishes (*cuisson sous vide*)

Storage and Preparation

Directions from the producer should be carefully followed. Depending on the production method, the convenience food should be stored cool, dry, chilled, or frozen. Portions and cook times should be followed accurately.

With imagination and care, convenience foods can be enhanced with the addition of selected ingredients.

4.8 Coffee and Tea

The beverages described here do not have any nutritional value and do not contribute to the building and maintenance of the human body. They contain substances that stimulate or calm the brain and nervous system, such as caffeine, theine, and theobromine. Coffee and tea must be fermented and roasted to be palatable.

4.8.1 Coffee – KAFFEE – *café*

Origin

Coffee originally came from the Kaffa region in Ethiopia. Coffee plants were transported via the Red Sea to Arabia and quickly spread all over Asia Minor. Not until 1615 was coffee introduced from Turkey into Europe. Coffee plants and coffee as a beverage crossed the oceans and was soon cultivated all over the world.

In the seventeenth and eighteenth centuries, the Dutch were an influential major seafaring power. In 1699 the Dutch had already planted coffee trees on the island of Java in Indonesia. Plantations were established soon afterward in India and Ceylon (Sri Lanka). The Dutch also brought coffee plants to South America and Dutch Guiana. From there coffee spread throughout the tropics of the New World, which now comprise the major coffee-producing countries of the world.

Coffee Beans

Approximately eighty different coffee tree varieties exist. Two species are of major importance: *Coffea arabica* and *Coffea robusta* (or *C. canephora*). Three-quarters of world pro- duction is arabica coffee. Arabica beans are long, with a smooth surface, and are bluish green after they have been washed. Generally arabica beans are of good quality. Robusta coffee trees grow very quickly, produce more beans, and are more pest-resistant than arabica trees. Robusta beans are round, irregular, and light brown to greenish when washed. One-quarter of world production is robusta coffee, but it is of only medium quality. The methods used to process the beans are shown in Table 4-54.

Coffee is sold from producer countries as green coffee beans, packed in bags of 125 to 150 pounds (60 to 70 kg), which are shipped all over the world.

Important Coffee-producing Areas

Central America: Mexico, Guatemala, El Salvador, Honduras, Nicaragua, Costa Rica, Cuba, Haiti, Dominican Republic

South America: Brazil, Venezuela, Colombia, Ecuador, Peru, Bolivia

Africa: Guinea, Ivory Coast, Ghana, Nigeria, Cameroon, Gabon, Angola, Congo, Tanzania, Uganda, Kenya, Ethiopia, Yemen, Madagascar

Asia: India, Malaysia, Indonesia, New Guinea

Cultivation

Growing wild, the coffee tree can reach a height of 20 to 24 feet (6.5 to 8 m). In plantations it is kept to 7 to 9 feet (2 to 3 m), to ease picking. The bush flowers two or three times a year; ripe and unripe fruit often are present at the same time. Coffee is hand-picked. The ripe fruit is dark red, and the flesh holds two beans, which are covered with a silvery skin and horn shell. If the fruit produces only one bean, it is round and known as pearl coffee. These pearl beans are removed and sold separately.

Roasting

Good coffee depends on high-quality beans and is often a mixture of coffee beans from several areas, of different varieties and characteristics. Central American and South American arabica beans are often blended with African or Asian robusta beans. When beans are blended, the final use is considered, for example, the blend may be designed for a latte, espresso, or mocha. The characteristic aroma

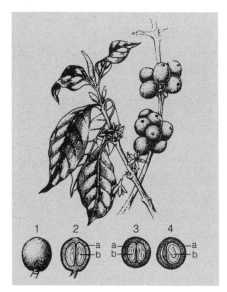

1 Fruit
2 Longitudinal section
3 Cross section
4 Cross section of a pearl bean
   a flesh
   b coffee bean

and color are developed during the roasting process; the etheric oils are released at a temperature of 390° to 480°F (200° to 250°C). Coffee loses about 20 percent of its weight during the roasting process but gains a quarter in volume. Roasted coffee attracts moisture and should be stored airtight. The aroma peaks a few days after roasting and diminishes thereafter. It is thus best if coffee is roasted for immediate use only.

Instant Coffee

The coffee blend is most important for good-quality instant coffee products. After roasting, the beans are immediately cooled and ground. Hot water is poured over the coffee powder to make a concentrate, which is either spray- or freeze-dried to remove the water.

Decaffeinated Coffee

Arabica coffee contains about 1 to 1.5 percent caffeine; robusta, about 2 to 2½ percent caffeine. Because caffeine is a mild stimulant, some people prefer decaffeinated coffee. Caffeine-free coffee is produced without negatively affecting the aroma. The green beans are treated with steam, and the caffeine is naturally removed from the soaked beans. The caffeine-free beans are then carefully dried and roasted and prepared as regular coffee is. Legally, decaffeinated coffee cannot contain more than 0.1 percent caffeine.

Coffee Substitutes

There is no real substitute for coffee. The stimulating properties and the aroma of roasted coffee cannot be matched by a surrogate product. However, for many years, other products have been introduced that are roasted and ground and brewed like coffee. Such products are:

• barley and the derived malt
• rye
• chicory and sugar beets
• figs
• sugar varieties

When coffee prices rise, coffee substitutes are sometimes used to stretch coffee; when prices are low, demand for substitute coffees is also low.

4.8.2 Tea – TEE – *thé*

Origin

No one knows how tea reached China. Written records of its use as a beverage there exist as far back as the tenth century B.C., and it may have been drunk there since perhaps the twenty-eighth century B.C. The tea bush arrived in Japan about 800 B.C., brought by Buddhist monks from China. The Dutch, not the English, brought tea to Europe in the seventeenth century. Shortly thereafter, tea was introduced to England, where it is highly prized and, as is also true in Japan, the service of tea is a ceremonial event.

The Tea Plant

Tea belongs to the tea family and is of the same genus as the camellia. Today the Assam hybrid is the most commonly grown tea plant. Though it does not require special soil, it does need a special climate. The best teas grow at high altitudes, up to 6,000 feet (2,000 m), especially on cloud-covered mountaintops. Plenty of light intensifies the aroma, and the constant shifting of sun and clouds is beneficial, regulating humidity. The clouds' cooling also promotes slow gowth.

Table 4-54. Processing of Coffee Beans

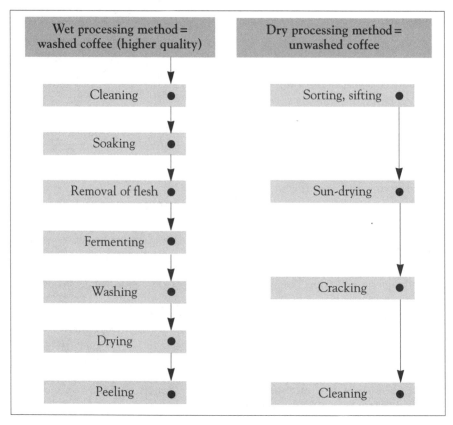

Wet processing method = washed coffee (higher quality)	Dry processing method = unwashed coffee
Cleaning ●	Sorting, sifting ●
Soaking ●	
Removal of flesh ●	Sun-drying ●
Fermenting ●	
Washing ●	Cracking ●
Drying ●	
Peeling ●	Cleaning ●

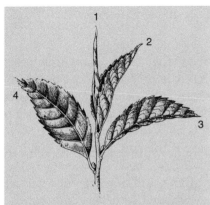

1 Flowery Orange Pekoe = tiniest, tender leaf tips, soft and covered with silky hairs
2 Orange Pekoe = tender, rolled leaves, sometimes with a light gray or golden tip
3 Pekoe = the second leaf from the top of the branch
4 Pekoe Souchong = the third, coarse leaf, long and open (Souchong signifies large leaves, round, coarsely rolled)

Tea Grades

Flowery Orange Pekoe (FOP)
Flowery orange pekoe tea is made from very young, tiny tea leaves, with many leaf tips and closed buds. *Orange* identifies the leaf, not the color, and is derived from the Dutch *oranje* ("royal"). These tender leaf tips do not completely darken during fermentation.

Orange Pekoe (OP)
Orange pekoe tea consists of very tiny tender leaves.

Pekoe (P)
Pekoe tea is made from young leaves, still covered with hairy fuzz.

Pekoe Souchong (PS) and Souchong
Of the sorted teas, these are made from the largest leaf, an open broad leaf that produces a weak brewed tea. *Souchong* is the Chinese designation for the coarsest tea leaf on the market.

Broken Pekoe Souchong
This is the name for north Indian teas, made from round, curled tea leaves.

Lapsang Souchong
This Chinese tea has a strong, smoky flavor. Connoisseurs consider today's Lapsang inferior to the Lapsang available prior to World War II, when the leaves were smoked only with wood from white-fir trees.

Broken Orange Pekoe (BOP)
This tea, made from broken leaves, is stronger but less fragrant.

Broken Pekoe (BP)
Broken larger leaves make up broken pekoe.

Pekoe Fannings (BF)
This tea consists of broken leaf bits; it contains no leaf edges or ribs.

Dust
Dust is the smallest tea bits, of poorest quality.

Quality Tea Production

In contrast to coffee, tea is completely processed on the plantation and exported, ready to brew, directly from the country of origin.

Wilting
After the tea leaves have been picked, they are placed in pans or spread on grates. They are then allowed to wilt naturally or with the aid of heated air. This process removes approximately 30 percent of water from the leaves.

Rolling
The somewhat wilted leaves are now mechanically rolled with the help of two table-size brass plates. This breaks the cell membranes, exposing them to oxygen, which aids in the development of the etheric oils. Depending on the pressure applied by the upper plates, the rolled teas are either whole leaves or broken.

Fermentation
The rolled leaves are placed in dark, humid rooms, where the leaves further oxidize and undergo fermentation. During fermentation, the leaf turns coppery red, the caffeine is activated, tannin content is reduced, and the flavor is developed.

Drying
Fermentation is interrupted to dry the tea leaves with 195°F (90°C) hot air. The leaves turn darker and become black tea. It takes 8.8 pounds (4 kg) of green tea to produce 2.2 pounds (1 kg) of black tea.

Sorting
Finally, the tea is sorted according to the market grades, with the help of various sifters.

In addition to the well-known black tea, green tea is also available on the market. For this tea, immediately after the leaves are picked, they are treated with steam or heated in large pans, so that the liquid in the leaves evaporates and the tea dries. Green tea is not fermented.

Sources of Tea

India and Sri Lanka (Ceylon) are the largest tea exporters in the world today. The important differences in the flavor of tea depend on the area of cultivation, climate, and soil, as well as the time of harvest and processing.

India, Darjeeling: High-altitude cultivation on the slopes of the Himalayas, 6,667 to 10,000 feet (2,000 to 3,000 m) above sea level. Excellent tea, very aromatic.

India, Assam: Grown in northern India along both sides of the Brahmaputra River; also in Doars and Nilgiri. A full-flavored, malty, strong, dark tea.

Sri Lanka (Ceylon): Ceylon teas have a characteristic tart taste with a rich golden color.

Kenya: Kenyan teas are very rich and are used extensively in tea bags.

China: Chinese teas (jasmine, Leechy, Lapsang Souchong) are usually used in tea mixtures.

Indonesia: Produces tea in Java and Sumatra.

Tea is also cultivated in Africa, Japan, Russia, Turkey, Bangladesh, Malaysia, Iran, and in some areas of South America.

4.9 Cocoa and Chocolate

4.9.1 Cocoa

The term *cocoa* refers to both the dried and roasted or unroasted seeds of the cacao tree and to the product that results from grinding the original or partially defatted cocoa mass. Cocoa powder must contain at least 20 percent cocoa butter. Cocoa is the basis for cocoa powder and the raw material for the manufacture of chocolate. Cocoa is considered both a stimulant and a nutritious food.

The Cacao Tree

The cacao tree grows only in tropical climates. The young trees, however, require shade to thrive, and large shade-providing trees, including bananas, breadfruit trees, and coconut palms, are called "cocoa mothers" in the trade. The tree's fruits are attached to the trunk or are in the forks of larger branches. Every cacao tree bears approximately twenty to thirty fruit pods. The hard, rough pod changes color from green or yellow to reddish brown. Inside the pod, embedded in white pulp and arranged in five rows, are about twenty to forty almond-shaped cocoa beans. Each tree bears from 1 to 5 pounds (0.5 to 2 kg) of beans.

Fermentation

The fruit is opened at the harvesting site or at collection points. The beans are scraped from the pods with some of the attached pulp (pulpa) and fermented. The fermentation process is key to producing high-quality cocoa. The processing technique varies by area of cultivation. The beans can be stacked in heaps or packed in large baskets. They are then covered with banana leaves or other plant materials, which smother the beans completely. The beans are left to ferment for two to six days. The fermentation process changes the bean fundamentally. The pulp disintegrates, and the resulting heat of about 122°F (50°C) destroys the seed germ. The beans lose a great deal of their bitter taste and new aromatic flavors develop. After the beans are dried and roasted, these aromatic substances give cocoa its characteristic flavor.

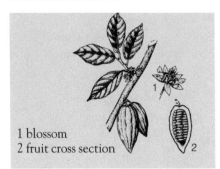

1 blossom
2 fruit cross section

Drying

The fermented raw beans still contain about 60 percent water. They are spread out on large floors or mats and dried with the help of the sun. After a week, the water evaporates, the beans turn a darker shade of brown, and their aroma is stronger. The beans are then packed in sacks.

Sources of Cocoa

Central America: Mexico, Costa Rica, Cuba, Haiti, Dominican Republic, Grenada, and Trinidad

South America: Colombia, Ecuador, Peru, Bolivia, Venezuela, and Brazil

Africa: Sierra Leone, Côte d'Ivoire, Ghana, Togo, Nigeria, Cameroon, Guinea, São Tomé, Gabon, and Congo

Asia: Sri Lanka, Malaysia, Indonesia, the Philippines, Papua-New Guinea

Processing

Upon their arrival at chocolate factories, the beans are washed and roasted at temperatures of 210° to 285°F (100° to 140°C) to develop their flavor and aroma. After roasting, the beans are shelled, degermed, cracked, and broken mechanically into nibs. Depending on their quality and price, crushed cocoa beans are blended as coffee and tea are, by their country of origin. These blends are ground into a smooth liquid paste. The finer the cocoa is ground, the better the quality of the final product. The processed cocoa mass consists of 50 percent fat, the cocoa butter. The high fat content prevents this mass from being pulverized, so part of the cocoa butter is removed under hydraulic pressure. The remaining hard cakes are then crushed and ground to a very fine powder. The cocoa butter is used primarily in the manufacture of chocolate.

Storage

Cocoa powder must be protected from light and changing temperatures. It is best stored dry and cool in sealed containers, to protect it from infestation by flour and cocoa moths.

4.9.2 Chocolate

Chocolate is a mixture of ground cocoa, sugar, and—depending on type—cocoa butter, flavorings, almonds, nuts, milk, and various other ingredients. Ingredients and their quantities determine the character, taste, and type of chocolate. Even though the cocoa mixture already contains 50 percent cocoa butter, more cocoa butter is added to develop a smoother chocolate with a milder taste.

The chocolate ingredients are thoroughly mixed: a process called conching. Rotating blades slowly blend the heated chocolate liquid for several hours to produce a creamy smooth chocolate bar.

Commercial Coating Chocolate –
ÜBERZUGSSCHOKOLADE–*couverture*

Coating chocolate contains about 50 percent sugar and 33 percent chocolate, with a 35 percent cocoa butter content. Coating chocolate is used to cover chocolate candy, cookies, tartlets, pastries, and cakes. In the United States, compound coating chocolate is only available commercially. The chocolate has a high gloss and must be tempered for use. It is generally sold in 10-pound blocks.

Keys to color pages

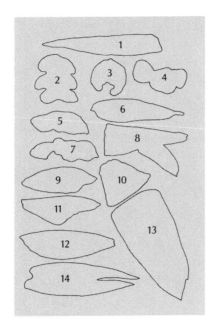

Saltwater Fish Fillets and Steaks (page C1)

1. Monkfish fillet
2. Monkfish steaks
3. Cod steak
4. Monkfish cheeks
5. Shark steak
6. Whiting fillet
7. Cod cheeks
8. Cod fillets
9. Lemon sole fillet
10. Tuna steak
11. Flounder fillet
12. Dover sole, skinned and boned
13. Tuna fillet
14. Dover sole fillets

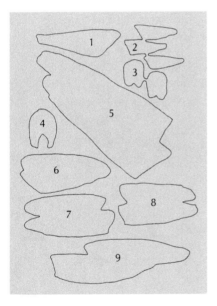

Freshwater Fish Fillets (page C2)

1. Pike perch fillet
2. River perch fillet
3. Pike steak
4. Salmon steak
5. Salmon fillet
6. Salmon trout fillet
7. Char fillet
8. Rainbow trout fillet
9. Whitefish fillet

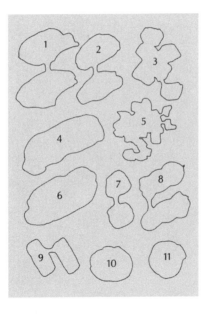

Veal (page C3)

1. Rib chops
2. Steaks
3. Stew meat
4. Paillards
5. Veal strips
6. Cutlet
7. Tenderloin steaks
8. Breast slices
9. Veal birds (paupiettes)
10. Shank steak (osso buco)
11. Rolled breast steak

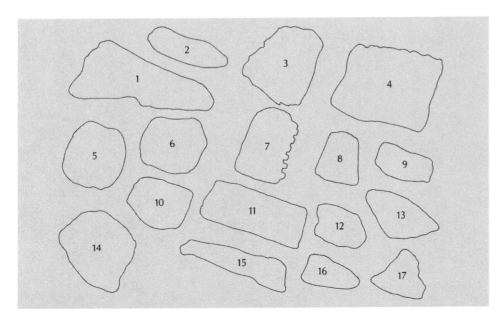

Veal (pages C4–C5)

1. Bottom round
2. Eye of round
3. Neck
4. Breast
5. Sirloin tip
6. Sirloin
7. Rack of veal
8. Veal shank
9. Shoulder clod
10. Bottom round
11. Boneless loin roast
12. Shoulder blade
13. Chuck arm roast
14. Top round
15. Tenderloin
16. Shoulder eye roast
17. Brisket

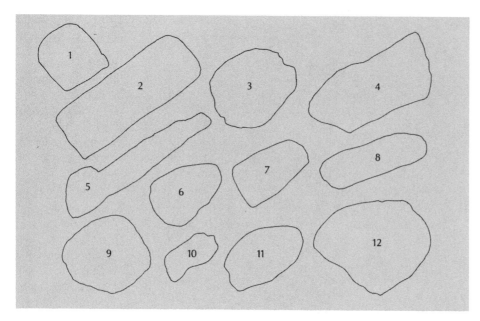

Beef Hindquarter (pages C6–C7)

1. Prime rib
2. Rib roast
3. Top round
4. Bottom round
5. Filet
6. Sirloin butt
7. Shank
8. Eye of round
9. Rump
10. Rump tip
11. Bottom round
12. Top round

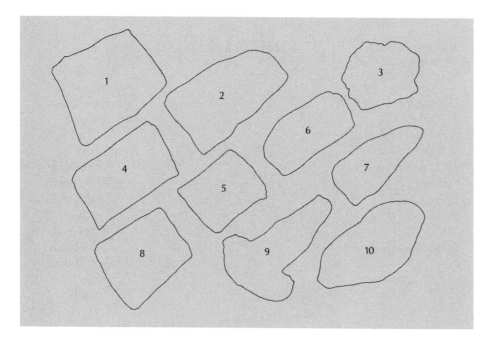

Beef Front Quarter (pages C8–C9)

1. Short plate
2. Clod tip
3. Foreshank without bone
4. Clod
5. Plate
6. Shoulder clod
7. Shoulder filet
8. Uncovered plate
9. Brisket
10. Chuck (thick shoulder)

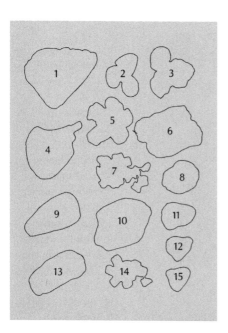

Beef (page C10)

1. Porterhouse steak
2. Marrow bones
3. Ox tail
4. Ribeye steak
5. Stew meat
6. Club steak
7. Stir-fry meat
8. Chateaubriand
9. Thick sirloin strip steak
10. Round steak
11. Tenderloin steak/filet steak
12. Tournedos
13. Sirloin steak
14. Tenderloin pieces
15. Filet mignon

Pork (page C11)

1. Rib chops
2. Boneless loin chops
3. Hocks
4. Tenderloin noisettes
5. Shoulder steak
6. Stir-fry meat
7. Boneless ham cutlets
8. Cutlets
9. Spare ribs (breast)

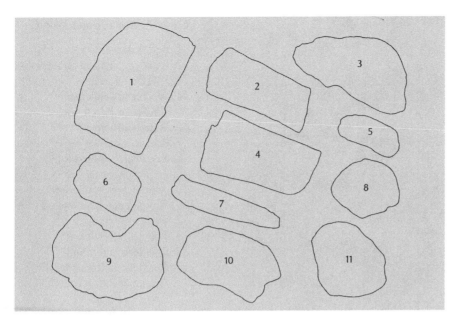

Pork (pages C12–C13)

1. Boneless breast
2. Boneless loin
3. Top round
4. Loin rib
5. Eye of round
6. Butt
7. Tenderloin
8. Boneless ham roast (nut)
9. Boneless shoulder
   (Boston butt)
10. Boneless neck
11. Boneless ham roast

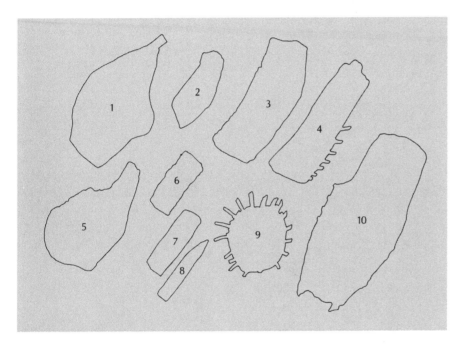

Lamb (pages C14–C15)

1. Leg of lamb
2. Neck
3. Breast
4. Frenched rack of lamb
5. Shoulder
6. Tied boneless loin
7. Boneless loin
8. Tenderloin
9. Crown roast
10. Saddle of lamb

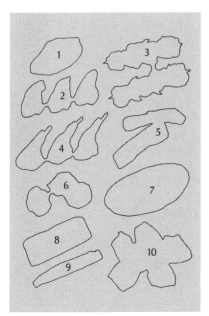

Lamb (page C16)

1. Saddle steak
   (double loin chop)
2. Loin chops
3. Kabobs
4. Rib chops
5. Breast slices
6. Boneless loin
   chops
7. Leg steak
8. Boneless loin
9. Tenderloin
10. Stew meat

Poultry (page C17)

1. Turkey thighs
2. Turkey cutlet
3. Turkey stew meat
4. Duck leg
5. Turkey strips
   (stir-fry)
6. Boneless chicken
   breast cutlet
7. Duck breast
8. Boneless chicken
   breast
9. Chicken tender
10. Guinea fowl leg
11. Chicken drumstick
12. Chicken thigh
13. Guinea fowl
    boneless breast
14. Chicken leg

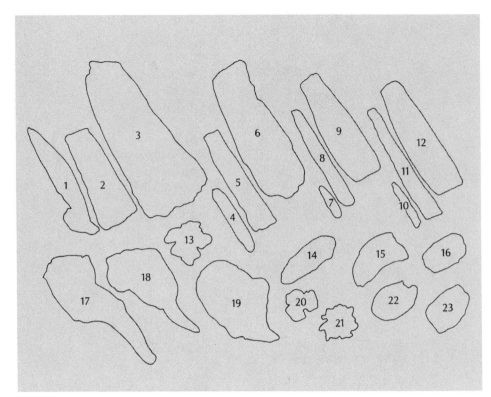

Game Animals (pages C18–C19)

1. Red deer, venison tenderloin
2. Red deer, venison boneless loin
3. Red deer, saddle of venison
4. Wild boar tenderloin
5. Wild boar loin, boneless
6. Wild boar loin
7. Roe deer, tenderloin
8. Roe deer, boneless loin
9. Saddle of roe deer
10. Alpine deer, tenderloin
11. Alpine deer, boneless loin
12. Saddle of alpine deer
13. Roe deer, stew meat
14. Roe deer, top round
15. Roe deer, bottom round
16. Alpine deer, top round
17. Roe deer, shoulder
18. Roe deer shoulder, boneless
19. Roe deer, haunch
20. Roe deer, cutlets
21. Roe deer, stir-fry meat
22. Roe deer, butt roast
23. Alpine deer, butt roast

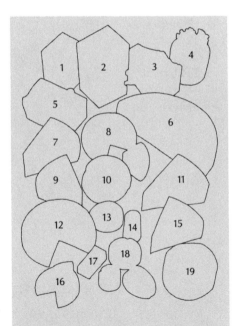

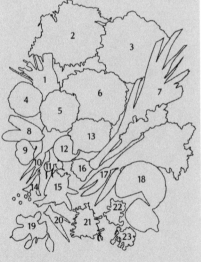

Cheeses (page C20)

1. Gruyère
2. Emmentaler, Swiss
3. Sbrinz
4. Tête de Moine
5. Hobelkäse
6. Raclette cheese
7. Appenzeller
8. Mutschli
9. Tilsiter
10. Swiss camembert
11. Freiburger Vacherin
12. Swiss brie
13. Tomme vaudoise
14. Glarner Schabziger
15. Bündner Bergkäse
16. Reblochon
17. Limburger
18. Formaggini
19. Vacherin Mont d'Or

Vegetables (page C23)

1. Fennel
2. Curly endive
3. Boston lettuce
4. Red cabbage
5. Cauliflower
6. Savoy cabbage
7. Leek
8. Zucchini
9. Garlic
10. White radish
11. Red radish
12. Beets
13. Caulibroc
14. Peas
15. Snow peas
16. Knob celery (celeraic)
17. Carrots
18. Winter squash
19. Spinach
20. Okra
21. Cress
22. Sprouts
23. Radish sprouts

Mushrooms (page C25)

1. Horns of plenty/black trumpets
2. Oyster mushrooms
3. White field mushrooms
4. Cultivated button mushrooms
5. Cèpe/porcini
6. Crimini mushrooms
7. Chanterelle
8. Black truffle
9. White truffle
10. Maronenröhrling
11. Morel

C1

C3

C10

C12

C13

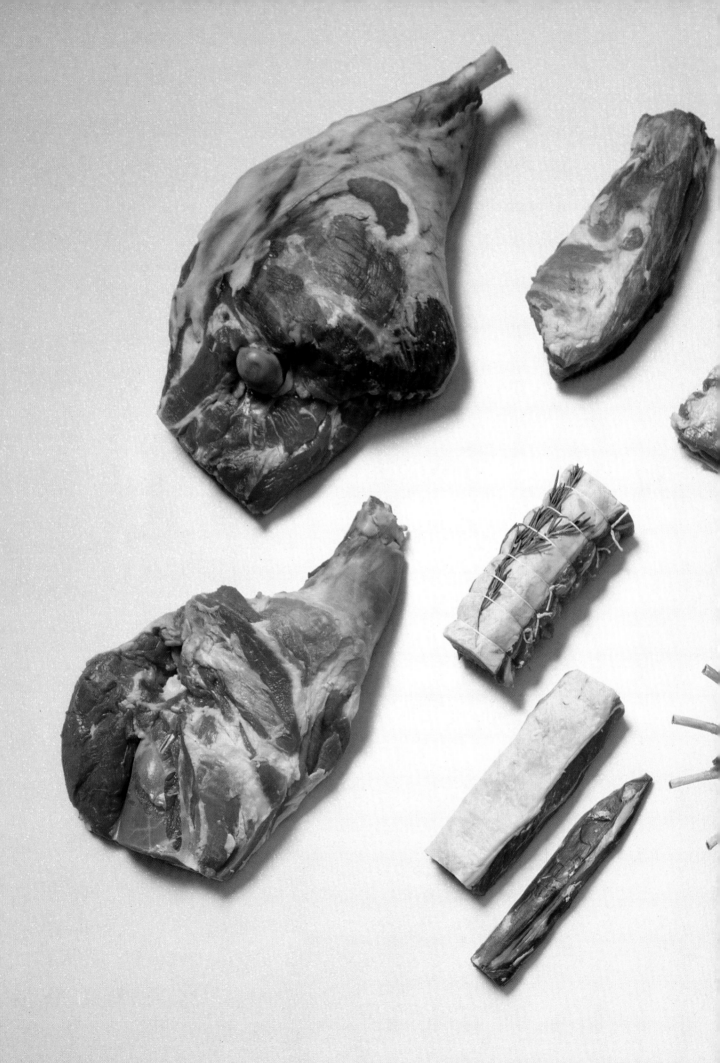

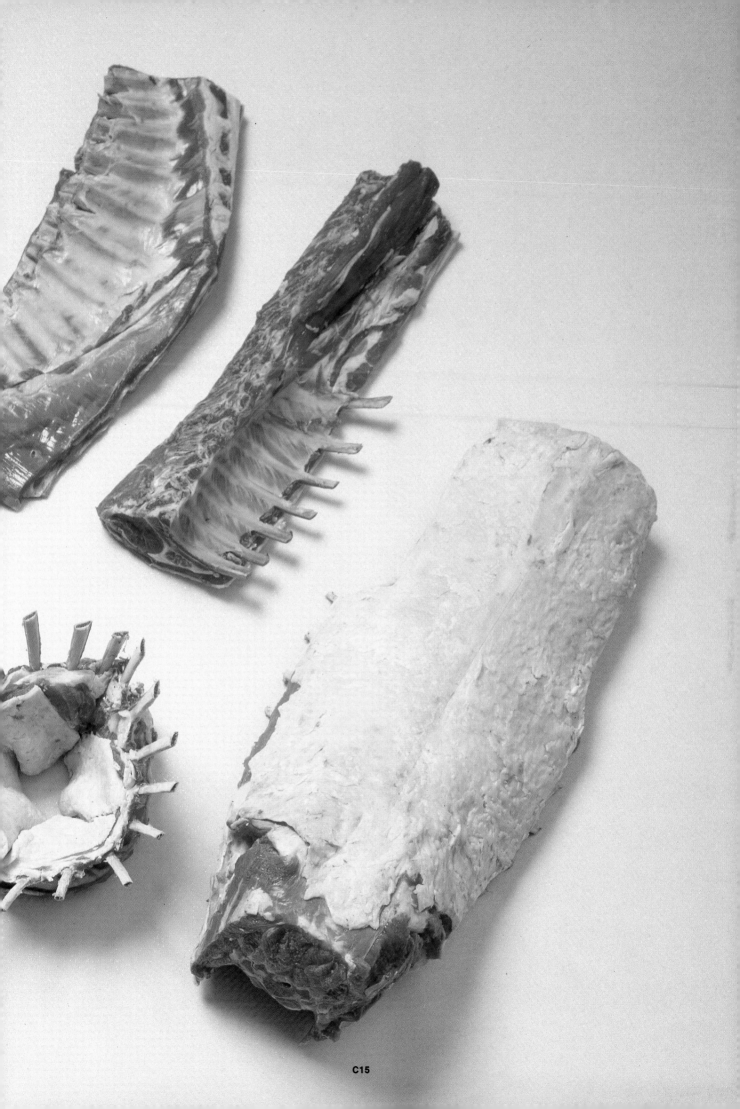

C15

Cheeses

Harzer Käse

Rondena de champagne

Edam

Provolone

Boursin

Taleggio

Cheddar

Gorgonzola

Danish blue

Saint-Paulin

Chavroux frais

Stilton

Mascarpone

Ricotta

Pecorino

Mozzarella

Fontina

Roquefort

Feta

Parmesan

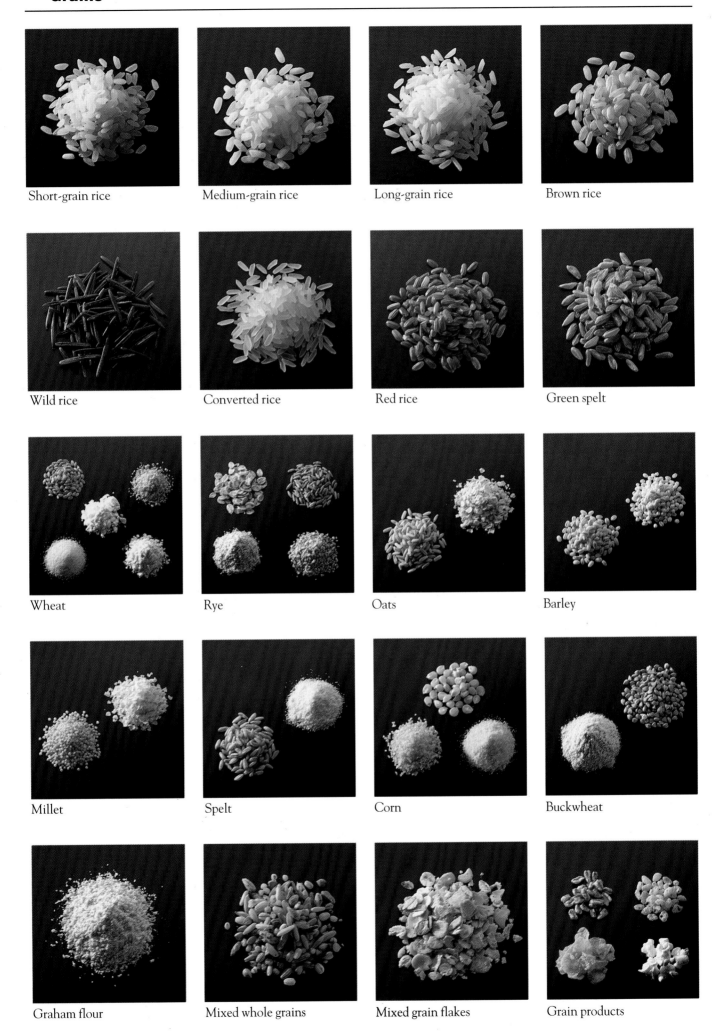

Short-grain rice

Medium-grain rice

Long-grain rice

Brown rice

Wild rice

Converted rice

Red rice

Green spelt

Wheat

Rye

Oats

Barley

Millet

Spelt

Corn

Buckwheat

Graham flour

Mixed whole grains

Mixed grain flakes

Grain products

Bell and chili peppers

Beans

Broccoli

Artichoke

Pattypan squash

Onions and shallots

Cress

Salsify

Leaf lettuce

Eggplant

Romaine lettuce

Sweet corn

Kohlrabi

Melons

Chinese cabbage

Turnips

Radicchio, Belgian endive

Swiss chard

Tomatoes

Cucumbers

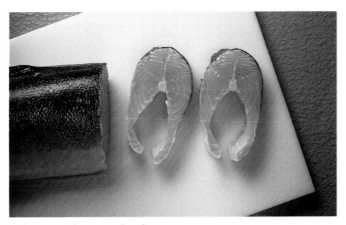

Salmon steaks – *tranches de saumon*

Remove the scales, cut off the fins, and gut and clean whitefish.

Salmon, center cut – *dame de saumon*

Make equidistant diagonal cuts across the body of the whitefish.

Salmon tail piece – *tronçon de saumon*

Make a cut behind a river perch's gills, and remove the fillet with a filleting knife, slicing along the backbone.

Salmon cutlet and salmon scaloppini – *côtelettes et escalopes de saumon*

Remove the skin by starting at the tail end.

Break open the shells of the Norway lobster tails.

Cut the spiny lobster tail (bottom) along both sides with scissors.

Carefully remove the meat.

Release the meat from the shell.

Devein the tail, pulling and removing the black intestinal tract.

Cut along the back (top), and remove the vein.

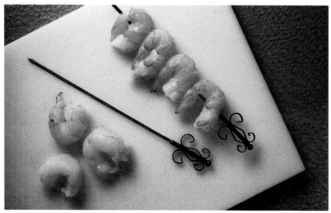

Skewer neatly.

Slice into medallions of equal size.

Tying a boneless pork neck roast

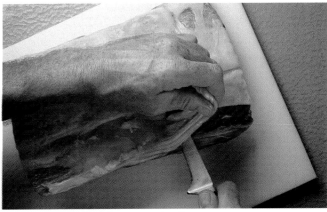

Removing cartilage from roast beef

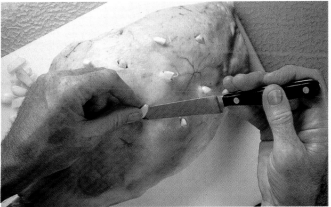

Inserting slit garlic cloves into a leg of lamb

Trimming silver skin of filet of beef

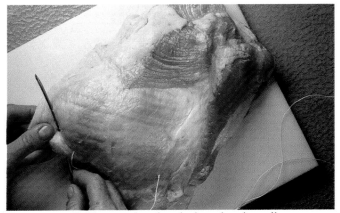

Sewing a stuffed breast of veal with thread and needle

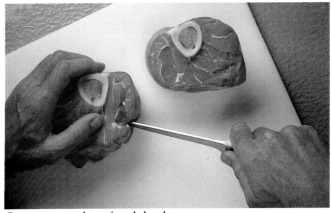

Cutting outer skin of veal shanks

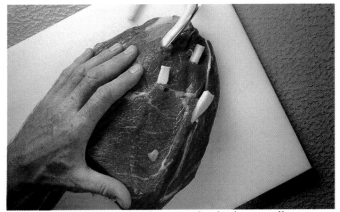

Inserting fatback into a beef roast with a larding needle

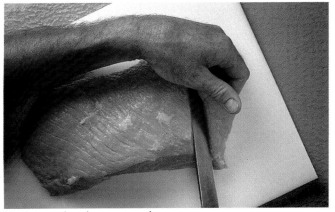

Cutting veal cutlets against the grain

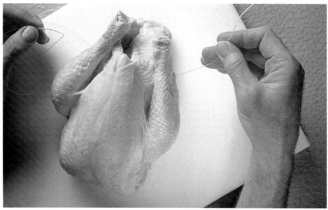

To roast: Truss the chicken. Place thread under the chicken.

To sauté: Cut off the chicken legs.

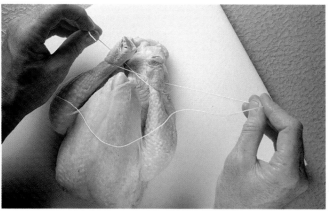

Cross the thread over the tucked legs.

Remove the breast meat from the carcass.

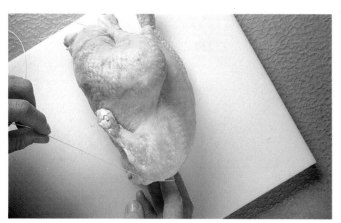

Place the chicken on its side, and bring the thread across the neck end.

Separate the drumstick from the thigh at the joint. Cut breasts in two pieces.

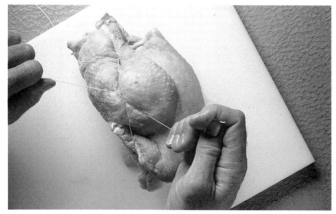

Tie firmly along the side, and make a knot.

A properly cut chicken, ready to be sautéed.

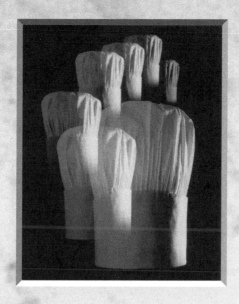

The Menu

Chapter Contents

5.1 History of the Culinary Arts

To understand classical culinary history, one must consider the culinary arts as they relate to important cultural eras of western civilization. None of the arts — architecture, literature, music, or the fine arts — can be fully appreciated without understanding the spirit of the age in which they were created. The same holds true for the culinary arts. The important events of an era are reflected in its food and culinary preferences.

5.1.1 Historical Developments

The important eras of European culture are shown in Table 5-1.

Antiquity
800 b.c. to a.d. 400
Food and eating were primarily for survival during this era. However, over time, they evolved to encompass eating for pleasure.

Ancient Greece (800 B.C. to A.D. 30) was the foundation of European and western civilization. To this day our thought processes, procedures, and creativity are modeled on and influenced by some of the principles the Greeks formulated as early as 600 B.C.

The renowned Greek teacher and physician *Hippocrates* (c. 460–377 B.C.) was an early promoter of a healthy diet. He understood the importance of proper food consumption to optimal health.

The ancient Romans (753 B.C. to A.D. 476) spread knowledge about the arts, including cooking styles. They learned from the Greek masters as they expanded their empire over most of Europe, north Africa, and the Middle East to the Red Sea and the Persian Gulf. Large, prosperous centers of commerce blossomed in the Middle East, which the Romans called the Orient. In addition to gold and silk, foodstuffs and spices played an important role in the marketplace.

The Middle Ages
5th to 15th Centuries
As the western world moved into the Dark Ages, little exploration took place and no culinary knowledge was gained. Only the monks and nuns in the cloisters preserved and passed on the culinary knowledge of the Romans, along with other treasures of previous centuries. Monks not only saved old manuscripts, they also copied and preserved recipes and cultivated the culinary arts.

By the end of the fifteenth century, however, Europeans once again had begun to develope a taste for delicacies and exotic foods. No new or significant culinary influence had reached most of Europe since Roman times. The marauding northern tribes contributed little to culinary knowledge.

The Italians, however, had explored the Orient as early as the thirteenth century. Various Italian principalities became wealthy merchant states, where culinary skills were constantly refined. They developed the first real western cuisine.

The Renaissance
16th and 17th Centuries
By 1500, a renaissance in learning and culture had begun to blossom and spread from Italy to all of Europe. In Florence, inquiry and experimentation flourished in an atmosphere of enlightenment. From Florence also came the culinary impulses that would exert a strong influence on later French cuisine. Catherine de Médicis (1519–1589) married the Duke of Orleans, later Henry II of France, and brought to the French court many of her Florentine cooks and pastry chefs.

In 1651 *Pierre de la Varenne* published *Le Cuisinier français*, which clearly recorded the changes that had taken place in French cuisine since the Middle Ages.

Baroque and Rococo
17th and 18th Centuries
French cuisine reached its first zenith during the reign of Louis XV (1710–1774). Chefs and master cooks worked in royal households and the homes of the nobility and wrote cookbooks that recorded their skills and recipes. Many newly invented recipes were named after famous people. The list of recipes dedicated to the "greats" of the time is endless. The best French chefs were recruited to work in royal palaces and the kitchens of the nobility all over Europe in the seventeenth and eighteenth centuries. They became the ambassadors of the classical French cuisine. Thanks to their records, we still know the famous chefs and "literary gourmets" of the time.

Industrial Revolution
Late 18th, 19th, and early 20th Centuries
The Industrial Revolution was a turning point that brought great changes to western civilization. Science and technology advanced significantly, as did travel and tourism. The first elegant restaurants had already been opened in Paris and other large cities by 1765, introducing the *haute cuisine* of the

Table 5-1. The Eras of European Culture

Antiquity	800 B.C. to A.D. 400
Middle Ages	5th to 15th centuries
Renaissance	16th and 17th centuries
Baroque and Rococo	17th and 18th centuries
Industrial Revolution	late 18th and 19th centuries
Modern	20th century

nobility to the wealthy bourgeoisie. As was true in all the arts, a few outstanding professionals dominated their contemporaries and introduced new concepts in the culinary arts. They were *Marie-Antoine Carême* and *Auguste Escoffier*. Escoffier's *Le Guide culinaire, the* reference book of classical cuisine, is the foundation for food preparation even today.

Modern Times

Late 20th century

A change in lifestyles has brought a change in eating habits. At the same time, modern communication and transportation has made seemingly distant cultures more accessible.

Examples of culinary changes in our time are *nouvelle cuisine* and *cuisine naturelle* (natural cooking), which have introduced changes in menu offerings and preparation methods.

The modern kitchen is based on classical cuisine but incorporates the newest nutritional information along with customers' preferences.

Development of Swiss Cuisine

As in Italy, so too in Switzerland, the culinary arts first were developed in the churches and cloisters, especially the cloister of St. Gallen, which took the lead in promoting the culinary arts that slowly found their way into the family home. The recipes passed down through generations appear on today's menus as favorite Swiss regional specialties. The many varied dishes reflect the diversity of Swiss customs and places.

The development of Swiss cuisine has been heavily influenced by its neighboring countries: in the east, Austria; in the north, the German state Baden-Württemberg; in the west, Alsace-Lorraine; and in the south, the Italian regions of Lombardy and Veltlin.

Swiss cuisine is based on classical cuisine, emphasizing food preparation and presentation that pleases the eye and the palate.

5.1.2 Important Individuals and Events

Both historical events and exceptionally skilled chefs shaped the culinary arts. Individual chefs recorded their knowledge in books and other publications and often showed off their talent in culinary salons.

Individuals

Marie-Antoine Carême (1784–1833)

A famous French chef, cook to princes and kings, Carême was the author of many well-known books about French cuisine. He recorded the French culinary trends of his time, which reached their peak in elaborate, ornate architectural and pictorial food presentations (*pièces montées*). Though these excessive presentations are dated, Carême left behind much valuable culinary knowledge, for example, his most famous book, *L'art de la cuisine française au XIXe siècle, 1833.*

Urbain Dubois (1818–1901)

The prolific Dubois wrote numerous books on cooking, including *La Cuisine de tous les pays* (1868) and *La Cuisine artistique* (1872). In 1856, with Emile Bernard, he published *La Cuisine classique*, a book that even today is famous and often used.

Auguste Escoffier (1847–1935)

Escoffier worked as a chef in Paris and in many luxury hotels in Europe, especially in London. His greatest accomplishment is his book *Le Guide culinaire*, in which he revised French cuisine and defined its principles, which today form the basis for classic French cuisine.

Escoffier based his work on the principles of the old classic French cuisine, but eliminated all the gauche excesses and, remarkably, included many international specialties. He is the founder of International Cuisine, which is today the basis of modern French cooking. Carême was the cook of kings, but Escoffier was the king of cooks.

Paul Bocuse (1926–)

Bocuse is considered the ambassador of modern French cuisine. He was honored in 1961 with the title *Meilleur ouvrier de France*. His father, George Bocuse, had been apprenticed to Fernand Point, a master of classic French cuisine, and Bocuse dedicated his first book to him.

In his restaurant near Lyons, Bocuse celebrates the cooking style *nouvelle cuisine*. His first cookbook, *Cuisine du marché*, has been translated into many languages. He stresses using seasonal fresh ingredients, last-minute preparation, and interesting new food compositions. Paul Bocuse is considered to be the first chef to embrace *nouvelle cuisine*.

Events

International Cooking Contests

Over the last hundred years, many countries have conducted regional and international cooking contests, with the goal of promoting the culinary arts and introducing them to a wider public. Even very small establishments can be exposed to and adapt new ideas.

Historical Events

Many historic events are permanently immortalized in the culinary arts, because dishes were named in honor of the event or a person associated with it. Indeed, some statesmen are more famous because of a dish named for them than because of their political exploits. Many famous musicians, poets, inventors, and others also have dishes named after them.

The culinary museums of such cities as Thun (Switzerland), Villeneuve-Loubet (France), and Frankfurt (Germany), contain much information about the history of the culinary arts.

5.2 Menu Planning

The menu is a planned order of courses in which the various dishes harmonize with each other. A menu is generally offered at a fixed price.

Function of the Menu

The printed menu for a specific meal period is an advertisement for the institution and is a symbol of quality for the guests. The meal plan is communicated to the guest through the menu.

A good menu not only pleases the eye and the palate but also reflects current nutritional knowledge.

An intimate knowledge and understanding of the individual establishment are important in planning a professionally accurate menu. Menu planning requires an extensive knowledge of foods and their preparation methods and an enjoyment of good food. It includes an understanding of

- ingredients
- basic preparation methods
- the institution
- cost calculations
- nutrition
- menu structure and writing (style and spelling)

Basic Rules in Menu Planning

Before the menu can be written, it is important to have the following information available:

1. Standardized recipes

2. Accurate cost calculations

3. Market analysis

When planning a menu, the following factors must be considered:

4. Type of establishment and personnel skills

5. Season and climate

6. Customer expectations

7. Up-to-date nutrition information

8. Variety

Menu preparation should include attention to:

9. Menu terminology (correctly written, no spelling errors)

10. Accurate descriptions and truth in advertising

1. Standardized Recipes
Standardized recipes are the basis for good menu planning. They guarantee consistent quality, accurate portion control and food cost calculations, and proper purchasing.

2. Accurate Cost Calculations
Accurate menu pricing is the most important factor in the success of a hospitality organization. Price, based on consumer demographics, is the starting point in financial calculations. Pricing also depends on such factors as type of establishment and targeted customer base.

Menu prices must be based on accurately calculated food costs of standardized recipes. Constant pre- and post-sales calculations are essential for good cost control.

Inventory, especially perishable foodstuffs, should be considered, as should delivery schedules and availability of ingredients. Maximum use of leftover foods, with minimum waste, contributes to lower food costs.

3. Market Analysis
Conducting frequent market surveys will measure customer satisfaction and track menu trends and customer preferences.

4. Type of Establishment and Employee Skills
The menu is influenced by the type of establishment and the skills of its employees. Considerations include:

- Type of establishment (four-star restaurant, ethnic restaurant, urban restaurant, cafeteria, etc.)
- Physical facilities (production and service space) and equipment
- Number of available employees and their culinary and service skills

- Balanced distribution of work among employees and equipment

5. Season and Climate
Excellent transportation and storage systems and modern preparation methods make it possible to have most food items year-round. Still, foods in season should be considered in menu planning. Many guests prefer a menu that reflects the seasons for economic, ecological, and health reasons. For example, in hot weather, light, cold dishes are preferred; when the weather is cool, hearty, warm dishes are welcome.

Important rule for the menu planner: Always be informed about specials offered by the supplier. A thorough knowledge of the market will make it easy to have a seasonal menu plan.

6. Customer Expectations
The wishes and expectations of the customer should be foremost in menu planning. This is especially true when menus are planned for festive occasions. The following factors should be considered:

- Age of guests
- Origin, nationality, and religion
- Social class
- Occasion

Children must be considered! Children are the customers of the future! It is therefore imperative to plan menus with children in mind.

7. Nutrition
The nutrition-conscious guest demands a varied, healthy, nutritionally sound menu. The quality of the food is more important than the quantity. To fulfill these expectations, the following points should be considered:

- Many fresh products should be used. Especially important are fresh vegetables, green salads, fruits, and fruit juices.
- High-fiber products should be included.

- Nutrient-saving preparation methods are preferable (such as poaching, steaming, braising, and grilling).
- Caloric content of meals should reflect customers' preference.
- Attention should be given to balance nutrients in the meal.
- Knowledge about nutrition should be applied in menu planning and food preparation (see Chapter 3).

8. Variety

The most important principle in menu planning is variety. Each course of the menu must differ in its composition from the other courses. Attention should be paid to:

- Ingredients
- Methods of preparation
- Shape and color of foods
- Taste
- Food presentation

Repetition of a previous day's menu should absolutely be avoided.

9. Menu Design and Text

The printed menu should contain:

- Accurate name and address of the establishment
- Date
- Description of meals offered (e.g. lunch, dinner)
- Price, if appropriate

10. Accuracy and Truth in Advertising

The menu must accurately describe and present all the relevant information a guest needs to evaluate the foods offered.

Swiss food laws protect the guest from false advertising and misleading information. This is especially important if the customer cannot easily verify if the food information offered is accurate.

An important facet of menu writing is the inclusion of detailed, accurate ingredient information. For example, it is not enough to write "Breaded Cutlet (*escalope*)"; the accurate menu description must read "Breaded Turkey Cutlet (*escalope*)."

Menu Planning

Menus are planned for specific time periods (cycles). Planning menus in this manner makes purchasing, *mise en place*, food preparation, and personnel planning more effective. Cycle menu planning allows for greater variety and avoids repetition.

Special banquets can be included in regular menu planning. For example, certain soups, appetizers, main dishes, and desserts from the regular menu can be offered on the banquet menu.

Menu-planning aids include: supplier offers and price lists, recipe files, menu collections, culinary texts, guest surveys and comments, and demographic statistics.

5.3   Meal Composition (Framework of the Menu)

5.3.1 Classical Meal Composition

The classical menu composition has its origin around 1650 at the courts of the aristocracy and in the cloisters. Great wealth gave cause for lavish feasts. In the classical cuisine of the eighteenth and nineteenth centuries dishes were grouped and presented together similar to menus (*table*), and, depending on the festive occasion, several would be offered consecutively. The classical menu composition evolved at the end of the nineteenth century. It typically had as many as thirteen courses, as shown in Table 5-2.

The menu shown here, with thirteen courses, has only nostalgic value. It could not be defended today from either an economic or a nutritional point of view. However, such a classic menu can serve as a guide for combining dishes on much shorter menus.

Cold Appetizer – KALTE VORSPEISE – *hors-d'œuvre froid*
Cold small dishes, light and wholesome compositions, are presented in an appetizing fashion. They should harmonize with the rest of the menu items.

If a cold appetizer is part of a menu, it should always be the first course.

Soup – SUPPE – *potage*
Soup is very often served at the beginning of a meal. Soup is often replaced with a fruit juice, cold fruit soup, vegetable juice, or a tossed salad.

Warm Appetizer – WARME VORSPEISE – *hors-d'œuvre chaud*
A hot appetizer is always served after the soup. The size of the appetizer should take into consideration the number of courses offered on the menu.

Fish – FISCH – *poisson*
All kinds of warm fish and seafood dishes are possible.

Main Course – HAUPTPLATTE – *grosse pièce/relevé*
Large roasts that are either carved in front of the guests or carved in the kitchen are presented on a large platter. The platter is usually presented with a classic garnish that names the dish.

Warm Entrée – WARMES ZWISCHEN-GERICHT – *entrée chaude*
This course consists of pieces of meat that have been sliced and portioned before preparation. They are usually served with a small side dish.

Table 5-2. Courses in a Complete Menu

1. Cold appetizer	KALTE VORSPEISE	*Hors-d'œuvre froid*
2. Soup	SUPPE	*Potage*
3. Warm appetizer	WARME VORSPEISE	*Hors-d'œuvre chaud*
4. Fish	FISCH	*Poisson*
5. Main course *Cooked whole then cut* HAUPTPLATTE		*Grosse pièce/relevé*
6. Warm entrée *Cut then sliced* WARMES ZWISCHENGERICHT		*Entrée chaude*
7. Cold entrée	KALTES ZWISCHENGERICHT	*Entrée froide*
8. Sherbet	SORBET	*Sorbet*
9. Roast with salad	BRATEN MIT SALAT	*Rôti avec salade*
10. Vegetable	GEMÜSE	*Légumes*
11. Sweets or dessert	SÜSSPEISE oder NACHTISCH	*Entremets ou dessert*
12. Savory	WÜRZBISSEN	*Savoury*
13. Dessert or sweets	NACHTISCH oder SÜSSPEISE	*Dessert ou entremets*

Oysters on ice
Huîtres sur glace
***
Double consommé
Consommé double
***
Potato gnocchi
Gnocchi piémontaise
***
Monkfish medallions on broccoli cream sauce
Médaillons de baudroie sur crème de brocoli
***
Roast beef with Yorkshire pudding
Roastbeef Yorkshire
***
Grilled veal kidney slices
Tranches de rognons de veau dijonnaise
***
Ham mousse with green asparagus
Mousse de jambon aux asperges vertes
***
Champagne sherbet
Sorbet de champagne
***
Butter-roasted pullet with morels
Bean-sprout salad
Poularde poêlée aux morilles
Salade de germes de soja
***
Stuffed, braised romaine
Laitue farcie
***
Camembert with rye bread
Camembert et pain de seigle
***
Blinis with caviar
Blinis au caviar
***
Figs with crème de cassis
Figues à la crème de cassis

Cold Entrée – KALTES ZWISCHENGERICHT – *entrée froide*

Cold dishes made from meat, poultry, game, fish and seafood, including aspics, galantines, pâtés, terrines, and mousse, constitute this course.

Today it is customary to serve such dishes as cold appetizers or as a cold main dish at a banquet.

Sherbet – SORBET – *sorbet*

Sherbets are served as a refresher or digestive during a menu with several courses. Granités, spooms (frothy sherbets with double amounts of Italian meringue), and similar concoctions are used for the same purpose.

The modern menu generally offers such items for dessert.

Roast with Salad – BRATEN MIT SALAT – *rôti avec salade*

Meats that are oven- or spit-roasted are offered with a simple salad for this course.

Vegetables – GEMÜSE – *légumes*

Vegetables of extraordinary quality are sometimes offered as a separate course, as are special vegetable dishes.

Sweets – SÜSSPEISE – *entremets*

All warm, cold, or frozen sweets, usually prepared in-house, make up this course. In the United States, it is generally considered dessert.

Savory – WÜRZBISSEN – *savoury*

This comprises highly flavored, small, warm dishes, for example, cheese pastries. Savories are popular with cocktails and as a snack.

Dessert – NACHTISCH – *dessert*

The classic ending of a meal includes:

- Cheese
- Fruits
- Dainty pastries
- Chocolates

All of these, except cheese, are offered after a sweet dessert has been served. Cheese is offered before a sweet dessert.

Dainty pastries (*petit fours*) and chocolates are now frequently served with coffee.

5.3.2 Modern Meal Composition

The more tempered eating habits of today and the busy life-style of today's customer requires a shorter modern menu.

The central focus of today's menu is the main course, which may be complemented by additional courses.

Today's menu features:

- Generally three to six courses
- Nutritional balance
- Smaller portions
- Service on plates

Table 5-3 demonstrates how the classic menu has been condensed to meet today's needs.

Table 5-3. Selection and Arrangement of Courses from the ClassicMenu

Modern Menu	Classic Menu
Cold appetizer	Cold appetizer
	Cold course
Soup	Soup
Warm Appetizer	Warm appetizer
	Fish
	Warm entrée
	Vegetable
	Savory
Main course	Fish
	Main course
	Warm entrée
	Cold entrée
	Roast with salad
	Vegetable
Sweets/Dessert	Sorbet
	Sweets/desserts
	Cheese, fruit, dainty pastries, chocolates

Menu Examples

GRIESS-SUPPE
Semolina soup with sorrel
Potage Léopold
***
Shredded veal, Zurich style
GESCHNETZELTES KALBFLEISCH ZÜRCHER ART
Emincé de veau zurichoise
Rösti potato cakes
RÖSTI
Rœsti
Seasonal Salad
SAISONSALAT
Salade de saison
***
Chocolate mousse
SCHOKOLADENMOUSSE
Mousse au chocolat

Seasonal salad with chicken livers
SAISONSALAT mit GEFLÜGELLEBER
Salade de saison au foie de volaille
***
Morel consommé with tapioca
MORCHELKRAFTBRÜHE mit TAPIOKA
Essence de morilles au tapioca
***
Poached fillet of sole with tomato
POCHIERTES SEEZUNGENFILET mit TOMATE
Filet de sole Dugléré
***
Rare roast beef
ROASTBEEF
Roastbeef Anglaise
Oven-roasted potatoes
BRATKARTOFFELN
Pommes rissolées
Vegetable garnish
GEMÜSEGARNITUR
Garniture de légumes
***
Fruit sherbet
FRÜCHTESORBET
Sorbet aux fruits

Smoked salmon roll
RÄUCHERLACHSROULADE
Roulade de saumon fumé
***
Chicken consommé with small dumplings
GEFLÜGELKRAFTBRÜHE DEMIDOW
Consommé Demidov
***
Butter-roasted filet of veal
POELIERTES KALBSFILET
Filet mignon de veau poêlé
Morel cream sauce
MORCHELRAHMSAUCE
Sauce aux morilles
Home-made noodles
HAUSGEMACHTE NUDELN
Nouilles maison
Broccoli with almonds
BROCCOLI mit MANDELN
Brocoli aux amandes
Boston lettuce
KOPFSALAT
Salade de laitue pomée
***
Cold sabayon
KALTE WEINSCHAUMSAUCE
Sabayon frappé

5.4   Types of Meals and Menus

The classic menu has changed not only in composition but also in the order of presentation. However, tradition still has a role in the way menus are planned and written. The types of meals and their importance vary from country to country. The life-styles and customs of international guests have affected how meals are served in Switzerland. Table 5-4 is an overview of the different types of meals and shows how they can be coordinated.

5.4.1   Types of Meals

Breakfast – FRÜHSTÜCK – *petit déjeuner*

Breakfast is the first meal of the day. It varies widely, depending on eating habits and nationality. The most distinctive difference in breakfast habits is between those of Great Britain and the United States and those of most continental European countries. The English and Americans enjoy a large breakfast, in the manner of a full meal, whereas the French and Italians have a very small breakfast. Asian and African countries, of course, have widely varying breakfast traditions.

Four types of breakfast have become the norm in the international hospitality industry.

Continental Breakfast

This is the most common breakfast on the European continent and is known in Switzerland as *Schweizer Frühstück, Swiss Zmorge, Petit déjeuner,* or *Complet.* It consists of the following:

Beverages: Fruit juices, coffee, café latte (coffee with hot milk), tea, hot chocolate, milk

Breads: A large variety of regional bread specialties, crispy rolls, croissants, zwieback, and toast

Butter: Butter and margarine, in portioned packages

Jams: Several varieties, in portioned packages or in bowls, often with honey

Miscellaneous: Soft-cooked eggs, cheese, cold cuts, and müesli

American or English Breakfast

This breakfast is often preferred by American and English guests, who like to start the day with a substantial meal. In addition to the continental breakfast items, the following foods are offered:

Fresh fruit: Grapefruits, apples, pears, bananas, oranges, etc.

Fruit juices: Orange, grapefruit, mango, etc.

Jams: Orange marmalade

Fruit compote: Prunes, apricots, pears, peaches, etc.

Cereals: Several varieties, including corn flakes and porridge

Egg dishes: Fried eggs, omelets, scrambled eggs with bacon or ham, poached eggs, etc.

Meat: Usually cold items, such as roast beef, sliced roasted meats, cold cuts, ham, salami, but also hot dishes such as pork links, ham slices, lamb chops, veal kidneys, etc.

Fish: Haddock, smoked salmon

Dairy products: Yogurt, cottage cheese, kefir, cream cheese, and other cheese varieties

Table 5-4. Overview of Meals

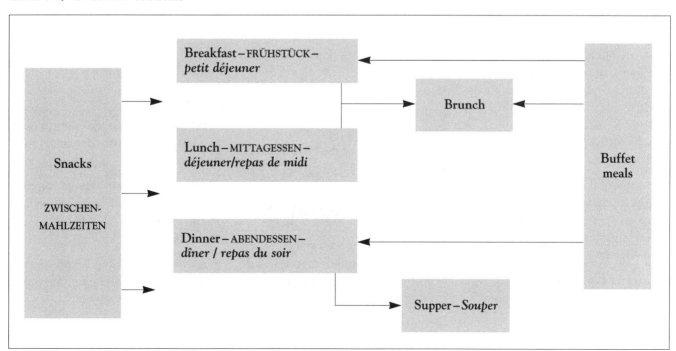

Table 5-5. Types of Menus

Traveler's Lunch	AUTO-LUNCH	*Auto-lunch*
Fast-food Menu	QUICK-LUNCH	*Quick-lunch*
Business Lunch	BUSINESS-LUNCH	*Business-lunch*
Gala Menu	GALAMENÜ	*Menu de gala*
Children's Menu	KINDERMENÜ	*Menu d'enfant*
Senior Citizen Menu	SENIORENMENÜ	*Menu de l'aîné*
Fasting Menu	FASTENMENÜ	*Menu maigre*
Vegetarian Menu	VEGETARISCHESMENÜ	*Menu végétalien et végétarien*
Spa/Whole-food Menu	VOLLWERTKOSTMENÜ	*Menu d'aliments complets*
Low-calorie Menu	ENERGIEARMESMENÜ	*Menu pauvre en énergie*
Therapeutic Diet Menu	DIÄTMENÜ	*Menu régime ou diététique*
Specialty Menu	SPEZIALMENÜ	*Menu spécial*
• Game Menu	JAGDMENÜ	*Menu de la chasse*
• Fish Menu	FISCHMENÜ	*Menu de pêcheur*
• Menu for Men	HERRENMENÜ	*Menu des messiers*
• Menu for Women	DAMENMENÜ	*Menu des dames*
Staff Menu	PERSONALMENÜ	*Menu pour le personnel*
Banquet Menu	BANKETTMENÜ	*Menu de banquet*

The Breakfast Buffet

The breakfast buffet, because of the large variety of items offered, is very similar to the American breakfast. The basic difference is in the style of service. The guests serve themselves; only hot beverages are served by wait staff.

Brunch

Brunch is a combination of *breakfast* and *lunch*. Brunch is in principle an expanded breakfast buffet. It could also be called a late breakfast or an early lunch. As a meal, brunch is becoming increasingly popular. The newly formed name combination is reflected in the variety of dishes offered from both meals. In addition to the basic breakfast buffet, various salads are offered, along with clear or cold soups, smoked fish, meat dishes, egg dishes, cakes, tarts, and cream desserts.

Lunch – MITTAGESSEN – *déjeuner*

In continental Europe, lunch is usually the main meal of the day. Lunch today is generally composed of lighter, simpler dishes and contains three courses:

Soup (often replaced with fruit or vegetable juice, salad, or an appetizer)

Main dish *plus*
Starch accompaniment *plus*

Vegetable or green salad
Dessert or sweets

Dinner – ABENDESSEN – *dîner/repas du soir*

In restaurants, including those in Europe, dinner is the main meal of the day, especially in seasonal establishments and in hotels offering meal plans. This practice is not consistent with today's nutritional knowledge, which cautions against causing stress on the digestive system with a late heavy meal. This should be considered when planning the dinner menu.

A dinner is usually composed of three to five courses:

Cold appetizer or salad
Soup
Warm appetizer or fish
Main dish *plus*
Starch accompaniment *plus*
Vegetable and/or green salad *plus*
Dessert or sweets

5.4.2 Types of Menus

In addition to professional considerations, the planned menu should reflect locale, time constraints, and guest preferences.

Menu types are classified in the following ways (see also Table 5-5).

Travelers' Lunch

Principle: Light, simple meals, which should not interfere with alertness or stress the digestive system.

Composition: The menu should consist of two or three courses.

• No gas-causing foods
• Low-fat dishes
• Nonspicy foods
• No alcoholic beverages or dishes containing alcohol
• Caloric content, including beverages, should not exceed 905 cal (3,800 kJ)

Application: This type of menu is suitable for highway rest stops and restaurants near major roads and those for and resorts, train stations, and airports.

Fast-food Menu

Principle: To provide appropriate food in a very short time at reasonable prices.

Composition: Plate service supplemented with soup, juice, or salad. Menu items can be quickly served and eaten.

Application: Food stands, self-service cafeterias, lunch restaurants, and fast-food establishments.

Business Lunch

Principle: Meals for businesspeople and their guests, who combine lunch with business discussions.

Composition: The menu is composed of three to four courses. It should include light, easily digested meals, with carefully prepared specialty dishes in a higher price range. Small portions, attractively presented, will be especially appreciated.

Application: Restaurants in the city or near commercial centers, with good food and good service.

Gala Menu (festive menu)

Principle: For special gala menus to honor an extraordinary occasion, dishes and foods should *not* be ordi-nary. Room decorations, music, and other special activities should underscore the festive nature of the event.

Composition: More courses than are commonly on the menu should be offered; at least four courses are rec-ommended. They should include:

• The best ingredients
• Exquisite specialties
• Light dishes

Application: Gala menus would be appropriate for:

• Family celebrations, such as bap-tisms, birthdays, and weddings
• Workplace celebrations such as anniversaries and promotions
• Holidays such as Christmas, New Year, Easter

Children's Menu

Principle: Children are important guests with special wishes who should not be ignored for reasons of profitability. Desserts should always be included on the children's menu.

Composition: Special attention should be given to simple ingredi-ents.

Favorite dishes are:

• Clear soups with garnishes
• Breaded cutlets, hamburgers
• Noodles, mashed potatoes, French fries
• Carrots
• Ice cream, pudding, other desserts

Unpopular are:

• Variety meats

Dîner de Noël
Christmas Dinner

Cocktail de melon au vin doux
Melon cocktail with sweet wine
***
Crème de morilles aux dés d'artichauts
Morel cream with diced artichokes
***
Filet de sandre sous croûte de grains de sésame et herbes fraîche
Fillet of pike perch in a crust of sesame seeds and fresh herbs
***
Aiguilettes de suprême de dinde poêlées
Butter-roasted strips of turkey breast
Jus de dinde au xérès
Turkey jus with sherry
Quartiers de pommes caramelisés
Caramelized apple quarters
Nouilles de pommes de terre au beurre
Potato noodles with butter
Choux de Bruxelles à la crème double
Brussels sprouts with double cream
***
Stilton cheese
Biscuits de grain complet
Whole-grain crackers
Gratin de myrtilles
Gratin of blueberries
Friandises
Small confections

Dîner de gala de Saint-Sylvestre
New Year's Eve Gala Dinner

Terrine de pintade au ris de veau et morilles
Terrine of guinea fowl with veal sweetbreads and morels
Sauce aux églantines
Sauce flavored with wild rose petals
Salade de céleri en branches et pommes à la sauce de séré
Celery salad with apples and fresh white cheese sauce
***
Elixir de queue de bœuf au vieux cognac
Clear oxtail soup with aged cognac
***
Pavé de suprême de sole sur feuilles d'épinards
Squares of sole with leaf spinach
***
Sorbet de champagne aux fines feuilles de menthe
Champagne sherbet with fresh mint leaves
***
Médaillons de filet de veau sauté au caviar
Veal medallions sautéed with caviar
Tartelette aux petits pois et concombres glacés
Tartlets with tiny peas and glazed cucumbers
***
Saint-Albray
Semi-soft cheese
Pain de seigle
Dark rye bread
***
Petite timbale de bavarois
Small timbales of Bavarian cream
Sauce de framboises à la crème
Raspberry Cream Sauce
Friandises et pralinés
Small confections and chocolates

- Rare meat
- Lamb and game
- Dishes that are difficult to eat, for example, whole fish, shellfish and crustaceans, meat with bones
- Very spicy dishes
- Dishes containing alcohol

Application: Especially family hotels, resort restaurants, and restaurants catering to families.

Senior Citizen Menu

Principle: Older people prefer familiar and regional dishes. These should be nutritionally adjusted for their life-style.

Composition: Small menus (three courses), with soup as a first course.

- Small portions
- Easily digested dishes
- No gas-causing foods
- Foods that are easy to eat (soft cooked foods, no bones in meat or fish)

Application: All restaurants with older clients.

Fasting Menu

Certain religious groups maintain strict dietary laws, including Muslims, Hindus, and Jews (kosher). Catholics observe fast days (Ash Wednesday, Good Friday), during which the consumption of animal flesh—meat, poultry, game—is prohibited. However, the consumption of fish, some water fowl, foods from plants, eggs, and dairy products is allowed.

Principle: A fasting menu generally consists of three courses.

Vegetarian Menu

Vegetarian menus are becoming increasingly popular. People choose a vegetarian (meatless) diet for various reasons. Even those who generally eat a regular diet enjoy an occasional vegetarian menu and choose it as a change of pace. Many guests especially enjoy the large variety of plant-based foods.

Because guests choose a vegetarian diet for many reasons, the vegetarian diet has several variations.

Composition: Vegan diets include *only* foods from plants. *Lacto-vegetarian* diets include plant foods and dairy products. *Ovo-vegetarian* diets allow plant foods and eggs. *Lacto-ovo vegetarian* diets include plant foods, dairy products, and eggs.

Whole-Food Menu

Principle: Primarily a lacto-ovo vegetarian diet.

Basic Requirements:

- Ingredients should be procured from controlled organic farms (seasonal).
- Preparation methods should conserve nutrients. This diet includes large amounts of raw foods and uses cold-pressed oils, whole grains, and whole-grain products.
- Highly processed foods, such as sugar, white flours, and junk food should be limited or omitted.
- The menu should include fewer protein and fatty foods, more high-fiber foods

Low-calorie Menu

Principle: The caloric content of all items on the menu is provided. Low- calorie menus are designed to maintain the normal body weight or to reduce it. To reduce body weight, one must eat fewer calories than are needed for energy. The demand for lower-calorie dishes and menus is increasing because more guests are weight- and nutrition-conscious.

A complete low-calorie menu with beverages should not exceed 690 cal (2,900 kJ).

By omitting any course on the low-calorie menu, the guests can further control their individual caloric intake.

Composition: High-fiber ingredients give a greater sense of satiety.

Application: This menu is especially useful in hospitals, spa restaurants, urban restaurants, and cafeterias.

Therapeutic Diet Menu

The therapeutic diet is planned by a dietitian, as prescribed by a doctor, to improve or control the illness of a patient.

Other Special Menus

Principle: Menus are composed of specialty ingredients and dishes that are characteristic of a special theme.

Composition: Foods reflect the theme or the occasion, for example, game for a hunting menu.

Application: Special theme restaurants as well as festive occasions in all restaurants.

Staff Menu

Employees in Switzerland expect a nutritionally balanced, high-quality, well-prepared, tasty lunch as part of the benefits. Here are several suggestions to fulfill this expectation:

- Only one menu is specially prepared for the staff (most common).
- A daily menu or a variety of dishes is offered at a very low cost; and the individual can choose.
- Employees receive a meal allowance.

Menus should be planned in writing and in advance.

Good cafeteria meals and menus for employees are important means of guaranteeing a good work environment!

Buffet Meals

Self-service Buffet, Cafeteria Style
Self-service buffets are used in many institutions, for various occasions. Self-service buffets are primarily found in department store restaurants, resort restaurants, staff cafeterias, and catering facilities.

Self-service buffets generally operate on a one-way principle: the guest picks up a tray and silverware, selects the menu items, and pays at the end of the line for the purchases.

Partial Self-service Buffet

For this type of buffet service, guests are seated at tables and the wait staff lays the tables and serves beverages. Customers serve themselves only from the dishes presented on the buffet.

These buffets are very popular. They allow for attractive food presentation and the large variety of dishes. Depending on the occasion, the buffet can be composed of simple foods or four-star cuisine. Cooks should be available to inform and help serve the guests. Well organized buffets can simplify the service, which is especially desirable with very large crowds.

Types of Buffets

- Cold buffets (only cold dishes)
- Combination buffets (cold and warm dishes)
- Special buffets (focused on certain foods, for example, breakfast buffet, cheese buffet, salad bar, smorgasbord)

Buffet Planning

Buffet planning follows the same guidelines as menu planning. Although it includes a large variety of dishes, the whole buffet should include a variety of presentations yet convey a unified theme. It should delight the eyes and present choices for every taste. Organizational chores include:

- Planning the menu
- Ordering required foods and decorations
- Controlling deliveries
- Planning the staff (*mise en place*, preparation, presentation, and service)
- Planning the room (buffet set-up, line space, table arrangements)
- Training the staff

Buffet Display

Effective buffets start with proper table arrangements. Tables should be set up to allow a smooth service flow and enough line space for the guests. Each buffet station should be able to handle about forty to fifty people). The buffet should be arranged in such a manner that all guests can serve themselves quickly and easily. The order of dishes should follow the menu format.

A clearly organized buffet, with some elevated plates and bowls, makes it easier for the customer to make choices. Sauces and salads and various side dishes should be placed near the dish that they complement.

Basic Rules

- Proper presentation ensures an attractive platter even after the first guests have been served. Major platters should be frequently replenished.
- Cooks serving at the buffet must know enough to be able to advise guests accurately.

Snacks – ZWISCHENMAHLZEITEN – *repas intermédiaires*

Today's eating habits, as well as nutritional recommendations to avoid heavy meals, have made snacks an important part of the modern diet. Snacks are generally small cold or warm dishes, such as sandwiches, appetizers, or small portions of entrées, which are combined with salads, yogurt, or cottage cheese. Small portions of cold cuts, ham, cold roasts, and the like can also be considered snacks. *Snack* is an American word meaning small meal. Snack stands and coffee shops are becoming more and more popular in Europe.

The importance of snack foods can be measured in the success of fast-food restaurants.

With alternative service, specialties, and tight organization, even a traditional restaurant can incorporate snack foods and gain a piece of that market.

5.4.3 Banquet Menus and Planning

In addition to skilled staff and proper facilities, banquet planning requires information about the type of festivity and the invited guests. It is important to know how many guests are expected, the cost per person, special food considerations, and more. The most important rule is to prepare an accurate and detailed banquet order.

Planning a banquet menu allows for far more personal vision and creativity than is possible in planning a regular or daily menu. Staff skills and the capacity of the facilities must be considered, however.

Thanks to technical advances, especially regenerating methods and equipment, it is possible to produce a high-quality banquet for large numbers of guests.

Necessary procedures include:

- Posting the banquet order in the kitchen and in all related departments
- Placing food orders on time and controlling food delivery
- Posting the staffing plan and providing necessary instructions
- Discussing the type and number of service dishes with the banquet chef
- Establishing guest counts and seconds policy
- Announcing the service schedule of courses to the kitchen in a timely fashion

The arrival of the banquet guests and the start of service should be conveyed to the kitchen staff.

5.5 Printed Menus

The specialty or daily menu offers dishes available for a brief time, in contrast to the printed menu, which is specific for a meal period and usually is in force for a longer period of time. Menus give guests the opportunity to compose small or large meals for themselves. They are generally the first impression the guest has of the establishment and should be treated accordingly. Menus also act as a binding agreement of the services offered.

5.5.1 Menu Organization

Before a menu is planned and printed, the following basic rules should be observed:

- A market analysis should be conducted, which should consider these points: *location* (rural, village, town, city, industrial center, suburbs, etc.); *make-up of local clientele* (businesspeople, employees, blue-collar workers, students, mixed clientele, etc.); *traffic patterns* (volume of traffic, public or private transportation, etc.); *operating hours* (desired or prescribed, operating hours of adjoining businesses, movie theaters, etc.)
- Number, type, and atmosphere of dining rooms
- Available storage and preparation areas
- Existing furnishings and appointments
- Number and skills of employees
- Climate and average daily seasonal temperatures
- Purchasing and procurement opportunities

Organization

A printed menu can be organized in one of two basic ways:

- Grouping meal components in a formal, technical manner, the so-called *classic menu*
- Grouping meal components based on marketing principles, the so-called *modern menu*

Table 5-6. Sequence of a Classic Menu

Cold appetizers	KALTE VORSPEISE	*Hors-d'œuvre froids*
Soups	SUPPEN	*Potages*
Warm appetizers	WARME VORSPEISE	*Hors-d'œuvre chauds*
Fish	FISCHGERICHTE	*Poisson*
Main dishes	ZWISCHENGERICHTE	*Entrées*
Daily specials	TAGESPLATTEN	*Plats du jour*
Roasts	BRATEN	*Rôtis*
Vegetables	GEMÜSEGERICHTE	*Mets de légumes*
Sweets	SÜSSPEISEN	*Entremets*
Dessert	NACHTISCH	*Desserts*

The menu sequence of a classic menu is not completely identical with the classical meal structure. Because daily specials can be warm entrées or a platter from the regular menu, this mixed group is listed after the entrées, in a separate section (daily specials – TAGESPLATTEN – *plats du jour*). They are generally dishes with a long preparation time. See also Table 5-6.

Professional Principles in Modern Menu Presentation

- The groupings should be clearly separate and the design pleasing.
- The selected groups should reflect the establishment's character.
- Cold and warm dishes should be presented separately.
- Light dishes are offered first, followed by the more substantial items.

Basic Rules of Menu Design

The following pointers should serve as guidelines to menu design.

The positions of items on a menu can increase their popularity. Guests' eyes usually move first to the upper center of the menu space. Here is where specialties and high-profit items should be listed.

In general, the menu should be designed to encourage sales. The following are important considerations.

- Menus must be clean and neat, without handwritten corrections.
- Menu items should be correctly spelled. Whenever appropriate, the menu should be written not only in the language of the country but also in French. But, most important, the menu should be written in the native language of the guests.
- Oversized menus annoy the guests and cause problems for the establishment.
- If the menu is short, the size of the type should be large. Avoid small type or writing and too many different fonts or styles.
- One menu should be provided for each guest.
- The menu should be printed on durable paper stock.
- Specialties should be highlighted, with bold or colorful print or colored pointers.
- Daily specials and meals that are part of the regular menu should be identified and easily exchangeable.
- Prices placed directly next to or under the text are most visible.
- Numbering dishes makes ordering and tabulation easier. Numbering is essential when an electronic data system is used.
- The caloric values of low-calorie dishes should be stated.
- Dishes that may take more time to prepare should be noted on the menu. Large meat portions to be served to more than one person should list the minimum number to be served.

Before the menu goes to the printer, the following questions should be answered:

- Does the design make a good impression on the staff and the customer?
- Is the menu easy to read and understand?
- Are all dishes popular and timely?
- Is each dish listed and well described?
- Does the paper stock meet the expectations?
- Are the graphics attractive?
- Can the kitchen and the service staffs deliver the expectations the menu offers?
- Are all sauces, side dishes, and garnishes listed for each dish?
- Are all prices correctly calculated?

- Are there absolutely no spelling errors?

5.5.2 Types of Printed Menus

Menu – MENÜKARTE
Planned menu of several courses, served in a specific order.

Daily Menu – TAGESKARTE
A selection of dated daily menu meals or daily specialty dishes.

Printed Menu – SPEISEKARTE
An assortment of (small or large) foods, offered for a limited time.

Specialty Menu – SPEZIAL-KARTE
An addition to the printed menu, for example, a specialty food offered for one week only.

Seasonal Menu – SAISON-KARTE
Timely dishes offered for foods in season.

Dessert Menu – SÜSS-SPEISENKARTE
The dessert menu can be part of the regular menu or printed separately.

Banquet Menu – BANKETT-KARTE
Printed menu suggestions for large groups, with several price structures.

5.6 Table Service

5.6.1 Organization

Good organization is as important to table service as it is to all other areas of the establishment. Good organization involves following these principles:

- Proper staff training
- Balanced workload
- Thorough knowledge of the menu
- *Mise en place* (preparation)
- Greeting of the guests
- Seating of the guests
- Taking of the orders
- Service
- Clearing
- Presentation of the check
- Farewell to the guest

5.6.2 Mise en place

As important as in the kitchen, preparation before service guarantees a smooth-running service. Preparation includes studying the regular and daily menus and setting up and assembling all necessary items in the service area:

- Extra tablecloths, napkins, etc.

- Dishes
- Glasses
- Silverware
- Condiment stands
- Specialty menu cards
- Ashtrays
- Plate warmers
- Service trays, order and tabulation pads, etc.

Both kitchen and service staff should have a basic knowledge of the other's department, to foster understanding and good relationships between the two.

5.6.3 Basic Table Setting

A basic table setting, which can be expanded or exchanged depending on the guest's order, is placed at each seat.

1. Napkins

Before the napkin is placed on the table, the server should check the cleanliness of the tablecloth and adjust the placement of chairs if necessary. The napkin is folded simply and placed, centered, before the seat, approximately ¼ inch (5 mm) from the edge of the table.

2. Silverware

The knife is placed first, to the right of the napkin, with the cutting edge facing in. The fork is placed on the left side of the napkin. The distance between the knife and fork must allow the placement of a large plate.

3. Glasses

The glass, usually a red-wine glass, is placed about ½ inch (1 cm) above the tip of the knife. Sometimes a second glass (white wine) is placed to the right, beside the first glass but a bit lower.

4. Condiment Stands

Salt and pepper shakers must be placed on all tables.

5.6.4 Service Rules

Basic rules, recognized internationally, exist for the service and the presentation of dishes.

From the Left Side of the Guest
- Platters are presented.
- Food is served with tongs from platters.
- Platters are offered from this side when guests serve themselves.
- Salad is placed on the left if it is part of the menu.
- Rolls or breads are offered to the guest.
- Finger bowls are placed to the left.
- Tablecloths are brushed from the left with a folded service napkin or crumb roller.
- Dishes served from the left are also cleared from the left.

From the Right Side of the Guest
- Plates are placed in front of the guest and cleared.
- Silverware is added or exchanged
- All beverages are served, and wine bottles presented for inspection.

Every rule has exceptions. The arrangement of tables, corner tables for example, may make it impossible to follow the service rules exactly. In such cases, it is important to disturb the guests as little as possible.

5.6.5 Food Presentation

Food presentation follows internationally recognized rules, which should be observed and followed.

Basic Rules
- Delicate soup garnishes are served separately or added at the last minute.
- Egg dishes are never served in direct contact with metal.
- Sauces are served in sauce boats or placed to the left of the meat or fish.
- Dishes that are cooked or finished in a sauce have the sauce served over the food.
- Composed butters are placed directly on the meat or are offered separately.
- During presentation of side dishes, the color combinations must be considered.
- Warm dishes should not have too many or complicated garnishes.

- Service platters and dishes should not look overloaded. The border of a platter or plate must be clear and clean. Food and garnishes should not be placed on the rim, and no spilled food drops should be present.
- Hot dishes are placed and served on very hot platters and plates; cold dishes are presented and served on chilled platters and plates.
- Silver platters with decorative borders and handles are never used for hot food presentations.
- Deep-fried dishes are never coated with sauce or covered with a warming dome. They are served blotted, on clean white paper napkins or doilies.
- Sauce or jus for breaded or rare meats is served separately in a sauce boat.
- All garnishes should be edible.

Platter service
- Meat and fish portions, steaks, and the like are placed neatly in the order they are to be served, first piece on top, for example.
- Garnishes and side dishes should be arranged on platters without hindering service.
- The number of garnishes must be equal to the number of portions on the platter.

Plate Service
- Meat is placed on the plate so that it is directly in front of the diner.
- The food on decorated or ornate plates should not obscure the design and should be placed in best view for the guest.
- When serving wedges of pies, cakes, or tarts, the point should be facing the guest.

5.6.6 Service Styles

Platter Service
- The guests serve themselves from a service platter.
- The guest is served from the service platter by wait staff.

Guéridon Service

The dishes are presented to the guest, placed on a service table on food warmers, plated, and served to the guest.

Plate Service

The food is placed and garnished on plates in the kitchen.

Self-service
- Complete self-service: the diner procures everything from silverware to beverages on a tray and carries it to the table.
- Partial self-service: The table is set, beverages are served, but the guests serve themselves from a buffet.

Room Service
- The food is served in a hotel room.

Party Service

Home delivery service without wait staff.

5.6.7 Types of Service

The type of service identifies how the guests will be served during a specified meal period.

There are four major service types:

- banquet service
- *table d'hôte* service
- *à part* service
- *à la carte* service

The Banquet Service

A banquet is served to a group of guests. For this type of service, all guests usually are served the same menu at the same time.

Appropriate service styles would be platter service, guéridon service, plate service, and self-service (for very large banquets).

The *Table d'Hôte* Service

In this type of service, meals are served at a specified time, and the same menu is served to all guests, who are not members of a group. This type of service is used in small hotels, guest houses, and residential foodservice establishments, where guests are offered the same menu within a specific time period.

Appropriate service styles are platter or plate service.

The *à Part* Service

Guests are served the same menu, without specified times, at their convenience. Platter, plate, and guéridon service styles are possible.

The *à la Carte* Service

Guests freely choose from a printed menu during business hours. The menu may, however, offer daily specials, and the wait staff may make recommendations, helping the guest choose menu items.

Appropriate service styles are: platter service, plate service, or guéridon service.

5.7 Menu Writing

Goal: Uniform menu writing, suitable to modern times, with correct spelling.

Correct Menu Writing

- The style should be congruent with current writing norms.
- It should be congruent with professional menu styles.

The style of a written menus should be current, because grammatical rules and spellings change with time. The following rules are a guide and provide help to the owner, chef, or any others responsible for writing the menu.

5.7.1 Basic Menu-writing Rules (all languages)

Menu Language

The language should reflect the local language or the language of the guests. Important, however, is the use of only one language for each menu. The old-fashioned so-called international menu language, in which nouns are capitalized or placed in quotation marks, should, in the interest of standardization, no longer be used.

Orthography

Correct spelling is dependent on the rules in each language. In addition, rules involving the spelling of technical words apply.

Authoritative essential guidebooks for correct spelling are:

For German: Duden, *Grosser Brockhaus*

For French: *Larousse*

For English: *The Concise Oxford Dictionary* (British); *Webster's Collegiate Dictionary* (American)

For all three languages: *Duboux Technical Dictionaries*

National Dishes

National or regional specialties can appear in their original language on the menu, especially such well-known dishes as pizza, minestrone, bouillabaisse, and Irish stew. If the dish is not widely known or from a region or country with a different writing style or even a different alphabet, the guest will appreciate a translation or explanation. For example:

Borscht (Beet soup)

Lesco (Hungarian vegetable stew)

Fiskebollars (Swedish fish balls)

Menu Text

The menu text is always addressed to *one person only*, even if it is a banquet menu.

Singular/Plural

Singular: If the portion per person is one piece only, or if several persons can be served from one large piece of food.

Examples:

Brook trout meunière
BACHFORELLE MÜLLERINART
Truite de rivière meunière

Leg of lamb, baker's style
LAMMKEULE BÄCKERINART
Gigot d'agneau boulangère

Artichoke
ARTISCHOCKE
Artichaut

Plural: If at least two or more pieces of food are served to each person.

Examples:

Perch fillets meunière
EGLIFILETS MÜLLERINART
Filets de perche meunière

Lamb cutlets, baker's style
LAMMKOTELETS BÄCKERINART
Côtelettes d'agneau boulangère

Green beans
GRÜNE BOHNEN
Haricots verts

Exceptions: Each language has words that are the same singular or plural, for example:

German: FENCHEL (fennel), ROSENKOHL (Brussels sprouts)

French: *tournedos* (tenderloin steak), *pois* (pea/s)

English: veal, venison

(Refer to the various food dictionaries).

Note: Many professional texts and cookbooks use the plural for dishes; however, on the menu, the above rules apply.

Presentation

The basic rule is the menu must be clean and free of errors.

Printing Options

Align left:

Cold appetizer

****

Soup

****

Main dish
Sauce
Starch
Vegetable
Salad

****

Dessert

Centered:

Cold appetizer

****

Soup

****

Main dish
Sauce
Starch
Vegetable
Salad

****

Dessert

Separation of Courses

Each course should be separated with type ornaments, rules, or extra space.

Initial Capital

The first letter of each line is capitalized:

Glazed chestnuts
Fresh strawberries

Exceptions:

- The initial word is not capitalized if the line is a continuation of the name of the dish (see next rule).

- The initial word is not capitalized if the word does not relate to the food item (such as *or, and*).

Turnover Lines

When copy takes up more than one line, the turnover should be sensible and not confusing.

Right:

Roast saddle of venison,
    forest style
GEBRATENER REHRÜCKEN
    FÖRSTERINART
*Selle de chevreuil rôtie
    forestière*

Wrong:

Roast saddle of veni-
son, forest style
GEBRATENER REH-
RÜCKEN FÖRSTERINART
*Selle de chevreuil
rôtie forestière*

Abbreviations

Abbreviations are confusing and should be avoided. For example, it would be wrong to write *sc.* instead of sauce.

Double Names

If a name already signifies the preparation method or an ingredient, the method or ingredient should not also be used.

Right:	Fruit salad with whipped cream or Fruit salad Chantilly
Wrong:	Fruit salad with Chantilly cream
Right:	Fillet of sole Colbert
Wrong:	Fried fillet of sole Colbert
Right:	*Féra meunière*
Wrong:	*Féra sauté meunière*

Beverages

On menus, all brand names are capitalized in every language.

Rémy Martin
    Consommé with Rémy Martin
    Consommé au Rémy Martin

Puschkin
    Sorbet with Puschkin
    Sorbet au Pouchkine

As with other nouns, all beverages are capitalized in German. In French and English they are capitalized only at the beginning of a sentence or menu line.

Sherbet with vodka
Sorbet mit Wodka
Sorbet à la vodka

Spelling of Russian Proper Names

In order to ensure a common way of spelling Russian proper names, those ending with *ov* or *of* take the ending *off* in English (Stroganoff), *ow* in German (Stroganow), and *ov* in French (Stroganov).

English Spelling

All words are written in lower-case letters, except for proper names and geographical names: Swiss cheese, Peter the Great. All adjectives derived from proper names are written with a capital letter: English style, French fries, Italian dressing. The phrase *à la* or *à la mode de* is usually translated as "style": Russian style, Milanese style, for example.

5.7.2 German Spelling

Chefs in Switzerland find it easier to write their menus in French, the professional culinary language. German translations are often clumsy and sound strange. Basic rule: the standard reference work is the Duden.

Upper- and Lower-case Words

Per standard German style rules, all nouns, as well as a word at the beginning of a sentence, are capitalized. Special rules apply when *nach Art von* ("in the style of") is used on the menu.

1. Geographical Names

Menu names are capitalized, as two words, if the name ends in *er*:

Kartoffeln Walliser Art (Potatoes in the style of Valais)

Adjectives are written in lower-case, as two words, when the word ends in *isch*:

Eier russische Art (Eggs Russian style)

2. Occupations

The preparation method is written as one word, with *art* added.

Kartoffeln Herzoginart (duchess potatoes)

Note: Female occupational names are always singular.

3. Personal Names and Towns

If a dish is named after a person or a town, *art* is omitted.

Names:
Kraftbrühe Carmen (consommé Carmen)
Lammkottelet Nelson (lamb cutlet Nelson)
Salat Emma (salad Emma)

Towns:
Kraftbrühe Monte Carlo (consommé Monte Carlo style)
Kalbskopf Orly (calf's head, Orly style)
Rehrücken Baden-Baden (saddle of venison, Baden-Baden style)

Compound Words

In German menu writing, geographical adjectives are joined with the noun they describe when the term is generic. However, if location is specific and the name ends in *er*, it should be written as two words. For example:

Schweizerkäse (Swiss cheese) is a generic term applied to cheese produced in different locations all over the world. It is written on the menu as one word.

Schweizer Käse (for example, Emmentaler cheese), written in two words, identifies a cheese that has been produced in Switzerland.

Hyphenation

On a German menu, words are hyphenated if a German word is paired with a foreign word, such as Mais-Gnocchi (cornmeal gnocchi), if two words end in the same name, such as Brunnen- und Gartenkresse (water- and garden cress), when three vowels occur together, as in Tee-Eis (tea ice cream), or if the adjective is identified with the main ingredient, such as Weisse-Bohnen-Suppe (white bean soup). The hyphenation clarifies that the soup is made with white beans, rather than that the bean soup is colored white.

5.7.3 French Menu Spelling

Upper- and Lower-case Words

On French menus, all words are written in lower-case except, of course, the first letter at the beginning of a line, *and* the following exceptions.

Proper Names
*Salade **E**mma*
*Sauce **R**obert*
*Filets de féra **E**ve*
*Côte de veau **N**elson*
*Œufs au plat **M**eyerbeer*
*Tournedos **R**ossini*

Fantasy Names
*Pommes **M**ont d'Or*

Towns and Regions
This rule is in effect if the word is the noun:

*Carottes **V**ichy*
*Consommé **M**onte-Carlo*
*Asperge du **V**alais*
*Melon de **C**availlon*

However, if the town or region is used as an adjective, it is written in lower-case:

The town Berlin
*Boules de **B**erlin*
Preparation Berlin style
Foie de veau berlinoise

Castles, Hotels, Restaurants
*Salade **W**indsor*
*Salade **W**aldorf*
*Beurre **C**afé de Paris*

Memorials
*Steak de veau **W**aterloo*
*Potage **S**olferino*

Names that used to indicate a special preparation method but have become commonplace are now written in lowercase:

une béchamel (une sauce Béchamel)
une soubise (une purée Soubise)

Singular and Plural Terms

Basic rule: The plural is usually indicated by the letter s added to the singular form and the adjective:

la pomme	*les pommes*
le champignon	*les champignons*
le haricot	*les haricots*

Exceptions
Singular words that end in s, x, or z are not changed.

Singular nouns and adjectives that end with *au, eau, eu* (and a few words ending in *ou*) are changed to the plural form with an *x*.

The one-portion menu rule applies in French.

Emincé de veau
Sauté de bœuf

Adjectives

The adjective is expressed in the same gender as the noun in the singular or plural state. This is also in effect if the adjective is used as a verb:

Singular Masculine
rôti de porc glacé (glazed pork roast)
fond blanc (white stock)

Singular Feminine
poitrine de veau glacée (glazed breast of veal)
sauce blanche (white sauce)

Plural Masculine
marrons glacés (glazed chestnuts)
haricots blancs (white beans)

Plural Feminine
carottes glaceés (glazed carrots)
asperges blanches (white asparagus)

If an adjective is attached to both a feminine and a masculine noun, the gender is always masculine:

Truite et saumon fumé (smoked trout [f] and salmon [m])

Carottes et petits pois sautés au beurre (carrots [f] and peas [m] with butter)

Tomate et piment farcis (tomato [f] and bell pepper [m] stuffing)

Prepositions

Preposition *en*

This signifies the preparation method:

Pomme en cage (apple in a puff-pastry cage)

Œuf en gelée (eggs in aspic)

Jambon en croûte (ham in pastry)

Preposition *de*

It is used in two ways:

1. The word *de* or *du* identifies the ingredient source:

Asperges du Valais

Melon de Cavaillon

2. If a dish contains an ingredient that is quantitative or dominates the taste, *de* replaces *à la*:

Cocktail de crevettes (shrimp cocktail)

Sauce aux crevettes (sauce with shrimp)

Beignets de fromage (cheese fritters)

Soufflé au fromage (souffle with cheese)

The Use of *à la*

To keep repetition in a menu to a minimum, the phrase *à la* or *à la mode*, as it should properly be written, is used as little as possible. The phrase *à la* is used in two ways:

1. "Prepared in the style of ..."

à la façon

à la mode

à la manière

Always eliminate *à la* when possible: Instead of *Truite à la meunière*, use *Truite meunière*.

Adjectives are always expressed as feminine when *à la* is used (*mode* is feminine), even when it has been omitted to avoid repetition:

le homard: *homard americaine* (lobster, American style)

le saumon: *saumon suédoise* (salmon, Swedish style)

2. "Served with"

If an ingredient is identified as served with the dish, *à la* is always written. It should be remembered that *à la* changes to *au* or *aux*, depending on the noun concerned:

au: masculine singular

à la: feminine singular

à l': in front of vowel or silent *h*

aux: masculine and feminine plural

le beurre: *carottes au beurre* (carrots with butter)

la vanille: *crème à la vanille* (cream with vanilla)

l'œuf: *consommé à l'œuf* (consommé with egg)

les câpres: *sauce aux câpres* (sauce with capers)

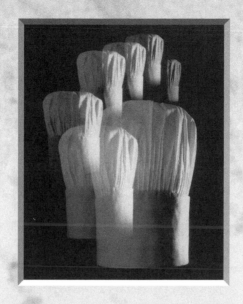

Kitchen Accounting

Chapter Contents

This chapter presents only the basic principles of cost calculation needed in the kitchen. Additional examples and exercises are taught in culinary training programs and hotel management schools, as are accounting principles, purchasing and inventory controls, and personnel costs. The following principles are necessary to calculate the costs of recipes and menus.

Organization

The foundations of effective cost calculation include:

- Appropriate purchasing
- Control of expenditures
- Accurate sales price calculation (initial calculation)
- Waste control
- Gross profit calculation

If these factors are managed properly, they not only guarantee a steady profit but are also a barometer of good kitchen management. If the gross profit is too high, the kitchen may be skimping on quality or quantity, which could cause a decline in sales volume. If the gross profit is too low, inadequate purchasing practices, inaccurate sales cost (low selling price), improper or underutilized use of leftovers, or lack of quantity controls may be the cause.

Maintaining accurate cost calculations and, at the same time, excellent and economical food preparation demands great skill. Only those who understand this relationship will be rewarded with good profits and satisfied guests. Obviously, the profitability of a kitchen must be based on exact and honest calculations.

The prices, quantities, and percentages used in the examples that follow are merely illustrations; they are not necessarily indicative of actual costs and profits.

6.1　Basic Kitchen Accounting Terms

Food costing in the hospitality industry is used to establish a selling price for the menu that covers all food, beverage, and payroll costs but is still competitive. With the help of cost information the chef can determine what food purchase prices he can afford, what the fixed organizational costs are, and at what selling price he can offer a dish and still make a reasonable profit. The costing information can also be used to institute a plan to reduce costs and keep an establishment profitable.

In addition to food cost calculations and establishing the selling price, food costing also encompasses the following areas:

Purchasing

When ordering food, the following must be considered:

- *Timeliness:* Foods are ordered on a timely basis, considering delivery time, storage capacity, and production needs.
- *Quality:* Good prices for standard food specifications suitable for the dishes to be prepared are sought *without* compromising food quality.
- *Quantity:* The right amounts of ingredients to prepare the menu,

which can be stored without spoilage, are ordered.

Receiving Controls

Receiving controls for delivered food should include:

- *Quantities:* The quantities listed on the invoice must be verified for price and amounts; the product should be inspected, counted, or weighed.
- *Quality:* The receiving clerk must be skilled and able to determine quality. Complaints at a later stage can rarely be resolved satisfactorily without some financial loss.

Storage Controls

The chef controls:

- *Storage conditions:* Proper storage for various foods in the right storage areas under the proper conditions.
- *Freshness:* Perishable foods need to be checked daily for freshness to avoid loss from spoilage.
- *Food requisitions:* First in, first out (FIFO) is the basic rule. Requisition slips identify what food has been issued to whom, and when.
- *Inventory:* To control storage and use, a perpetual inventory must be

periodically checked with a physical inventory.

Production Controls

To ensure that the food used corresonds to its forecasted cost, the following factors are important:

- *Recipes:* Standardized recipes should be developed and used in the production and finishing kitchens.
- *Waste:* Trimming and cooking losses must be checked and controlled to prevent increased costs due to wasteful preparation methods.
- *Portions:* Portion size is determined by the standardized recipe. The plated portion size must be checked periodically to assure compliance with portion size standards.
- *Food cost after sales calculation:* Food cost must be recalculated with actual costs after sales to make adjustments and correct problems immediately if necessary.

Price Quotation List

To calculate costs accurately in a kitchen, it is necessary to have a current price list of all ingredients available. This should include special sale offers.

The quotation list must be updated daily to reflect price changes. A computerized quotation price list is of invaluable assistance here, as the list can be kept current with minimal effort.

6.1.1 Glossary of Terms

Contribution factor: The calculation factor to determine sales price. The factor can vary depending on labor intensity ± 3.0.

Expenses: Food cost plus fixed costs; the sum of all expenses.

Fixed costs/operating expenses: Payroll costs, benefits, insurance, interest, energy costs, rent, mortgage, equipment, dishes, linens, etc.

Food cost: Total cost of all ingredients needed in the production of a dish.

Gross profit: Operating expenses plus profit; the difference between food cost and sales price. The percentage added to the food cost to cover all other expenses and provide a margin of profit.

Gross weight: Purchase weight (vegetables: includes packaging [tare]; meat: dead weight; fish: whole or alive).

Net profit: Percentage added to operating expenses to guarantee a profit to pay off investment. This protects the existence of the business and provides funds for further investment.

Net weight: The weight of foods after they have been cleaned, boned, trimmed, etc.

Pan-ready: Products that are ready to use and incur no trimming losses.

Purchase price: The price of raw ingredients (gross price), or of partially prepared ingredients or convenience foods (net price).

Sales price: Benefit/ratio of a dish, or a menu. Expenses plus profit **or** food cost plus expenses plus profit **or** food cost contribution factor.

Sales volume: Same amount as sales price. Sales volume (cash intake) for a day, month, year.

Tare: The weight of packaging materials, boxes, crates, etc.

Usable trimmings: Trimmings that can be used in food production, e.g., meat trimmings, bones, fish carcasses, trimmings from shaping vegetables.

Waste: Waste from raw ingredient preparation.

6.2   Yield, Waste, Gross Weight

Calculating Net Weight

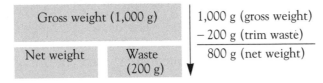

Calculating Waste

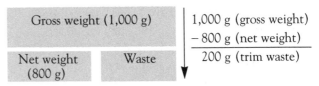

Calculating Net Weight Percentages

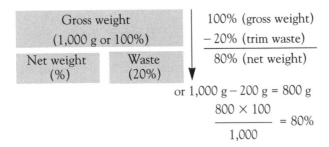

Calculating Waste Percentages

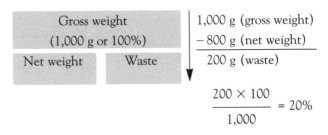

From Raw Product to Finished Product in Several Steps

After they have been cleaned and trimmed, many vegetables must be cut a certain way or cut into barrel shapes (turned). In this case, the food cost is calculated in two steps, starting with the raw product (gross weight):

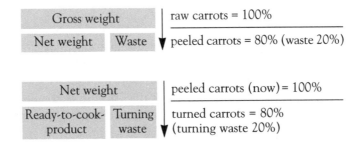

Example: The vegetable cook has 2.5 kg (5 lb., 8 oz.) raw, unpeeled carrots. The cook wants to prepare barrel-shaped (turned) glazed carrots. Peeling the carrots produces 20% waste and shaping the carrots, another 20%. How many carrots can be glazed?

$$100\% = 2.5 \text{ kg}$$
$$80\% = \frac{2.5 \times 80}{100} = 2.0 \text{ kg}$$

$$100\% = 2.0 \text{ kg}$$
$$80\% = \frac{2.0 \times 80}{100} = 1.6 \text{ kg}$$

1.6 kg (3 lb., 8 oz.) of carrots can be glazed.

The waste and trim losses cannot be added together; always do the calculations in two steps.

From Prepared Product to Raw Product in Several Steps

The amount of pan-ready product is known, but the trim waste percentage and the gross weight needs to be calculated.

The gross weight is calculated starting with the amount of pan-ready product:

Gross weight		raw carrots = 100%
Net weight	Waste	peeled carrots = 80% (waste 20%)

Net weight		peeled carrots (now) = 100%
Ready-to-cook product	Turning waste	turned carrots = 80% (turning waste 20%)

Example: The vegetable cook needs 1.6 kg barrel-shaped (turned) carrots for a special event; 20% of the carrots is lost on average by the shaping process, and an additional 20% is lost by peeling the carrots. How many carrots should the cook order from the produce purveyor?

$$80\% = 1.6 \text{ kg}$$
$$100\% = \frac{1.6 \times 100}{80} = 2.0 \text{ kg}$$

$$80\% = 2.0 \text{ kg}$$
$$80\% = \frac{2.0 \times 100}{80} = 2.5 \text{ kg}$$

2.5 kg (5 lb., 8 oz.) of carrots must be ordered.

The losses cannot be added together; they must always be calculated separately, in two steps.

6.2.1 Loss Percentages of Vegetables

Vegetables as a rule are delivered in their natural state. Trimming and peeling causes waste, which must be considered when calculating food costs. Table 6-1 lists the average percentage lost from various vegetables as a result of trimming and peeling; these figures can vary, depending on quality, use, season, and origin.

Table 6-1. Vegetable Trim Losses

Artichoke for bottoms	80%
Asparagus, green	10%
Asparagus, white	30%
Beet root, cooked	15%
Beet root, raw	20%
Belgian endive	10%
Broccoli	30%
Brussels sprouts	15%
Carrots	20%
Cardoon	20%
Cauliflower	25%
Celeriac knob celery	30%
Celery	20%
Chanterelles	5%
Chestnuts, fresh	20%
Cucumber	5%
Dandelion greens	10%
Eggplant	10%
Fennel	20%
Garden cress	10%
Garlic	5%
Green beans	5%
Green cabbage	15%
Kohlrabi	30%
Leeks, green	10%
Leeks, white part only	5%
Lettuce, packaged cut	10%
Lettuce, frisée	10%
Lettuce, head	15%
Lettuce, iceberg	15%
Lettuce, loose leaf, green/red	5%
Lettuce, sugarloaf	10%
Mâche, corn salad	5%
Mushrooms, brown	10%
Mushrooms, white	5%
Napa cabbage	10%
Onions	10%
Peppers	15%
Porcini	5%
Potatoes, peeled by hand	25%
Potatoes, machine peeled	30%
Pumpkin	20%
Radicchio	15%
Radish	10%
Rhubarb	15%
Romaine	15%
Salsify	30%
Snowpeas	5%
Spinach	10 %
Swiss chard	20%
Tomatoes	5%
Tomato concassé	50%
Watercress	10%
Zucchini	10%

6.2.2 Loss Percentages of Fruits

The percentage of trim loss for various fruits, shown in Table 6-2, are average values, which may vary depending on quality, use, season, and origin.

6.2.3 Loss Percentages of Fish and Shellfish

The preparation of fish and shellfish creates waste, including intestines, fish bones, carcasses, heads, and skin, which must be included in the calculation of food costs. The waste percentages in Table 6-3 are average values, which may vary depending on origin, spawning time, time of year, and use.

6.2.4 Loss Through Cooking

Different cooking methods incur different weight losses. The amount of the weight loss depends on the following factors:

- quality of the ingredient
- condition and composition
- surface of food
- preparation and cooking method
- use of correct temperatures
- use of appropriate cooking equipment

When standardizing and calculating the cost of a recipe, the weight loss must be included; hence, percentages of loss must be known. The percentages in Table 6-4 are average values.

Table 6-2. Fruit Trim Losses

Apples, 1st choice, eating	15%
Apples, cooking	20%
Apricots	10%
Avocados	25%
Bananas	20%
Cherries	5%
Clementines	30%
Currants, red	5%
Currants, black	5%
Dates	10%
Figs, fresh	5%
Grapefruit	45%
Grapes	10%
Quince	25%
Italian plums	15%
Kiwi fruit	10%
Mangos	20%
Mandarin oranges	30%
Melons	20%
Nectarines	15%
Oranges, segments	45%
Papayas	15%
Passion fruits	40%
Peaches	15%
Pears	15%
Pineapple	45%
Plums	15%
Strawberries	5%

Table 6-4. Weight Losses for Meat and Poultry

Whole Roasts	Tender Meat	Less Tender Meat
Roast, cooked rare (*saignant*)	15–20%	—
Roast, cooked well done (*bien cuit*)	about 25%	about 30%
Low-temperature cooking	about 10%	about 15%
Braising (dark meat)	about 30%	about 35%
Glazing (white meat)	about 25%	about 30%
Boiling/simmering	about 35%	about 40%
Poaching	about 10%	about 15%
Vacuum-cooking (*cuisson sous vide*)	about 5%	about 10%
Portioned meat (meat cut into portions before cooking)		
Sautéing	about 10%	about 10%
Grilling	about 10%	about 10%
Poaching	about 10%	about 10%
Boiling/simmering	about 10%	about 10%
Stewing	about 10%	about 10%
Glazing	about 10%	about 10%
Braising	about 10%	about 10%
Vacuum-cooking (*cuisson sous vide*)	about 10%	about 10%
Poultry		
Duck	about 30%	about 40%
Goose	about 35%	about 40%
Chicken, pullet	about 15%	about 20%

Table 6-3. Waste Percentages for Fish and Shellfish

Freshwater fish		Saltwater fish		Seafood	
Carp	50%	Cod	50%	Crab	75%
European river perch	65%	Gold bream	45%	Crayfish	85%
Grayling	30%	Hake	40%	Lobster	70%
Pike	60%	John Dory	70%	Mussel, Spanish	80%
Pike perch	40%	Monkfish, w/o head	20%	Prawns, w/ heads	75%
Saibling	30%	Red mullet	50%	Prawns, w/o heads	20%
Salmon	35%	Sole	50%	Shrimp, w/ heads	75%
Sheatfish	50%	Turbot	60%	Shrimp, w/o heads	15%
Trout	30%	White ocean perch	55%	Spiny lobster	80%
Whitefish	30%	Whiting	50%	Squid/octopus	20%

6.3 Purchase Price and Food Cost

The difference between purchase price and actual food cost is called the *yield factor* and is expressed in percentages.

This percentage is never identical to trim waste or loss.

To calculate the actual cost, the following information must be available:
* purchase price
* percent of loss **or**
* net weight percentages (gross weight minus trimming/losses)

$$\frac{\text{purchase price} \times 100\%}{100\% - \text{weight loss \%}} = \text{net price}$$

$$\frac{\text{purchase price} \times 100\%}{\text{net weight \%}} = \text{net price}$$

Example

1 kg (2 lb., 2 oz.) whitefish, with head, costs	fr. 14.40	purchase price
Loss due to filleting	28%	weight loss in %
Usable fish (fillets)	72%	net weight in %

Solution

$$\frac{14.40 \text{ (fr.)} \times 100\%}{72\%} = \text{fr. } 20.00$$

The actual cost of 1 kg (2 lb., 2 oz.) is 20.00 francs.

Net price	fr. 20.00
− Purchase price	− fr. 14.40
Yield factor (in francs)	fr. 5.60

The yield factor in francs is the difference between the net price and the purchase price.

Yield Factor in Weight Percentages

$$\frac{\text{loss in percentages} \times 100\%}{\text{net weight \%}} = \text{additional cost \%}$$

$$\frac{28\% \times 100}{72\%} = 38.89\%$$

Additional Cost in Francs in Percentages

$$\frac{\text{additional cost fr.} \times 100}{\text{purchase price}} = \text{additional cost \%}$$

$$\frac{5.60 \times 100\%}{14.40} = 38.89\%$$

6.4 Price Calculations for Menus and Recipes

Costing a Menu for Ten People

Barley soup

Veal stew with spring vegetables

Mashed potatoes

Cucumber salad

Baked apples

Costing a Standardized Recipe

The U.S. prices are 1997 market prices. The costs for fish *fumet* and *beurre manie* are educated guesses.

Ingredients	Gross Amounts	Purchase Price	Cost	Total
Barley Soup				
Butter	0.04 kg (1⅓ oz.)	14.90	0.60	
Onions	0.08 kg (3 oz.)	1.40	0.12	
Carrots	0.08 kg (3 oz.)	2.00	0.16	
Leeks. white part	0.08 kg (3 oz.)	3.20	0.26	
Knob celery	0.05 kg (1⅔ oz.)	2.40	0.12	
All-purpose flour	0.03 kg (1 oz.)	1.90	0.06	
Veal stock. white	2.5 L (2 qt., 21 oz.)	0.90	2.25	
Heavy cream	300 ml (10 oz.)	13.05	3.92	
Seasoning			0.20	
Chives	0.05 kg (1⅓ oz.)			7.77
Veal Stew				
Veal shoulder	1.8 kg (4 lb)	22.00	39.60	
Salt/spices for meat			0.40	
All-purpose flour	0.025 kg (1 oz.)	1.90	0.05	
Peanut oil	100 ml (3½ oz.)	4.90	0.49	
Garlic	0. 01 kg (⅓ oz.)	8.90	0.09	
Tomato paste	0. 05 kg (1⅔ oz.)	2.00	0.10	
White wine	200 ml (6¾ oz.)	6.90	1.38	
Veal stock. brown	1 L (1 qt., 2 oz.)	1.65	1.65	
Demi-glace	500 ml	2.55	1.28	
Bouquet garni	0.3 kg (10½ oz.)	1.80	0.54	
Sachet bag	1		0.50	
Cornstarch	0.02 kg (⅔ oz.)	3.10	0.06	46.14

continued on next page

continued from previous page

Ingredients	Gross Amounts	Purchase Price	Cost	Total
Vegetable Garnish				
Carrots	0.2 kg (7 oz.)	2.00	0.40	
Turnips	0.2 kg (7 oz.)	2.20	0.44	
Knob celery	0.2 kg (7 oz.)	2.40	0.48	
Pearl onions	0.15 kg (5⅓ oz.)	2.50	0.38	
Peas, extra-fine	0.15 kg (5⅓ oz.)	3.80	0.57	
Butter	0.05 kg (1⅔ oz.)	14.90	0.75	
Veal stock, white	300 ml (10 oz.)	0.90	0.27	
Sugar	0.01 kg (⅓ oz.)	1.25	0.02	
Salt/pepper			0.20	3.51
Mashed Potatoes				
Potatoes	2.0 kg (4 lb., 6 oz.)	0.95	1.90	
Water	2 L (2 qt., 4 oz.)			
Salt	0.02 kg (⅔ oz.)	0.95	0.02	
Butter	0.075 kg (2⅔ oz.)	14.90	1.12	
Milk	400 ml (13½ oz.)	1.75	0.70	
Nutmeg			0.10	
Salt /pepper			0.20	4.04
Cucumber Salad				
Cucumbers	1.2 kg (2 lb., 10 oz.)	3.90	4.68	
Sauce				
Dill, fresh	0.01 kg (⅓ oz.)	1.60	0.02	
Dry mustard	0.005 (⅙ oz.)	29.00	0.15	
Salt/pepper			0.20	
Herb vinegar	100 ml (3½ oz.)	2.00	0.20	
Yogurt, plain	0.1 kg (3½ oz.)	3.25	0.33	
Sunflower oil	100 ml (3½ oz.)	4.80	0.48	
Dill, fresh			0.10	6.16
Baked Apples				
Apples	1.2 kg (2 lb., 10 oz.)	2.60	3.12	
Sugar	0.1 kg (3½ oz.)	1.25	0.13	
Raisins	0.1 kg (3½ oz.)	6.30	0.63	
Cinnamon	0.001 kg (⅓ oz.)	8.90	0.02	
Butter	0.1 kg (3½ oz.)	14.90	1.49	
White wine	300 ml	6.90	2.07	
Confectioners' sugar	0.02 kg (⅔ oz.)	2.10	0.05	7.51
Food cost (10 people)				75.13
Food cost (1 person)				7.50
Contribution factor 3.5				
Sales price (1 person)				26.25

Whitefish Fillets, Zuger Style

Ingredients	Amount (U.S.)	Amount (metric)	Price/lb.	Price/kg	Total Cost	Total Cost
Whitefish fillets	2 lb., 14 oz.	1.30 kg	3.50	18.50	10.06	24.05
Butter	1⅔ oz.	0.05 kg	2.10	14.90	0.22	0.75
Shallots	2 oz.	0.06 kg	1.10	3.90		0.24
Fresh herbs (parsley)					0.50	1.50
Lemon	½	½	0.20	0.30		
White wine	10 oz.	300 ml	8.50	6.90	2.65	2.07
Fish *fumet*	10 oz.	300 ml	3.20	2.80	2.00	0.84
Seasoning					0.10	0.20
Beurre manie	1⅔ oz.	0.05 kg	2.50	8.00	0.26	0.40
Heavy cream	5 oz.	150 ml	1.50	13.05	0.49	1.96
Total food cost 10 portions					$16.28	32.16
Contribution factor 3.2					$52.096	102.912
Selling price, 1 portion					$ 5.21	10.30

6.5 Cost Calculations

Costs are organized into two main categories: food cost and fixed cost. In addition to these two categories it is also important to place costs in direct or indirect cost categories for billing calculations. Direct costs are those resulting from the purchase of one specific ingredient. This is the case for the *raw material cost*. Indirect costs result from several factors and cannot be billed individually. They are calculated using the contribution factor. This is the case for *operating expenses*.

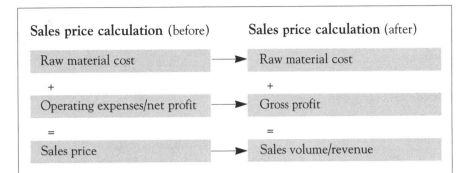

Sales price calculation (before)	Sales price calculation (after)
Raw material cost	Raw material cost
+	+
Operating expenses/net profit	Gross profit
=	=
Sales price	Sales volume/revenue

The columns above show that before- and after-sale calculations are essentially identical. Differences may occur as a result of waste, leftovers, theft, higher salary or operating costs, and the like. To make quick sale price calculations possible, a ratio of operating costs to raw food cost, the contribution factor is established. To calculate the contribution factor the following formula is used:

Structure of Sale Price	Structure of Contribution Factor
Food cost	1
+	+
Fixed costs + net profit	1.9
=	=
Sale price / sales volume	2.9

Sale price/income or sales volume always equals 100%.

6.5.1 Calculating Selling Price

To determine the selling price, the following information must be available:

- actual food cost
- contribution factor

Actual food cost	×	Contribution factor	=	Sales price
12.50	×	2.9	=	36.25

6.5.2 Calculating Food Costs of a Fixed Sales Price

In order to calculate the food cost, the following information is needed:

- sales price
- contribution factor

Sales price	÷	Contribution factor	=	Food cost
36.25	÷	2.9	=	12.50

6.5.3 Calculating Food Costs in Percentages

To calculate the food cost in percentages, the following information is needed:

- sales price
- food cost *or*
- contribution factor

$$\frac{(\text{Food cost})\ 12.50 \times 100\%}{(\text{Sales price})\ 36.25} = 34.48\%$$

The sales price is always 100 percent.

$$\frac{(\text{Sales price})\ 100\%}{(\text{Contribution factor})\ 2.9} = 34.48\%$$

6.5.4 Calculating Gross Profits in Percentages

To calculate gross profits in percentages, the following information is needed:

- sales price
- food costs

$$\begin{array}{c} \text{Sales price} \\ - \text{Food costs} \\ \hline \text{Gross profits} \end{array} \longrightarrow \frac{\text{Gross profits} \times 100 \ (\%)}{\text{Sales price}} = \text{Gross profits \%}$$

Example

The food cost for ten portions of Baked Apples is fr. 9.80. The contribution factor is 3.5.

a. What is the sales price?

b. What are the food cost percentages?

c. What is the gross profit?

Solutions

a. 9.80 (food cost) × 3.5 (contribution factor) = fr. 34.30

The sales price is fr. 34.30.

b. $\dfrac{9.80 \ (\text{food cost}) \times 100\%}{34.30 \ (\text{sales price})} = 28.57\%$

The food cost is 28.57%.

c. $\begin{array}{l} \text{fr. } 34.30 \ (\text{sales price}) \\ \text{fr. } \ \ 9.80 \ (\text{food costs}) \\ \hline \text{fr. } 24.50 \ (\text{gross profit}) \end{array} \longrightarrow \dfrac{24.50 \ (\text{gross profit}) \times 100 \ (\%)}{34.30 \ (\text{sales price})} = 71.43\%$

The gross profit is 71.43%.

6.5.5 Calculating the Contribution Factor

To calculate the contribution factor, the following information is required:

- sales price
- food cost

Sales price ÷ food costs = contribution factor

$$\frac{34.30 \ (\text{sales price})}{9.80 \ (\text{food cost})} = 3.5 \ (\text{contribution factor})$$

$$\frac{100\% \ (\text{sales price})}{28.57\% \ (\text{food cost})} = 3.5 \ (\text{contribution factor})$$

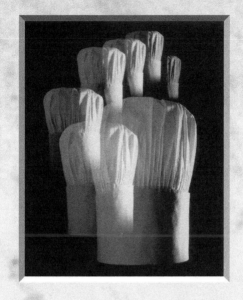

CHAPTER

7

Cooking

Chapter Contents

7.1   Introduction

The history and art of cooking is best understood and appreciated when viewed in relationship to the cultural, economic, and political circumstances of the times, as Table 7-1 illustrates. The art of cooking begins with the Italian Renaissance, the most influential cultural development in modern times. The bombastic nature of the Baroque is reflected in the presentation style of the old French cuisine. It finally changed with the cultural realism of the early nineteenth century to the clearly structured classical cooking of French cuisine. Modern cuisine reflects the changing life-styles of today, especially the knowledge that wellness and health are influenced by a nutritious, well-balanced daily diet. Table 7-2 outlines the features of these culinary trends.

Table 7-1. Important Historical Culinary Trends

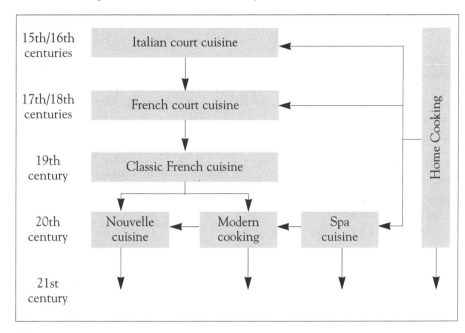

Table 7-2. Culinary Trends and Their Characteristic Features

Home Cooking	Home cooking evolved over the centuries in private kitchens. The simple, tasty dishes are prepared with local ingredients. Regional or national specialties that are widely accepted are basically home-cooked dishes unique to that region or country.
Italian Court Cuisine	Italian courts had developed a high degree of culinary skills and table culture, far more advanced than other European principalities. The marriage of Catherine de Medici to the future Henry II transferred that culinary culture to France.
French Court Cuisine	French cuisine was limited to the king and the nobility during the Baroque period, when France was feudalistic. In this decadent, gluttonous society, meals were viewed as entertainment rather than nutrition, forcing kitchen chefs to create bizarre culinary monstrosities.
	The nationalism of the Enlightenment at the end of the eighteenth century brought changes. Defined and recorded by **Marie-Antoine Carême,** a clearly structured cuisine with standard preparation methods and variations evolved, which became the basis of classical French cuisine.
Classical French Cuisine	Beginning at about mid-nineteenth century, the growing hotel and restaurant industry freed itself from elaborate, inedible structures and focused on the pleasures of the palate, basically refining most dishes.
	New recipes were created, preparation methods recorded, instructions defined, and kitchenware, cooking utensils, and equipment developed. Many chefs contributed to this valuable work, none more than **Auguste Escoffier.** Classical French cuisine was the standard in all international hotel and restaurant kitchens until 1960.
Nouvelle Cuisine	Nouvelle Cuisine is based on classical cooking but is not limited by its structure. Nouvelle cuisine is timely, celebrates creativity and spontaneity, and seeks absolute perfection in taste and presentation. This type of cuisine depends strongly on the personality of the chef and can be subject to fads.
Modern Cooking	Modern cooking is the further development of classical cuisine. It incorporates nutritional science and ecological principles, pays attention to societal changes, and selectively includes dishes from other culinary trends.
	Modern cooking based on classical principles is the standard today and will continue to be the standard of the future for the international hospitality industry.
Whole-food/Spa Cuisine	Diet and ecology strongly influence this style of cooking. Meats are reduced in favor of unprocessed grains and foods that have been produced with environmental sensitivity.

The Art of Cooking

Superior performance in the preparation of foods is the sign of the culinary artist. As is true for all art forms, the culinary arts are constantly changing and being influenced by contemporary trends. Current culinary trends can be found and examined at culinary conferences (salons), which display culinary talents and serve as a platform from which to inform the public about the enormous possibilities and strength of the culinary arts.

7.2   Cooking Techniques

Some foods can be eaten raw and unprepared, but most must be cooked. The cooking process:

- causes fibers to soften
- destroys pathogenic microorganisms
- creates flavors and aromas
- facilitates chewing and increases digestion
- allows the absorption of foods indigestible in their raw state
- changes texture, taste, and color and thereby increases eating pleasure

Before consumption and even before cooking, most foods must be prepared:

- Fruits and vegetables should be washed thoroughly to remove dust, dirt, disease-causing microorganisms, and possible pesticide residue.
- Fruits and vegetables are trimmed; for example, peels, stems, leaves, and seeds are removed.
- Fish is scaled and filleted, meat is dressed and portioned.
- Dried foods are reconstituted in water to allow the starch and protein molecules to expand.
- Large food is cut into smaller pieces to speed up cooking and digestibility.

It is necessary to understand the chemical and physical processes that affect food preparation, to produce consistently excellent food with minimal taste and nutrient loss.

7.2.1 Physical and Chemical Processes

Effects of Water in Cooking

The effects of the properties of water on cooking are discussed below and summarized in Table 7-5 in this section.

Water Can Dissolve and Infuse

Each water molecule consists of two atoms of hydrogen and one atom of oxygen (H_2O). The atoms are aligned to form positive and negative opposite poles. Therefore, water molecules are called bipolar. This makes it possible for the hydrogen to interact with many substances, to either combine or dissolve. Solubility is enhanced with heat, a property used ex-

Table 7-3. Water Properties at Change of State

Steaming	Change from liquid to gaseous state at boiling point: water evaporates.
Condensation	Change from gaseous to liquid state, the reverse of boiling. Both processes take place at about 212°F (100°C). Condensation is visible when steam cools on a pan lid or when warm moist air contacts cold window panes.
Evaporation	Change from fluid to gaseous state below the boiling point. For example: foods dry up, wet streets dry, sweat on the skin cools and evaporates.
Sublimation	Direct change from solid to gaseous state; for example: "freezer burn," icy streets drying even at below-freezing temperatures. This process enables freeze-drying.
Resublimation	Opposite process, direct change from gaseous to solid state. For example: snow, frost, man-made snow, ice formation in freezer.
Melting	Change from ice to water with the application of heat.
Freezing	Change from water to ice by reducing temperature. For example: deep-freezing, hail. Melting and freezing take place at 32°F (0°C).

Table 7-4. Changes of State of Water

Condition (State)	Addition/Reduction	Transition	New Condition (State)
Solid (ice)	Heat added	Melting	Liquid (water)
Solid (ice)	Heat added	Sublimation	Gaseous (vapor)
Liquid (water)	Heat added below boiling point	Evaporation	Gaseous (vapor)
Liquid (water)	Heat added to boiling point	Steaming	Gaseous (steam)
Liquid (water)	Heat reduced	Freezing	Solid (ice)
Gaseous (steam)	Heat reduced	Condensation	Liquid (water)
Gaseous (steam)	Heat reduced	Resublimation	Solid (ice, snow)

Table 7-5. Synopsis of Water Properties

Water Characteristic	Usage, Notes
Dissolves foods when cold or hot, depending on product	Salt, sugar, instant products, proteins; possible nutrient losses
Infuses foods only when hot	Meat and fish bones, meats, spices and herbs, vegetables, tea, coffee
Expands (swells) proteins and starches	Legumes, dried vegetables, dried fruit, dried mushrooms, whole grains, dough, batters
Conducts heat in form of hot water or steam	Between 148°F (65°C) and about 248°F (120°C): poaching, boiling, stewing, blanching, steaming, braising, and glazing; the boiling point depends on barometric pressure
Cleans	Dissolves, loosens, and removes dirt particles
Sanitizes	Hot steam kills bacteria
Acts anomalously	Greater density at 40°F (4°C) causes ice to float; freezing point is lowered with the addition of salt, sugar, and alcohol.

tensively in the kitchen when working with salt, sugar, instant products, and certain proteins.

Infusion of color, flavors, and aromatics can occur only in hot water. Meat and fish bones, meats, spices, vegetables (including soup vegetables and *mirepoix*) are infused into various stocks, soups, and sauces. Coffee and tea are also infusions.

Improper preparation methods can destroy large amounts of nutrients, as proteins, minerals, and some vitamins are water soluble.

Water Can Expand
Proteins and starches swell when they attract and absorb water. They expand and become less dense, which shortens and eases the cooking process. This is practiced in the kitchen when legumes, grains, dried fruits, mushrooms, or vegetables are soaked, and when water is incorporated into dough and batters.

Water Conducts Heat
The heat conductivity of water is used in the kitchen when hot water or steam is used in the cooking process (blanching, poaching, simmering, stewing, braising, glazing, steaming). As a rule, the higher the temperature, the shorter the cooking time.

Heating water sets the molecules in rapid motion until they evaporate as steam at high temperature. Water boils at normal barometric (1 bar) pressure at 212°F (100°C). Increased

air pressure (as, for example, in a steamer) results in a higher boiling point (adding pressure of 0.5 bar increases the temperature to 232°F [111°C]; adding 1 bar pressure, to 248°F [120°C]). If air pressure is lowered, as in a pressure cooker (where some of the air is removed) or at high altitudes, water will boil below 212°F (100°C) (with 0.5 bar less air pressure, water boils at 178°F [81°C]; at 1,500 to 1,800 feet (500 to 600 m) above sea level, water will boil at 205°F [96°C]).

Water Cleans and Sanitizes
Water is used to clean and wash away dirt. Steam can be used to sanitize (see chapter 1 for more information).

Water is Anomalous
Water changes in ways unlike other substances when exposed to temperature changes, which is called the anomalous nature of water. (The changes of state that water undergoes through temperature change are shown in Tables 7-3 and 7-4.) Water expands when it freezes, whereas other substances contract. In a mixture of ice and water, the surface temperature will be 32°F (0°C); below the surface, it will be about 40°F (4°C). All other liquids will be cooler below, with the surface temperature higher. Ice floats on top of water; all other frozen substances would sink. Consequently, plants and fish can survive in frozen waters: the ice surface protects the lower levels from getting too cold.

Consequences of the Anomalous Properties of Water
- At 40°F (4°C), water is most dense, and 1 liter weighs exactly 1,000 grams; at 68°F (20°C), only 998 grams; and at 32°F (0°C), 999 grams.
- At the moment water freezes at 32°F (0°C), the volume increases and 1 liter ice weighs 917 grams.
- The addition of salt, sugar, and alcohol will lower the freezing point of water. Some foods, because of high mineral content, will not freeze at 32°F (0°C), but freeze at a lower temperature. An ice soufflé with a high sugar and alcohol content may not freeze properly. Freezers should operate at below 0°F (-18°C).
- When water freezes, it expands very little but with enormous pressure. It can cause full bottles that are put in the freezer to break.

Effects of Carbohydrates in Cooking

The effects of the properties of carbohydrates on cooking are discussed below and summarized in Table 7-6.

Carbohydrates are Partially Water Soluble
Simple sugar and disaccharides, as well as dextrose and glycogen (animal starch), are water soluble. Warm water dissolves more sugar than cold water. Highly concentrated hot sugar solutions tend to crystallize when chilled.

Table 7-6. Synopsis of Carbohydrate Properties

Simple Sugars	Disaccharide	Dextrin	Starch	Starch Gel	Pectin	Pyrodextrin	Flour
Sweet	Sweet	Develops when starch is hydrolyzed by dry heat	Not water-soluble	Pudding consistency when cold	Thickens when cooked with acid and sugar	Simple sugars and protein combine to form nicely browned pyrodextrins with dry heat	Used as a thickener, it should be cooked for at least 15 min. at 203°F (95°C) or above
Water soluble	Water soluble		Begins to swell at 103°F (40°C)	High concentration of starch prevents curdling of egg yolk	Gels when chilled		
Hydrates (attracts moisture)	Caramelizes	Water-soluble				Gives color and taste to baked products	
	Hydrates (especially powdered sugar)	Easier to digest than starch	Thickens at 140°–177°F (60°–80°C)				
Ferments (alcohol and milk fermentation)		Reduced liquid absorption and thickening properties	Thickening qualities diminish at temperatures above 203°F (95°C)	Should not be stirred when cold			
				Prolonged storage causes weeping			
		Gives flavor and color to baked goods					

The creation of a sugar solution can be hastened by

- *Pulverizing:* Confectioners' sugar, as in the preparation of cold fruit sauces or desserts.
- *Heating:* Hot sugar syrup, as in the preparation of Italian meringue.
- *Agitation:* Stirring sugar into tea, coffee, sauces, and creams.

Water-soluble dextrin will give a sheen to hot baked goods if they are brushed immediately with water.

Carbohydrates Have Various Sweetening Properties

Simple sugars and disaccharides taste sweet but have different sweetening power. If the sweetening strength of cane and beet sugar (sucrose) is measured at 100, then fructose would be measured at 120, invert sugar (equal parts of glucose and fructose) at 80, malt sugar at 65, glucose at 50, and lactose at 35.

Carbohydrates Attract Moisture (Hygroscopic)

Simple sugars (glucose, fructose) strongly attract moisture. To keep baked goods soft and moist, honey is added, because it contains the most simple sugars of all the sweeteners. Confectioners' sugar is also very moisture absorbent.

The ability to absorb large amounts of moisture makes sugar an excellent preservative (jams, jellies, candied fruits), because spoiling agents, such as yeast and microbes, are deprived of moisture and cannot grow.

Carbohydrates Can Thicken (Gel)

The ability to thicken is especially high in starches and the edible fibers hemicellulose and pectin (see also chapter 3). Pectin expands when boiled with acid and sugar, and it gels when cooled. This property is used in the preparation of jams and jellies.

Starch (flour, arrowroot, corn, potato) is not water soluble and will sink to the bottom in a liquid solution. Therefore it is imperative that all cold starch solutions be stirred just before they are added to thicken sauces or stocks. Starch will start to swell in warm water at about 103°F (40°C). Above 140°F (60°C), starch granules rupture and bind liquid (soups, sauces, and creams). Thickening is usually complete at 177°F (80°C). Different starches thicken at different temperatures. When chilled, the starch mixture achieves a pudding-like firmness. Chilled starch mixtures have formed additional bonds, which will tear when beaten, releasing water and causing the mixture to become thin and runny. Chilled crèmes should never be whipped in a mixer to smooth them; they should be passed through a fine sieve instead.

When starch-thickened foods are cooked beyond 203°F (95°C), the starch bonds weaken. Hence, soups and sauces are thinned by letting them cook for a period of time.

Long storage of starch-thickened dishes will cause water to be released from the gel. This process is called *syneresis,* or more commonly, *weeping.* Release of moisture from the starch in breads and baked goods causes them to dry out and become stale.

The inclusion of starch in thick white sauces or vanilla crèmes can prevent egg yolk from curdling, even if the product boils. However, in thin sauces or crèmes, egg yolk will curdle at 177°F (80°C).

Liquids thickened with *flour* should cook slowly for at least fifteen minutes at about 203°F (95°C) or above, to ensure a smooth, creamy product and complete gelatinization.

Carbohydrates Can Brown

Heating carbohydrates causes them to develop aroma, flavor, and color.

Sugar heated to 302°F (150°C) will melt into a transparent liquid, which soon turns a caramel color when heated further. The darker the color, the less sweet it becomes.

If starch is heated without water to 302°F (150°C) or above, dextrin forms. Dextrin has a slight sweet taste and is more digestible than starch. Dextrins develop in the crusts of breads and pastries, in zwieback, and in brown *roux*. Darker browning reduces the starch's liquid absorption and thickening properties.

Pyrodextrins (browning flavors) develop in the crusts of baked goods, breakfast cereals, and fried batter-dipped foods when simple sugars combined with proteins are subjected to temperatures greater than 248°F (120°C).

Carbohydrates Can Ferment

Simple sugars (glucose and fructose) can be fermented with the addition of yeast, to produce alcohol and carbon dioxide. This process is used to make yeast dough, ferment wine, and brew beer.

Bacterial action in milk changes simple sugars (*lactose*) to lactic acid, a useful process in the production of yogurt, sour cream, cheese, sauerkraut, and raw sausages.

Effects of Fat in Cooking

The effects of the properties of fat on cooking are discussed below and summarized in Table 7-7.

Fat Dissolves Certain Substances

Fat is not water soluble and thus cannot be mixed with water, since it contains no water-binding molecules. Fat can, however, be dissolved with certain solutions (gasoline, alcohol). This process is applied when fats or oils are extracted. Fats themselves are capable of absorbing the fat-soluble vitamins A, D, E, K, and some color pigments. This process is applied in kitchens when seafood shells are boiled and made into lobster and shrimp butter or crab oil. The human body also absorbs carotenoids better in the presence of fat.

Fat Improves Taste

Most dishes can be improved with the addition of fats (e.g., fats with noodles, potatoes, rice, or vegetables, oil with salads, cream with some sauces, soups, and crèmes), because most flavor substances are fat-soluble. Doughs become smoother and more elastic with added fat, and pastries become moister and shorter in texture.

Fat Is Lighter than Water

Fats are less dense than water; therefore, fat floats as small droplets in stocks, soups, and sauces. Hot fat is removed by careful skimming; in order to defat a product completely, it must be thoroughly chilled. The hardened fat can then be passed though a sieve and removed.

Fat Has a High Smoke Point

Fats are ideal to produce nicely browned food (pyrodextrins) at above 248°F (120°C). Not all fats, however, can be used to roast, sauté, grill or deep-fry, because they heat differently.

All fats start to smoke and break down at a certain temperature, which is called the *smoke point*. Fats that are allowed to disintegrate above the smoke point can cause health problems, and their by-products are considered carcinogens.

Table 7-7. Synopsis of Fat Properties

Fat Characteristic	Usage, Notes
Absorbent	Fat-soluble vitamins, red color of crustacean shells, greater absorption of carotene.
Improve flavor	In the preparation of meat, fish, pasta, vegetables, sauces, and salads.
Lighter than water	Defat stocks, sauces, and soups; need to stir vinaigrette sauce.
High smoke point	Avoid overheating.
Conducts heat evenly	Fried food browns evenly and quickly.
Separates substances	Oiled forms; puff pastry rises.
Melting points	Fats with various fatty acids and different melting points are combined.
Prevention of proper egg-white foam	Bowls and whisks should be absolutely free of fat.
Emulsions	Proteins and lecithin act as fat amalgamators.
Rapid spoilage	Protect from light, oxygen, moisture, and heat.

Fat Conducts Heat Evenly

This characteristic of fats is demonstrated in the deep-fat fryer, where the product browns evenly.

Fat Separates Substances

This quality is useful in the kitchen when molds and sheet pans are oiled. Puff-pastry layers are created when fat separates the various dough layers. The water in the fat turns to steam and forces the dough apart. If the dough is rolled out too thin or unevenly, and the fat layers are too thin or damaged, they will no longer separate the layers, and the puff pastry will be uneven or only partially puffed.

Fat Has a Melting Point

The temperature at which fat changes from a solid to a liquid is called the *melting point*. Cooking fats and oils are often mixtures of fatty acids with different melting points. They do not melt at a specific point but at several. In specialized commercial fats, this is accomplished through hydrogenation to increase the smoke point of fats.

Fat Inhibits Egg Whites from Foaming Perfectly

Fatty acids destroy the formation and stability of beaten egg-white foams. Bowls and whips should be immaculately clean and free of fat. Egg yolk, which is high in fat, should be completely separated from the egg white. Even a minute residue of detergent can influence the formation of perfectly beaten egg whites.

Fat Can Be Emulsified

A permanent mixture of fat and water is called an emulsion. The creation of an emulsion requires the presence of amalgamators. In the production of mayonnaise or hollandaise, the lecithin and proteins of egg yolk act as amalgamators; the protein in meats is the amalgamator for pâtés and farces. Milk, cream, butter, and margarine are also emulsions.

Fat Spoils Easily

Fat spoils when fatty acids and glycerol separate. This process occurs when fat is exposed to light (ultraviolet rays), heat, moisture, air (oxygen), minerals (iron and copper), and microorganisms. Fats with a high water content and polyunsaturated fatty acids spoil especially rapidly.

Effects of Protein in Cooking

The effects of the properties of proteins on cooking are discussed below and summarized in Table 7-8.

Proteins Are Soluble

- *In water* (for example, albumin): This property is useful when clarifying broth with lean ground meat and when soaking sweetbreads, brains, and marrow. Protein foods should never be left in water for long periods of time.
- *In 2 to 3 percent salt solutions* (for example, globulin): When chopping and blending meat or fish for a farce, salt is needed to extract globulin to facilitate proper binding of the mixture.
- By *simmering in hot water* (for example, collagen): Bones, cartilage, tendons, rinds, fish bones, and the like contain large amounts of collagen, a gluelike protein, which can be infused into the stock through long simmering. Cooking time can be shortened when acid is added to the stock.

Proteins Swell

Proteins can bind with water (for example, globulin, gluten, collagen):

- *Through water absorption*: Legumes must expand to become soft. For this reason, legumes must be started off in cold water when cooking or must be soaked first. Yeast breads, pâté dough, and spätzle dough are kneaded or beaten hard to strengthen the gluten and improve the absorption of water. Farces and boiled sausages become juicy when cooked in water. Meats with a high percentage of connective tissue absorb liquid during the slow cooking (stewing, braising, simmering), so that the collagen is softened into gelatin. For this reason, goulash made with hindquarter meat (high in connective tissue) is juicy and tender.
- *Through acidic action*: Marinating with vinegar or wine mixtures (for example, sauerbraten, game stews, fish) causes muscle fiber to become firm, while the collagen in the connective tissue expands and becomes gelatinous and tender.

Proteins Foam

(For example, albumin and globulin.)

When egg white is beaten it will foam, which is useful in the preparation of sponge cake, sabayon, whiped egg white in dessert creams, and puddings.

Proteins Emulsify

(For example, albumin and globulin.)

In the preparation of sausage mixtures, farces, buttercreams, mayonnaise, and hollandaise, it is essential that fat and water be combined into an emulsion. In the preparation of sauces, the lecithin and proteins in egg yolks act as amalgamators. Emulsions are very sensitive to heat (especially albumin) and should usually not be heated above 103°F (40°C).

The final temperature—depending on the type of farce or sausage mixture—should not be higher than 58°F (15°C).

Proteins Coagulate

- *With heat*, starting at about 140°F (60°C), for example, albumin, globulin, gluten: This can be observed as skin forms on milk and foam develops when cooking legumes, potatoes, meat, bones, and the like. Proteins form foam when butter is heated. When proteins coagulate, they absorb water. Coagulation cannot be reversed. When proteins coagulate, they lose the ability to absorb or bind any other foods. This property is helpful:
  - Hard-cooked eggs become firm.
  - Farces and boiled and blood

Table 7-8. Synopsis of Protein Properties

Characteristic	Albumin	Globulin	Gluten	Casein	Collagen	Usage, Notes
Soluble:						
• in water	•					Leaches from meats to clarify; useful in soaking sweetbreads, brains, marrow.
• in salt solution		•				Without salt, farces and fillings do not bind properly.
• through simmering					•	Gelatin from bones, tendons, rinds, and fish bones dissolves; acid hastens this process.
Swells with:						
• water absorption			•			Preparation of dough, batters: working the dough increases water absorption.
• water absorption		•				Farces and sausage mixtures become juicy.
• water absorption					•	Meat high in connective tissue becomes juicy and tender through slow cooking.
• acidic action					•	Vinegar and wine marinades tenderize connective tissue.
Foaming	•	•				Sponge cake, sabayon, beaten egg whites, etc., become lighter, with more volume.
Emulsion	•	•				Fat and water emulsify in fillings, crèmes, sausage mixtures, mayonnaise, and hollandaise.
Coagulation						
• with heat	•	•				Farces firm up, eggs become hard when cooked, consommés clarify, ice creams, crèmes, and savory egg custard thicken.
• with heat			•			Gives texture to breads and pastries.
• with acid				•		Production of sour cream, cheese, yogurt.
• with rennet				•		Milk curdles to produce most cheeses.
Browning	•	•	•	•	•	When roasting, sautéing, grilling, frying, broiling, or baking meat, fish, seafood, potatoes, vegetables, cheese, etc.
Spoiling	•	•	•	•	•	Microorganisms and enzymes break down quickly in protein-rich foods.

sausages can be sliced (the coagulated protein traps fat and water).
– Gluten gives structure to breads and baked goods.
– Cooking methods for meat, fish, vegetables, and grain products.
– Crèmes, ice creams, savory egg custards (soup garnish), puddings can be bound.
– Soups and sauces and blood in *pfeffer* (jugged game), a European game stew specialty, will thicken.
– Consommé and aspics can be clarified (when the protein coagulates, it binds impurities).
• *With acid*, for example, casein: This process is helpful in the production of yogurt, sour cream, some cheeses, and other sour-milk products.

• *With rennet*, for example, casein: This quick method of coagulation is used in the production of most cheeses.

Because enzymes can break down coagulated proteins more quickly, the human body digests them more easily.

Disadvantages of Protein Coagulation

• At temperatures above 177°F (80°C), protein can curdle or disintegrate, for example, in soups or sauces and crèmes made with egg yolk, liaison, or blood; also savory egg custards and flans collapse.
• Meat proteins coagulate between 140° and 166°F (60° and 75°C) and give off moisture. Meats with little connective tissue (short-

order cuts) will become dry if cooked too long.

Proteins Brown at High Temperature
When meat, fish, or fowl is roasted, sautéed, grilled, deep-fat fried, or gratinéed, flavor and browning agents form.

The protein content of butter makes it possible to brown butter at about 248°F (120°C).

Proteins Spoil Rapidly
Foods with a high protein content spoil rapidly through enzyme action and the presence of microorganisms. Decomposed proteins can be harmful, even poisonous.

7.3 Preservation Methods

Preservation means prolonging the shelf life of foods for short or long periods. The goal of the various preservation methods is to kill the microorganisms that cause spoilage, fermentation, and mold growth and to kill or slow down the food's own enzymes. Several methods may be used at the same time or one after the other. Depending on the type of preservation, the process can be physical or chemical. Table 7-11 summarizes the different methods.

Physical Processes

Lowering of temperature
• refrigeration, freezing

Heating
• pasteurizing, hot-packing, sterilizing, UHT

Dehydration
• drying, heat-drying, freeze-drying, reducing

Oxygen removal
• vacuum-packing, coating

Filtering

Radiation

Chemical Processes

Salting

Curing

Smoking

Sugaring

Pickling and souring

Alcohol preservation

Chemical preservatives

7.3.1 Lowering Temperature

Refrigeration

Effect: Freezing temperatures (for most foods, below 23°F [-5°C]) stop microorganisms from growing and prevent enzyme activity (see Table 7-9).

Use: Most foods, except nonperishables and canned goods.

Refrigeration Rules
• Cooked foods must be chilled quickly and held at refrigerator temperatures; otherwise sanitation laws are violated (see chapter 1).
• Temperature and relative humidity should be regulated, or quality will be affected.
• Storage time should be monitored, or spoilage will occur.
• Temperature fluctuation should be avoided. Refrigerator and freezer doors should not be opened unnecessarily to prevent condensation (also increases energy costs), which may cause growth of microorganisms.
• Foods that easily absorb flavors and foods with strong odors should be refrigerated separately or stored in tightly sealed containers to prevent flavor absorption.
• Stocks, soups, and sauces should be covered and placed in shallow containers to chill them rapidly, to prevent evaporation and bacterial growth.
• To protect against loss of quality, foods that dry out easily should be covered or vacuum-packed.

Freezing

Freezing is the most sparing long-term preservation method for fresh or prepared foods. The food should be blast-frozen at no less than 0°F (18°C) to rapidly chill the food to its core. Water is the major ingredient in most foods that are to be frozen. The water is present in unsaturated solutions of salt, sugar, acids, and other soluble materials, and is partially available free in cells or cell membranes. It is important to freeze the water molecules as rapidly as possible to form tiny ice crystals. If the freezing process is slow, water forms large crystals that rupture cell structure. The thawed product will lose valuable nutrients, flavor, and texture.

The activity of microorganisms stops when the water in foods freezes. Even cold-loving bacteria stop growing at 5°F (-15°C).

Table 7-9. Effects of Temperature on Microorganisms and Enzymes

Temperature		Effect on Microorganisms and Enzymes
-40° to -4°F	(-40 to -20°C)	All enzymes affecting fats are barely active.
-4° to 32°F	(-20° to 0°C)	All enzymes are somewhat active.
5°F + colder	(-15°C + colder)	Microorganisms are no longer active and cannot reproduce.
5° to 32°F	(-15° to 0°C)	Microorganisms reproduce very, very slowly.
32° to 50°F	(0° to 7°C)	Microorganisms and enzymes become slowly active.
50° to 122°F	(10° to 50°C)	Microorganisms are very active and reproduce very rapidly, enzymes are very active.
122° to 140°F	(50° to 60°C)	Yeasts and molds are killed.
122° to 158°F	(50° to 70°C)	Enzymes become inactive in moist heat, no longer affect food.
148° to 177°F	(65° to 80°C)	Most bacteria are killed.
177° to 193°F	(80° to 90°C)	Enzymes become inactive in dry heat.
250°F	(121°C)	Spores of bacteria are killed in moist heat.
355°F	(180°C)	Spores of bacteria are killed in dry heat.

Prerequisites for Good Frozen Products

- The food product must be suitable for freezing.
- Only very fresh raw ingredients should be used.
- Correct preparation methods ensure that the foods are appropriately partially or fully fried and cooked before freezing. It is important to use nutrient-saving methods and work under strict sanitary conditions.
- Portioned and individually frozen products are easier to use than large pieces.
- Vacuum-sealed packaging protects foods from drying out and prevents freezer burn.
- Volume freezing requires very cold temperatures, -22°F (-30°C) or colder. Quick freezing at very low temperatures prevents the formation of large ice crystals, which occurs at temperatures between 22° and 32°F (-5° and 0°C).
- From the moment of freezing to the time of usage, frozen foods should be continuously kept at temperatures between -10° and 0°F (-22° and -18°C).
- Properly thawed frozen foods should be used immediately and cannot be frozen again, for reasons of quality and sanitation.

Guidelines for Proper Freezing
Pre-preparation
- Vegetables should be harvest fresh. They are trimmed, blanched, drip-dried, and chilled. Blanching destroys enzymes that may cause discoloration or off-flavors. Vegetables that are not blanched are cucumbers, zucchini, bell peppers, tomatoes, and fresh herbs.
- Fruit should be ripe. Berries can be individually quick-frozen (IQF) or frozen with sugar and sugar syrup (possibly with a small amount of ascorbic acid). Stone fruits are usually blanched in water, to which sugar and lemon juice have been added. Peaches are peeled and cut. Apricots and plums are cut into halves and individually frozen.
- Meat, poultry, and game should be aged when necessary and stored and handled the same as freshly prepared meats. It is best to freeze in pan-ready portion sizes.
- Fish should be freshly caught. They are scaled, gutted, and washed. They can be frozen whole, portioned, or filleted and glazed to prevent drying. (Individual pieces are partially frozen and dipped in cold water, which causes a thin sheet of ice to form).
- Partially or fully prepared foods should be prepared with little fat, since fat affects the storage time. Flour-thickened sauces will become runny and should be bound after thawing or with freeze-resistant emulsifiers. Prepared foods should be quickly chilled and frozen immediately.
- The dough recipes of baked goods need not be altered, except for yeast dough. The amount of yeast must be increased, since it loses some of its strength when frozen. Small pastries should be frozen within thirty minutes, larger baked goods within two hours.

Packaging
All foods should be wrapped carefully. The wrapping material must be approved for food use, of freezer strength, resistant to fat and acid, pliable, strong, and impermeable to water vapors and oxygen. The best method is vacuum packing. Air pockets insulate and prevent quick freezing. In addition, air contains microorganisms that will become active when the food is thawed.

Correct Freezing
- Freezing equipment is set at lowest possible temperature.
- Freezing capacity should not be exceeded.
- Frozen goods are shaped into flat packages to promote rapid freezing.
- Packages are placed directly on cooling coils or surfaces.
- Packages are spaced to allow air to circulate around each product. Stack only after freezing.
- All packages are labeled with content and date.

Storage Times
Most foods can be frozen successfully. Storage time depends largely on the type and fat content of the food (See Table 7-10). High-fat foods become rancid after a short while, because fat-destroying enzymes are still

Table 7-10. Storage Times for Some Frozen Foods

Food	Storage Time in Months
Peas, spinach, beans	10–12
Raspberries, strawberries	10–12
Fruit juice	10–12
Beef, veal	9–12
Poultry	7–12
Prepared foods	6–12
Cherries, peaches	8–10
Game birds, lean	8–10
Frozen whole eggs	8–10
Pork, lean	6–9
French fries	6–8
Butter	6–8
Game, lean	5–7
Fish, lean	5–7
Seafood	4–6
Bread	4–6
Pork, fatty	4–5
Fish, fatty	2–4
Ground beef	up to 3
Baked pastries	up to 1

active at freezing temperatures. A minimum temperature of 0°F (18°C) must be maintained and should be checked daily.

Thawing of Frozen Products

Principally for sanitary reasons, all frozen foods should be thawed under refrigeration. Poultry wrappers are removed before thawing, and poultry is placed in pans to prevent dripping (salmonella danger) and cross contamination of other food products.

Water conducts heat more quickly than air and will thus thaw food products much faster. This method, however, can only be used with cold running water, for vacuum-packed products.

Preparation of Frozen Foods

Vegetables frozen in a solid block must be fully or at least partially thawed. Individually frozen vegetables are best cooked unthawed. Cooking times for frozen vegetables should be reduced by 30 to 50 percent, because they have already been blanched.

Fruits used in cooking and baking should remain unthawed. Fruits that are consumed uncooked should be covered while thawing.

Meat, game, and poultry are best when thawed slowly under refrigeration. The cooking process can be better controlled this way. Very small pieces can be used frozen or partially or fully thawed, depending on the preparation method.

Fish should be partially thawed to make the separation of fillets or portioning possible. Breaded frozen fish portions should not be thawed.

Cooked potatoes, for example, French fries, should be deep fried while still frozen. Defrosting adds water to the deep fryer, which causes the fat to foam and spatter. Baskets should not be overfilled.

7.3.2 Heating

Microorganisms that destroy foods reproduce rapidly at temperatures of 68° to 102°F (20° to 40°C). If moist-

heat temperature is raised to 140°F (60°C), yeasts and molds are killed. At 178°F (80°C), almost all bacteria are killed. However, to destroy spores, it is necessary to raise the temperature to above 248°F (120°C) (high-pressure canning). The enzymes contained in foods are inactive at 212°F (100°C), because their proteins become denatured (see Table 7-9).

Pasteurization

Pasteurizing is a process whereby foods are rapidly heated to temperatures of 148° to 193°F (65° to 90°C) for a short period of time and then quickly chilled. The higher the temperature, the shorter the heating time. Pasteurization deactivates enzymes and destroys disease-causing bacteria. Pasteurizing foods is a sparing method; however, it does not preserve the food as well as other preservation methods. Pasteurized foods should be stored refrigerated.

Usage: Milk, cream, fruit and vegetable juices, caviar, fish in marinades, salads, *sous-vide* products (vacuum-packed cooked dishes), prepared and vacuum-packed foods (rolled smoked ham, *Schüfeli* [smoked, cooked pork shoulder], and fully prepared foods).

Hot-pack Canning

As the name already implies, in this process foods are heated to boiling, placed in containers, and immediately sealed airtight. This method kills most bacteria, with the exception of spores.

Usage: Jam, jelly, and fruit compote.

Sterilizing

Depending on the process, sterilizing temperatures reach 212° to 275°F (100° to 135°C). (Temperatures above 205°F [96°C] can be achieved only under high pressure.) Temperatures this high destroy all disease- and spoilage-causing bacteria. Sterile products can therefore be stored for a relatively long time at room temperature. However, due to

the high heat, some unwanted side effects may include a loss of vitamins and changes in color, flavor, and consistency of food products.

Usage: Evaporated milk, partially or fully cooked meals, canned meat, poultry, fish, vegetables, mushrooms, fruit, and more.

UHT Method

Foods are heated for a few seconds at ultra-high temperatures of 265° to 302°F (130° to 150°C) and then chilled rapidly, to create products free of microorganisms. The results are comparable to sterilized products.

Usage: Milk and various creams.

7.3.3 Dehydration

When foods are air-, heat-, or freeze-dried, water, which is essential for enzymes and microorganisms to survive, is removed, sharply reducing their activity. Dried foods attract moisture and must be stored in a low-humidity environment or, preferably, they should be vacuum-packed to protect against mold. Foods with a very low moisture content can be stored without refrigeration. Dehydrated foods have a different final texture, color, flavor, and caloric content, and proteins are denatured.

Air-drying

Foods are dried in warm moving air.

Usage: Grains, pasta, coffee beans, legumes, mushrooms, herbs, spices, meat jerky, *coppa* (northern Italian specialty: salted and air-dried pork neck), fish, grapes.

Cylinders and Sprayers

These are used in food manufacturing for pastes or liquids. Foods are dried in hot rotating cylinders or are pressure-sprayed with a hot air stream and then pulverized.

Usage: Milk powder, dry eggs, and fruit juice extracts.

Heat-drying

Foods are dehydrated in mechanical

Table 7-11. Synopsis of Preservation Methods

Preservation Method	Effect	Usage
Refrigeration from 30° to 42°F (-1° to 5°C)	Cold inhibits microbial and enzyme activity.	All foods
Freezing, minimum, -18°F (-30°C); storage minimum -0°F (-18°C)	Freezing stops microbial growth and slows enzyme activity.	All foods
Pasteurizing, between 148° and 193°F (65° and 90°C)	At these temperatures, most bacteria are killed, and enzymes become inactive.	Dairy products, fruit juices, vacuum-packed foods
Hot-pack canning, about 212°F (100°C)	Boiling temperatures kill most microorganisms; enzymes are no longer active.	Jam, jelly, fruit compote
Sterilizing, 212° to 275°F (100° to 135°C)	At these temperature, all microorganisms and spores are destroyed; enzymes are no longer active.	Canned meat, fish, mushrooms, vegetables
UHT Method, 265° to 302°F (130° to 150°C)	All microorganisms and spores are destroyed; enzymes are no longer active.	Milk and cream
Air-drying	Reduces microbial and enzyme activity, due to lack of moisture.	Meat, fish, pasta, grains, spices, vegetables
Heat-drying	Reduces microbial and enzyme activity, due to lack of moisture.	Fruit, vegetables
Freeze-drying	Reduces microbial and enzyme activity, due to lack of moisture.	Instant beverages, vegetables, mushrooms, dry milk, herbs
Reducing	Reduces microbial and enzyme activity, due to lack of moisture.	Extracts, such as *glace de viande*, *glace de poisson*, tomato paste
Vacuum-packing	Reduces oxygen-dependent microorganisms, protects from bacteria, prevents drying.	Refrigerated and frozen foods
Coating	Reduces oxygen-dependent microorganisms, protects from bacteria.	Terrines, cheese, rutabagas
Filtration	Microorganisms and residue are filtered away through fine cellulose fibers.	Fruit juice, wine, beer, cooking oil
Radiation (not legal in Switzerland)	Radioactive rays destroy microorganisms; enzymes are no longer active.	Spices, potatoes, poultry, onions, grains
Salting	Reduces microbial growth due to lack of available moisture.	Fish, meat, vegetables
Curing	Strong reduction of microbial activity (no available moisture), nitrates strongly inhibit bacterial growth.	Meats, sausages, ham, *gnagi* (pig's tail)
Smoking	Same as curing; smoke further destroys microorganisms.	Bacon, spare ribs, raw ham, sausages, fish, poultry
Sugaring	Reduces microbial growth, due to lack of available moisture.	Jam, jelly, candied fruit, sweetened condensed milk
Pickling and souring	Lowering pH values below 5 reduces spoilage-causing bacteria.	Sauerkraut, sour cream, salads, mushrooms, sauerbraten, *Wildpfeffer* (jugged game)
Alcohol preservation	Microorganisms cannot survive in an alcohol concentration of 15%.	Rum pot, Maraschino cherries, brandied fruit
Chemical preservation	Chemical preservatives destroy spoilage-causing microorganisms.	Many manufactured foods

food dryers or in convection ovens/combi ovens.

Usage: Fruit and vegetables.

Freeze-drying

Freeze-drying is a most sparing drying method. The food is first frozen, and then the water is evaporated in a pressure vacuum.

Usage: Instant coffee, instant tea, citrus juice, milk powder, mushrooms, herbs, vegetables.

Reducing

Reduction removes water and concentrates liquids, while at the same time stopping enzyme activity. The water from tomato puree and fruit concentrate is removed gently, often under vacuum pressure. Microbial activity is very low, because water has been removed and some of the available liquid is bound to other materials, such as proteins and minerals.

Usage: Tomato paste, fruit concentrate, and in the production of extracts such as *glace de viande* (veal glaze), and *glace de poisson* (fish glaze).

7.3.4   Removal of Oxygen

Vacuum-packing

Vacuum-packing alone is not a preservation method. Dry foods are vacuum-packed to protect them from moisture. Air-sensitive foods are protected from oxygen and microorganisms. Refrigerated and frozen foods are protected from loss of water due to evaporation (and, hence, loss of weight and freezer burn). Vacuum-packing preserves flavor and protects against flavor absorption.

Pressure-sensitive vacuum-packed products are mechanically inflated with inert gas (nitrogen).

Usage: Frozen products, chilled foods, dried foods, and prepared *sous-vide* (vacuum-packed) dishes.

Coating

Foods are coated with an airtight fat or wax cover to improve storage time.

Usage: Wax coating for Edam cheese; fat on top of terrines; sugar coating for sweets.

7.3.5   Filtration

Liquids are filtered through fine cellulose fibers to remove microorganisms and substances causing cloudiness. Cold foods are sanitized by this method without any effect on the nutritional value.

Usage: Fruit juice, beer, wine, oils.

7.3.6   Radiation

Ultraviolet rays can kill microorganisms present in the air of storage rooms or on the skins of fruits and vegetables.

In some countries foods are treated with ionized radiation, which kills microorganisms and prevents sprouting (for example, potatoes, onions, poultry, spices, grains, strawberries).

Unwanted side effects are:
- Some vitamins are destroyed.
- Fatty acids and proteins are changed.
- Hydrogen peroxide may form.

Usage: Ionized radiation of foods is not permitted in Switzerland, since many factors relating to human health are still unknown.

7.3.7   Salting

Salt reduces freely available water when it is absorbed in foods. This causes a reduction of microbial growth and enzyme activity.

Usage: Fish, cheese, bacon, caviar, butter, capers.

7.3.8   Curing

In addition to salt curing requires additional materials, such as sugar, saltpeter, or nitrates. Curing provides more protection from bacterial activity than salting does. It creates a hostile environment for microbes. Curing produces the characteristic pink color and cured flavor. The cur-

ing room should be kept at a temperature of 43° to 47°F (6° to 8°C).

The most common curing methods are:
- *Dry-salting:* Foods are rubbed with a mixture of salt, sugar, and saltpeter or nitrate.
- *Brining:* Foods are placed in a brine of curing salts.
- *Quick-curing:* Foods are injected with a brine of curing salts.

Usage: All types of ham, sausages, meat products, bacon, smoked tongue.

7.3.9   Smoking

Smoked products are generally also cured. Smoke kills microorganisms. Smoke, especially hot smoke, dries out the surface. Today the desirable flavor and color imparted by smoke are the main reasons for smoking foods, rather than preservation. Smoke temperatures vary from 58° to 212°F (15° to 100°C).

Usage: Fish, sausages, ham, bacon, spare ribs, poultry, game.

7.3.10   Sugaring

In small quantities, sugar is an excellent growth medium for microorganisms. Large quantities of sugar, however, can kill bacteria or at least reduce their activity, because sugar, like salt, reduces the available moisture in foods.

Usage: Jam, jelly, citron, candied orange peel, candied fruits, marzipan, and sweetened condensed milk.

7.3.11   Pickling and Souring

Acids reduce the activity of microorganisms. Lowering pH values below 5 kills spoilage-causing microorganisms and prevents other bacteria from growing. Two different acid preservations are used: lactic acid fermentation, which is caused by enzyme action in lactic acid bacteria, and the addition of acid to foods, usually in the form of vinegar. The latter method causes a loss of some nutrients.

Usage: Lactic acid fermentation products include sauerkraut and several dairy products. Products that have vinegar added include pickles, olives, mushrooms, salads, onions, sweet-sour fruits, fish, and sauerbraten.

7.3.12 Alcohol Preservation

Solutions that contain more than 15 percent alcohol destroy bacteria. The taste of the preserved food is the major reason for using this method.

Usage: Rum pot, brandied fruit, Maraschino cherries.

7.3.13 Chemical Preservatives

Chemical preservatives are used in very small quantities. They affect microorganisms like poison: they either destroy the membranes or attack the organism's metabolism.

Usage: How, when, and in what quantities chemical preservatives can be added to foods are all legally regulated (Swiss ZuV/U.S. GRAS list). Generally, additives are used only in the commercial manufacture of foods. Today, the trend is toward reduced use of additives. Accumulated amounts of food additives and other environmental hazards are a problem. It is not possible to know how these chemicals affect human health, especially since the knowledge of how additives interact is limited. Chemical preservatives may also cause allergies.

7.3.14 Convenience Foods

The trend toward the use of prepared and manufactured food products has strongly increased, as life-styles change. These are the convenience foods—foods that make food preparation easier and are convenient to use. These food products reduce labor by already being washed, trimmed, cooked, spiced, and preserved.

Convenience foods are not really new. Even earlier generations relied on others to do some of the work, for example, the grinding of grain, the baking of bread, the production of pasta.

Working with Convenience Foods

Convenience Foods as Basic Ingredients

Many convenience foods are basic products that can and should be individually improved, refined, and spiced.

Follow Directions Carefully

Preparation instructions should be read carefully. Information about measures, cooking times, and preparation should be followed exactly.

Short Cooking Times

Convenience sauces and soups have a very short cooking time. Long, unnecessary cooking will affect quality and cause them to thin.

Precise Measures

Proportions between mass and water must be exactly measured or weighed. Guesses are not appropriate and will produce poor results.

Solubility of Powdered Sauces and Soups

Sauces and soups, depending on instructions, can be dissolved in cold or hot water, and then cooked.

Instant Foods

Instant foods will not lump and can be easily dissolved in hot or cold liquid. Paste products can be used to taste.

Partial Use

It is important to mix the ingredients thoroughly if only a partial package is needed. Partially used packages must be properly sealed and stored in a dry, cool space.

Convenience foods are helpful in the kitchen. Used sparingly and individually refined, they are a help and a challenge to the cook. However, establishments that primarily use convenience foods are not places to teach professional cooking skills to apprentices. In Switzerland apprentices are not allowed to train in these facilities.

The various costs associated with different convenience foods are compared in Table 7-12.

Table 7-12. Profitability of Convenience Foods

Raw ingredients	Partially prepared ingredients	Ready-to-cook foods	Ready-to-heat foods	Ready-to-serve foods
Purchase price	Purchase price	Purchase price	Purchase price	Purchase price
Food Waste				
	Food Waste			
Labor Cost		Food Waste		
	Labor Cost	Labor Cost	Food Waste	
Overhead	Overhead	Overhead	Labor Cost	
			Overhead	Overhead
Profit	Profit	Profit	Profit	Profit

7.4 Basic Cooking Methods

Thorough knowledge of basic cooking methods guarantees error-free mastery of all cooking processes. Only after understanding and using these basic techniques can one create more complicated dishes.

Every recipe includes one or several of the following basic cooking methods in some form:

→ Blanch – *blanchir* 100°C Moist
→ Poach – *pocher* 70°C Moist
→ Simmer – *bouillir*
→ Steam – *cuire à la vapeur* 100-120°C Moist
→ Deep-fry – *frire* 160-170
→ Sauté – *sauter* 160°C-200°C Dry
Grill – *griller* 190-230 Dry
Gratinate/au gratin – *gratiner* 240-300 Dry
→ Bake – *cuire au four* 170-240 Dry
→ Roast – *rôtir* 170-200 Dry
Braise – *braiser* 120-200°C Wet then 85°C
Glaze – *glacer*
Poêlé/butter-roast – *poêler*
→ Stew – *etuver* 120-160°C Dry Wet after 58°C

7.4.1 Blanching

Blanching leaf vegetables cooks them completely. All other food products remain only partially cooked when blanched.

	Starting with cold or hot water	In boiling water		With steam (high-pressure or convection steamer)		In oil (deep-fat fryer)
Where	Starting with cold or hot water	In boiling water		With steam (high-pressure or convection steamer)		In oil (deep-fat fryer)
What	Bones in cold water; fowl, in hot water	Potatoes	Vegetables	Potatoes	Vegetables	Potatoes, vegetables, fruit, fish
How	Add bones or fowl to water. Bring quickly to a boil, skim to remove fat, drain. Then rinse first with hot water, then with cold.	Add to plenty of salted water, return quickly to a boil, drain. Let cool on sheet pan for further preparation.	Add to plenty of salted water, bring quickly to a boil. Chill in cold or ice water.	Partially steam in steamer unit according to directions. Let cool on sheet pan for further preparation.	Partially steam in steamer unit according to directions. Chill at once in cold or ice water.	Blanch in deep-fat fryer at 270°–300°F (130°–150°C).
Why	Removes impurities (fat, bone fragments). Fresh meat should not be blanched.	Destroys enzymes. Potatoes are cooked and dry, ready for use in other dishes.	Diminishes bitter taste. Preserves green color. Enzymes become inactive. To freeze product.	Retains vitamins and minerals. Steam leaches less flavor. Product stays dry and ready to use in other dishes.	Retains vitamins and minerals. Steam leaches less flavor. Product stays dry and ready to use in other dishes.	The fried product is pre-cooked. A labor-saving device for quantity production.

7.4.2 Poaching

Poaching is a very gentle cooking process that uses carefully monitored temperatures, generally between 150° and 175°F (65° and 80°C).

Where	In stock or with a small amount of liquid	Floating in water or stock	In a water bath, while stirring	In a water bath, without stirring	In a combi oven or a steamer with accurate steam temperature regulator
What	Whole fish, fish fillets, poultry breasts, seafood	Eggs, galantines, sausages, poultry, dumplings, gnocchi, brains, sweetbreads, fillings, smoked or brined pork, large fish, and fish steaks	Crèmes, sabayon, sponge cakes, sauces (hollandaise), desserts, and parfait mixtures	Egg royal, custard and unmolded crèmes, terrines, timbales, vegetable flans, puddings, and other desserts	Egg royal, whole fish, fish fillets, vegetable flans, terrines, custard and unmolded crèmes, and other desserts
How	In a little stock, covered with buttered parchment paper, in the oven.	Depending on the individual product, in liquid at 160°–175°F (70°–80°C).	Beat product in large bowl for maximum whipping action.	Set molds on paper (protects against contact heat that is too high, increases stability).	Depending on the food product, at different temperatures
Why	Use small amounts of poaching liquid in sauce. A safe method for foods without much connective tissue.	Guarantees slow cooking. Too much heat negatively affects the consistency of the food.	The water bath transfers heat evenly.	Safe, even cooking with controlled temperatures.	Safe, even cooking with accurate temperatures. Even heat distribution. Easy application.

(handwritten annotations: "wine" with arrow pointing to "In stock or with a small amount of liquid"; "+ Vinegar" with arrow pointing to "Floating in water or stock" column)

7.4.3 Boiling, Simmering

Boiling means cooking at or near the boiling point.

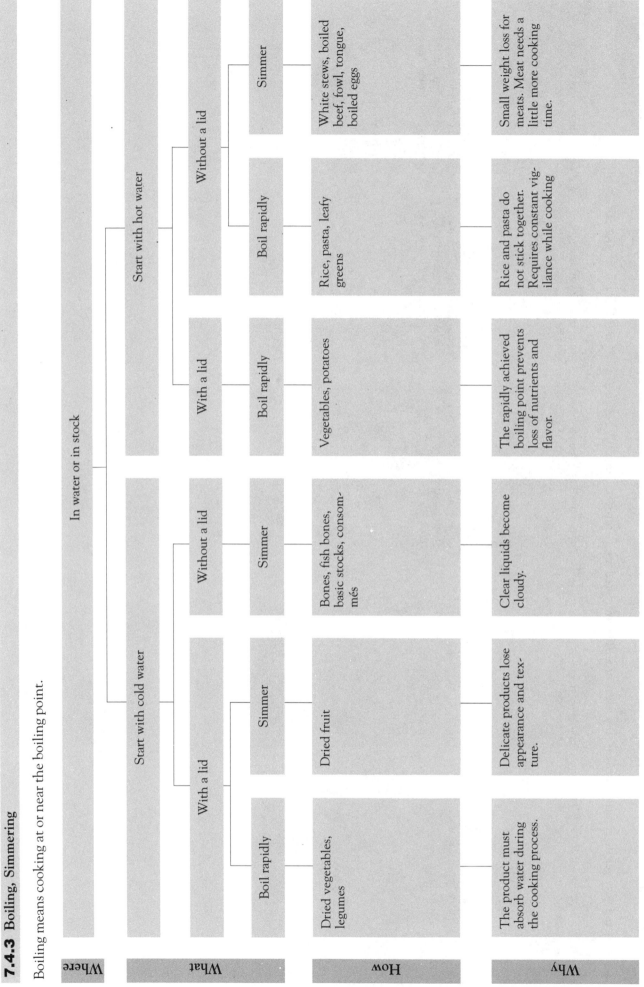

Where	What			How	Why
In water or in stock	**Start with cold water**	With a lid	Boil rapidly	Dried vegetables, legumes	The product must absorb water during the cooking process.
			Simmer	Dried fruit	Delicate products lose appearance and texture.
		Without a lid	Simmer	Bones, fish bones, basic stocks, consommés	Clear liquids become cloudy.
	Start with hot water	With a lid	Boil rapidly	Vegetables, potatoes	The rapidly achieved boiling point prevents loss of nutrients and flavor.
		Without a lid	Boil rapidly	Rice, pasta, leafy greens	Rice and pasta do not stick together. Requires constant vigilance while cooking
			Simmer	White stews, boiled beef, fowl, tongue, boiled eggs	Small weight loss for meats. Meat needs a little more cooking time.

7.4.4 Steaming

Steaming is a cooking process that uses dry or wet steam, with or without pressure.

	Pressure steamer	Convection steamer	Pressure cooker	Pot with lid and perforated insert	Universal steamer unit	Vacuum steamer for packed foods
Where	Pressure steamer	Convection steamer	Pressure cooker	Pot with lid and perforated insert	Universal steamer unit	Vacuum steamer for packed foods
What	Vegetables of all kinds, potatoes, meat, fish, seafood, organ meats, grain products, legumes. Reconstitution of prepared dishes. Steam at the same time: • Food pieces of same size • Foods with similar cell structures				Quantities of vegetables, potatoes, grain products, legumes, meat, etc.	Vegetables, meat, fish, seafood, potatoes, terrines
How	With or without pressure. Controlled gradual steam temperatures of 140° to 250°F (60° to 120°C), "dry steam."	Without pressure. Gradual temperature regulation of 140° to 210°F (60 to 98°C), "wet steam."	With pressure and wet steam.	Without pressure and with wet steam.	With pressure and dry steam.	Without pressure, with accurate gradual temperatures of 140° to 210°F (60° to 98°C), "wet steam."
Why	Reduces cooking time to about two-thirds (only with pressure above 212°F/100°C). Steam dissolves fewer nutrients, retains flavor and color. Foods stay drier and can immediately be prepared further. No agitation, preserves product appearance.				Large quantity, minimal space requirement. General application.	No stale "reheating" flavors. Maximum color retention for vegetables. Longer cooking times. Demands strict sanitation.

7.4.5 Deep-frying

Deep-frying is a process that cooks food in a hot fat bath at increasing or constant temperatures.

Where	In deep fat in the deep-fryer.
What	Meat dishes, fish dishes, seafood, cheese dishes, potatoes, vegetables, fruits, mushrooms, pastries, etc.
How	Blanching (pre-frying), from 265° to 300°F (130° to 150°C). Deep-frying (finish frying) at about 355°F (180°C).

Special Requirements for Deep-fat Fryers

• Use only nonfoaming, very heat-resistant fats.
• The thermostat should be set correctly, and temperature must be checked periodically for accuracy.
• Never heat fats above 390°F (200°C).
• Fats that are high in polyunsaturated fatty acids break down at frying temperatures, which ruins the fat.
• Reduce temperature by half during service lulls.

Adding Product to Fat

• Add only small quantities of the product to the hot fat. Otherwise, the temperature drops too much, and the food becomes greasy.
• Drain wet product well (fat will bubble up and escape, increasing the danger of burns).
• Shake off loose breading or excess batter to prevent breakdown of the fat.

Removing Product from Fat

• Drain grease from foods on toweling or paper.
• Do not salt, sugar, or add spices to foods above the fat.
• Never cover deep-fried foods, or they will become soggy (condensation).

Frying is Finished

• Strain fat and clean if needed.
• Check if fat is clean and can be used again.
• Shut down deep-fryer and cover.

Signs of Spoiled Frying Fat

• Strong foaming, small bubbles (beerlike foam) that increase during the frying process
• Low smoke point (below 340°F/170°C). Lots of smoke at 355° to 375°F (180° to 190°C).
• Eye- and lung-irritating smoke
• Bad smell and poor taste of fried product
• Viscous, dark-colored fat
• Fat-testing devices give negative reading

7.4.6 Sautéing

Sautéing is a quick cooking process that uses a small amount of very hot fat, without liquid. The food is flipped or turned and removed before any liquid is added to the pan drippings if a sauce is desired.

Where	Frying pan, saucepan, sauté pan, tilting skillet	Frying pan, tilting skillet	Frying pan, saucepan, non-stick frying pan	Frying pan, nonstick frying pan	Griddle top
What	Tender meat cuts	Small fish, fish fillets, steaks, sticks, etc.	Vegetables, mushrooms	Potatoes, fruits	Tender meat cuts and fish fillets
How	• Sauté meat pieces in hot fat, shaking the pan constantly or turning the food. • Deglaze pan drippings, add appropriate basic sauce or stock.	• Sauté fish or fish pieces in hot fat, shaking the pan constantly or turning the fish. • Pour a small amount of foamy butter over finished product.	• Sauté vegetables (blanched or raw) and mushrooms in hot butter or vegetable oil. Shake product in pan; brown if desired.	• Brown boiled or steamed potatoes in hot fat. Turn or flip until fried. • Sauté fruit in hot butter but do not brown.	• Oil griddle plate lightly, brown meat or fish on both sides.
Why	• Sautéing both sides quickly in hot oil sears the surface and seals in the juices. • Salt meat at the very last moment.	• Make incisions in whole fish to cook evenly. • Sauté the flesh side of fish fillets first, present this side after the fish is turned.	Sautéed vegetables retain their color, taste, and texture.	Pros: • Small amounts of fat • Ideal for larger quantities • Excellent method for steaks Cons: • No sauce production • Not suitable for finely cut meats	

7.4.7 Broiling, Grilling

Food is grilled or broiled on or below heated racks. Grill racks can be heated electrically, with gas, or with charcoal.

Where	Electric grill, gas grill, or in a special grill pan on top of the stove	Charcoal grill

What

Small to medium-size meat pieces (cutlets, steaks, chops, sirloin strip, chateaubriands, kabobs, tournedos, filet mignon, etc.)

Poultry (cut-up pieces, bone-in breasts, boneless breasts, cutlets, etc.)

Small whole fish and fish fillets and steaks (freshwater and saltwater fish)

Seafood (shrimp, lobster, Norwegian lobster (langouste/prawn), squid, etc.)

Potatoes (in aluminum foil)

Vegetables and fruits (may be wrapped in aluminum foil)

How

Grilling is done with contact heat.

Marinating some foods lightly can tenderize.

Use high heat at the beginning to sear the meat and then lower the temperature, cook until done.

Turn the meat (do not use a fork, it will pierce the meat) to create the characteristic grilled pattern.

Adjust temperature to thickness of the food (thin pieces, high heat; thick pieces, moderate heat).

Use a spatula to apply light pressure to test for doneness.

Why	Oil marinades protect the spices from burning. The aromatic flavors transfer from the oil to the meat.	Meat should not be placed over the hot coals but near them (fat gets caught in a drip pan). Fat that drips on the coals burns, and its smoke contains carcinogenic particles (benzo-a-pyrenes).

7.4.8 Gratinating, au Gratin

Food is gratinated, using high temperatures, from above only.

Where

In a salamander or in the oven with broiler unit (radiated heat)

What

Raw food:
- tomatoes

Cooked foods:
- egg dishes, soups, and cheese dishes
- fish and seafood
- meat and poultry
- pasta dishes and pastry dishes
- vegetable dishes and potatoes
- a variety of desserts

How

To gratinate a dish, at least one of the following ingredients is needed alone or as part of a mixture, for example, a sauce or cream custard:
- cheese
- *mie de pain* (soft bread crumbs)
- heavy cream
- butter or other fats
- eggs
- egg batter

Sauces suitable for au gratin are:
- white cheese sauce (*sauce Mornay*)
- white onion sauce (*soubise*)
- white sauces

Why

- To achieve a crisp crust, the food is sprinkled with grated cheese, dry bread crumbs, or *mie de pain* (soft bread crumbs).
- A tender juicy topping is produced when the food is covered with a cream or cheese sauce (*sauce Mornay*).

7.4.9 Baking

Food is baked in dry heat, without fat and without liquid.

	In the oven (on sheet pan, rack, or in baking pans)	Combination steamer oven	Convection oven, rack oven	Compartment convection oven with extra heating elements
Where	In the oven (on sheet pan, rack, or in baking pans)	Combination steamer oven	Convection oven, rack oven	Compartment convection oven with extra heating elements
What	Baked goods (tarts, cakes, small pastries) Potatoes (baked potatoes, duchess potatoes) Pasta dishes, choux paste (*gnocchi parisienne*), quiche, pizza Soufflés (with cheese, ham, mushrooms, vegetables) Puddings (hot baked almond pudding/Frankfurter, Saxon pudding, all English puddings) Meat (ham in pastry, beef Wellington, pâté) Poultry (chicken in pastry) Game (pheasant *Suworoff*)			All the dishes listed in the left column, but especially designed for: • cakes, all kinds • pastry • puff pastry • Swiss *Wähen* (sheet cakes with a sweet or savory filling), pizza • Pasta dishes
How	On sheet pans, in baking pans, or on the rack. Temperature dependent on baked goods, 260°–485°F (140°–250°C). The heat requirement can change during the baking process and heat may need to be increased or decreased.			On the rack with varied temperatures. Heat elements can be adjusted to create better browning.
Why	Advantages to baking meat in pastry dough: • Meat is hermetically sealed and stays juicy. • Volatile flavors are retained and cannot escape. • Food stays hot for a long period. • Starch side dish already provided by dough.			The separate heating elements are useful in creating nicely colored cakes, tarts, and small pastries.

7.4.10 Roasting

Roasting is a process of cooking foods using medium dry heat, basted frequently with fat but without liquid and uncovered.

	In the oven		On the spit	Slow roasting oven
Where	Combination steamer oven	Convection oven or compartment convection oven	On the spit	Slow roasting oven
What	• Meat: beef (filet, roast beef, prime rib, rump), veal (loin, rack, filet, veal kidney roast, crown roast), pork (neck, loin, ham), lamb (leg, saddle, rack, baron crown roast) • Poultry: all chicken (not soup fowl), turkey, duck, goose, pigeon, guinea fowl • Game: loin and haunch of venison, game birds • Potatoes: oven-roasted potatoes, oven-roasted potato balls, oven-roasted potato slices, oven-roasted potatoes with onions		All meat listed in the left column (except crown roasts). All poultry and game and also suckling pig.	All meat, poultry, and game listed in the left column.
How	• Sear at medium heat, uncovered (exception: roasts with a thick fat cover, such as prime rib). • Roast at lowered heat, basting and turning frequently. • Let roasted meat rest in a warm place for 15–30 minutes.		• Start with high heat. • Lower heat and baste frequently. • Let roasts rest.	In slow roasting oven exactly at manufacturer's prescribed temperature.
Why	Resting the roasted meat before carving evens out the meat temperature, which reduces the loss of juices when the meat is sliced. A sharp carving knife gives best results.			The slow cooking process at low temperatures tenderizes the meat. Weight loss is minor. Disadvantages: • Poor temperature regulation may cause meat to spoil • No crisp outer skin

7.4.11 Braising

Food is cooked with a small amount of liquid, covered in the oven or in a pressure cooker.

	Dark meat (= braising)	Light meat and poultry (= glazing)	Round steak, stews, poultry	Vegetables	Fish
Where	In a covered braising pan in the oven or in a pressure cooker				In a braising pan or a fish cooker
What	Dark meat (= braising)	Light meat and poultry (= glazing)	Round steak, stews, poultry	Vegetables	Fish
How	• Brown meat well. • Add mirepoix, tomato purée. • Deglaze with wine or marinade. • Add stock to cover food by ⅓. • Braise in oven, basting often. • Remove meat. • Reduce sauce, strain, remove fat, and season. • Slice meat and cover with sauce.	• Brown meat lightly. • Add mirepoix. • Deglaze with wine, reduce. • Add stock to cover food by ¼. • Braise, covered, in oven. • Remove lid toward the end and let stock reduce to a syrup-like consistency. • Glaze meat. • Remove meat. • Make a sauce with wine, etc. • Slice meat. • Serve sauce separately.	• Brown meat. • Add mirepoix. • Deglaze with wine, reduce to a syrup-like consistency. • Completely cover with stock and braise until tender. • Cut meat to shape. • Strain the sauce, season and flavor, or add garnishes. • Return meat to the sauce.	• Sauté (bacon, matignon). • Add prepared vegetables. • Cover ⅓ of vegetables with bouillon or other liquid. • Bring to a simmer and cook until tender. • Let cool in the liquid. • Slice and dress when needed.	• Sauté (matignon). • Add fish. • Cover ¼ of fish with wine and fish stock. • Cover and bring to a simmer. • Braise in the oven, basting and glazing the fish often. • Remove fish. • Use remaining stock to make sauce.
Why	Beef: from hind quarter, shoulder Lamb: leg and shoulder Game: shoulder	Veal kidney roast, veal shank, veal shoulder, veal breast, lamb shoulder, ham, pork shoulder. Boneless stuffed chicken, veal breast, osso buco, veal birds (paupiettes)	Sauté de veau, de bœuf, de porc; poulet (veal, beef, pork, poultry) navarin d'agneau (lamb stew), civets (game stew), sauté au curry (curry), carbonade (stew)	Romaine lettuce, knob celery, fennel, sauerkraut, red cabbage, pole beans, Bavarian cabbage, Belgian endives	Large fish, and fish pieces from salmon, sea trout, halibut, carp (often larded and stuffed)

7.4.12 Glazing

Cooked vegetables are glazed with their own reduced (syrup-like) juices. See also braising white meats, later in this chapter.

7.4.13 Butter-roasting

Butter-roasting cooks food in fat at low temperature, in the oven, covered, without liquid.

7.4.14 Stewing

The stewing process cooks food in its own juices, with little or no liquid added.

	7.4.12 Glazing	7.4.13 Butter-roasting	7.4.14 Stewing
Where	In a sauté pan (*sauteuse*), larger amounts in a braising pot (*rondeau*)	In a braising pan (*braisiere*), saucepan with lid (*sautoir*), braising pot with lid (*rondeau*)	Deep saucepan (*casserole*), sauté pan (*sauteuse*), saucepan with lid (*sautoir*), braising pot with lid (*rondeau*)
What	Mostly vegetables high in sugar: • carrots, turnips • chestnuts, pearl onions • knob celery, cucumbers • zucchini, kohlrabi	Poultry: all types Meat: tender pieces, such as filet, leg of lamb, veal kidney roast, pork loin	Meat: fricassee, goulash Vegetables: tomatoes, cucumbers, zucchini, leaf spinach, mushrooms Fruit: apples, pineapples, apricot, peaches
How	• Do not blanch vegetables. • Cook vegetables in light broth or water with butter, salt, and sugar (best glazing effect). • Braise covered. • Toss vegetables in reduced cooking liquid, glaze under broiler.	• Place flavoring vegetables and possibly bacon cubes in braising pan. • Set rolled and spiced meat on top. • Pour hot melted butter over meat. • Cover, cook at 285°–320°F (140°–160°C), basting frequently. • Near the end of the cooking time, uncover and brown the meat quickly. • Use flavoring vegetables and dripping for the sauce.	• Heat fat lightly. • Add food product and any additional ingredients. • Depending on the food product, add liquid if necessary. • Continue to cook, generally with the lid on.
Why	Why are vegetables not blanched? Blanching causes unnecessary vitamin and mineral loss. Pronounced vegetable flavor is lost.	Cooking meat at temperatures around 320°F (160°C) spares nutrients and is more easily digestible (no brown crust).	Because browning flavors are weak, the product's own flavor is most pronounced.

7.5 Bases and Ingredients

7.5.1 Marinades—MARINADEN—marinades

The purpose of immersion in marinades, or marinating, is:

- to tenderize tough meats
- to flavor foods (fish, meat, vegetables, fruit)
- to preserve and prevent spoilage

There are three types of marinades:

Quick marinades—KURZMARINADEN—marinades rapides (see Table 7-13)

Marinades for meat and game—MARINADEN FÜR SCHLACHTFLEISCH UND WILDBRET—marinade pour viande de boucherie et pour gibier

Brines—SALZLAKEN—saumures

Marinades for Meat and Game—MARINADEN FÜR SCHLACHTFLEISCH UND WILDBRET—marinade pour viande de boucherie et pour gibier

YIELD: 5 QT, 9 OZ (5 L)		
Onions	14 oz	400 g
Carrots	7 oz	200 g
Knob celery	5⅓ oz	150 g
Garlic	⅔ oz	20 g
Clove	1	1
Bay leaves	2	2
Thyme and rosemary		
Juniper berries (game)		
Red or white wine	4 qt, 24 oz	4.5 L
Red or white wine vinegar	1 pt, 1 oz	500 ml

Mise en place

- Clean vegetables and cut into mirepoix (coarse cubes).

Method

- Place the spices, mirepoix, and trimmed, sliced meat in a proper-size stainless-steel pan.
- Mix the wine with the wine vinegar and pour over the meat.
- Place weight on top to keep meat submerged.
- Marinate for a few days in the refrigerator.

Notes

To shorten the marinating time, bring the mixture to a boil, chill, and pour cold over the meat. This is called a cooked marinade (marinade cuite).

Brine—SALZLAKE—saumure

YIELD: 2 GAL, 2½ QT (10 L)	
Salt	Water
10% brine 2 lb, 3 oz (1 kg)	9½ qt (9 L)
12% brine 2 lb, 11 oz (1.2 kg)	9⅓ qt (8.8 L)
15% brine 3 lb, 6 oz (1.5 kg)	9 qt (8.5 L)
18% brine 3 lb, 15 oz (1.8 kg)	8⅔ qt (8.2 L)
20% brine 4 lb, 6 oz (2 kg)	8⅓ qt (8 L)

To each 1 qt., add 2 oz. (1 L) of brine, ¼ oz. (5 g) potassium nitrate, ⅓ oz. (10 g) sugar, and ⅛ oz. (2 g) sodium citrate. Any noncorrosive vessel that does not absorb flavors can be used. Brining should be done at a temperature of 43° to 48°F (6° to 8°C).

Table 7-13. Quick Marinades—KURZMARINADEN—marinades rapides

	Oil	Spices, Herbs, Lemon Juice															Alcoholic Beverages			
	Peanut oil	Basil	Sage	Parsley	Chervil	Dill	Lemon balm	Thyme	Marjoram	Rosemary	Tarragon	Paprika	Pepper, freshly ground	Garlic	Pâté spice	Lemon juice	Madeira	Port	Cognac	Kirsch
Fish				●	●	●	●	●			●		●			●				
Grilled beef	●							●		●			●							
Grilled veal	●	●					●	●					●			●				
Grilled lamb	●	●						●	●				●	●						
Grilled poultry	●		●							●			●	●						
Grilled pork	●								●				●	●						
Pâtés and terrines								●	●						●		●	●	●	
Fruit																●				●

Note: All quick marinades should be prepared without salt. The length of time that foods are marinated depends on the thickness of the pieces and on the desired strength of flavor.

7.5.2 Aspics – SULZEN/GELEES – gelées

In the pantry/larder/cold kitchen (*garde manger*), aspics are used in gelatin dishes, pâtés, and mousse, and are used to line forms. Cold dishes covered with aspic have a nice shine and are protected from drying out and discoloration. Silver platters are often covered with aspic to protect them from scratches.

Aspics are grouped as follows:

Meat aspic – FLEISCHSULZE – *gelée de viande*

Poultry aspic – GEFLÜGELSULZE – *gelée de volaille*

Fish aspic – FISCHSULZE – *gelée de poisson*

Aspic powder – FERTIGSULZE – *gelée de . . . en poudre*

Working with aspic is discussed in section 7.19.2.

Meat Aspic – FLEISCHSULZE – *gelée de viande*

YIELD: 5 QT, 9 OZ (5 L)		
Veal bones	11 lb	5 kg
Calves' feet	6 lb, 10 oz	3 kg
Pork rind, fresh	1 lb, 2 oz	500 g
White veal stock, fat free	2 gal, 2½ qt	10 L
Salt	1 oz	30 g
White bouquet garni	1 lb, 5 oz	600 g

Clarification		
Lean beef	1 lb, 12 oz	800 g
Matignon	7 oz	200 g
Egg whites	3 oz	90 g

Spice sachet
Marjoram, thyme, peppercorns, bay leaves, cloves

Mise en place
• Chop veal bones and blanch with calves' feet and pork rind.
• Grind beef using coarse disk of meat grinder. Mix ground beef with *matignon*, egg whites, and a little ice water.
• Prepare white *bouquet garni* and spice sachet.

Method
• Combine blanched bones, calves' feet, and pork rinds with cold veal stock. Bring slowly to boiling point.
• Skim and add salt.
• Simmer carefully for 4 to 5 hours.
• Skim off fat occasionally.
• Add *bouqet garni* and spice sachet after 4 hours. Simmer 1 hour longer.
• Strain through a double layer of cheesecloth.
• Let cool. Remove fat.
• Add beef clarification mixture and bring to a simmer, stirring carefully occasionally.
• Simmer, without further stirring, for about 1½ hours.
• Strain through a double layer of cheesecloth, and remove any remaining fat.
• Flavor with Madeira or port wine.
• If necessary, add a little caramel color.

Note
Test the aspic strength by pouring a small amount of liquid onto a chilled plate. If necessary, correct the consistency with a few gelatin leaves. For a high-quality aspic, no more than 6 to 8½ oz.) gelatin leaves may be added to 1 qt., 2 oz. (1 L) of consommé. The aspic should be the color of amber.

Poultry Aspic – GEFLÜGELSULZE – *gelée de volaille*

YIELD: 5 QT, 9 OZ (5 L)		
Veal bones	11 lb	5 kg
Poultry necks and backs	8¾ lb	4 kg
Calves' feet	6 lb, 10 oz	3 kg
Pork rind, fresh	1 lb, 2 oz	500 g
Chicken stock, fat free	2 gal, 2½ qt	10 L
Salt	1 oz	30 g
White bouquet garni	1 lb, 5 oz	600 g

Clarification		
Lean poultry meat	1 lb, 12 oz	800 g
Matignon	7 oz	200 g
Egg whites	3 oz	90 g

Spice sachet
Marjoram, thyme, peppercorns, bay leaves

Mise en place
• Chop veal bones and blanch together with calves' feet, poultry necks and backs, and pork rind.
• Grind lean poultry meat, using the coarse plate of a meat grinder. Mix ground poultry with *matignon*, egg whites, and a little ice water.
• Prepare white *bouquet garni* and spice sachet.

Method
• Combine blanched bones, poultry necks and backs, calves' feet, and pork rinds with cold chicken stock. Bring slowly to boiling.
• Skim and add salt.
• Simmer carefully for 3 to 4 hours.
• Skim off fat occasionally.
• Add *bouqet garni* and spice sachet after 4 hours. Simmer 1 hour longer.
• Strain through a double layer of cheesecloth.
• Let cool. Remove fat.
• Add poultry clarification mixture and bring to a simmer, stirring carefully occasionally.
• Simmer, without further stirring, for about 1½ hours.
• Strain through a double layer of cheesecloth, season, and remove any remaining fat.

Note
The color of poultry aspic should be light golden.

Fish Aspic – FISCHSULZE – *gelée de poisson*

YIELD: 5 QT, 9 OZ (5 L)		
Fish fumet	6 qt, 28 oz	6.5 L
Dry white wine	8½ oz	250 ml
Salt	⅔ oz	20 g
Leaf gelatin	4⅓ oz	125 g
Dry vermouth	1⅔ oz	50 ml

Clarification		
Whiting fillets	1 lb, 5 oz	600 g
Pike fillets	1 lb, 5 oz	600 g
Matignon	7 oz	200 g
Egg whites	1⅔ oz	50 g
Fresh mushroom trimmings	1⅔ oz	50 g

Spice sachet
Peppercorns, bay leaves, dill

Mise en place
- Bone and skin fish fillets, and grind fish using the coarse plate of a meat grinder.
- Mix ground fish with *matignon*, egg whites, and a little ice water.
- Prepare spice sachet.
- Soak gelatin in cold water.

Method
- Blend clarification mixture with the fish fumet and white wine.
- Add fresh mushroom trimmings, and bring slowly to boiling.
- Skim and add salt and spice sachet.
- Simmer carefully for 30 minutes.
- Strain through a double layer of cheesecloth.
- Squeeze the soaked gelatin, and add to hot fond.
- Remove all fat and flavor with dry vermouth.

Note
Fish aspic should be very clear. Test the aspic strength by pouring a small amount of liquid onto a chilled plate. If necessary, correct the consistency with a few gelatin leaves. The amount of gelatin needed varies according to the gelatin content of the fish used.

Aspic Powder – FERTIGSULZE – *gelée de . . . en poudre*

Aspic powders in various flavors and colors are commercially available. Aspic powders combined with correctly measured water will produce a good product. The aspics can be enhanced with the addition of Madeira or Cognac; instead of water, salt-free stocks can be used. An infusion of fresh herbs can also enhance the taste.

7.5.3 Forcemeats – FÜLLUNGEN – *farces*

Forcemeats are puréed mixtures of raw or cooked meat, game, poultry, fish, seafood, vegetables, mushrooms, and the like. They are used in warm and cold meat, fish, or poultry dishes, added to soups, and used to stuff vegetables and more.

Forcemeats are grouped as follows:

Mousseline forcemeat (raw) – ROHE MOUSSELINE-FARCE – *farce mousseline*

Game forcemeat – WILDFARCE – *farce de gibier*

Mousseline forcemeat for fish (raw) – ROHE MOUSSELINE-FARCE FÜR FISCHGE-RICHTE – *farce mousseline de poisson*

Mousseline Forcemeat (Raw) – ROHE MOUSSELINE-FARCE – *farce mousseline*

YIELD: 2 LB, 3 OZ (1 KG)		
Veal shoulder, boneless	1 lb, 14 oz	850 g
Salt	¼ oz	7 g
Ice cubes	3½ oz	100 g
Heavy cream (36%)	15 oz	450 ml
Seasoning (white pepper)	1 x	1 x
Nutmeg (pinch)	1 x	1 x

Mise en place
- Remove sinew and fat from veal, cut into small cubes, and refrigerate.

Method
- Grind veal through the medium-size plate of the meat grinder.
- Add salt and ice, and grind into a smooth mixture in a food chopper.
- Pass through a fine wire-mesh sieve (tamis), and put into a stainless-steel bowl.
- Place bowl on ice, and add heavy cream in small amounts with a spatula.
- Season with pepper and nutmeg. Add additional salt if necessary.

Note
All ingredients must be kept chilled during preparation, or the fat and proteins of the meat tend to separate, curdle, and lose the ability to bind.

Truffles, pistachio nuts, goose liver, mushrooms, and diced smoked tongue can be added to this forcemeat.

Game Forcemeat – WILDFARCE – *farce de gibier*

YIELD: 2 LB, 3 OZ (1 KG)		
Game (shoulder, trimmings)	1 lb, 2 oz	500 g
Pork (neck)	5⅓ oz	150 g
Shallots	2 oz	55 g
Apple	3½ oz	100 g
Chicken livers	5⅓ oz	150 g
Butter	⅔ oz	20 g
Cognac (40%)	1⅓ oz	40 ml
Madeira	1⅓ oz	40 ml
Back fat, unsalted	5⅓ oz	150 g
Heavy cream (36%)	3½ oz	100 ml
Seasoning (salt, pepper)	1 x	1 x

Mise en place
- Remove sinews from game and pork, cut into small cubes, and refrigerate.
- Peel and chop shallots.
- Peel and core apples, and cut into thin slices.

Method
- Sauté shallots, apples, and chicken livers briefly in butter.
- Add Cognac and flame, douse with Madeira and chill.
- Grind game using the coarse plate of the meat grinder.
- Grind pork separately using the coarse plate.
- Add salt and place the ground meat in a food chopper. Turn into a smooth mixture, adding the back fat and the shallot/apple/liver mixture at intervals.
- Push through a fine wire-mesh sieve (tamis) into a bowl.
- Place bowl on ice, and fold in heavy cream gently with a spatula.
- Season with freshly ground pepper.

Note
Keep all ingredients well chilled during preparation to prevent curdling. A curdled farce loses liquid and becomes grainy. The mixture must not be blended too long in the chopper, or it will become warm and start to curdle.

Mousseline Forcemeat for Fish (Raw) – ROHE MOUSSELINE-FARCE FÜR FISCHGERICHTE – *farce mousseline de poisson*

YIELD: 2 LB, 3 OZ (1 KG)		
Pike fillets	1 lb, 5 oz	600 g
Whiting fillets	10½ oz	300 g
Egg whites	1⅔ oz	50 g
Heavy cream (36%)	12 oz	350 ml
Seasoning (salt, cayenne, white pepper)	1 x	1 x
Dry vermouth (Noilly Prat)	1⅔ oz	50 ml

Mise en place
- Trim, skin, and remove bones from fish fillets, cut into small dice. Refrigerate.
- Lightly beat egg whites.

Method
- Chop fish into a fine purée in a food chopper, with a little cream and salt.
- Pass through a fine wire-mesh sieve into a stainless-steel bowl. Refrigerate.
- Place bowl on ice and fold in remaining cream in small amounts with a spatula.
- Carefully fold in the beaten egg whites.
- Season with salt, cayenne, white pepper, and dry vermouth.

Note
At least one-third of the fish should be pike, because it binds well and makes for a very smooth farce.

The amount of cream used depends on the fish and the desired consistency.

All ingredients should be kept as cold as possible during preparation.

Always test a small sample before poaching.

7.5.4 Duxelles – DUXELLES – *duxelles*

Duxelles are finely chopped mixtures, mainly mushrooms, shallots, and herbs, which are used as stuffings.

Duxelles are grouped as follows:

Dry duxelles (mushroom filling) – TROCKENES DUXELLES – *duxelles sèche*

Duxelles to stuff vegetables – DUXELLES FÜR GEMÜSEFÜLLUNGEN – *duxelles pour légumes farcis*

Duxelles to fill tartlets – DUXELLES FÜR TÖRTCHENFÜLLUNGEN – *duxelles pour tartelettes farcis*

Dry Duxelles (Mushroom Filling) – TROCKENES DUXELLES – *duxelles sèche*

YIELD: 2 LB, 3 OZ (1 KG)		
Shallots	6 oz	170 g
Parsley, Italian, fresh	1⅔ oz	50 g
Mushrooms, fresh	2 lb, 14 oz	1.3 kg
Butter	3½ oz	100 g
Lemon juice	½ oz	15 ml
Salt, freshly ground pepper	1 x	1 x

Mise en place
- Peel and chop shallots.
- Wash parsley, remove stems, and chop fine.
- Trim and wash mushrooms, and chop fine.

Method
- Sauté shallots briefly in butter, without color. Add chopped mushrooms.
- Add lemon juice. Season with salt and pepper.
- Cook, uncovered, until all liquid has evaporated.
- Taste, and add chopped parsley.

Mushroom Stuffing for Vegetables – DUXELLES FÜR GEMÜSEFÜLLUNGEN – *duxelles pour légumes farcis*

YIELD: 2 LB, 3 OZ (1 KG)		
White bread	5⅓ oz	150 g
Tomato purée	1⅔ oz	50 g
Butter	1 oz	30 g
Dry duxelles (see above)	1 lb, 12 oz	800 g
Dry white wine	1 pt, 1 oz	500 ml
Glace de viande	1⅔ oz	50 g
Salt, pepper	1 x	1 x

Mise en place
- Remove crusts from bread, and make fresh bread crumbs (*mie de pain*).

Method
- Cook tomato purée in melted butter briefly, to reduce acidity.
- Add dry duxelles.
- Add white wine and *glace de viande*.
- Add bread crumbs and blend well; cook to desired consistency.
- Season to taste.

Mushroom Stuffing for Tartlets – DUXELLES FÜR TÖRTCHENFÜLLUNGEN – *duxelles pour tartelettes farcis*

YIELD: 2 LB, 3 OZ (1 KG)		
Dry duxelles (see above)	1 lb, 2 oz	500 g
Mousseline farce, raw	1 lb, 2 oz	500 g
or Boiled ham	1 lb, 2 oz	500 g

Mise en place
- Prepare dry duxelles.
- If using ham, cut it into a very small dice (*brunoise*).

Method
- Mix dry duxelles with either raw mousseline farce or diced ham.

7.5.5 Ingredients for Stocks, Sauces, and Soups – ZUTATEN FÜR FONDS, SAUCEN UND SUPPEN – *ingrédients pour fonds, sauces, et potages*

Only the freshest ingredients should be used in the preparation of stocks, soups, and sauces, to create the fullest flavors. Ingredients with strong flavors should be used sparingly, or they will dominate and destroy the harmony of flavors.

Ingredients are grouped as follows:

Vegetable bundle for white stocks – GEMÜSEBÜNDEL FÜR WEISSE FONDS – *bouquet garni pour fonds blanc*

Vegetable bundle for clear beef stock – GEMÜSEBÜNDEL FÜR BOUILLON – *bouquet garni pour bouillon*

Mirepoix for brown stock – MIREPOIX FÜR BRAUNE FONDS UND BRAUNE SAUCEN – *mirepoix pour fonds bruns et sauces brunes*

Flavoring vegetables for meat – MATIGNON FÜR FLEISCHGERICHTE – *matignon pour mets de viande*

Flavoring vegetables for fish stock and soups—MATIGNON FÜR FISCHFONDS UND SUPPEN—*matignon pour fonds de poisson et potages*

Herb bouquet—KRÄUTERBÜNDEL—*bouquet aromatique*

Spice sachet—GEWÜRZSÄCKLEIN—*sachet d'épices*

Vegetable Bundle for White Stocks
—GEMÜSEBÜNDEL FÜR WEISSE FONDS—*bouquet garni pour fonds blanc*

Vegetable Bundle for Clear Beef Stock—GEMÜSEBÜNDEL FÜR BOUILLON—*bouquet garni pour bouillon*

Notes

Vegetables are tied together into a neat bundle, and spices are added, depending on end use. Trimmings and small pieces can also be tied into a cloth. The combinations and amounts vary but should produce a balanced flavor (see Table 7-14).

Amounts

Use about 5 percent of the volume of the end product; for example, for 2 gallons, 2 ½ quarts (10 L) of clear beef broth, use 1 pound, 2 ounces (500 g) of vegetables.

Mirepoix for Brown Stock—MIREPOIX FÜR BRAUNE FONDS UND BRAUNE SAUCEN—*mirepoix pour fonds bruns et sauces brunes*

Notes

A *mirepoix* is a mixture of large vegetable cubes with spices: the combination of vegetables and spices used depends on the end product. If desired, leeks and garlic can be added after the vegetables are browned. Clean, washed vegetable trimmings can be used when making mirepoix (see Table 7-15).

Amount

Use about 5 percent of the volume of the end product for broth, and about 10 percent of the raw weight of the meat for meat dishes.

Flavoring Vegetables for Meat—MATIGNON FÜR FLEISCHGERICHTE—*matignon pour mets de viande* Flavoring Vegetables for Fish Stocks or Soups—MATIGNON FÜR FISCHFONDS UND SUPPEN—*matignon pour fonds de poisson et potages*

Notes

In a *matignon*, vegetables are sliced thinly or cut into small cubes and mixed with spices. The combination of vegetables and spices used varies, depending on the end product (see Table 7-16). The shorter the cooking time, the smaller the vegetable should be sliced. If desired, leeks and garlic can be added after the vegetables are browned.

Herb Bouquet—KRÄUTERBÜNDEL—*bouquet aromatique*

The basic ingredients for an herb bouquet are parsley, thyme, and bay leaf. Depending on the end product, additional herbs can be added.

Spice Sachet—GEWÜRZSÄCKLEIN—*sachet d'épices*

A spice sachet contains a combination of spices and herbs wrapped in cheesecloth, to keep the product to-

Table 7-14. Ingredients for a Vegetable Bundle

Vegetable Bundle	Vegetables							Spices			
	Roasted onions	Onions	Whole leeks	Leeks, white part only	Carrots	Celeriac	Green cabbage	Bay leaf	Cloves	Peppercorns	Parsley stems
For white stocks		•		•	○	•		•	•	•	•
For beef stocks	•		•		•		○	•	•	•	•

Table 7-15. Ingredients of a *Mirepoix*

Mirepoix	Vegetables			Spices				
	Onions	Celeriac	Carrots	Peppercorns	Bay leaf	Thyme	Marjoram	Parsley stems
For brown stocks	•	•	•	•	•	•	•	•

Table 7-16. Ingredients for a *Matignon*

Matignon	Vegetables					Misc.		Spices				
	Whole leeks	Leeks, white part only	Carrots	Celeriac	Onions	Bacon trimmings	Ham trimmings	Garlic	Bay leaf	Cloves	Thyme	Parsley stems
For meat dishes			•	•	•	•	•	•			•	
For fish stocks		•		•	•				•	•		•
For consommés	•		•	•	•							•
For cream soups			•	•	•				•	•		

gether and facilitate easy removal after the food is cooked. The combination varies, depending on end use. The standard spice sachet contains parsley stems, dried thyme, bay leaf, and cracked peppercorns. A spice sachet is used when cooking red cabbage, sauerkraut, game stews, ragouts, braised roasts, and stocks, for example.

7.5.6 Composed Butters– BUTTERMISCHUNGEN–*beurres composés*

Composed butters are made by creaming butter with other ingredients (see Table 7-17). These very popular butters are offered with grilled meats or used to finish a sauce. However, they can serve as an excellent growth medium for bacteria and must therefore be used quickly and kept refrigerated at all times.

It is illegal to add margarine or other substitutes to composed butters. However, if in the menu, the word *sauce* is used, rather than *composed butter*, substitutes are permissible.

Shrimp Butter–DANIELI-BUTTER– *beurre Danieli*

YIELD: 2 LB, 3 OZ (1 KG)		
Shallots	2⅓ oz	65 g
Butter, soft	1 lb, 7 oz	650 g
Shrimp, cooked and peeled	4½ oz	130 g
Red peppers	5⅓ oz	150 g
Anchovy fillets, in oil, drained	½ oz	15 g
Egg yolk, pasteurized	2⅓ oz	65 g
Cognac (40%)	⅓ oz	10 ml
Lemon juice	⅓ oz	10 ml
Salt and freshly ground pepper	1 x	1 x

Table 7-17. Composed Butters

Ingredients for 2 lb, 3 oz (1 kg)	Seasonings, Fresh Herbs, and Spices								Other Ingredients						
	Salt	Pepper, freshly ground	Dill	Basil	Tarragon	Parsley	Garlic	Cilantro	Glace de viande	Dijon mustard	Horseradish	Truffle broth	Black truffles	Lemon juice	Anchovies
Garlic butter– KNOBLAUCHBUTTER– *beurre d'ail*	½ oz (15g)	●					7 oz (200g)							●	
Anchovy butter– SARDELLENBUTTER– *beurre d'anchois*														●	7 oz (200g)
Dill butter– DILLBUTTER– *beurre d'aneth*	½ oz (15g)	●	5⅓ oz (150g)											●	
Basil butter– BASILIKUMBUTTER– *beurre de basilic*	½ oz (15g)	●		5⅓ oz (150g)										●	
Colbert butter– COLBERT-BUTTER– *beurre Colbert*	½ oz (15g)	●			1⅔ oz (50g)				1⅔ oz (50g)					●	
Herb butter– KRÄUTERBUTTER– *beurre maître d'hôtel*	½ oz (15g)	●				7 oz (200g)								●	
Mustard butter– SENFBUTTER– *beurre de moutarde*	½ oz (15g)	●								5⅓ oz (150g)				●	
Horseradish butter– MEERRETTICHBUTTER– *beurre de raifort*	½ oz (15g)										7 oz (200g)			●	
Truffle butter– TRÜFFELBUTTER– *beurre de truffes*	½ oz (15g)	●										3½ oz (100g)	1 oz (25g)		
Cilantro butter– KORIANDERBUTTER– *beurre de coriandre*	½ oz (15g)	●						4¼ oz (120g)							

Mise en place
- Peel and chop shallots. Sauté in 1 ounce (30 g) butter, and let cool.
- Seed red pepper, wash, and cut into a very small dice (*brunoise*). Sauté peppers with a little butter, and let cool.
- Chop anchovy fillets.

Method
- Cream egg yolk with remaining butter.
- Add all other ingredients and blend well.
- Season with salt and pepper.

Note
Shrimp butter is served with grilled crustaceans and mussels.

Lobster Butter – HUMMERBUTTER – *beurre de homard*

YIELD: 2 LB, 3 OZ (1 KG)		
Lobster shells	1 lb, 12 oz	800 g
Lobster trimmings	7 oz	200 g
Thyme twig, fresh	1	1
Dill, fresh	⅔ oz	20 g
Butter	2 lb, 10 oz	1.2 kg
Matignon	5⅓ oz	150 g
Tomato purée	1⅔ oz	50 g
Freshly ground pepper	1 x	1 x
Cognac (40%)	⅔ oz	20 ml
Dry white wine	6¾ oz	200 ml
Fish fumet	10 oz	300 ml

Mise en place
- Crush lobster shells and trimmings.
- Wash thyme and dill.

Method
- Sauté lobster shells and trimmings slowly in butter, to release the red pigment into the fat.
- Add *matignon*, and continue cooking.
- Add tomato purée, herbs, and pepper and continue cooking.
- Add Cognac, and ignite.
- Add wine, and reduce liquid until almost evaporated.
- Add fish fumet, and simmer for 30 minutes.
- Strain, and press through fine-mesh china cap.
- Strain resulting stock through

double layer of cheesecloth and refrigerate.
- Lift solidified lobster butter from top.
- The remaining stock can be used to make a fumet of crustaceans or a bisque.

Note
Lobster butter can be enhanced with puréed lobster coral. Lobster butter is used to flavor sauces and soups. This recipe can also be used to make crab butter, substituting crab shells for lobster shells. Lobster butter is commercially available.

Red-wine Butter – ROTWEIN-BUTTER – *beurre au vin rouge*

YIELD: 2 LB, 3 OZ (1 KG)		
Shallots	7 oz	200 g
Butter	1 lb, 9 oz	700 g
Red wine	1 pt, 9 oz	750 ml
Parsley, Italian, fresh	1⅔ oz	50 g
Salt, freshly ground pepper	1 x	1 x

Mise en place
- Peel and chop shallots. Sauté in a small amount of butter.
- Add red wine, and reduce to about 3⅓ oz (100 ml). Let cool.
- Wash parsley, remove stems, and chop fine.

Method
- Cream remaining butter.
- Add wine reduction and chopped parsley.
- Season with salt and pepper.

Note
Red-wine butter is especially good with grilled beef.

7.5.7 Thickening Agents – BINDEMITTEL – *liaisons*

Thickeners bind liquids, cream sauces, and soups, and they enhance flavors. Modern dietary guidelines advise against high-calorie thickening agents. Today's consumer demands tasty but lighter dishes.

Thickeners are grouped as follows:

Starches – STÄRKEMEHLE – *amidon de blé*

Flours – MEHLE – *farines*

Roux – MEHLSCHWITZE – *roux*

Beurre manié – MEHLBUTTER – *beurre manié*

Heavy cream – RAHM – *crème*

Egg yolk – EIGELB – *jaune d'œuf*

Egg yolk and cream – EIGELB UND RAHM – *liaison*

Butter – BUTTER – *beurre*

Blood – BLUT – *sang*

Starches – STÄRKEMEHLE – *amidon de blé*

Starches must be dissolved in cold liquid before they can be added to hot foods. Undissolved starch cannot expand when it comes into contact with hot liquid and will form lumps. Starches bind liquids best at 177°F (80°C), but lose some of their binding capacity at 203°F (95°C). Soups and sauces that have been thickened with cornstarch will thin when cooked too long. Cornstarch is the most commonly used starch in the United States; other starches are potato, arrowroot, and tapioca. The texture of the thickened product changes with the type of starch used. The food industry has developed some new starch flours that are void of digestible carbohydrates based on guar gum and carob fruit.

Flours – MEHLE – *farines*

Soups and sauces can be thickened with flour (all-purpose flour). The flour is stirred into milk, water, or wine (slurry), and added to the hot liquid. Soups and sauces thus thickened have fewer calories than those thickened with *beurre manié*, because the butter has been eliminated. However, liquids thickened with a slurry must cook for at least 15 minutes, to reduce the taste of raw flour and achieve perfect creaminess.

Roux – MEHLSCHWITZE – *roux*

There are three types:

White *roux*: Sauté flour in fat without coloring it

Blond *roux*: Sauté flour in fat until pale golden

Brown *roux*: Sauté flour in fat until light brown

Amount for 1 qt, 2 oz (1 L) soup	Amount for 1 qt, 2 oz (1 L) sauce
⅔ oz (20 g) fat	1⅓ oz (40 g) fat
1 oz (30 g) flour	1⅔ oz (50 g) flour

When flour is heated, its starch changes to dextrine, and the raw flour taste is eliminated. Consequently, soups and sauces thickened with flour are simmered for at least 15 minutes. That amount of cooking time is also needed to achieve full thickening strength.

Beurre Manié – MEHLBUTTER – *beurre manié*

Soft butter and flour are kneaded together in equal amounts (1:1). *Beurre manié* is used to thicken *à la minute* dishes. To achieve a full thickening strength, *beurre manié* must be cooked for several minutes.

Heavy Cream – RAHM – *crème*

Warm sauces: Generally, the heavy cream is reduced along with the sauce, or double cream (not available in the United States) is used. Sauces thickened with cream are thin, which is consistent with mod-

ern eating habits, but have more calories.

Soups: Cream is added at the end of the cooking process and is not heated, to preserve the cream flavor.

Sour cream can also be used to thicken some soups and sauces, but it must always be added after the liquid has been removed from the heat.

Egg Yolk – EIGELB – *jaune d'œuf*

Egg yolk is added to *salpicon* (diced meat and vegetable mixtures bound with sauce) for croquettes, fritters, or duchess potatoes. The egg yolks must be vigorously beaten into the still-hot mixture to achieve proper thickening.

Egg yolks are used to thicken ice-cream mixtures, custards, cream fillings, and Bavarian creams. The egg yolks are beaten into hot milk and brought to a temperature of no more than 177°F (80°C) to prevent the egg from curdling, and then chilled immediately.

Egg Yolk and Cream – EIGELB und RAHM – *liaison*

Blend the *liaison* with a small amount of hot soup and sauce, and pass through a fine-mesh china cap. Add the tempered mixture to the liquid while stirring constantly. Soups, sauces, or creams with little or no

starch should be heated only to about 177°F (80°C), as egg yolk curdles at about 182°F (83°C). Do not keep the product in a boiling hot-water bath. Foods bound with cream and egg yolk cannot be reheated.

Amount for 1 qt, 2 oz (1 L) soup	Amount for 1 qt, 2 oz (1 L) sauce
1 egg yolk	2–4 egg yolks
3½ oz (100 ml) heavy cream	6¾ oz (200 ml) heavy cream

Butter – BUTTER – *beurre*

Butter is the most elegant thickener. Cold butter in small nuggets is stirred into the finished soup or sauce. The sauce or soup should not be heated further at this point and should be served immediately. If the product is too hot, the butter will separate, causing fat to float on the top, and the product will become thin.

Blood – BLUT – *sang*

Blood (usually pig blood) is used to thicken game stews (jugged game). Because blood is a protein-rich substance, it can spoil easily; only very fresh blood should be used. (The sale of blood is prohibited in the United States).

Cream is often blended into blood; the same steps as for a *liaison* should be followed.

7.6   Stocks

Careful and proper preparation of stocks guarantees the quality and taste of the foods derived from them.

The following guidelines are especially important:

• Select only good-quality, blemish-free raw ingredients (bones, trimmings, vegetables).

• Select the right-size pot of good-quality material.
• Know how the various stocks are started and properly handled.
• Simmer all stocks very slowly.
• Never cover the pot while cooking.
• Frequently remove foam and fat.
• Limit spices.
• The bones for brown stock should

be chopped quite small. After they have been browned, the pan should be deglazed with small amounts of water two or three times and reduced each time to a syrup-like stage before the rest of the liquid is added.

7.6.1 Plain Beef Stock –
BOUILLON – *bouillon d'os*

YIELD: 2 GAL, 2½ QT (10 L)		
Beef bones	17 lb, 10 oz	8 kg
Water	4 gal	15 L
Bouqet garni	1 lb, 2 oz	500 g
Spice sachet	1	1
Salt	1⅔ oz	50 g

Mise en place
• Chop and blanch the beef bones.

• Rinse the bones, first with hot water, then with cold water.
• Prepare the *bouquet garni*.
• Prepare a spice sachet, consisting of bay leaves, cloves, peppercorns, and thyme.

Method
• Cover blanched bones with cold water and bring to a boil.
• Add salt. Skim occasionally.
• Simmer for 3 to 4 hours.
• After 2 hours, add *bouquet garni* and spice sachet.
• Strain carefully through a double layer of cheesecloth.

Notes
Depending on the end use of the stock, green cabbage, tomatoes, and the like can be added to the *bouquet garni*.

If beef brisket or chuck is simmered with the bones, the stock will be much richer (*bouillon de viande*).

7.6.2 Vegetable Stock – GEMÜSE-
BOUILLON – *bouillon de légumes*

YIELD: 2 GAL, 2½ QT (10 L)		
Leeks, green tops	1 lb, 5 oz	600 g
Onions	10½ oz	300 g
Garlic (optional)	⅓ oz	10 g
Carrots	1 lb, 5 oz	600 g
Green cabbage	10½ oz	300 g
Fennel bulb	7 oz	200 g
Celery	10½ oz	300 g
Tomatoes	7 oz	200 g
Margarine	3½ oz	100 g
Water	3 gal, 22 oz	12 L
Spice sachet	1	1
Salt	1⅔ oz	50 g

Mise en place
• Clean and trim all vegetables, and cut into medium dice (*matignon*).

Method
• Sauté leeks, onions, and garlic in margarine.
• Add remaining vegetables, and continue to cook.
• Add water, bring to a boil, and skim.
• Add spice sachet and salt.
• Simmer for no more than 30 minutes.
• Strain carefully through a double layer of cheesecloth.

Notes
Vegetable combinations and amounts can be varied, depending on the end use of the stock.

Vegetable stock is primarily used in vegetarian cooking but is also excellent in fish dishes.

7.6.3 White Veal Stock –
WEISSER KALBSFOND –
fond de veau blanc

YIELD: 2 GAL, 2½ QT (10 L)		
Veal bones	13 lb, 4 oz	6 kg
Spice sachet	1	1
White bouquet garni	1 lb, 12 oz	800 g
Water	3 gal, 3 qt	14 L
Salt	1⅔ oz	50 g

Mise en place
• Chop the veal bones and blanch.
• Rinse the bones, first with hot water, then with cold water.
• Prepare a spice sachet consisting of bay leaves, cloves, peppercorns, and thyme.
• Prepare a white *bouquet garni*.

Method
• Add water to the bones, and bring to a slow simmer.
• Add salt. Skim frequently, and remove fat.
• Simmer for 2 to 3 hours.
• Add the spice sachet and *bouquet garni* after 2 hours.
• Strain carefully through a double layer of cheesecloth.

Notes
Depending on the end use, carrots may be added. The stock will be more flavorful if blanching is omitted; however, it will probably have an undesirable gray color.

7.6.4 Chicken Stock –
GEFLÜGELFOND – *fond de volaille*

YIELD: 2 GAL, 2½ QT (10 L)		
Chicken necks, backs, and carcasses	11 lb	5 kg
Fowl	2 lb, 3 oz	1 kg
Spice sachet	1	1
White bouquet garni	1 lb, 7 oz	600 g
Water	3 gal, 22 oz	12 L
Salt	1⅔ oz	50 g

Mise en place
• Blanch chicken necks, backs, carcasses, and fowl.
• Prepare spice sachet consisting of bay leaves, cloves, peppercorns, and thyme.
• Prepare a white *bouquet garni*.

Method
• Add cold water to chicken parts, and bring to a slow simmer.
• Add salt. Skim frequently, and remove fat.
• Simmer for 1 to 2 hours.
• Add spice sachet and *bouquet garni* after 1 hour.
• Strain carefully through a double layer of cheesecloth.

Notes
If the bones and fowl are very fresh, blanching is not needed, and a better flavor results. The bones must be soaked in water first, and the stock frequently skimmed. The boiled meat of the fowl can be used in other dishes.

7.6.5 Fish Stock – FISCHFOND – *fond de poisson*

YIELD: 2 GAL, 2½ QT (10 L)		
Fish bones and trimmings from saltwater fish	13 lb, 4 oz	6 kg
Matignon	1 lb, 5 oz	600 g
Spice sachet	1	1
Water	2 gal, 2½ qt	10 L
Dry white wine	1 qt, 2 oz	1 L
Mushroom trimmings, fresh	3½ oz	100 g
Salt	1 oz	25 g

Mise en place
- Remove heads and bloody parts from fish bones.
- Chop bones and trimmings. Soak in cold water.
- Prepare the *matignon*.
- Prepare a spice sachet consisting of peppercorns, bay leaves, cloves, and parsley stems.

Method
- Cover the fish bones with cold water.
- Bring to a slow simmer, and skim.
- Add the *matignon*, spice sachet, white wine, mushroom trimmings, and salt.
- Simmer for 30 minutes.
- Strain carefully through a double layer of cheesecloth.

Notes
The spices can be varied, depending on end use of stock; dill, chervil, or fennel can be added.

7.6.6 Fish Fumet – FISCHFUMET – *fumet de poisson*

YIELD: 2 GAL, 2½ QT (10 L)		
Fish bones and trimmings from saltwater fish	13 lb, 4 oz	6 kg
Flavoring vegetables	1 lb, 5 oz	600 g
Shallots	1⅔ oz	50 g
Butter	1⅔ oz	50 g
Mushroom trimmings, fresh	3½ oz	100 g
Dry white wine	1 qt, 2 oz	1 L
Fish stock	2 gal, 2½ qt	10 L
Salt, spices, herbs		to taste

Mise en place
- Remove heads and bloody parts from fish bones.
- Chop bones and trimmings. Soak in cold water.
- Prepare the *matignon*.
- Peel the shallots and slice finely.

Method
- Sauté the shallots in butter.
- Add the *matignon* and mushroom trimmings, and continue cooking.
- Add the fish bones and trimmings, and continue cooking.
- Deglaze with the wine, and add the fish stock. Bring to a simmer, and skim.
- Add the salt and spices. Simmer for 30 minutes, skimming frequently.
- The fish stock should not simmer longer than 30 minutes with the fish bones, or the resulting fumet will have an unpleasant taste.
- Strain carefully through a double layer of cheesecloth.

Notes
Reducing the *strained* fish fumet will create a more intense flavor. Spices and herbs may be varied, depending on end use.

7.6.7 Brown Veal Stock – BRAUNER KALBSFOND – *fond de veau brun*

YIELD: 2 GAL, 2½ QT (10 L)		
Veal bones	13 lb, 4 oz	6 kg
Calves' feet	4 lb, 7 oz	2 kg
Mirepoix	2 lb, 3 oz	1 kg
Spice sachet	1	1
Peanut oil	5 oz	150 ml
Tomato paste	3½ oz	100 g
Water	4 gal	15 L
Dry white wine	1 qt, 2 oz	1 L
Salt	1⅔ oz	50 g

Mise en place
- Chop the veal bones as small as possible.
- Chop the calves' feet
- Prepare a *mirepoix*.
- Prepare a spice sachet consisting of peppercorns, cloves, thyme, bay leaves, and rosemary.

Method
- Roast the veal bones and calves' feet slowly in the peanut oil. Use a tilting frying pan, or a convection or regular oven.
- Add the *mirepoix*, and continue roasting.
- Pour off all excess fat and discard (not down the drain).
- Add the tomato paste, and roast carefully (do not scorch).
- Deglaze with a little water two to three times, reducing the liquid each time to a syrup-like consistency.
- Deglaze with the wine, and add the rest of the water.
- Bring to a simmer, and add salt. Skim and defat the surface frequently.
- Simmer for 3 to 4 hours. Add the spice sachet during the last hour.
- Strain through a double layer of cheesecloth.

Notes
If the bones are roasted in a convection oven, the peanut oil can be omitted.

The smaller the size of the bones, the greater the surface area for browning, which makes the stock darker and more flavorful. The roasting of the bones with the tomato paste must be done slowly at lower temperature, or the stock will become bitter.

7.6.8 Veal Jus – KALBSJUS – jus de veau

YIELD: 2 GAL, 2½ QT (10 L)		
Veal breast bones	11 lb	5 kg
Veal bones	6 lb, 10 oz	3 kg
Calves' feet	4 lb, 7 oz	2 kg
Veal trimmings	2 lb, 3 oz	1 kg
Mirepoix	2 lb, 3 oz	1 kg
Spice sachet	1	1
Peanut oil	5 oz	150 ml
Tomato paste	3½ oz	100 g
Water	4 gal	15 L
Dry white wine	1 qt, 2 oz	1 L
Brown veal stock	5 qt, 9 oz	5 L
Salt	1⅔ oz	50 g

Mise en place
- Chop the veal breast bones and the veal bones as small as possible.
- Chop the calves' feet into small pieces. Chop the veal trimmings.
- Prepare a *mirepoix*.
- Prepare a spice sachet consisting of peppercorns, bay leaves, cloves, marjoram, and thyme.

Method
- Roast the veal breast bones, veal bones, calves' feet, and trimmings slowly in the peanut oil. Use a tilting frying pan or a convection or regular oven.
- Add the *mirepoix*, and continue roasting.
- Pour off excess fat.
- Add the tomato paste, and roast carefully.
- Deglaze with a little water two to three times, reducing the liquid each time to a syrup-like consistency.
- Deglaze with the wine, and add the rest of the water and the brown veal stock.
- Bring to a simmer, and add salt. Skim and defat the surface frequently.
- Simmer for 3 to 4 hours. Add the spice sachet during the last hour.
- Strain through a double layer of cheesecloth.
- Reduce to 10 ½ qt (10 L). Season to taste.

Notes
The many quality ingredients enrich the veal jus and give it the deep, intense flavor. Veal jus is the basis for many exquisite sauces.

7.6.9 Roasting Juices – BRATENJUS – jus de rôti

To complement the inherent flavor of a roast, the roast is removed, excess fat is discarded, and a *matignon* is sautéed in the pan drippings. The pan is then deglazed with wine or an appropriate brown stock. Roasting juices are offered clear or occasionally thickened with a little cornstarch.

7.6.10 Game Stock – WILDFOND – fond de gibier

YIELD: 2 GAL, 2½ QT (10 L)		
Game bones	11 lb	5 kg
Mirepoix	2 lb, 3 oz	1 kg
Spice sachet	1	1
Game trimmings	2 lb, 3 oz	1 kg
Peanut oil	5 oz	150 ml
Tomato paste	3 oz	80 g
Water	3 gal, 3 qt	14 L
Dry red or white wine	2 qt, 4 oz	2 L
Salt	1⅓ oz	50 g

Mise en place
- Chop the game bones as small as possible.
- Prepare a *mirepoix*.
- Prepare a spice sachet consisting of peppercorns, juniper berries, bay leaves, cloves, and thyme.

Method
- Roast the game bones and trimmings slowly in the peanut oil. Use a tilting frying pan or a convection or regular oven.
- Add the *mirepoix*, and continue roasting.
- Pour off excess fat.
- Add the tomato paste, and roast carefully.
- Deglaze with a little water two to three times, reducing the liquid each time to a syrup-like consistency.
- Depending on end use, deglaze the pan with red or white wine, and add the rest of the water.
- Bring to a simmer, and add salt. Skim and defat the surface frequently.
- Simmer slowly for 3 to 4 hours. Add the spice sachet during the last hour.
- Strain through a double layer of cheesecloth.

Notes
Game stock can be enriched with game bird carcasses. The selection of herbs and spices depends on the end use.

7.6.11 Meat Glazes/Extracts – EXTRAKTE – glaces

Glazes or extracts are prepared by reducing stocks to a syrup-like consistency. The basic stock is salt-free. For example:

Chicken stock –
fond de volaille ➤ glace de volaille

Fish stock –
fond de poisson ➤ glace de poisson

Brown veal stock –
fond de veau brun ➤ glace de viande

Game stock –
fond de gibier ➤ glace de gibier

It is necessary to skim the boiling stock frequently, to pass the reduced stock through cheesecloth layers several times, and to change the size of the pot every time, to produce an extract of excellent quality. The still-warm extract is best spooned into an artificial sausage casing, so that thick disks can be sliced and added to sauces when needed.

7.7   Sauces

Joseph Favre, the author of *Dictionnaire universel de cuisine pratique*, defined sauce as "an aromatic substance, more or less liquid, gelatinous, that can be thickened with flour, starch, egg yolks, or blood."

The History of Sauces

Sauce preparation reached new heights of quality and creativity at the zenith of classical French cuisine. It often took as much labor, time, and ingredients for sauce production as it did for the entire main dish. These flavorful sauces were not thickened with flour but with highly concentrated stock that was enriched with fatty ingredients such as butter, goose liver, or bone marrow.

In the lean years following the two world wars, cooks had to be more thrifty. Consequently, starchy thickeners were used more often, to the detriment of flavor.

Sauce production over the last thirty years has been influenced by nutritional knowledge and the growing awareness of health-conscious customers. Although today's sauces are based on classical principles, they have undergone fundamental changes as different ingredients and modern kitchen machines are used. They are of a lighter consistency, not so heavily spiced, and are characterized by a delicate, clearly defined aroma.

The Purpose of Sauces

Depending on the cooking method used, cooked foods lose more or less flavor. Lost flavors must be captured and restored to the dish. Conversely, some foods have little flavor of their own and must be enhanced with added flavors. Hence, the two basic functions of sauces are:

1. To restore flavors lost during cooking. The sauce in this case is made from the cooking stock or the pan drippings (e.g., brown and white sauces).

2. To serve as a flavorful complement and enhancement of a dish. The sauce in this case need not be based on the flavors of the food with which it is served (e.g., tomato, butter, oil, or specialty sauces).

Prerequisites of a Good Sauce

In addition to the professional proficiency of the cook, the following requirements must be met:

- First-class quality ingredients in sufficient quantity
- Flavorful, rich basic stocks with a clean taste
- Fresh herbs whenever possible
- High-quality wines and liqueurs

Characteristics of a Good Sauce

- The color is appetizing, and the sauce shows no signs of fat.
- The consistency is light.
- The flavor is distinct and is not overpowered by spices.

7.7.1 Classification and Summary of Sauces

Table 7-18 shows the types of basic sauces and derivatives thereof.

7.7.2 Brown Sauces – BRAUNE SAUCEN – *sauces brunes*

Brown sauces are known for their deep, full flavor, a result of the bitter aromatic roasting particles that form when protein-containing foods (bones, meat) are browned, and of sugars contained in flavoring vegetables and tomato purée. Taking care to brown the basic ingredients well is essential for good color and great flavor.

The roasting flavors combine during the simmering of the sauce with the gelatinous substances from the bones.

Structure of Brown Sauces

1. Preparation of basic brown stock (see section 7.6.7).

2. Preparation of basic brown sauce: brown stock is enriched with the addition of pan drippings, reduced, strained, and thickened.

3. Preparation of derivative sauce: the basic sauce is enriched with additional drippings of the meat from which it is to be served, to give it the integral taste. A garnish is frequently added.

Uses for Brown Sauces

Brown sauces are usually served with sautéed meat. However, they can complement warm egg dishes or various warm appetizers, braised vegetables, romaine lettuce, celery, Belgian endives, and other vegetables.

Brown sauces served with braised or glazed meats are not derived from a stock-based sauce but are derived from meat juices released during the cooking process; these are called *integral sauces*.

Basic Brown Sauces

Demi-glace

YIELD: 2 GAL, 2½ QT (10 L)		
Veal bones	20 lb	9 kg
Calves' feet	2 lb, 3 oz	1 kg
Mirepoix	2 lb	900 g
Spice sachet	1	1
Peanut oil	3⅓ oz	100 ml
Tomato purée	7 oz	200 g
Dry white wine	1 qt, 2 oz	1 L
Brown veal stock	6 gal, 44 oz	24 L
Butter	10½ oz	300 g
All-purpose flour	12½ oz	360 g

Mise en place

- Chop the veal bones and calves' feet into small pieces (to provide greater surface area for roasting, to improve flavor).
- Prepare *mirepoix* without leeks (leeks burn and cause bitterness when the bones are browned).
- Prepare a spice sachet consisting of thyme, bay leaves, parsley stems, and peppercorns.

Table 7-18. Sauces

Classification	Basic Sauce	Examples of Derivatives	
Brown sauces — BRAUNE SAUCEN — *sauces brunes*	Demi-glace — DEMI-GLACE — *demi-glace*	Garlic sauce — *sauce à lail* Orange sauce — *sauce à l'orange* Marrow sauce — *sauce bordelaise* Hunter's sauce — *sauce chasseur* Cream sauce — *sauce crème* Duxelle sauce — *sauce duxelles* Italian sauce — *sauce italienne*	Onion sauce — *sauce lyonnaise* Madeira sauce — *sauce madère* Truffle sauce — *sauce Périgueux* Piquant sauce — *sauce piquante* Brown mustard sauce — *sauce Robert*
	Veal jus, thickened — GEBUNDENER KALBSJUS — *jus de veau lié*		
	Game demi-glace — WILD DEMI-GLACE — *demi-glace de gibier*	Game cream sauce — *sauce à la crème gibier* Pepper sauce — *sauce poivrade*	

White sauces — WEISSE SAUCEN — *sauces blanches*

	Grand Sauces	Small Sauces	
	Veal velouté — KALBS-VELOUTÉ — *velouté de veau*	Creamed veal velouté — DEUTSCHE SAUCE — *sauce allemande*	White mustard sauce — *sauce à la moutarde* Tarragon sauce — *sauce à l'estragon* Horseradish sauce — *sauce raifort*
	Chicken velouté — GEFLÜGEL VELOUTÉ — *velouté de volaille*	Chicken cream sauce — GEFLÜGELRAHMSAUCE — *sauce suprême*	Chicken cream sauce with red pepper coulis — *sauce Albuféra*
	Fish velouté — FISCH-VELOUTÉ — *velouté de poisson*	White-wine sauce — WEISSWEINSAUCE — *sauce au vin blanc*	Shrimp sauce — *sauce aux crevettes* Lobster sauce — *sauce homard*
	Béchamel sauce — BECHAMEL-SAUCE — *sauce Béchamel*	Cream sauce — CREMESAUCE — *sauce à la crème*	Mornay sauce/Cheese sauce — *sauce Mornay*
	Sauces that can be derived from all basic small sauces:		Mushroom sauce — *sauce aux champignons* Fresh herb sauce (tarragon, basil, dill) — *sauce aux fines herbes (estragon, basilic, aneth)*

Classification	Basic Sauce	Examples of Derivatives	
Tomato sauces — TOMATENSAUCEN — *sauces tomate*	Tomato sauce — TOMATENSAUCE — *sauce tomate*	Neapolitan sauce — *sauce napolitaine*	
	Tomato concassé — TOMATENWÜRFELSAUCE — *tomates concassées*	Portuguese sauce — *sauce portugaise* Provençale sauce — *sauce provençale*	
Butter sauces — BUTTERSAUCEN — *sauces au beurre*	Hollandaise sauce — HOLLÄNDISCHE SAUCE — *sauce hollandaise*	Mustard sauce — *sauce dijonnaise* Sauce Malta — *sauce maltaise* Mousseline sauce — *sauce mousseline*	
	Béarnaise sauce — BEARNER SAUCE — *sauce béarnaise*	Choron sauce — *sauce choron* Foyot sauce — *sauce Foyot*	
Oil sauces — ÖLSAUCEN — *sauces à l'huile*	Herb vinaigrette — ESSIG-KRÄUTER-SAUCE — *sauce vinaigrette*	Ravigote sauce — *sauce ravigote* Vegetable vinaigrette — *sauce vinaigrette aux légumes*	Tomato vinaigrette — *sauce vinaigrette aux tomates* Salad dressings, see section 7.14
	Mayonnaise — MAYONNAISE-SAUCE — *mayonnaise*	Chantilly sauce — *sauce Chantilly* Cocktail sauce — *sauce cocktail* Mayonnaise with fresh white cheese — *sauce mayonnaise au séré*	Rémoulade sauce — *sauce rémoulade* Tartar sauce — *sauce tartare* Green sauce — *sauce vert*

Method
- Heat the peanut oil in a tilting frying pan or roasting pan (browning the bones on all sides imparts color and flavor). Pour off excess oil.
- Add the *mirepoix*, and continue roasting.
- Add the tomato purée, and continue to roast (to reduce acid and intensify flavor and color).
- Add the white wine with a little brown stock, and reduce until the liquid becomes syrupy.
- Pour into a large stock pot, add the brown veal stock, and bring to a boil. Skim off fat and foam.
- Simmer for about 3 hours.
- Add the spice sachet and simmer for an additional 30 minutes.
- Strain through cheesecloth.
- Prepare a roux from the butter and flour. Add the roux to the strained liquid, and boil until reduced to about 10½ quarts (10 L).
- Salt lightly, and pass through a fine-mesh china cap.

Note
When browning bones for brown stock, do not dredge them in flour, as the coating prevents the bones from fully imparting their flavor and nutrients to the stock. In addition, the sauce is more likely to scorch.

Red wine can be substituted for white wine. White wine has a better flavor, but red wine gives a better color.

Thickened Veal Jus – GEBUNDENER KALBSJUS – *jus de veau lié*
In many of today's kitchens, an alternative to demi-glace is thickened veal jus. Veal jus (see section 7.6.8) is reduced more and slightly thickened with starch (such as cornstarch) dissolved in cold liquid.

In the same manner, thickened game jus (*jus de gibier lié*) or thickened chicken jus (*jus de volaille lié*) can be prepared.

Game Demi-glace – WILD-DEMI-GLACE – *demi-glace de gibier*
This sauce is made in the same way as demi-glace, with the following different ingredients:

- Substitute game bones and trimmings for veal bones and veal trimmings.
- Add juniper berries and dried porcini to the spice sachet.

Brown Sauce Derivatives

Classical cuisine developed many derivative sauces from the basic brown sauce (see Table 7-19). They are all prepared using three basic steps.

Preparation
1. Remove excess fat from the pan and deglaze drippings with flavoring vegetables and wine. Reduce.
2. Add the appropriate basic sauce, and boil briefly.
3. Pass the sauce through a fine sieve and enhance. Add appropriate garnishes.

Example: Marrow Sauce
1. Remove excess fat and add finely chopped shallots to the pan drippings. Sauté briefly and deglaze with red wine. Reduce to a syrup-like consistency.
2. Add demi-glace, and boil briefly.
3. Pass the sauce through a fine sieve. Stir in small bits of butter, season, and add blanched marrow slices or cubes.

Notes
- Pan drippings are an essential part of a derivative brown sauce. It provides the characteristic flavor.
- Only good-quality wines should be used in the reduction. The sauce must be cooked down very well to reduce acidity.
- Sweet wines are not reduced and are added only toward the end of the cooking process, to preserve their delicate flavor.
- Brown sauces should not be beaten with a whisk, or their color will lighten.

Table 7-18. Sauces - *continued*

Subdivision		Sauce Examples	
Puréed sauces – PÜREESAUCEN – *coulis*		*Coulis d'écrevisses* (shrimp) *Coulis de homard* (lobster) *Coulis de myrtilles* (blueberry) *Coulis de poivrons* (bell peppers) *Coulis de tomates* (tomato)	
Specialty sauces – SPEZIAL-SAUCEN – *sauces spéciales*	Warm specialty sauces	Apple sauce Horseradish sauce Lobster sauce – *sauce armoricaine* Sauce curry	Sour cream sauce – *sauce smitane* Onion purée – *sauce soubise* Sweet-and-sour sauce Fish specialty sauces
	Cold specialty sauces	Horseradish cream sauce – *raifort Chantilly* Garlic sauce – *sauci ailloli* Cranberry sauce – *sauce aux airelles rouges*	Cumberland sauce Mint sauce – *sauce menthe* Mustard-dill sauce – *sauce moutarde à l'aneth*

- The sauce should not be heated after the garnishes have been added, or the flavor of the basic sauce will change.

7.7.3 Tomato Sauces – TO-MATENSAUCEN – *sauces tomate*

Because of their beautiful color and fruity acidic flavor, tomato sauces stimulate the appetite. The best tomatoes for sauce are fully ripe, meaty tomatoes or the small, oval, Italian plum tomatoes. Tomato concassé can be prepared when tomatoes are in season locally and at their peak and can be frozen for future use.

Two Basic Tomato Sauces
There are two basic tomato sauces:

Tomato sauce – TOMATOSAUCE – *sauce tomate*

Tomato concassé – TOMATEN CONCASSÉ – tomates concassées

Examples of Use
Tomato sauce: Served with pasta, in noodle dishes, with vegetables, added to brown sauce derivatives, as a base for short-order tomato cream soups.

Tomato Concassé: Served with grilled or sautéed meat, fish or crustaceans, fritters, pasta, noodle dishes, vegetables.

Tomato sauce – TOMATOSAUCE – *sauce tomate*

YIELD: 1 QT, 2 OZ (1 L)		
Tomatoes	1 lb, 12 oz	800 g
Spice sachet	1	1
Matignon	5⅓ oz	150 g
Butter	3 oz	80 g
Garlic, crushed	⅙ oz	5 g
Tomato purée	8¾ oz	250 g
All-purpose flour	⅓ oz	10 g
White veal stock	1 pt, 8 oz	700 ml
Salt (pinch)	1 x	1 x
Sugar	1 x	1 x
Seasoning	1 x	1 x

Mise en place
- Prepare a spice sachet (basil, thyme and crushed peppercorns).
- Peel and cut tomatoes into halves, seed and quarter.

Method
Braise *matignon* in butter without browning it, or the sauce may get a brownish tint.
- Add garlic and tomato purée and continue cooking.

- Dust with flour, stir well, and cook briefly.
- Add quartered tomatoes and veal stock. (Flavor gets concentrated and acid is reduced.)
- Bring to a simmer and skim. Add spice sachet, salt and sugar.
- Simmer for 1 hour.
- Season to taste and strain through fine mesh china cap.

Tomato Concassé – TOMATEN CONCASSÉ – *tomates concassé*

YIELD: 1 QT, 2 OZ (1 L)		
Tomatoes	4 lb, 7 oz	2.0 kg
Shallots	1⅓ oz	50 g
Garlic	⅙ oz	5 g
Olive oil	1⅓ oz	50 ml
Tomato purée	3 oz	80 g
Seasoning	1 x	1 x

Mise en place
- Peel tomatoes, cut in half, remove seeds, and cut into small dice.
- Chop shallots.
- Crush garlic into a fine paste.

Method
- Sauté shallots in oil.
- Add garlic and tomato purée and continue cooking.
- Add diced tomatoes and cook briefly. (The tomato cubes should keep their shape and not become mushy.)
- Season.

Variations of the Basic Tomato Sauce

Tomato sauce variations are prepared by adding chopped herbs, sautéed sliced mushrooms, olives and other ingredients to the basic tomato sauce. Classic tomato sauce variations are, for example:

Neapolitan sauce – NEAPOLITAN-ISCHE SAUCE – *sauce napolitaine*
Tomato sauce and tomato concassé are mixed in a 1:2 ratio.

Portuguese Sauce – PORTUGIESISCHE SAUCE – *sauce portuguaise*
Tomato concassé is prepared with a large amount of chopped onions and finished with *glace de viande* (meat extract) and chopped fresh herbs.

Table 7-19. Brown Sauce Derivatives

Sauce	Reduce Drippings with:	Basic Sauce Garnish	Refining, Garnish
Orange sauce – ORANGENSAUCE – *sauce à l'orange*	Port, orange juice	Demi-glace	Curaçao, orange zest
Marrow sauce – MARKSAUCE – *sauce bordelaise*	Shallots, peppercorns, herbs, red wine	Demi-glace	Cubes of marrow
Hunter's sauce – JÄGERSAUCE – *sauce chasseur*	Shallots, white wine	Demi-glace	Mushrooms, parsley
Piquant sauce – PIKANTE SAUCE – *sauce piquante*	Shallots, peppercorns, white wine	Demi-glace	Gherkins, herbs
Brown mustard sauce – SENFSAUCE – *sauce Robert*	Onions, white wine	Demi-glace	Mustard butter or Dijon mustard and lemon juice
Game cream sauce – WILDRAHMSAUCE – *sauce à la crème gibier*	Shallots, white wine	Game demi-glace	Heavy cream, currant jelly, gin
Game pepper sauce – WILD-PFEFFERSAUCE – *sauce poivrade*	Shallots, peppercorns, game marinade	Game demi-glace	Cold butter cubes

Provençale Sauce – PROVENZALISCHE SAUCE – *sauce provençale*
Tomato concassé is prepared with sliced black olives and chopped herbs.

7.7.4 White Sauces – WEISSE SAUCEN – *sauces blanches*

The flavor of white sauces depends on the natural flavor of the basic stock or poaching liquids. Excellent, pure-flavored stocks are a prerequisite in the production of white sauces.

The basic sauce can be refined with a liaison (egg yolk and cream) or with cream. The use of a liaison produces a better flavor; however, the egg yolks increase the cholesterol content and the sauce will curdle if reheated.

The Flavor Basics of White Sauces

White sauces are generally named for their garnishes. It is important to the structure of the sauce to select the right stock to complement the dish with which it is to be served. This means:

Veal stock: for meat dishes

Chicken stock: for poultry dishes

Fish stock: for fish and seafood dishes

Milk: for pasta, vegetable, mushroom, and egg dishes

Special Preparation of Curry and Paprika Sauces

When preparing a curry or paprika sauce derived from a white sauce, it is essential that the delicate flavor of the basic sauce be enhanced but not overpowered. Two techniques are especially useful here:

- A small basic white sauce is flavored with part curry sauce or a bell pepper coulis.
- Curry or paprika powder is lightly sautéed in butter, placed in a spice sachet, and simmered in the basic sauce for a short time.

Grand White Sauces

The grand white sauces are the bases for the small white sauces and also serve as thickeners for fillings.

Structure of Grand White Sauces

Roux + veal stock = veal velouté – KALBS-VELOUTÉ – *velouté de veau*

Roux + chicken stock = chicken velouté – CHICKEN-VELOUTÉ – *velouté de volaille*

Roux + fish stock = fish velouté – FISCH-VELOUTÉ – *velouté de poisson*

Roux + milk = béchamel sauce – BECHAMEL-SAUCE – *sauce béchamel*

Example: Veal Velouté – KALBS-VELOUTÉ – *velouté de veau*

YIELD: 1 QT, 2 OZ (1 L)		
Butter	1⅔ oz	50 g
All-purpose flour	2 oz	60 g
White veal stock	1 qt, 8 oz	1.2 L
Salt		

Method
- Make a blond roux with butter and flour. (The starch changes to dextrin, which destroys the floury taste.)
- Cool the roux. Add the hot stock. (Cold roux prevents the formation of lumps.)
- Bring to a boil, stirring constantly.
- Simmer for about 30 minutes, season, and strain through a fine-mesh china cap.

Small White Sauces

The small white sauces are the bases for derivative white sauces.

Structure of Small White Sauces

Veal velouté + reduced stock + cream = creamed veal velouté – DEUTSCHE SAUCE – *sauce allemande*

Chicken velouté + reduced stock + cream = chicken cream sauce – GEFLÜGELRAHMSAUCE – *sauce suprême*

Fish velouté + reduced stock + cream = white wine sauce – WEISS-WEINSAUCE – *sauce au vin blanc*

Béchamel sauce + cream = cream sauce – CREMESAUCE – *sauce á la crème*

Example: Creamed Veal Velouté – DEUTSCHE SAUCE – *sauce allemande*

YIELD: 1 QT, 2 OZ (1 L)		
Veal stock	13½ oz	400 ml
Veal velouté	1 pt, 11 oz	800 ml
Egg yolks	2	2
Heavy cream	6¾ oz	200 ml
Lemon juice	1 x	1 x
Salt, cayenne	1 x	1 x
Butter, cold	1⅔ oz	50 g

Method
- Reduce the veal stock *rapidly* to a syrupy consistency.
- Add the velouté, and bring to a simmer.
- Combine egg yolks with the cream (liaison). Remove the sauce from the heat and stir in the liaison. Do not allow to boil, or the egg yolk will curdle.
- Season with lemon juice, salt, and cayenne to taste, and strain through a fine-mesh china cap.
- Stir in small cold butter nuggets.

Derivatives of White Sauces

The derivative white sauces are structured in the same way as the brown sauces and follow the basic three preparation steps. Unlike the derivative brown sauces, however, the flavor of derivative white sauces is not based on drippings. The characteristic flavor is derived from the reduced poaching or braising liquid in which the product has been cooked (see Table 7-20).

Preparation Steps
1. The poaching or braising liquid is reduced.
2. A small white sauce is added and briefly simmered.
3. The sauce is strained, refined, briefly mixed, and garnished.

Example: Chervil Sauce for Fish
1. Remove poached fish from the pan and keep warm. Reduce the poaching liquid to a syrupy consistency.
2. Add white wine sauce, and bring to a simmer.
3. Strain the sauce, and season. Refine with cold butter nuggets. Mix briefly, and add freshly chopped chervil.

Notes

- The reduced poaching or braising liquid is an essential component of a derivative sauce.
- Garnishes in the sauce should not be heated. (The basic taste would be altered).

7.7.5 Butter Sauces – BUTTERSAUCEN – *sauces au beurre*

Butter sauces are an emulsion of warmed beaten egg yolks and liquid clarified butter. Because the egg yolks have a high cholesterol content and the butter is high in calories, cholesterol, and fat, these sauces should be used sparingly and served primarily with low-fat dishes, for example, steamed vegetables, poached fish, or lean grilled meat and fish.

Holding butter sauces at temperatures of 105° to 120°F (40° to 50°C) not only allows microorganisms to grow but also causes the flavor to change.

Butter sauces should always be freshly prepared for each serving period.

Basic Butter Sauces

In classical cooking, the two basic butter sauces are differentiated by their taste, though their ingredients and preparation methods are identical:

1. **Hollandaise sauce** (mild and neutral in flavor)
2. **Béarnaise sauce** (highly spiced and flavorful): tarragon vinegar is replaced with white-wine vinegar in the reduction and tarragon and chervil are added to the sauce.

If both sauces are needed, it is sensible to prepare hollandaise sauce first and use a part of it to create béarnaise sauce, adding the flavorful reduction before straining and the chopped herbs after straining, to save labor.

Sauces derived from the basic butter sauces are outlined in Table 7-21.

Hollandaise Sauce – HOLLÄNDISCHE SAUCE – *sauce hollandaise*

YIELD: 1 QT, 2 OZ (1 L)		
Reduction		
Shallots	1⅔ oz	50 g
White peppercorns	10	10
White-wine vinegar	1 oz	30 ml
Dry white wine	⅔ oz	20 ml
Water	3⅓ oz	50 ml
Other Ingredients		
Water	3⅓ oz	50 ml
Egg yolks	8	8
Butter	1 lb, 12 oz	800 g
Salt, cayenne, lemon juice		

Mise en place

- Clarify the butter slowly by placing it in a water bath. (This gentle clarification process preserves the butter flavor.)
- Carefully pour off the butter fat from the milky residue. (Milky residue ruins the flavor.)
- Cool the clarified butter to 115°F (45°C). (Egg yolk proteins would curdle at a higher temperature.)

Table 7-20. Derivative White Sauces

Sauce	Reduction	Small White Sauce	Enrichment, Garnish
Tarragon sauce – ESTRAGONSAUCE – *sauce à l'estragon*	Braising liquid from sweetbread slices	Creamed veal velouté – *sauce allemande*	Butter nuggets, chopped tarragon
Chicken cream sauce with red pepper coulis – ALBUFERA SAUCE – *sauce Albuféra*	Poaching liquid from a chicken breast	Chicken cream sauce – *sauce suprême*	*Glace de viande* and red pepper coulis
Lobster sauce – HUMMERSAUCE – *sauce homard*	Poaching liquid from filets of sole	White wine sauce – *sauce au vin blanc*	Lobster butter
Cream sauce with fresh porcini – STEINPILZRAHMSAUCE – *sauce aux cèpes*	Porcini braising liquid	Cream sauce – *sauce à la crème*	Braised porcini and chopped parsley
Mornay sauce – MORNAY-SAUCE – *sauce Mornay*	None	Cream sauce (with little cream) – *sauce crème*	Egg yolks and grated cheese

Table 7-21. Derivative Butter Sauces

Sauce	Basic Sauce	Refinement/Garnish	Usage
Mousseline sauce – SCHAUMSAUCE – *sauce mousseline*	Hollandaise sauce	Lemon juice and whipped cream (served on top or folded in)	Poached fish and blanched vegetables
Mustard sauce – DIJON-SAUCE – *sauce dijonnaise*	Hollandaise sauce	Dijon mustard (warmed slightly)	Poached flatfish fillets
Choron sauce – CHORON-SAUCE – *sauce choron*	Béarnaise sauce (without herbs)	Tomato *coulis* or slightly warmed tomato paste	Grilled beef and fish
Foyot sauce – FOYOT-SAUCE – *sauce foyot*	Béarnaise sauce	*Glace de viande* (liquid); *caution:* sauce will become thick.	Grilled beef and artichoke bottoms

Method

- Simmer all the reduction ingredients together until almost evaporated. (Flavorings are first dissolved and then concentrated.)
- Thin the reduction with a little water. (The aggressive acidity of the reduction would affect the emulsion strength of the lecithins in the yolks.)
- Add the egg yolks to the reduction, and beat over a 180°F (80°C) water bath until thick and foamy.
- Add the clarified butter in a thin stream, whipping vigorously. (The lecithin cannot emulsify too much fat at once.)
- Season with salt, cayenne, and lemon juice. Strain the sauce through dry cheesecloth.

7.7.6 Oil Sauces – ÖLSAUCEN – sauces à l'huile

Cold sauces based on oil fall into this category. Oil sauces are divided into two groups, derived from two basic sauces:

Clear Oil Sauces

Herb Vinaigrette – ESSIG-KRÄUTESAUCE – sauce vinaigrette

Mayonnaise-based Sauces

Mayonnaise – MAYONNAISE-SAUCE – sauce mayonnaise

Clear Oil Sauces

Clear oil sauces are ideal media for the volatile (etheric) oils in herbs and spices.

As salad dressings, they are versatile with cold or lukewarm dishes. They can also be used as imaginative marinades for cooked vegetables, mushrooms, fish, or seafood (see Table 7-22).

Herb Vinaigrette – ESSIG-KRÄUTER-SAUCE – sauce vinaigrette

YIELD: 1 QT, 2 OZ (1 L)		
Onions	5⅓ oz	150 g
Fresh herbs (chives, basil, parsley, chervil, tarragon)	3½ oz	100 g
Sunflower oil	1 pt, 4 oz	600 g
Herb vinegar	8½ oz	250 g
Salt, freshly ground pepper		

Mise en place

- Chop the onions finely.
- Wash the herbs, and chop or slice them.

Method

- Combine the oil and vinegar with the onions and herbs in a bowl, and whip.
- Season to taste.

Notes

- The types of oil and the vinegar used depend on the end use of the sauce.
- Possible oil varieties are: corn oil, canola oil, olive oil, walnut oil, grape-nut oil. Possible vinegar

varieties are: red-wine vinegar, balsamic vinegar, sherry vinegar, herb vinegar.

- Because onions ferment easily, and herbs rapidly lose their color, it is advisable to prepare only enough dressing for one service period.
- Stir the sauce before each use.

Mayonnaise-based Sauces

Mayonnaise is an homogeneous emulsion of beaten egg yolks and vegetable oil. Table 7-23 lists derivative sauces based on it.

Standards for Mayonnaise

The composition of mayonnaise is regulated by law (federal standards). By Swiss standards, mayonnaise must contain at least 75 percent vegetable oil, whole eggs or egg yolks, and vinegar, salt, spices, mustard, sugar, and lemon juice.

Raw egg yolks can cause salmonella contamination. Using pasteurized egg yolks is recommended.

Lecithin in Egg Yolk as Emulsifier

Lecithin is a fatlike substance with molecules that are capable of simultaneously binding water and fat molecules. Lecithin therefore acts as a stabilizer for these two insoluble liquids.

Butter sauces and mayonnaise will curdle only if the basic rules for handling the delicate lecithin in egg yolks have not been followed.

Table 7-22. Derivative Clear Oil Sauces

Sauce	Oils/Vinegars	Flavorings	Usage
Vegetable vinaigrette – GEMÜSE-VINAIGRETTE – vinaigrette aux légumes	Olive oil, balsamic vinegar	Soy sauce, blanched vegetables brunoise	Sautéed fish on a bed of lettuce
Tomato vinaigrette – TOMATEN-VINAIGRETTE – vinaigrette aux tomates	Olive oil, white-wine vinegar	Diced tomatoes with additional basil	Marinade for a lukewarm fish salad
Egg vinaigrette – EIER-VINAIGRETTE – vinaigrette aux œufs	Sunflower oil, white-wine vinegar	Chopped eggs	White or green asparagus salad
Ravigote Sauce – RAVIGOTE SAUCE – sauce ravigote	Sunflower oil, herb vinegar	Chopped cornichons, chopped capers	Cold boiled beef

The strength of a lecithin emulsion is weakened when:

- denatured proteins (too hot, too acid) encapsulate the lecithin (never add vinegar or acid reduction directly to egg yolks)
- viscous oil (very cold) is added
- the mixture is not beaten vigorously enough, or too much oil is added at once

Mayonnaise – MAYONNAISE-SAUCE – *sauce mayonnaise*

YIELD: 1 QT, 2 OZ (1 L)		
Egg yolks	4	4
Water	⅔ oz	20 ml
Prepared mustard	⅔ oz	20 g
Salt	1 x	1 x
Sunflower oil	1 pt, 11 oz	800 ml
White-wine vinegar	1 oz	30 ml
White pepper, lemon juice		

Method

- Combine the egg yolks, water, mustard, and salt; whisk until foamy.
- Add the oil in a fine, steady stream, while whipping vigorously.
- Add the vinegar after all the oil has been incorporated.
- Season with pepper and lemon juice.

Notes

- The egg yolks and oil must be at room temperature.
- The oil should be neutral in taste and high in polyunsaturated fatty acids. The neutral taste makes it possible to use the mayonnaise in various ways, and the polyunsaturated fatty acids keep mayonnaise at the right consistency when refrigerated.

7.7.7 Purée Sauces/Coulis – PÜREESAUCEN – *coulis*

A *coulis* is a delicate, pure-tasting, semiliquid purée of fruit, vegetables, meat, fish, and seafood. Even though it is expensive to prepare, it is perhaps the lightest and tastiest of the sauces. *Coulis* are always pure products, thickened by the main ingredient, not by starch or flour.

Important Purée Sauces

Fruit purées are generally used for desserts. However, fruit *coulis* can accompany game and poultry entrées, when the sugar is reduced and a meat glaze is incorporated.

Vegetable purées are important in warm meals. Almost any vegetable can be made into a purée. Unless the purée is used in a vegetarian dish, the flavor of vegetable purées can also be refined with the addition of reductions from fish, veal, poultry, or game.

Crustacean coulis are strong concentrates made from the shells and innards of lobster or crayfish. The *coulis* is further refined with coral butter and cream.

Usage of Purées

Purées are extremely versatile. They are mainly used in food preparation:

- *as sauces:* because of their firm consistency, they are frequently used as a base for plate presentations.
- *as a flavoring:* adding a little *coulis* to small white sauces creates very delicate derivative sauces, due to the pure, concentrated flavor of purées.
- *as soups: coulis* are an ideal basis for light, flavorful soups.

Example: Tomato *Coulis* – TOMATEN-COULIS – *coulis de tomates*

YIELD: 1 QT, 2 OZ (1 L)		
Onions	7 oz	200 g
Garlic clove	1	1
Tomatoes	5 lb, 8 oz	2.5 kg
Olive oil	1⅔ oz	50 ml
Tomato purée	3½ oz	100 g
Meat glaze	1⅔ oz	50 g
Butter	1⅔ oz	50 g
Salt, sugar, ground pepper		

Mise en place

- Chop the onions and grate the garlic.
- Peel the tomatoes, cut in half, seed, and dice.

Method

- Sauté the onions in the olive oil. Add the garlic.
- Add the tomato purée, and continue cooking.
- Add the diced tomatoes, cover, and braise in the oven for 15 minutes.
- Strain through a fine-wire china cap.
- Add the appropriate meat glaze, browned butter, salt, sugar, and pepper.

Serving Suggestions for Warm Coulis

Tomato coulis – TOMATEN-COULIS – *coulis de tomates:* serve with sautéed or grilled meat, fish kabobs, sautéed or grilled seafood; with vegetables, pasta, whole-grain patties, fritters, or batter-fried meat, poultry or fish.

Table 7-23. Derivative Mayonnaise-based Sauces

Sauce	Flavorings, Garnishes	Usage
Rémoulade sauce – REMOULADENSAUCE – *sauce rémoulade*	Chopped cornichons, anchovy fillets, capers, fresh herbs, onions	Fried fish
Tartar Sauce – TATARENSAUCE – *sauce tartare*	Chopped eggs, chopped cornichons, chives	Cold meat dishes
Cocktail sauce – COCKTAILSAUCE – *sauce cocktail*	Grated horseradish, tomato ketchup, brandy, Tabasco sauce	Cold seafood dishes
Green sauce – GRÜNESAUCE – *sauce verte*	Smooth purée of blanched spinach and fresh herbs (cress, parsley, etc.)	Poached cold fish

Blueberry *coulis* – HEIDELBEEREN-COULIS – *coulis de myrtilles:* serve with sautéed game, for example, venison medallions, and with sautéed or fried game birds and poultry.

Lobster *coulis* – HUMMER-COULIS – *coulis de homard:* serve with sautéed or grilled seafood, fish dumplings, and use in derivative white-wine sauces.

7.7.8 Specialty Sauces – SPEZIAL-SAUCEN – *sauces spéciales*

All warm and cold specialty sauces that are not derived from a basic sauce are grouped together as specialty sauces (see Tables 7-24 and 7-25).

Many of these sauces are highly spiced, to contrast the sauce with the food it accompanies. However, contrast should not be the main focus; it is more important to construct a sauce that will add missing flavor components and complement the dish to its fullest potential.

Many cold sauces have their roots in English cuisine or the cuisines of former English colonies.

These sauces are used as condiments, and high-quality products are commercially available, for example, ketchup, chili sauce, Worcestershire sauce, soy sauce, mango chutney, and sweet-and-sour sauce.

Table 7-24. Examples of and Pointers for Warm Specialty Sauces

Sauce	Pointers	Usage
Apple sauce – APFELSAUCE	Apple sauce should be thick; otherwise it will become runny on the plate when it mingles with the roasting juices, which are served alongside the apple sauce.	Roast goose or duck and pork roast
Curry sauce – *sauce curry*	Curry powder should be sautéed lightly, or it will develop a bitter taste.	Curry dishes; to flavor soups and derivative sauces
Horseradish sauce – MEERRETTICHSAUCE		Roast or boiled beef
Sweet-and-sour sauce	The commercially available sweet-and-sour sauces are prepared from basic ingredients and as a rule are of high quality.	Deep-fried dishes in Asian cuisine

Table 7-25. Examples of and Pointers for Cold Specialty Sauces

Sauce	Pointers	Usage
Mint sauce – MINZSAUCE – *sauce menthe*	Spooned hot into jars, tightly closed, and kept in a cool place, this sauce can be stored for a month.	Roast lamb
Cumberland sauce – *sauce cumberland*	This sauce should rest refrigerated for a few days before service.	Cold game dishes, pâtés and terrines
Whipped cream with horseradish – MEERRETTICHRAHM – *raifort Chantilly*	Horseradish must be finely grated. Variation: with walnuts, dill, etc.	Smoked fish

7.8 Soups

7.8.1 Classification and Summary of Soups

Table 7-26 shows the basic types of soups and their variations.

Soup through History

During the sixteenth and seventeenth centuries, solid, stewlike soups were the norm at mealtime, because of the very primitive cooking facilities (open hearth). Including soups as a part of a menu was basically unknown. Only in the eighteenth century, when classical cuisine was developed and a formal menu was served, did soup become a constant feature on the menu. In the households of the upper classes, offering a choice of a clear and a thickened soup to guests was considered the height of elegance. This custom is responsible for the many soup varieties in today's repertoire.

The Functions of Soup

Within the menu, soup serves to prepare the stomach for the food that follows:

- It activates the digestive juices because of its aroma, flavor, and of course, appetizing presentation.
- It warms the stomach.

Soups are often high in calories and nutrients and have a strong satiety value. This is especially important when costs are a factor, as in home cooking, for example.

Soups are also used to advantage in special diets (for example, low-fat puréed grain soups or double consommés), either a weight-reduction diet or a diet to strengthen a recovering patient.

Important Principles

1. Choosing the Right Soup
   The soup must complement the appetizer or the main course. Repetition of color, texture, or main ingredient should be avoided.

Table 7-26. Types of Soups

Class.	Main Groups	Subgroups	Variations	
Clear soups – KLARE SUPPEN – *potages clairs*	Consommés – KRAFTBRÜHEN – *consommés*	Consommé Consommé de gibier (game) Consommé de poisson (fish) Consommé de volaille (chicken)	*à la moelle* (marrow) *aux pailettes* (pastry straws) *quenelles de semoule* (semolina dumplings) *Demidov* (chicken dumplings) *Dubarry* (royal custard and cauliflower) *madrilène* (chilled) *princesse* (barley and chicken strips)	
	Meat broth – FLEISCHBRÜHE – *bouillon de viande*			
Thickened Soups – GEBUNDENE SUPPEN – *potages liés*	Cream soups – CREMESUPPEN – *potages crème*	Meat, poultry, fish, and grain cream soups *Crème de viande, de volaille, de poisson, et de céréales*	*Crème de volaille* (chicken) *Crème dieppoise* (fish and mussels) *Crème d'orge* (barley)	*Crème Agnès Sorel* (chicken with calf's tongue, mushrooms) *Crème Marie Stuart* (chicken with vegetable garnish)
		Vegetable cream soups – GEMÜSECREMESUPPEN – *crèmes de légumes*	*Crème d'artichauts* (artichokes) *Crème d'asperges* (asparagus) *Crème de brocoli* (broccoli) *Crème de concombres* (cucumber)	
	Purée soups – PÜREESUPPEN – *potages purés*	Purée vegetable soups – GEMÜSEPÜREESUPPEN – *crémes de légumes*	*Purée Crécy* (carrots) *Purée florentine* (spinach) *Purée Parmentier* (potato)	
		Puréed legume soups – HÜLSENFRÜCHTE-PÜREESUPPEN – *purées de légumineux*	*Purée Condé* (with pastry strips) *Purée Faubonne* *Purée St.Germain* (green split pea) *Purée Victoria* (yellow split pea)	
	Vegetable soups – GEMÜSESUPPEN – *potages aux légumes*		*Potage bonne femme* (creamed potato soup) *Potage cultivateur* (garden vegetable) *Potage paysanne* (farmer's soup)	
	Grain soups – GETREIDESUPPEN – *potages aux céréales*		*Potage à l'orge perlé* (barley) *Potage aux flocons d'avoine* (oatmeal) *Potage Léopold* (semolina with sorrel)	

2. Amount to Serve

If the soup is intended to help satiate the guest, the serving should be about 8½ ounces (250 ml) per person. In menus with four or more courses, the serving size should be no more than 5 ounces (150 ml) per person.

7.8.2 Clear Soups – KLARE SUPPEN – *potages clairs*

Consommés – KRAFTBRÜHEN – *consommés*

Table 7-27 shows the components of the basic consommés.

Preparing the Clarification

1. Grind the lean meat from older animals with the coarse plate of the meat grinder. (Ground meat releases nutrients quicker. Meat from older animals has more flavor.)

Table 7-26. Types of Soups – *continued*

Classification	Sub groups	Variations
National soups – NATIONALSUPPEN – *potages nationaux*	Switzerland	*Bündner Suppe* (barley cream soup), *Basler Mehlsuppe* (old-fashioned onion soup), *potée vaudoise*
	France	*Bouillabaise marseillaise, petite marmite Henri IV, soupe à l'oignon gratinée*
	Italy	Minestrone, *busecca* (vegetable/dry bean), *zuppa pavese* (egg with parmesan bread), *zuppa mille-fanti* (parmesan/egg drop)
	England	Clear oxtail soup, chicken broth
	Others	Gazpacho (Spain), Polish borscht (Poland), *gulyas* (Hungary), mulligatawny (India)
Special soups – SPEZIALSUPPEN – *potages spéciaux*		*Bisque d'écrevisses* (crayfish bisque), *crème au citron vert* (cream of lime soup), *soupe au vin d'Auvernier* (wine soup), *potage* Germiny (egg cream soup with sorrel)
Cold soups – KALTE SUPPEN – *potages froides*		*Consommé en gelée* (jellied consommé), *crème d'avocat froide* (cold avocado soup), *crème de tomates froide* (cold tomato soup), *vichyssoise* (cold potato and leek soup)

Table 7-27. Structure of Consommés

Basic Stock	+	Clarification	=	Consommé
Beef bouillon	+	Beef, egg white, *matignon*, tomato trimmings and water	=	Consommé – KRAFTBRÜHE – *consommé*
Fish stock	+	Fish, egg white, diced shallots, white part of leeks, common mushrooms, and ice	=	Fish consommé – FISCHKRAFTBRÜHE – *consommé de poisoon*
Chicken stock	+	Beef and chicken (1:2), browned chicken carcasses, egg white, *matignon*, and water (ice)	=	Chicken consommé – GEFLÜGELKRAFTBRÜHE – *consommé de volaille*
Game stock	+	Beef and game (1:2),browned game trimmings, egg white, *matignon*, tomato trimmings, and water (ice)	=	Game consommé – WILDKRAFTBRÜHE – *consommé de gibier*

2. Add browned bones and trimmings. (Browning adds roasting flavors.)

3. Add the rest of the ingredients, and mix well. Refrigerate for several hours. (Proteins are leached into the liquid.)

Clarification

The proteins in meat and egg white clarify consommés. The proteins disperse in the cold stock when mixed. When the stock is heated, they begin to coagulate at about 160°F (70°C) and encapsulate the impurities. When the liquid comes to a boil, the protein rises to the top in a solid layer.

Notes

Using more egg white than is necessary to clarify the consommé will negatively affect the taste, as the egg white will remove not only impurities but also flavor particles.

Consommé – KRAFTBRÜHE – *consommé*

YIELD: 2 QT, 20 OZ (2.5 L)		
Clarification meat	1 lb	450 g
Matignon	8½ oz	250 g
Tomatoes	1⅔ oz	50 g
Egg whites	2	2
Water	6¾ oz	200 ml
Bouillon	3 qt, 5 oz	3 L
Salt		

Mise en place

• Combine the meat, tomatoes, egg whites, and water, and refrigerate this clarification mixture for several hours or overnight.

Method

• Mix cold bouillon with the clarification mixture (hot bouillon would cause the protein to coagulate instantly, and no clarification would take place).

• Bring to a slow simmer, stirring occasionally (stirring stops the proteins from sinking to the bottom, where they could scorch).

• After the mixture has come to a simmer, reduce the heat and do not stir (stirring would cause the clarification to break up and release impurities).

• Skim the fat occasionally, and let the stock simmer for about 1 hour (fish stock, only 30 minutes).

• Push the coagulated protein layer gently to one side, and pour or ladle the consommé through a double layer of cheesecloth.

• Season, and remove any remaining fat with absorbent paper.

Double Consommés – DOPPELTE KRAFTBRÜHEN – *consommés doubles*

Double consommés are made with double the amount of clarification meat and no egg whites.

Double consommés are prepared only for special occasions, and in French they are called *essence (de bœuf, de volaille, de gibier)*. Double consommés are the basis for chilled consommés.

Consommé Variations

Variations are created by:

• adding one or more garnishes
• flavoring the consommé with sweet wines
• serving appropriate accompaniments separately

Examples of Garnishes and Accompaniments

Eggs: Whole egg yolk, egg drops, egg custard, quail eggs

Meat: Marrow slices, strips or cubes of cooked meat, small dumplings

Vegetables: Vegetable slices, strips, and cubes; mushroom slices

Doughs: Strips of crêpes, small ravioli or tortellini, soup pastas, *choux* peas

Grains: Rice, barley

Accompaniments: Puff pastry, grated cheese, bread croutons

Identification

The name *consommé* always refers to enriched, clarified beef stock. Consommés made from poultry, fish, or game must be identified as such.

The consommé should be identified not only by the basic stock but also by the garnish:

CONSOMMÉ	CONSOMMÉ
with liver dumplings	*aux noques de foie*
with strips of vegetables	*julienne*
with Madeira	*au madère*
with cheese toast	*aux diablotins*
with egg custard	*royale*
with marrow	*à la moelle*
with strips of crêpes	*Célestine*

Table 7-28. Differences Between Bouillons and Consommés

Regarding	Meat Bouillon	Consommé
Basic stock	Beef bone bouillon	Beef bone bouillon, poultry, game, or fish stock
Enrichment	Beef brisket or fowl	Ground meat type depends on consommé
Flavoring	*Bouquet garni*	Matignon
Clarification	None	Completely clear, through clarification
Fat removal	May have small amount of fat	Completely fat-free
Color	Golden	Dependent on variety, from very light (fish) to dark amber (game)

Table 7-29. Thickened Soups

Basic Stock	Finishing	Refinement
Cream soups		
Meat, poultry, fish, and grain cream soups	White *matignon*	Wheat flour or other flours
Vegetable cream soups	White *matignon* and base vegetable	A little wheat flour or rice flour and the base vegetable
Purée soups		
Vegetable and legume purée soups	White *matignon* and base vegetable or legume	Potatoes
Grain soups	Diced vegetables or chopped onions	Base grain in the form of fine meal, flakes, or coarse meal
Vegetable soups	Chopped onions and sliced vegetables	Sliced potatoes or a little flour

Bouillons – FLEISCHBRÜHEN – *bouillons de viande*

When meat is cooked in stock, the resulting enriched liquid is called *bouillon*. The meat is removed and used either in cold or warm dishes. The bouillon is passed through a double layer of cheesecloth, the fat is partially removed, and the bouillon is seasoned and used in the preparation of soups. The same garnishes that are listed for consommés can be added to bouillon. Table 7-28 compares bouillons and consommés.

7.8.3 Thickened Soups – GEBUNDENE SUPPEN – *potages liés*

Soups that contain starches, starch products, vegetables, grains, or legumes are called thickened soups. Unlike clear soups, which are appropriate for most menus, thickened soups have more limited applications and are often on a daily menu.

Cream Soups – CREMESUPPEN – *potages crème*

Cream soups include all soups that are lightly thickened, strained, and enriched with cream or a liaison. These soups are further differentiated by their various preparation methods and ingredients, and they are classified as meat, poultry, fish, grain, and vegetable cream soups (Table 7-30).

Use of the Liaison

Dilute and warm the liaison first with a little hot soup to temper it, and then stir it into the rest of the soup. Heat, stirring constantly, to about 175°F (80°C), and serve at once.

Low-calorie Preparation

Reducing calories involves reducing fat. Replace the roux with a cold rice-flour slurry, and beat into the hot stock. Decrease the amount of cream.

Grain Cream Soups

Grain cream soups are prepared in the same way as meat cream soups. The flour is replaced with flour of the base grain but is only dusted over the soup, not incorporated as a *roux*.

Meat, Poultry, Fish, and Grain Cream Soups – FLEISCH-, GEFLÜGEL-, FISCH-, UND GETREIDECREMESUPPEN – *crèmes de viande, de volaille, de poisson, et de céréales*

Table 7-30. Examples of Meat, Poultry, Fish, and Cereal Cream Soups

Soup	Garnish
Curried cream of chicken soup – CURRY- GEFLÜGELCREMESUPPE – *crème Lady Hamilton*	Finely diced vegetables (brunoise)
Fish and shellfish soup with cream – FISCHCREMESUPPE – *crème dieppoise*	Mussels and shrimp
Cream of chicken with mushrooms and calves' tongue – GEFLÜGELCREMESUPPE – *crème Agnès Sorel*	Mushrooms, calves' tongue, and chicken meat
Cream of chicken with vegetables GEFLÜGELCREMESUPPE MARIE STUART – *crème Marie Stuart*	Finely diced carrots, celeriac, and leeks (brunoise)
Cream of barley soup – GERSTENCREMESUPPE – *crème d'orge*	Finely diced vegetables, for example
Cream of green spelt soup – GRÜNKERN-CREMESUPPE – *crème de blé vert*	Finely diced artichoke bottoms, for example
Cream of oat soup – HAFERCREMESUPPE – *crème d'avoine*	Strips of vegetables (julienne), for example
Cream soup with rice and tomatoes – KALBSCREMESUPPE MIT RICE – *crème Carmen*	Firm cooked rice and diced tomatoes
Cream of almond soup – MANDELMILCH-GEFLÜGELCREMESUPPE – *crème dame blanche*	Chicken dumplings and cubed chicken meat
Cream of rice soup, German style – CREMESUPPE – *crème allemande*	None

YIELD: 2 QT, 20 OZ (2.5 L)		
White matignon	5 oz	150 g
Butter	1⅔ oz	50 g
All-purpose flour/ grain flour	3 oz	80 g
Stock	2 qt, 20 oz	2.5 L
Salt and spices		
Heavy cream or liaison	10 oz	300 ml
Cold butter nuggets	⅔ oz	20 g

Basic Stock	Finishing	Refinement
Bouillon, veal, poultry, fish, or vegetable stock	Strain through cheesecloth	Heavy cream or liaison, cold butter nuggets
Bouillon or vegetable stock	Purée and strain through a fine-mesh china cap	Heavy cream
Bouillon or vegetable stock	Purée in a blender or food mill and strain through a coarse-mesh china cap	Heavy cream
Bouillon, veal, poultry, or vegetable stock	As is or strained	Heavy cream or liaison
Bouillon or vegetable stock	As is	Varies with the style of soup

Method

- Sweat the *matignon* in the butter (increases the flavor).
- Add the flour, and continue to cook (raw flour taste is diminished).
- Cool. Add the hot stock (less stirring), and bring to a simmer, while stirring.
- Simmer for about 30 minutes (cooks flour completely), skimming occasionally.
- Strain through cheesecloth or a fine-mesh china cap, and return to a simmer.
- Season, and enrich with the cream or liaison.
- Add the butter nuggets and separately cooked garnishes.

Vegetable Cream Soups–GEMÜSE-CREMESUPPE–*crèmes de légumes*

In contrast to meat-based cream soups, which depend on the quality and flavor of the stock, vegetable cream soups get their characteristic flavor from cooking and blending the ingredients of the soup (see Table 7-31.

Vegetable Cream Soup–GEMÜSE-CREMESUPPE–*crèmes de légumes*

YIELD: 2 QT, 20 OZ (2.5 L)		
White matignon	7 oz	200 g
Vegetables	1 lb, 10 oz to 2 lb, 3 oz	750 g to 1 kg
Butter	1⅓ oz	40 g
All-purpose flour / rice flour	1⅓ oz	40 g
Stock	2 qt, 20 oz	2.5 L
Salt and spices		
Heavy cream or liaison	10 oz	300 ml
Fresh herbs		

Method

- Sauté the *matignon* and the vegetables in the butter (increases the flavor and reduces acidity).
- Add the flour, and continue to cook (the amount of flour depends on the starch content of the vegetables). Cool.
- Add the hot stock (less stirring), and bring to a simmer, while stirring.
- Simmer for about 30 minutes (cooks flour completely), skimming occasionally.
- Strain through cheesecloth or a fine-mesh china cap, and return to a simmer.
- Season with salt and spices, and enrich with the cream or liaison.
- Add separately cooked garnishes.
- Sprinkle with the fresh herbs.

Notes

Use a mild-flavored stock, such as bouillon, for vegetable cream soups when no vegetable stock is on hand.

Purée Soups–PÜREESUPPEN–*potages purées*

In the past, it was customary to serve puréed meat, poultry, game, and seafood soups in addition to purée soups made from vegetables and legumes. In today's cuisine, those puréed soups no longer play a role. On the contrary, the fiber-rich, satisfying vegetable and legume purée soups are now the favorites, especially those cooked in the home. The biggest difference between purée soups and vegetable cream soups is the substitution of potatoes for the flour, giving them a thicker consistency.

Vegetable Purée Soups–GEMÜSE-PÜREESUPPEN–*purées de légumes*

YIELD: 2 QT, 20 OZ (2.5 L)		
White matignon	7 oz	200 g
Butter	2 oz	60 g
Vegetables	1 lb, 12 oz	800 g
Stock	2 qt, 20 oz	2.5 L
Potatoes	10½ oz	300 g
Heavy cream	10 oz	300 ml
Cold butter nuggets	⅔ oz	20 g
Fresh herbs	⅔ oz	20 g
Salt, spices		

Method

- Sauté the *matignon* in the butter.
- Add the vegetables, and continue to cook (increases the flavor and reduces acidity).
  Add the hot stock, and skim (removes impurities).
- Simmer for about 20 minutes. Add the potatoes, and cook another 20 minutes.
- Purée the soup with a food mill. Strain through a fine-mesh china cap, and return to a simmer. (Use of a blender is optional).
- Season, and enrich with the cream and butter nuggets.
- Add separately cooked garnishes. Sprinkle with the fresh herbs.

Table 7-31. Vegetable Cream Soups

Soup	Examples of Garnishes
Cream of artichoke soup–ARTISCHOCKENCREMESUPPE–*crème d'artichauts*	Cubed artichoke bottoms
Cream of broccoli soup–BROCCOLICREMESUPPE–*crème de brocoli*	Broccoli florets
Cream of mushroom soup–CHAMPIGNONCREMESUPPE–*crème de champignons*	Mushroom strips
Cream of cucumber soup–GURKENCREMESUPPE–*crème de concombres*	Poached cucumber cubes
Cream of carrot soup–KAROTTENCREMESUPPE–*crème de carottes*	Carrot pearls (tiny melon baller), tapioca, chervil leaves
Cream of pumpkin soup–KÜRBISCREMESUPPE–*crème de potiron*	Porcini mushroom strips, artichoke bottom cubes, pumpkin seeds (toasted)
Cream of leek soup–LAUCHCREMESUPPE–*crème de poireaux*	Finely cut strips of leek, chives
Cream of asparagus soup–SPARGELCREMESUPPE–*crème d'asperges*	Green asparagus tips, chicken dumplings, chopped pistachios
Cream of tomato soup–TOMATENCREMESUPPE–*crème de tomates*	Diced tomatoes, rice, bread croutons

Notes

The same garnishes used for vegetable cream soups are suitable for purée soups.

Classic Vegetable Purée Soups

Purée of chestnut soup – KASTANIEN-PÜREESUPPE – *purée Clermont*

Purée of carrot soup – KAROTTEN-PÜREESUPPE – *purée Crécy*

Purée of potato soup – KARTOFFEL-PÜREESUPPE – *purée Parmentier*

Purée of cauliflower soup – BLUMEN-KOHL-PÜREESUPPE – *purée Dubarry*

Legumes Purée Soup – HÜLSEN-FRÜCHTE-PÜREESUPPEN – *purée de légumineux*

YIELD: 2 QT, 20 OZ (2.5 L)		
White matignon	7 oz	200 g
Butter	2 oz	60 g
Legumes	12 oz	350 g
Stock	3 qt, 5 oz	3 L
Bacon (optional)	1⅔ oz	50 g
Potatoes	7 oz	200 g
Salt and spices		
Heavy cream (optional)	7 oz	200 ml
Cold butter nuggets	⅔ oz	20 g
Fresh herbs	⅔ oz	20 g

Method

- Sauté the *matignon* in the butter.
- Add the legumes, and continue to cook (increases the flavor and reduces acidity).
  Add the hot stock, and skim (removes impurities). If desired, add the bacon.
- Simmer for about 20 minutes. Add the potatoes, and cook another 20 minutes.

- Purée the soup with a food mill. Strain through a fine-mesh china cap, and return to a simmer. (Use of a blender is optional).
- Season, and enrich with the cream and butter nuggets.
- Add the separately cooked garnishes. Sprinkle with fresh herbs.

Notes

Hot bread croutons are an excellent garnish.

Classic Legume Purée Soups

Purée of red kidney beans – PÜREE-SUPPE VON ROTEN BOHNEN – *purée Condé*

Purée of lentils – LINSENPÜREESUPPE – *purée Esaü*

Purée of navy beans – PÜREESUPPE VON WEISSEN BOHNEN – *purée Faubonne*

Purée of green split peas – GRÜNERBSEN-PÜREESUPPE – *purée St-Germain*

Purée of yellow split peas – GELBERB-SEN-PÜREESUPPE – *purée Victoria*

Vegetable Soups – GEMÜSESUPPEN – *potages aux légumes*

Vegetable soups originated in domestic kitchens. They consist of one or more *sliced* vegetables and are *not* strained.

Especially suitable vegetables are: onions, leeks, celery, carrots, Savoy cabbage, turnips, and potatoes. Zucchini, green beans, diced tomatoes, or asparagus tips can be added to the soup later in the cooking process, as they cook quickly. Table 7-32 lists common vegetable soups.

Vegetable Soups – GEMÜSESUPPEN – *potages aux légumes*

YIELD: 2 QT, 20 OZ (2.5 L)		
Smoked slab bacon	1⅔ oz	50 g
Butter	1 oz	30 g
Vegetables	1 lb, 10 oz	750 g
Flour (optional)	⅔ oz	20 g
Vegetable bouillon	2 qt, 2 oz	2.5 L
Salt and spices		
Chopped fresh herbs	⅔ oz	20 g

Method

- Sauté the diced bacon in the butter.
- Add onions, Savoy cabbage, and turnips, if they are among the vegetables being used, and continue to cook (high in acidity).
- Add the rest of the vegetables (except potatoes), and sauté carefully (concentrates flavor).
- Dust with flour if desired.
- Add the hot boullion and simmer for 15 minutes. Add potatoes if used, and cook 10 minutes more.
- Season.
- Just before service, sprinkle with the chopped fresh herbs (herbs taste stronger).

Garnishes

Vegetable soup garnishes include grated cheese, toast, and cheese topped bread slices.

Grain Soups – GETREIDESUPPEN – *potages aux céréales*

The main ingredient of these soups are grains, in the form of coarse or fine meal, flakes, or groats. This type of soup rarely appears on the menu, but it is likely that its popularity will increase as interest in whole foods and spa cuisine continues to grow.

Table 7-32. Vegetable Soups

Soup	Ingredients	Garnishes or Accompaniments
Creamed potato soup – GEMÜSESUPPE HAUSFRAUENART – *potage bon femme*	Leeks, potatoes, enriched with cream	Chives, toast pieces
Farmer's Vegetable Soup – GEMÜSESUPPE BAUERNART – *potage paysanne*	Onions, leeks, carrots, celery, Savoy cabbage, potatoes, a little flour	Chopped parsley, grated cheese
Garden Vegetable Soup – GEMÜSESUPPE PFLANZERART – *potage cultivateur*	Diced bacon, onions, leeks, carrots, turnips, potatoes	Chopped parsley, grated cheese
Vegetable soup, village style – GEMÜSESUPPE DÖRFLICHE ART – *potage villageoise*	Leeks, Savoy cabbage, vermicelli	Chervil leaves, grated cheese

Basic Technique for Grain Soups

Start: Sauté chopped onions or diced vegetables in butter. Add grains and continue to sauté.

Finish: Add hot meat broth or chicken stock, and simmer until done. Strain if desired, or leave as is.

Enrich: Add garnish according to recipe directions. If desired, enrich with heavy cream or a liaison, and add chopped fresh herbs.

Classic Grain Soups

Semolina soup with sorrel—GRIES-SUPPE LEOPOLD—*potage Léopold*

Toasted semolina soup—GERÖSTETE GRIESS-SUPPE—*potage à la semoule grillée*

Barley soup—GERSTENSUPPE—*potage à l'orge perlé*

Oatmeal soup—HAFERFLOCKENSUPPE—*potage aux flocons d'avoine*

7.8.4 National Soups—NATIONAL-SUPPEN—*potages nationaux*

National soups are soups that were originally regional specialties, which because of their ingredients and preparation method became famous beyond their region. The preparation methods vary widely: There are clear, thick, and cold national soups (see Table 7-33).

National soups reflect the native eating habits of their homeland and, on the menu, should therefore be written in the language of that country.

Characteristics of National Soups

Function: Many national soups are stewlike casseroles and take the place of a meal. Extra consideration should be given to these factors when they are added to the menu, and the portion size should reflect the composition.

Ingredients: The ingredients generally are common to the region and low in cost. Exotic ingredients should be used with discretion; the same may be true for certain coarse cuts of meat.

Recipe: Even in the original country, various interpretations of the same soup recipe may exist. A claim to the "original recipe" should therefore not be made.

7.8.5 Special Soups—SPEZIAL-SUPPEN—*potages speciaux*

Some of the special soups are clear, others thick, but all are made with special ingredients.

Expensive and sometimes exotic ingredients give these soups an extraordinary taste, making them ideal for a multicourse meal for special occasions or as an *à la carte* soup.

Small quantities highlight the exclusiveness of the soup. It is therefore important to incorporate them carefully into a menu. Depending on the intensity of the taste, not more than 3½ to 4 ounces (100 to 120 ml) should be served per person.

Examples of Special Ingredients

Shells from crustaceans: Soups made with shells are called by their French name *bisque* and are further identified by the type of crustacean used, for example, *bisque de homard* (lobster), *bisque d'écrevisse* (crayfish). Other crustacean shells do not have enough flavor.

The basis for a bisque is a fragrant concentrated stock made from the shells. The soup follows the preparation structure of a fish cream soup. The garnish is diced lobster or crayfish meat.

Shark fins, kangaroo tail, abalone, birds' nests, trepang (sea cucumber): These ingredients are impossible for most restaurants to obtain fresh. These types of soup are generally produced commercially and sold canned. They are reconstituted in the kitchen following the manufacturer's directions. These usually clear soups can be topped with a curry, for example, and glazed under the broiler, or they can be enriched

Table 7-33. Well-known National Soups

Country	Soup	Description
Switzerland	*Bündner Suppe*	Barley soup with diced vegetables, air-dried beef, white beans, and smoked raw ham. Enriched with a liaison.
	Basler Mehlsuppe	Brown *roux*-based soup with lots of onions, puréed, and flavored with red wine and grated cheese.
France	*Bouillabaisse*	Fish soup with mussels, crayfish, vegetable strips and diced tomatoes. Flavored with saffron and Pernod, and served with garlic bread.
	Petite marmite Henri IV	Meat broth with chicken, boiled beef, marrow bones and vegetables. Toast served separately.
	Soupe à l'oignon gratinée	Meat broth with sautéed onions. Served with cheese toast au gratin.
Italy	Minestrone	Tomato-based vegetable soup with beans and pasta. Flavored with pesto.
	Busecca	Vegetable soup with diced tomato, borlotti beans, and strips of tripe. Flavored with pesto.
	Zuppa mille-fanti	Bouillon with beaten eggs, fresh bread crumbs, Parmesan cheese, and chopped parsley.
England	Clear oxtail soup	Oxtail and calves' feet are made like a jus. The jus is clarified with beef and flavored with sherry. The oxtail meat is removed from the bone, pressed, diced, and added as a garnish.
Others	Gazpacho (Spain), Borscht (Poland), *Gulyas* (Hungary), Mulligatawny (India), Chicken broth (England)	

Table 7-34. Popular Cold Soups

Basic Soup	Cold Soup	Pointers and Description
Consommé	Chilled consommé– *consommé en gelée*	A double consommé is needed to create a satisfying cold consommé. The cold, richly flavored consommé is spooned into cups and chilled for about 5 hours.
Variations:	*à l'estragon* (tarragon), *aux poivrons* (allspice), *aux tomate* (tomato), *au vin* (wine)	Cold consommé should gel only lightly; no extra gelatin is necessary.
Cream soup	Cold cream of tomato soup– *crème de tomates froide*	A thin cream of tomato soup is lightly flavored with Tabasco sauce. As a garnish, diced tomatoes and basil could be used.
Purée soup	Vichyssoise	Potato purée soup is cooked with lots of leeks (white part only). Garnished with chives, enriched with cream, and served very cold.
National soup	Gazpacho	Cucumbers, tomatoes, green peppers, onions, garlic, soft bread crumbs, and a little consommé are puréed in a blender with some olive oil and vinegar. Diced vegetables are added as a garnish.
Special soup	Cold avocado soup– *crème d'avocat froide*	Puréed avocados are thinned with a little cream or yogurt and consommé. Spiced liberally and garnished with finely diced shrimp.

and thickened with a liaison. *Note:* Due to the Washington endangered species agreement, it is no longer legal to import turtle meat and turtle meat products into Switzerland as of June 1, 1988.

Truffle fond: The extremely fragrant canned liquid can be poured cold over a finely cut cooked vegetable garnish in an oven-proof cup, topped with puff pastry, and baked (*fumet de truffes en croûte*).

Sorrel: Shredded sorrel (*chiffonade*) is cooked in a bouillon, enriched with a liaison, and heated to below 185°F (85°C)–*potage Germiny*.

Lime juice: A double consommé is enriched with a liaison, heated to below 185°F (85°C), seasoned with lime juice, and garnished with soft boiled rice (*créme au citron vert*).

Extraordinary wines: A veal cream soup is cooked and finished with wine and garnished with seeded, peeled, halved grapes (*crème au vin d'Auvernier*).

7.8.6 Cold Soups – KALTE SUPPEN – *potages froids*

In warm weather, cold soups are a pleasant change on the menu. They are served in well-chilled soup cups. It is important to remember that cold soups must be seasoned more strongly than warm soups. Cold fruit soups and fruit and vegetable juices are important alternatives to classic cold soups. They are refreshing, stimulate the appetite, and aid digestion; consequently, they are gaining greatly in popularity. Table 7-34 lists some popular cold soups.

Cold Fruit Soups – FRUCHTKALT-SCHALEN – *soupes froides aux fruits*

Cold fruit soups can be prepared from one or more fruits. Especially good are cherries, peaches, mangos, and all types of berries. Melons can also be used.

Method

* *Basic syrup:* Bring sugar (amount depending on type of fruit), water, vanilla bean, and orange and lemon peel to a boil, cool, and pass through a sieve.
* *Thickener:* Purée some of the fruit and add to syrup.
* *Garnish:* Finely dice the rest of the fruit, and add to the syrup purée. If desired, cooked tapioca can be added.
* *Refinement:* If desired, a liqueur (Curaçao, Grand Marnier, Framboise, etc.) or, immediately before service, champagne can be added.

Note

Cold fruit soups are served in chilled glasses with small spoons and drinking straws.

7.9 Appetizers

The History of Appetizers

Cold and warm appetizers were introduced in the courts of the early czars in Russia. These tiny delicacies, called *zakouski,* were offered not to satiate but rather to stimulate the appetite.

The French phrase *hors-d'œuvre* is derived from offering these tidbits "outside" (*hors*) the dining room where the food "presentation" (*œuvre*) usually took place. The cold and warm appetizers of that time are not unlike the cocktail canapés offered today.

Influenced by classical French cuisine, appetizers became more elaborate, were divided into two groups, and were made a part of the menu. Cold appetizers were served before the soup; warm appetizers, after the soup.

7.9.1 Cold Appetizers – KALTE VORSPEISEN – *hors-d'œuvre froids*

Purpose of Cold Appetizers

The purpose of cold appetizers is to stimulate the appetite, and thus they should always be served first. They are often no longer followed by soup. However, if a soup is served, it is best to select a flavorful, clear soup, such as a consommé, *oxtail claire*, or *essence de faison*, to stimulate the appetite further.

Depending on the occasion, the cold appetizer can be a single food or a combination of several select foods. The number of appetizers does not matter; the important considerations are the taste and color combination. Table 7-35 provides an overview of the various types of cold appetizers.

Basic Service Principles

The saying "one eats with one's eyes" is especially true for appetizers. An appealing presentation entices the taste buds. The elegant simplicity of modern cuisine should serve as a guideline here.

Attention should be paid to:

- careful selection of serving dishes
- small amounts, of exceptionally high quality
- a presentation style that does not require complicated hand work
- appropriate simple garnishes

Presentation Styles for Cold Appetizers

Plates – AUF TELLER – *sur assiette*
Individual appetizers or a selection of appetizers are placed on small plates. This service method is practical for the guest as well as the kitchen. It is a very effective service style for daily menus and banquets.

Bowls – IN SCHALEN – *dans raviers*
Each cold appetizer is placed in a glass dish, usually square. The dishes can be assembled on large silver platters or arranged on a refrigerated hors d'œuvre cart and placed in the dining room. This service style is especially useful in à la carte service. It traditionally divides cold appetizers into two types:

Mixed Cold Appetizers –
GEMISCHTE KALTE VORSPEISEN –
hors-d'œuvre variés
A selection of popular cold appetizers, accompanied by complementary sauces, breads (toast), and butter.

Cold Gourmet Appetizers –
SPEZIELLE KALTE VORSPEISEN –
hors-d'œuvre riches
Mixed cold appetizers are enhanced by a few very exclusive items, such as lobster, prawns, or caviar.

Cocktail Snacks

Cocktail snacks are generally served with apéritifs and cocktails. They both buffer the stomach from the impact of alcohol and they help shorten the waiting time for the first course.

Cocktail snacks are classified into three main groups:

Canapés – BELEGTE BROTSCHNITTCHEN – *canapés*

Savories – DELIKATESSENHÄPPCHEN – *gourmandises*

Dips – DIPS – *dips*

Presentation: Cocktail snacks should be neatly arranged on napkin- or paper-covered platters or trays (dips are an exception). The trays can be placed on small tables for self-service or can be offered by service personnel to standing guests.

Canapés – BELEGTE BROTSCHNITTEN – *canapés*
Canapés, also called *amuse-bouche*, are made from white bread with the crust removed, sometimes toasted. Sliced about ¼ inch (5 mm) thick, the bread can be cut into various shapes with a knife or hors-d'oeuvre cutters. For large quantities of canapés, it is more efficient to cut slices from the whole loaf of bread, place the topping and garnish, glaze with gelatin, and then cut into shapes.

Canapés taste best when freshly made, just before service. If this is not possible, an additional layer of gelatin will prevent drying and discoloration.

Instead of white bread, such specialty breads as rye crisps, black bread, pumpernickel, or whole-grain bread can be used. A variety of toppings and garnishes is possible (see Table 7-36).

Savories – DELIKATESSEN-HÄPPCHEN – *gourmandises*
Savories are small appetizers with high-quality, expensive ingredients. Production is often very labor-intensive and demands professional skill. A light gelatin glaze is often applied for additional eye appeal.

In contrast to canapés, which generally have a bread base, savories need not have a base. A toothpick holds the savory in place to make it easier for the guests to eat those without a stable base.

A selection of savories are called *frivolités*.

Examples of Savories
- Tartlets filled with chicken mousse and garnished with a black truffle slice
- Small pastries filled with smoked salmon mousse and garnished with caviar
- Small éclairs filled with a Roquefort cheese–chive butter mixture
- Small cooked artichoke bottoms filled with lobster mousse and garnished with lobster tail slices
- Pastry boats with rolled smoked salmon, filled with a horseradish cream
- Fritters filled with game mousse, garnished with fresh figs and glazed figs.

Dips – DIPS – *dips*
The English word *dip* is used in French and German as well. Small pieces of meat, seafood, or vegetables are dipped into a complementary sauce. Vegetable dips in particular are increasing in popularity.

Table 7-35. Cold Appetizers

Classification	Major Groups	Examples
Cocktail snacks	Finger sandwiches–BELEGTE BROTSCHNITTCHEN–*canapés*	Ham finger sandwiches–*canapés au jambon* Smoked salmon canapés–*canapés au saumon fumé*
	Savories–DELIKATESSENHÄPPCHEN–*gourmandises*	Cream puffs with game mousse–*éclairs Saint-Hubert*
	Dips–DIPS–*dips*	Curry dip–*dip au curry* Orange dip–*dip à l'orange*
Cocktails	Cocktails–COCKTAILS–*cocktails*	Shrimp cocktail–*cocktail de crevettes roses* Cold fillet of sole with mango sauce–*cocktail de sole à la mangue* Grapefruit cocktail with ginger–*cocktail de pample-mousse au gingembre*
Appetizers from the second course	Galantines–GALANTINEN–*galantines*	Chicken galantine with fruits–*galantine de volaille aux fruits (fruitière)* Game pâté with cranberry sauce–*pâté de gibier à la compote d'airelles rouges* Vegetable terrine with tomato vinaigrette–*terrine de légumes à la vinaigrette de tomates* Ham mousse with green asparagus–*mousse de jambon aux asperges*
	Pâtés–PASTETEN–*pâtés*	
	Terrines–TERRINEN–*terrines*	
	Mousses–MOUSSEN–*mousses*	
Fish and fish products	Raw and marinated fish–ROHE, MARINIERTE FISCHE–*poissons crus et marinés*	Carpaccio of salmon trout and turbot–*carpaccio de truite saumonée et de turbot* Gravlax–*gravad lax*
	Smoked fish–GERÄUCHERTE FISCHE–*poissons fumés*	Smoked salmon roses with sour cream–*rosettes de saumon fumé à la crème acidulée*
	Combinations–KOMBINATIONEN–*combinaisons*	Fish fillets sauté vinaigrette–*rouget et saint-pierre sur feuilles de salade*
	Caviar–KAVIAR–*caviar*	Osetra caviar–*caviar Oscètre Malossol*
Shellfish	Crustaceans–KRUSTENTIERE–*crustacés*	Lobster appetizer with artichokes–*avant-goût de homard et d'artichauts*
	Mollusks–WEICHTIERE–*mollusques*	Oysters on the half shell–*huîtres sur glace*
Meat, meat products, and poultry	Meat and poultry appetizers–VORSPEISEN MIT FLEISCH, FLEISCHWAREN, GEFLÜGEL–*viande de boucherie et volaille*	Steak tartare–*tartare* Chicken salad with pineapple–*salade de volaille à l'ananas*
Vegetables	Raw vegetables–ROHE GEMÜSE–*légumes crus*	Raw vegetable salad with three sauces–*crudité maraîchère aux trois sauces*
	Cooked vegetables–GEKOCHTE GEMÜSE–*légumes cuits*	Bouquet of white asparagus with herb cheese–*bouquet d'asperges au fromage frais*
Fruits	Fruits–FRÜCHTE–*fruits*	Avocado and shrimp salad–*avocat aux crevettes*

Presentation: Trimmed cut vegetables or meat on toothpicks are placed in square glass dishes (*raviers*) or glasses. They are arranged in the center of large platters, with assorted sauces around them.

Foods to Serve with Dips
- small carrots or carrot sticks
- radishes with a bit of greenery left on
- tender celery stems
- leaves of Belgian endive
- cucumber sticks
- sliced heart of fennel
- cauliflower florets
- roasted (rare) beef cubes
- cubed, roasted (medium-rare) filet of venison
- poached cubes of Norway lobster tail (Dublin prawn)

Dips: Egg, orange, cheese, herb, and curry dip are some examples.

Cocktails

Appetizer cocktails may consist of several ingredients, for example, fruits, vegetables, mushrooms, fish, seafood, and poultry (see Table 7-37). They are generally served in stemmed glasses. Fruit cocktails are often served in hollowed out fruits (grapefruit, papaya, small melons), placed atop crushed ice.

The key considerations is that the cocktail ingredients harmonize in color and flavor. Toast and butter are traditionally served with appetizer cocktails, except fruit cocktails.

Appetizers from Cold Second Courses

Preparation of cold second courses is discussed in detail in section 7.19.

Presentation: Cold second courses are best presented by themselves. A neatly cut slice, placed on a neutral plate and garnished appropriately, will generally have the most appeal. Toast, brioche, and butter are served with such dishes.

Appetizers are selected from these four groups:

Pâtés — PASTETEN — *pâtés*

Terrines — TERRINNEN — *terrines*

Galantines — GALANTINEN — *galantines*

Mousses — MOUSSEN — *mousses*

Examples of Cold Second-course Appetizers
Game pâté with cranberry sauce — WILDPASTET MIT PREISSELBEERKOMPOTT — *pâté de gibier à la compote d'airelles rouge*

Vegetable terrine with tomato vinaigrette — GEMÜSETERRINE MIT TOMATEN-VINAIGRETTE — *terrine de légumes à la vinaigrette de tomates*

Chicken galantine with fruits — GEFLÜGELGALANTINE MIT FRÜCHTEN — *galantine de volaille aux fruits (fruitière)*

Ham mousse with green asparagus — SCHINKENMOUSSE MIT GRÜNEN SPARGELN — *mousse de jambon aux asperges*

Fish Appetizers

The preparation of cold fish appetizers is discussed in detail in section 7.19.

In contrast to French classical cuisine, which limited such appetizers to an exquisite few, the Scandinavian and Japanese influences on today's cuisine have resulted in a large variety of cold fish appetizers.

Fish appetizers are classified into these four main groups:

Raw and marinated fish — ROHE UND MARINIERTE FISCHE — *poissons crus et marinés*

Smoked fish — GERÄUCHERTE FISCHE — *poissons fumés*

Combinations — KOMBINATIONEN — *combinaisons*

Caviar — KAVIAR — *caviar*

Appetizers from Raw and Marinated Fish

Gravlax — GRAVAD LAX
This Scandinavian salmon specialty is made by marinating a whole salmon fillet with salt, sugar, spices, and fresh dill. Sliced thinly, gravlax is served with a mustard-dill sauce. Large fillets of salmon trout or sea trout can be prepared in the same way.

Fish Carpaccio
Fresh fish can taste quite wonderful when sliced paper thin and lightly salted and spiced. This concept, influenced by the traditional Japanese *sashimi*, is being more and more appreciated. European cooks have taken the name originally used for raw, thinly sliced marinated beef, *carpaccio*, and added the name of the fish variety, for example, Salmon Carpaccio.

Table 7-36. Canapés

Type of Bread	Topping	Garnish
White bread	Asparagus tips	Mayonnaise and radish slices
	Cooked ham	Cherry tomato half
	Shrimp and cocktail sauce	Tomato fan
	Egg salad with chives	Radish fan
	Sliced tomato and chopped egg	Chopped fresh herbs
Toast	Spicy steak tartar mixture	Stuffed green olive slices
	Smoked salmon slices	Sweet onion rings and capers
Pumpernickel	*Tomme vaudoise* (Swiss soft cheese) and herbs	Fresh herbs
Whole-grain bread	Bündner meat (Swiss air-dried beef)	Fresh fig slices

Fish Tartare – FISCH TATAR

Another way to enjoy raw fish is to prepare fish tartare. Again, this is a variation of the classic steak tartare, in which raw, very fresh fish is chopped and well seasoned.

The best fish for fish carpaccio and fish tartare are salmon, trout, halibut, and John Dory.

Smoked-Fish Appetizers

The best-known and best-liked smoked fish is smoked salmon. The color varies from light pink to dark red, depending on the salmon variety and its diet. Wild salmon are much more expensive but have a better flavor than farm-raised salmon. Smoked salmon is most flavorful when sliced very thin.

Since small commercial smokers have become widely available, it is now possible to offer freshly smoked trout or saibling (char) fillets. Combined with a small green salad or with traditional classic garnishes, smoked fish fillets make an excellent appetizer.

Other important smoked fish are eel, sturgeon, sprats, mackerel, and flounder.

Garnishes: chopped onions, capers, olives, whipped cream with horseradish, lemons, toast, or blinis.

Fish Appetizer Combinations

Warm poached, fried, or grilled fish pieces can be combined with vegetables or green salad. Served in this manner, small fish portions flavored with a complex vinaigrette can be used in a multitude of flavorful and easily digested summer appetizers.

Example

Salad of monkfish and green asparagus – KLEINER SALAD MIT SEETEUFEL UND GRÜNEN SPARGELN – *petite salade de baudroie et asperges vertes*

Caviar – KAVIAR – *caviar*

Caviar is the most renowned of the cold fish appetizers. Served by itself or as a garnish for a special *hors-d'œuvre*, it lends any gathering an exclusive note.

Served from the Original Container

Before and after the service, the can must be weighed to be able to bill correctly for the amount of caviar served.

The original can is placed on a block of ice or placed in a crystal bowl filled with crushed ice. The lid should be leaned against the can, so that the name of the caviar type is visible. The server scoops the requested amount for the guest with a caviar spoon (usually made from mother of pearl).

Toast or blinis and butter are served separately.

Caviar of the best quality does not need lemon juice or chopped onions; they distort the delicate flavor.

Service by Weight

The desired amount, usually 1 to 1⅔ ounces (30 to 50 g), is scooped from the original can, shaped into an egg, and served on a flat crystal plate. Toast or blinis and butter are served separately.

Shellfish Appetizers

Long-time favorites such as shrimp and lobster cocktails will always find a place on the menu. However, the future belongs to the lighter, complex, brilliantly flavored and imaginatively presented shellfish appetizers, combined with garden-fresh vegetables (see Table 7-38).

Table 7-37. Appetizer Cocktails

Cocktail	Description
Shrimp cocktail – RIESENCREVETTENCOCKTAIL – *cocktail de crevettes roses*	Sliced, poached large shrimp. Mixed with finely sliced strips of celery, and small quartered mushrooms. Seasoned. Served in a cocktail glass, with shredded lettuce beneath, coated with cocktail sauce to which fresh tomato cubes and whipped cream have been added. Garnished with diced avocado and tomato.
Fresh fig cocktail with port wine – FEIGENCOCKTAIL MIT PORTO – *cocktail de figues au porto*	Marinated fresh figs in port wine syrup. Cut into wedges and arranged in cocktail glasses. Napped with yogurt, flavored with port wine syrup and black pepper.
Vegetable cocktail with yogurt – GEMÜSECOCKTAIL MIT JOGHURT – *cocktail de légumes au yogourt*	Cauliflower, tomatoes, fennel, mushrooms, avocado, and cooked artichoke bottoms are cut into neat pieces and marinated. Mixed with a yogurt sauce (with horseradish, Tabasco, ketchup), arranged in glasses, and garnished.
Grapefruit cocktail with ginger – GRAPEFRUIT COCKTAIL MIT INGWER – *cocktail de pamplemousse au gingembre*	Grapefruit sections, flavored with grated fresh ginger. Garnished with raspberries and a sprig of mint.
Melon cocktail – MELONENCOCKTAIL CREMONA – *cocktail de melon Crémona*	Melon pieces and chopped pickled mustard fruits are marinated in a rum and port wine syrup. Served in cocktail glasses, garnished with a sprig of mint.
Cold fillet of sole with mango sauce – SEEZUNGENCOCKTAIL MIT MANGO – *cocktail de sole à la mangue*	Poached fillet of sole strips are mixed with mango and mayonnaise. Arranged in cocktail glasses with leaf lettuce and celery strips, and garnished with mango slices and green peppercorns.
Wild mushroom salad (cocktail) – WALDPILZ-COCKTAIL – *cocktail de champignons des bois*	Wild mushrooms are sautéed with shallots and marinated with vinegar and parsley. Arranged in cocktail glasses on leaf lettuce and garnished with scallion rings.

Most important is the absolute freshness and quality of the ingredients. Adding the *still-warm* shellfish to the other ingredients should produce a fabulous taste experience.

Shellfish prepared as cold appetizers are best poached in fish stock or sautéed. It is important to let the shellfish cool in the stock to keep it moist.

Meat and Poultry Appetizers

Using meat or poultry as the main ingredient in an appetizer is not the best idea, since they do not have a stimulating effect on the appetite and tend to be too filling. They are much more suited as a partial component in a more appetite-arousing combination of vegetables, fresh herbs, condiment sauces, and fruits.

Steak Tartare – TATAR – *tartare*

(Swiss laws governing steak tartare and sanitation are discussed in section 4.2.3.) First-quality beef, either filet or sirloin, without fat and tendons, is used for tartare. The meat is ground with a medium plate of the meat grinder or chopped with a knife at the moment the guest places an order. Tartare is sharply seasoned with a raw egg yolk, salt, and various spices or condiment sauces. (Today's chefs prefer to omit the raw egg yolk, because of the danger of salmonella bacteria.) The mixture is formed into a flat patty and served on lettuce leaves. Toast and butter are served separately, or the tartare can be spread directly onto buttered toast.

Carpaccio – CARPACCIO – *carpaccio*

A northern Italian specialty, filet of beef is sliced paper thin, placed on a plate, seasoned with salt and freshly ground pepper, and marinated *à la minute* with olive oil and lemon juice. The beef is usually sprinkled with shaved Parmesan.

Depending on regional preference, differently marinated versions of carpaccio may be served, or a whole filet may be marinated for a length of time and then sliced.

Examples of Meat and Fruit Combinations

Smoked pork loin with fresh figs – LACHSSCHINKEN MIT FRISCHEN FEIGEN – *jambon saumoné aux figues fraîches*

Smoked duck breast with kumquats – GERÄUCHERTE ENTENBRUST MIT ZWERG-ORANGEN – *magret de canard fumé aux kumquats*

Ham of young wild boar with mustard fruits – FRISCHLINGSSCHINKEN MIT SENFFRÜCHTEN – *jambon de marcassin aux fruits moutardés*

Chicken salad with pineapple – GEFLÜGELSALAT MIT ANANAS – *salade de volaille à l'ananas*

Examples of Meat and Vegetable Combinations

Smoked breast of goose with whipped horseradish cream – GERÄUCHERTE GÄNSEBRUST MIT MEER-RETTICHSCHAUM – *poitrine d'oie fumée au raifort parisienne*

Veal sweetbread salad with chanterelle mushrooms – SALAT MIT KALBS-MILKEN UND EIERSCHWÄMMEN – *salade au ris de veau et aux chanterelles*

Small salad with chicken livers and croutons – KLEINER SALAT MIT GEFLÜGEL-LEBER UND BROTWÜRFELCHEN – *petite salade au foie de volaille et aux croûtons*

Vegetable Appetizers

Because they are not filling, have a wide variety of colors, and are high in acid flavor, vegetables naturally stimulate the appetite.

Nutritionally conscious menus should offer vegetable appetizers, because vegetables are high in minerals, vitamins, and fiber.

Simple or tossed green salads are not, strictly speaking, appetizers in the classical sense. However, they can function as an appetizer on a small menu, for example, that for a business lunch.

Raw Vegetables

Raw vegetable salads are a new addition to the appetizer category, influenced by whole-food cuisine. These appetizers consist of either shredded or neatly cut raw vegetable combinations, arranged on a plate and often served with additional fruits and nuts.

Salad sauces are given special attention. Specialty vinegars and oils, yogurt, honey, and fruit juices are preferred ingredients.

Examples of Raw Vegetable Appetizers

Celery salad with fruits – STANGENSEL-LERIE-ROHKOST MIT FRÜCHTEN – *crudité de céleri en branches aux fruits*

Raw shredded salsify with tomatoes – SCHWARZWURZEL-ROHKOST MIT TOMAT-EN – *crudité de scorsonères aux tomates*

Table 7-38. Cold Shellfish Appetizers

Example	Description
Lobster appetizer with artichokes – SALATVORSPEISE MIT HUMMER UND ARTISCHOCKEN – *avant-goût de homard et d'artichauts*	Combination of artichoke bottoms and poached lobster
Oysters on the half shell – AUSTERN AUF EIS – *huîtres sur glace*	Raw oysters on the half shell are set in crushed ice. Served separately with lemon, butter, dark rye or pumpernickel bread.
Assorted cold shellfish – ALLERLEI MIT AUSTERN UND JACOBSMUSCHELN – *panaché d'huîtres et de coquilles Saint-Jacques*	A combination of poached oysters and scallops with broccoli and leeks, served with a walnut-oil vinaigrette.

Shredded raw vegetables with three sauces – ROHKOST MIT DREI SAUCEN – *crudité maraîchère aux trois sauces*

Melon half with smoked salmon and celeriac – HALBE MELONE MIT RÄUCHER-LACHS UND SELLERIE – *demi-melon au saumon fumé et au céleri*

Carved melon boats with dates and honey – MELONENMUSCHELN MIT DAT-TELN UND HONIG – *coquilles de melon aux dattes et au miel*

Melon with port – MELONE MIT PORTWEIN – *melon au porto*

Cooked Vegetables

Some vegetables are indigestible if they have not been cooked, including artichokes, beans, potatoes, and white asparagus. But cooking does not mean overcooking. Over-cooking vegetables not only ruins their texture but destroys nutrients, color, and flavor.

These appetizers taste best when served at room temperature.

Examples of Cooked Vegetable Appetizers

Artichoke bottoms with marinated wild mushrooms – ARTISCHOKENBODEN MIT MARINIERTEN WALDPILZEN – *fond d'artichaut aux champignons des bois marinés*

Asparagus salad with orange and ham – SPARGELSALAT MIKADO – *salade d'asperges mikado*

Salad Niçose – NIZZA-SALAT MIT THUN-FISCH – *salade niçoise au thon*

Greek salad with saffron – GRIECHIS-CHER SALAT MIT SAFRAN – *salade grecque au safran*

Fruit Appetizers

Fruits, like vegetables, have appetite-stimulating properties (acidity and color) and are ideal appetizer ingredients. Fruits are often stuffed with various salads or are combined with vegetables, meat, poultry, fish, seafood, or dairy products (see Table 7-39).

7.9.2 Warm Appetizers – WARME VORSPEISEN – *hors-d'œuvre chauds*

Classic Warm Appetizers

In classical cuisine, warm appetizers were small, standardized, well-flavored dishes served between the soup and the fish course. One forgets how very small these appetizers must have been in the elaborate classical menus. The puff pastries (*bouchées*), for example, were no bigger than one mouthful (*bouche* means "mouth").

The shorter menus of today, as well as nutritional considerations, have caused a great number of the classic warm appetizers to disappear.

Classic Groups of Appetizers Still on the Menu

- Soufflés – AUFLÄUFE – *soufflés*
- Turnovers – TEIGKRAPFEN – *rissoles*
- Fritters – KRAPFEN – *beignets*
- Croquettes – KROKETTEN – *croquettes*
- Quiche – KUCHEN – *quiches*
- Patty shells – PASTETCHEN – *bouchées*
- Fried bread slices – SCHNITTEN – *croûtes*

Warm Appetizers on the Short Menu

Items that were once part of the classical menu but are no longer served can be listed as warm appetizers on the shorter menu. However, they must be:

- not filling
- light and delicately prepared
- well seasoned
- presented appetizingly
- served hot

Depending on the composition of the main entrée, the following dishes could be included as warm appetizers on the menu (see also Table 7-40):

- classic warm appetizers
- vegetable or mushroom dishes
- pasta or rice dishes
- warm egg dishes

Fish and shellfish are also served before the main entrée. However, the fish course is separate from the warm

Table 7-39. Fruit Appetizers

Dish	Description
Avocado fans with mushrooms – AVOCADOFÄCHER MIT PILZEN – *eventail d'avocat aux champignons*	Peeled avocado halves, sliced and fanned, are lightly coated with a red bell pepper vinaigrette and garnished with sautéed, marinated mushrooms and radishes.
Avocado stuffed with shrimp – AVOCADO MIT KREVETTEN – *avocat aux crevettes*	Avocado halves are filled with shrimp salad and garnished with a slice of egg, radish, and black olive.
Sweet-and-sour fruit fans – FRÜCHTEFÄCHER – *eventail de fruits à l'aigre-doux*	A variety of soft fruits (strawberries, kiwis) are sliced, fanned, arranged on a plate, and drizzled with a marinade of honey, port wine, lemon, and cinnamon. Seasoned with pepper.
Nectarine salad with mint – NECTARINENSALAT MIT PFEFFERMINZE – *salade de nectarines à la menthe*	Thin nectarine wedges are arranged in a circle on a plate. The center is covered with a pool of peppermint-flavored yogurt and garnished with a purslane salad.
Grapefruit salad with cottage cheese – GRAPEFRUITSALAT MIT QUARK – *salade de pamplemousse au séré*	Grapefruit wedges are combined with blanched fennel strips and marinated. Two scoops of cottage cheese are placed on a plate and surrounded with grapefruit salad and garnished with chervil leaves.

Table 7-40. Warm Appetizers

Classification	Group	Examples
Soufflés	Soufflés–AUFLÄUFE–*soufflés*	*Soufflé de homard* (lobster), *au fromage* (cheese), *au jambon* (ham), *aux épinards* (spinach)
Fritters	Fritters–KRAPFEN–*beignets*	*Fritot de légumes* (vegetable) *Beignets soufflés au fromage*, (cheese), *au jambon* (ham), *de cervelle* (brains)
Croquettes	Croquettes–KROKETTEN *croquettes*	*Croquettes de crevettes* (shrimp), *de légumes* (vegetables), *de volaille* (chicken)
Fried bread slices or toast	Fried bread slices or toast–SCHNITTEN–*croûtes*	*Croûte aux champignons* (mushrooms), *à la moelle* (marrow), *au foie de volaille* (chicken liver), *au fromage* (cheese)
Pastry appetizers	Turnovers–TEIGKRAPFEN–*rissoles*	*Rissoles forestière* (wild mushrooms), *aux fruits de mer* (seafood), *au salpicon de gibier* (venison)
	Puff-pastry pillows–BLÄTTERTEIGKISSEN–*feuilletés*	*Feuilletés jardiniere* (spring vegetables), *au saumon et au basilic* (salmon with basil)
	Patty shells–PASTETCHEN–*bouchées*	*Bouchées à la reine* (chicken, mushroom, and tongue), *au ris de veau* (sweetbreads), *fermière* (fine vegetables)
	Quiche–KUCHEN —*quiche*	*Quiche lorraine, marseillaise* (seafood), *aux poireaux* (leeks)
Vegetable and mushroom appetizers	Gratin–GRATIN–*gratin*	*Gratin de légumes* (vegetables), *de brocoli et de crevettes* (shrimp and broccoli)
	Stuffed–GEFÜLLT–*farcis*	*Fonds d'artichauts farcis* (filled artichoke bottoms) *courgettes farcis* (stuffed zucchini), *champignons de Paris farcis* (stuffed mushrooms)
	Asparagus–SPARGEL–*asperges*	*Asperges milanaise* (parmesan cheese), *maltaise* (orange), *aux morilles* (morels)
	Artichoke–ARTISCHOCKEN–*artichauts*	*Artichaut bouilli à la vinaigrette* (marinated), *hollandaise*
Starch appetizers	Pasta–EINFACHE TEIGWAREN–*pâtes alimentaires simples*	Examples are listed in the text.
	Pasta dishes–TEIGWAREN-GERICHTE–*mets aux pâtes alimentaires*	
	Gnocchi–GNOCCHI–*gnocchi*	
	Risotto–RISOTTO–*risotto*	
Egg Appetizers	Shirred eggs–EIER IM TÖPFCHEN–*œufs en cocotte*	Examples are listed in the text.
	Omelets–OMELETTEN–*omelettes*	
	Scrambled eggs–RÜHREIER–*œufs brouillés*	
	Poached eggs–VERLORENE EIER–*œufs pochés*	
	Cooked eggs–WACHS-WEICHE EIER–*œufs mullets*	

appetizer course, and so fish and shellfish are considered separately.

Soufflés

Soufflés are very temperature-sensitive dishes. They will collapse very quickly after being taken from the oven. Complete cooperation between the kitchen and service staffs is necessary to provide guests with a satisfactory soufflé. Soufflés are best served in individual-portion molds (*cocottes*) and are served with a complementary sauce.

Basic Preparation of Soufflés

Although all soufflés are prepared in essentially the same way, it is still difficult to give a basic all-purpose recipe. Small variations in water and fat content of the various purées must be considered and the recipe adjusted accordingly. The recipe for spinach soufflé that follows is an example of how soufflés are prepared, but a different primary ingredient could not be substituted for the spinach with good results. Table 7-41 does list the basic components of a variety of soufflés.

Spinach Soufflé – SPINATAUFLAUF – soufflé aux épinards

YIELD: 10 SERVINGS		
Butter	3 oz	80 g
All-purpose flour	3 oz	80 g
Milk	6¾ oz	200 ml
Garlic clove	1	1
Salt, freshly ground pepper, nutmeg		
Spinach, defrosted	4 oz	120 g
Egg yolks	6	6
Egg whites	6	6

Mise en place

- Butter soufflé molds and dust with flour (helps the soufflé to rise during baking). Gently knock out excess flour.
- Squeeze the defrosted spinach dry, and purée with 3 egg yolks.
- Purée or crush the garlic clove.

Method

- Prepare a thick béchamel sauce with the butter, flour, and milk. Cool slightly.
- Season the sauce with the garlic, salt, and spices.
- Beat the rest of the yolks into the béchamel.
- Add the spinach purée.
- Beat egg whites until firm.
- Fold about one-quarter of the beaten egg whites into the spinach mixture.
- Gradually fold in the rest of the beaten egg whites.
- Fill the prepared soufflé molds about three-quarters full.
- Place the molds in a water bath for 30 minutes to prewarm the mixture.
- Bake first at 320°F (160°C), and finish at 400°F (200°C).
- The baking time for small *cocottes* (one portion) is 10 to 15 minutes.
- Place the soufflé on a paper doily, and serve at once.

Fritters – KRAPFEN – beignets

Dishes that can be categorized as fritters are divided into three groups:

Fritters – KRAPFEN – *beignets*

Puffed fritters – AUFLAUF KRAPFEN – *beignets soufflés*

Turnovers – TEIGKRAPFEN – *rissoles*

(discussed with pastry appetizers later in this section)

Fritters are foods that are dipped into batter and deep-fried. The name reflects the main ingredient, for example, broccoli fritter, zucchini fritter. If a combination of fritters is offered, then the dish is called *frito misto*, an Italian term.

Fritters made with a choux-paste base are puffed fritters and are fried without being dipped in batter. Depending on the main ingredient, they may be served with a warm tomato sauce or a cold tartar or rémoulade sauce.

Basic Ingredients for Fritters

Pieces, sticks, or florets of cooked vegetables or meat: cauliflower, broccoli, artichoke bottoms, celeriac, salsify, sweetbreads, veal brains, and calves' heads

Strips, slices, pieces of raw fish fillet, shrimp, cultivated mushrooms, porcini, eggplant, zucchini

Choux-paste balls with ham cubes, tongue, mushrooms, cheese, chicken, sardines, and/or fresh herbs

Batter-fried Vegetables/Frito misto of Vegetables – FRITOT VON GEMÜSE – fritot de légumes

YIELD: 10 SERVINGS		
Cooked vegetables	1 lb, 12 oz	800 g
Lemon	1	1
Chopped herbs	3½ oz	100 g
Salt and pepper		
All-purpose flour	1⅘ oz	50 g
Frying batter	1 lb, 5 oz	600 g

Table 7-41. Soufflé Components

Soufflé	Flavoring of Thick Béchamel Sauce	+ Egg Yolks	+ Cooked, Puréed Basic Ingredient	+ Beaten Egg Whites	Serve With
Lobster soufflé	Béchamel with lobster butter	+ Egg yolks	+ Puréed and diced lobster meat	+ Beaten egg whites	Lobster sauce
Cheese soufflé	Béchamel with pepper and nutmeg	+ Egg yolks	+ Grated cheese and diced cheese	+ Beaten egg whites	Tomato *coulis*
Ham soufflé	Béchamel with shallots and paprika	+ Egg yolks	+ Purée of lean ham	+ Beaten egg whites	Madeira sauce
Spinach soufflé	Béchamel with a little garlic	+ Egg yolks	+ Purée of blanched spinach	+ Beaten egg whites	Cream sauce

Method

- Marinate the vegetables for 10 minutes in the lemon juice and chopped herbs (basil, chervil).
- Season with salt and pepper, dust with flour.
- Dip in the batter, and deep-fry at 360°F (180°C) until crisp.
- Drain the vegetables on absorbent paper.
- Serve tomato concassé separately.

Ham Puffs – SCHINKENAUFLAUFKRAPFEN – *beignets soufflés au jambon*

YIELD: 10 SERVINGS		
Choux paste	1 lb, 12 oz	800 g
Salt, nutmeg, paprika		
Ham, diced very fine	8¾ oz	250 g

Method

- Season the choux paste with salt, nutmeg, and paprika. Cool a little.
- Add the diced ham.
- With a pastry bag, using a smooth tip, pipe the fritters, ⅔ oz (20 g) in weight, onto oiled strips of parchment paper.
- Deep-fry at 325°F (160°C). The fritters will double in size.
- Drain on absorbent paper.
- Serve on a doily-lined plate, garnished with parsley sprigs.
- Serve with Madeira sauce on the side.

Croquettes – KROKETTEN – *croquettes*

The basic ingredients for croquettes are diced cooked vegetables, poultry, game, fish, or shellfish, to which chopped, cooked, cultivated mushrooms, porcini, ham, and minced herbs may be added (see Table 7-42). The thickeners are a reduced brown (*espagnol*) or white sauce (*velouté*) and egg yolk.

The mixture is spread ¾ inch (1½ cm) thick on an oiled sheet pan and chilled. After heating the bottom of the sheet pan a bit, the chilled mixture is easily transferred to a cutting board. The croquettes can be cut into various shapes with a knife or cookie cutters.

The pieces are breaded and fried in oil or clarified butter. A suitable sauce (depending on the primary ingredient) is served separately.

If the menu lists a warm appetizer as "cutlet" (e.g., *côtelet de volaille*), a breaded and fried croquette mixture shaped like a cutlet is meant. The bone is symbolized by a piece of macaroni.

Poultry Croquettes – GEFLÜGELKROKETTEN – *croquettes de volaille*

YIELD: 10 SERVINGS		
Butter	1⅓ oz	40 g
Shallots, chopped	1 oz	30 g
Mushrooms, chopped	3½ oz	100 g
Cooked poultry, diced	1 lb, 5 oz	600 g
Ham, diced	3½ oz	100 g
Poultry velouté	1 pt, 1 oz	500 g
Semolina	⅔ oz	20 g
Heavy cream	1⅔ oz	50 ml
Egg yolks	4	4
All-purpose flour	⅔ oz	20 g
Eggs, whole	2	2
Bread crumbs	3½ oz	100 g

Method

- Heat the butter, and sauté the shallots until soft.
- Add the mushrooms, and sauté until dry.
- Add the diced poultry and ham, and continue to cook.
- Add the velouté, season. Stir in the semolina. Cook for 2 to 3 minutes. Season to taste.
- Stir in cream and egg yolks. Simmer until thick.
- Spread the croquette mixture about ¾ inch (1.5 cm) thick on an oiled sheet pan. Refrigerate.
- Turn the sheet pan upside down to drop the croquette mixture onto a cutting board.
- Cut into shapes. Bread with flour, egg, and bread crumbs.
- Fry, and drain on absorbent paper.
- Present on a doily-covered platter. Serve sauce separately.

Fried Bread Slices/Toast – SCHNITTEN – *croûtes*

Both appetizers have white bread as a base. The difference is that fried bread slices are fried in clarified butter, whereas the other is simply toasted. Another difference is found in the topping. Fried bread slices are an ideal base for sauced ingredients, since the fried bread will not turn soggy (see Table 7-43). Toast is generally topped with dry ingredients, and often baked with cheese. In the United States, no such distinctions are made in culinary terms.

In contrast to fried bread slices, toast plays only a minor role as a warm appetizer. However, it can serve as an

Table 7-42. Croquettes

Croquette	Basic Ingredient	Additions	Thickeners	Served with
Poultry croquettes– GEFLÜGELKROKETTEN– croquettes de volaille	Diced poultry meat	Chopped mushrooms, porcini, and ham	Poultry velouté, semolina, egg yolk	Truffle sauce
Shrimp croquettes– KREVETTENKROKETTEN– croquettes de crevettes	Diced shrimp	Chopped mushrooms, braised leeks	Fish velouté, shrimp butter, egg yolk	Dill sauce
Vegetable croquettes– GEMÜSEKROKETTEN– croquettes de légumes	Diced vegetables	Chopped mushrooms, porcini	Semolina, béchamel sauce, egg yolk	Tomato concassé

excellent snack, since it can be prepared quickly and without much effort, requiring only a salamander or broiler as a heat source.

Preparation

For round slices, use a round toasting bread; if that is not available, slice square white bread into a cylinder shape, 2⅓ inches (6 cm) in diameter. The slices should be about ⅓ inch (8 mm) thick. Traditionally the bread was hollowed out slightly, but that technique has been eliminated to save labor.

Frying

Bread slices are fried in clarified butter in a fry pan until golden brown and then placed on a rack to cool.

Presentation

The bread slices are placed on an oven-proof plate and briefly warmed. The hot topping is poured over the slices. The topping may run over the edge of the bread.

Pastry Appetizers

All baked pastries (puff pastry, mock puff-pastry, pie pastry, and the like) that contain a fully cooked filling with finely cut ingredients are considered pastry appetizers. The filling can be very varied and, as a rule, is thickened with a sauce or an egg custard.

Pastry appetizers are classified as follows:

Turnovers – TEIGKRAPFEN – *rissoles*

Puff pastry pillows – BLÄTTERTEIG-KISSEN – *feuilletés*

Patty shells – PASTETCHEN – *bouchées*

Quiches – KUCHEN – *quiches*

Basic Information

- The size of the pastry depends on the size of the menu. Two small pieces per person are usually preferable to one large piece.
- The appetizer is named for its dominant ingredient, for example, *rissoles aux chanterelles* (chanterelle turnovers), *bouchées aux crevettes* (patty shells filled with shrimp).
- The fat content of the sauce in an oven-baked pastry, for example, turnovers, must not be too high, or the sauce will break down, and the fat will separate.

The Main Pastry Groups

Turnovers are half-moon pastry pockets made from puff pastry or pie dough and baked in the oven. In the United States, they are often pastry triangles. They should be served with an additional refined filling or a complementary sauce.

Patty shells are small, round, hollow puff-pastry cups, which are first baked and then filled with a savory creamy filling. A large patty shell (for three to four persons) is called a *vol-au-vent*.

Puff-pastry pillows are flatter and smaller than patty shells and usually square or oval. The filling does not have to be sauced and can be any creative combination.

Quiches are large pastries made from mock puff pastry or pie dough. The filling is usually composed of cooked ingredients that are baked in an egg custard. A smaller version is called a tartlet.

Mushroom Turnovers –
TEIGKRAPFEN MIT PILZEN – *rissoles aux champignons*

YIELD: 10 SERVINGS (10 PIECES AS APPETIZER)		
Mock puff pastry	1 lb, 12 oz	800 g
Prepared mushroom filling	1 qt, 2 oz	1 L
Egg	1	1

Method

- Roll out the mock puff pastry ¹⁄₁₆ inch (2 mm) thick. With a fluted cutter, cut into 5½-inch (14-mm) circles.
- Fill the center of each circle with a heaping spoonful of cold filling. Brush the edges with beaten egg.
- Fold the dough over filling to form half moons. Seal well with the blunt side of a cutter.
- Brush with beaten egg, and decorate with pastry strips if desired.
- Let rest 1 hour. Bake at 395°F (200°C) for about 15 minutes.

Puff Pastry Pillow with Spring Vegetables – BLÄTTERTEIGKISSEN MIT FEINEM GEMÜSE – *feuilletés jardinière*

YIELD: 10 SERVINGS (10 PIECES AS APPETIZER)		
Baked puff pastry pillows, 4 × 2½ inches (10 × 6 cm)	10	10
Vegetables in light cream sauce	1 qt, 2 oz	1 L
Fresh asparagus tips	20	20
Butter	⅔ oz	20 g
Chervil, chopped	⅓ oz	10 g

Method

- Remove the top layer from each baked pillow, to make a lid, and set aside.

Table 7-43. Fried Bread Appetizers

Fried Bread Slices-Toast	Topping
Mushroom toast – CHAMPIGNONSCHNITTEN – *crouté aux champignons à la crème*	Fresh mushrooms (mushrooms, porcini, chanterelles, or morels) are sautéed in butter. Cream sauce is added and reduced to desired consistency. Garnished with fresh herbs.
Poultry liver toast with green peppercorns – GEFLÜGELLEBERSCHNITTE MIT GRÜNEM PFEFFER – *crouté au foie de volaille et au poivre vert*	Shallots are sautéed in butter with pieces of poultry livers and fried until rare. Madeira sauce is added, reduced, and seasoned with green peppercorns.
Grilled cheese toast with tomato – KÄSESCHNITTE MIT TOMATEN UND PEPERONI – *crouté au fromage portugaise*	Toast is sprinkled with a little white wine and topped with Gruyère cheese slices. It is baked under a broiler or salamander. The center of the toast is garnished with stewed tomatoes and bell peppers.

- Heat the puff pastry pillows.
- Fill the bottoms with hot vegetables.
- Heat the asparagus tips in the butter, and garnish each pillow with two tips.
- Sprinkle with chopped chervil.
- Place lid on top at a 45-degree angle.

Sweetbreads in Patty Shells –
KALBSMILKENPASTETCHEN –
bouchées au ris de veau

YIELD: 10 SERVINGS (20 PIECES AS APPETIZER)		
Baked patty shells, 2½ inches (6 cm)	20	20
Prepared sweetbreads	1 qt, 2 oz	1 L

Method
- Slice the tops from the patty shells, and reserve.
- Heat the patty shells.
- Fill the hot patty shells with the sweetbreads (can overflow).
- Place the reserved lids on top.

Seafood Quiche – MEERESFRÜCHTE-
KUCHEN MIT SAFRAN – *quiche marseillaise*

YIELD: 10 SERVINGS (1 QUICHE, 12 INCHES [30 CM])		
Mock puff pastry	14 oz	400 g
Poached fish and shellfish	1 lb, 5 oz	600 g
Sautéed vegetable strips	7 oz	200 g
Saffron egg custard	10 oz	300 ml

Method
- Roll out the mock puff pastry ¹⁄₁₆ inch (2 mm) thick, and fit into a baking pan.

- Spoon the cold seafood and vegetables evenly over the dough.
- Pour the saffron custard over the filling.
- Bake in the oven at 425°F (220°C), for about 30 minutes.
- If desired, serve with a white-wine sauce.

Vegetables and Mushroom Appetizers

Asparagus

Green and white asparagus are popular vegetable appetizers. Classic preparation methods include:

Asparagus with hollandaise sauce (*asperges hollandaise*)

Asparagus with orange sauce (*asperges maltaise*)

Asparagus with grated Parmesan cheese (*asperges milanaise*)

Asparagus with morels (*asperges aux morilles*)

Asparagus with hard-cooked eggs and buttered bread crumbs (*asperges polonaise*)

Artichokes

Artichoke bottoms are as popular as asparagus as a warm vegetable appetizer. They are stuffed or are included in gratinated preparations (see next section). They can also be served whole: after removing the straw, the artichokes are served warm, accompanied by a sauce (for example, hollandaise sauce or vinaigrette variations).

Stuffed Vegetables and Mushrooms

Vegetables can be stuffed in many ways (see Table 7-44). They are often finished by topping them with a sauce, cheese, or soft buttered bread crumbs and broiling. The *mise en place* for stuffed vegetable preparations is discussed in detail in section 7.15.

Vegetable and Mushroom Gratins

Main Ingredients
- Vegetables, coarsely cut, to which other ingredients, such as mushrooms, sweetbreads, or shrimp can be added
- Sliced mushrooms, to which other ingredients have been added

Preparation
The two basic cooking methods are stewing and sautéing, which best preserve the individual vegetable flavors. The vegetables should not be soft.

Sauce Preparation
Vegetable cooking liquids are reduced, mixed with Béchamel sauce, and enriched with egg yolk. Before baking vegetable gratins, they should be further enriched with cream and, if desired, with grated cheese (cream and cheese add the necessary fat and proteins for successful browning).

Finishing
Warm prepared vegetables are topped with an enriched sauce and placed under a salamander or broiler until golden brown.

Table 7-44. Stuffed Vegetables and Mushrooms

Vegetable	Filling Options	Finished Presentation
Artichoke bottoms	Mushroom duxelle, leaf spinach, creamed mushrooms, purée of peas, asparagus tips, ratatouille	Glazed with a mixture of whipped cream and hollandaise; baked gratinated with cheese or onion sauce
Eggplant, bell peppers, zucchini, onions	Stuffed with a separately prepared spicy rice/meat filling, to which the vegetable flesh has been added, and braised in the oven until tender	Baked au gratin with cheese or onion sauce; baked sprinkled with Parmesan cheese and drizzled with butter
Mushroom caps	Mushroom duxelle, poultry liver filling	Baked au gratin with cheese or onion sauce

Table 7-45. Starch Appetizers

Pasta	Macaroni, home-made noodles (white or green), spaghetti, bows, etc.	
	In butter:	with Parmesan, with herbs and garlic, with zucchini, etc.
	With cream:	with Parmesan, with white truffles, with strips of cold cuts
	In tomato sauce:	with tomato concassé and variations
	As meat stew	with small, roasted meat cubes in demi-glace
Pasta dishes	Canneloni, lasagna, tortellini, ravioli	
	Fillings:	Fresh cheese and fresh herbs, mushrooms, meat, fish, shellfish, and vegetables
Gnocchi	Potato gnocchi (*piedmontaise*), semolina gnocchi (*romanaise*), puff-paste gnocchi (*parisienne*)	
	Garnish:	for semolina gnocci, chicken-liver stew, mushroom stew, tomato concassé, ratatouille, etc.
Risotto	Garnish:	Chicken-liver stew, mushrooms (porcini, white truffles), seafood, saffron, tomato concassé, etc.

• Starch Appetizers

Basic starch preparation methods are discussed in detail in section 7.17.

As warm appetizers, starch dishes are especially popular in Italian cuisine. Their neutral taste makes pasta and risotto ideal bases for strong-flavored ingredient combinations. However, their high satiety value must be considered in menu planning. Examples of starch appetizers are shown in Table 7-45.

Starch appetizers are classified into the following groups:

Pasta – EINFACHE TEIGWAREN – *pâtes alimentaires simples*

Pasta dishes – TEIGWARENGERICHTE – *mets aux pâtes alimentaires*

Gnocchi – GNOCCHI – *gnocchi*

Risotto – RISOTTO – *risotto*

Egg Appetizers

Basic egg preparation methods are discussed in section 7.10. Eggs are fairly neutral in taste and lend themselves to many flavor combination. Many classic egg appetizers are well known. Changes in eating habits, however, have led to a reduced use of egg dishes as appetizers. The major groups of egg dishes still used in today's menus are:

Shirred eggs – EIER IM TÖPFCHEN – *œufs en cocotte*

Omelets – OMELETTEN – Omelettes

Scrambled eggs – RÜHREIER – *œufs brouillés*

Poached eggs – VERLORENE EIER – *œufs pochés*

Coddled eggs – WACHSWEICHE EIER – *œufs mollets*

Portion Size

Portion size is determined by the number of menu items. One egg per person is the general rule, with the exception of an appetizer omelet, which is made from two eggs.

7.10 Egg Dishes

Eggs are very nutritious, low in price, and generally easy to digest. At the turn of century, egg dishes were routinely on the midday menu as a second course, but today's menus seldom include eggs. (Although eggs are the food of choice on American breakfast and brunch menus.) Concern over the amount of cholesterol in the diet is will likely reduce the use of egg dishes even further. Table 7-46 lists the various types of egg dishes.

Uses for Egg Dishes

As a breakfast dish: soft-cooked eggs, poached eggs, fried eggs, scrambled eggs, omelets, eggs on toast with bacon, ham, or sausages.

As a warm appetizer (1 to 2 eggs) or *as a snack* (2 eggs): shirred eggs (eggs in cocotte), omelets, scrambled eggs, poached eggs, fried eggs, soft-cooked eggs (many variations, generally served with a delicate garnish)

As an entrée (2-3 eggs): shirred eggs (eggs in cocotte), omelets, scrambled eggs, poached eggs, fried eggs, soft-cooked eggs (many variations, generally served with a delicate garnish)

As a dessert: sabayon, omelette soufflé, pancakes, jam-filled omelets, French pastry creams, etc.

Notes

- Many egg dishes are prepared at low temperatures. Consequently, they may pose a health risk (salmonella) unless great care is taken in purchasing and handling the eggs. Only top quality eggs, without damage, should be used; for some dishes, only pasteurized eggs are advised.
- Egg dishes cannot be served in silver dishes, as they blacken surfaces they touch.

7.10.1 Cooked Egg Dishes

- Eggs often have invisible hairline fractures that will split further during the cooking process, releasing egg white. To test for such fractures, tap two eggs together lightly: a clear, strong sound indicates undamaged eggs.
- Abrupt changes in temperature may cause eggs to crack. Protect refrigerated eggs against cracking by putting them in lukewarm water before cooking.
- Eggs are always cooked in boiling hot water. Large quantities are best cooked by placing them in wire baskets in batches.
- The cooking time is calculated from the moment the water returns to a simmer (see Table 7-47). After cooking, the cooked eggs must be placed immediately in cold water. The cooked egg will separate from the shell membrane and be easier to peel.

Notes
When eggs are overcooked or kept in hot water, the egg yolk develops iron sulfates, which cause the outer layer of the yolk to turn green.

Suggestions for Using Soft-cooked Eggs
Warm dishes: Place the eggs on filled tartlet shells or puff pastry pil-

Table 7-46. Egg Dishes

Classification	Main Group	Examples
Cooked egg dishes	Coddled eggs— WEICHE EIER— *œufs à la coque*	
	Soft-cooked eggs— WACHSWEICHE EIER— *œufs mollets*	*Œufs mollets indienne* (curried eggs)
	Hard-cooked eggs— HARTE EIER— *œufs durs*	*Œufs russe* (eggs on Russian vegetable salad)
Poached egg dishes	Poached eggs— POCHIERTE EIER— *œufs pochés*	*Œufs pochés florentine* (with spinach)
	Shirred eggs— EIER IM TÖPFCHEN— *œufs en cocotte*	*Œufs en cocotte chasseur* (with chicken livers)
	Scrambled eggs— RUHREIER— *œufs brouillés*	*Œufs brouillés portugaise* (with diced tomatoes)
Sautéed eggs	Omelets— OMELETTEN— *omelettes*	*Omelette bonne femme* (Plain omelet)
	Fried Eggs— SPIEGELEIER— *œufs sur le plat*	*Œufs sur le plat au jambon* (ham and eggs)

lows, and cover with an appropriate sauce. Possible toppings are: ragout of fish, chicken, sweetbreads, seafood, creamed vegetable strips, mushrooms, leaf spinach, rice combinations.

Cold dishes: Place eggs on filled artichoke bottoms or tomatoes, and cover them just before service with a mayonnaise-based sauce. Garnish with anchovy fillets, fresh herbs, or paprika. Possible fillings are: piquant chicken, seafood, mushroom, or vegetable salads.

Suggestions for Using Hard-cooked Eggs

Hard-cooked eggs are used predominantly for cold dishes:

As a garnish: slices or wedges for salads and cold plates

As an ingredient: chopped in cold sauces, or sliced for canapés or egg salad

Stuffed: cut in half vertically or horizontally, and stuffed with crab cocktail, smoked salmon, or an egg yolk–butter mixture, and garnished creatively.

As a stand-alone dish: halved and served on Russian salad, coated with a thin mayonnaise. Garnish possibilities are smoked fish, sardines in oil, asparagus, or salami.

7.10.2 Poached Egg Dishes

Poached egg dishes are easily digested and tender; the low cooking temperature is gentle on the protein and preserves nutrients. Poached eggs and scrambled eggs are suitable for a soft-food medical diet.

Egg dishes poached without movement:

Poached eggs – POCHIRTE EIER – *œufs pochés*

Shirred eggs – EIER IM TÖPFCHEN – *œufs en cocotte*

Egg dishes poached with movement:

Scrambled eggs – RÜHREIER – *œufs brouillés*

Poached Eggs – POCHIERTE EIER – *œufs pochés*

Poached eggs are cooked by cracking them into hot water with vinegar. The vinegar's acidity immediately coagulates the egg white and holds it together. Salt is not added to the water, as it has the opposite affect of vinegar on egg white.

Freshness of the eggs is essential. Fresh eggs poach well and keep their shape: old eggs run in poaching liquid and are not usable. Poached eggs are served immediately.

Method
- In a saucepan, bring the vinegar and water to a simmer.
- Crack the eggs, without damaging the yolk, into small dishes.
- Carefully slide the eggs into the simmering water (loosen any that stick to the pan with a wooden spoon).
- Poach for 3 to 4 minutes (the egg white should be firm, and the yolk liquid).
- Lift the eggs out with a strainer. Use at once, or shock in ice water for later use. Trim any ragged whites.
- Reheat for warm presentation in 125°F (50°C) salted water.

- Drain on a cloth napkin before service.

Shirred Eggs – EIER IM TÖPFCHEN – *œufs en cocotte*

Shirred eggs are poached in small casseroles, called cocottes, that are set in a water bath in the oven. They are named for the garnish they contain.

Method
- Butter individual cocottes.
- Pour in a little cream.
- Add the garnish (creamed chicken or seafood, truffles, creamed mushrooms, vegetables, etc.).
- Top with a cracked egg.
- Salt the egg white, and dot with bits of butter.
- Place in a paper-lined water bath, and poach in the oven for about 5 minutes. (The egg white should be firm at the edges, but the yolk only warm.) This method of cooking may not destroy all salmonella bacteria.
- Pour a complementary sauce or some cream over the egg white but not the yolk, which should remain visible.
- Serve the cocottes on a napkin covered plate.

Scrambled Eggs – RÜHREIER – *œufs brouillés*

Scrambled eggs are cooked in a saucepan or frying pan. It is necessary to stir the beaten eggs constantly with a wooden spoon and poach the eggs over low heat to create the desirable soft texture and creamy consistency. Adding a little cream, milk, or bits of butter stops the poaching process and enriches the scrambled eggs at the same time.

Table 7-47. Main Groups of Cooked Eggs

Eggs	Cooking time	Preparation
Soft-cooked eggs	2–5 minutes, depending on the guests' wishes	Shock the cooked eggs in cold water, and serve immediately in an egg cup.
Cooked eggs	6 minutes	Shock cooked eggs, and cool in cold water. Carefully peel eggs in water. Store in water until needed. To serve warm, heat in hot salted water.
Hard-cooked eggs	10 minutes	Shock cooked eggs, and completely cool in cold water. Peel, and slice, quarter, or chop.

Preparation

- Crack the eggs into a bowl, and beat well with a whip.
- Heat butter in frying pan.
- Add the beaten eggs, and slowly cook over low heat, stirring with a wooden spoon.
- Add cream or milk, and season.
- Enrich with small bits of butter.

Variations

Add smoked salmon, truffles, diced ham and tomato, chives, croutons, or chicken livers.

Presentation Options

Service in a cocotte, on toast, in a tartlet shell, or in a hollowed brioche bread are all possibilities.

7.10.3 Sautéed Egg Dishes

Omelets – OMELETTEN – *omelettes*

Omelets are cooked in restaurants in specially reserved pans (Lyoner pan) or in nonstick pans. Omelets are cooked in butter over medium heat to prevent browning.

Method

- Crack the eggs into a bowl, and beat well with a whip.
- Heat butter in a frying pan; do not brown.
- Add the beaten eggs, and slowly cook over low heat, shaking the pan constantly and stirring the egg mixture with a fork (no metal with nonstick pans).
- Tilt the pan and let the mixture slide toward its front rim.
- Roll the egg mixture with a fork or spatula toward the rim, into an oval shape.
- Rap the handle sharply with the fist to loosen the omelet from the pan.
- Use a fork to fold in the ends.
- Slide omelet onto a warm plate.
- Brush the top with melted butter.

Characteristics of a Correctly Prepared Omelet

- Oval, completely closed shape
- Tender, smooth surface
- Soft interior

Fillings

- Mushrooms, diced tomatoes, leaf spinach, zucchini, asparagus tips, cheese, ham, bacon
- Creamy stews of chicken, sweetbreads, crustaceans

These ingredients can be added in various ways:

- cooked and added to the uncooked egg mixture
- as a filling in the center of the omelet before it is rolled (creamy ragouts)
- inside the omelet, through a split in its top (usually creamy ragouts)
- as a garnish, arranged like a bouquet next to the omelet.

Fried Eggs – SPIEGELEIER – *œufs sur le plat*

Fried eggs in European restaurants are frequently prepared and served in small pans or heat-resistant special egg plates. Fried eggs should not have browned edges, which makes them less digestible. A perfectly fried egg has a firm white, with a hot, shiny, but still slightly runny yolk. Only the egg white is salted, because salt leaves white spots on the egg yolk. In the United States, these eggs are called "sunny-side up"; "over-easy" or "over hard" eggs are flipped and cooked on both sides.

Method

- Crack the eggs into a shallow bowl without damaging the egg yolk.
- Heat butter in the desired dish or pan.
- Slide the eggs gently into the dish or pan.
- Sprinkle the egg white with salt.
- Cook over medium heat without browning the edges.
- It is convenient to cook the egg in the oven with top heat.
- If the eggs are not cooked in heat-proof serving dishes, serve on a warmed plate and garnish appropriately.

Variations

Garnish with fried ham or bacon, fried sausages, chicken liver ragout, sautéed mushrooms, or sautéed diced tomato.

7.11 Fish Dishes

Even though the flesh of fish does not differ from that of other animals in chemical composition, because of their environment and feeding habits, fish provide a very different taste experience.

Nutritionally, fish are major protein providers. The generally low fat content is high in polyunsaturated fatty acids, and the flesh is low in connective tissues and so is easily digested (also see chapter 4).

A delicious fish dish depends not only on the skill of the cook but also on the freshness and quality of the fish. Well-developed transportation and distribution systems have made it possible to buy freshly caught fish even miles from the coast.

Its nutritional value and the creativity cooks display in the preparation of fish has increased its popularity, so that the demand for fish dishes is constantly growing. Table 7-48 shows the many ways fish can be included on the menu, and Table 7-49 summarizes the methods of preparing it.

7.11.1 Basic Preparation Methods for Fish

See Table 7-49.

7.11.2 Warm Fish Dishes – WARME FISCHGERICHTE – *poissons chaud*

The basic preparation methods for fish are similar to those of meat.

Table 7-48. Uses of Fish on the Menu

Usage	Characteristic	Examples
Canapés	Mainly smoked or marinated fish and caviar; served on small toasts, specialty breads, blini, or pastry.	*Canapé de saumon fumé* (smoked salmon) *Tartlette au caviar* (caviar-filled tartlet)
Cold appetizer	Cooked cold or lukewarm fish (e.g., in salad combinations), smoked or marinated fish, and cold second-course fish dishes.	*Variation de saumon suédoise* (poached salmon variations). *Rouget à la vinaigrette de légumes* (marinated red snapper with vegetables)
Soup	Fish consommé, fish cream soups, national or specialty soups.	*Crème dieppoise* (fish and mussel soup) *Bouillabaise*
Warm appetizer	In classical cuisine, fish plays a minor role in warm appetizers, generally used only as a filling.	*Vol-au-vent du pêcheur* (large pastry with fish filling) *Quiche marseillaise* (seafood quiche)
Fish course	If fish is the main ingredient in a dish, it should be listed on the menu as a fish course. A fish course can also be listed as the main entrée if no meat dish is to follow.	*Mèdaillons de baudroie au Sauterne* (monkfish slices in white wine) *Escalope de saumon écossaise* (salmon scaloppini Scottish style) *Filets de sole Marguèry* (fillet of sole with mussels and shrimp)
Cold second course	Fish in a terrine, pâté, galantine, or mousse	*Terrine de loup de mer au fenouil* (terrine of sea bass and fennel) *Galantine de brochet à l'aneth* (galantine of pike with dill)
Buffet platters	Whole fish or fish slices poached in stock and chilled, then decorated and placed on a pool of gelatin with appropriate garnishes.	*Saumon en bellevue* (decorated cold salmon) *Turbotin farci* (stuffed young turbot)

Since fish have fewer tough connective tissues, temperatures are generally lower. In practice, this means that the internal temperature of 150°F (65°C) needed to kill bacteria is also the correct degree of doneness. Higher internal temperatures cause the protein to become dry.

Poaching – POCHIEREN – *pocher*

To poach means to cook fish or fish pieces in hot liquids at about 165°F (75°C).

Two different types of poaching are used:

Poaching in stock – *pocher au court-bouillon*

Poaching in wine – *pocher au vin*

Basic Poaching Principles
• Very large fish are placed in *cold* stock.
• Pieces of fish and fish to be poached "blue" are placed in *hot* stock.

• Fish that are part of a cold preparation should be allowed to cool in the stock to prevent them from drying out.

Table 7-51 lists fish commonly poached in stock and basic preparation methods.

Side Dishes/Garnishes
A suitable starch side dish is boiled potatoes. For a fish entrée, spring vegetables, leaf spinach, snow peas, green peas, and green asparagus are all good side dishes. Lemon halves or lemon wedges should always be offered separately.

Sauces
Butter: fresh butter, melted butter, composed shallot butter, etc.

Butter sauces: hollandaise, mousseline sauce, mustard sauce, etc.

Fish sauces: specialty sauces with basil, leeks, etc.

Salmon Steaks Poached in Fish Stock

YIELD: 10 SERVINGS (APPETIZER)		
Water	3 qt, 19 oz	3 L
Matignon	8¾ oz	250 g
Parsley stems	1 oz	30 g
Bay leaf	1	1
Peppercorns	⅓ oz	10 g
Fresh thyme	1 sprig	5 g
Salt	1⅓ oz	40 g
White wine	8½ oz	250 ml
White-wine vinegar	5 oz	150 ml
Salmon steaks (10)	2 lb, 14 oz	1.3 kg

Method for Small Fish and Fish Pieces
• Bring water to a simmer. Add the vegetables, herbs, and spices, and simmer for 10 minutes.
• Add the wine and vinegar.
• Add the prepared fish or fish pieces (fish to be poached "blue" should be drizzled with vinegar to improve the blue color).

Table 7-49. Basic Perparation Methods for Fish

Classification	Main groups	Examples of Dishes
Poaching–POCHIEREN–*pocher*	in stock–*au court bouillon*	*Truite au bleu* ("poached blue" brook trout) *Darne de saumon pochée hollandaise* (center piece or filet of salmon with hollandaise) *Tranche de colin pochée aux câpres* (poached hake steak with capers)
	in wine–*au vin*	*Omble chevalier zougoise* (saibling, Zürich style) *Filets de sole Marguèry* (fillet of sole with mussels and shrimp) *Turbot aux fleurs de safran* (turbot with saffron)
Braising–SCHMOREN–*braiser*		*Loup de mer braisé au Noilly Prat* (sea bass braised in dry vermouth) *Turbotin braisé aux champagne* (young turbot braised in champagne)
Steaming–DÄMPFEN–*cuire à la vapeur*		*Escalope de saumon à la moutarde* (salmon scallopini with mustard)
Sautéing–SAUTIEREN–*sauté*	floured–*meunière*	*Filet de limande sole belle meunière* (floured flounder)
	with egg–*à la œuf*	*Tranche de colin sauté à la œuf* (hake in beaten egg)
	breaded–*pané*	*Filets de sole panés, aux bananes* (breaded sole with bananas)
Deep-frying–FRITIEREN–*frire*	in flour–*nature*	*Goujons de poisson frites, au citron* (deep-fried strips of fish, resembling small whole fish)
	breaded–*pané*	*Solette Colbert* (sole with lemon-tarragon sauce)
	in batter–*en pâte à frire*	*Filets de perchettes Orly* (batter-fried perch fillets with tomato sauce)
Grilling–GRILLIEREN–*griller*		*Tranche de baudroie grillée sur lit de poireaux* (monkfish steak grilled with leeks)
Baking–BACKEN IM OFEN–*cuire au four*		*Filet de turbot farci en croûte* (stuffed turbot fillet in pastry)
Roasting in a salt crust–*cuire en croûte de sel*		*Truite saumonée en croûte de sel* (salmon trout)
Cooking in parchment paper–*cuire en papillote*		*Filets de rouget de roche en papillote* (striped mullet baked in parchment paper)

Special Methods

Broiling–*cuire sous la salamandre*		*Baudroie au grins de coriandre* (monkfish broiled with coriander seeds)
Cooking in vacuum–*cuire sous vide*		

Table 7-50. Poaching in Stock

Type of Poaching	Ingredients	Use
Poaching in fish stock – *pocher au court-bouillon ordinaire*	Water, vinegar, white wine, salt, *matignon*, herbs and spices	For whole fish, fish pieces, and freshwater fish steaks. *Pocher au bleu:* The slimy covering of the skin turns blue when submerged in acidulated liquid. Only whole fish that have been killed minutes before can be poached "blue." When handling the fish care must be taken not to touch the slimy skin with a towel or paper, which would remove the slime. The *matignon* should be cut neatly if it it is to be served with the fish.
Poaching in milk stock – *pocher au court-bouillon blanc*	Water, milk, salt, spices, and lemon slices	For whole fish or flatfish steaks. Other saltwater fish can be poached in milk stock or in salted water with peeled lemon slices.

Table 7-51. Dishes with Fish Poached in Stock

Dish	Description
Trout "blue" – FORELLE BLAU – *truite au bleu*	Kill trout and clean. Drizzle lightly with vinegar. Slide trout into hot vinegar stock, and poach several minutes. Serve with boiled potatoes and melted butter and lemon on the side.
Poached cod with anchovy butter – POCHIERTER KABELJAU MIT SARDELLENBUTTER – *cabillaud pochéau beurre d'anchois*	Poach cod in milk stock or salted water with lemon slices. Serve with boiled potatoes, and offer anchovy butter (compound butter) and lemon separately.
Poached salmon – LACHS IM SUD – *darne de saumon à la nage*	Start the center piece of salmon in cold stock; poach. Serve with boiled potatoes, and offer a complementary sauce and lemon separately.
Hake steak with hollandaise – MEERHECHTSCHNITTE HOLLÄNDISCHE ART – *tranche de colin hollandaise*	Same method as for cod; however, serve with hollandaise sauce.

- Reduce the temperature to 165°F (75°C).
- Cook for about 5 minutes at 165°F (75°C).

Method for Large Fish
- Place *matignon*, herbs, and spices in the bottom of a fish-poaching kettle.
- Place prepared fish on the perforated kettle insert, and place insert atop vegetables.
- Cover with cold water, white wine, and vinegar, and bring to a simmer.
- Reduce temperature to 165°F (75° C).
- Poach. Cooking time per 2 pounds, 3 ounces (1 kg) fish is about 15 minutes at 165°F (75°C).

Halibut Poached in Milk Stock

Lemon	½	½
Water	3 qt, 19 oz	3 L
Milk	10 oz	300 ml
Bay leaf	1	1
Peppercorns, crushed	⅓ oz	10 g
Salt	1⅓ oz	40 g
Halibut steaks (10)	3 lb, 5 oz	1.5 kg
Dill, fresh	10 sprigs	5 g

Method
- Peel the lemon and cut into slices.
- Bring the water, milk, bay leaf, peppercorns, and salt to a simmer.
- Add the halibut steaks.
- Reduce temperature to 165°F (75°C).
- Place the lemon slices and dill sprigs on the fish.

- Cook for about 5 minutes at 165°F (75°C).

Poaching in Wine
This is the most often used poaching method for fish. It is especially suitable for poaching fish steaks, fish fillets, and fish scaloppini (see Table 7-52).

Important Differences from Poaching in Stock
- The poaching liquid is composed of a concentrated fish stock (fumet) and a very good wine.
- The fish is shallow-poached in very little liquid (prevents loss of flavor).
- The poached fish is always served in a sauce.

Table 7-52. Dishes with Fish Poached in White Wine

Dish	Description
With crayfish, mushrooms, and truffles— *joinville*	Nap poached fish with crayfish sauce. Garnish with peeled crayfish tails, quartered mushrooms, and truffle slices.
Glazed with diced tomato— *dugléré*	Top poached fish with sautéed diced tomato. Cover with a white-wine sauce and glaze under the broiler.
With whiskey sauce and smoked salmon— *écossaise*	Prepare a white-wine sauce with finely diced vegetables and whiskey. Nap poached fish, and garnish with a smoked salmon rosette, salmon caviar, and dill.
With saffron— *aux fleurs de safran*	Place poached fish on sautéed julienne of vegetables. Cover with a saffron-flavored white-wine sauce. Garnish with sautéed diced tomato.
With vodka sauce and caviar— *moscovite*	Flavor a white-wine sauce with vodka, add caviar, and nap the fish immediately. Garnish with dill.
Zurich style— *zougoise*	Add chopped fresh herbs (6 or 7 kinds) to a white-wine sauce. Enrich by beating in cold butter nuggets. Nap fish and serve.

The poaching liquid is always used in the sauce preparation. Any flavor leached from the fish during the process is returned to the dish in the sauce.

Side Dishes/Garnish

Because the fish is sauced, steamed rice is an excellent accompaniment. For a fish entrée, spring vegetables, leaf spinach, snow peas, and green asparagus are all good side dishes.

Fish poached in white wine are often garnished with small puff-pastry crescents (*fleurons*).

Fish Fillets Poached in White Wine

YIELD: 10 SERVINGS (APPETIZER)		
Butter	1⅔ oz	50 g
Shallots, minced	2 oz	60 g
Fish fillets (10)	1 lb, 12 oz	800 g
Salt, freshly ground white pepper		
Lemon	½	½
White wine	10 oz	300 ml
Fish fumet	10 oz	300 ml
Beurre manié (1:1)	1⅔ oz	50 g
Heavy cream	6¾ oz	200 ml

Method

- Butter a flat saucepan.
- Sprinkle the bottom with the minced shallots.
- Place the fish fillets in the pan, and season with salt and pepper.

- Brush with butter (to prevent sticking).
- Drizzle with lemon juice, and add the white wine and fish fumet.
- Cover with parchment paper.
- Bring to just below simmering.
- Place in the oven to finish poaching.
- Remove fillets, and keep warm in a little stock.
- Add the *beurre manié* to the poaching liquid, and cook to desired consistency for at least 15 minutes.
- Add cream, and reduce again.
- Season the sauce, and pass through a fine-mesh china cap.
- Add any garnishes to the sauce.
- Drain fish well, and plate.
- Serve napped with sauce.

Notes

- The garnishes in the sauce should always be cooked, with the exception of fresh herbs.
- When preparing large quantities, it is customary to reduce the poaching liquid and add it to an already prepared white-wine sauce.

Glazing Fish Dishes

To glaze a fish dish, the surface of a fully prepared fish dish is exposed to the full heat of a salamander (broiler). In addition to the added eye appeal, glazing imparts additional flavor and enhances the quality of the dish.

After glazing, the sauce surface should have an even, light brown color. Dark brown or black spots on the surface are not acceptable.

The glazing capacity of a white-wine sauce depends on its protein and fat content. Adding a little hollandaise sauce and heavy cream or only heavy cream *immediately* before glazing will increase the fat and/or protein content and therefore the glazing ability.

Poaching in Red Wine—*pocher au vin rouge*

Very few fish are poached in red wine, because red wine overpowers most delicately flavored fish. In addition, the white fish flesh may become discolored and turn gray when poached in red wine. Suitable fish for red-wine poaching are listed in Table 7-53.

Fish Fillets Poached in Red Wine

YIELD: 10 SERVINGS (APPETIZER)		
Butter	1⅔ oz	50 g
Shallots, minced	2 oz	60 g
Fish fillets (10)	1 lb, 12 oz	800 g
Salt, freshly ground white pepper		
Red wine	14 oz	400 ml
Red-wine fish fumet	14 oz	400 ml
Beurre manié (1:1)	1⅔ oz	50 g
Butter nuggets	1⅔ oz	50 g
Lemon	½	½

Method

- Poach fish fillets using the same method as described under white-wine poaching, using red wine and red-wine fish fumet.
- Remove the fish, cover, and keep warm.
- Reduce the poaching liquid, and add *beurre manié*. Cook to the desired consistency for at least 15 minutes.
- Season, and pass through a fine-mesh china cap.
- Beat in cold butter nuggets.
- Season with lemon juice.
- Add any garnishes to the sauce.
- Drain fish well, and plate.
- Serve napped with sauce.

Notes

Poach fish in white-wine stock to preserve the white color of the fish. The red wine can be added to the poaching liquid after the fish has been removed and reduced. To enrich a red wine fish sauce, a little double cream (concentrated heavy cream) can be added at the end.

Braising – SCHMOREN – *braiser*

Usually large fish or fish pieces are braised, such as medium-sized turbot, turbot backs, and the center piece of salmon (darnes). Table 7-54 lists some braised fish dishes.

The technique for braising fish lies somewhere in between braising vegetables and braising meat. Like vegetables, fish is not browned, but like meat, fish must be frequently basted and is fully cooked when most of the liquid has evaporated. After the fish has been removed, the braising liquid is passed through a fine-mesh sieve, reduced, and added to a prepared white-wine or red-wine sauce. Both a white- and a red-wine sauce can be served with braised fish at the same time.

Presentation and Service

Braising is used only when the whole piece is placed on a platter and presented to the guests. The fish is then properly portioned in front of the guests and served.

Side Dishes / Garnishes

Boiled potatoes, steamed rice or pilaf, sautéed fennel strips, and vegetables julienne or green spring vegetables braised in butter are all appropriate side dishes.

Braised Whole Turbot in White-Wine Sauce

YIELD: 10 SERVINGS (APPETIZER)		
Turbot, whole	8 lb, 3 oz	4 kg
Salt, freshly ground white pepper		
Butter	3 oz	80 g
Matignon	10½ oz	300 g
Dill, fresh	⅓ oz	10 g
Tarragon, fresh	⅓ oz	10 g
Bay leaf	1	1
White wine	1 pt, 1 oz	500 ml
Fish fumet	1 qt, 2 oz	1 L
White-wine sauce	1 pt, 1 oz	500 ml

Method

- Wash and clean the turbot.
- Butter the insert of a turbot poaching kettle, season the turbot, and place, white side up, on the insert.
- In a saucepan, sauté the *matignon* (onion, leeks, celeriac, fennel) in butter, and place in the bottom of turbot poaching kettle.
- Sprinkle the herbs on top.
- Place the insert with the fish on top of the vegetables.
- Add the wine and fish fumet. The fish should be about one-quarter submerged.

Table 7-53. Dishes with Fish Poached in Red Wine

Dish	Description
Turbot fillets in red-wine sauce with sesame seeds – STEINBUTTFILETS MIT ROTWEINSAUCE UND SESAM – *filets de turbotin au vin rouge et au sésame*	Toast sesame seeds under the broiler and sprinkle over sauced fish.
Monkfish fillet, sailor style – SEETEUFELFILETS MATROSENART – *baudroie en matelote*	Glaze pearl onions and sauté crayfish tails. Place on the fish fillets, and nap with red-wine sauce.

Table 7-54. Braised Fish Dishes

Dish	Description
Braised sea bass with vermouth – GESCHMORTER WOLFSBARSCH MIT NOILLY PRAT – *loup de mer braisé au Noilly Prat*	Braise fish in dry vermouth. Remove skin. Reduce stock, and enrich with double cream (concentrated heavy cream) and hollandaise. Nap fish. Garnish with sautéed vegetable and truffle strips.
Turbot with champagne sauce – STEINBUTT MIT CHAMPAGNERSAUCE – *turbotin au champagne*	Braise turbot in champagne. Remove skin. To make a sauce, reduce the braising liquid, and enrich with double cream. Nap the fish with a little sauce, and serve the rest separately.

- Bring to a simmer, and cover partially (part of the stock should evaporate).
- Braise in the oven at low temperature. Baste the fish occasionally with its own juices.
- Remove the fish and insert when done, cover, and keep warm.
- Strain the stock through a fine-mesh china cap, reduce until almost syrupy, and add to the prepared white-wine sauce.
- Arrange the turbot on a pretty platter, and brush with butter.
- Serve sauce and garnish separately.

Notes

If the white wine is a very good wine or champagne, after stirring and reducing, the stock can be enriched by whisking in cold butter nuggets to make a sauce (*monté au beurre*).

The reduced stock can also be incorporated into a prepared red-wine sauce.

Steaming – DÄMPFEN – *cuire à la vapeur*

Fish is also steamed without pressure. Pressure-steaming causes the temperature to rise too high, drying out the fish and toughening its protein. Appropriate steaming equipment is listed in Table 7-55.

Fish that are suitable for poaching can also be steamed: fillets, steaks, and pieces are better than whole fish. Unlike poaching, in steaming, the fish is never in contact with liquid. This preserves flavor and nutrients but has the disadvantage of not providing any stock for sauce making.

Adddding wine, herbs, and spices to the steaming liquid will help flavor the fish. It is important to salt the fish and not the steaming liquid, be-

cause salt cannot dissolve in steam.

Steaming in a Commercial Steamer

If fish is steamed in a commercial steamer, no added flavoring is possible. The steam is automatically injected from a water source. The steam should be without pressure (convected), and the temperature should be 160° to 180°F (70° to 80°C). If the fish is placed in a pan, with fumet and wine and then cooked in a commercial steamer, the method is then poaching in wine, not steaming.

Sauces and Garnishes

Since steaming does not produce stock for sauces, steamed fish is generally served with sauces to which reduced fish fumet (fish extract) has been added. For example:

- Special fish sauces
- Tomato or red pepper *coulis*
- White-wine or red-wine fish sauces

The same side dishes and garnishes for poached fish can be used for steamed fish.

Steamed Fillets of Fish

Yield: 10 servings (appetizer)		
Fish fumet	1 qt, 19 oz	1.5 L
White wine	1 pt, 1 oz	500 ml
Fresh herbs	3 oz	100 g
Fish fillets (10)	1 lb, 12 oz	800 g
Salt, freshly ground white pepper		
Butter	1⅔ oz	80 g
Prepared fish sauce	13½ oz	400 ml

Method

- Place the fish fumet, wine, and herbs into fish steamer, and bring to a boil.

- Season the fish fillets.
- Butter the steamer insert (to prevent sticking), and place fillets in it, neatly in a row.
- Brush lightly with butter.
- Place insert above liquid, and cover with a lid.
- Keeping the liquid near simmering, steam the fillets until just done.
- Serve on a pool of sauce, or serve napped with sauce.

Notes

The amount of fumet depends on the size of the steamer. The fumet can also be used to make fish sauces.

Sautéing – SAUTIEREN – *sauté*

To sauté means to cook food in a small amount of fat. Sautéing is always done on top of the stove.

Fish suitable for sautéing are:

- small, whole round or flat fish
- fillets, cutlets, and steaks from all fish

Fish are sautéed in special fish sauté pans (long oval) and in frying pans (Lyon pan) or in nonstick pans. They are coated with flour and/or other coatings before frying (see Table 7-56.)

Three steps are necessary to sauté whole fish or thick pieces of fish:

Step 1: Clean the fish, fillets, or steak, marinate in pepper and lemon juice, and salt at the very last moment. Dredge in flour, removing excess flour by tapping the fish lightly.

Step 2: Brown the fish in a fat with a high smoke point until almost cooked through. (The heat denatures the released proteins, which form a crust. The crust prevents juices from escaping. At the same time flavor and color are added to the fish.)

Step 3: Finish the almost cooked fish by sautéing it in fresh butter, and plate. (This step can be omitted for thin fish pieces.) Garnish appropriately, and pour foaming butter over the fish. Serve the fish at once, while the butter is still foaming.

Table 7-55. Steaming Equipment

Steamer	Source of Steam
Steamer and convection steamer	Water from an external source
Sauce pots with perforated inserts and lids Couscous steamers (*couscoussière*) Special fish steamers or poachers	Water or fish stock; if desired, enhance with wine, fresh herbs, spices

Table 7-56. Sauté Styles

Name	Mise en place	Method
Floured– MÜLLERINART– *meuniére* (whole fish, steaks, fillets)	Slash whole fish several times, marinate in lemon juice and pepper. Season with salt, dredge in flour, tap off excess flour	Sauté and plate. Drizzle with *jus meuniére* (a mixture of veal jus, Worcestershire sauce, and lemon juice), sprinkle with chopped parsley, and pour on foaming butter. Garnish.
Sauté in beaten egg– IM EI SAUTIEREN– *sauter à l'œuf* (fillets, cutlet)	Prepare as for floured sautéing, but then dip into egg and wipe off excess.	Do not sauté too hot. Plate. Garnish appropriately. Pour on foaming butter before service.
Breaded– PANIERT SAUTIEREN– *sauter pané* (fillets, cutlet)	Prepare as for beaten egg sautéing, but then dredge in fresh bread crumbs, pressed lightly into the fish.	Sauté in hot clarified butter. Garnish appropriately. Pour on hot foaming butter before service.

Table 7-57. Dishes with Sautéed Fish

Name	Type	Description
With capers and lemon–*grenobloise*	Floured–*meuniére*	Add diced lemon flesh, capers, and chopped parsley to the butter, and pour over fish.
With tomatoes and capers–*lucernoise*	Floured–*meuniére*	Add finely chopped sautéed onions, capers, and fresh herbs to a tomato concassé, and pour over the fish.
With artichokes and potatoes–*murat*	Floured–*meuniére*	Garnish with sautéed quartered artichoke bottoms, small barrel-shaped potatoes, *jus meuniére*, chopped parsley, and foaming butter.

Some common garnishes are listed in Table 7-57.

If the sautéed fish fillets are served without foaming butter, they are listed on the menu as fried golden brown–*sauté doré*.

Side Dishes and Garnishes
A popular side dish is potatoes, especially steamed potatoes tossed with melted butter and fresh herbs (dill, chives, parsley). For a fish entrée, spring vegetables, leaf spinach, snow peas, and green asparagus are all good side dishes. Lemon should be served separately.

Basic Principles for Sautéing Fish
Incisions in Whole Fish
Making incisions in whole fish allows the marinade and the hot butter to penetrate better. The result is a more flavorful fish and a shorter cooking time.

Sauté the Presentation Side First
Always place the side that is to be presented to the guest in the hot fat first. The proteins brown better, and the first side will be more presentable.

Breading without Egg
This breading method is a bit difficult. The fish is floured and dipped in clarified butter rather than egg. (The protein released during sautéing makes the breading stick.)

Sautéed Floured Sole–SEEZUNGEN MÜLLERINART–*sole meunière*

YIELD: 10 SERVINGS (APPETIZER)		
Fillets of sole (10)	4 lb, 14 oz	2.2 kg
Lemon	1	1
Freshly ground white pepper, salt		
Flour	1⅔ oz	50 g
Peanut oil	3⅓ oz	100 ml
Parsley, chopped	1⅓ oz	40 g
Jus meuniére	½ oz	15 g
Butter	3 oz	100 g
Lemon (separate)	2½	2½

Method
- Clean and portion the sole.
- Marinate in lemon juice and pepper.
- Season with salt. Dredge in flour, and tap lightly to remove excess flour.
- Sauté in oil until golden brown.
- Plate on a warm dish.

- Drizzle with jus meuniére.
- Sprinkle with chopped parsley.
- Pour foaming butter over the fish.

Fish Sautéed in Beaten Egg–FISCH IM EI SAUTIEREN–*sauter à l'œuf*

YIELD: 10 SERVINGS (APPETIZER)		
Fish fillets (10)	2 lb, 3 oz	1 kg
Lemon	1	1
Freshly ground white pepper, salt		
Flour	1⅔ oz	50 g
Eggs	2	2
Peanut oil	3⅓ oz	100 ml
Butter	3 oz	100 g
Lemon (separate)	2½	2½

Method
- Marinate fish in lemon juice and pepper
- Season with salt. Dredge in flour, tapping lightly to remove excess flour.
- Dip into beaten egg, wipe off excess.
- Sauté in oil or clarified butter until golden brown.
- Plate on a warm dish.
- Pour foaming butter over the fish.

Sautéed Breaded Fish – PANIERT SAUTIEREN – *sauter pané*

YIELD: 10 SERVINGS (APPETIZER)		
Fish fillets (10)	2 lb, 3 oz	1 kg
Lemon	1	1
Freshly ground white pepper, salt		
Flour	1⅔ oz	50 g
Eggs	2	2
Fresh bread crumbs	7 oz	200 g
Clarified butter	7 oz	200 g
Butter	3 oz	100 g
Lemon (separate)	2½	2½

Method

Prepare as for fish sautéed in beaten egg, but:

- After dipping in egg, dredge in fresh bread crumbs, pressing the crumbs lightly onto the fish.
- Instead of oil, sauté in clarified butter until golden brown.

Deep-frying – FRITIEREN – *frire*

Deep-fried products have an intense flavor, which is partially caused by the evaporation of water during high-temperature frying. The temperature of the fat should always be about 355°F (180°C) to guarantee a crisp end product.

Lean fish are best suited for deep-frying:
- small, whole round or flat fish
- steaks, fillets, or strips.

Fish should be fried in a separate fryer to produce a clean taste and protect other foods from tasting fishy. The various ways to deep-fry fish are listed in Table 7-58.

Fish with a large number of fine bones, for example, pike and carp, benefit from deep frying. Some of the bones turn crisp during the process and become edible.

Use in the Daily Menu

If deep-fried fish is offered and large quantities are to be served in a relatively short time, the fish can be partially deep-fried at about 285°F (140°C) and then finished to order at about 355°F (180°C).

Presentation

After deep-frying the fish, place it on absorbent paper to remove fat. Serve deep-fried fish on a warm platter lined with a paper napkin. Garnish with parsley and lemon if desired.

As with all deep-fried products, it is very important not to cover the fish or the steam will make the fried coating soggy. The fish should be served at once.

Garnish with lemon.

Side Dishes

No starch is necessary, but steamed or boiled potatoes are suitable if a starch side dish is desired.

Sauces

Mayonnaise, rémoulade, tartar, and tomato sauce or tomato concassé all go well with deep-fried fish. The classic dish of deep-fried fish Orly is still accompanied by a tomato *coulis*.

Deep-fried Floured Fish – FISCH IM MEHL FRITIERT – *poisson frit nature*

YIELD: 10 SERVINGS (APPETIZER)		
Fish fillets	2 lb, 3 oz	1.0 kg
Lemon	1	1
Freshly ground white pepper, salt		
Flour	1⅔ oz	50 g
Oil (about 10% loss)	3 oz	100 g
Lemon (separate)	2½	2½

Method

- Marinate the fish in lemon juice and pepper.
- Season with salt. Dredge in flour, tapping lightly to remove excess flour.
- Depending on the thickness of the fish, deep-fry in oil at about 340° to 355°F (170° to 180°C), until crisp.
- Place on absorbent paper. Salt lightly.
- Place on a warm platter with paper napkin, and garnish with parsley.
- Serve lemon quarters, side dishes, and sauces separately.

Grilling – GRILLIEREN – *griller*

Food is grilled on or below heated racks. Grill racks can be heated electrically, with gas, or with charcoal. More detailed information is given in section 7.4.7.

Properly grilled fish is juicy and marked by the characteristic rhombic grill pattern.

Fresh, firm-fleshed fish are suitable for grilling, such as:

Table 7-58. Methods for Deep-frying Fish

Name	Suitable for	Method
Deep-fried floured – IM MEHL FRITIERT – frit nature	Whole fish, steaks, fillets, strips	Marinate, salt, flour, tap off excess flour, deep-fry
Deep-fried breaded – PANIERT FRITIERT – frit pané	Fillets, strips, sole Colbert (with lemon-tarragon butter)	Marinate, salt, flour, tap off excess flour, dip in beaten egg, then in fresh bread crumbs, press lightly, deep-fry
Batter-fried – IM BACKTEIG FRITIERT – frit à la pâte à frire	Fillets, strips	Marinade, flour, tap off excess, dip in batter, deep fry

Fish may be marinated several hours in advance but must be salted at the very last minute.

- small, whole round or flat fish
- steaks and fillets

Just as in sautéing, whole fish should be slashed several times before being marinated.

Nutritional Considerations

Grilled fish are important components of medical diets:

- Grilling is a low-fat preparation method.
- Nutrients are retained because of the very short cooking time.
- The strong flavors developed by the high temperatures make it possible to enjoy grilled fish without salt.

Presentation

Grilled fish is generally served plain. To improve eye appeal, it can be brushed with butter.

Side Dishes and Sauces

An appropriate starch side dish is steamed or boiled potatoes; in the United States, baked potatoes are popular. Complementary sauces include béarnaise, rémoulade, compound butters, tomato *coulis*, and special fish sauces.

Grilled Fish

YIELD: 10 SERVINGS (APPETIZER)		
Salmon steaks	2 lb, 14 oz	1.3 kg
Lemon	1	1
Freshly ground pepper, salt		
Peanut oil	3 oz	100 g
Lemon (separate)	2½	2½
Watercress	3 oz	100 g

Method

- Marinate the fish for a few minutes in the lemon juice and pepper.
- Season the fish with salt, and dip completely in oil.
- Place diagonally on a clean, hot grill rack (presentation side first).
- Change the position on the grill after one-third of the expected cooking time, to create cross pattern.
- Turn after another third of the cooking time; finish cooking.
- Plate on a heated dish.

- Brush with clarified butter.
- Garnish with watercress.
- Serve lemon quarters, sauces, and side dishes separately.

Notes

Fish with white or dry flesh can be floured before being dipped in oil. The thin flour coating forms a light crust and prevents the juices from escaping. The grill pattern is also more prominent, turning a golden brown color.

Examples of Grilled Fish Dishes

Grilled salmon cutlet with white butter sauce and green asparagus—*escalopes de saumon grillées au beurre blanc et aux asperges vertes*

Grilled fillet of sole with homemade noodles—*filets de sole grillées aux nouillettes fraîches*

Grilled monkfish steak on a bed of sautéed leeks—*tranche de baudroie grillée sur lit de poireaux.*

Baking—BACKEN IM OFEN—*cuire au four*

This method is used for fish that are baked in dough. Because baking in a dough crust takes time, whole, large fish (without head and scaled, or even skinned, boned, and stuffed) are prepared in this manner.

To make it easier to serve fish in a crust, the skinned fillet can be slit and stuffed, or the stuffing can be sandwiched between two fillets and then wrapped in the dough.

Protected by the dough crust from the high heat, the fish cooks slowly, retaining its flavor and nutrients. Released juices are absorbed by the dough and combine with the flavor of the dough to make a tasty treat.

Suitable Doughs

Puff pastry is excellent from a labor point of view, as the dough is commercially available and easy to work. It also produces an excellent taste.

Yeast dough provides excellent flavor harmony but is difficult to work.

Pie dough is frequently used in the United States.

Presentation and Service

Fish in pastry should be placed on a doily-covered platter, presented to the guests, and sliced properly in front of them.

Side Dishes

No side dishes are necessary for fish baked in pastry. Spring vegetables can be the garnish if the fish is the main entrée.

Sauces

- White-wine sauces and variations
- Special fish sauces

Baked in Puff Pastry— IM BLÄTTERTEIG GEBACKEN— *cuit en feuilletage*

YIELD: 10 SERVINGS (APPETIZER)		
Fish fillets (2)	1 lb, 5 oz	600 g
Lemon	½	½
Freshly ground pepper, salt		
Fish stuffing	1 lb, 2 oz	500 g
Puff pastry	1 lb, 5 oz	600 g
All-purpose flour	1 oz	30 g
Egg yolks	2	2

Method

- Marinate the skinless fish fillets in lemon juice and pepper.
- Place the fish stuffing (and any garnish) atop the interior side of one fillet.
- Place the second fillet, exterior side up, on top of the filling. Chill.
- Roll out half the puff pastry on a flour-covered board ⅛ inch (3 mm) thick, 1½ inches (4 cm) bigger than the fish.
- Position the fish on pastry. Brush the dough edges with beaten egg yolk.
- Roll out the other half of the pastry, place atop fish, and press the edges together tightly, to seal.
- Brush the dough with beaten egg yolk (to which a little water has been added), and decorate with pastry.
- Chill for 30 minutes. Prick the surface two or three times with a fork.
- Bake at 395°F (200°C) for about 25 minutes.

Baked in Yeast Dough – IM HEFETEIG GEBACKEN – *cuit en brioche*

Use the same ingredients, in the same quantities, as for "Baked in Puff Pastry," but use yeast dough instead of puff pastry.

Method
- Wrap the fish in the yeast dough. Seal tight.
- Brush the dough with beaten egg yolk (to which a little water has been added), and decorate with pastry.
- With kitchen shears, carefully pinch scales into the dough.
- Chill for 30 minutes.
- Bake at 465°F (240°C) for about 25 minutes.

Special Preparation Methods

Special Preparation in the Oven
Cooking fish wrapped in salt, aluminum foil, roasting foil, or parchment paper is not a basic baking method, because the flavor that results from direct baking is absent. These special methods are designed to have eye appeal and at the same time trap the volatile flavors of the fish, creating an intense individual fish flavor.

The two basic methods are:

Roasting in a salt crust: for whole fish in their skin

Roasting in foil: (aluminum foil, roasting foil, parchment paper), for very small whole fish, steaks, fillets, and scaloppini. Fish in foil are generally single portions.

Presentation and Service
Present the cooked fish in the salt crust on a paper napkin or in the foil in a hot gratin dish directly to the guest. Open the crust or foil in front of the guest, and portion if necessary. Serve on a plate.

Side Dishes
For fish baked in foil, side dishes are often created by cooking the side dish ingredient along with the fish in the foil.

A suitable side dish for fish in a salt crust is spring vegetables.

Sauces
White-wine sauces and variations, as well as some special fish sauces, are appropriate.

Roasting in a Salt Crust – *cuire en croûte de sel*

YIELD: 10 SERVINGS (APPETIZER)		
Salmon trout	3 lb, 15 oz	1.8 kg
Lemon	1	1
Freshly ground pepper, salt		
Chervil, fresh	⅔ oz	20 g
Dill, fresh	1 oz	30 g
Parsley, fresh	⅔ oz	20 g
Egg white	2	2
Salt, kosher	2 lb, 3 oz	1 kg
Sea salt, coarse	2 lb, 3 oz	1 kg
Water	1⅔ oz	50 ml

Method
- Clean and wash the fish. Season with lemon, pepper, and salt inside.
- Rub with chopped fresh herbs.
- Mix the egg white, salt, and water for 2 to 3 minutes.
- Coat the fish with salt mixture, ½ to ¾ inch (1 to 2 cm) thick.
- Bake at 395°F (200°C) for 20 to 25 minutes.

Cooking in Parchment Paper – *cuire en papillote*

YIELD: 10 SERVINGS (APPETIZER)		
Salmon cutlets	1 lb, 12 oz	800 g
Lemon, freshly ground pepper, salt		
Clarified butter	5 oz	150 g
Spinach leaves, blanched, seasoned	10½ oz	300 g
Mushroom duxelles	10½ oz	300 g
Chives, finely chopped	1⅔ oz	50 g

Method
- Marinate the salmon cutlets in lemon juice, pepper, and salt.
- Briefly sauté in some of the clarified butter.
- Fold round parchment paper, 12 inches (30 cm) in diameter, in half.
- Brush the center of the bottom half with some clarified butter.
- Layer spinach, salmon, mushroom duxelles, and chives atop the bottom of the paper.
- Fold the top half of the parchment over the fish. Fold in and crimp the edges to create an air-tight seal.
- Brush the surface with some clarified butter.
- Place in a gratin dish, and bake in a hot oven for a few minutes. The paper wrapper will puff up when it fills with steam.
- Serve at once. Open in front of the guest.

Broiling under the Salamander – *cuire sous la salamandre*

This method is advantageous in that the fish can be cooked on the plate on which it is to be served.

Thin slices of fish are seasoned and cooked directly under the salamander (broiler) or are covered with a thin sauce (glazed) and then broiled (see Table 7-59).

The degree of doneness must be *constantly* monitored to prevent the fish from drying. The fish should not brown and must be just barely cooked. This method can be used for all fish. However, only one portion can be prepared at a time.

Sauces
Separately prepared using concentrated fish fumet (glace), enriched variations of a white-wine sauce, or any of the special fish sauces are appropriate.

Cooking in a Vacuum – *cuire sous vide*

This is not a new basic technique but rather a production method, and reconstitution is necessary before service (see Table 7-60). Cooking in vacuum bags makes sense only in kitchens that are based on a reconstitution system and are equipped accordingly (a more detailed discussion is found in section 7.4.4).

Table 7-59. Broiled Fish

Mise en place	No Glazing	Glazing
• Brush plate lightly with butter. • Season with salt and freshly ground pepper. • Fillet fish, skin, and remove bones. • Cut into ⅟₁₆-inch (2-mm) slices. • Arrange on a plate.	Brush lean fish with clarified butter (prevents drying). Drizzle fatty fish with a little fish fumet. • Cook under broiler. • Remove, sauce lightly, and sprinkle with fresh herbs. • Serve at once. Generally served without a starch side dish.	Brush lean fish with clarified butter (prevents drying). Drizzle fatty fish with a little fish fumet. • Cook under broiler. • Remove, sauce lightly, and sprinkle with fresh herbs. • Serve at once. Generally served without a starch side dish.

Table 7-60. Vacuum Production Processes for Fish

Preparation method	Vacuum process					
	1.	2.	3.	4.	5.	6.
Poaching in stock or wine	Prepare fish as usual.					
Steaming Roasting in foil	Put raw fish and all other ingredients (and little liquid) in a vacuum bag, and vacuum-seal.	Cook in steamer at 165°F/70°C (about 20% longer than normal cooking time).	Chill at once in ice water to 34°F/1°C.	Identify, date, and refrigerate.	Reheat in the bag in a steamer or in a hot water bath.	Plate and serve with a suitable sauce, side dish, and/or garnish.
Sautéing Grilling	Marinate, season. Score with grill marks or sauté briefly, let cool, and vacuum-seal. Refrigerate.					

Special Fish Sauces

Several fish preparation methods, for example, steaming, broiling, roasting in a salt crust, in parchment paper, or in vacuum bags, produce no cooking liquids with which to prepare a sauce. For these instances, special fish sauces have been developed, which are not based on a fish velouté but on concentrated fish fumet , or fish extract *(glace de poisson)*.

In contrast to the common white-wine sauce, which is thickened with carbohydrates (flour in *roux*), a special fish sauce is thickened with protein (in extract and egg yolk) or with fat (double cream or butter).

These sauces cannot be surpassed in flavor and complexity by any other sauce preparation method. However, the sauces are very sensitive to heat, expensive to prepare, high in calories, and must be prepared at the very last minute. Sauces based on fish extract are listed in Table 7-61.

Fish Extract – FISCHGLACE – *glace de poisson*

YIELD: 1 QT, 12 OZ (1 L)		
Fish bones (sole)	10 lb, 15 oz	5 kg
Shallots	1 lb, 2 oz	500 g
Leeks, white part	1 lb, 5 oz	600 g
Parsley stems	7 oz	200 g
Clarified butter	3 oz	80 g
dry white vermouth	1 pt, 11 oz	800 ml
White wine	1 qt, 22 oz	1.6 L

Mise en place
- Soak fish bones in water.
- Chop shallots, leeks, and parsley stems to make a *matignon*.

Method
- Sauté the *matignon* in clarified butter.
- Add the fish bones, and continue to cook for 15 minutes.
- Add the dry white vermouth and white wine. Simmer for 25 minutes, skimming occasionally.
- Strain through a double layer of cheesecloth, and reduce to 2 quarts, 2 ounces (1 L).

Notes
Stored in the refrigerator in small plastic containers, the fish extract can be kept until needed.

Use of a fish extract is not limited to special fish sauces. It can enrich any fish cream soup or sauce.

Variations
Adding chopped fresh herbs, such as tarragon, dill, or basil, or compound butters, such as sea urchin butter, lobster coral butter, or lobster butter (red), to a fish specialty sauce allows for many variations of the basic sauce.

Table 7-61. Special Fish Sauces

Sauce	Description
Special fish sauce with cream – FISCH-SPEZIALSAUCE MIT RAHM – *sauce poisson spéciale à la crème*	Reduce fish extract and double cream. Remove from heat and beat in cold butter nuggets. Season.
Special fish sauce for glazing – FISCH-SPEZIALSAUCE ZUM GLASIEREN – *sauce poisson spéciale à glacer*	Special fish sauce with cream. Remove from heat and carefully fold in egg yolks and whipped cream. Season.
Fish sabayon – FISCH-SABAYON – *sabayon de poisson*	Reduce white wine, extract, chicken stock, chopped shallots and herbs. Strain. Beat the reduction with egg yolks until thick and creamy. Gently beat in soft butter bits. Season.
White butter sauce – WEISSE BUTTERSAUCE – *beurre blanc*	Cook the fish extract with a little white wine and chicken stock. Remove from heat and beat in cold butter nuggets. Season with salt, freshly ground pepper, and lemon juice.
Red butter sauce – ROTE BUTTERSAUCE – *beurre rouge*	Prepare in the same way as white butter sauce, but add heavy, flavorful, reduced red wine.

Preparation Methods for Freshwater Fish

Main criteria for selection:

- Texture of fish flesh
- Flavor
- Fat content
- Cut of fish
- Size

	Poach in court bouillon	Poach in milk stock	Poach in white wine	Poach in red wine	Braise	Steam	Sauté floured	Sauté in beaten egg	Sauté breaded	Deep-fry in flour	Deep-fry in beaten egg	Deep-fry breaded	Batter-fry	Grill	Bake	Bake in salt crust	Bake in parchment paper	Broil under salamander
River eel – FLUSSAL – *anguille*	●		●							●				●				
Young pike – GRASSHECHT – *brocheton*			●	●			●											
Young pike fillets						●	●			●				●				
Young pike steaks							●			●				●				
Carp – KARPFEN – *carpe*	●		●	●														
Sturgeon – STÖR – *estugeon (filet)*							●							●				
Whitefish – FELCHEN – *féra*			●				●											
Whitefish fillets			●			●	●		●	●			●					
Sheatfish fillet – WELSFILET – *glanis (filet)*				●			●				●							
Lake char – SAIBLING – *omble chevalier*	●		●	●			●											●
Lake char fillet			●	●		●	●											
Grayling – ÄSCHE – *ombre*			●				●							●				
Grayling fillets			●			●	●											
River perch – EGLI – *perche*							●			●								
River perch fillets			●				●	●		●	●		●					
Pike perch – ZANDER – *sandre*			●				●							●			●	
Pike perch fillet			●			●	●			●	●		●	●				
Salmon – LACHS – *saumon*	●															●	●	
Salmon fillet			●	●		●	●											●
Rainbow trout – REGENBOGENFORELLE – *truite arc-en-ciel*	●		●			●	●			●							●	
Trout fillet			●	●		●	●	●		●								●
Lake trout – SEEFORELLE – *truite du lac*	●			●		●										●	●	
Lake trout fillet			●	●		●	●											●
Brook trout – BACHFORELLE – *truite de rivière*	●		●				●			●							●	

Preparation Methods for Saltwater Fish

Main criteria for selection:

- Texture of fish flesh
- Flavor
- Fat content
- Cut of fish
- Size

	Poach in court bouillon	Poach in milk stock	Poach in white wine	Poach in red wine	Braise	Steam	Sauté floured	Sauté in beaten egg	Sauté breaded	Deep-fry in flour	Deep-fry in beaten egg	Deep-fry breaded	Batter-fry	Grill	Bake	Bake in salt crust	Bake in parchment paper	Broil under salamander
Haddock – SCHELLFISCH – *aglefin*		●	●				●											
Monkfish fillet – SEETEUFELFILLET – *baudroie (filet)*		●	●			●	●							●				●
Monkfish steak			●			●	●							●			●	
Sea bream – GOLDBRASSE – *dorade royale*					●		●							●		●	●	
Plaice fillet – SCHOLLENFILET – *carrelet (filet)*			●				●	●	●	●	●	●	●					
Atlantic cod – KABELJAU – *cabaillaud*		●	●															
Hake – MEERHECHT – *colin*		●	●			●												
Swordfish – SCHWERTFISCH – *espadon*					●		●							●				
Flounder fillet – FLUNDERFILET – *flet (filet)*			●				●	●	●	●	●	●						
Halibut fillet – HEILBUTFILET – *flétan*	●	●		●		●	●							●				●
Halibut steak	●	●												●				
Lemon sole – ROTZUNGENFILET – *limande sole (filet)*			●				●	●	●	●	●	●						
White ocean perch – WOLFSBARSCH – *loup de mer*					●									●	●	●		
White ocean perch fillet			●			●	●							●				
Mackerel – MAKRELE – *maquereau*							●							●				
Whiting – WEISSLING – *merlan*							●							●				
Whiting fillet								●	●	●	●	●						
European mullet – MEERÄSCHE – *mulet*	●						●			●				●				
Skate wing – ROCHENFLÜGEL – *raie (aile)*	●						●											
Red ocean perch – ROTBARSCH – *racasse du nord*		●					●			●								
Red mullet – ROTBARBE – *rouget barbet*							●							●				
Red mullet/barbel fillet						●	●							●				
Sole – SEEZUNGE – *sole*	●	●	●			●		●	●		●		●					
Sole fillets		●	●			●	●	●	●	●	●	●	●	●				
Turbot – STEINBUTT – *turbot*	●				●													
Turbot fillet		●				●	●							●			●	●
Turbot steak	●	●					●							●				
Tuna – THUNFISCH – *thon*							●			●				●				

7.12 Crustaceans and Mollusks

Biologically speaking, there are numerous varieties of shellfish. Only a few are of culinary importance, however, and most of them live in the ocean.

Shellfish are usually grouped with fish as *seafood* on the menu (see Table 7-62 for uses on the menu). Seafood is nutritionally important and contributes large amounts of protein and minerals. It is also very tasty. However, some shellfish are high in cholesterol, and some are not easily digested. Crustaceans and mollusks should be prepared as soon as they are killed and kept refrigerat-

ed. Dead shellfish develop high levels of bacteria rather quickly, and the toxins are not destroyed through cooking.

7.12.1 *Mise en place* for Crustaceans

Killing Crustaceans

Ethical and animal-rights considerations make it necessary to kill crustaceans before they are prepared. Crustaceans die quickly if they are thrown head first into a pot of boiling salted water or stock and left to boil for one minute. In the past, it

was customary to split and sever live lobsters; this method is no longer acceptable.

For the following preparation methods, crustaceans are:

- briefly plunged in salted water or stock: *braising*, *sautéing*, and *grilling*
- Plunged in stock and left to poach: *poaching*, *deep frying*, and *cold preparations*

Removing Meat from Lobsters and Spiny Lobsters

1. Remove the legs and break at the middle joint. With a skewer or lob-

Table 7-62. Uses for Crustaceans and Mollusks

Usage	Characteristics	Examples
Cold appetizers	**Raw:** mostly oyster varieties, and some mussels and clams; served opened on crushed ice with lemon, butter, and black bread.	*Fines de claires sur glace* (*fines de claires* on crushed ice) *Salade d'huîtres au caviar* (oyster salad with caviar)
	Cooked: Crustaceans and mollusks in salads and appetizer cocktails	*Homard et coquilles Saint-Jacques en salade* (lobster and scallop salad) *Variation de fruits de mer aux avocat* (seafood with avocado) *Cocktail de crevettes* (shrimp cocktail)
Soups	Cold or hot fish consommés with seafood garnish, seafood cream soups (bisques), mussel soups (clear, creamy, or au gratin)	*Bisque de homard* (lobster bisque) *Germiny aux crevettes* (sorrel soup with shrimp) *Soupe aux moules gratinée* (gratinated mussel soup)
Warm appetizers	Warm appetizers in the classical culinary sense are of minor importance	*Risotto aux langoustines et au basilic* (spiny lobster risotto with basil) *Soufflé de homard* (lobster soufflé) *Bouchées aux crevettes Nantua* (patty shells with shrimp, crayfish tails, and truffles)
Fish course	On the menu, crustaceans and mollusks are listed under the fish course; small portions emphasize their gourmet character	*Fricasée de homard au Sauternes* (lobster stew with wine) *Ecrevisse bordelaise* (crayfish in bordelaise sauce) *Langoustines à la crème au caviar* (Norway lobster in cream with caviar) *Coquilles Saint-Jacques à la ciboulette* (creamed scallops with chives) *Moules marinière* (steamed mussels with wine and herbs) *Fines de Belon chaud au xérès* (warm Belon oysters with sherry)
Shellfish entrees	Larger portions of items listed in the fish course can be served as entrées or a separate course	
Cold second course	Crustaceans and mollusks as used in terrines, pâtés, mousses, and aspic	*Mousse de homard* (lobster mousse) *Aspic de crustacés au Riesling* (crustacean aspic with Riesling wine)
Buffet platter	Crustaceans poached in stock and cooled, peeled, and neatly arranged on large platters with appropriate garnishes; platters of open oysters on ice.	*Langouste bellevue* (Norway lobster) *Homard parisienne* (lobster with crayfish and truffles)

ster pick, remove the thin strips of flesh.

2. Depending on the preparation method, split lobsters in half, crack the lobster claws, or remove claws from the body and remove the meat.

3. Place the tip of a knife between the upper body and the tail and, with swift pressure, cut the upper body and the tail in half.

4. Remove offal. Liver, roe, and coral can be used in compound butters or for sauces.

5. Do not split crustaceans if medallions are wanted. Remove the tail from the upper body, and cut the inside of the tail with scissors. Remove the tail meat. Shallowly slice the upper side of the tail, and remove the intestinal tract.

Preparing Dublin Prawns / Scampi

Prawns are generally sold without upper bodies. They arrive as tails with shells in the kitchen, and the tail meat must be removed:

1. Press the shell firmly to break open the horny layer.

2. From the inside, press the shell apart, and remove the meat carefully.

3. Remove the intestinal tract; sometimes a cut with the tip of a knife is necessary to remove the black vein.

Cutting Crustaceans

Different forms are:

• *Half:* Small spiny lobsters, lobsters, and prawns (with or without shells)

• *Medaillons:* Spiny lobster and lobster

• *Stews:* Small spiny lobsters and lobsters (first split in half, then cut into even-sized large pieces).

For more information on crustaceans for cold preparations, see section 7.19.

7.12.2 Warm Dishes with Crustaceans – WARME KRUSTEN-TIERGERICHTE – *mets chauds de crustacés*

Most of the meat of crustaceans is found in the tail and in the claws, and in large animals also in the legs.

The texture of tail meat differs greatly from the flesh of the claws and legs. Leg and claw meat tend to be soft and stringy, but tail meat is toothy and tender. If the tail meat is crumbly and dry, it is a sign that the crustacean was dead before cooking, and it should not be eaten.

Crustaceans should not be cooked too long nor at too high a temperature. While the leg and claw meat will not seem to be affected, the tail meat will become tough and dry. The basic preparation methods used for crustaceans are shown in Table 7-63.

Poaching in Fish Stock – POCHIEREN im SUD – *pocher au court-bouillon*

This basic preparation method is used for all live crustaceans, whether they are to be served in stock or prepared cold.

If crustaceans are served in fish stock, the *matignon* is cut precisely; for shellfish destined for cold preparation, a basic fish stock is sufficient. The compositon of the stock is different from that for fish only in that, for crustaceans, dill seeds or caraway seeds may be added. To ensure that animals die quickly, they must be plunged head first into rapidly boiling water. The temperature is then lowered to about 165°F (75°C) to continue poaching.

For cold preparations, crustaceans are left to cool in the stock. Crustaceans become bright red when cooked, because the surface pigmentation that hides the red color is destroyed.

Poaching Times
• For animals weighing 1 pound, 2 ounces to 2 pounds, 3 ounces (500 g to 1 kg), cook 12 to 20 minutes.
• For Dublin prawns, shrimp, and crabs, cook 5 minutes.

Presentation and Service
Take the crustaceans from the poacher, and place in a service dish, usually a fish kettle (*poissonniere*), with some stock and vegetables. Garnish the top with lemon slices and fresh dill. Freshwater crayfish are not sliced but served the guest with a perforated ladle, directly from the stock to the plate. Remove small lobsters and spiny lobsters from the stock in front of the guest, split in half, loosen the tail meat, remove the intestinal tract, and crack the legs and claws. The guests will remove the meat him/herself. For lobster and spiny lobster, crackers and pick plus a finger bowl should be provided.

Table 7-63. Basic Preparation Methods for Crustaceans

Preparation method	Examples
Poaching in fish stock – POCHIEREN IM SUD – *pocher au court-bouillon*	*Homard à la nage* (poached lobster)
Stewing – DÜNSTEN – *etuver*	*fricassée de homard au Noilly Prat* (lobster stew) *Homard américaine* (lobster in wine and tomato sauce) *Ecrevisses bordelaise* (crayfish in bordelaise sauce)
Sautéing – SAUTIEREN – *sauter*	*Langoustines aux fleurs de safran* (spiny lobster with saffron)
Deep-frying – FRITIEREN – *frire*	*Scampi Orly* (batterfried prawns with tomato sauce)
Grilling – GRILLIEREN – *griller*	*Homard grillé provençale* (grilled lobster with tomato, garlic, and olives)

Side Dishes

Steamed or boiled potatoes, French bread, and lemon are suitable.

Sauces

Butter (fresh or melted), butter sauces (for example, hollandaise), and *beurre blanc* (with dill or basil) are good choices.

Boiled Lobster – HUMMER IM SUD – *homard au court-bouillon*

YIELD: 10 SERVINGS (MAIN COURSE)		
Water	5 qt, 9 oz	5 L
Matignon	1 lb, 2 oz	500 g
Parsley stems	¾ oz	25 g
Bay leaf	1	1
White peppercorns	⅓ oz	10 g
Caraway/dill seeds	¹⁄₁₆ oz	1 g
Salt	2⅔ oz	75 g
White wine	1 pt, 11 oz	800 ml
White-wine vinegar	8½ oz	250 ml
Live lobsters (10)	10 lb	4.5 kg

Method

- Simmer the *matignon*, herbs, and spices in the water for 10 minutes.
- Add wine and vinegar, and continue to cook.
- Plunge the lobsters, head first, into the boiling stock.
- Bring to a quick boil.
- Poach at 165°F (75°C) for 12 minutes.
- Serve the lobster in a copper fish kettle with some stock and *matignon* vegetables. Garnish if desired with a little dill and peeled lemon slices.

Stewing – DÜNSTEN – *etuver*

This preparation method is used for crustaceans in the shell that are served with a sauce. Especially suit-able are freshwater crayfish, lobster, and spiny lobster. The special trick is to fry the shell in hot oil quickly, which develops intense roasting flavors (important in sauce making).

Glazing Crustacean Dishes

As for other fish dishes, the sauce is enriched with a little hollandaise sauce, heavy cream, or a liaison of heavy cream and egg yolks just before placing the dish under the salamander.

Presentation and Service

Crayfish, lobster, and spiny lobster claws or tails can be served cracked in their shells or removed from their shells. It is recommended that the crusteaceans be completely removed from their shells for banquet service. Side dishes are not necessary for such delicate dishes.

Lobster Stew – HUMMERFRICASSEE – *fricassée de homard*

YIELD: 10 SERVINGS (MAIN COURSE)		
Lobsters (10)	10 lb	4.5 kg
Butter	5 oz	150 g
Salt, pepper		
Olive oil	3½ oz	100 ml
Shallots	5 oz	150 g
Cognac	1⅓ oz	100 ml
Dry white vermouth	5 oz	150 ml
Fish fumet	8½ oz	250 ml
Double cream	1 pt, 1 oz	500 ml
Salt, cayenne pepper, lemon juice		

Mise en place

- Kill the lobsters by plunging them into boiling water head first, remove, and cut into pieces.
- With a fork, combine the coral, liver, and half, or 2⅔ ounces (75 g) of the butter. Strain through a fine sieve.

Method

- Season the lobster pieces in the shell with salt and pepper.
- Sauté the pieces in hot olive oil briefly.
- Drain the oil, and replace with the remaining 2⅔ ounces (75 g), butter.
- Add the shallots, and continue to cook.
- Add the cognac, and ignite.
- Add the vermouth, and reduce. Remove the lobster pieces.
- Add the fish fumet and double cream, and cook to the desired consistency.
- Strain and season.
- Return the lobster pieces to the sauce. Heat briefly. Remove from the sauce, and arrange on a plate.
- Remove the sauce from the heat, whip in the coral butter, and pour the sauce over the lobster pieces.

Notes

Double cream is not available in the United States. An equivalent can be produced by reducing 36 percent heavy cream over medium heat until thick.

Variations

Many variations of the basic recipe can be prepared by using different:

- wines (sauternes, white port wine, champagne, etc.)
- herbs (basil, dill, chervil, tarragon, etc.)
- reductions (lobster extract, red pepper *coulis*, English mustard, etc.)

Sautéing – SAUTIEREN – *sauter*

Shelled crustacean tails are usually sautéed, especially lobster tails,

Table 7-64. Other Stewed Crustacean Dishes

Dish	Description
Lobster, American style – HUMMER AMERIKANISCHE ART – *homard américaine*	Sauté lobster pieces with chopped shallots, herbs, and diced tomatoes. Remove lobster pieces, and keep warm. Add meat extract (*glace de viande*) to the pan liquid, and reduce. Add lobster coral butter, and pour over the reserved warm lobster pieces.
Crayfish bordelaise – KREBSE BORDELESER ART – *ecrevisses bordelaise*	Kill the crayfish, remove the intestines, and prepare in the same way as lobster, American style. Remove the tail meat. Enrich the sauce not with lobster coral butter but with double cream. Pour sauce over tail meat, and sprinkle with chopped chervil.

Dublin prawns, and giant shrimp.

In contrast to stewing, sautéing involves fat. The higher temperatures seal the uncovered surfaces, retaining the juices, and browning adds additional flavor.

Mise en place
- Pull away the shells, remove the tail.
- Cut along the back, and remove the intestinal tract with the tip of a knife.
- Wash away any intestinal matter.
- The tails are often rolled and skewered to shape before being sautéed.

Sautéing and Saucing
Sautéing leaves no pan liquids. To prepare a sauce, the pan is deglazed with fish stock, which forms the base for a sauce.

It is *extremely* important to sauté the tails without browning them. Brown particles decrease the sauce's eye appeal (dark spots) and overpower the delicate flavor of the tails.

An excellent side dish is steamed rice.

Dublin Bay Prawns with Saffron—
SCAMPI MIT SAFRANSAUCE—*scampi au safran*

YIELD: 10 SERVINGS (MAIN COURSE)		
Dublin Bay prawns with shells	4 lb, 14 oz	2.2 kg
Olive oil	3½ oz	100 ml
Salt, freshly ground pepper		
Dry white vermouth	3½ oz	100 ml
White wine	5 oz	150 ml
Fish fumet	6¾ oz	200 ml
Saffron threads		
Double cream	10 oz	300 ml
Butter nuggets	3 oz	100 g
Garnish		
Almonds, sliced, toasted	1⅔ oz	50 g
Pistachios, blanched, chopped	1⅔ oz	50 g

Method
- Remove prawns from their shells, and devein.

- Heat the olive oil in a straight-sided saucepan.
- Add the prawns, and season.
- Sauté till about three-quarters done, without browning.
- Remove the prawns from the pan, and keep warm.
- Drain the excess oil, deglaze the pan with the vermouth and white wine, and reduce.
- Add the fish fumet, and strain through a fine-mesh china cap.
- Add the saffron, and reduce the liquid.
- Add the double cream, and continue to cook.
- Add the prawns, and heat.
- Remove the prawns from the sauce, and arrange on a plate.
- Whip cold butter nuggets into the sauce, season, and pour lightly over prawns.
- Sprinkle with toasted almonds and chopped pistachios.

Notes
Double cream is not available in the United States. An equivalent product can be produced by reducing 36 percent heavy cream over medium heat until thick.

Variations
Many variations of the basic recipe can be prepared by using different:

- wines (sauternes, white port wine, champagne, etc.)
- herbs (basil, dill, chervil, tarragon, etc.)
- reductions (lobster extract, various *coulis*, English mustard, etc.).

Sautéed and Served without Sauce
This preparation method is very much like the floured version discussed in the fish section.

Method
- Marinate shelled and deveined tails.
- Flour lightly, and sauté in oil until golden brown.
- Serve (for example, on green and white home-made noodles, leaf spinach, ratatouille, tomato concassé, steamed rice, or risotto variations).
- Pour foaming butter and, if desired, chopped fresh herbs over all.

Deep-frying—FRITIEREN—*frire*
Shelled giant shrimp, prawn tails, and the claw meat of crabs are best suited for this method. It is important to protect the delicately flavored meat from direct contact with the hot oil by coating it to protect it.

Suitable Coatings
- Batters or similar dough
- Egg and fresh bread crumbs

Preparation of Tails
For eye appeal (as well as to identify the crustacean type to the guest) and for practical purposes (when guests handle them as appetizers, for example), it makes sense to peel the tails partially and leave the tail fin in place.

Presentation
- Place the fried tails on a warm platter lined with absorbent paper, to blot excess fat.
- *Do not cover!* Steam will make the crisp crust soggy.
- Garnish with lemon and parsley.

Sauces
- Mayonnaise (rémoulade, dill mayonnaise with fresh cheese [quark], etc.)
- Asian special sauces (sweet and sour sauce or soy sauce)

Deep-fried, Breaded—PANIERT FRITIEREN—*frire pané*

YIELD: 10 SERVINGS (MAIN COURSE)		
Giant shrimp with shells	4 lb, 7 oz	2 kg
Lemon	1	1
Freshly ground pepper, salt		
All-purpose flour	1⅔ oz	50 g
Eggs	3	3
Fresh bread crumbs	10½ oz	300 g
Oil (about 10% loss)	7 oz	200 g
Lemon (separate)	5	5

Method
- Remove the shells from tails, leaving tail fins in place.
- Cut along the backs, and remove intestinal tracts with the tip of a knife.

- Wash away any intestinal matter. Dry with paper towels.
- Marinate the shrimp in lemon juice and pepper.
- Season with salt, and dredge in flour. Shake off excess flour.
- Dip into beaten egg. Wipe off excess.
- Dip in bread crumbs, pressing crumbs lightly in place.
- Fry in small quantities at 335° to 355°F (170° to 180°C) until crisp.
- Drain well, and place on absorbent cloth or paper.
- Serve on a heated platter lined with a paper napkin. Serve garnished with lemon and parsley.
- Serve lemon wedges and sauce separately.

Deep-fried in Batter – IM BACKTEIG FRITIERN – *frire en pâte*

YIELD: 10 SERVINGS (MAIN COURSE)		
Dublin Bay prawns with shells	4 lb, 13 oz	2.2 kg
Lemon	1	1
Freshly ground pepper, salt		
All-purpose flour	1⅔ oz	50 g
Batter	1 lb, 5 oz	600 g
Oil (about 10% loss)	7 oz	200 g
Lemon (separate)	5	5

Method
Same preparation method as for deep-fried breaded, however after the tails have been dredged in flour they are dipped in batter.

Notes
If a deep-fried food is offered Orly-style it is served with a tomato *coulis*.

Grilling – GRILLIEREN – *griller*

Crustaceans can be grilled with or without their shell.

Live animals such as lobster and spiny lobster are killed and grilled in the shell (see *mise en place* page 303–304).

Dublin prawns and giant shrimp are basically only prepared as tails and can be grilled in the following ways:

- Cut in half in the shell and grill
- Remove the shell except the tail fin and grill
- Remove tail completely and grill.

Notes
The meat of a briefly (1–2 minutes) poached lobster stays juicier and plumper when it is grilled. Crustacean flesh grilled raw will shrink considerably.

Sauces
Grilled crustaceans should always be served with a separate sauce. These are especially suited:

- melted butter (e.g. with shallots or dried herbes de Provence)
- various cold compound butters
- warm butter sauces (e.g. bearnaise sauce)
- special sauces (e.g. *beurre blanc* with basil)
- *coulis* (e.g. tomato, or red pepper)

Side Dishes
Starch side dishes are not necessary, but steamed or wild rice is suitable. Crustaceans without shells can also be served atop side dishes.

Garnish
Garnish grilled crustaceans with lemon and fresh herbs (for example, a sprig of parsley, a bouquet of cress, dill, or basil).

Grilled Lobster, Provençal Style – GRILLIERTER HUMMER PROVENZAL-ISCHE ART – *homard grillé provençale*

YIELD: 10 SERVINGS (MAIN COURSE)		
Lobster (10)	11 lb	5 kg
Lemon juice	1 oz	30 ml
Freshly ground pepper, salt		
Olive oil	5 oz	150 ml
Lemon	1	1
Watercress	⅔ oz	20 g
Tomato coulis	8½ oz	250 g
Butter provençale	8½ oz	250 g

Method
- Kill the lobster by plunging it into boiling water head first; poach for 1 to 2 minutes.
- Remove, cut into pieces, and clean (see 7.12.1).
- Marinate the exposed meat in lemon juice and pepper.
- Just before grilling season with salt and brush with oil.
- Place meat side down on a hot grill, and create grill marks carefully on both sides.
- Arrange meat side up on a warm platter. Garnish with lemon and watercress.
- Serve the tomato *coulis* and butter provençale separately.

Notes
Frozen lobster or spiny lobster tails are not poached. The tails are marinated, brushed with oil, and placed meat side down directly on the hot grill.

7.12.3 *Mise en place* for Mollusks

Mussels

Mussels are frequently prepared in the shells and served to the guest that way. Mussels should therefore be thoroughly cleaned: all sand and attached parasites should be scrubbed off under running water with a stiff brush. The hairy beard must be removed before preparation.

Opening Mussels
Mussel shells are normally tightly closed. If they are open and remain open even when sharply rapped, then the mussel is very likely dead and should not be prepared. Unlike oysters, which are opened with a special oyster knife, mussels are opened with heat.

Scallops

Opening Scallops
Scallops can be opened by hand or with heat. Hold the shell with a cloth in your cupped hand. Move the tip of a blunt knife along the rim of the shell, probing for an opening. Push the blade inside, and sever the muscle. Remove the scallop, and use.

Scallops can also be placed in a hot oven until they open.

Oysters

Opening Oysters

A special oyster knife is available for prying open oysters. Between the handle and the sharp, pointy blade is a metal protector. If the knife slips, the metal shield will hit the oyster, preventing injury. In the Unites States, a metal mesh glove is used for protection.

Place the oyster with the flat side up on a cloth on a cutting board. Cover the oyster with the cloth, keeping the hinge section visible. Insert the sharp point of the oyster knife into the hinge, and with a sharply twisting movement, push the oyster against the knife to lift off the upper shell.

Oysters must offer strong resistance; if the shell is easy to open, the oyster is very likely dead and should not be eaten.

Preparation of Oysters

Most oysters are eaten chilled and raw. After the upper shell has been lifted off, any shell fragments are brushed off. With the tip of a knife, the oyster is severed from the muscle by which it is attached to the lower shell. The oyster should not be touched, and the briny liquid should remain inside the oyster. Set the oysters in crushed ice.

For warm dishes, oysters are removed from the shell and used immediately.

7.12.4 Warm Mollusk Dishes – WARME WEICHTIERGERICHTE – mets chauds de mollusques

Bivalves are the most popular of the mollusks. Bivalves not only taste wonderful but can be used in many ways. Bivalves can be eaten raw or cooked. They are very nutritious but may not to be easily digested and are high in cholesterol.

It is important to use only tightly closed bivalves. Partially open shells may signify the creature inside is dead, and consumption can cause food poisoning.

Squid, periwinkles, and land snails also belong to the mollusk family but are of minor importance in the kitchen and are only rarely offered as specialty dishes. See Table 7-65 for examples of dishes using them as well as more popular mollusks.

Oysters – AUSTERN – huîtres

Though the quality and excellent taste of oysters are most appreciated when they are eaten raw, delicious oyster dishes can be prepared hot as well. The best cooking method is poaching (in their own juice). Careful poaching is essential: oysters must never be fully cooked, or they will become tough (maximum 20 seconds).

Presentation
- Return the poached oyster to its own half shell. Cover with a sauce made partially from the poaching liquid, and glaze according to recipe under the salamander.
- Serving dishes are often small porcelain casseroles or small copper dishes, which highlight the exclusive quality of the dish.

Oysters Florentine – GLASIERTE AUSTERN AUF BLATTSPINAT – huîtres florentine

YIELD: 10 SERVINGS (MAIN COURSE)		
Special fish sauce	1 pt, 9 oz	750 ml
Shallots	3½ oz	100 g
Butter	3½ oz	100 g
Leaf spinach (thawed)	14 oz	400 g
Salt, pepper		
Oysters	40	40

Mise en place
- Prepare the special fish sauce for glazing.
- Chop the shallots, and sauté in the butter. Add the spinach, and cook until soft. Season.
- Open the oysters, and remove beards.
- Strain the oyster liquid into the saucepan.
- Clean the deep half-shell thoroughly, and place on small gratin plates or special oyster plates.

Method
- Divide the spinach mixture among the shells, and make a hollow in the center.
- Bring the oyster liquid to a boil, remove from the heat, add the oysters, and poach a few seconds.

Table 7-65. Mollusk Dishes

Mollusk	Dishes
Oysters – AUSTERN – huîtres	Fines de Belon chauds au xérès (warm Belon oysters with sherry) Huîtres florentine (oysters with spinach)
Scallops – JAKOBSMUSCHELN / PILGERMUSCHELN – coquilles Saint-Jacques, grandes peignes	Coquilles Saint-Jacques grillées (grilled scallops) Coquilles Saint-Jacques à la ciboulette (creamed scallops with chives)
Mussels and clams – MIESMUSCHELN, HERZMUSCHELN, VENUS MUSCHELN – moules, coques, clams	Brochette de moules frites (fried mussels on a skewer) Moules marinière (steamed mussels with wine and herbs Clams orientale (clams, oriental style) Coques aux tomatoes et au basilic (clams with tomato and basil)
Snails – SCHNECKEN – escargots	escargot au Riesling (snails with Riesling wine) escargots bourguignonne (snails, Burgundy style)
Cephalopods – TINTENFISCH – seiches	Sépioles frites en pâte à frire (fried battered cuttlefish)

- Set the oysters atop the spinach.
- Reduce the oyster liquid, and add it to the special fish sauce.
- Cover the oysters with the sauce, and glaze immediately.

Variations
The sauces prepared for glazing can be varied by using champagne (*au champagne*) or sherry (*au xérès*).

Scallops – JAKOBSMUSCHELN, PIL-GERMUSCHELN – *coquilles Saint-Jacques, grandes peignes*

Scallops, members of the fan-shell group of mussels, are gourmets' favorite bivalves. The tender, ivory-colored muscle (called NUSS in German, *noix* in French) and the orange-colored coral can be prepared in many different ways.

Market Forms
In the shell: As for all bivalves, make sure the shells are tightly closed.

Removed from the shell: The muscle and coral, packed in their own liquid in plastic, must be placed on ice or refrigerated immediately.

Basic Preparation Methods
The best basic method is stewing; other possibilities are sautéing lightly floured, grilling (on skewers), steaming, and broiling (review basic methods in the fish section).

Stewing is an especially good method for scallops that are prepared in a sauce. Scallops can be left whole or sliced into ¼-inch-thick (5-mm) slices.

When heating in sauce, it is important to keep the scallops from boiling, or they will at once become tough and dry and will thin the sauce immediately.

Stewed Scallops with Chives – GEDÜNSTETE JAKOBSMUSCHELN MIT SCHNITTLAUCHSAUCE – *coquilles Saint-Jacques à la ciboulette*

YIELD: 10 SERVINGS (MAIN COURSE)		
White-wine sauce	10 oz	300 ml
Chives	½ oz	15 g
Butter	3½ oz	100 g
Scallops without shells	2 lb, 10 oz	1.2 kg
Salt, freshly ground pepper		
Dry white vermouth	1⅔ oz	50 ml
Fish fumet	6¾ oz	200 ml
Butter nuggets	3½ oz	100 g

Mise en place
- Prepare a white-wine sauce.
- Finely chop the chives.

Method
- Heat the butter in a saucepan.
- Add the scallops, and stew briefly. Season.
- Deglaze pan with dry vermouth.
- Add the fish fumet, and poach the scallops until done.
- Remove the scallops.
- Reduce the poaching stock by half.
- Add the white-wine sauce, and cook briefly (if necessary, thicken with *beurre manie*).
- Whip cold butter nuggets into sauce; season.
- Just before service, carefully heat the scallops and add the chives.

Variations
Many variations of the basic recipe can be prepared by using different:

- wines (sauternes, white port wine, etc.)
- herbs (basil, chervil, tarragon, etc.)
- special sauces (special fish sauces, curry suce, *coulis*, lobster sauce, etc.)

By changing the presentation (different garnishes, glazing), many more variations of the basic recipe can be produced.

Mussels and Clams – MIESMUSCHELN, HERZMUSCHELN, VENUS MUSCHELN – *moules, coques, clams*

Unlike oysters and scallops, which are generally opend before they are cooked, mussels and clams are opened by heat, that is, when they are cooked.

Steaming is the ideal cooking method, because the heat is high enough to quickly open the shells, but its moistness protects the tender meat. Steaming in the shell can be used as a basic preparation method or as *mise en place* (for example, for mussels or clams in salad, on skewers, or as an ingredient in other dishes); Table 7-66 lists various clam and mussel dishes.

The liquid must be made to steam quickly, so that the mussels or clams open quickly, and long cooking times are avoided. A tight-fitting lid and a good heat source are necessary.

Using the Pan Liquid
- Never salt mussels or clams, as their liquid contains enough salt.
- Always strain stock through a napkin to filter any shell particles or sand.

Poached Mussels – POCHIERTE MIES-MUSCHELN – *moules pochées*

YIELD: 10 SERVINGS (MAIN COURSE)		
Shallots	3½ oz	100 g
Butter	3½ oz	100 g
Mussels	8 lb, 13 oz	4 kg
White wine	1 pt, 1 oz	500 g
Thyme, sprig	1	1

Method
- Chop the shallots, and sauté in butter.
- Add the cleaned mussels.
- Cover with white wine, add the thyme sprig, and put on the pan lid.
- Steam for 3 to 5 minutes, shaking the pot on occasion, until the mussels open.
- Pour the liquid off (strain the stock through a cloth napkin).
- Remove the hot mussels from their shells.

Mussel Dishes with Sauce
These dishes are prepared in the following manner:

- Thicken the mussel stock lightly.
- Flavor as desired (e.g., saffron, curry).
- Enrich with unsalted butter, cream, or a liaison.

- Add garnish (e.g., chopped fresh herbs, cooked vegetable strips, diced tomato).
- Add the mussels, and heat carefully.

Presentation

- Arrange mussel shells on a plate, and fill them lightly with mussel stew.
- Spoon mussel stew into patty shells or pastry boats.

Snails – SCHNECKEN – *escargots*

Although snails are one of the largest varieties in the mollusk family, only the European vineyard snail and East Asian achat snail are of culinary importance. Periwinkles are limited to regional specialties. Table 7-67 lists a few snail recipes.

Preparation of Snails

Snails for the kitchen are now specially bred and raised in snail gar-

dens. On the market, they are available canned or frozen. The cleaned snail shells are sold separately. The snails are generally prepared and packaged by the grower. Only fresh closed snails are used.

Mise en place for fresh (live) snails:

- Wash and brush the shells.
- Kill the snails by immersing them in boiling water and poaching them for 10 minutes to open the shell.
- Chill under running water, and remove the snail with a pick.
- Apply several salt and vinegar rubs to remove the slime.
- Cut off the head and the black section of the tail.
- Sauté the tails briefly in shallots and garlic, and simmer for about 3 hours in white wine and veal stock until they are tender.
- Clean the empty snail shell.

Snails, Burgundy Style – SCHNECKEN BURGUNDER ART – *escargots bourguignonne*

YIELD: 10 SERVINGS (MAIN COURSE)		
Snails, cooked and without shells	120	120
Snail shells	120	120
Snail butter		
Shallots	1½ oz	40 g
Garlic	½ oz	15 g
Parsley, fresh	1 oz	30 g
Marjoram, fresh	¼ tsp	5 g
Thyme, fresh	¼ tsp	5 g
Butter	3½ oz	100 g
Cognac	½ oz	15 g
Heavy cream (not too cold)	3½ oz	100 ml
Freshly ground pepper, salt		

Preparation of Snail Butter

- Finely chop the shallots.
- Grate the garlic.
- Chop the parsley.

Table 7-66. Clam and Mussel Dishes

Dishes	Description
Mussels with herb sauce – MIESMUSCHELN MIT KRÄUTERSAUCE – *moules marinè*	Slightly thicken reduced mussel stock. Add shallots and chopped fresh parsley. Whip in cold butter nuggets.
Mussels in saffron sauce – MIESMUSCHELN MIT SAFRANSAUCE – *moules marseillaise*	Same method as poached mussels, but flavor with saffron, and add stewed strips of vegetables and diced tomatoes.
Fried mussels on a skewer – GEBACKENE MIESMUSCHELN AM SPIESS – *brochette de moules frites*	Space large mussels properly on skewers. Bread in flour, egg, and fresh bread crumbs. Fry in clarified butter until golden. Serve rémoulade sauce separately.
Clams, Oriental style – VENUSMUSCHELN ORIENTALISCHER ART – *clams orientale*	Place clams in warmed shells. Enrich a curry white-wine sauce with reduced clam juice, heavy cream, and hollandaise, and glaze.
Clams with tomatoes and basil – HERZMUSCHELN MIT TOMATEN/BASILIKUM – *coques aux tomatoes et au basilic*	Same method as for poached mussels but flavor with additional tomato cubes and chop basil

Table 7-67. Additional Snail Recipes

Dish	Description
Snails, Newburg style – SCHNECKEN NEUENBURGER ART – *jacquerie neuchâteloise*	Heat cooked snails in butter and white wine, serve on sauerkraut, pour snail butter over all, and glaze under the broiler.
Snails with riesling (white wine)sauce – SCHNECKEN MIT RIESLING SAUCE – *escargots au riesling*	Stew cooked snails in riesling and cover with a riesling double cream sauce. Enrich sauce by whipping in cold snail butter nuggets, glaze under broiler

- Chop the marjoram and thyme leaves.
- Cream the butter.
- Combine all the ingredients and mix well, but do not beat.
- Season with salt and pepper.

Preparation of Snails
- Place a little snail butter in each snail shell.
- Place one snail in each shell (if very small, use two).
- Fill house with plenty of snail butter.
- Place in special snail pan.
- Bake at 395° to 425°F (200° to 220°C), until the butter boils and foams.
- Serve with 2-inch-long (5-cm) French bread strips, for dipping into the snail butter.

Squid — TINTENFISCHE — *seiches*

Squid (cuttlefish, octopus) play a larger role in Mediterranean and Asian cuisine, where they are served in seafood salads, fish soups, fried in batter and are braised (as stew or stuffed).

The dark brown fragrant ink, found inside the squid in an ink sac, is used to color soups, sauces, and pastas.

Squid spoil quickly and must be prepared immediately.

The bag-like body and the tenacles are the meat. Squid has a mild, sweet taste and is excellent blended with exotic spices and vegetables from the southern hemisphere. In contrast to fish, squid is not considered easy to digest.

Notes
Small tender squid cooks very quickly; older larger specimens must be cooked for much longer times; the older the longer the cooking time. Squid should be served quickly, as the flesh tends to get tougher when kept warm.

Deep-fried Squid in Beer Batter — GEBACKENE SEPIA IN BIERTEIG — *sépioles frites en pâté à frire*

YIELD: 10 (ENTREE)		
Small sepia	5 lb, 8 oz	2.5 kg
Lemon	1	1
Freshly ground pepper, salt		
All-purpose flour	1⅔ oz	50 g
Batter	14 oz	400 g
Oil (about 10% loss)	3½ oz	100 g
Lemon (separate)	2½	2½
Parsley bouquet	1 oz	30 g
Remoulade sauce	10½ oz	300 g

Mise en place
- Remove head from the mantle.
- Remove skin from mantle, pull out the quill.
- Cut away the eyes, ink sack, intestines, and beak

Method
- Slice squid in pieces.
- Marinade with lemon juice and pepper.
- Salt and flour lightly.
- Dip in beer batter.
- Fry in small quantities at 335° to 355° F (170° to 180°C) until crisp.
- Drain well and drop on absorbent paper.
- Serve on a heated platter lined with a paper napkin.
- Garnish with lemon and parsley.
- Serve lemon wedges and rémoulade sauce separately.

7.13 Meat, Game, and Poultry Dishes

Meat is an important part of the human diet because of its high nutritional and satiety value. Meat dishes constitute the focal point and main entrée of most menus. The other courses are generally selected to complement the meat course in taste and color.

As a rule, meat is one of the most expensive items in the kitchen budget. Proper use and preparation of meat are very important to an establishment's profitability.

From the Cooking Process to the Basic Preparation Method

The following basic preparation methods have developed over time and are still in use today.

The best results are achieved by the cook who can select the right meat for the best method, or who can choose the best method for the meat on hand.

The cook must therefore:

- be able to tell the degree of tenderness of meat

- depending on the tenderness of the meat select the best suited method to derive the best flavor

Cooking Method

Meats with Little Connective Tissue
If the meat contains little or no visible connective tissues, the meat will be tender, and it becomes more important to heighten the flavor and to preserve the juiciness of the meat.

Two points should be given consideration.

- Flavors (roasting flavors) develop on the meat surface when proteins are denatured through heating and turn brown. *Conclusion:* Since browning occurs only at about 325°F· (165°C), no liquid should be added.
- At temperatures of 140° to 162°F (60° to 72°C) proteins in the meat start to loose water and the meat becomes dry. *Conclusion:* Tender meat should never be cooked to an internal temperature above 162°F (72°C). The *internal temperature* of poultry (to kill salmonella bacteria) and pork (to kill parasites) should reach 162°F (72°C) and be kept at that temperature for 10 minutes.

Therefore, *use dry-heat cooking methods for tender meat.*

Meats with Much Connective Tissue

If the meat contains large amounts of visible or invisible connective tissue, the meat will be less tender and the main objective is to produce a tender meat.

The following point should be given consideration:

- Connective tissue has the ability to absorb water when exposed to moist heat near the boiling point (208°F [97°C]) for long periods of time. The collagen swells and dissolves into chewable, easily digested gelatin. The gelatin replaces the lost meat juices that have been released into the liquid during the long cooking process. *Conclusion:* Since the long exposure to heat would cause the meat to dry out, liquid must be part of the cooking process.

Therefore, *use moist-heat cooking methods with temperatures just below the boiling point for less tender meats.*

7.13.1 Basic Meat Preparation Methods

See Table 7-68.

Sautéing – SAUTIEREN – *sauter à la minute*

Sautéing, like grilling, is a basic preparation method for tender meat cuts, which as a rule are cooked in a few minutes. For this reason, they are also known as *à la minute* dishes. Sautéed meats should be served immediately, as any delay results in drying and a severe loss of quality (tough meat). Since the meat is too thin to be tested with a thermometer the degree of doneness must be tested with finger pressure, as outlined in Table 7-69. An overview of sautéing is shown in Table 7-70.

Notes

Sautéed meat is often served with a sauce. It may be a lightly thickened jus or a derivative of a basic brown sauce. In both cases, the pan drippings are incorporated into the sauce. The meat can be served plain/ *nature* (sauce served separately), napped with sauce, or in the sauce.

Basic Rules for Sautéing

1. Salt meat at the very last moment.

Salt draws moisture from foods. When placed into the hot fat, the moistness on the meat produces steam, which prevents the meat surface from sealing, so that juices are lost; moreover, no browning occurs. The result is a dry, poorly browned piece of meat.

2. Dust white meat with flour.

White meat has a higher water content than dark meat. A thin flour coating will combine with the meat juices as soon as the meat is placed in the hot oil. The meat surface stays dry, the meat stays juicier and browns evenly and faster.

3. Start with very high temperature, then lower the temperature.

Sautéing both sides of the meat in very hot oil causes the surfaces to seal and prevents juice loss. For thicker pieces, the temperature is reduced after browning to prevent a hard crust from forming (drying of surface).

4. Cook uncovered.

Condensation on the lid would drip into the pan and cause stewing, rather than sautéing.

5. Do not pierce the meat with a fork.

After the meat is browned, it should not be turned frequently. Most important, it should not be pierced with a fork, or the juices will gush out through the fork punctures.

6. Meat should not rest in its own juices.

Meat pieces that are removed from the pan during sauce preparation should be held on a warm surface that allows for drainage of the meat juices. Thicker meat pieces are often refried in hot butter; thinner pieces, reheated under the broiler. If the sauce is served separately, hot foaming butter is poured over the meat.

7. Do not boil in the sauce.

Àla-minute meat pieces that are served in a sauce, for example, Swiss Geschnetzeltes (shredded veal in a cream sauce), should not simmer or boil in the sauce. The meat would become dry and the sauce, thin. The meat should be carefully reheated just before service.

Sautéing White Meat

Veal Cutlets in Cream Sauce –
KALBSSCHNITZEL MIT RAHMSAUCE – *escalope de veau à la crème*

YIELD: 10 SERVINGS (MAIN COURSE)		
Veal top round (20 cutlets)	3 lb, 5 oz	1.5 kg
Salt, pepper		
All-purpose flour	1⅓ oz	50 g
Peanut oil	3½ oz	100 ml
Butter	5 oz	150 g
Shallots	5 oz	150 g
White wine	6¾ oz	200 ml
Brown veal jus	10 oz	300 ml
Heavy cream	6¾ oz	200 ml
Heavy cream, lightly whipped	6¾ oz	200 ml

Method
- Season the cutlets and dust with the flour.
- Sauté the cutlets in hot peanut oil on both sides until light golden.
- Remove the cutlets and keep warm. Pour off excess oil.

Table 7-68. Basic Cooking and Preparation Methods for Meat

Meat Type	Cooking Method	Basic Preparation Method	Classification
Meat low in connective tissue (tender)	*Dry-heat cooking methods* (no liquids)	Sautéing— SAUTIEREN— *sauter à la minute*	Sautéing dark meat Sautéing white meat Sautéing meat in a wrapper
		Grilling— GRILLIEREN— *griller*	
		Roasting— BRATEN— *rôtir*	Roasting in the oven Roasting in the convection oven Roasting on the spit Low temperature roasting
		Baking meat— BACKEN IM OFEN— *cuire au fou*	Baking meat in dough Cooking in special wrappers
		Butter-roasting— POELIEREN— *poêler*	
	Moist-heat cooking methods: at temperatures from 160° to 165°F (70° to 75°C)	Poaching— POCHIEREN— *pocher*	Poaching variety meats (organs) Poaching poultry Poaching brined meat
Meat high in connective tissue (~~tender~~) *less Tender*	*Moist-heat cooking methods*: temperatures at just below boiling (liquid added)	Braising— SCHMOREN *braiser*	Braising large meat pieces Braising meat portions Braising stews Braising tender meat pieces
		Stewing— DÜNSTEN— *étuver*	Stewing white meat Stewing red meat
		Simmering— SIEDEN— *cuire par ébullition*	Simmering large meat pieces Simmering blanquettes Simmering brined meats

- Add chopped shallots, and sauté in pan drippings.
- Add the wine, and reduce completely.
- Add the veal jus and heavy cream. Strain the sauce through a fine-mesh china cap.
- Season and fold the whipped cream into the sauce. If desired, add lemon juice.
- Plate cutlets, slightly napped with sauce, and serve the rest of the sauce on the side.

Sautéed White-meat Dishes
Veal
Shredded veal liver with Madeira sauce—GESCHNETZELTE KALBSLEBER MIT MADEIRASAUCE —*eminé de foie de veau au madère*

Veal filet mignon with porcini cream sauce—SAUTIERTE KALBSFILET-MIGNONS MIT STEINPILZRAHMSAUCE—*mignons de veau sautés aux cèpes à la crème*

Veal scallopini with ham and sage—KALBSSCHNITZEL MIT ROHSCHINKEN UND SALBEI—*saltimbocca alla romana*

Veal cutlet Holstein (with fried egg and anchovies)—SAUTIERTES KALB-SCNITZEL MIT SPIEGELEI—*escalope de veau Holstein*

Pork

Porkchop with mustard sauce—SAUTIERTES SCHWEINSKOTELETT MIT SENF-SAUCE—*côte de porc sautée Robert*

Pork cutlets with paprika cream sauce—SAUTIERTES SCHWEINSSCHNITZEL MIT PAPRIKARAHMSAUE—*escalope de porc sautée à la crème au paprika*

Pork medallions with apples and calvados—SAUTIERTE SCHWEINS-FILETMEDAILLONS AUF APLFELSCHNITTEN

—*médaillons de filet mignon de porc sautés normande*

Pork cutlets, gypsy style—SAUTIERTES SCHWEINSSTEAK ZIGEUNERART—*steak de porc sauté zingara*

Lamb

Lamb chops with mushrooms and tomatoes—SAUTIERTE LAMMCHOPS PROVENZALISCHE ART—*chops d'agneau sautés provençale*

Lamb filet chops with thyme—SAUTIERTE LAMMNÜSSCHEN MIT THYMI-AN—*noisettes d'agneau sautées au thym*

Poultry

Shredded breast of chicken, Indian style—GESCHNETZELTES GEFLÜGELFLEISCH INDISCHE ART—*eminé de volaille indienne*

Sautéed breast of chicken with cucumbers—SAUTIERTES GEFLÜGEL-BRÜSTCHEN MIT GURKEN—*suprême de volaille sauté Doria*

Sautéing Red Meat

Sirloin Steak with Red-Wine Sauce—ENTRECÔTE MIT ROTWEIN-SAUCE—*entrecôte au vin rouge*

YIELD: 10 SERVINGS (MAIN COURSE)		
Sirloin steaks	3 lb, 5 oz	1.5 kg
Salt, pepper		
Peanut oil	3½ oz	100 ml
Shallots	1⅔ oz	50 g
Strong red wine	10 oz	300 ml
Demi-glace	13½ oz	400 g
Butter	3½ oz	100 g

Method
- Season the steaks.
- Sauté the steaks quickly on both sides in hot peanut oil.
- Remove steaks and keep warm. Pour off excess oil.
- Add chopped shallots, and sauté in pan drippings.

only for tender cuts

Table 7-69. Testing for Doneness with Finger Pressure

°F/°C	German	French	English	Usage	Response to Finger Pressure
115°F (45°C)	Stark blutig	Bleu	Rare	Beef	Meat is spongy.
125°F (50°C)	Blutig (bloody)	Saignant	Underdone	Beef	Meat springs back strongly.
140°F (60°C)	Mittel / rosa	A point / rosé	Medium	Beef, game, lamb, duck, guinea fowl	Meat springs back lightly.
155°F (68°C)	Hell rosa		Medium well	Veal	
160°F (72°C)	Durch	Bien cuit	Well-done	Chicken, pork	Meat is firm.

Table 7-70. Sauté Styles

	Sautéing Red Meat	Sautéing White Meat	Sautéing Coated Meat
Cutting method	• 1–2 person portion • Stir-fry • Diced • Strips	• 1–2 person portion • Stir-fry • Diced • Strips	Individual portions
Mise en place	Season	Season, dust with flour	• Season, dust with flour • Dip in egg • Dip in egg/cheese mixture • Bread
Pan	• Shallow pan with straight sides (*sautoir*) • Shallow pan with sloping sides (*sauteuse*) • Stainless-steel frying pan	• Shallow pan with straight sides (*sautoir*) • Shallow pan with sloping sides (*sauteuse*) • Stainless-steel frying pan	• Frying pan (Lyon) • Nonstick frying pan
Cooking temperature	400°F (200°C), brown 355°F (180°C), cook	355°F (180°C), brown 320°F (160°C), cook	Sauté in clarified butter at 320°F (160°C), brown
Finishing	Remove meat, use pan drippings when making sauce	Remove meat, use pan drippings when making sauce	Plate and serve covered with foaming butter

- Add the wine, and reduce completely.
- Add the demi-glace, and bring to a simmer. Strain the sauce through a fine-mesh china cap.
- Season, and whip half the butter, in small nuggets, into the sauce.
- Heat the remaining butter, and turn steak in the butter until hot.
- Plate the steaks. Slightly nap with sauce, and serve the remaining sauce separately.

Sautéed Red-meat Dishes
Beef
Beef Stroganoff—RINDSFILETGOULASCH STROGANOW—*filet de bœuf Stroganov*

Club steaks with herb ·butter— SAUTIERTES RUMPSTEAK MIT KRÄUTER- SAUCE—*rumpsteak maître d'hôtel*

Beef tournedos with crushed pepper —SAUTIERTES TOURNEDOS MIT ZERDRÜCK- TEM PFEFFER—*tournedos sauté au poivre écrasé*

Game
Venison chop with blueberries— SAUTIERTES HIRSCHKOTELETT MIT HEIDEL- BEEREN—*côtelette de cerf sauté aux myrtilles*

Venison cutlets with apples— SAUTIERTE REHNÜSSCHEN MIRZA— *noisettes de chevreuil Mirza*

Venison cutlets with mushrooms and Brussels sprouts—SAUTIERTE REHNÜSSCHEN JÄGERART—*noisettes de chevreuil sautées chasseur*

Sautéing Coated White Meat
Basic Rules
1. **Season, dredge in flour, tap off excess flour, and coat well.**
Without the flour, the coating would fall off. See Table 7-71 for types of coatings.

2. **Instead of oil, use clarified butter.**
Depending on the composition of the coating, the coating tends to absorb more or less of the frying fat. For the best flavor, it is better to use clarified butter instead of oil. Clarified butter has the additional advantage to be free of milk proteins and is more heat resistant.

3. **Sauté at lower temperatures.**
Because the meat is covered with a protective coating, the hot searing of the meat is no longer needed to retain juices. To prevent burning of the coating, temperatures for thinner pieces can be higher, but thicker pieces should be cooked at lower temperatures.

4. **As a rule, serve coated meat without sauce.**
This method does not provide pan drippings, and the meat is usually served covered with only foaming butter. If a sauce is desired, it should be served separately.

7.13.3 Grilling—GRILLIEREN—*griller*

The same basic rules for sautéing, discussed in the previous section, also apply to grilling. Grilling is a cooking method that employs radiant heat from an electric, gas, or charcoal-heated rack below the food.

Most important is an absolutely clean, very hot grill. The meat surfaces must sear, to seal in the juices, as soon as they come into contact with the grill. Grilled foods are juicy, and they show the characteristic rhombic markings of the grill.

Nutritional Considerations
Grilled veal and poultry meat plays a role in special diets, because:

- Grilling cooks these easily digested meats in a very low-fat way.
- The short cooking time retains nutrients.
- The intense flavor of grilled foods makes them tasty without salt.

Service
Grilled meat is usually served as is (*au nature*). The surface can be brushed with a little butter for eye appeal and garnished with lemon slices and watercress bouquets.

Sauces
Because of the strong roasted flavor of grilled meats, most guests prefer just a little piece of lemon as an accompaniment. Other suitable items are:

- *Poultry and veal:* compound butters such as lemon butter, orange butter, thyme butter, or a tomato *coulis*
- *Pork:* flavorful herb butter or barbecue sauces
- *Beef:* béarnaise sauce, Choron sauce (tarragon-tomato-hollandaise), Foyot sauce (tarragon, chervil, meat extract, vinegar, hollandaise), flavorful herb butters, or tomato concassé
- *Lamb:* Shallot butter, garlic butter, flavorful herb butters, or tomato concassé.

Basic Rules for Grilling

1. **Marbled meat is preferred.**
Meat marbled with fat will not dry out quickly and is thus preferable to lean meat. Very lean game is rarely grilled.

2. **Marinate first, then salt.**
Thicker pieces of meat are generally marinated in oil and herbs. Because salt attracts moisture, no salt is added to the marinade. The meat is seasoned with salt just before it is grilled.

Table 7-71. Coatings

Coatings	Dishes
Beaten egg (can be flavored with fresh chopped herbs, grated cheese, etc.)	Veal piccata
Beaten egg and soft bread crumbs (instead of soft bread cumbs, light dry bread crumbs can be used)	Veal cutlet cordon bleu— *escalope de veau cordon bleu*

3. Never grill over an open flame.

4. Meat type and thickness must be considered.

White meat dries out quicker and should be grilled at lower temperature. The basic rule is: the thicker the meat, the lower the temperature.

5. Never press on the meat.

The high heat on the outside causes the inside of the meat to develop pressure. Any external pressure or a puncture with a fork causes the meat juices to gush out and be lost.

6. Thicker pieces should be basted frequently and allowed to rest before carving.

Thick pieces of meat, for example, chateaubriand, could form a hard crust. To prevent this, the meat should be brushed frequently with oil or a marinade. Thick pieces also need to rest, so that the temperature can equalize throughout the meat and meat juice loss is kept to a minimum during carving.

Grilling Meat

Grilled T-bone Steak – GRILLIERTES T-Bone-Steak

YIELD: 10 SERVINGS (MAIN COURSE)		
Marinade		
Thyme, sprig	1	3 g
Rosemary, sprig	1	3 g
Peppercorns	1 tsp	3 g
Peanut oil	3 oz	80 ml
T-bone steaks	7 lb, 12 oz	2.5 kg
Salt		
Peanut oil	3½ oz	100 ml
Watercress	3½ oz	100 g
Lemon	1	1

Mise en place
- Chop the thyme and rosemary, crush the peppercorns, and mix with the marinade oil.
- Brush the steaks with the marinade, and chill for 1 to 2 hours.

Method
- Scrape off the marinade from the steaks, and season with salt.
- Dip into fresh peanut oil.

- Place the meat, best side down, on a hot grill, and carefully create grill marks.
- Turning the steak carefully, create grill marks on the other side.
- Arrange the meat best side up on a warm platter. Garnish with watercress and lemon.
- Serve a compound herb butter or a complementary sauce (e.g., béarnaise) separately.

Grilled Meat Dishes
Veal
Calves' liver brochettes with bacon, Zurich style – ZÜRCHER LEBERSPIESSLI – *brochette de foie de veau grillée*

Grilled veal chops with basil butter – GRILLIERTES KALBSKOTELETT MIT BASILIKUMBUTTER – *côte de veau grillée au beurre basilic*

Grilled veal paillards with lemon – GRILLIERTES KALBS-PAILLARD MIT ZITRONE – *paillard de veau grillée au citron*

Grilled veal kidneys with mustardé – GRILLIERTE KALBSNIERENSCHNITTE MIT SENF – *tranche de rognon de veau grillée dijonnaise*

Beef
Grilled chateaubriand with béarnaise sauce – CHATEAUBRIAND MIT BEARNER SAUCE – *chateaubriand béarnaise*

Grilled sirloin steak with herbes de Provence – GRILLIERTES ENTRECÔTE MIT PROVENZALISCHEN KRÄUTERN – *entrecôte grillée aux herbes de Provence*

Grilled club steak with tomatoes and fried onion rings – GRILLIERTES RUMPSTEAK MIT TOMATEN UND GEBACKENEN ZWIEBELRINGEN – *rumpsteak grillé maître d'hôtel*

Pork
Grilled spare ribs – GRILLIERTE SCHWEINSBRUSTRIPPCHEN – *spare-ribs*

Lamb
Grilled loin lamb chops with thyme – GRILLIERTE LAMMCHOPS MIT THYMIAN – *chops d'agneau grillés au thym*

Grilled lamb rib chops in the style of Provence – GRILLIERTE LAMMKOTELETTS PROVENZALISCHE ART – *côtelettes d'agneau grillées provençale*

Poultry
Grilled chicken, American style – GRILLIERTES HÄHNCHEN AMERICANISCHER ART – *poulet grillé américaine*

Grilled spicy chicken – GRILLIERTES HÄHNCHEN TEUFELSART – *poulet grillé diable*

Mixed Grill

A mixed grill is a variety of small grilled meat pieces, for example, a piece each of:

- beef, veal, *and* pork fillet medallions
- lamb rib chop *or* lamb medallion *or* lamb loin chop
- slice of veal liver
- veal sweetbread or slice of veal brain
- slice of bacon
- sausage (chipolata)

Herb butter is served separately with mixed grill.

7.13.4   Roasting – BRATEN – *rôtir*

Roasting is a dry-heat cooking method for tender, large pieces of meat or poultry (see Table 7-72 for different methods of roasting).

In contrast to sautéing and grilling, in roasting the meat is exposed to radiant heat from all sides. Because such large surface areas are browned, roasting is one of the most flavorful cooking methods for tender meats. Roasts are always served with clear or lightly thickened pan juices.

Correct Internal Meat Temperature

The best means of gauging the internal temperature of meat correctly (see Table 7-69) is to use one of the various meat thermometers on the market. Follow instructions accompanying the instrument.

It is important to remember that the internal temperature will increase as the meat rests after roasting.

Chicken has been completely cooked when the juices run clear; for duck and game birds, the juices may have a tinge of pink.

Resting the Roast

With the exception of small poultry (which should be served at once), all roasts should rest for about 10 to 15 minutes before they are carved (thin pieces, such as rack of lamb, only 5 minutes). The importance of resting meat can be illustrated by using a beef roast for example:

Just before a rare beef roast is perfectly roasted, if the temperature on the surface of the roast is about 212°F (100°C), in the center, it is only about 105°F (40°C). If the meat were to be carved at this moment, the outer surface would be disappointingly gray, while the center would be cold and raw. However, if the roast is left to rest on a rack (the meat should not rest in its own juice) in a warm place at about 115°F (45°C) for 15 minutes, a heat exchange will take place. The outer layer will reabsorb some of the juices and become red. The result is a completely evenly cooked roast that can be carved without much loss of juice.

For health reasons, in the United States, the internal temperature of beef must register 130°F (54°C).

Basic Rules for Oven-roasting

1. Bard game birds.
Game birds (pheasant, partridge, quail) should be barded with fatback, since the breast meat contains little fat and needs protection. Remove the fat when the cooking is nearly complete; baste frequently to make sure the barded places brown properly.

2. Tie poultry and roasts.
Tying poultry and meat helps them retain their shape, which might otherwise change during roasting.

3. Meat should not be cold when placed in the oven.
The meat should be removed from refrigeration about 1 hour before roasting. The meat temperature will thus be room temperature, and the roasting time will be shorter.

4. Prevent a tough burnt crust.
It is essential to sear the meat when roasting in conventional ovens.

In a preheated convection oven, the meat is sealed automatically when it comes in contact with the hot air. The initial temperature, however, should be reduced as soon as the meat is sealed to prevent a hard crust from forming. This crust could act like insulation, preventing the heat from penetrating the meat properly, and causing the surface to burn.

5. Roast poultry lying on its side.
Placing poultry on its side has two advantages:

- The delicate breast meat is prevented from drying out, because the meat juices will baste the meat.
- In this position, the thighs and drumsticks cook at the same rate as the breast.

Turn the poultry on its back during the last roasting phase, to give the breast good color, basting frequently.

6. Open the vent – baste frequently.
A perfect roast has a nice, crisp exterior but should not show signs of dryness.

In the conventional oven, opening the vents prevents steam from building up in the oven, and frequent basting prevents the surface from drying out.

In the convection oven, where the air in the oven tends to be much drier, an occasional squirt of water (steam in the combination oven) during roasting is necessary. During the last phase of roasting, this should be eliminated, to create a crisp crust.

Table 7-72. Roasting Methods

Roasting Method	Type of Heat	Description
In the oven	Contact heat (below) Radiant heat (above)	• Season meat, and brown in hot oil. • Place in a roasting pan or on a rack with pan, baste frequently until done.
	Combination heat	• Remove meat. • Use pan drippings and brown particles for the jus.
In the convection oven or combination oven	Convection heat (hot air)	• Season meat, and place in roasting pan. • Drizzle with oil and place in preheated oven. • Roast, spraying the meat with water occasionally. • Use pan drippings and brown particles for the jus.
On a spit	Radiant heat (conventional, charcoal, today mostly electric)	• If desired, marinate meat, season, brush with oil. • Fit meat on the spit. • Hang in the oven or self-contained unit, start rotating device. • Baste constantly with drippings in the catch basin. • Use pan drippings for the jus.

Oven-roasting Meat

Roast Beef, English style –
ROASTBEEF ENGLISCHER ART –
roastbeef anglaise

YIELD: 10 SERVINGS (MAIN COURSE)		
Beef roast, boneless, tied	4 lb, 6 oz	1.8 kg
Salt, pepper		
Peanut oil	3 oz	80 g
Matignon	7 oz	200 g
Red wine	6¾ oz	200 ml
Brown veal stock	1 pt, 5 oz	600 ml
Yorkshire pudding	10	10

Method
- Season the roast with salt and pepper.
- Brown in the oil in hot oven, about 450°F (230°C), on all sides.
- Basting frequently, continue to roast at 350° to 400°F (180° to 200°C).
- Remove from oven at 50° to 60°F (10° to 20°C) below the desired internal temperature. ("English" means more pink than rare). Pour off excess fat from drippings.

Preparation of Roasting Juices
- Add *matignon* to the pan drippings, and sauté.
- Add the red wine (white wine for white meat), and reduce completely.
- Add brown veal stock (preferably a stock that has been enriched with the beef trimmings), bring to simmer, and strain through a double layer of cheesecloth.
- Reduce to the desired consistency, skim off fat, season, and if necessary, thicken lightly with cornstarch.
- Serve roasting juices and Yorkshire pudding separately.

Roasted Meat Dishes
Veal
Roast rack of veal with bouquet of vegetables – GEBRATENES KALBSKAREE MIT GEMÜSE – *carré de veau rôti bouqueyière*

Veal kidney roast, home style – KALBS-NIERENBRATEN BÜRGERLICHE ART – *rogonnade de veau rôtie bourgeoise*

Beef
Roast beef tenderloin with glazed vegetables – GEBRATENES RINDSFILET MIT GLASIERTEM GEMÜSE – *filet de bœuf rôti*

English roast beef – ROASTBEEF ENGLISCHE ART – *roastbeef anglaise*

Pork
Roast pork loin with dried prunes – SCHWEINSBRATEN MIT DÖRRPFLAUMEN – *rôti de porc suédoise*

Lamb
Roast rack of lamb, Provence style – GEBRATENES LAMMKAREE PROVENZAL-ISCHE ART – *carre d'agneau rôti provençale*

Lamb with oven-roasted potatoes, olives, and onions – GEBRATENE LAMM-KEULE BÄCKERINART – *gigot d'agneau rôti boulangére*

Poultry
Roast duckling with oranges – GEBRATENE JUNGE ENTE MIT ORANGEN – *caneton à l'orange*

Roast chicken with artichokes and olives – GEBRATENES MASTHUHN MIT ARTISCHOCKEN UND OLIVEN – *poularde rôtie Beaulieu*

Game
Roast leg of venison with fresh figs – GEBRATENE REHKEULE MIT FRISCHEN FEIGEN – *gigue de chevreuil rôtie aux figues fraîches*

Roast saddle of venison with cranberry-stuffed pear – GEBRATENER REH-RÜCKEN MIT PREISSELBEERBIRNE – *selle de chevreuil Baden-Baden*

Game birds
Roast quail with grapes – GEBRATENE WACHTELN MIT TRAUBEN – *cailles rôties vigneronne*

Roasted pheasant with sauerkraut – GEBRATENER FASAN MIT TRAUBEN – *faisan rôti à la choucroute*

Spit-roasting Meat

The difficult operation and high labor cost of the traditional charcoal-heated roasting spit has resulted in a decline in its use and replacement of the charcoal heat with automated electric roasting spits. However, the flavor from electric spits cannot compare to the wonderful taste produced by the traditional charcoal spit.

Well-marbled, aged meat is best suited for the roasting spit, for example:
- sirloin of beef
- whole racks of veal or lamb
- leg of lamb
- medium-sized chicken

Basic Rules for Traditional Spit-roasting
(See also Table 7-72 for roasting methods.)

1. Use only charcoal or pitch-free wood.

Only charcoal is legal; other coals give off noxious fumes. Wood with pitch should be avoided, as it causes an unpleasant taste.

2. Use only solid starters.

Working with a charcoal spit brings with it the danger of fire, and only experienced staff should be working the unit.

Starter liquid should not be used; only solid cubes and starter paste are safe.

3. Place meat in front not above coals.

If the meat is above the coals, the drippings could not be caught in a pan and would drip on the coals, causing flames and heavy smoke. This could make the meat inedible. The drippings are also needed to baste the meat.

4. Increase the distance from the coals during roasting.

When roasting large pieces, the meat must be moved farther from the heat to prevent a tough crust from forming.

Low-temperature Roasting

Low-temperature roasting is not a basic preparation method. It is limited in use and requires special equipment. It is just another variation of the basic roasting method.

Special low-emperature roasting ovens (slow roasting should only be done with this equipment) are fully automated, computerized with internal temperature sensors.

This cooking method retains nutrients and produces high-quality results even when the meat is held for several hours at low temperatures.

Each unit is different, and operating instructions should be carefully followed.

Basic Principles of Low-temperature Roasting

Meat that has not been aged is very high in enzymes, which only become inactive during the aging process. If unaged meat is heated at temperatures of about 250°F (120°), to be cooked slowly, the enzyme activity becomes very intense and creates many chemical changes within the meat, resulting in a tender, juicy product.

Meat Requirements
- Meats high or low in connective tissues can be low-temperature-roasted; both domestic animals and game are suitable.
- The meat should be fresh and barely aged.
- The meat should be at room temperature when placed in the oven.

Advantages
- No weight loss due to aging.
- Weight loss of low-temperature-roasted meat is about 10 percent; conventional roasting losses are about 20 to 25 percent.
- Nutrients are retained.
- Internal temperature can be exactly controlled, for tender, juicy meat.

- Long holding time without loss of quality.

Disadvantages
- Meat is not too flavorful, since most meat flavors develop during the aging process.
- No roasting juices or browning particles for sauce making.
- Meat must be browned after roasting if roasting flavor is desired.
- Aged meat becomes overaged during the process and has an off flavor (soured).
- The equipment requires superb sanitation control, since meats are cooked below sterilizing temperatures.

7.13.5 Baking – BACKEN IM OFEN – *cuire au four*

Baking meat in the oven is a dry-heat method used for tender, whole pieces of meat or game.

Typically, meat to be baked in the oven is boneless, browned in oil, stuffed or layered with a filling (farce), covered with back fat, and wrapped in dough (see Table 7-73). An exception is brined and/or smoked meats, such as ham or smoked ribs, which are usually poached and then wrapped in pastry without fat or filling.

It is important to remember that the internal temperature will increase during the resting period of the meat.

Resting

(See also section 7.13.4.)

To allow the outer and inner temperature of the baked meat to equalize

and to facilitate the redistribution of juices, the baked meat must rest. For baked meats, a resting time of 5 to 10 minutes is generally sufficient. It is important to keep the door of the holding unit ajar to prevent steam from collecting and the crust from turning soggy.

Presentation and Service

Baked meat should be served on a platter or a cutting board and carved in front of the guests.

Side Dishes

Because every piece of meat is served with baked dough, a starch side dish is not needed.

Sauces

Complementary sauces are derivitave sauces with a demi-glace base.

Basic Rules for Baking Meat in Dough

1. Proportion of meat : farce : dough. Neither the dough nor the farce should be predominant; the main ingredient should be the meat. If small meat pieces are baked in dough, it is better to use two layers, separated by a layer of farce.

2. Baking time is related to size. The baking time for the dish is based on its diameter. The meat and filling should reach the right degree of doneness at the same time the pastry is fully baked.

3. Consider the temperature of the composition. Another way to accomplish simultaneous doneness of dough and filling,

Table 7-73. Baking Meat in Dough

Meat Cut	Filling	Meat *mise en place*	Dough
Beef tenderloin	Duxelles–ground meat–liver–gratin filling	Season and brown in oil on all sides, let cool resting on a rack	Puff pastry
Veal tenderloin	Duxelles–spinach filling		Mock puff pastry
Pork tenderloin	Duxelles–spinach filling		Pie dough
Leg of spring lamb	Duxelles–herb filling		Brioche dough
Boneless lamb loin	Duxelles–herb filling		
Boneless venison loin	Duxelles–game–liver–gratin filling		
Ham	Sautéed onions, leeks, or cabbage	Poach, let cool in stock	Bread dough
Smoked ribs, sausages			Brioche dough

without affecting the baking time, is to chill the meat (thin pieces) or to bring the meat to room temperature (thicker pieces).

Baking Meat in Dough

Veal Filet Mignon with Morels in Puff Pastry – KALBSFILET MIT MORCHELN IN BLÄTTERTEIG – *filet mignon de veau aux morilles en croûte*

YIELD: 10 SERVINGS (MAIN COURSE)		
Morels, dried	1⅔ oz	50 g
Onions	5⅓ oz	150 g
Butter	1 oz	30 g
Chives	1 oz	30 g
White bread	10½ oz	300 g
Eggs	4	4
Heavy cream	5 oz	150 ml
Veal fillet	3 lb, 8 oz	1.6 kg
Salt, pepper		
Peanut oil	3 oz	80 ml
Fatback, smoked	3½ oz	100 g
Puff-pastry dough	1 lb, 5 oz	600 g

Mise en place

- Soak the morels, cut in quarters, rinse well.
- Chop the onions, and sauté in the butter. Add the morels, and continue to cook. Season, and cool.
- Finely chop the chives.
- Remove the crust from the white bread and grate finely. Mix with 3 eggs, the cream, the sautéed morels, and the chives to make a farce. Season well.
- Season the veal fillet, and brown quickly on all sides in the hot peanut oil. Place on a rack to cool.
- Cut the fatback into thin slices.
- Separate the last egg.

Method

- Roll the puff pastry out (not too thin), and place half of the fatback slices in center the dough.
- Place half of the farce on the fatback, to form a base.
- Set the veal fillet on top of the farce, and cover with the other half of the farce.
- Add the rest of the fatback slices along the length of the fillet, atop the filling.

- Brush the puff pastry with lightly beaten egg white.
- Fold the puff pastry around fillet, and place seam side down on a sheet pan.
- Brush with lightly beaten egg yolk, and decorate with pastry strips, leaves, and the like.
- Chill. Prick with a fork several times.
- Bake in a preheated oven at about 350°F (175°C) for 40 minutes.
- Serve Madeira sauce separately.

Baked Meat-and-Pastry Dishes

Pork

Ham in bread dough – SCHINKEN IM BROTTEIG – *jambon en croûte*

Sausage in brioche dough – SAUCISSON IN BRIOCHE-TEIG – *saucisson en brioche*

Beef

Beef Wellington – RINDSFILET WELLINGTON – *filet bœuf Wellington*

Special Oven Wraps or Coatings

Cooking meat that is coated in salt or wrapped in aluminum foil, roasting foil, or parchment paper is not a baking method, because the flavor developed by direct baking is absent.

Dishes of Meat Baked in Special Coatings

Roast beef in a salt crust – ROASTBEEF IN DER SALZKRUSTE – *roastbeef en croûte de sel*

Veal cutlet in parchment paper – KALBSKOTELETT IN DER PAPIERHÜLLE – *côte de veau en papillote*

7.13.6 Butter-roasting (poêléing) – POELIEREN – *poêler*

Butter-roasting is an excellent cooking method for whole pieces of tender meat and poultry.

The meat is cooked, covered, in the oven at about 285° to 320°F (140° to 160°C) *without browning*, with butter and flavoring vegetables (*mirepoix* or *matignon*).

The lid is removed just before the meat is fully cooked so that its surface can brown.

Although any meat that can be roasted can also be butter-roasted, meats with a high fat content (duck, goose) or strong flavor (lamb, beef, game) are better roasted conventionally.

Benefits of Butter-roasting

- The mild browning flavors do not overpower the mild taste of the meat; rather, they tend to intensify it, which is preferable for veal, poultry, and game birds.
- At temperatures of only 320°F (160°C), the method retains nutrients, and because there is no brown crust, the meat is more easily digested.

The Correct Degree of Doneness

See section 7.13.4.

Preparation of Pan Drippings

When meat is butter-roasted, butter-rich, flavorful meat juices collect in the bottom of the pan, which form the base for the stock:

- Remove the butter-roasted meat, and keep warm.
- Add white wine to the pan drippings, reduce, and add a good brown veal stock (if poultry, brown chicken stock).
- Simmer for about 5 minutes.
- Skim off the fat, and reduce somewhat.
- If desired, thicken with cornstarch, and season.

Presentation

- Butter-roasted meat is generally presented on a platter and carved in front of the guest.
- Butter-roasted poultry is also carved in front of the guest and served with skin.
- Pour the sauce in a pool around the meat, or serve separately.

Basic Rules for Butter-roasting

1. **Tie the meat or poultry as for roasting.**

2. **Slice the vegetables to suit the dish.**

If the vegetables accompany meat that has a short cooking time (e.g., pheasant, fillet of veal), cut the vegetables into small dice (*matignon*). If the vegetables accompany meat that has a long cooking time (e.g., rack of veal, whole turkey), cut the vegetables into large dice (*mirepoix*).

3. Add no liquid.

With the exception of game birds, which may be flamed with cognac, no liquid is added, or the special flavor will be compromised.

4. Baste occasionally.

Basting not only prevents the meat from drying, but it also flavors the surface of the meat.

Butter-roasting Meat

Butter-roasted Rack of Veal with Madeira – POELIERTES KALBSKAREE MIT MADEIRA – *carré de veau poêlé au madère*

YIELD: 10 SERVINGS (MAIN COURSE)		
Matignon	10½ oz	300 g
Thyme, rosemary, bay leaf		
Veal roast, tied	4 lb	1.8 kg
Salt, pepper		
Clarified butter	3½ oz	100 g
White wine	1⅔ oz	50 ml
Brown veal stock	1 pt, 5 oz	600 ml
Cornstarch	⅓ oz	10 g
Madeira	1⅔ oz	50 ml

Method

- Put the *matignon* and herbs in a deep roasting pan with a lid (*rondeau*) or Dutch oven.
- Place the tied and seasoned meat on top.
- Pour hot clarified butter over the meat.
- Roast briefly in a preheated oven without lid, 325°F (165°C).
- Cover and roast at 285° to 320°F (140° to 160°C), basting the roast with the butter drippings.
- Remove the lid for the last 10 minutes of cooking time, so the meat can color lightly.
- Remove the meat, and keep warm.
- Add the wine to the pan drippings, and scrape the bottom of the pan.
- Add the veal stock, and boil for about 5 minutes.
- Strain, and remove excess fat.
- Dissolve the cornstarch in the Madeira, and bring to a simmer. Reduce a little. Season.
- Add the Madeira to the strained stock.
- Slice meat, plate, and pour a little sauce around the slices; or serve sauce separately.

Butter-roasted Meat Dishes
Veal

Butter-roasted fillet of veal with porcini – POELIERTES KALBSFILET MIT STEINPILZEN – *filet mignon de veau poêlé aux cèpes*

Butter-roasted saddle of veal – POELIERTER KALBSRÜCKEN ORLOW – *selle de veau poêlée Orlov*

Poultry

Butter-roasted guinea hen with spring vegetables – POELIERTES PERLHUHN MIT KLEINEM GEMÜSE – *pintadeau poêlé aux petites légumes*

Butter-roasted chicken with morels – POELIERTES MASTHUHN MIT PORSCHELN – *poularde poêlée aux morilles*

Game Birds

Butter-roasted partridge in cocotte – POELIERTES REBHUHN IN DER COCOTTE – *perdreau poêlé en cocotte*

Table 7-74. Poaching Meats

Meat	Mise en place	Blanch	Poach	Finish
Variety meats (brain and sweetbreads)	Soak in water to remove blood (brain must also be skinned). Soak again.	Do not blanch *brain*.	Start cooking *brain* in cold vinegar–salt–water (with thyme, bay leaf and peppercorns). Poach 10 minutes.	Serve brain poached.
		Start in cold water, bring to a quick boil, blanch *sweetbreads*, drain, rinse, first in hot, then in cold water.	Cook *sweetbreads* in hot veal stock (with white wine and studded onion). Poach about 20 minutes.	Serve *sweetbreads* in a derivative creamed veal velouté, or let cool in stock.
Whole poultry (chicken)	Singe, gut, rinse, and tie chicken.	Start with hot water, bring to a boil with additional poultry trimmings; drain, rinse, first in hot, then in cold water.	Poach in hot white chicken stock (with the blanched trimmings and a white vegetable bundle). Poach about 50 minutes.	Remove skin, slice, and serve with a derivative chicken cream sauce.
Brined and smoked meat (ham and spare ribs)	Soak ham, depending on size, about 12 hours.	Do not blanch.	Start to cook in cold water without salt. Poach about 40 minutes per 2 lb, 3 oz	Serve hot or let cool in stock.

Butter-roasted pheasant with truffle cream sauce – POELIERTER FASAN MIT TRÜFFELRAHMSAUCE – *faisan poêlé à la crème aux truffes*

7.13.7 Poaching – POCHIEREN – *pocher*

Poaching is a moist-heat cooking method for tender white meat.

With this method, meat is cooked in liquid at temperatures of 155° to 165°F (70° to 75°C), which is a very sparing way to cook food.

Although all meats low in connective tissues could be poached, in reality it is more practical to limit poaching to brains, sweetbreads, and tender brined pork and poultry. Table 7-74 lists the various meats that are commonly poached and the preparation methods used for each.

Poaching is useful when browning flavors are not wanted or when meat must be precooked for use in another preparation method.

Browning flavors are not desired:

- in medical diets (poultry and veal) when a nourishing but low-fat, easily digested diet is prescribed
- in the preparation of a light, easily digested evening meal (poached chicken dishes have been specially developed in hotel restaurants for this reason)
- in poaching tender brined and smoked pork (here the browning flavors are superfluous)

Veal brains and veal sweetbreads must be poached, because their raw texture is too difficult to handle when sautéing, grilling, or braising.

Poaching Variety Meats

Brain should rarely be included on the menu because of nutritional considerations. It belongs to the group of very perishable foods, and it is very high in cholesterol (3½ ounces [100 g] contains ten times the daily requirement).

Veal Sweetbreads in Cream Sauce with Cucumbers and Mushrooms – KALBSMILKEN MIT RAHMSAUCE, GURKEN UND CHAMPIGNONS – *ris de veau à la crème aux concombres et aux champignons*

YIELD: 10 SERVINGS (MAIN COURSE)		
Veal sweetbreads	3 lb, 5 oz	1.5 kg
Butter	1⅓ oz	40 g
All-purpose flour	1⅔ oz	50 g
White veal stock	2 qt, 20 oz	2.5 L
White wine	6¾ oz	200 ml
Onion	1⅔ oz	50 g
Clove, bay leaf	1 each	1 each
Egg yolk	1	1
Heavy cream, 36 percent	3½ oz	100 ml
Salt, pepper		
Garnish		
Mushrooms	5⅓ oz	150 g
Butter	1⅔ oz	50 g
Lemon	½	½
Cucumbers	5⅓ oz	150 g

Mise en place

- Soak the sweetbreads in water. Place in cold water, bring to a simmer, and blanch. Rinse, first hot, then cold.
- Make a *roux* with the butter and flour, add 1 quart, 2 ounces (1 L) of the veal stock, and prepare a velouté. Strain.

Method

- Bring remaining veal stock, white wine, and studded onion (clove/bay leaf) to a simmer.
- Add the blanched sweetbreads, and bring to a boil.
- Reduce the temperature to 155°F (70°C), and poach for 15 minutes. Skim.
- Quarter the mushrooms, and sweat in a little butter and lemon juice.
- Peel cucumbers, seed, and dice neatly. Cook in the rest of the butter.
- Reduce very quickly 1 pint, 1 ounce (500 ml) of the poaching stock to a syrup, and add to the velouté.
- Mix the cream and egg yolk, and add the liaison to enrich the velouté. Reheat, but do not boil. Season.
- Cut the sweetbreads in slices, and plate.
- Pour a little of the sauce over the sweetbreads, top with the mushrooms and cucumbers.
- Serve rest of sauce separately.

Poached Variety-meat Dishes
Veal

Poached veal brain with capers – POSCHIERTES KALBSHIRN MIT KAPERN – *cervelle de veau pochée aux câpres*

Sweetbreads with porcini au gratin – ÜBERBACKENE KALBSMILKEN MIT STEINPILZEN – *gratin de ris de veau aux cèpes*

Poaching Poultry

Poached Chicken with Tarragon Sauce – POSCHIERTES MASTHUHN MIT ESTRAGONSAUCE – *poularde pochée à l'estragon*

YIELD: 10 SERVINGS (MAIN COURSE)		
Chicken (1)	3 lb, 8 oz	1.6 kg
Butter	1⅓ oz	40 g
All-purpose flour	1⅔ oz	50 g
White chicken stock	3 qt, 22 oz	3.5 L
Tarragon, fresh	⅓ oz	10 g
White vegetable bundle	8½ oz	250 g
Heavy cream, 36 percent	3½ oz	100 ml
Salt, pepper		

Mise en place

- Singe, gut, rinse, and tie the chicken.
- Place the chicken and poultry trimmings in hot water; blanch.
- Rinse, first with hot, then cold water.
- Make a *roux* with the butter and flour. Cook a little. Measure 1 pint, 5 ounces (600 ml) chicken stock, and prepare a basic velouté.
- Heat the rest of the chicken stock.
- Remove the tarragon leaves from stem and chop.

Method

- Put the blanched poultry trimmings and chicken in a large pot, and cover with the hot chicken stock.

- Bring to a boil, and add the vegetable bundle. Reduce heat to 155°F (70°C), and poach for 50 minutes. Skim.
- Reduce very quickly 1 pint, 1 ounce (500 ml) of the poaching stock to a syrup, and add to the velouté.
- Add the cream and reheat, but do not boil. Season.
- Add the chopped tarragon.
- Pour a little of the sauce over the chicken, and serve rest of the sauce separately.

Notes
Pan-ready chicken breasts can be poached directly in chicken stock, without the vegetable bundles.

Poached Poultry Dishes
Chicken
Poached chicken with cream sauce— POSCHIERTES MASTHUHN ALBUFERA— *poularde pochée Albuféra*

Poaching Brined, Smoked Meat

Ham and spare ribs are generally poached. Since these meats have a very strong flavor, a stock is not necessary. They tend to be also quite salty, and so the poaching water should therefore not be salted.

Ham: A large ham is brined much longer than ribs. Depending on its size, the ham should be soaked in water about 12 hours. If the ham is also baked, the poaching time should be reduced by 30 minutes.

Poached Meat Dishes
Pork
Spare ribs with sauerkraut—RIPPCHEN MIT SAUERKRAUT—*carré de porc fumé à la choucroute*

7.13.8 Braising—BRAISIREN/ SCHMOREN—*braiser*

Braising is a demanding and labor-intensive cooking method but has many applications.

Braising combines dry-heat cooking and moist-heat cooking. The principle techniqes of this basic preparation method are as follows:

- In the *first* phase, the meat is seared to seal in the juices and browned to develop roasting flavors
- In the *second* phase, the meat is covered with a little dark stock and simmered in the oven, which changes the connective tissues to soft gelatin.

Usage
The second phase of this preparation method makes it suitable for less tender meats, such as some veal, beef, pork, and lamb cuts, as well as poultry and game.

Note
The braising of tender meats, such as pullets, sweetbreads, and ham, is not really used as a basic preparation method, but as more of a finishing process, after the pullets have been sautéed, or ham or sweetbreads have been poached.

Glazing
White meat (meat of young animals) contains more gelatinous matter than that of older animals. This collects in the braising liquid and is added to the meat when the meat is braised, giving the meat a glossy surface. This gelatinous surface is very desirable, since it protects white meat from drying out.

The gelatin content can be increased by adding a small amount of stock to the braising liquid. Only after frequent basting and after the braising liquid has been reduced to a syrup should more stock be added.

These liquids that form when white meats are braised (with the exception of stews) are called glazes, and dishes cooked this way are referred to as *glazed*, for example, glazed shoulder of lamb—*épaule d'auneau glacée*.

Classification of Braising Methods
Methods used for braising can be divided into four groups, based on the type and cut of meat being braised:

- *large pieces,* for example, beef shoulder clod, stuffed breast of veal, lamb shoulder (see Table 7-75).
- *portioned meat,* for example, *osso buco,* veal slices from the leg (grenadins), beef rolls, pork cutlets (see Table 7-76).
- *stews,* for example, lamb stew, beef stew, jugged game, veal stew (see Table 7-77).
- *tender meat pieces,* for example, poultry, ham, sweetbreads (see Table 7-78).

Basic Rules for Braising Meat

1. Do not marinate white meats. White meat should not be placed in a wine marinade. White meat has little connective tissue and does not need a marinade to tenderize it. The marinade could overpower the delicate flavor of the meat.

2. Brown white meat only lightly. A seared, brown surface is desirable for red meats to seal the juices and flavors. A dark crust on white meat is not appealing, and glazing protects the white meat from juice and flavor loss.

3. Add red wine to red meat, white wine to white meat.
Red wine enhances the flavor of red meat but interferes with white meat. Red wine also gives good color to red-meat braising juices, whereas the juices from white meat should be more golden.

4. Red-meat slices should be covered with sauce; white-meat slices have the sauce around them.
The muscle color (from myoglobin) and blood color (from hemoglobin) change from red to gray at a temperature of 160°F (70°C). Braised meat is always cooked to this temperature, and it contains large amounts of myoglobin and hemoglobin, which gives braised red meat an unattractive color.

5. Test doneness with a fork.
No specific cooking times can be given for braised meats, as the timing depends on the meat, the size of the piece, the age of the animal, and the degree the meat has been aged.

Table 7-75. Braising Large Pieces of Meat

	Red Meat	White Meat
Mise en place	• Lard lean meat pieces, and tie them. • Marinate meat pieces in a red-wine marinade.	• Tie meat pieces securely.
Start	• Season and sear in hot oil on all sides to form a brown crust. • Remove meat, pour off excess oil. • Add *mirepoix* and sauté. • Add tomato paste, and continue to cook.	• Season, and brown lightly in hot oil on all sides. • Remove meat, pour off excess oil. • Add *mirepoix*, and sauté. • Add tomato paste, and continue to cook.
Deglaze	• Return meat to braising pan. • Deglaze with red wine, reduce. • Add ⅔ brown veal stock and ⅓ demi-glace to cover a third of the meat.	• Return meat to braising pan, and deglaze with white wine. • Add a little veal stock, and reduce to a syrup, basting the meat continuously. • Add veal stock to cover a quarter of the meat.
Cook	• Add a spice sachet, and cook, covered, in the oven, turning and basting the meat from time to time until done. • Add more stock to replenish evaporated stock.	• Add a spice sachet, and cook, covered, in the oven, basting the meat from time to time. • Baste very frequently during the final cooking phase.
Finish	• Remove meat, and keep warm. • Strain sauce, reduce, and thicken with cornstarch if desired. • Slice meat, and pour sauce on top.	• Remove meat and keep warm. • Add more veal stock to the reduced braising liquid, and bring to a simmer. • Thicken lightly with cornstarch, strain, and skim off fat. • Slice meat, pour sauce around meat, serve rest of sauce separately.

Table 7-76. Braising Portioned Meat

Mise en place	• Prepare meat according to the recipe in portions, such as cutlets, shank slices, rolls, veal birds, etc.
Start	• Season in batches (dust white meat with flour), and sear in hot oil on both sides. • Remove meat, pour off excess oil. • Add a *mirepoix* and, depending on the recipe, also chopped onions or tiny diced vegetables (brunoise), and sauté lightly. • Add tomato paste, and continue to cook.
Deglaze	• Return meat to braising pan. • Deglaze with wine, and reduce. • Add brown veal stock to top of meat. • Add only a small amount of stock to white meat, reduce, and glaze meat.
Cook	• Add spice sachet, and cook, covered, in the oven, turning and basting the meat from time to time, until done. • Add more stock to replenish evaporated stock. • Glaze white meat with the syrupy braising liquid to give it a glossy sheen.
Finish	• Remove meat pieces, and cover immediately with foil. • Thin the braising liquid and, depending on the recipe, strain the sauce and skim off the fat. • If desired, thicken with cornstarch. • Plate meat pieces. • Cover red meat with sauce; pour a pool of sauce around white meat. • Garnish according to recipe.

Table 7-77. Braising Stews

Mise en place	• Cube meat. • Marinate game in a red-wine marinade.
Start	• Season in batches (dust white meat with flour), and sear in hot oil in braising pan on all sides. • Pour off excess oil. • Add a *mirepoix* and, depending on the recipe, also tiny diced vegetables (brunoise) or chopped onions, and sauté well. • Add tomato paste, and continue to cook.
Deglazing	• Deglaze with wine, and reduce. • Add ⅔ brown veal stock (for game, use the reduced marinade and game stock), and ⅓ demi-glace to cover the meat.
Cooking	• Add a spice sachet and cook, covered, in the oven, turning and basting the meat from time to time, until done. • Add more stock to replenish evaporated stock.
Finish	• Remove meat pieces, and cover immediately with foil. • If desired, strain sauce and reduce. • If desired, thicken with cornstarch. Season (the sauce for game is usually enriched with a mixture of pig blood and cream). • Return meat pieces to the sauce, and serve in sauce. • Garnish according to recipe.

Table 7-78. Braising Tender Meat Pieces

	Chicken	Ham	Sweetbreads
Mise en place	• Prepare chicken (pullet) for sautéing. • Season. • Brown lightly in shallow skillet until pieces are ¾ done. • Pour off excess oil. • Flame with cognac. • Remove chicken, and keep warm.	• Poach until ¾ done; do not cool. • Remove rind and knuckle bone. • Cut a diamond pattern into the fat.	• Poach sweetbreads until ¾ done. • Let cool in the stock.
Start	• Add a little butter, shallots, and finely diced vegetables (brunoise) to the pan, and sauté.	• Brown a *matignon* in the braising pan. • Place ham on top.	• Sauté chopped shallots in braising pan. • Place sweetbreads on top.
Deglazing	• Deglaze with white wine, and reduce. • Add thickened chicken or veal jus. • Simmer briefly. • Strain sauce, and season.	• Deglaze with madeira or port wine. • Add brown veal stock to cover ¼ of meat.	• Deglaze with white vermouth or port wine. • Add a little veal jus, and baste meat until liquid is reduced to a syrup. • Add brown veal stock to cover ¼ of meat.
Cooking	• First place the legs in the sauce; a little later, add the breasts. Simmer slowly until juicy and done.	• Basting frequently, braise until juicy and done. • Remove ham and keep warm.	• Basting frequently, braise until juicy and done. • Remove sweetbreads, and keep warm.
Finish	• Place chicken in a ramekin dish. • Pour sauce over chicken, and garnish.	• Strain braising liquid, reduce, and thicken with a little cornstarch. • Dust ham with powdered sugar, and glaze under the broiler. • Serve sauce separately.	• Strain braising liquid, and season. • Whip in cold butter nuggets to enrich. • Add garnish to sauce. • Slice sweetbreads, plate, and pour a pool of sauce around sweetbreads.

The purpose of braising is to achieve tenderness. Doneness can be measured by these two methods:

- When a fork is inserted in the thickest part of the meat, the juices should run clear.
- A fork can be pushed easily into the meat without any significant resistance.

Test braised stew meats by tasting a piece.

Braised Meat Dishes

Veal

Stuffed breast of veal – GEFÜLLTE KALBS-BRUST – *poitrine de veau farcie*

Glazed veal shanks, home style – GLASIERTE KALBSHAXE BÜRGERLICHE ART – *jarret de veau glacé bourgeoise*

Beef

Braised shoulder clod with vegetables – GESCHMORTER RINDSHUFTSPITZ MIT GEMÜSE – *pointe de culotte de bœuf à la mode*

Braised beef, Burgundy style – RINDERSCHMORBRATEN BURGUNDER ART – *pièce de bœuf bourguignonne*

Lamb

Stuffed lamb shoulder – GEFÜLLTE LAMMSCHULTER – *epaule d'agneau farcie*

Pork

Glazed pork shoulder roast with apples – GLASIERTE SCHWEINSSCHULTER MIRZA – *epaule de porc glacée Mirza*

Braising Portioned Meat
Red and White Meat

All basic principles of braising apply.

Braised Portioned Dishes

Veal

Osso buco (braised veal shanks) – OSSOBUCO CREMOLATA

Breast of veal slices with ratatouille – GLASIERTE KALBSBRUSTSCHNITTE MIT RATATOUILLE – *tendron de veau glacé à ratatouille*

Beef

Braised beef rolls with tomatoes – GESCHMORTE RINDSRÖLLCHEN MIT TOMATEN – *paupiettes de bœuf braisées aux tomates*

Pork

Pork cutlets braised in beer (Flemish style) – KARBONADE VON SCHWEINE-FLEISCH FLÄMISCHE ART – *carbonade de porc flamande*

Poultry

Stuffed poultry leg with pistachio cream sauce – GEFÜLLTER GEFLÜGEL-SCHENKEL MIT PISTAZIENRAHMSAUCE – *ballottine de volaille glacée aux pistaches*

Braising Stews

Red and White Meat

All basic principles of braising apply

Braised Meat Stew Dishes

Veal

Veal stew with spring vegetables – KALBSVORESSEN MIT FRÜHLINGSGEMÜSE – *sauté de veau aux primeurs*

Veal stew, grandmother's style – KALBSVORESSEN GROSSMUTTERART – *sauté de veau grand-mère*

Beef

Beef stew with mushrooms – RIND-SRAGOUT MIT PILZEN – *sauté de bœuf aux champignons*

Lamb

Brown lamb stew with vegetables – LAMMRAGOUT MIT KLEINEM GEMÜSE – *navarin d'agneau aux petits légumes*

Game

Jugged game, hunter's style – REHPFEF-FER JÄGERART – *civet de chevreuil chasseur*

Braising Tender Pieces of Meat

For tender meat, braising is a finishing method, used after another basic preparation method has been used to cook the meat.

Braised Tender Meat Dishes

Chicken

Braised chicken in red wine – GESCHMORTER HAHN IN ROTWEIN – *coq au vin rouge*

Braised curried chicken – GESCHMORTER HAHN MIT CURRYRAHM-SAUCE – *coq à la crème au curry*

Ham

Braised ham in madeira sauce – GES-MORTER SCHINKEN MIT MADEIRA – *jambon braisé au madère*

Sweetbreads

Glazed veal sweetbreads with tarragon – GLASIERTE KALBSMILKEN MIT ESTRAGON – *ris de veau glacés à l'estragon*

7.13.9 Stewing – DÜNSTEN – *étuver*

Stewing is a moist-heat cooking method used for less tender meats, which are usually cubed. Although very similar to braising, with this method the meat is not browned in hot oil (the meat is only stewed lightly), giving it a distinctively different taste.

The principles of this preparation method are:

- In the *first* step, the meat and onions are cooked in a little fat without browning, until the meat and onion juices have been reduced to a syrup-like consistency.
- In the *second* step, the meat and onions are deglazed with white or red wine, covered with a white or brown stock, and simmered until done.

Stewing is used for:

- white meats, for example, all fricassées and Vienna goulash (veal)
- red meats, for example, all stews and beef goulash

See Table 7-79 for methods used to stew both red and white meats.

Stewing Meats

Veal Fricassee – KALBSFRIKASSEE – *fricasée de veau*

YIELD: 10		
Veal shoulder	3 lb, 8 oz	1.6 kg
Onion	10½ oz	300 g
Spice sachet	1	1
Salt, pepper		
Butter	3½ oz	100 g
All-purpose flour	2½ oz	70 g
White wine	10 oz	300 ml
White veal stock	1 qt, 19 oz	1.5 L
Heavy cream, 36%	6¾ oz	200 ml
Lemon	½	½

Table 7-79. Stewing Meats

	White Meat (veal, lamb, poultry, rabbit)	Red Meat (beef)
Mise en place	• Cut veal and lamb meat into cubes weighing 1⅓ oz (40 g).	• Cut beef into 1⅓ oz (50 g) cubes (longer cooking = greater weight loss)
Pan	• Shallow braising pan (*rondeau*)	• Shallow braising pan (*rondeau*)
Start	• Heat clarified butter. • Season, dust lightly with flour, and add with chopped onions to pan. • Stew together until a syrupy liquid (*glace*) forms. • Depending on recipe, add curry or paprika, and continue to cook. • Dust with the rest of the flour.	• Heat clarified butter. • Season meat, add with chopped onions and garlic to pan. • Stew together until a syrupy liquid (*glace*) forms. • Add tomato paste, and continue to cook. • Depending on recipe, add paprika, and continue to cook. • If desired, dust lightly with flour (except goulash).
Deglaze	• Deglaze with white wine. • Barely cover meat with white veal or chicken stock, simmer, and skim. • Add spice sachet.	• Deglaze with red wine, and reduce. • Barely cover meat with brown veal stock or bouillon, simmer, and skim. • Add spice sachet.
Cooking	• Stew, covered in the oven or on top of stove. • Add more liquid if needed.	• Stew, covered, 1½ hours in the oven or on top of stove. • Add more liquid if needed.
Finish	• Remove meat and spice sachet with a skimmer, and cover meat immediately with foil (prevents drying). • Purée the stewing liquid, and strain. • Reduce a little, and thicken if needed. • Add cream and season. • Return meat to sauce and add any garnishes, per recipe.	• Remove meat and spice sachet with a skimmer, and cover meat immediately with foil (prevents drying). • Purée the sauce for goulash; for stews, the sauce may be strained. • Reduce a little, and thicken if needed. • Return meat to sauce and add any garnishes, per recipe.

Mise en place

• Cut veal shoulder meat into cubes weighing 1½ oz (40 g).
• Dice or slice onions.
• Make a spice sachet.

Method

• Heat butter in a shallow braising pan.
• Season the meat, dust with some flour and add, with the onions, to the pan.
• Stew together until a syrupy liquid (*glace*) has formed.
• Add the rest of the flour.
• Deglaze with the white wine.
• Pour in the veal stock, and bring to a simmer.
• Skim, and add the spice sachet.
• Cover, and simmer slowly on top of the stove for about 1 hour.
• Remove the meat with a skimmer, place in a bowl, and cover. Discard spice sachet.
• Purée the stewing liquid with the onions, and strain through a fine-mesh china cap.
• Bring to a simmer, and thicken with a little cornstarch if needed.
• Stir in the heavy cream, and season with lemon juice and salt.
• Return meat to sauce.

Stewed Meat Dishes

Veal

Veal fricassée with mushrooms—KALBSFRIKASSEE MIT CHAMPIGNONS—*fricassée de veau aux champignons de Paris*

Viennese veal goulash—WIENER GULASCH—*goulache viennoise*

Poultry

Chicken fricassée with vegetables—GEFLÜGELFRIKASSEE MIT GEMÜSE—*fricassée de volaille aux de légumes*

Chicken fricassée with tarragon—GEFLÜGELFRIKASSEE MIT ESTRAGON—*fricassée de volaille à l'estragon*

Lamb

Lamb fricassée with curry—LAMMFRIKASSEE MIT CURRY—*fricassée d'agneau au curry*

Beef

Beef stew with vegetables—RINDSDÜNSTRAGOUT MIT KLEINEM GEMÜSE—*estouffade de bœuf aux petits de légumes*

Beef stew with tomatoes and olives—RINDSDÜNSTRAGOUT MIT TOMATEN UND OLIVEN—*estouffade de bœuf aux tomates et aux olives*

Hungarian goulash—UNGARISCHES GULASCH—*goulache hongroise*

Goulash

The classic Hungarian goulash is an unstrained paprika goulash, composed of beef, lots of sliced onions, fresh tomatoes, and potatoes. Today the sauce, with the onions, is often puréed in a blender or with a food mill. For practical and service reasons, a new way of preparing Hungarian goulash has evolved in restaurant kitchens. Goulash is started as a basic stew, but with more onions and spiced with paprika. Diced tomatoes are added after the sauce has been strained, and the potatoes are served separately as steamed potatoes.

7.13.10 Boiling – SIEDEN – cuire par ébullition

Boiling and simmering are moist-heat cooking methods used for less tender meats.

With this basic preparation method, the meat is cooked just below the boiling point, 208°F (about 98°C), in an appropriate stock. During this process, tough connective tissue is softened and changed into edible gelatin.

In addition to the stock and the meat, such dishes are flavored by vegetable bundles and spice sachets.

Usage

This method is best suited to meats that are flavorful, because no roasting flavors are added during this cooking process. For example:

- veal from older animals
- beef
- lamb or mutton
- fowl
- cured meats.

Boiling/simmering is used for:

- whole pieces of meat, for example, beef loin choice (2nd quality), leg of mutton, fowl, calf's head, veal tongue (see Table 7-80)
- white stews (blanquettes), for example, veal, mutton, and chicken

- cured meats, for example, bacon, spare ribs, cured beef tongue

Basic Rules for Boiling Meat

1. Tie large pieces and fowl with twine.
Tying large pieces of meat prevents them from becoming misshapen.

If various sizes of meat pieces must be simmered at the same time, it is best to attach meat pieces with a string to the pot handles. This makes it easier to control doneness in the individual pieces.

2. Blanch, and start large pieces with hot water.
With the exception of cured meats, all meat to be simmered should first be blanched. Blanching not only seals the surface and retains flavors, but it also removes surface contaminants. The blanched meat is rinsed, first hot and then cold, to make sure all contaminants are washed off. The blanched meat is always started in hot stock to keep the surface sealed.

3. Check doneness with meat fork.
No specific cooking times can be given for simmered meats. The timing depends on the meat, the size of the piece, the age of the animal, and the degree the meat has been aged. The purpose of simmering meats is to make them tender. Doneness can be measured by these two methods:

- When a fork is inserted into the thickest part of the meat, the juices run clear.
- A fork can be pushed into the meat easily without any significant resistance. Cubed meats are best tested by tasting.

4. The meat should cool in the stock if the boiled meat is to be used in a cold dish.
Meat that is taken warm from the stock dries out very rapidly.

Boiled Meat Dishes

Veal
Boiled calf's head, turtle style – KALBSKOPF SCHILDKRÖTEN ART – *tête de veau en tortue*

Boiled calf's tongue with cream sauce – KALBSZUNGE MIT WEISSER SAUCE – *langue de veau allemande*

Beef
Boiled beef with sauerkraut and bacon – SIEDFLEISCH ELSÄSSER ART – *bœuf bouille alsacienne*

Boiled beef au gratin with onion sauce – ÜBERBACKENES SIEDFLEISCH IN ZWIEBELSAUCE – *miroton de bœuf*

Lamb
Boiled leg of lamb with vegetables and caper sauce – LAMMKEULE ENGLISCHE ART – *gigot d'agneau anglaise*

Simmering White Stews

Veal Blanquette, German Style – KALBSBLAKETT DEUTSCHE ART – *blanquette de veau allemande*

YIELD: 10 SERVINGS		
Veal shoulder	3 lb, 8 oz	1.6 kg
Bouquet garni	10½ oz	300g
Spice sachet	1	1
White veal stock	1qt, 19 oz	1.5 L
White wine	10 oz	300 ml
Salt		
Butter	1⅓ oz	40 g
All-purpose flour	1⅔ oz	50 g
Egg yolk	3	3
Heavy cream, 36 percent	6¾ oz	200 ml

Mise en place

- Cut veal shoulder meat into cubes weighing 1⅓ oz (40 g). Blanch in hot water.
- Drain; rinse first with hot water, then with cold water.
- Prepare a *bouquet garni* for white stock
- Prepare a spice sachet with bay leaf, parsley stems, peppercorns, and thyme.

Method

- Bring the veal stock and white wine to a simmer. Add the blanched meat, return to a simmer, and skim.
- Season lightly with salt.
- Add the *bouquet garni* and spice sachet. Simmer just below boiling for about 1 hour.

Table 7-80. Boiling Whole Pieces of Meat

	Beef, Lamb, and Mutton	Veal Head and Veal Tongue
Mise en place	• Blanch bones. • Start blanched bones in cold water, bring to a simmer, and cook, skimming and removing fat from time to time, for about 1½ hours. • Tie meat, place in hot water, blanch, drain, rinse, first hot, then cold.	• Add meat (boned calf's head) to hot water, blanch, drain, rinse first hot, then cold. • Have a white veal stock ready to use.
Flavorings	• For boiled beef and mutton, add a vegetable bundle with roasted onions and a spice sachet. • For fowl and lamb, add a white vegetable bundle and spice sachet.	• Use a white vegetable bundle and spice sachet.
Start	• Put blanched meat into the slowly simmering stock.	
Cooking	• Add flavorings, and simmer just below the boiling point, occasionally skimming and removing fat, until done.	
Finish	*Boiled beef* Slice, plate, and cover with a little broth. Serve with zesty garnishes such as vegetable salads, mixed pickles, horseradish-flavored whipped cream, cranberries, plus steamed potatoes. *Lamb and mutton* Slice, and surround with cooked potatoes and vegetables. Prepare a caper sauce with the stock and serve separately.	*Calf's head* Let cool in the stock, and cut into cubes. Serve lukewarm with a fresh herb vinaigrette, or deep-fry the meat and serve with a tomato sauce. *Veal tongue* Peel the tongue, and cut into thin long slices (the length of the tongue). Make a derivative cream sauce from the stock, and pour sauce over tongue slices.

• Remove the meat with slotted spoon, and keep warm in a little stock.
• Heat the butter, and add the flour to make a white *roux*.
• Cool the *roux* slightly, and stir in 1 quart, 2 ounces (1 L) of stock.
• Bring to a boil, stirring constantly, and cook for 20 minutes.
• Strain through a double layer of cheesecloth.
• Mix the egg yolks with the heavy cream (liaison).
• Remove the pan from the heat, and stir the liaison into the sauce.
• Reheat, but do not boil.
• Add the reserved warm meat to the sauce, and heat briefly.

White Stews
Veal
Veal blanquette with mushrooms and pearl onions—KALBSBLANKETT MIT CHAMPIGNONS UND PERLZWIEBELN—*blanquette de veau ancienne*

Poultry
Chicken blanquette with chives—GEFLÜGELBLANKETT MIT SCHNITTLAUCH—*blanquette de volaille á la ciboulette*

Lamb
Lamb stew, Emmenthal style—EMMENTALER LAMMVORESSES—*blanquette d'agneau emmentaloise*

White lamb stew with tomatoes and herbs—LAMMBLANKETT MIT TOMATEN UND KRÄUTERN—*blanquette d'agneau aux tomates et aux fines herbs*

Irish stew

Boiling/Simmering Cured and Smoked Meats

Meats that are simmered are usually:

• pork: brined fatback, ham hocks, cured ears, pigs' feet, snout, and smoked tail
• beef: cured tongue

Method
• Soak cured meat for 6 to 12 hours in cold water.
• Bring to a simmer in plenty of cold water, with no other ingredients. Simmer until done.
• Bacon is done when the pork rind can be pulled off easily.
• Beef tongue is done when the tip of the tongue is soft.
• Remove beef tongue when done, rinse with cold water, and peel. Store the peeled tongue, refrigerated, in lightly salted water.

Boiled Cured and Smoked Meat Dishes
Beef
Smoked beef tongue with white beans—GERÄUCHERTE RINDSZUNGE AUF WEISSEN BOHNEN—*langue de bœuf fumée bretonne*

Beef tongue with madeira sauce—RINDSZUNGE MIT MADEIRASAUCE—*langue de bœuf, sauce madère*

7.14 Salads

A wide variety of foods can be used to make salads. From a nutritional point of view, leaf lettuce and raw vegetable salads with fresh herbs, fruits, and nuts are the most valuable. Cooked vegetable salads and combination salads with vegetables, meat, poultry, fish, rice, legumes, and pasta can be valuable as whole-food salads, if they are prepared with a complementary light dressing and fresh herbs.

Salads can be served as a garnish, side dish, appetizer, appetizer cocktail, or exquisite salad entrée.

Classification of Salads

Salads from Plant Foods

These salads are served as side dishes to main courses or as a separate course in a menu. Included in this group are:

- *simple salads* of:
  - green leaf lettuce
  - raw vegetables
  - sprouts (sprouted seeds)
  - raw shredded vegetables
  - cooked vegetables
  - legumes
- *composed salads*: various combinations of salad ingredients, such as leafy greens, raw and cooked vegetables, sprouts, legumes, rice, or pasta, garnished with fruits and nuts.
- *salad plates*: A variety of dressed salads, arranged like a bouquet: mixed green salad, raw and cooked vegetable salads, mushroom salads, legume salads.

Salads from Plant and Animal Foods

These composed salads are always served as a separate course, never as a side dish to a main course.

Salad Variations as Appetizers – *variations de salade pour hors-d'œuvre*

Mixed greens, raw vegetable salads, or cooked vegetable salads, combined with cooked or roasted meat, poultry, game, variety meats, fish, or shellfish (usually added at room temperature), are garnished with additional fruits and nuts.

7.14.1 Salad Dressings – SALAT-SAUCEN – *sauces à salade*

The terms salad *sauce, dressing*, or *marinade* are often used interchangeably. The term used often depends on the origin of the recipe, the composition, and the application.

The main salad dressings are standard recipes, consisting of basic ingredients (see Tables 7-81 and 7-82). Skill is demonstrated in the ability to enhance these sauces and combine them with salad ingredients into a tasty salad.

For use in kitchens, the dressings are bottled and kept cool. Before each service, the sauce must be shaken thoroughly.

Salad dressings with fresh onions, garlic, and shallots should be prepared for daily use, as the fresh ingredients ferment.

Emulsions made with egg yolks must be stored refrigerated. For health reasons, it is best to use pasteurized egg yolks, to avoid salmonella contamination.

To prevent oxidizing, salad dressings should be prepared in nonreactive containers. The same is true for storing prepared salads. Salad utensils should also be from nonreactive materials.

Salad dressings should be low in calories for nutritional reasons. Fatty thickeners can often be fully or partially replaced with lower-fat alternatives.

The use of fresh herbs depends on the salad ingredients. Onions and garlic should be used sparingly, since they are not enjoyed by all guests. See Table 7-82.

7.14.2 Simple Salads – EINFACHE SALATE – *salades simples*

A simple salad contains one salad green. Depending on type, it is dressed just before service or marinated in advance.

Examples of salad greens

Leaf Lettuce Salads

Catalonia (dandelion-like green) – *salade de catalogne*

Red and green radicchio (cicorino rosso e verde) – *salade de chicorée amère*

Curly endive – *salade de chicorée frisée*

Escarole – *salade de chicorée scarole*

Napa cabbage – *salade de chou Chine*

Cress – *salade de cresson*

Dandelion greens – *salade de dent-de-lion*

Belgian endive – *salade de chicorée*

Endive (Batavian) – *salade de laitue batavia*

Iceberg lettuce – *salade de laitue iceberg*

Boston lettuce – *salade de laitue pommée*

Loose-leaf lettuce (lattughino/lollo) – *salade de lattughino/lollo*

Corn salad/mâche – *salade de mâche/doucette*

Romaine lettuce – *salade de laitue romaine*

Purslane – *salade de pourpiere*

Raw Vegetable Salads

Avocado

Beet

Bell pepper

Carrot

Celery

Cucumber

Fennel

Table 7-81. Major Ingredients in All Salad Dressings

Acid: gives dressing a refreshing taste	• A variety of vinegars, such as red-wine vinegar, white-wine vinegar, balsamic vinegar, sherry vinegar, raspberry vinegar, cider vinegar, lemon vinegar, herb vinegar • Lemon juice, orange juice, yogurt, buttermilk, cottage cheese, and sour cream
Oils and fats: heighten flavors, thicken, and absorb fat-soluble vitamins	• Oils from sunflower seeds, corn kernels, peanuts, olives, thistle, rape seeds, soybeans, hazelnuts, walnuts, grape seeds • Heavy cream, double cream, creamed cottage cheese, sour cream • Egg yolks, mayonnaise
Flavorings	• Finely minced, such as shallots, onions, garlic, horseradish, capers. • Fresh herbs, such as parsley, chervil, tarragon, dill, basil, lovage, peppermint, wild garlic • Mustard, condiment sauces, wine, honey, and liqueurs
Garnishes	• Fresh fruits, such as apples, pears, sectioned citrus fruit, pineapple, mango, dates, figs, grapes, and dried fruits • Nuts and seeds, such as almonds, sunflower seeds, pine nuts, pistachios, walnuts, hazelnuts, sesame seeds and poppy seeds

Table 7-82. Salad Dressings

Salad Dressing	Safflower oil	Olive oil	Specialty oils	Heavy cream	Light sour cream	Sour cream	Creamed cottage cheese	Egg yolk (pasteurized)	Roquefort	Low-fat cottage cheese	Yogurt	White-wine vinegar	Red-wine vinegar	Cider vinegar	Lemon juice	Orange juice	Shallots/onions	Garlic	Fresh herbs	Mustard	Spices/condiment sauces	Salt/pepper	Sugar	Apple horseradish
Basic dressing	●											●									●	●		
Vinaigrette	●											●					●		●	●		●		
French dressing	●							●				●			●		●				●	●	●	
Italian dressing		●												●			●	●				●		
Heavy cream dressing				●	●	●						●			●							●	●	
Sour cream dressing						●	●					●							●			●		
Roquefort dressing	●							●	●		●				●				●			●		
Cottage cheese dressing							●					●			●				●			●		
Yogurt dressing											●				●	●			●			●		
Low-calorie dressing					●		●			●	●			●	●							●		
Apple dressing	●													●				●						●

Green cabbage	**Cooked Vegetable Salads**	Knob celery
Knob celery	Artichoke	Leeks
Radish	Asparagus	Mushrooms
Red cabbage	Beets	Potato
Sauerkraut	Broccoli	
Spinach	Carrot	**Legume Salads**
Tomato	Cauliflower	Beans (black beans, borlotto, great northern, lima, kidney)
White radish	Corn	Lentils (red, green, and brown)
Zucchini	Green beans	

Sprout Salads

Mung bean sprouts

Lentil sprouts

Radish sprouts

Mustard sprouts

Soybean sprouts

Salads with Raw Ingredients

Mise en place
Leafy Green Salads

- Trim lettuce; remove wilted parts, large stems, and leaf veins.
- Wash carefully in large quantities of water to remove dirt and sand. Do not bruise the leaves.
- Do not keep lettuce soaking in water, or valuable vitamins and minerals will be lost.
- Place in a salad spinner to remove excess water.
- Keep loosely spread in the refrigerator until use.

Raw Vegetable Salads

- Thoroughly wash vegetables.
- Peel root vegetables.
- For nutritional reasons, do not peel tender cucumbers, zucchini, and tomatoes.
- With a vegetable peeler, peel only the very outer stems of celery and fennel.
- Remove outer leaves from red and green cabbage, quarter, and remove core and any thick ribs.
- Wash and blanch sprouts.

Shredded Raw Vegetable Salads (ROHKOST)

- Shredded raw vegetable salads are an important component of a healthy diet . They contribute vitamins, minerals, and fiber.
- To trim, clean, and cut, follow the same principles as for raw vegetable salads.
- Use only first-quality unblemished vegetables in season.
- To retain as many vitamins as possible, the vegetables are cut or shredded immediately before service.

Cutting and Tearing

Raw vegetables must be cut into small pieces to be eaten. How small depends on the cell structure of the vegetable:

- *Tear into bite-size pieces:* Leaf lettuce
- *Cut into thin strips:* Cabbage varieties and root vegetables, also fennel
- *Cut into strips:* Bell peppers
- *Cut into thin slices (slicer or mandoline):* Radishes, white radishes, cucumbers, zucchini
- *Cut into slices:* Tomatoes
- *Shred (mostly in whole-food or spa cuisine):* Carrots, knob celery, beets

Method

- The prepared salad ingredients are carefully dressed in a large bowl. Tossing must be thorough but gentle, so that the salad ingredients are covered with dressing but not bruised. Mixing should be done with salad utensils or, for large quantities, with plastic gloves.
- All leaf lettuce and tender vegetable salads, such as those with tomatoes or cucumbers, are dressed *just before service*, to keep them crisp. Salt will draw moisture from the greens if they are dressed too early, and the salad will wilt.
- All salads from more solid vegetables, such as carrots, knob celery, and bell peppers, can be prepared *in advance*. The dressing will have time to penetrate and make the salad tastier.
- Cabbage salads are dressed with a warm marinade and tossed well, to help break down the cell structure and soften the salad.
- Raw shredded salads, for whole-food or spa cuisine, are usually served with cold-pressed oils, dairy products, fruit juices, honey, or fruit vinegars. Salt is used sparingly. Additions or garnishes are fresh herbs, nuts, fresh fruit, or dried fruits.

Cooked Vegetable and Legume Salads
Mise en place

- The cooked or raw vegetables are cut into eye-appealing shapes. Knob celery and carrots can be shaped with melon ballers, hors d'oeuvre cutters, or knives.
- Cut surfaces of some white vegetables, such as artichoke bottoms, knob celery, and salsify, discolor in the presence of oxygen and so must be placed in acidulated water until use. (For more detailed discussions of cutting, cooking methods, and cooking times see section 7.15.)
- Steam, simmer, or stew the cut vegetables according to the recipe directions. Vegetables should be crisp-tender, not too soft.
- The cooked vegetables should cool in the cooking liquid to retain their flavor. However, the vegetables will continue to cook in the hot liquid and so should be removed from the heat before the desired texture is achieved.
- Fully cooked legumes should be cooled in the cooking liquid, to which a little vinegar should be added. The legumes are then drained, and possibly rinsed, before adding the rest of the ingredients.

Method

- Salads made with cooked vegetables or legumes should be mixed while still hot or warm with the dressing, to allow the dressing to penetrate the vegetables or legumes.
- The well drained vegetables are tossed gently but thoroughly with the dressing in a large bowl.
- If the dressing is mayonnaise-based, the vegetables should be very dry and well chilled. Wet vegetables cause the sauce to become runny, and loss of flavor is also a problem.
- Vegetable salads must be stored covered and chilled to keep them safe.
- Fresh herbs that would discolor from the acids should be added only at the moment of service.

7.14.3 Composed Salads – GEMISCHTE SALATE – *salades mêlées*

Composed salads can be prepared in as many ways as creativity and a good sense of taste and color allow. Table 7-83 lists a few examples, to illustrate the endless variety possible, along with a few classic examples.

Table 7-83. Composed Salads

Salad	Description
Rice and pepper salad— SALAT ANDALUSISCHE ART— *salade andalouse*	Quartered tomatoes, strips of bell peppers, and cooked long-grain rice are mixed with a salad dressing made from olive oil, sherry vinegar, garlic, and fresh herbs.
Fruit salad with curry— SALAT AUS FRÜCHTEN MIT CURRY— *salade de fruits au curry*	Peel and cut fresh fruit, such as apples, pineapple, bananas, oranges, papayas. Mix with a dressing made from sour cream, mayonnaise, curry, ginger, and lemon juice. Garnish with toasted pine nuts and peppermint leaves.
Vegetable salad with ham— SALAT ITALIENISCHE ART— *salade italienne*	Dice carrots, turnips, and potatoes . Cut beans into ½-inch (1–2-cm) pieces. Cook until crisp-tender, cool, drain. Mix with chopped anchovies, ham, and capers. Mix with a zesty mayonnaise sauce. Garnish with egg quarters and parsley.
Black beans, corn, and pepper salad— SALAT MEXICANISCHER ART— *salade mexicaine*	Mix black beans, corn, bell pepper strips, and crisp green beans. Toss with a salad dressing made from white-wine vinegar, garlic, sunflower oil, savory, and chili sauce.
Shredded carrot salad with raisins— ROHKOSTSALAT MIT ÄPFELN, KAROTTEN UND ROSINEN— *salade de pommes et de carottes aux raisin secs*	Shred sour apples and carrots, and marinate in freshly squeezed orange juice. Soak raisins in orange juice, and add to carrots. Place in glasses or bowls. Garnish with Belgian endives. Top with a rosette of whipped cream with horseradish and toasted sunflower seeds.
Russian salad— GEMÜSESALAT RUSSISCHE ART— *salade russe*	Dice carrots, knob celery, and potatoes, and cook until crisp-tender. Cut beans into ¼-inch (1-cm) pieces, and cook with peas; cool and drain. Mix mayonnaise with plain yogurt; season well.
Red cabbage salad with grapes— ROHKOSTSALAT MIT ROTKRAUT, UND WEINTRAUBEN— *salade de chou rouge et de pommes aux raisins*	Cut red cabbage and apples into fine strips, and marinate in lemon and apple juice. Cut green grapes in half, and add to cabbage. Mix salad with currant jelly and walnut oil. Arrange in glass bowls, and garnish with chopped walnuts.
Waldorf salad— SELLERIESALAT MIT ÄPFELN UND BAUMNÜSSEN— *salade waldorf*	Cut raw knob celery into fine strips, and dice apples. Mix mayonnaise with sour cream and lemon juice, season. Combine with apples and knob celery salad. Garnish with walnut halves and canned pineapple chunks.
Chicken, tongue, and celeriac salad— WINDSOR SALAT— *salade Windsor*	Cut knob celery, boiled tongue, and poached chicken breast into thin strips. Sauté mushrooms, and mix. Mix mayonnaise with plain yogurt and mushroom liquid. Season, and add to salad. Place on a crown of dressed mâche.

7.14.4 Salad Plates— ZUSAMMGESTELLTE SALATE— *salades de composées*

The salads in Table 7-84 all originated in classical cuisine. But today they are prepared with contemporary ingredients, for example, special vinegars, oils rich in polyunsaturated fatty acids, cottage cheese, yogurt, sour cream, and fruit juices. In today's cuisine, the main consideration is season and market availability. It is left to the chef's creativity and preference to compose the salads in the classic way or follow a modern trend.

Many of the trendy composed salads made from fish, meat, poultry, fruits, and cheese are often salads that are more like appetizers, and these are discussed in section 7.9.1.

7.14.5 Salad Presentation

Basic Principles
- All salad ingredients should be in bite-sized pieces, as only a fork is used as an eating utensil.
- Cleaned or dressed salads should always be refrigerated or stored in a salad cooler at 40°F (4°C) and should not be kept longer than one day.
- However, salads will taste better if not ice cold. When they are not prepared to order, salads should be removed from refrigeration a few minutes before service.
- Plate salad greens loosely and neatly. Use plastic gloves or salad forks to serve salad. Salad should not be drowned in dressing.
- Leafy green salads taste better if they are carefully tossed before service, rather than drizzled with sauce.
- Taste variations are achieved with several lettuce and vegetable varieties and especially with tossing the salad with various dressings.
- Colors stimulate the appetite. It is therefore important when arranging salads to appeal not only to the sense of taste, but also the sense of color. Attention to proper garnishes can further increase the eye appeal.
- Plates, bowls, and glass platters are all excellent for salad presentations. They all bring out the freshness, color, and shapes in the salad to their best advantage.

Table 7-84. Salad Plates

Salad	Description
Artichoke and tomato salad— SALAT AIDA: ENDIVIENSALAT MIT ARTISCHOCKEN UND PEPERONI— *salade Aïda*	Arrange curly endive, peeled tomato wedges, bell pepper strips, and cooked, thinly sliced artichoke bottoms into a vegetable bouquet. Sprinkle with chopped hard-cooked egg, and drizzle with a simple salad dressing (the salad components could also be dressed individually before assembly).
Salad of green beans, tomatoes, and mushrooms— SALAT SPANISCHE ART— *salade espagnole*	Cut cooked fresh green beans into 1¾- to 2-inch (4- to 5-cm) pieces, and mix with tomato wedges. Place on bite-size pieces of leaf lettuce. Arrange bouquets of pepper salad and stewed mushrooms around them. Garnish with thin onion rings, and drizzle with desired salad dressing.
Imperial salad— SALAT KÄISERLICHE ART: BOHNEN-, KAROTTEN-, UND APFELSALAT MIT TRÜFFELN—	Arrange apple salad with creamy salad dressing, cooked green beans, and fine strips (julienne) of cooked carrots on Boston lettuce leaves. Drizzle beans and carrots with an herb vinaigrette. Sprinkle apple salad with truffles cut julienne.
Celery and cauliflower salad with walnuts— SALAT MARIE-LOUISE— *salade Marie-Louise*	Mix finely sliced celery stalks with a walniut salad dressing. Mix crisp-cooked cauliflower florets with a sour cream dressing. Quarter tender hearts of head lettuce. Arrange all bouquet fashion. Drizzle salad hearts with herb vinaigrette. Garnish with chopped walnuts.

7.15 Vegetables

7.15.1 Basic Preparation Methods for Vegetables

It is the role of vegetables to provide the body with enough vitamins, minerals, and fiber. Vegetable preparation methods should keep losses of these important nutrients to a minimum. Table 7-85 illustrates how these losses occur and how they can be prevented.

Vegetables are generally cooked with moist heating methods, because these methods preserve and enhance the vegetables' own flavor. For some special vegetable preparations, dry and moist heating methods are combined. Table 7-86 outlines the appropriate preparation methods for specific vegetables.

Blanching—BLANCHIEREN—*blanchier*

- *Mise en place* for many cooking methods
- Cooking method for leafy greens

Boil/Simmer—SIEDEN—*cuire*

- Boiling in acidulated water with flour and veal kidney fat—*cuisson des légumes dans un blanc*
- Simmering dry vegetables (legumes) —*cuisson des légumineuses*

Steaming—DÄMPFEN—*cuire à la vapeur*

- Steaming in a pan with perforated insert
- Steaming in a steamer
- Pressure-steaming—*cuisson sous vide*

Braising—SCHMOREN—*braiser*

Stewing—DÜNSTEN—*étuver*

Glazing—GLASIEREN—*glacer*

Baking au gratin—GRATINIEREN—*gratiner*

Deep-frying—FRITIEREN—*frire*

Sautéing—SAUTIEREN—*sauter*

Grilling—GRILLIEREN—*griller*

Table 7-85. Nutrient Losses and Prevention When Preparing Vegetables

Vitamins and minerals are lost	through contact with water	Cleaning Soaking Boiling
	through contact with oxygen	Storage
	through contact with heat	Cooking Holding
Vitamin and mineral losses are minimized when these steps are observed:	<ul><li>Prepare vegetables as soon as possible. Do not store long.</li><li>Store in the dark and refrigerated</li><li>Wash vegetables before cutting them into smaller pieces.</li><li>Do not leave cleaned vegetables in water. Cover with a damp cloth instead.</li><li>Blanch vegetables only when necessary.</li><li>Steam or stew vegetables. Boiling causes greater losses.</li><li>When boiling vegetables, start them in hot water.</li><li>Cook only small amounts in advance. Keeping vegetables warm will cause loss of nutrients, color, and texture.</li><li>The soaking liquid of legumes should be used in the cooking process, since it contains soluble nutrients.</li></ul>	

Table 7-86. Vegetable Preparation Methods

(The preparation methods printed in **bold** are especially well-suited for a particular vegetable.)

Vegetable	*Mise en place*	Preparation Methods
Artichokes– ARTISCHOCKEN– *artichauts*	Wash artichokes. Carefully break off stems, pulling tough fibers from the flower bottom. Remove the small lower leaves and cut off leaf tips. Cut a little off the bottom (to make it flat), rub with lemon juice.	• **Simmer** • Steam • Pressure steam
Artichoke bottoms– ARTISCHOCKEN-BÖDEN– *fonds d'artichauts*	See photo series later in this chapter	• **Simmer in acid/flour water** • **Pressure-steam**
Asparagus (white)– SPARGEL– *asperges*	Start peeling *white* asparagus near the tip with an asparagus peeler, and peel thinly all around. Rinse in cold water, bundle, and cut off ends so they are uniform in length. Use end cuts to make asparagus stock for soups. *Green* asparagus needs little peeling; see photo series later in this chapter	• **Simmer** • Pressure steam • Gratinate • Steam
Belgian endive– BRÜSSELER-ENDIVIE– *chicorée*	Remove outer leaves if discolored or wilted. Remove core, which contains most of the bitter taste, with a sharp, pointed knife. Rinse.	• Blanch • **Simmer in acid/flour water** • **Pressure steam** • Braise • **Sauté** • Gratinate
Beets– RANDEN– *betteraves rouges*	Peel raw beets with a peeler. Cut into barrel shapes (turn) or sticks. Rub skin off boiled beets with your hands. Cut whole beets into slices or sticks.	• Glaze • Simmer • Steam
Broccoli– SPARGELKOHL– *brocoli*	Remove leaves. Separate the head from the stem. Cut into 2-inch (5–6-cm) pieces (peel if necessary). Wash carefully. Stem and long side branches can be peeled, trimmed, and used in soups.	• Blanch • Simmer • **Steam** • **Pressure-steam** • Deep-fry • Gratinate
Brussels sprouts– ROSENKOHL– *chou de Bruxelles*	Remove bruised or wilted leaves. Cut base short to keep the leaves together. Cut a cross in stem to facilitate even cooking.	• Blanch • Simmer → **Sauté** • **Steam** • Stew
Carrots– KAROTTEN– *carottes*	*Tender young carrots:* Remove tops. Blanch in boiling water 2 minutes. Drain, and rub off loose skin under cold running water. *Stored carrots:* Peel with vegetable peeler or scraper. Cut into barrel shapes (turn), slices, or sticks.	• Blanch • Simmer • Pressure steam • Steam • **Glaze**
Cardoons– KARDY– *cardons*	Remove any leaves and thorns, cut out dark spots. Peel from stem end upward to remove tough strings with vegetable peeler. Wash, and place in lemon juice and water.	• Blanch • **Simmer in acid/flour water** • Gratinate
Cauliflower– BLUMENKOHL– *chou-fleur*	Cut off bottom stem and leaves. Place whole heads in salted cold water to remove any insects; rinse well. Cut a cross into stem for whole heads. Or separate the head into small florets (soaking in salt water not necessary).	• Blanch • Simmer • **Steam** • **Pressure-steam** • Deep-fry • Gratinate
Celeriac/knob celery– SELLERIE– *céleri-rave*	Brush well with a stiff brush in lots of water. Peel with a vegetable peeler, trim roots with knife, and place immediately into lemon juice and water, to prevent oxidizing. Knob celery can also be cooked in the skin. Cut knob in half and cook, or cut into barrel shapes (turning) or sticks.	• Blanch • **Simmer** • **Pressure-steam** • Simmer in acid/flour water • **Glaze**

Table 7-86. Vegetable Preparation Methods (continued)

(The preparation methods printed in **bold** are especially well-suited for a particular vegetable.)

Vegetable	Mise en place	Preparation Methods
Celery— BLEICHSELLERIE— céleri en branches	Remove leaves and reserve (for vegetable bundles/mirepoix). Cut across bottom end. Remove any strings from the outer stems with vegetable peeler. Spread the stalks, and rinse well. Cook bunches whole or cut into halves.	• Blanch • **Braise** • Simmer • Pressure-steam • Gratinate
Corn— ZUCKERMAIS— epi de maïs	Remove leaves and silk from fresh cobs, break off stem ends. Rinse well. Corn on the cob can also be cooked very well in the microwave without removing leaves or silk. To remove kernels, remove leaves and silk. Hold onto the stem end, and cut off kernels with a sharp chef's knife.	**Cobs:** • Simmer • Steam • Wrap in foil, grill **Kernels:** • Simmer • Steam
Cucumber— GURKEN— concombres	Wash. If used as a vegetable, peel, cut in half, and scoop out seeds. Peel cucumbers from the center toward the blossom end and stem end. Check ends for bitterness. Cut into barrel shapes (turn) or sticks or prepare for stuffing.	• **Glaze** • **Stew** • Gratinate (stuffed)
Eggplant— AUBERGINEN— aubergines	Rinse, cut off stem end (peel if desired). Cut into slices, cubes, or sticks. To stuff: Cut small eggplants in half, make several incisions in the cut surface, brush with olive oil. Bake. Scoop out soft flesh with a spoon, and use for stuffing.	• Stew • Deep-fry • **Sauté** • Gratinate (stuffed)
Fennel— FENCHEL— fenouil	Cut stems ½ inch (1–2 cm) above bulb. Use fennel leaves as a flavoring. Cut slice off stem end, and cut cross into bottom. Use an asparagus peeler to peel away outer layer. Wash well. Cut large bulbs in half.	• Blanch • **Braise** • Simmer • **Pressure-steam** • Gratinate
Green beans— GRÜNE BOHNEN— haricots verts	Trim both ends, remove any strings, pulling from stem to top. Rinse. Cut large beans into pieces.	• Blanch • **Braise** • **Simmer → Sauté** • **Steam → Sauté**
Green cabbage— WEISSKOHL— chou blanc	Remove tough outer leaves. Cut heads into wedges, starting at the core. Remove cores from wedges, and trim or cut out any thick ribs. Rinse wedges. Cut according to recipe	• Braise • Steam • Stuff → Braise
Jerusalem artichoke— TOPINAMBOUREN— topinambours	Brush under running water, and clean well. Peel with an asparagus peeler. Scratch peel out of cracks with a knife. Keep in water until needed.	• Simmer • Sauté (cooked, coarsely grated) • Gratinate
Kohlrabi— KOHLRABI— chou-raves	Remove leaves from bulb. Stem tender leaves and reserve for other uses. Peel from root end to top. Cut off any woody parts. Cut into barrel shapes (turn), slices (cut large bulbs in half), or sticks.	• **Simmer** • **Steam** • Pressure-steam • **Glaze** (tender small bulbs)
Leeks— LAUCH— poireaux	Cut off root end, and remove outer leaves. Split in half lengthwise. Rinse well under running water.	• Blanch • **Simmer** • Stew • **Braise** • Gratinate
Onions— ZWIEBELN— oignons	Remove root end and tip of pearl onions, blanch 1 minute in boiling water to loosen the peel. Drain and cool, pull off peel, and remove thin skin covering. Peel large onions; blanch and core for stuffing.	• Blanch • Glaze • Braise (stuffed)
Parsnips— PASTINAKEN— panais	Wash and peel, same as carrots.	• Simmer • **Glaze**

Table 7-86. Vegetable Preparation Methods (continued)

(The preparation methods printed in **bold** are especially well-suited for a particular vegetable.)

Vegetable	*Mise en place*	Preparation Methods
Peas— ERBSEN— *petits pois*	Shell peas, and rinse. Fresh peas undergo color and flavor changes rapidly when in contact with oxygen and should be prepared immediately.	• Blanch • **Simmer** • **Steam** • Stew
Peppers— PEPERONI— *piments doux*	Wash, cut in half, remove stem and seeds. Rinse. For stuffing, choose large, thick-walled peppers.	• **Stew** • Steam • Gratinate (stuffed)
Red cabbage— ROTKOHL— *chou rouge*	Remove tough outer leaves. Cut heads into wedges, starting at the core. Remove cores from wedges, and trim or cut out any thick ribs. Cut into fine strips or use a mandolin; marinate if desired.	• **Braise**
Romaine— LATTICH— *laitue romaine*	Remove tough outer leaves. Trim stem end short to keep leaves attached. Dip into water, holding head at stem end. Repeat several times to be sure all sand has been rinsed out.	• Blanch • **Braise** (stuffed) • Steam
Savoy cabbage— WIRSING— *chou frisé*	Remove tough outer leaves. Cut heads into wedges, starting at the core. Remove cores from wedges, and trim or cut out any thick ribs. Rinse very well, as the loose-leaf head and curly leaf structure make good hiding places for pests.	• Blanch • Braise • Steam • Stuff → Braise
Salsify— SCHWARZWURZELN— *scorsonères/salsifis*	Wash roots in cold water with a stiff brush to remove dirt. Peel with vegetable peeler, and place at once into lemon juice and water, to prevent oxidizing. Cut into 2-inch (4–5-cm) pieces.	• **Simmer in acid/flour water** • Gratinate • Deep-fry
Snow peas— KEFEN— *pois mange-tout*	Trim at both ends. If necessary, pull strings from stem end to tip. Rinse. Large (full) snow peas need to be shelled, and only the peas should be used.	• **Stew** • Steam • Pressure-steam • **Sauté**
Spinach— SPINAT— *epinards*	Clean spinach. Remove wilted or bruised leaves, tough stems, and any weeds. Wash several times in large amounts of water to remove pests and dirt. Drain well.	• Blanch • Stew • Sauté • Gratinate
Swiss chard— KRAUTSTIELE— *côtes de bette*	Place leaf side up, and cut off the green leaves, reserve, blanch, and prepare the same way as spinach. Cut stem at leaf top and pull off inside skin. Repeat on other side of stem. Wash the peeled stems, and cut into same-size rectangles.	• Blanch • **Simmer in acid/flour water** • Gratinate
Turnips— WEISSRÜBEN— *navets*	Use only tender, small turnips. Remove leaves and root ends. Wash and peel with vegetable peeler. Cut into barrel shapes (turn) or sticks	• Blanch • Simmer • **Glaze**
Zucchini— ZUCCHETTI— *courgettes*	Wash zucchini, and trim stem end. Tender young zucchini need no peeling. Large specimens must be peeled, because the skin tastes bitter. They also need seeding. Cut into barrel shapes (turn), slices, or sticks.	• Glaze • Sauté • Stew • Gratinate (stuffed) • Deep-fry

7.15.2 Blanch—BLANCHIEREN—*blanchir*

Blanching is not a classic basic preparation method but is used as a first step for further preparation of vegetables (freezing, short storage, or cooking).

Blanching can used for *mise en place* or for cooking certain vegetables.

Blanching as *mise en place:*
- to preserve the color (chlorophyll) or enhance it in green vegetables
- to reduce the volume of leafy greens (spinach, romaine)
- to change strong taste to milder (cabbage and root vegetables, fennel, celery, onions)
- to peel tomatoes
- to soften texture (cabbage and peppers for stuffing)
- to prevent oxidizing and discoloration during the cooking process (celery, cauliflower, fennel, cardoons)

Blanching to cook tender green vegetables (for example, leaf spinach, snow peas, and very tender young beans): This method is much the same as simmering, because the thin vegetables are cooked almost at once, and the same changes occur as when vegetables with a firmer structure are cooked. To enhance the taste of blanched vegetables, they are usually briefly sautéed in butter.

Mise en place for Freezing

Green Beans

YIELD: 10 SERVINGS		
Water	1 gal, 1¼ qt	5 L
Salt	1⅔ oz	50 g
Green beans	2 lb, 3 oz	1 kg

Method
- Bring lightly salted water to a boil.
- Add the trimmed beans.
- Return to a boil. Drain.
- Chill the beans quickly in ice water.
- Drain well.
- Spread on sheet pans, chill in cooler briefly, then freeze.
- Vacuum-package, and store properly.

Salting the water prevents leaching.

Vegetables with a firmer texture should be blanched in 5 parts water to 1 part vegetables.

Prevention of Oxidation

Cardoons

YIELD: 10 SERVINGS		
Water	1 gal, 1¼ qt	5 L
Salt	1⅔ oz	50 g
Lemon juice	¾ oz	25 ml
Cardoons	2 lb, 3 oz	1 kg

Method
- Bring lightly salted water to a boil.
- Add the lemon juice and prepared cardoons.
- Return to a boil. Drain.
- Chill the cardoons quickly in cold or ice water.
- Drain well.
- Keep chilled until needed.

As a Cooking Process

Spinach

YIELD: 10 SERVINGS		
Water	2 gal, 2½ qt	10 L
Salt	1⅔ oz	50 g
Spinach	2 lb, 3 oz	1 kg

Method
- Bring lightly salted water to a boil.
- Add the cleaned, well-drained spinach
- Return to a boil. Drain.
- Chill the spinach quickly in cold or ice water.
- Drain well.
- Keep chilled until needed.

7.15.3 Boiling/Simmering
–SIEDEN–*cuire*

Boiling/simmering is a moist-heat cooking method, which causes vegetables to

- change texture, making digestion of nutrients possible
- retain their inherent flavor or reduce strong flavors

The shortest cooking time preserves the most flavor and nutrients. Therefore:

- Add the vegetables to boiling water.
- Return to a full boil as quickly as possible
- Reduce temperature immediately to below boiling to preserve color and texture.

The vegetable is cooked when it is crisp-tender and has "bite" (*al dente*). Overcooking causes vegetables to lose large amounts of vitamins and minerals and reduces flavor. When determining the point of doneness, remember to consider whether the vegetable will be cooked further for the final preparation of a dish.

Cauliflower, white asparagus, knob celery, and carrots are kept in cooking liquid and tend to continue to cook. Further cooking can be interrupted with the addition of ice cubes.

Broccoli and caulibroc, if not immediately prepared further, must be removed from the hot liquid, and placed in cold salted water to chill. They can be returned to the cooled cooking liquid when chilled.

Tender vegetables should not be cooked in large quantities, as it takes too long to bring them back to a full boil, resulting in nutrient and flavor loss. Blanch such vegetables in batches.

Cooking liquids should be used. For example they can be added to soups or used for reheating vegetables. Mild flavored liquids can be reduced and added to flavor a vegetable sauce (cauliflower with a cream sauce, kohlrabi with a white sauce [velouté] with herbs).

Check legumes for stones and blemishes. Rinse well. Soaking is not essential with fresh product but still helpful. They will absorb liquid if soaked for 2 to 8 hours, covered with two to three times their volume of cold water. Soaking shortens the cooking time, allows starch to expand properly, and makes legumes more digestible. The soaking liquid, which contains nutrients, is used for cooking.

Frozen vegetables such as cauliflower, broccoli, peas, beans, etc. are cooked in their frozen state.

The three ways to boil/simmer vegetables:

Boiling/Simmering in Salt Water

Kohlrabi

YIELD: 10 SERVINGS		
Kohlrabi	2 lb, 10 oz	1.2 kg
Water	3 qt, 5 oz	3 L
Salt		

Mise en place
- Clean and peel kohlrabi.
- Cut according to recipe requirements or leave whole.

Method
- Bring lightly salted water to a boil.
- Add kohlrabi, bring quickly to a boil, skim.

- Reduce to simmer and cook until done.
- Cool in cooking liquid.

Boiling/Simmering in Acid/Flour Water

Swiss Chard Stems

YIELD: 10 SERVINGS		
Swiss chard	4 lb	1.8 kg
Water	2 qt, 4 oz	2 L
Salt		
Lemon juice	¾ oz	25 ml
All-purpose flour	1⅔ oz	50 g
Veal kidney fat	1⅔ oz	50 g

Mise en place
- Remove leaves from Swiss chard.
- Blanch leaves and reserve.
- Peel off skin from stems, from leaf top to bottom.
- Cut stems into same-size rectangles.
- Blanch in salted boiling water with a little lemon juice.
- Stir the flour into a little water to make a slurry.

Method
- Bring the acidulated water and kidney fat to a boil.
- Stir in the flour slurry.
- Add the chard stems, and bring to a boil.
- Reduce to a simmer, and cook until done.
- Leave in liquid until needed.

Boiling/Simmering Legumes

Lentils

YIELD: 10 SERVINGS		
Lentils	1 lb, 5 oz	600 g
Water	2 qt, 21 oz	2.5 L
Bouquet garni	7 oz	200 g
Onion, studded with 1 bay leaf and 3 cloves	1	1
Bacon rinds		
Salt		

Mise en place
- Check lentils for stones, and rinse.
- Soak for 4 to 8 hours.
- Prepare a *bouquet garni*.

Method
- Start to cook lentils in soaking liquid.

- Bring to a boil. Skim.
- Add the *bouquet garni*, studded onion, and bacon rinds.
- Cover, and simmer until soft.
- Add salt, and let cool in the liquid.
- Rinse the lentils in lukewarm water before further preparation.

Simmered Vegetable Dishes

White asparagus with Parmesan cheese – SPARGELN MAILÄNDER ART – *asperges milanaise*

Artichokes with hollandaise sauce – ARTISCHOCKEN MIT HOLLÄNDISCHER SAUCE – *artichauts à la sauce hollandaise*

Knob celery with fresh herbs – SELLERIE MIT FRISCHEN KRÄUTERN – *céleri-rave aux fines herbes*

Brussels sprouts with butter – ROSENKOHL MIT BUTTER – *choux de Bruxelles anglaise*

Kohlrabi with butter – KOHLRABI MIT BUTTER – *choux-raves au beurre*

Corn kernels with butter – MAISKÖRNER MIT BUTTER – *grains de maïs au beurre*

7.15.4 Steaming – DÄMPFEN – *cuire à la vapeur*

Steaming vegetables retains many of their nutrients, because the vegetables are not in direct contact with water. Steaming under pressure reduces cooking time, resulting in even lower vitamin and mineral losses. Convection steaming reduces cooking times only marginally.

Holding and preparation methods for steamed vegetables are the same as for simmered vegetables.

Suitable for steaming are all vegetables with a firm cell structure, for example, carrots, knob celery, kohlrabi, cauliflower, broccoli, fennel, artichokes, artichoke bottoms, and peas. Less suitable are romaine, spinach, bell peppers, white asparagus, eggplant, zucchini, and mushrooms.

Almost all fresh vegetables can be

cooked in vacuum bags, except leafy vegetables.

Steaming without Pressure
- Steaming in a pot with a perforated insert
- Steaming in a combi unit (convection oven with steam)
- In the United States atmospheric steamers – convection steamers without pressure – are also used
- Steaming in vacuum bags (*cuisson sous vide*).

Steaming with Pressure
- Steaming in a pressure cooker
- Steaming in a commercial steamer

More and more kitchens take advantage of steam equipment today. When using commercial steamers, it is important to pay close attention to the manufacturers' instructions. Steamers use various methods and operate with different pressures, which affect cooking temperature and timing.

Steaming Vegetables in a Commercial Steamer

Cooking in a steamer is done with higher temperatures and various degrees of pressure.

Pressure and cooking temperatures:

Low-pressure steamer, U.S. 5 psi (0.5 bar) = 225° to 230°F (108° to 110°C)

High-pressure steamer, U.S. 15 psi (1.0 bar) = 225° to 248°F (108° to 120°C)

Method
- Properly prepared vegetables are put into inserts (4-inch-deep or 2-inch-deep solid or perforated) and seasoned.
- They are steamed until they reach the desired consistency. Manufacturer's directions should be followed closely.

The Cooking Time is Affected by
- The *quality of product*: vegetables are fresh, dried, or frozen, tender or mature.
- the *cut size*: the smaller the size, the more quickly the vegetable will be cooked; equal size is important

- the *texture:* dense or open cell structure, plus the water content of the vegetable
- the *selected pressure:* low-pressure steamers operate at 5 psi, high-, at 15 psi.

Finishing

The steamed vegetables can be finished with various basic preparation methods, for example, sautéing, deep-frying, or baking au gratin.

Cooking with steam equipment requires a mental adjustment on the part the cook. To get good results, the cook has to follow manufacturer's instruction but at the same time use the equipment appropriately to meet the special needs of the operation. This may mean experimenting with methods and times that serve the operation to its best advantage. *The cook must control the equipment, and not the equipment the cook.*

Cooking in Vacuum Bags

This method cooks and preserves (pasteurizes) foods in boil-safe vacuum bags at food-specific temperatures.

The cooking temperature for vegetables, fruits, mushrooms, and potatoes is 203° to 208° F (95° to 98°C).

Process

- The properly prepared raw vegetables are seasoned, packed with a little butter into the boil-in bags, and vacuum-sealed.
- The bags are cooked at about 205°F (96°C) in a water bath or combi steamer.
- Cooking the vegetables in the vacuum bags takes about 10 to 15 percent longer because the temperature is below the boiling point.
- The bags are chilled quickly in ice water, to about 34° to 37°F (1° to 3°C).
- The vacuum-cooked vegetables can be stored in their bags at 34° to 37°F (1° to 3°C) for up to two weeks.

Finishing/Reconstituting

Reconstituting the vegetables is best

done in the vacuum bag, using the same equipment that was used in the bagging process. However, the vegetables can also be finished using any suitable basic preparation method, such as sautéing, deep-frying, or baking au gratin.

To use vacuum-packing effectively, it is essential that the chef experiment intensely with it, in order to fit it to the needs of the operation with best results.

Keeping careful records of the steps used and their results is vital to achieving consistent success.

7.15.5 Braising–SCHMOREN–*braiser* Stewing–DÜNSTEN–*étuver*

Braised and stewed vegetables are cooked slowly in very small amounts of liquid.

Unlike the boiling or steaming process, in which vegetables are supposed to cook as quickly as possible to retain nutrients, taste, and texture, braising and stewing are slow cooking methods, in which the flavors of individual ingredients blend with each other to produce a unified taste. The cooking liquid will absorb most of the vegetables' flavor; however, this is not detrimental, because the liquid is an integral part of the whole vegetable dish.

Flavorings

Braised or stewed vegetable dishes require additional flavorings. Romaine, fennel, and Belgian endive are cooked with a *matignon*, bacon, and veal kidney fat, which impart not only a great taste, but also a lovely gloss. Other vegetables may be flavored with finely chopped onion, garlic, or fresh herbs. These ingredients can be used alone or in combination. A touch of sugar is sometimes added to reduce bitter flavors and to glaze the vegetables.

Cooking Liquids

The choice of cooking liquid influences the final flavor of the dish. Veal stock, vegetable stock, or light-col-

ored bouillon is used for fennel, romaine, and celery stalks. Wine and bouillon are used to braise red cabbage and sauerkraut. Brown stock and bouillon are used to braise and stew stuffed vegetables, such as bell peppers, cabbage, onions, and tomatoes.

Usage

Braising is frequently used to cook cabbage varieties, romaine lettuce, celery stalks, Belgian endive, and fennel. It is also the method most often used for stuffed cabbage, cabbage rolls, stuffed peppers, onions, and patty-pan squash.

Stewing is mainly used for vegetable varieties with a high water content, such as tomatoes, mushrooms, zucchini, cucumbers, snow peas, and peppers.

The distinction between braised and stewed vegetables is fluid. The choice depends mostly on the texture of the vegetable.

Braising–SCHMOREN–*braiser*

Fennel–FENCHEL–*fenouil*

YIELD: 10 SERVINGS		
Fennel	4 lb, 6 oz	2 kg
Matignon	7 oz	200 g
Veal kidney fat	1⅔ oz	50 g
Butter	⅔ oz	20 g
Bacon rind	1⅔ oz	50 g
Salt, pepper		
Bouillon	1 qt, 2 oz	1 L

Mise en place

- Wash the fennel, trim, peel, and cut a cross into the stem bottom. Cut in half if large.
- Blanch in lightly salted water.
- Prepare the *matignon.*
- Dice the veal kidney fat.

Method

- Butter a suitable shallow saucepan.
- Add the *matignon,* veal kidney fat, and bacon rind. Sauté briefly.
- Place the fennel on top.
- Season, and add the bouillon to cover fennel by about one-third.
- Place buttered foil on top, and weigh it down with a plate. Bring to a boil.

- Cover, and bake in the oven at 320°F (160°C) until done.
- Transfer the fennel to a shallow pan if not using immediately. Strain and cool the stock.

Stewing – DÜNSTEN – *étuver*

Snow Peas – KEFEN – *pois mange-tout*

YIELD: 10 SERVINGS		
Snow peas	3 lb, 5 oz	1.5 kg
Shallots	3½ oz	100 g
Bacon	3½ oz	100 g
Butter	3 oz	80 g
Salt, pepper		
Vegetable bouillon	6¾ oz	200 ml

Mise en place
- Wash and trim the snow peas.
- Blanch if desired, chill in ice water, and drain.
- Finely chop the shallots.
- Dice the bacon into small cubes.

Method
- Sauté the shallots and bacon in the butter in a suitable shallow pan.
- Add the snow peas, cook briefly, and season.
- Add the vegetable bouillon.
- Cover, and cook slowly over medium heat.
- The snow peas should stay crisp. Serve at once or chill, or they will lose their bright green color.

Braised Vegetable Dishes

Braised fennel with beef marrow – GESCHMORTER FENCHEL MIT MARK – *fenouil braisé à la moelle*

Braised fennel with cheese – GESCHMORTER FENCHEL MIT KÄSE – *fenouil milanaise*

Cardoons with toasted bread crumbs – KARDY POLNISCHE ART – *cardons polonaise*

Braised red cabbage – GESCHMORTES ROTKRAUT – *chou rouge braisé*

Braised sauerkraut – GESCHMORTES SAUERKRAUT – *choucroute braisée*

Braised Belgian endive – GESCHMORTE BRÜSSELER ENDIVIEN – *endives braisées*

Stewed Vegetable Dishes

Carrots Vichy – VICHY-KAROTTEN – *carottes Vichy*

Baby peas with lettuce and pearl onions – JUNGE ERBSEN MIT ZWIEBELN UND SALAT – *petits pois française*

Fresh stewed tomatoes – GEDÜNSTETE TOMATENWÜRFEL – *tomates concassés*

Zucchini Provençale – ZUCCHETTI MIT KRÄUTERN – *courgettes provençale*

Okra with tomatoes – OKRA MIT TOMATEN – *gombos aux tomates*

Ratatouille – GEMISCHTES GEMÜSE-GERICHT – *ratatouille*

Stuffed Braised Vegetables

Stuffed peppers – GEFÜLLTE PEPERONI – *poivrons doux farcis*

Stuffed cabbage – GEFÜLLTER KOHL – *chou farci*

Stuffed nappa cabbage roll – CHINA-KOHLROULADE – *roulade de chou chinois*

Stuffed Stewed Vegetables

Stuffed cucumbers – GEFÜLLTE GURKEN – *concombres farcies*

Stuffed tomatoes Provençale – GEFÜLLTE TOMATEN MIT KRÄUTERN UND MIE DE PAIN – *tomates farcies provençale*

Stuffed morels – GEFÜLLTE MORSCHELN – *morilles farcies*

7.15.6 Glazing – GLASIEREN – *glacer*

Vegetables are glazed with butter, sugar, and a small amount of liquid over low temperature. The vegetables become juicy and slightly sweet, with a glossy syrup clinging to them that remains even if all liquid is evaporated.

Glazing is suitable for firm vegetables that are high in carbohydrates (starch and dextrose), such as carrots, knob celery, parsnips, turnips, zucchini, pearl onions, and chestnuts.

Vegetables that have been boiled in salted water can be glazed in minutes in a skillet, tossed with butter and a little sugar. This quick method is especially suitable for zucchini, kohlrabi, turnips, and soft mixed vegetables. The taste of the classic method, of slowly glazing the vegetables, is of course far superior to the results of this quick method.

- Blanch older or stronger-flavored vegetables, as well as those that may oxidize. Use only small, unpeeled zucchini.
- For taste reasons, neither onions nor shallots are used for glazing vegetables. The liquid of choice is water. Reduced stock may discolor white vegetables and carrots.
- The goal of glazing is to intensify the vegetables' own flavor, not to introduce another.
- Onions can be glazed golden brown by first roasting them with a little sugar and then adding bouillon.
- When glazing chestnuts, the sugar is first caramelized and then dissolved in vegetable stock or water. The chestnuts and the butter are added and cooked until the chestnuts are tender and glazed.

Glaze with as little liquid as possible. Eliminate the water if the vegetable contains a lot of liquid and the cooking temperature is very low.

Glazed Carrots – GLASIERTE KAROTTEN – *carottes glacés*

YIELD: 10 SERVINGS		
Carrots	4 lb	1.8 kg
Butter	1⅓ oz	40 g
Sugar, pinch	1	1
Water	1 pt, 1 oz	500 ml
Salt		

Mise en place
- Clean and peel carrots and cut into barrel shapes (turn), slices, or sticks.
- Blanch if desired.

Method
- Butter a shallow skillet.
- Add the carrots and sugar.
- Sauté briefly.
- Add water just to cover the carrots.
- Season, and cover.

- Cook until tender; remove lid.
- Cook the liquid rapidly to a syrup, tossing carrots to glaze.

Glazed Vegetable Dishes

Glazed chestnuts – GLASIERTE KASTANIEN – *marrons glacés*

Glazed onions – GLASIERTE ZWIEBELN – *petits oignons glacés*

Glazed cucumbers – GLASIERTE GURKEN – *concombres glacés*

Glazed spring vegetables – KLEINE GLASIERTE GEMÜSE – *petits légumes glacés*

Glazed knob celery with herbs – GLASIERTER SELLERIE MIT KRÄUTERN – *céleri-rave glacé aux herbes*

Glazed patty-pan squash – KLEINE GLASIERTE BISCHOFSMÜTZEN – *petits patissons glacés*

Glazed parsnips with chives – GLASIERTE PASTERNAKEN MIT SCHNITTLAUCH – *panais glacés á la ciboulette*

7.15.7 Gratinating – GRATINIEREN – *gratiner*

Vegetable dishes that are gratinated in the oven or placed under the broiler at 480° to 575°F (250° to 300°C) have a crisp brown surface. Many cooked vegetable dishes are browned as a finishing touch. However, for many dishes, the crispy brown crust becomes its major attraction.

- To achieve a dry crisp topping, the vegetables are sprinkled with cheese and fresh bread crumbs *(mie de pain)* that are flavored with fresh herbs. They are then drizzled with melted butter and baked au gratin in the salamander (broiler) or a very hot oven.
- A juicy soft crust produced by topping the vegetable dish with a Mornay sauce (cheese) and then placing it in the oven. A better crust results from placing the dish in the oven, rather than under the broiler. Cooked cold vegetables can be used with this method.
- When a butter sauce is poured over cooked broccoli, cauliflower, or asparagus, the process is called glazing.

Variations of the Browning (Gratinating) Method

Dry Gratinating

Grated cheese, fresh bread crumbs, chopped herbs, and butter are used to gratinate cauliflower, celery, and stuffed vegetables (zucchini, eggplant, cucumbers, tomatoes, mushrooms).

Moist Gratinating or Glazing under the Broiler

Mornay sauce (cheese), tomato concassée with cheese, or butter sauces are used to gratinate cooked vegetables such as cauliflower, knob celery, kohlrabi, broccoli, Belgian endive, celery, and asparagus.

Gratinated Vegetable Casseroles

Here the sauce is a major ingredient. The base is a cream sauce or a white vegetable sauce, which is enriched with heavy cream, cheese, egg yolk, or hollandaise sauce. The vegetables are generally folded into the sauce. Gratinated vegetables are cooked at medium heat in the oven and broiled briefly at the end. Examples include gratinated Swiss chard stems, gratinated salsify, and gratinated Belgian endive.

Stuffed Tomatoes Provençale – TOMATEN MIT KRÄUTERN UND MIE DE PAIN – *tomates farcies provençale*

YIELD: 10 SERVINGS		
Tomatoes (10)	*2 lb, 10 oz*	*1.2 kg*
Butter	*⅔ oz*	*20 g*
Salt and pepper		
Stuffing		
Anchovy fillets, canned, drained	*⅔ oz*	*20 g*
Onions	*3½ oz*	*100g*
Garlic	*⅓ oz*	*10 g*
Parsley	*1 oz*	*30 g*
Thyme, fresh	*⅓ oz*	*10 g*
Oregano, fresh	*⅓ oz*	*10 g*
Olive oil, cold pressed	*3⅓ oz*	*100 ml*
Fresh bread crumbs	*5⅓ oz*	*150 g*
Salt, pepper		
Gratin		
Grated cheese (Sbrinz)	*1⅔ oz*	*50 g*
Butter	*1⅔ oz*	*50 g*

Mise en place

- Soak the anchovy fillets, dry, and chop.
- Wash the tomatoes, remove the stem ends, and halve cross-wise.
- Scoop the pulp out lightly.
- Season. Place cut side up in an oven-proof buttered dish.
- Finely chop the onions and garlic.
- Wash the herbs, strip the leaves from the stems, and chop finely.

Method

- Sauté the onions and garlic in the olive oil.
- Add the fresh bread crumbs *(mie de pain)*, herbs, and anchovies. Season.
- Stuff the tomatoes with the mixture.
- Sprinkle with the grated cheese, and dot with bits of butter.
- Bake with high heat from above until done.

Gratinated Swiss Chard Stems – KRAUTSTIEL GRATIN – *gratin de côtes de bette*

YIELD: 10 SERVINGS		
Swiss chard	*4 lb, 7 oz*	*2 kg*
Shallots	*¾ oz*	*25 g*
Garlic	*1 tsp*	*5 g*
Lemon juice	*¾ oz*	*25 ml*
All-purpose flour	*1⅔ oz*	*50 g*
Veal kidney fat	*1⅔ oz*	*50 g*
Salt		
Butter	*¾ oz*	*25 g*
Sauce		
Béchamel sauce	*10 oz*	*300 ml*
Heavy cream	*3½ oz*	*100 ml*
Grated cheese (Sbrinz)	*1⅔ oz*	*50 g*
Salt, pepper, nutmeg		
Gratin		
Grated cheese (Sbrinz)	*1⅔ oz*	*50 g*
Butter	*1⅔ oz*	*50 g*

Mise en place

- Wash the Swiss chard.
- Trim the leaves of the chard. Blanch leaves, chill in ice water, drain, chop coarsely, and reserve.
- Chop the shallots and garlic.
- Peel the skin from the chard stems from leaf top to bottom. Cut the stems into same-size rectangles.

- Simmer the stems in acid/flour water with veal kidney fat until done. Drain.
- Sauté the chopped leaves in the butter, garlic, and shallots. Season.

Method
- Butter a gratin dish.
- Enrich the béchamel sauce with the cream and cheese.
- Add the drained stems to the sauce, and season with salt, pepper, and nutmeg.
- Pour half the sauced stems in the gratin dish, top with the sautéed leaves, and cover with the rest of the sauce.
- Sprinkle with the cheese, and dot with the butter.
- Bake slowly in the oven.

Gratinated Vegetable Dishes
Cauliflower au gratin – GRATINIERTER BLUMENKOHL – chou-fleur Mornay

Leeks au gratin – GRATINIERTER LAUCH – poireaux gratinés

Belgian endive au gratin – BRÜSSELER-ENDIVIEN-GRATIN – gratin de chicorée

Eggplant au gratin – AUBERGINEN-GRATIN – gratin d'aubergines

7.15.8 Deep-fry – FRITIEREN – frire

Firm vegetables, such as cauliflower, broccoli, salsify, and knob celery, must be cooked before they can be deep-fried. Vegetables with a soft texture and a high water content, such as zucchini, eggplant, and mushrooms, can be deep-fried raw. Table 7-87 lists various ways to deep-fry different vegetables.

- The vegetables are cut into slices, pieces, or rings, and are patted dry.
- To increase their flavor, they are marinated or seasoned.
- To handle large quantities during a very short service time, the vegetable can be partially fried at 285°F (140°C) beforehand. Finish cooking them to order at 355°F (180°C) until crisp.
- Deep-fried vegetables are drained well and served at once. Keeping them warm would make the coating soggy and less tasty. Serve deep-fried vegetables with lemon wedges and parsley.

Deep-fried Salsify – GEBACKENE SCHWARZWURZELN – scorsonéres frites

YIELD: 10 SERVINGS		
Salsify, cooked	2 lb, 3 oz	1 kg
Parsley	1 oz	30 g
Lemon juice	⅔ oz	20 ml
All-purpose flour	1⅔ oz	50 g
Salt, pepper		
Beer batter	1lb, 10 oz	750 g
Peanut oil for frying (10% oil loss)	3½ oz	100 ml

Mise en place
- Cut the cooked salsify into even pieces, and marinate in lemon juice.
- Wash the parsley, select 10 pretty sprigs for a garnish, and chop the rest.
- Mix flour with salt and pepper.

Method
- Flour the salsify pieces, and dip into the batter.
- Drip off the excess, and deep-fry at

355°F (180°C) until crisp. Drain well.
- Deep-fry the parsley sprigs until crisp, drain, and salt lightly.

7.15.9 Sautéing – SAUTIEREN – sauter

Vegetables that are sautéed in a shallow skillet (sauté pan – sauteuse) retain most of their taste and color. The vegetables must be carefully prepared and watched during cooking, because they are exposed to very high heat during sautéing.

Suitable pans for sautéing are frying pans, nonstick pans, and for flipping vegetables while sautéing, a sauté pan with sloping sides (sauteuse).

The methods for sautéing vegetables are oulined in Table 7-88.

Moist Sautéing
Steel pans should be avoided, or a great deal of vitamin C will be destroyed.

- Sautéing blanched or already cooked vegetables (leafy vegetables, tender green beans, snow peas, Brussels sprouts): Blanch first or cook until almost tender.
- Sautéing raw vegetables or mushrooms: Wash mushrooms, trim, drain, cut into strips or slices. Cut eggplant and zucchini into barrel shapes (turn) or slices.

Dry Sautéing
- Sautéing raw vegetables: Sauté vegetables cut into barrel shapes (turn), cubes, or slices in hot fat,

Table 7-87. Various Ways to Deep-fry Vegetables

Coating	Use for	Method
Flour	Eggplant slices, bell pepper rings, onion rings	Marinate, season with salt, flour, tap off excess, deep-fry
Egg	Eggplant and zucchini slices	Marinate, season with salt, flour, tap off excess, dip into beaten egg, drip off excess, deep-fry
Fresh or dry bread crumbs	Mushrooms, knob celery,* asparagus*	Marinate, season with salt, flour, tap off excess, dip into egg white, bread, press firmly, deep-fry
Batter (beer or wine)	Broccoli,* green asparagus,* salsify,* cauliflower,* mushrooms	Marinate, flour, tap off excess, dip in batter, drip off excess, deep-fry

*Cook before deep-frying.

Table 7-88. Sautéing Vegetables

Principle	Suitable for	Method
Sauté without browning		Sauté in butter, clarified butter, olive oil.
Moist sautéing	Leaf spinach,* snow peas,* chard stems,* Brussels sprouts,* green beans*	Sauté shallots (garlic) in fat, add vegetables, sauté briefly, and season.
Dry sautéing	Zucchini, eggplant, carrots	If desired, sauté shallots and garlic, add vegetables, and sauté quickly; by constantly flipping the vegetables, they should stay dry.
Sauté with browning		
Sautéing coated		Butter only (slowly), clarified butter, or first oil and then butter.
Floured	Belgian endives,* knob celery,* eggplant, zucchini	Season or marinate, dry, flour, tap off excess, do not sauté too hot, brown lightly.
Dip in egg or egg with cheese	Knob celery,* fennel,* eggplant, zucchini, pumpkin	Marinate, flour, tap off excess, dip into beaten egg, drip off excess, sauté slowly.
Fresh bread crumbs or dry bread crumbs	Knob celery,* fennel,* carrots,* leeks*	Marinate, salt, flour, tap off excess, dip into beaten egg white, dip into fresh bread crumbs, press firmly, sauté slowly until crisp.

*Precooked or blanched vegetables

flipping constantly, to intensify flavor through light browning. The vegetables should stay crisp.

- Sautéing dipped or breaded vegetables: Vegetables (raw or cooked) should be dried well before sautéing, to produce a crisp crust (moisture would prevent the crust from forming).

Moist Sautéing

Sautéed Leaf Spinach with Pine Nuts — SAUTIERTER BLATTSPINAT MIT PINIEN — *feuilles d'épinards aux pignons*

YIELD: 10 SERVINGS		
Spinach	4 lb, 7 oz	2 kg
Shallots	2⅔ oz	75 g
Garlic	⅓ oz	10 g
Butter	3 oz	80 g
Salt, pepper, nutmeg		
Pine nuts	3½ oz	100 g
Butter	1 oz	30 g

Mise en place
- Wash and blanch the leaf spinach, chill in ice water, and drain well.
- Finely chop the shallots and garlic.

Method
- In a shallow skillet, sauté the shallots and garlic in butter.
- Add the blanched spinach, sauté until hot, and season.

- Toast pine nuts in butter, and sprinkle over the plated spinach.

Dry Sautéing

Zucchini and Carrots with Thyme — ZUCCHETTI UND KAROTTEN MIT THYMIAN — *courgettes et carottes sautés au thym*

YIELD: 10 SERVINGS		
Tender carrots	2 lb, 3 oz	1 kg
Small zucchini	1 lb, 10 oz	750 g
Thyme	½ oz	15 g
Olive oil	3½ oz	100 ml
Salt, pepper		

Mise en place
- Wash and peel carrots, cut thinly, and blanch briefly.
- Wash the zucchini, trim, and cut into ⅛-inch (3-mm) disks.
- Remove the thyme leaves from the stems.

Method
- Heat the olive oil, and add the carrots.
- Sauté, flipping constantly, for 5 minutes.
- Add the zucchini and thyme, season, and sauté until done.
- The vegetables can brown lightly but must not draw liquid.

Sautéing Coated Vegetables

Knob Celery Piccata — SELLERIE-PICCATA — *piccata de céleri-rave*

YIELD: 10 SERVINGS		
Knob celery	3 lb, 5 oz	1.5 kg
Lemon	½	½
Salt, pepper		
All-purpose flour	1⅔ oz	50 g
Eggs	3	3
Grated cheese (Sbrinz)	2⅔ oz	75 g
Butter	3 oz	80 g
Tomato concassée	1 pt, 1 oz	500 ml

Mise en place
- Wash and peel the knob celery; cut in half.
- Slice the knob celery into ⅕-inch (5-mm) pieces, or use cutters for different shapes if desired.
- Cook in lemon juice and water until crisp-tender.
- Chill in ice water, and drain well; dry.
- Beat the eggs with the grated cheese until smooth.

Method
- Season the celery slices, and flour.
- Dip into egg/cheese mixture, and drip off any excess.
- Sauté slowly in the butter until crisp on both sides.
- Serve arranged atop hot tomato concassé.

Sautéed Vegetable Dishes

Sautéed Brussels sprouts – SAUTIERTER ROSENKOHL – *choux de Bruxelles sautés*

Sautéed cèpe mushrooms, Provençal syle – STEINPILZE MIT KNOBLAUCH – *cèpes provençale*

Sautéed spinach with sardines – SAUTIERTE BLATTSPINAT MIT SARDELLEN – *epinards italienne*

Sautéed green beens – SAUTIERTE BOHNEN – *haricots verts sautés*

Sautéed snow peas with bacon – SAUTIERTE KEFEN MIT SPECK – *pois marge-tout sautés au lard*

Sautéed pepper quarters – SAUTIERTE PEPERONI-ECKEN – *quartiers de poivrons doux sautés*

Egg-dipped eggplant with herbs – AUBERGINEN IM EL MIT KRÄUTERN – *aubergines romaine aux herbes*

Breaded celeriac with pepper purée – PANIERTE SELLERIE AUF PEPERONI-COULIS – *célerie-rave pane sure coulis de poivrons doux*

7.15.10 Grilling – GRILLIEREN – *griller*

Vegetables are exposed to a high, dry heat during grilling, which produces a crisp, brown surface and lovely flavor from the caramelized vegetable sugars.

Grilled vegetables are a popular side dish with charcoal-grilled meats during the summer months, but they play a minor role in classical cuisine.

- Cooking is done with charcoal, gas, or electric grills, and special grill pans.
- Vegetables that grill well are zucchini, eggplant, peppers, large flat mushroom caps, tomatoes, and corn on the cob, as well as scallions and large garlic cloves in foil.
- Regardless of which method is used, the vegetable must be prepared in such a way that it can cook fully without burning on the surface.

Mise en place

- Cut *zucchini* and small eggplant in half lengthwise, cut larger vegetables at an angle into approximately ½-inch (1.5-cm) slices. Slash the surface lightly to allow the heat to penetrate evenly. Sprinkle surfaces with fresh herbs, and drizzle with olive oil.
- Remove the stem end of *tomatoes*, cut a deep cross into the top, and push the quarters outward. Fill the opened center with chopped herbs and spices, and drizzle with olive oil.
- Wash, halve, stem, and seed *bell peppers*. Cut again into halves, and brush the inside with olive oil.
- Sprinkle *mushroom caps* with pepper, and brush with olive oil.
- Pull down the leaves of fresh *corn cobs*, remove silk, and pull leaves back up; secure with string at the top (to prevent the kernels from touching the grill). Place the corn cobs in water for 30 minutes to ensure that the kernels stay moist and juicy. Drain well, and grill, turning several times. Another method is to remove the leaves, brush the corn with oil, and wrap in foil.
- Peel small *onions* and large *garlic cloves*, season, brush with oil, and wrap in foil.

Method

- Blot excess oil or marinade. Season.
- Place the better side of the vegetable face-down on the hot grill rack.
- Adjust the position with a spatula after a few moments at about a 60-degree angle, to create grill markings.
- Brush the top with oil, and turn over; repeat marking procedure.
- Cook the vegetables over medium heat until a knife point can be easily inserted. Larger and thicker pieces may need to be placed on foil to finish cooking.

Table 7-89. Finishing Vegetables

English style, with butter – *anglaise*	Dot the cooked vegetables with bits of butter.
With butter – *au beurre*	Pour foaming hot butter over finished vegetables.
With marrow – *bordelaise*	Pour a little red-wine sauce over vegetables, top with blanched marrow slices or cubes, sprinkle with parsley.
Stuffed with peas – *Clamart*	Fill with creamed peas or a green pea purée.
With cream sauce – *à la crème*	Pour a liitle cream sauce or reduced seasoned cream over vegetables.
With fried bread cubes – *aux croûtons*	Top cooked vegetables with croutons.
With veal jus reduction – *demi-glace*	Finish by pouring a little demi-glace over vegetables.
With puff-pastry crescents – *aux fleurons*	Arrange puff-pastry crescents around plated vegetables.
With grated cheese – *milanaise*	Sprinkle with grated cheese (Sbrinz, Parmesan), drizzle with melted butter, and glaze.
With cheese sauce – *Mornay*	Pour Mornay sauce (cream- and cheese-enriched white sauce) over vegetables, dot with butter, and bake au gratin.
Polish style – *polonaise*	Sauté fresh bread crumbs (*mie de pain*) in butter, add chopped eggs and fresh herbs, pour over vegetables.
With fresh herbs – *provençale*	Combine chopped parsley and other fresh herbs with garlic, fresh bread crumbs, and olive oil. Either stuff vegetables with this mixture and broil, or sauté the mixture and sprinkle over vegetables.
With white sauce – *au velouté*	Reduce vegetable cooking liquids, add to white sauce, and pour over vegetables or fold in.

346 M E T H O D S   A N D   T E C H N I Q U E S

7.15.11 Basic Vegetable Preparation and Presentation Methods

Table 7-89 lists classical ways to finish vegetable dishes. Table 7-90 lists the vegetables to use with each finishing method.

Stuffed Vegetables — GEFÜLLTE GEMÜSE — *légumes farcis*

Vegetables are cleaned, trimmed, and sliced. They can be left raw or they can be blanched or partially cooked, and then stuffed. To complete cooking, they can be braised, stewed, or baked au gratin.

There are many ways to stuff vegetables. Table 7-91 provides some suggestions.

Table 7-90. Finishes for Vegetable Dishes

	anglaise	au beurre	bordelaise	à la crème	aux croûtons	demi-glace	aux fleurons	gratiné	milanaise	Mornay	polonaise	au velouté	Clamart	provençale	farci
Artichoke — ARTISCHOKE — *archaut*			●										●		●
Asparagus — SPARGEL — *asperge*	●	●		●				●	●	●	●	●			
Belgian endive — BRUSSELER ENDIVIE — *endive/chicorée*								●		●	●				
Beet roots — RANDEN — *betteraves rouges*	●	●													●
Broccoli — BROCCOLI/SPARGELKOHL — *brocoli*	●	●								●	●				
Brussels sprouts — ROSENKOHL — *choux de Bruxelles*	●	●		●											
Cabbage — WEISSKOHL/WEISSKABIS — *chou blanc*														●	
Carrots — KAROTTEN — *carottes*	●	●		●											
Cardoons — KARDY — *cardons*		●	●	●		●		●	●	●		●			
Cauliflower — BLUMENKOHL — *chou-fleur*	●	●						●	●		●				
Celeriac (knob celery) — KNOLLENSELLERIE — *célerie-rave*	●	●		●		●		●	●	●	●				●
Celery stalk — STANGENSELLERIE — *célerie en branches*	●	●	●			●		●		●					
Chinese cabbage — CHINAKOHL — *chou de chinois*															●
Corn kernels — SÜSSMAISKÖRNER — *sweet corn*		●		●								●		●	
Corn on the cob — MAISKOLBEN — *épis de mais*		●													
Cucumbers — GURKEN — *concombres*		●		●								●			●
Eggplant — AUBERGINEN/EIERFRUCHT — *aubergines*								●		●					●
Fennel — FENSCHEL — *fenouil*		●	●			●		●	●		●	●			
Green beans — BOHNEN — *haricots vert*	●	●													
Jerusalem artichokes — TOPINAMBUR — *topinambours*		●		●				●			●				
Kohlrabi — KOHLRABI — *chou-raves*	●	●		●								●	●		●
Leeks — LAUCH — *poireaux*				●					●	●					●
Mushrooms, button — CHAMPIGNONS — *champignons*												●		●	●
Morels — MORSCHELN — *morilles*				●											●
Okra — LADYFINGER — *gombo*		●													
Onions — ZWIEBELN — *oignons*															●
Parsnips — PASTINAKEN — *panais*		●													
Peas — ERBSEN — *petits pois*	●	●										●			
Peppers — PEPERONI — *poivrons doux*															●
Porcini — STEINPILZE — *cèpes*			●	●								●		●	
Romaine — LATTICH — *laitue*			●			●		●							●
Salsify — SCHWARZWURZELN — *scorsonères*		●						●	●	●	●	●			
Snow peas — KEFEN — *pois mange-tout*		●													
Spinach — SPINAT — *épinards*		●		●	●		●	●				●			
Swiss chard — KRAUTSTIELE — *côtes de bette*								●	●						●
Tomatoes — TOMATEN — *tomates*									●				●	●	●
White turnips — WEISSRÜBEN — *navets*	●	●													●
Zucchini — ZUCHETTI — *courgettes*		●												●	●

Table 7-91. Stuffings for Vegetables

Vegetable/*Mise en place*	Stuffing	Finishing
Artichoke bottoms Prepare correctly and simmer, place in a buttered casserole.	With broccoli in cheese sauce Duxelles topped with onion purée Clamart style: purée of fresh peas	Gratinate Gratinate Drizzle with butter
Mushroom caps 2-inch (5-cm) caps, raw or cooked. Place bottom up in a buttered dish. Add chopped stems to stuffing.	Uncooked mousseline farce (meat or fish) mixed with herbs Chopped spinach and ricotta	Top with bread crumbs. Bake in oven until browned. Top with a mixture of bread crumbs and grated cheese.
Cucumbers Peel, cut off ends. Cut into thick rounds, and seed with melon baller. Or split peeled cucumbers in half, and remove seeds.	Uncooked mousseline farce (meat or fish) mixed with herbs. Use a pastry bag to fill. Cover ends with foil. Fill with stuffing, and brush with melted butter. Or fill with regular meat stuffing.	Place stuffed cucumbers in a buttered casserole, add a little vegetable stock. Cover and braise in oven. Reduce braising liquid, whip in cold butter nuggets, and pour over cucumber pieces.
Onions Peel and cut off a quarter from the top and bottom. Cook partially in salt water, cool. Hollow out with a spoon, leave two rings.	Fill with regular meat stuffing to which sautéed onions and herbs have been added.	Butter a casserole, add bacon rind and a *matignon*, set onions on top. Add a little bouillon, cover, and braise in the oven until done.
Cabbage *Green and red cabbage* Core, wash, and cook in salted water until the first layer of leaves is soft. Put in ice water, remove leaves. Repeat until leaves are too small to fill. *Napa and Savoy cabbage* Remove leaves, blanch, and cool a little in ice water.	Chop the rest of the cabbage leaves. Sauté onions and garlic in finely diced bacon. Add cabbage, season, and cook. Add cream if desired. Or stuff with thickened cooked lentils. *To form little heads:* Remove ribs from large leaves. Lay flat on surface, add 1 or 2 smaller leaves. Season with salt and pepper. Place filling in center, fold leaves around it, twist with a cloth into small heads.	Butter a casserole, add bacon rind and a *matignon*, set cabbage heads on top. Add a little bouillon, cover, and braise in the oven until done. Reduce braising liquid and pour over cabbage heads.
Kohlrabi and knob celery Peel and cut off the top to level. Simmer or steam, chill in ice water, and hollow out. Or blanch, chill, and hollow out.	Fill with regular meat stuffing to which the chopped and sautéed vegetables (from hollowing) have been added.	Butter a casserole, add bacon rind and *matignon*, set the vegetables on top. Add a little bouillon, cover, and braise in the oven until done. Sprinkle with grated cheese, brown in the oven. Reduce the braising liquid and pour over vegetables.
Bell peppers Select large, evenly formed, thick-walled peppers. Wash, slice off stem side to use as lid. Seed, blanch pepper and lid.	Fill with regular raw meat stuffing. Or mix cooked rice with sautéed mushrooms and finely diced vegetables. Stuff peppers. Or fill with a lightly thickened cooked ground beef and rice mixture.	Butter a casserole, add filled peppers. Pour either bouillon or a tomato sauce around peppers. Braise covered in the oven.
Tomatoes Wash same-size tomatoes. Remove stem ends. Cut large tomatoes in half, hollow out. Cut tops off small tomatoes, seed or hollow out carefully.	Duxelles for vegetable fillings Cauliflower florets Sautéed leaf spinach Provençale style With mushrooms and cream sauce	Sprinkle with grated Sbrinz, drizzle with butter, and place under salamander. Pour cheese sauce (Mornay) or a hollandaise sauce over cauliflower. Glaze under the salamander. Drizzle with butter. Bake au gratin in the oven with high upper heat. Bake, keep warm.

Table 7-91. Stuffings for Vegetables (continued)

Vegetable/Mise en place	Stuffing	Finishing
Zucchini and eggplant Wash and halve lengthwise. Criss-cross fruit flesh, salt, and brush with olive oil. Place on a sheet pan, and bake until barely tender, so flesh can be removed with a spoon but the walls are still firm. Chop flesh and add to stuffing. *Raw zucchini*	Fill with small diced ratatouille, or mushroom stew with cream sauce. Or fill with cooked rice and tomato concassé or a finely cut stew (meat or poultry) with vegetables and mushrooms. Same as stuffed cucumbers.	Sprinkle with parmesan, drizzle with butter and bake au gratin in the oven. Same as stuffed cucumbers.

7.16 Potato Dishes

Potatoes play a major role in the diet, because they:

- are neutral in taste
- can be prepared in many ways
- harmonize with many other dishes
- are a nutrient-balanced food.

Potatoes are first peeled (except potatoes boiled or baked in the skin), then cut into the desired shape or scooped with a melon baller. Waste should be kept to a minimum and, when possible, used for other preparations. Table 7-92 lists the amount of waste produced by various cutting methods.

Potatoes should be peeled as close to preparation time as possible to prevent nutrient loss, which occurs when potatoes are held in water. Starch, protein, minerals, and vitamins leach from potatoes when they are left in water.

Large potatoes have less waste when they are cut into shapes. Potatoes that are cut the same size will cook evenly and have more eye appeal on the plate.

When potatoes are cut, the cells emit starch, which attaches to the surface and causes uneven browning. Therefore, potatoes are always rinsed before they are deep-fried.

7.16.1 Basic Preparation Methods

Blanching — BLANCHIEREN — *blanchier*

- Frying until partially cooked in oil
- Blanching in boiling salted water

Boiling/Simmering — SIEDEN — *cuire*

- Boiling in salted water
- Simmering in bouillon

Steaming — DÄMPFEN — *cuire à la vapeur*

- Steaming in a pan with perforated insert
- Steaming in a pressure steamer

Baking in the oven — BACKEN IM OFEN — *cuire au four*

- Baking
- Stuffed and baked
- Baking and unmolding

Frying/Roasting — BRATEN — *rissoler*

- In a frying pan
- In a sauté pan
- In a roasting pan
- In a tilting skillet
- In a convection oven
- In a regular oven

Frying/Sautéing — SAUTIEREN (RÖSTEN) — *sauter à la poêle*

- Boiled potatoes
- Raw peeled and trimmed potatoes
- Mashed potatoes

Deep-frying — FRITIEREN — *frire*

- Raw potatoes, oil-blanched
- Raw potatoes without prior blanching
- Mashed potatoes: with egg yolk (*duchess*) or with choux pastry (*dauphine*)

Gratinating — GRATINIEREN — *gratiner*

- Raw potatoes
- Baked stuffed potatoes
- Mashed-potato mixtures

7.16.2 Blanch — BLANCHIEREN — *blanchir*

Blanch in Salt Water

Potatoes	1 part
Water	5 parts
Salt (per quart)	⅓ oz

Method

- Select the right size pot for the amount of potatoes to be cooked.
- Bring the salted water to a boil.

Table 7-92. Waste Percentages from Cutting Potatoes

Waste from	Percentage
Potatoes boiled in the skin	about 15%
Potatoes peeled by hand	about 25 %
Potatoes peeled with a machine	about 30%
Potatoes cut into barrel shapes (turning)	about 35%
Potatoes scooped with a melon baller	about 45–50%

- Add the potatoes.
- Return to a boil, and blanch according to size. Stir.
- Drain, and pour onto a sheet pan to stop the cooking process.

Notes

- Consecutive batches of potatoes can be blanched in the same water with the help of a basket.
- Change the water when it becomes sticky from starch.
- Potatoes that are not blanched long enough will turn black.
- Potatoes can also be blanched in a commercial steamer, with no salt.

Blanching in Oil

Potatoes		
Peanut oil	265°–300°F	(130°–150°C)

Method

- Rinse and dry potatoes that have been cut the same size, for example, French fries.
- Fill the frying basket, not too full.
- Potatoes should be cooked (tender) but without color after they have been blanched in oil.
- Shake the basket from time to time during frying to prevent the potatoes from sticking together.
- After blanching, allow the oil to drip off by keeping the basket above the deep-fryer (shake).
- Spread the potatoes on sheet pans to cool and to prevent further cooking.

7.16.3 Boiling/Simmering –SIEDEN– *cuire*

Table 7-93 lists some of the dishes in which boiled and simmered potatoes are used.

Boiling/Simmering in Salted Water

Boiled Potatoes

YIELD: 10 SERVINGS		
Potatoes	4 lb	1.8 kg
Water		
Salt		

Method

- Peel medium-size potatoes.

- Cut them into even barrel shapes (turn), or halve.
- Add potatoes to boiling salted water.
- Return quickly to a boil (the surfaces would otherwise close, and the center would not become tender).
- Skim, reduce heat, and cover.
- Simmer slowly until done.
- Drain, and serve or keep warm in a water bath until needed.

Simmering in Bouillon

YIELD: 10 SERVINGS		
Potatoes	3 lb, 5 oz	1.5 kg
Onions, chopped	1⅔ oz	50 g
Vegetables, finely diced	3½ oz	100 g
Butter	1⅔ oz	50 g
Bouillon	1 qt, 2 oz	1 L
Salt, pepper, nutmeg		
Parsley, chopped	⅓ oz	10 g

Method

- Peel the potatoes, and cut into about ¾-inch (2-cm) cubes; blanch. (Blanching closes the surfaces with starch, which protects the potato from falling apart during the simmering process.)
- Sauté the onions and finely diced vegetables in butter. Add the blanched potatoes.
- Cover barely with hot bouillon, bring to a boil, and skim.
- Reduce the heat, cover, and simmer slowly.
- Season.
- Sprinkle with chopped parsley just before serving.

7.16.4 Steaming –DÄMPFEN– *cuire à la vapeur*

Steaming allows potatoes to retain nutrients. Moreover, the potatoes are already dry when they need to be mashed.

Potatoes in the jacket can also be steamed. It is important to wash the potatoes well and that they be of even size. Pour cooked potatoes onto a sheet pan, and peel while still warm. The peel is easier to remove this way.

Potatoes that are to be sautéed or puréed should be steamed.

Steaming in a steamer

Potatoes		
Salt		

Method

- Steam evenly sliced or turned potatoes in the steamer.
- Salt after the potatoes have been steamed. (Steam would blow the salt crystals against the steamer walls and damage them.)
- Cooking time depends on the size of the potatoes and the pressure of the steam.

Steaming in a Pan with a Perforated Insert

Potatoes		
Water		
Salt		

Method

- Put water into the pot to reach just below the perforated insert (should not touch insert).
- Add cut or turned potatoes; salt lightly.
- Place a heavy lid on top, and start to steam.
- Carefully watch the cooking process; add water if necessary.

7.16.5 Oven-baking –BACKEN IM OFEN– *cuire au four*

Oven-baking is a dry cooking method, which is especially good for whole unpeeled potatoes or potato mixtures. Raw sliced potatoes can also be baked in the oven, usually arranged in special molds with butter. The starch binds with the butter, making it possible to unmold the baked potatoes when done. Table 7-94 lists various baked potato dishes.

Baked Potatoes

YIELD: 10 SERVINGS		
Potatoes	2 lb, 10 oz	1.2 kg
Salt	1 lb, 2 oz	500 g
Sour cream	10 oz	300 ml
Chives	1⅔ oz	50 g
Salt, pepper		

Table 7-93. Dishes with Boiled or Simmered Potatoes

Turned or cut potatoes

Boiled potatoes with melted butter— KARTOFFELN MIT BUTTER— *pommes anglaise*	Toss boiled potatoes in melted butter.
Boiled potatoes with fresh herbs— SALZKARTOFFELN MIT KRÄUTERN— *pommes aux fines herbes*	Toss boiled potatoes carefully with melted butter and fresh chopped herbs, such as parsley, chervil, and chives.
Creamed potatoes— MILCHKARTOFFELN— *pommes maître d'hôtel*	Peel potatoes boiled in their jackets while hot. Slice. Carefully fold them into a light cream sauce. Sprinkle with chopped parsley.
Parslied potatoes— PETERSILIENKARTOFFELN— *pommes persilées*	Toss boiled potatoes carefully with melted butter and fresh chopped parsley.

Mashed potatoes

Potato snow— SCHNEEKARTOFFELN— *pommes en neige*	Drain boiled peeled potatoes, briefly heat to dry. Put through a potato press while hot, and serve dotted with bits of butter.
Mashed potato balls baked with cheese— GRATINIERTE KARTOFFELKUGELN— *pommes Byron*	Mash dry, boiled potatoes. Fold in onions that have been sautéed in butter with chopped parsley and nutmeg. With a ladle, scoop out mounds and make a hollow in the top. Set in a buttered oven-proof dish. Pour heavy cream over potato mounds, sprinkle with grated cheese, and bake until brown in the oven.
Mashed potatoes glazed with cheese— GRATINIERTES KARTOFFELPÜREE— *pommes Mont-d'Or*	Mound mashed potatoes on an oven-proof plate. Sprinkle with grated Sbrinz, drizzle with melted butter, and brown under a broiler or salamander.
Mashed potatoes with cream— KARTOFFELPÜREE MIT RAHM— *pommes mousseline*	Add heavy cream to hot mashed potatoes.
Mashed potatoes— KARTOFFELPÜREE— *pommes purées*	Drain boiled potatoes, briefly heat to dry. Put hot through a potato press. Add butter and hot milk, beat until smooth, season with salt and nutmeg.

Potatoes cooked in bouillon

Bouillon potatoes with paprika— BOUILLONKARTOFFELN MIT PAPRIKA— *pommes hongroise*	Cut potatoes in slices or cubes, blanch. Sauté diced onions and tomatoes in butter, dust with mild paprika. Add potatoes, barely cover with bouillon, and cook until tender. Sprinkle with chopped parsley.
Bouillon potatoes with fresh mint— BOUILLONKARTOFFELN MIT MINZE— *pommes à la menthe*	Add a few leaves of fresh mint when cooking the potatoes in bouillon.
Potatoes with leeks— LAUCHKARTOFFELN— *pommes*	Cut potatoes into slices or cubes; add finely cut strips of leeks.
Bouillon potatoes with bacon— BOUILLONKARTOFFELN MIT SPECK— *pommes paysanne*	Sauté onions with finely diced bacon; add to potatoes with bouillon.

Oven-baked potatoes with bouillon

Melted potatoes— SCHMELZKARTOFFELN— *pommes fondantes*	Cut large potatoes into barrel shapes (turn). Place in a heavily buttered baking pan. Cover with hot bouillon. Brush often with stock from pan. The surfaces should be golden when the potatoes are done. Brush with melted butter before service.
Potatoes au gratin— GRATINIERTE KARTOFFELSCHEIBEN— *pommes savoyarde*	Shape large halved potatoes (lengthwise), cut into thin ⅛-inch (2-mm) slices (keep shape). Place in a buttered baking pan. Barely cover with hot bouillon. Bake uncovered in oven. Sprinkle with Sbrinz, drizzle with butter, place under salamander or broiler. The potatoes must stay very moist.

Table 7-94. Baked Potato Dishes

Baked potatoes with caraway seeds – KÜMMELKARTOFFELN – *pommes au cumin*	Wash potatoes well, halve lengthwise. Brush the cut surfaces with olive oil, sprinkle lightly with salt and caraway seeds. Bake on a bed of salt or in foil.
Baked potatoes with rosemary – ROSMARINKARTOFFELN – *pommes au romarin*	Wash potatoes well, halve lengthwise. Brush the cut surfaces with peanut oil, sprinkle lightly with salt and fresh rosemary. Bake on a bed of salt or in foil.
Baked potatoes, unmolded	
Potatoes Anna – GESTÜRZTE KARTOFFELN – *pommes Anna*	Cut small potatoes into thin slices; do not rinse. Season with salt and pepper. Grease a metal mold (conducts heat better than ceramic) with clarified butter. Layer in overlapping circles along the bottom and sides. Fill in center with slices, press down. Pour clarified butter over potatoes, bake in oven. Let rest a few minutes, press down, pour off excess butter, and unmold.
Stuffed potatoes	
Baked potatoes stuffed with spinach – MIT SPINAT GEFÜLLTE KARTOFFELN – *pommes florentine*	Remove a slice from the flat side of a baked potato. Remove ⅔ of potato pulp (mix with spinach, if desired). Fill with sautéed leaf spinach. Cover with cheese sauce (Mornay), sprinkle with grated Sbrinz. Bake au gratin in the oven.
Baked potatoes stuffed with vegetables – MIT GEMÜSE GEFÜLLTE KARTOFFELN – *pommes fermière*	Same *mise en place* as above. *Filling:* Mix potato pulp with sautéed finely diced vegetables. Enrich with egg yolk, butter, and parsley. Fill potato boats heaping full. Sprinkle with grated Sbrinz. Gratinate in the oven.
Mashed potatoes with egg yolk	
	Mix 2 lb, 3 oz (1 kg) of puréed potatoes with 1 oz (25 g) butter, 3 egg yolks, and a little nutmeg.
Duchess potatoes – GEBACKENE KARTOFFELROSETTEN – *pommes duchesse*	With a pastry bag, form large rosettes on a buttered sheet pan; brush with beaten egg yolk. Bake in a hot oven.
Tomato-flavored duchess potatoes – GEBACKENE KARTOFFELROSETTEN – *pommes marquise*	Add tomato purée to potato mixture. With a pastry bag, form large rosettes on a buttered sheet pan; brush with beaten egg yolk. Bake in a hot oven.

Method
- Cover a baking or sheet pan with a ¼-inch (0.5-cm) layer of salt.
- Set washed, dried, whole, unpeeled potatoes on top.
- Bake at about 335°F (170°C) (test for doneness with a needle).

or

- Wrap cleaned, dried potatoes in aluminum foil (foil may be oiled).
- Bake on a sheet pan with or without salt.

Advantage: Potatoes baked in foil stay moister and retain their shape better when they have to be kept warm for a lengthy period.

Service
Present baked potatoes on a plate lined with a napkin or in a specialty basket.

Garnishes
- Sweet butter
- Sour cream or cottage cheese with chives.
- Crisp bacon strips.

Potatoes Baked in a Mold

YIELD: 10 SERVINGS		
Potatoes	4 lb	1.8 kg
Butter	3½ oz	100 g
Salt, pepper		

Method
- Cut peeled potatoes into matchstick shapes. Do not rinse, but towel dry.
- Sauté in clarified butter but do not brown. Season with salt and pepper.
- Grease small frying pans, cocottes, or metal molds with clarified butter.
- Fill with potatoes, pressing down hard.
- Bake in a hot oven, 425°F (220°C).
- Let stand a few minutes, then unmold upside down onto a warmed plate.

7.16.6 Roasting – BRATEN – *rissoler*

Potatoes for roasting should be
- cut evenly
- cut into barrel shapes (turned)
- scooped out with a melon baller.

They are blanched before they are roasted to ensure the starch stays in the potato to prevent sticking. Table 7-95 lists various roasted potato dishes.

Oven-roasted Potatoes with Onions – BÄCKERINKARTOFFELN – *pommes boulangèr*

YIELD: 10 SERVINGS		
Potatoes	4 lb	1.8 kg
Peanut oil for frying	3½ oz	100 ml
Salt, pepper		
Onions	8½ oz	250 g
Peanut oil for frying	1⅔ oz	50 ml
Butter	1⅔ oz	50 g
Parsley	⅔ oz	20 g

Method
- Cut potatoes into slices; blanch.
- Heat peanut oil in a baking pan or large cast-iron frying pan.

Table 7.-95. Oven-roasted Potato Dishes

Name	Description
Château potatoes– SCHLOSSKARTOFFELN –*pommes château*	Cut potatoes into barrel shape (turn) 2 inches (5 cm) long, with flat ends.
Roasted potato cubes– MAXIME-KARTOFFELN –*pommes maxime*	Cubes about ⅔ inch (1.5 cm).
Hazelnut potatoes– HASELNUSSKARTOFFELN –*pommes noisettes*	With a melon baller, cut out balls about ⅓ inch (1 cm) in size.
Oven-roasted potato balls– GEBRATENE KARTOFFELKUGELN – *pommes parisienne*	With a melon baller, cut balls ⅔ to ¾ inch (1.5 to 2.0 cm) in size.
Roasted diced potatoes– GEBRATENE KARTOFFELWÜRFEL – *pommes Parmentier*	Cut potatoes into ¼-inch (5-mm) cubes.
Oven-roasted potatoes– BRATKARTOFFLEN –*pommes rissolées*	Cut potatoes into ⅓-inch (1-cm) cubes or use small peeled new potatoes.
Oven-roasted potatoes with bread crumbs and parsley– BRÖSELKARTOFFELN –*pommes sablées*	Cut potatoes into ⅓-inch (1-cm) cubes. Sprinkle with fresh bread crumbs and continue to roast until done. Sprinkle with parsley.

Table 7-96. Fried and Sautéed Potato Dishes

Name	Description
Rösti potatoes–RÖSTI–*rœsti*	Peel boiled potatoes, grate, sauté in butter, turn upside down like a cake onto a heated platter. Brush with butter.
Rösti potatoes, Bernese style– BERNER RÖSTI–*pommes bernoise*	Peel boiled potatoes, grate, sauté in butter with bacon and onions, turn upside down like a cake onto a heated platter. Brush with butter.
Rösti potatoes (with raw potatoes)– RÖSTI AUS ROHEN KARTOFFELN – *pommes crues sautés*	Peel raw potatoes, grate or cut into fine strips, rinse, and dry. Sauté in clarified butter on all sides. Season with salt and pepper. Form a crust on top and bottom. Turn upside down like a cake onto a heated buttered platter.
Sautéed potatoes–RÖSTKARTOFFELN– *pommes sautés*	Peel boiled potatoes, slice, and sauté in butter.
Variations of sautéed potato mixtures	
Potato cakes–KARTOFFELGALETTEN– *galettes de pommes de terre*	Form duchess potato mixture into a 2-inch-diameter (5-cm) log; chill. Cut into about ⅓-inch (1-cm) slices, press grate pattern on top, flour lightly. Sauté in clarified butter.
Small potato cakes– KARTOFFELKÜCHLEIN–*pommes Macaire*	Bake potatoes or use leftover baked potatoes; mash. Season with salt and pepper. Shape into small cakes, and sauté in clarified butter on both sides.

- Add the potatoes: they should cover the bottom of the pan; season.
- Roast until golden brown in the oven, turning occasionally.
- Pour off excess fat.
- Add the onions, sliced and sautéed in peanut oil.
- Add butter and finish roasting. Sprinkle with parsley.

Notes

- Roasted potatoes can also be cooked with a specially formulated frying butter (*Bratbutter*). There is no such product in the United States, but ghee or clarified butter can be used.

- Roasted potatoes are not covered during cooking, as steam formation would cause them to soften.

7.16.7 Frying/Sautéing–SAU-TIEREN (RÖSTEN)–*sauter à la poêle*

Potatoes for sautéing can be

- boiled in their jacket, grated, sliced, or cubed
- small new potatoes
- finely grated raw potatoes
- mashed potato mixtures

See Table 7-96 for examples of sautéed potato dishes.

Fried Potatoes–LYONER KARTOFFELN –*pommes sautés*

YIELD: 10 SERVINGS		
Jacketed Potatoes	3 lb, 5 oz	1.5 kg
Clarified butter	3½ oz	100 ml
Salt, pepper		
Butter	1⅔ oz	50 g
Onions	8½ oz	250 g
Butter	1⅔ oz	50 g
Parsley	⅔ oz	20 g

Method

- Peel boiled or steamed potatoes.
- Cut into slices.
- Heat the clarified butter in a frying pan.

Table 7-97. Deep-fried Potato Dishes

Without oil blanching

Potato chips—*pommes chips*	Slice potatoes very thinly with a mandolin or machine. Rinse and dry well. Deep-fry, stirring all the time. Serve warm or cold. Salt, or dust with curry or paprika.
Waffle potatoes—WAFFELKARTOFFELN—*pommes gaufrettes*	Cut potatoes with the fluted blade of the mandoline that cuts a waffle pattern into the slices. Rinse, and dry well. Deep-fry, stirring constantly.
Straw potatoes—STROHKARTOFFELN—*pommes paille*	Slice potatoes into thin strips (julienne) or grate. Rinse, and dry well. Deep-fry, stirring constantly.

With oil blanching

Shoestring potatoes—ZÜNDHOLZKARTOFFELN—*pommes allumettes*	Cut potatoes into matchsticks. Rinse starch off well.
Home fries—FRITIERTE KARTOFFELWÜRFEL—*pommes bataille*	Cut potatoes into ⅓-inch (1-cm) cubes.
French fries—POMMES FRITES—*pommes frites*	Cut potatoes into ⅓-inch-thick (1-cm), 2- to 2½-inch-long (5–7-cm) sticks.
Steak fries—FRITIERTE KARTOFFELSTÄBE—*pommes Pont-neuf*	Cut double the size of French fries. Can also be baked in the oven.
Thin french fries—FRITIERTE KARTOFFELSTÄBCHEN—*pommes mignonnettes*	Cut potatoes ¼-inch-thick (¼-cm) and 1¾-inch-long (4-cm) sticks.

Duchess potatoes

	Mix 2 lb, 3 oz (1 kg) of puréed potatoes with 1 oz (25 g) butter, 3 egg yolks, and a little nutmeg.
Fried potato croquettes with almonds—FRIETIETE MANDELKARTOFFELKUGELN—*pommes Berny*	Soak dried horn-of-plenty mushrooms (classic version, chopped truffles), chop finely, add to duchess potato mixture. Form tiny balls, roll in sliced, crushed almonds.
Potato croquettes—KARTOFFELKROKETTEN—*pommes croquettes*	With a plain tube in a pastry bag, pipe rows ¾ inch in diameter (1.5 cm) on a board. Cut into 1¾ inch (4 cm) pieces. Bread.
Potato croquettes with spinach—KARTOFFELKROKETTEN MIT SPINAT—*pommes croquettes florentine*	Mix finely chopped sautéed spinach into the duchess potato mixture.
Fried potato balls with ham—FRITIERTE KARTOFFELKUGELN MIT SCHINKEN UND FIDELI—*pommes Saint-Florentin*	Mix finely chopped ham into the duchess potato mixture. Form into small balls, and roll in crushed vermicelli noodles.
Pear-shaped potato croquettes—BIRNENKARTOFFELN—*pommes Williams*	Form pears from duchess potato mixture. Bread. Use a piece of almond or spaghetti for a stem.

Dauphine potatoes

	Add 14 oz (400 g) choux paste to 2 lb, 3oz (1 kg) of hot, boiled, riced potatoes.
Fried potato puffs—FRITIERTE KARTOFFELKRAPFEN—*pommes dauphine*	With two tablespoons, form small oval shapes from dauphine potato mixture, and place on oiled parchment paper.
Fried potato puffs with cheese—FRITIERTE KARTOFFELKRAPFEN—*pommes lorette*	Mix shredded cheese with dauphine potato mixture. Shape into mounds or rings on oiled parchment paper.

- Add the potato slices. They should cover the bottom of the pan well.
- Sauté lightly, and season.
- Turning frequently, cook until golden brown.
- Add half the butter and the chopped onions; sauté.
- Add the rest of the butter, and finish sautéing.
- Sprinkle with chopped parsley.

7.16.8 Deep-frying—FRITIEREN—*frire*

Potatoes that are deep-fried should be well drained and towel dried. Excess water can cause the fat to spatter, increasing the danger of burns and making the fat spoil faster.

Small cut potatoes are cooked in one step; they are not blanched in oil first. They are deep-fried to a golden brown at 320° to 335°F (160° to 170°C).

Large cut potatoes are first blanched at 265°F (130°C); they will cook but not brown. They are deep-fried to order at 335°F (170°C). The outside will be golden brown and crisp, and the inside, soft.

Duchesse or *dauphine mixtures* are deep-fried in small batches until crisp.

- Deep-fried potatoes must be allowed to drain well. They are tossed with salt in a separate bowl or in the basket (not above the fat, or it will spoil rapidly).
- Do not salt deep-fried mashed potato products, because the mixture is already seasoned.
- Do not cover deep-fried potatoes, or they will become soggy.

Frozen blanched French fries are deep-fried, unthawed, at 335°F (170°C) until they are brown and crisp. Thawed French fries are covered with condensed water, which causes the fat to spatter and spoil rapidly. Keep the amounts in the fry basket small to prevent the fat temperature from dropping too low. Table 7-97 lists various deep-fried potatoes.

French-fried Potatoes – *pommes frites*

YIELD: 10 SERVINGS		
Potatoes	4 lb	1.8 kg
Peanut oil for frying (10% oil loss)		
Salt		

Method

- Rinse the evenly cut potatoes, and dry well.
- Fill the fry basket about half full.
- Blanch at 265°F (130°C) until the potatoes are cooked but not browned.
- Remove the basket, draining the oil from it.
- Spread the potatoes on a sheet pan until needed.
- Deep-fry to order at 335°F (170°C).
- Drain on absorbent paper.
- Salt lightly.
- Serve on paper-lined plates.

7.16.9 Gratinating – GRATINIEREN – *gratiner*

Many prepared potato dishes are finished by gratinating them, for example, stuffed potatoes. Such dishes are classified by their basic preparation method. Gratinating only adds to and completes the taste of the dish. For some potato dishes, however, gratinating is the basic preparation method.

Potatoes au Gratin – KARTOFFEL-GRATIN – *gratin daupinois*

YIELD: 10 SERVINGS		
Potatoes	3 lb, 5 oz	1.5 kg
Milk	1 pt, 5 oz	600 ml
Heavy cream	10 oz	300 ml
Salt, pepper, nutmeg		
Gruyere cheese, grated	3½ oz	100 g
Sbrinz, grated	3½ oz	100 g
Butter	1⅔ oz	50 g
Garlic	⅓ oz	10 g

Method

- Slice peeled potatoes.
- Bring the milk and cream to a boil.
- Season.
- Fold in the potatoes.
- Bring to a boil.
- Fold half of the cheese into the potatoes.
- Butter a casserole, sprinkle with chopped garlic, and add the potatoes.
- Sprinkle the rest of cheese on top, and drizzle with melted butter.
- Bake slowly at 320°F (160°C) for 40 minutes.
- Brown top at 425°F (220°C).

Baking at low temperatures increases the cooking time but ensures a moist, juicy gratinated dish.

7.17 Grain Dishes

The huge variety of grain products allows us to produce many types of dishes that enrich our diets in many ways.

Grain dishes can be appetizers or entrées, but they are more frequently used on the menu as a starch side dish.

Grains are classified into these groups:

- Pasta dishes
  - made with commercial dry pasta
  - made with home-made fresh pasta
- Gnocchi Varieties
- Rice dishes
- Corn dishes
- Whole grain dishes

7.17.1 Pasta

Pasta is differentiated as being commercial or freshly made. Commercial pasta has as its advantage a large variety of shapes. Home-made pasta has a fresh taste and a delightful, unique texture—"bite." However, home-made pasta is only excellent if the ingredients are of first quality and if the product is consumed very fresh and not allowed to dry.

Table 7-98 lists various dishes made with fresh and commercially prepared pastas.

Cooking Pasta

- Cook pasta in large amounts of salted boiling water. The minimum ratio is 1:5.
- Each 1 quart, 2 ounces (1 L) of water is salted with ⅓ ounce (10 g) of salt.
- Adding a little oil prevents foaming (grain protein) and prevents the pasta from sticking together.
- Never cover pasta.
- Cook in rapidly boiling water, which keeps the pasta in constant motion and prevents it from sticking to the bottom of the pot.
- Pasta is drained when it is still *al dente* and has bite. Overcooked pasta sticks to the teeth and tastes gooey.
- Pasta is often cooked in advance and held for later use. Pasta that will be reheated should be cooked for a shorter time.
- Cooking time and absorption of water varies from product to product.

Amounts

Commercial dry pasta absorbs 150 percent of its weight in water.

Table 7-98. Pasta Dishes

Name	Description
Macaroni au gratin— GRATINIERTE MAKKARONI— *gratin de macaroni*	Mix macaroni cooked *al dente* with a light cream sauce. Put in a buttered dish, sprinkle with grated Sbrinz, and drizzle with melted butter. Bake au gratin in the oven.
Spaghetti with ham and mushrooms— SPAGHETTI MAILÄNDER ART— *spaghetti milanaise*	Toss cooked spaghetti in butter, season. Top with mushrooms and ham sautéed in butter. Sprinkle with freshly grated cheese (Sbrinz).
Spaghetti with Gorgonzola sauce— SPAGHETTI MIT GORGONZOLA SAUCE— *spaghetti au gorgonzola*	Melt Gorgonzola in a cream sauce. Mix with a tomato concasée, and toss with sphagetti.
Spaghetti with tomatoes— SPAGHETTI MIT TOMATEN— *spaghetti napolitaine*	Toss cooked spaghetti with butter. Mix with a tomato concasée, and season. Serve topped with extra tomato concasée. Serve grated cheese separately (Sbrinz).
Home-made noodles with ham— NUDELN WESTFÄLISCHE ART— *nouilles westphalienne*	Toss noodles with sautéed ham strips, cream sauce, and grated cheese. Gratinate in the oven.
Home-made noodles with vegetables— NUDELN MIT GEMÜSE STREIFEN— *nouilles á la julienne de légumes*	Toss noodles with butter and very briefly sautéed fresh vegetable strips.

The amount needed per person is:

Appetizer:	1 ounce (30 g)
Side dish:	1⅓ to 2 ounces (40 to 60 g)
Entrée:	2½ to 3½ ounces (70 to 100 g)

Storing Cooked Pasta

- Rinse the drained pasta in cold water until cool; drain well.
- Toss with a little oil.
- Place in a flat insert, covered, in the refrigerator at 35° to 42°F (2° to 5°C) for a short time.
- Or seal in vacuum bags, and store at 35° to 42°F (2° to 5°C).

Reheating Cooked Pasta

- Reheat cooked pasta in boiling salted water, drain, toss with butter, season with salt and a little nutmeg.
- Or season when cold, dot with butter, and heat in a combi steamer or in the microwave oven.

Basic Recipe for Fresh Pasta

YIELD: 10 SERVINGS		
All-purpose flour	1 lb, 5 oz	600 g
Hard-wheat semolina, fine	3½ oz	100 g
Eggs, beaten	8½ oz	250 g
Egg yolk	1⅔ oz	50 g
Olive oil	1 oz	25 g
Water, if needed		

Method
Variation 1

- Form a ring with the sifted flour and semolina.
- Put the rest of ingredients in the center of the ring, and mix everything into a very firm but smooth dough.
- Knead for at least 20 minutes to make the dough elastic. (If finishing with a noodle machine, only brief kneading is necessary.)
- Let rest for 1 hour.

Variation 2

- Place all ingredients in a mixer bowl, and with a dough hook, work into a smooth, elastic dough.
- Knead for about 5 minutes,
- The dough can be used immediately.

Never add salt to home-made noodle or ravioli dough, or it will crack when rolled out.

Variations for this basic recipe are listed in Table 7-99.

Cutting Pasta

Method 1 (by Hand)

Divide the elastic, well-kneaded, rested dough into quarters. Dust the pieces with flour, and place on a floured marble slab. Roll out very thinly with a rolling pin, constantly lifting and re-applying the rolling pin to maintain a rectangle. If the dough is almost translucent, sprinkle the top with a little more finely ground semolina to prevent sticking. Fold both sides of the rectangle toward the middle, so that the edges touch. Do not press down, or it might stick. Cut into strips of any size, as desired.

Slide a long knife under the dough at the folded edge. Slide the whole blade under it, and tip up the dull edge. The noodles should unroll, and hang down from the knife on both sides. Slide them into a loosely formed nest; sprinkle with more semolina to prevent sticking.

Method 2 (with Machine)

Briefly kneaded dough is made elastic with the machine. Cut the dough into quarters, and press each into a flat rectangle with the palms of the hand. Set the rolls of the machine at a greatest distance. Dust the rectangles with semolina, and crank through the rolls. Fold the dough together to be as thick as at the beginning. Turn the dough 90 degrees, and repeat the process at least six to eight times, until the dough glistens.

Machine-kneaded dough is immediately rolled out. Cut the dough into quarters, and press each into a flat rectangle with the palms of the hand. Set the rolls of the machine at a greatest distance. Dust the rectangles with semolina, and crank through the rolls. Repeat, reducing the distance between the rolls each time by two notches. Turn the dough 90 degrees and repeat the process until the dough is thin enough. Let the rolled dough strips dry briefly. Use the cutter roll to cut the dough into ribbons. Catch the noodles with the hands, and slide them into a loosely formed nest. Sprinkle with more semolina to prevent sticking.

7.17.2 Pasta Dishes

Pasta dishes contain home-made freshly prepared noodle dough combined with filling and sauces of various types. They are often gratinated or served with foaming hot butter. Stuffed pastas and spaetzle also belong in this category. Table 7-100 lists some common stuffed pastas.

Basic Ravioli Dough

YIELD: 10 SERVINGS		
All-purpose flour	1 lb, 5 oz	600 g
Eggs, beaten	8½ oz	250 g
Sunflower oil	1⅔ oz	50 g
Water (approx.)	3½ oz	100 ml

Method

- Sift flour, and form a ring.
- Place the eggs, oil, and water in the center.
- Mix flour gently into the center until a firm dough has been formed.
- Knead the dough until it is very elastic. Wrap in plastic.
- Let rest 1 to 1½ hours before use.

Making Ravioli

Table 7-101 lists some common ravioli dishes.

Without Ravioli Board

- Roll the dough out very thinly into two large pieces.
- With a pastry bag, pipe the filling into evenly spaced separate mounds on one dough piece. Brush the space around the filling with egg white or a little water.

- Place the second dough piece carefully on top.
- With a stick, press the dough down between the filling mounds.
- With a pastry wheel, cut out the individual ravioli.

With Ravioli Forms (Board)

- Roll the dough out very thinly into two large pieces.
- Dust the form with flour, and place one sheet of dough on it.
- With the fingers, gently push the dough into the hollows.
- With a pastry bag, pipe the filling into the hollows.
- Brush the spaces between the hollows with a little water.
- Place the second piece of dough on top, and press down carefully with a rolling pin.
- Turn the whole over and release onto a marble slab. Cut the individual ravioli with a pastry wheel.

Making Tortellini

See Table 7-101 for a dish made with tortellini.

- Roll out the dough very thinly.
- Cut into small disks, about 1⅛ inch (3 cm) in diameter.
- With a pastry bag, pipe on desired filling. Brush the borders with water.
- Fold each disk into a crescent shape.
- Pinch the border closed with thumb and forefinger.
- Hold the crescent with both hands, and carefully bend it around one finger to form a ring whose ends almost touch. At the same time, fold the pressed-together dough edges upwards, so that a ditchlike channel forms around the filling.
- With the thumbs, pinch the ends of the crescents tightly together to form a closed ring.
- Set the finished tortellini on a floured cloth. Keep them apart, to prevent sticking.

Making Cannelloni

- Cook dough pieces, 2½ inches by 3¼ inches (6 by 8 cm), in plenty of salted water with a little oil until *al dente*.
- Drain, cool, and air-dry.

- With a pastry bag, pipe on desired filling, and roll up.
- Butter an oven-proof dish. Pour in the desired sauce. Place the filled canelloni in neat rows on top of the sauce.
- Cover with a little more sauce, sprinkle with grated cheese (Sbrinz), drizzle with melted butter, and bake au gratin.

Making Lasagne

See Table 7-101 for a dish that includes lasagne noodles.

- Cook dough pieces, 2½ inches by 3¼ inches (6 by 8 cm), in plenty of salted water with a little oil until *al dente*.
- Drain, cool, and air-dry.
- Butter an oven-proof dish. Pour in the desired sauce.
- Place a layer of lasagne on top of the sauce.
- Fill the dish alternately with sauce and lasagne noodles.
- Cover the top layer with a cream sauce.
- Sprinkle with grated cheese (Sbrinz). Dot with bits of butter.
- Bake in the oven, and brown the lasagne top lightly under the broiler.

Basic Spaetzle Dough
(SPÄTZLI/ KNÖPFLI)

YIELD: 10 SERVINGS		
All-purpose flour	14 oz	400 g
Fine semolina (dunst)	3½ oz	100 g
Eggs, beaten	8½ oz	250 g
Milk	3½ oz	100 ml
Water (approx.)	3½ oz	100 ml
Salt	⅓ oz	10 g

Method

- Sift the flour and semolina into a bowl.
- Add the rest of the ingredients.
- Beat quickly together into a very smooth, not-too-thin batter. Beat until the dough forms bubbles, a sign that the gluten is fully developed.
- Push through a spaetzle mill into boiling salted water.
- Remove the spaetzle as soon as they rise to the surface. Drop the spaetzle into cold salted water to chill them rapidly; drain at once.

Table 7-99. Variations of Home-made Pasta

Leaf noodle prints— NUDELBLÄTTER— *feuilles de nouilles*	Roll out the pasta dough very thinly. Place small Italian (flat) parsley leaves on top. Cover with another sheet of thinly rolled out pasta dough. Roll out together with a pasta machine. Cut out round disks or squares, each with one leaf pressed inside.
Basil pasta— BASILIKUMNUDELN— *nouilles au basilic*	Add fresh, finely chopped basil to the basic pasta recipe.
Beet pasta— RANDENNUDELN— *nouilles aux betteraves rouges*	Use beet juice instead of water to color the basic dough.
Whole-wheat pasta— VOLLKORNNUDELN— *nouilles de farine complète*	Instead of white flour, use finely milled and sifted whole-grain flour.
Black pasta— TINTENNUDELN— *nouilles noires*	Color the basic dough with octopus or squid ink.
Saffron pasta— SAFRANNUDELN— *nouilles safranées*	Color the basic dough with saffron that has been dissolved in a little hot water.
Tomato pasta— TOMATENNUDELN— *nouilles aux tomates*	Add tomato paste to the basic dough, omitting the water.
Spinach pasta— SPINATNUDELN— *nouilles vertes*	Add chopped cooked spinach to the basic dough. Press the spinach to remove liquid, and omit water from the basic dough.

Table 7-100. Stuffed Pastas

Pasta	Fillings	Suitable Sauces
Ravioli	Meat, vegetables, spinach, ricotta, mushrooms, fish, crustaceans, tofu	Tomato sauce, pesto, cream sauce, basil sauce, lobster sauce
Tortellini	Meat, mushrooms, ricotta, tofu	Tomato sauce, cream sauce, Gorgonzola sauce, pepper *coulis*
Lasagne	Stewed vegetables, Bolognese sauce (meat/tomato), stewed mushrooms	Cream sauce, tomato sauce
Cannelloni	Same as ravioli fillings	Tomato sauce, pesto, cream sauce

Table 7-101. Pasta Dishes

Dish	Description
Ravioli with sage— RAVIOLI MIT SALBEI— *ravioli à la sauge*	Arrange ravioli in a buttered oven-proof dish. Cover with ravioli chopped shallots and finely cut fresh sage that have been sautéed in butter.
Fresh cheese (ricotta) ravioli— QUARKRAVIOLI— *ravioli au séré*	Ravioli with a spinach-ricotta filling.
Ravioli, Nice style— RAVIOLI NIZZAART— *ravioli niçoise*	Ravioli baked in a tomato concassée.
Fish ravioli— FISCHRAVIOLI— *ravioli de poisson*	Ravioli filled with a fish mousseline and served with a white-wine sauce.
Tortellini with pesto— *tortellini al pesto*	Tortellini (any filling), cooked fresh, are tossed in a sauce with pine nuts, garlic, basil, Parmesan, and olive oil.
Green lasagne— *lasagne verdi*	Layer Bolognese sauce with green lasagne noodles in a buttered baking dish. Cover with cream sauce, sprinkle with cheese, dot with butter, and bake.

Table 7-102. Variations of Basic Spaetzle Dough

Spinach spaetzle— SPINATSPÄTZLI— *spaetzli aux èpinard*	Mix basic dough with 5⅓ oz (150 g) well-pressed, finely chopped spinach (reduce water in dough).
Saffron spaetzle— SAFRANSPÄTZLI— *spaetzli safrané*	Dissolve two pinches of saffron in the liquid to be added to the basic dough.
Tomato spaetzle— TOMATENSPÄTZLI— *spaetzli aux tomates*	Mix 1⅔ oz (50 g) tomato paste into the basic dough.
Whole-wheat spaetzle— VOLLKORNSPÄTZLI— *spaetzli de farine complète*	Substitute finely sifted whole-wheat flour for the all-purpose flour.
Ricotta spaetzle— QUARKSPÄTZLI— *spaetzli au séré*	Substitiute 5⅓ (150 g) oz low-fat ricotta cheese for water in the basic dough recipe.
Spaetzle, Glarus style— GLARNER SPÄTZLI— *spaetzli glaronaise*	Sauté spinach spaetzle with soaked golden raisins in butter, sprinkle with grated cheese (sapsago).
Mixed spaetzle, Tessin style— TESSINER SPÄTZLI— *spaetzli tessinoise*	Sauté a mixture of spinach, saffron, and tomato spaetzle in butter.

Table 7-103. Dishes with Gnocchi

Dish	Description
Choux-paste gnocchi with ham— BRANDTEIGNOCKEN MIT SCHINKEN— *gnocchi parisienne au jambon*	Sauté finely diced ham in butter, cool. Mix with minced parsley, add to choux paste. Finish as for plain choux-paste gnocchi.
Potato gnocchi with porcini— KARTOFFELNOCKEN MIT STEINPILZEN— *gnocchi piémontaise aux cèpes*	Place gnocchi in a buttered oven-proof dish. Cover with fresh porcini and cream sauce, sprinkle with grated cheese (Sbrinz), and gratinate in the oven.
Semolina gnocchi with braised chicken livers— GRIESSNOCKEN MIT GEFLÜGELRAGOUT— *gnocchi romaine au foie de volaille*	Place gnocchi in a circle around the edge of a round oven-proof dish and gratinate in the oven. Fill the center with braised chicken livers in a Madeira sauce, and sprinkle with chopped parsley.

7.17.3 Gnocchi

Table 7-103 lists dishes made with the three types of gnocchi.

Choux-paste Gnocchi—BRANDTEIGNOCKEN—*gnocchi parisienne*

YIELD: 10 SERVINGS		
Choux paste	1 lb, 2 oz	800 g
Cream sauce	1 pt, 11 oz	800 ml
Grated cheese (Sbrinz)	1⅔ oz	50 g
Butter	1⅔ oz	50 g

Method
- With the pastry bag and a plain tube and with the help of a larding needle, press nut-size choux-paste pieces into simmering salted water.
- Poach the gnocchi.
- Remove with a wire skimmer, and cool in cold water.
- Drain well.
- In a buttered oven-proof dish, pour a thin layer of the cream sauce.
- Place a layer of gnocchi on top—not too close together.
- Pour the rest of sauce on top.
- Sprinkle with grated cheese (Sbrinz), and drizzle with melted butter.
- Bake in the oven with increasing heat to form a golden brown crust.
- Baking time is about 20 minutes, at 355° to 425°F (180° to 220°C).
- The gnocchi should expand like a soufflé in the oven and must be served immediately, as they will collapse as they cool.

Potato Gnocchi—KARTOFFELNOCKEN—*gnocchi piémontaise*

YIELD: 10 SERVINGS		
Potatoes in their skin	2 lb, 10 oz	1.2 kg
Eggs, beaten	5⅓ oz	150 g
Salt, pepper, nutmeg		
All-purpose flour	7 oz	200 g
Tomato concassé	1 pt, 8 oz	700 ml
Grated cheese (Sbrinz)	1⅔ oz	50 g
Butter	1⅔ oz	50 g

Method
- Mix in the eggs, season, and let cool.
- Work in the flour.
- With the pastry bag, using a plain tube, press long rows on a floured marble slab. With a knife, cut into even pieces.

- Form nut-size balls, and roll them over the tip of a dinner fork.
- Poach the gnocchi for 5 minutes in salted water.
- Let drain in a sieve.
- In a buttered oven-proof dish, pour a thin layer of the tomato concassé sauce.
- Place a layer of gnocchi on top.
- Sprinkle with grated cheese (Sbrinz) and freshly ground pepper, and drizzle with melted butter.
- Bake in oven with increasing heat to form a golden brown crust.
- Gnocchi can also be tossed in butter or sautéed lightly.

Notes

- Use older mealy potatoes (such as Idaho baking potatoes), because they are very starchy.
- The amount of eggs and flour depends on the moisture in the pressed potatoes. The mixture should be dry. For moist potatoes, use egg yolk only.

Semolina Gnocchi – GRIESSNOCKEN – *gnocchi romaine*

YIELD: 10 SERVINGS		
Milk	1 qt, 2 oz	1 L
Salt, nutmeg		
Butter	3 oz	80 g
Hard-wheat semolina	7⅓ oz	220 g
Grated cheese (Sbrinz)	3½ oz	100 g
Egg yolk	2⅔ oz	75 g

Method

- Bring the milk, salt, nutmeg, and 1⅔ oz (50 g) butter to a boil.
- Stirring constantly, pour the semolina slowly into the hot milk.
- Reduce heat to low, cover, and simmer about 15 minutes.
- Mix in 1⅔ oz (50 g) of grated cheese (Sbrinz) and the egg yolk; season.
- Spread mixture about ¾ inch (2 cm) thick on an oiled sheet pan; cover with oiled parchment paper and let cool.
- Cut the dough into crescents or circles.
- Place gnocchi, slightly overlapping, in a buttered oven-proof dish.

- Sprinkle with remaining cheese, drizzle with melted butter. Bake in oven with increasing heat to form a golden brown crust.

Notes

- The semolina should swell, or the mixture will not bind, and the gnocchi will fall apart while gratinating. The cooking time must be complete.
- Another method is to brush the chilled mixture with butter, sprinkle with grated cheese, and drizzle again with butter; then cut shapes and bake au gratin on a sheet pan. With this method, each piece can be served separately.

7.17.4 Rice Dishes

Three different preparation methods are used to produce rice dishes:

- rice pilaf – PILAW-REIS – *riz pilaf*
- boiled rice – TROCKENREIS – *riz créole*
- risotto

They are compared in Table 7-104. Table 7-105 lists various rice dishes.

Rice Pilaf

YIELD: 10 SERVINGS		
Onion	4¾ oz	140 g
Butter	1⅓ oz	40 g
Carolina-Rice	1 lb, 5 oz	600 g
Bouillon about	1 qt, 2 oz	1 L
Bay leaf	1	1
Butter	1⅓ oz	40 g

Method

- Sauté onions in the butter until opaque.
- Add the rice, and sauté briefly with the onions.
- Add the bouillon and bay leaf, and bring to a boil.
- Cover, and cook in the oven for about 15 minutes.
- Remove from the oven, and pour into another pan to interrupt the cooking process.
- Mix the remaining butter with rice using a two-pronged fork (carving fork).

Boiled Rice – TROCKENREIS – *riz créole*

YIELD: 10 SERVINGS		
Water	3 qt, 22 oz	3.5 L
Salt	1⅓ oz	40 g
Siam-Patna rice	1 lb, 2 oz	500 g
Butter	1⅔ oz	50 g

Method

- Bring water to a boil; add salt.
- Add the rice, and boil vigorously for 10 to 12 minutes.
- Drain, rinse with cold water, drain well.
- Spread in a buttered shallow dish.
- If necessary, add a little more salt, and dot with the butter.
- Cover with buttered parchment paper.
- Warm rice in the oven or microwave, fluffing with a fork occasionally.

Risotto

YIELD: 10 SERVINGS		
Onion	5⅓ oz	150 g
Garlic cloves	2	2
Olive oil	1⅔ oz	50 ml
Vialone rice	1 lb, 5 oz	600 g
Bouillon	about 2 qt	1.8 L
Bay leaf	1	1
Sage leaves, fresh	2	2
White wine	5 oz	150 ml
Butter	1⅓ oz	40 g
Grated cheese (Sbrinz)	1⅔ oz	50 g
Salt, pepper		

Method

- Sauté the onions and garlic in the olive oil until translucent.
- Add the rice, and sauté briefly.
- Add a bit of bouillon, the bay leaf, and chopped sage leaves.
- Add the hot bouillon in small amounts, bringing to a simmer each time and stirring with a wooden spoon.
- Simmer for 17 to 18 minutes, until all liquid is absorbed, stirring frequently.
- Fold in white wine, cold butter, and grated cheese (Sbrinz) carefully.
- Season to taste with salt and pepper.

Table 7-104. Comparison of Rice Preparation Methods

Rice Pilaf	Boiled Rice	Risotto
Ratio, rice to liquid = 1:1.5	Ratio, rice to liquid = 1:5	Ratio, rice to liquid = 1:3
Siam-Patna, Carolina, converted rice	Siam-Patna, Carolina, Basmati, converted rice	Vialone, Arborio
Butter		Butter, olive oil, poultry fat, marrow
Onion, bay leaf		Onion, garlic Fresh sage leaves, bay leaf
Light bouillon, veal stock, vegetable stock	Salted water	Light bouillon, chicken stock, vegetable stock
Butter	Butter	Butter, grated cheese (Sbrinz), white wine
Slightly moist, without any excess liquid; bound by its own starch and butter	Separate kernels, dry and fluffy	Grainy, but slightly liquid; the remaining liquid combines with the unglazed rice starch; adding cheese and butter at the end makes the risotto even creamier

The amount of liquid varies depending on the rice variety and the amount of rice to be cooked.
Basic principle: The greater the amount of rice, the less liquid used.

Table 7-105. Rice Dishes

Dish	Description
Rice pilaf with morels— PILAW-REIS MIT MORCHELN— *riz pilaf aux morilles*	Add sautéed morels and strips of vegetables (julienne) to rice pilaf.
Rice wih fruit— REIS MIT FRÜCHTEN— *riz aux fruits*	Add sautéed cubes of bell peppers, apples, peaches, pineapple, and soaked currants to rice pilaf. Sprinkle with toasted pine nuts or almonds.
Yellow rice— GELBER REIS— *riz jaune*	Start Basmati rice with the pilaf method. Dust with turmeric before adding bouillon.
Ginger rice— INGWERREIS— *riz au gingembre*	Start Basmati rice with the pilaf method. Add a little grated fresh ginger and chopped lemon grass, simmer. Fold small cubes of candied ginger into rice.
Risotto with green asparagus— RISOTTO MIT GRÜNEM SPARGEL— *risotto aux asperges vertes*	Add blanched green asparagus tips and pieces to risotto after one-third of the cooking time; finish cooking. Garnish with green asparagus tips.
Risotto with tomatoes— RISOTTO MIT TOMATEN— *risotto aux tomates*	Flavor risotto with tomato paste, and fold in diced tomato cubes at the end.
Risotto with porcini— RISOTTO MIT STEINPILZEN— *risotto aux cèpes*	Soak dried porcinis, remove sandy residue. Slice into strips, and sauté with the onions; if desired, flavor with saffron. Cook risotto as usual.
Risotto with saffron— SAFRANRISOTTO— *risotto milanaise*	When the risotto is almost finished, add powdered saffron or saffron threads (saffron flavor will be more intense).
Red-wine risotto— ROTWEINRISOTTO— *risotto au vin rouge*	Use a strong red wine for the first phase of the risotto, continue with bouillon, finish the risotto with red wine.

7.17.5 Cornmeal Dishes

Cornmeal dishes are most popular in southern Europe and in South America. Depending on the dish, a coarse meal (*bramata*) or a very finely milled semolina-style cornmeal is used. In Europe, polenta is the primary cornmeal dish (see Table 7-106 for polenta dishes). In South America, it is used for tortillas and related dishes. In the southern United States, it is used for corn pone and hush puppies.

Table 7-106. Polenta Dishes

Dish	Description
Cornmeal timbales– MAISKÖPFCHEN– timbale de maïs	Prepare polenta using medium-fine cornmeal. Add 4 egg yolks, and pour into buttered timbale molds. Bake in the oven, let rest, and unmold.
Cornmeal gnocchi– MAISNOCKEN– gnocchi de maïs	Prepare polenta using medium-fine cornmeal. Add 4 egg yolks, and spread onto an oiled sheet pan; cool. Cut out shapes or slice. Gratinate in the oven, or dip in egg and sauté.
Breaded polenta slices– PANIERTE MAISSCHNITTEN– polenta panée	Cut polenta in slices, bread, and sauté in butter until crisp.
Cornmeal souffle– MAISAUFLAUF– soufflé de maïs	Prepare polenta using medium-fine cornmeal; let cool a little. Add egg yolks. Beat egg white, and fold in gently. Place in buttered soufflé forms sprinkled with cornmeal. Poach to warm in a water bath, and finish by baking in the oven.
Polenta slices with cheese– GESCHMOLZENE MAISSCHNITTEN– polenta piémontaise	Prepare polenta using coarse cornmeal, and fold in diced cubes of Fontina cheese. Spread mixture on an oiled sheet pan about ¾ inch (2 cm) thick. Cut out shapes, sprinkle with grated cheese (Sbrinz), drizzle with melted butter, and gratinate in the oven.

Table 7-107. Whole Grains and Uses

Grain	Uses
Whole oats	Whole-grain risotto, soufflé
Spelt	Whole-grain risotto, whole-grain cakes
Rye	Whole-grain risotto, whole-grain cakes
Wheat	Whole-grain risotto, whole-grain cakes
Barley	Barley risotto, whole-grain risotto
Buckwheat	Mixed only with other whole grains
Millet	Millet risotto, millet ring, whole-grain risotto
Brown rice	Rice pilaf, boiled rice, risotto, whole-grain risotto
Red wild rice	rice pilaf, boiled rice, risotto, whole-grain risotto
Wild rice	Combined creatively with other rice varieties, whole-grain risotto

Basic Recipe for Polenta

YIELD: 10 SERVINGS		
Onion	3½ oz	100 g
Garlic	⅓ oz	10 g
Olive oil	1⅔ oz	50 ml
Bouillon	1 qt, 2 oz	1 L
Cornmeal, coarse	8½ oz	250 g
Bay leaf	1	1
Salt, pepper		
Grated cheese (Sbrinz)	3½ oz	100 g

Method
- Sauté the onions and garlic in the olive oil until translucent.
- Add the bouillon, and bring to a boil.
- Drizzle in the cornmeal slowly, stirring constantly.
- Cook over very low heat for about 5 minutes, stirring frequently, until all liquid is absorbed.
- Add bay leaf, season with salt and pepper, cover, and let expand over the lowest possible heat.
- Do not stir.
- Fold cheese into polenta.

Notes
If desired, the polenta can also be cooked in 1 pt, 5 oz (600 ml) of bouillon and 13½ oz (400 ml)milk

7.17.6 Whole-grain Dishes

Whole-grain dishes should not be reserved only for whole-grain or health spa menus. They make great side dishes with other items on the standard menu. Table 7-107 lists various whole grains and their uses. Table 7-109 lists dishes that contain whole grains.

Preparing Whole-grain Dishes
- Unrefined grain kernels are rinsed before preparation.
- Soaking kernels in water or vegetable stock shortens the cooking time. It is important to use the soaking liquid in the cooking process.
- Grains combine well with legumes.

Cooking Whole Grains

Washing
Rinse the measured amount of grains in cold water, drain.

Pour boiling water briefly over buckwheat groats.

Drying/Toasting
Place the rinsed, still wet kernels on a sheet pan and bake for 60 minutes

Table 7-108. Basic Directions for Cooking Grains

Ingredient	Soaking	Cooking	Expanding	Special Notes
Spelt	3 to 8 hours	1 to 1½ hours	30 minutes	
Barley	up to 8 hours	1 to 2 hours	30 minutes	
Unripe spelt	up to 8 hours	½ to 1½ hours	30 minutes	
Oats	up to 8 hours	1 to 1½ hours	15 minutes	
Rye	5 to 8 hours	1 to 1½ hours	30 minutes	Toast before soaking
Brown rice	not necessary	1½ to 2 hours	10 minutes	Long-grain rice needs less water and cooks faster
Wheat	5 to 8 hours	¾ to 1 hour	30 minutes	
Millet	not necessary	25 minutes	15 minutes	

in a regular or convection oven at 140° to 178°F (60° to 80°C). The flavor and digestibility of the grain improves because some of the starch is changed to dextrose.

Soaking

The longer the kernels soak, the shorter the cooking time. The water-soluble nutrients will leach into the liquid; hence, the grains are always cooked in the soaking liquid. The grains must be refrigerated if they are soaking in vegetable stock.

Cooking

Whole kernels are cooked starting in cold liquid, which is brought to a boil and skimmed. Keep at a simmer and cook without stirring until done.

Grains can be cooked in a pressure cooker, which reduces the cooking time by half, with less liquid.

Meal and flakes are added to simmering liquid.

Coarse meal is started in cold water and brought to a boil with constant stirring.

Salting

After the grain has come to a boil, add a little salt. Add a little salt to the water if the grain is cooked in a pressure steamer.

Expanding

Let covered grains expand over a very low flame or in a low-temperature oven. Grains that have had time to expand are tastier and more easily digested.

Amounts and Times

The figures in Table 7-108 are guidelines only. They vary with age, type of cooking liquid (hardness of water), and the desired consistency. Larger quantities of grain need less liquid.

Basic Recipes for Cooked Grains

Table 7-109 lists dishes made with cooked grains.

Wheat/Rye – WEIZEN/ROGGEN

YIELD: 10 SERVINGS		
Wheat, whole kernel	7 oz	200 g
Rye, whole kernel	7 oz	200 g
Vegetable bouillon	1 qt, 8 oz	1.2 L
Bouquet garni	5⅓ oz	150 g
Onion studded with 3 cloves	1	1
Thyme, sprig	1	1
Salt		

Method

- Rinse the wheat and rye.
- Let soak about 8 hours in vegetable bouillon, in the refrigerator.
- Bring the kernels and soaking liquid to a boil.
- Skim, and add the *bouquet garni*, studded onion, and thyme.
- Simmer, and add salt after 1 hour.
- Cover, and let simmer over very low heat for 1½ hours.
- Let expand for 30 minutes.

Unripe Spelt – GRÜNKERN

Unripe spelt	14 oz	400 g
Vegetable bouillon	1 qt, 2 oz	1 L
Bouquet garni	5⅓ oz	150 g
Onion studded with 3 cloves	1	1
Thyme, sprig	1	1
Salt		

Method

- Rinse the unripe spelt.

- Let soak about 6 hours in vegetable bouillon, in the refrigerator.
- Bring the kernels and soaking liquid to a boil.
- Skim, and add the *bouquet garni*, studded onion, and thyme.
- Simmer, and add salt after ½ hour.
- Cover, and let simmer over very low heat for 1 hour.
- Let expand for 10 minutes.

Brown-rice Risotto – VOLLREIS-RISOTTO

Brown rice, round kernel	1 lb, 2 oz	500 g
Onion	3½ oz	100 g
Garlic cloves	2	2
Olive oil	1⅔ oz	50 g
Vegetable bouillon	1 qt, 8 oz	1.2 L
Sage leaves	2	2
White wine	3½ oz	100 ml
Grated cheese (Sbrinz)	3½ oz	100 g
Butter	1 oz	30 g
Salt, pepper		

Method

- Rinse the brown rice.
- Sauté the finely chopped onion and garlic in olive oil.
- Add the rice, and continue to sauté.
- Add the vegetable bouillon.
- Add chopped sage leaves.
- Do not salt, or the rice will remain hard.
- Simmer for 30 to 35 minutes.
- Do not stir, or the rice may become mushy.
- Remove from the heat, and let expand for 10 to 15 minutes.
- Carefully fold in the white wine, cheese, and butter.
- Season to taste with salt and pepper.

Table 7-109. Whole-grain Dishes

Dish	Description
Spelt croquettes— GRÜNKERNKROKETTEN— *croquettes de blé vert*	Cool cooked unripe spelt. Stir together with whole-wheat flour, eggs, and chopped fresh herbs into a dough that holds its shape. Form into logs, cut into small pieces, and dredge in whole-grain semolina. Deep-fry until crisp.
Whole-grain Rösti— GETREIDE RÖSTI— *roesti de cérealés*	Sauté chopped onions and garlic in butter until translucent. Add cooked whole grains (wheat, rye, unripe spelt), and sauté well, until a crisp crust forms. Moisten with vegetable stock if necessary.
Wheat soufflé with vegetables— WEIZENAUFLAUF MIT GEMÜSE— *soufflé de froment aux légumes*	Sauté chopped onions until translucent, add blanched seasonal vegetables, and continue to sauté. Mix with cooked wheat kernels. Beat in egg yolks and cream. Beat egg whites, and fold gently into mixture. Butter an oven-proof dish, sprinkle with whole-grain semolina, and pour in batter. Poach to warm in a water bath, and finish baking in the oven for 35 minutes, using increasingly higher heat.
Millet ring with wild mushroom stew— HIRSERING MIT PILZRAGOUT— *bordure de millet aux champignons des bois*	Fill a buttered ring mold with cooked millet, and press down. Let stand for a time; then unmold. Fill center with wild mushroom stew.
Barley risotto— GERSTOTTO	Soak whole barley for 5 hours. Prepare as for whole-grain risotto. Add tomato paste, and sauté before adding liquid. Cooking time, about 2 hours. Let expand for 30 minutes more.

7.18 National Dishes

The origin of a dish is not easily assigned to a specific country. Throughout history, as people migrated, they brought ingredients and dishes with them into many different regions, so that it is almost impossible to pinpoint the country of origin for many dishes. Many national dishes are foreign creations that, with slight changes, became national favorites. For example, Wiener Schnitzel, or Viennese veal cutlets, supposedly were introduced by the noted gourmet field marshall Radetzky in Vienna. They are actually a variation of the Italian *cotoletta*, which came to Italy from Spain, via Arabia, from the Byzantine empire.

As recipes are passed along, changes are made to suit the eating habits of the region, so that often several versions of the same "original" recipe exist.

The selection of recipes offered in *Classical Cooking the Modern Way: Recipes* is limited to dishes offered in foodservice operations.

7.18.1 Swiss Cuisine

When Switzerland's stony fields pro-duced little, and steep mountains isolated the people living in the valleys, the basic ingredients for simple dishes were milk, cream, butter, and cheese, with some pork and lamb. Poor cooking facilities limited preparation to simple methods.

Better transportation brought increased commerce and the exchange of foods with surrounding countries. Italian, French, German, and Austrian influences became more and more apparent. The original Swiss cuisine developed into an international cuisine, based on classical principles, with a few Swiss specialties.

Typical Swiss Specialties

Bündner Gerstensuppe – Barley soup (page 51)

Basler Mehlsuppe – Old-fashioned onion soup (page 48).

Buseca ticinese – Italian vegetable soup with tripe (page 52)

Fondue – Swiss fondue (page 308)

Ramequin – Small puff pastry shells filled with cheese

Raclette – Cheese raclette (page 238)

Schaffhauser Bölletünne – Onion cake, Schaffhausen style

Basler Zwiebelwähe – Basel Onion Tart (page 132)

St. Galler Käsekugeln – St. Galler cheese fritters (page 155)

Omble chevalier genevoise – Poached char with a cream and white-wine sauce

Felchenfilets Luzerner Art – Whitefish fillets, Lucerne style (page 161)

Saibling auf Zuger Art – Poached saibling (char) with herbs (page 341)

Luzerner Chügelipastete – Vol-auvent, Lucerne style

Geschnetzeltes Zürcher Art – Shredded veal in cream sauce, Zürich style

Urner Kabisfleisch – Lamb, goat, pork, and beef ragout with green cabbage

Potée fribourgeoise – Thick one pot soup, Friburg style

Berner Platte – Poached smoked meats and sausage, Bernese style

Capuns – Stuffed Swiss chard rolls

Rösti – Rösti potatoes (page 321)

Aargauer Rüeblitorte – Aargau Carrot Cake

Zuger Kirschtorte – Kirsch torte, Zug style (page 399)

St. Galler Klostertorte – St. Gallen convent cake

7.18.2 French Cuisine

Paris and Surroundings – Ile de France

The region around Paris is viewed as the birthplace of *haute cuisine*. Here in the court kitchens of many kings and princes, innumerable dishes were invented and perfected. And, of course, specialties from many regions of France were introduced and integrated.

Typical Dishes
Civet de lièvre – Jugged rabbit stew

Coquetlet à la crème à la ciboulette – Poulet with cream sauce and chives

Bretagne

In Bretagne, the ocean provides the basic ingredients for many fish and seafood specialties. *Crêpes*, French pancakes, also originated in this region.

Typical Dishes
Crêpes des moines – Crepes filled with seafood

Normandy

Normandy is an agricultural region, and its cuisine uses many dairy products. In addition, there are many apple recipes, and recipes that use Calvados (apple brandy).

Typical Dishes
Tripes à la mode de Caen – Braised tripe with apple wine and Calvados

Douillons de pommes normande – Apple in puff pastry with apricot jam and cream

Alsace-Lorraine

For a long time, this area was part of Germany, which is reflected in its cuisine. Alsatian specialties are sausages and sauerkraut. Lorraine is the home of one the most famous French specialties, *quiche lorraine*.

And in the countryside, a *potée*, a sauerkraut soup with pork and vegetables, is very popular. The fruity white Rhine wines from Alsace are close relatives of the German Rhine wines.

Typical Dishes
Faisan alsacienne – Butter-roasted pheasant with sauerkraut

Quiche lorraine – Egg, bacon, and onion tart

Burgundy

Burgundy is world-famous for its great wines. Wine also plays an important role in their regional cuisine. Red wine, for example, is the most important ingredient in *bœuf bourguignonne*.

Every year Dijon, renowned as the mustard capital of France, hosts the gastronomical world's fair for gourmets.

Burgundy is also the home of the famous Charolais beef.

Typical Dishes
Bœuf bourguignonne – Beef stew or roast cooked in a Burgundy red-wine sauce

Bordeaux

The Bordeaux wines are as famous as the wines of Burgundy. The cooks in Bordeaux gave *haute cuisine* the wonderful gift of *sauce bordelaise*.

At the northern edge of the Bordeaux region lies Cognac, the brandy capital of the world, and Périgueux, where black truffles are used in many recipes.

Typical Dishes
Pâté de foie gras truffé – Liver pâté with truffles

Confit d'oie salardaise – Goose legs roasted in goose fat, served with truffle sauce.

Languedoc

Languedoc was the French outpost of the Roman empire, and the regional populace still enjoys *cassoulet*, which originated in old

Roman cuisine. *Cassoulet* is a combination of white beans, sausage, goose, duck, and pork or lamb. Languedoc is also the home of the best-known sheep's cheese, Roquefort.

Along the Pyrenees, in Foix and Rouissilon, the culinary influences are from neighbor Spain, especially noticeable in the omelets, which are filled with green peppers, tomatoes, and ham.

Typical Dishes
Cassoulet de mouton – Lamb stew with bacon and white beans

Andouilette braisée – Braised pork sausages in natural casings.

Provence

Provence is France's favorite vacation region.

Like that of many other regions of the northern Mediterranean, the cuisine of Provence is based on garlic, olives, olive oil, and tomatoes. One dish that includes all of these ingredients is *bouillabaisse*, from Marseilles, a fish stew that often contains a dozen types of fish and shellfish from the Mediterranean Sea.

The dishes from Provence are spicier than those from northern France.

Typical Dishes
Bouillabaisse – Fish stew

Ratatouille – Vegetable stew

Salade niçoise – Potato, green bean, tuna, olive, and tomato salad

Other French National Dishes

Petite marmite Henri IV – Vegetable soup with beef, chicken, and marrow bones

Soupe à l'oignon gratinée – Gratinated onion soup

Crème dieppoise – Fish and mussel soup with cream

Crème au vin d'Auvergne – Grape soup with leeks, onions, and wine from Auvergne

Filets de sandre Joinville – Poached

pike perch fillet with crayfish sauce

Coquilles Saint-Jacques parisienne – Gratinated scallops

Bœuf bouilli alsacienne – Boiled beef with sauerkraut

Coq au vin rouge – Chicken braised in red wine

Escargots bourguignonne – Snails with garlic and butter

Crêpes Suzette – Crepes with glazed orange sauce

7.18.3 Italian Cuisine

Italian cuisine is a hearty, colorful cuisine that awakens vacation fantasies. Connoisseurs appreciate the wonderful raw ingredients: white truffles from Piedmont, Parma hams from Emilia, great beef from Romagna, and the simple pasta dishes and pizzas from the South and Naples. Flavorful olive oils and vinegars, and strong wines complete the culinary picture.

Piedmont

The truffle capital of Piedmont is Alba. The season for white truffles stretches from November to January. Using a very sharp mandolin, the truffles are shaved almost translucently thin over many dishes.

Typical Dishes
Fettuccine ai tartufi – Fettuccini with white truffles

Gnocchi piemontese – Gnocchi au gratin with tomato sauce

Venice

The cuisine of Venice is based on a large variety of fish and shellfish.

Typical Dishes
Zuppa di pesce – Fish soup

Scampi alla griglia – Grilled prawns

Milan, Lombardy

The cuisine of Milan is known for its slowly braised meats *brasati* and *osso buco*. The cooks of Milan sauté in a lot of butter, just as the French do.

Panettone and the pickled mustard fruits are from Lombardy.

Typical Dishes
Manzo brasato lombardese – Braised beef roast in red wine sauce

Osso buco – Glazed veal shanks

Panettone – Sweet yeast bread studded with candied fruit

Risotto milanaise – Risotto with butter and grated cheese

Genoa, Liguria

The cuisine of Liguria is full of fish and shellfish dishes. In addition, very good pasta dishes are a part of the diet in this coastal region.

Typical Dishes
Ravioli alla ricotta – Ravioli with ricotta cheese

Pesto genovese – Basil, pine nut, garlic, and grated cheese (Pecorino) sauce

Bologna, Emilia Romagna

Here one finds Italy's most sumptuous and plentiful cuisine: wonderful veal and beef dishes, Parma ham, excellent pasta dishes, and great cheese.

Typical Dishes
Spaghetti bolognese – Spaghetti with meat sauce

Involtini cacciatore – Glazed veal birds with chicken liver stuffing

Tuscany

The food in Tuscany is true home cooking. Dishes are prepared from first-class ingredients. Lovely wines from the region include the classic Chianti.

Typical Dishes
Bistecca fiorentina – Grilled Porterhouse steak

Crostini ai funghi – Garlic cheese and mushroom toast

Rome

As one might expect of a capital, one finds both northern and southern Italian cuisines in Rome. But it has a few specialties of its own as well.

Typical Dishes
Gnocchi alla romana – Semolina gnocchi

Saltimbocca – Veal cutlet with sage and smoked ham

Naples

The cuisine of Naples is very hearty: many spaghetti and macaroni dishes with interesting sauces, fish, and shellfish. Pizza, and all its variations, is probably Naples' best-known export.

Typical Dishes
Pizza napoletana – Pizza with tomatoes, mozzarella, oregano, and garlic

Spaghetti napoletana – Spaghetti with tomato sauce

Sardinia and Sicily

The cuisine of these two islands is quite different from that of the rest of Italy. It is influenced by the Middle East and north Africa. Their desserts are world-renowned.

Typical Dishes
Pomodori siciliana – Baked tomatoes with anchovies

Zabaione – Frothy Marsala custard sauce (zabaglione)

Other Italian National Dishes

Busecca – Italian vegetable soup

Minestrone – Italian vegetable noodle soup

Zuppa pavese – Bread, egg, and cheese soup

Zuppa mille-fanti – Italian egg-drop soup

Bollito misto – Assorted boiled meats

Carpaccio – Marinated, thinly sliced raw beef

Canneloni – Gratinated stuffed noodle rolls

Lasagne – Layered noodle casserole

Piccata – Veal cutlets sautéed in egg and cheese batter

Vitello tonnato–Cold veal with tuna sauce

Cassata siciliana–Sicily's Easter cake: rum-soaked sponge cake, layered with a ricotta, candied orange, and chocolate chip filling

7.18.4 German Cuisine

Southern Germany

Rhine

The famous Rhine wines are served with various simple stews of cabbage, turnips, and smoked ham in many variations. The Rhine area also has many creative potato dishes.

Typical Dish
Eisbein mit Sauerkraut–Cured pig knuckles with sauerkraut

Baden

Baden is known for having the best regional cuisine in Germany. From here comes the famous Black Forest cake, which is served in every restaurant or bakery, made from the "original" recipe.

Typical Dishes
Rehschnitzel Baden-Baden–Venison cutlet (marinated), served with a cranberry-stuffed pear

Schwarzwälder Kirschtorte–Black Forest cherry cake

Württemberg

Württemberg is the home of many spaetzle varietes. Large, filled pasta squares called *Maultaschen*, potato noodles, and Schwetziger white asparagus are all from this region.

Typical Dishes
Leberspätzle–Liver spaetzle

Dampfnudeln–Yeast dumplings poached in milk

Bavaria

Bavarians believe in the maxim "Meat is the best vegetable." Beloved are hearty pork dishes, boiled meats and sausages of all kinds, and veal and pork shanks. Usually beer is the beverage of choice, and a clear brandy follows these rather high-fat dishes.

Typical Dishes
Weisswürste–White veal sausages

Leberknödel–Liver dumplings

Central Germany

Westphalia

The famous smoked Westphalian ham is from pigs raised on acorns. A traditional ham platter also contains paprika ham, smoked hard sausages, butter balls, and pumpernickel (black whole-grain and coarse-rye bread; the dough rises for twenty-four hours and is baked as long).

Typical dish
Grüne Sauce–Mayonnaise with chopped fresh herbs and hard-cooked eggs

Saxony, Silesia

Saxony is famous for its sweet doughs, such as in *Bienenstich* (yeast sheet cake covered with caramelized almonds), and *Streusselkuchen* (sweet yeast cake covered with streusel). Silesia is known for its country-style stews.

Typical Dishes
Schnitzel Holstein–Veal cutlet topped with an egg, sunny side up, and crossed with anchovy fillets

Hefekranz–Yeast Bundt cake

North Germany

The harsh, cold climate of northern Germany has inspired hearty meals, such as cabbage and bacon soups, dishes with pickled or smoked fish, roast goose and duck, halibut and flounder, eel and herring.

North Sea and Baltic Coasts
Herring is the most popular fish. It is offered as "Matjes" or Bismark herring (brined raw) or is fried or pickled. Delicacies are Katen (farm-cured and -smoked) ham and sausages.

Typical Dishes
Geräucherter Aal–Smoked eel

Brathering–Fried herring pickled with vinegar and onions

Lüneburg Heath
Best known are the regional sheep known as *Heidschnucken*.

Typical Dishes
Graupensuppe mit Backpflaumen–Barley soup with prunes

In Butter und Dill gedünstete saure Gurken–Braised sour cucumbers in butter and dill

7.18.5 Austrian Cuisine

The origin of Austrian cuisine can be found in the former realm of the greater Bohemian emperors.

Typical Dishes
Wiener Schnitzel–Breaded veal cutlet

Rahmgoulash–Braised veal stew with cream

Wiener Backhendle–Breaded and deep-fried chicken

Rostbraten–Sirloin steak sautéed or braised with onions

Kaiserschmarrn–Oven-baked soufflé dumplings

Marillenknödel–Apricot dumplings

Salzburger Nockerln–Sweet baked soufflé dumplings

Palatschinken–Pancakes stuffed with a sweet filling

Wiener Apfelstrudel–Viennese apple strudel

Sacher Torte–Chocolate layer cake

Linzer Torte–Almond-macaroon raspberry tart

7.18.6 Spanish and Portuguese Cuisine

The cuisine of the Iberian peninsula is as diverse as its population. However, garlic and olive oil are unmistakably asssociated with most Spanish and Portuguese dishes.

During the day, the Spanish people eat many small delicate snacks, found on *tappas* buffets. Often as many as thirty of these snacks are offered, from marinated olives, small meatballs, rice salad, pickled fish, and salted anchovies to canned peppers and more.

Typical Dishes

Cochinillo asado – Roast suckling pig

Sopa de ajo – Garlic soup

Cocido madrileno – Meat casserole

Gazpacho – Cold vegetable soup

Paella – Rice with fish, mussels, and chicken

Salsa ali-oli – Garlic sauce

Zarzuela de mariscos – Seafood stew

Pollo a la chilindrón – Roasted chicken with bell peppers

7.18.7 British Cuisine

British cuisine includes the cooking of England, Scotland, Ireland, Northern Ireland, and Wales.

British cuisine is not known for being imaginative but has wonderful basic ingredients, great fish and shellfish, and Aberdeen beef and lamb.

As one of the greatest colonial empires, England could once afford to import the very best. British dishes are plain and uncomplicated and rely on the food's inherent taste.

Typical Dishes

Scotch broth (barley soup with vegetables)

Cock-a-leekie (chicken broth with leeks and prunes)

Scotch woodcock (toast with anchovies, capers, and scrambled eggs)

Welsh rarebit/rabbit (melted cheese and beer on toast)

Smoked haddock

Aberdeen Angus beef

Yorkshire pudding (egg batter pudding baked in roast beef drippings)

Boiled leg of lamb

Roast leg of lamb with mint sauce

Irish stew (lamb stew with vegetables)

Roast grouse

Scottish haggis (Scottish pudding of oatmeal and variety meats cooked in a sheep's stomach)

Bread and butter pudding

Gingerbread

Muffins

Chicken broth

Clear oxtail soup

7.18.8 East and South Asian Cuisine

East and South Asia have a wide variety of delightful and intriguing delicacies. Asian dishes are generally very tasty and at the same time easily digested and very healthy. Although these dishes are based on thousand-year-old traditions, they nevertheless meet modern nutritional requirements. The foundation of Asian cuisine is the use of fresh ingredients. Rice is a staple of the Asian diet and the main food at each meal.

Different nations have different traditions, ingredients, and eating habits. For example, an Indonesian meal is not eaten from plates but from small bowls, and instead of fork and knife, chopsticks are used.

India, Pakistan, Sri Lanka

Typical Dishes

Vegetarian dishes

Curry dishes

Dishes with chutney

Mulligatawny (meat or vegetable broth with apples and curry spices)

China

Typical Dishes

Spring rolls (vegetables and/or cooked meat strips wrapped in noodle dough and deep-fried until crisp)

Sweet-and-sour pork (batter-fried pork cubes mixed with onions, green peppers, and pineapple chunks in a red sweet-and-sour sauce.

Peking duck (very crisp roasted duck with several side dishes)

Japan

Typical Dishes

Maguro, sashimi (thin slices of raw tuna served as an appetizer)

Sukiyaki – Thin slices of beef and vegetables, cooked in broth, prepared tableside

Tempura – Batter-fried fish, shellfish, and vegetables

Thailand, Indonesia, Philippines

Typical Dishes

Bami – Very spicy meat and fish with noodles and onions

Nasi goreng – Very spicy meat and fish with rice and onions

7.19 Cold Dishes

The term *cold dishes* refers to all cold dishes on the menu, from small snacks to elaborate cold buffets. On the menu, cold dishes are offered as appetizers, salads, or, especially in the summer, cold entrées. The most important aspect of a cold dish is its presentation. Clean, neat work habits and an appreciation for form and color are prerequisites for success. Of course, exquisite taste is of primary importance.

Cold soups – KALTE SUPPEN – *potages froids* (see section 7.8.6)

Cold sauces – KALTE SAUCEN – *sauces froids* (see section 7.14.1)

Cold appetizers – KALTE VORSPEISEN – *hors-d'œuvre froids* (see section 7.9.1)

Salads – SALATE – *salades* (see section 7.14)

Cold second courses – KALTE ZWIS-CHENGERICHTE – *entrées froides*
Pâtés – PASTETEN – *pâtés*

Terrines – TERRINNEN – *terrines*

Galantines – GALANTINEN – *galantines*

Mousses – MOUSSEN – *mousses*

Aspics – ASPIKS – *aspics*

Cold Fish Dishes – KALTE FISCH-GERICHTE – *poissons froids*
Cold seafood dishes – KALTE KRUSTEN-UND WEICHTIERGERICHTE – *met de crustacés et de mollusques froids*

Cold Meat Dishes – KALTE FLEISCH-GERICHTE – *plats de viande froide*
Beef – RIND – *bœuf*

Veal – KALB – *veau*

Pork – SCHWEIN – *porc*

Lamb – LAMM – *agneau*

Poultry – GEFLÜGEL – *volaille*

Game animals – HAARWILD – *gibier à poil*

Game birds – FEDERWILD – *gibier à plume*

Cold garnishes – KALTE GARNITUREN – *garnitures froides*

7.19.2 Working with Aspic

Aspic plays an important role in the preparation of cold dishes.

Aspic is needed:

- to line silver plates
- to line molds
- to decorate and flavor ingredients for savory pâtés and terrines
- as a major ingredient in mousses
- as *the* major ingredient for aspics
- to glaze cold dishes

Aspic prevents dishes from drying out and prevents undesirable color changes. However, it would be wrong to consider aspic a preservative; because it contains large amounts of protein, it is considered a perishable food. Aspic must be kept in sanitary containers and stored refrigerated at about 34° to 35°F (1° to 2°C). Hands should not come into contact with it.

Regardless of whether aspic is produced from scratch or from a commercial product, the color and taste must be matched to the dish.

Aspics are grouped as follows:

- *Meat aspic:* Amber colored
- *Game aspic:* Amber colored, flavored with Madeira or port wine
- *Chicken aspic:* Light, pale yellow
- *Fish aspic:* Crystal clear

The production of aspic is described in section 7.5.2 in detail.

The flavor of an aspic is generally enhanced with wine and liqueurs, for example, white wine, port wine, Madeira, Cognac, or vermouth.

With the exception of aspic used for silver platters, all aspic should be liquid but cold. To keep aspic for a long period at the perfect temperature requires sanitary handling and a proper *mise en place*.

Mise en place for Working with Aspic

The following should be on hand when preparing to work with aspic:

- plenty of warm and cold aspic in pans
- bowls free of fat
- ice cubes
- racks and sheet pans
- cheesecloth and paper towels
- small and large ladles
- brushes free of fat
- rubber and metal spatulas
- wooden skewers

Pouring a Mirror of Aspic

Aspic pools protect expensive silver platters and also makes a dish more attractive. The aspic for pools should contain about ⅓ oz (10 g) more aspic powder for 1 qt, 2 oz (1 L) liquid, than regular aspic does. Pour onto the absolutely clean silver platter the not too hot aspic, starting in the center; make sure that no bubbles form.

Lining molds with Aspic

The molds should be stainless steel, and the inside walls must be immaculately clean and free of fat.

Chill the molds in ice water. Fill them with cold but liquid aspic, let set for a few seconds, and pour off the excess aspic. The aspic lining should not be thicker than ⅛ of an inch (3 to 4 mm). Chill the mold well before continuing to work with it.

Glazing Dishes with Aspic

Brush the cold but still liquid aspic onto the cold food or pour over food that has been placed on a rack with a sheet pan below. The aspic layer should be thin and even and show no sign of drips. When working with aspic, the cold aspic can be made more liquid with the addition of warm aspic. To glaze fruits, fruit juice or white-wine aspics are used. Gelatin (12 to 18 leaves per 2 quart, 2 ounces [1 liter] liquid) is added to a filtered clear liquid from poached fruit.

Any aspic drips can be removed with a warm metal spatula.

7.19.3 Pâtés, Terrines, Galantines – PASTETEN, TERRINNEN, GALANTINEN – *pâtés, terrines, galantines*

Definitions

Pâtés: Filling wrapped in dough and baked in the oven

Terrines: Filling cooked in a mold in a water bath in the oven or poached in a steamer.

Galantines: Deboned fish, meat, or poultry, filled with a forcemeat, rolled in a skin and poached in stock.

Farces (Fillings)

In the production of pâtés, terrines, and galantines, the farces are of utmost importance.

Different farces are grouped as follows:

- *Meat farces:* Veal, game, mixed meats, calves' liver
- *Poultry farces:* chicken, game birds, chicken liver
- *Fish farces:* freshwater and saltwater fish
- *Shellfish farces*

Composition of Farces
The classic meat farce is composed of three parts:

- meat (veal, game, poultry, liver)
- pork
- fatback (unsalted, unsmoked)

To produce a light and airy filling, as well as to bind the components, the following ingredients are needed:

- egg
- egg white
- milk
- cream
- salt

Only first-quality, fresh products are used for farces.

Flavorings for Farces
In addition to the inherent flavors of the various meats or fish, additional ingredients are added to create farces with a singular taste:

- *Spices:* Herbs, spices, and pâté spices
- *Vegetables:* Shallots, onions, garlic, *mirepoix,* flavorful mushrooms
- *Fruits:* Apples, orange zest, lemon juice, lemon zest
- *Spirits:* White wine, red wine, Cognac, Madeira, port wine, sherry, Pernod

Farce Ingredients
Depending on the recipe, the amounts of farce can vary from large (as in a vegetable terrine) to very small (as in a liver pâté).

- *Meat:* Tender meat pieces, such as filet of veal, rabbit, or game, or breast of chicken

- *Fish:* Caviar, salmon fillet, trout fillets, turbot fillets, lobster tails
- *Vegetables:* Green beans, spinach leaves, Swiss chard, broccoli, knob celery, carrots
- *Miscellaneous:* Pistachio nuts, pumpkin seeds, walnuts, dried fruits
- *Mushrooms:* Cultivated mushrooms, porcini, truffles, black trumpets, morels

Preparation of Farces
Types of farces are classified according to their preparation method:

- *Raw mousseline farce* for meat and fish
- *Raw mousseline farce with panade* (a thick paste of bread crumbs or rice, liquid, and butter or egg)
- *Game farce* (sautéed shallots, apples and liver)
- *Au gratin farce* (sautéed ingredients)

The preparation of farce requires the chopping of meat, poultry, game, or fish in pieces small enough that the protein can bind the rest of the ingredients during the cooking process. Careful attention must be given to the following points:

- All ingredients and utensils should be well chilled.
- The well-trimmed meat or fish is cut into small cubes.
- The ingredients are measured according to specific recipes.
- The cut meat is seasoned before it is ground.
- The grinding or cutting in the meat grinder or chopper must be rapid. Knives in machines should be sharp.
- Very delicate forcemeat is passed through a fine-mesh sieve.
- Garnishes are added at the very last moment to prevent discoloration.
- Alcohol is used in marinades or to deglaze but is never added directly to a forcemeat.

The preparation of farces requires skill and knowledge. A farce is a delicacy and is high in calories. Pâtés, terrines, and galantines should always be served in small portions.

Farce for Veal Pâté

YIELD: 10 SERVINGS		
Shallots	1⅔ oz	50 g
Fatback, fresh, unsalted	7 oz	200 g
Veal, pan-ready	8¾ oz	250 g
Veal liver, pan-ready	8¾ oz	250 g
Salt, pepper		
Pâté spice	⅓ oz	10 g
Sodium nitrite	1 tsp	5 g
Heavy cream, 36 percent	3½ oz	100 ml

Mise en place
- Chop the shallots, cube the fatback into ⅓-inch (1-cm) cubes.
- Cut the veal into medium-size cubes and the veal liver into larger cubes. Chill.

Method
- Melt the fatback slowly in sauté pan.
- Sauté the chopped shallots and the veal liver cubes briefly, season, and place on a sheet pan to chill completely.
- Grind the chilled ingredients, the veal cubes, the spice, and the sodium nitrite quickly in a food chopper, and chill again.
- Pass through a fine-mesh sieve, and chill again. Set in a bowl of ice cubes, and fold in the chilled cream. Season to taste.

Pâtés

Pâtés are classified as:

Fish pâtés—FISCHPASTETEN—*pâtés de poisson* (e.g., salmon pâté—LACHSPASTETE—*pâté de saumon*)

Veal pâtés—KALBFLEISCHPASTETEN—*pâtés de veau* (e.g., house pâté—HAUSPASTETE—*pâté maison*)

Game pâtés—WILDPASTETEN—*pâtés de gibier*

(e.g., Venison pâté—REHPASTETE—*pâté de chevreuil;* rabbit pâté—HASENSPASTETE—*pâté de lièvre*)

Game bird—WILDGEFLÜGELPASTETEN—*pâtés de gibier à plume* (e.g., quail pâté—WACHTELPASTETE—*pâté de caille;* partridge pâté—REBHUHNPASTETE—*pâté de perdrix*

Liver pâté–LEBERPASTETEN–*pâtés de foie* (e.g., liver pâté with truffles–GETRÜFFELTE LEBERSPASTETE–*pâté de foie truffé*)

A pâté consists of dough, forcemeat with garnishes, and aspic. Composition and preparation of forcemeats are discussed in section 7.5.3.

Pâté Dough
The pastry wrapping around the filling gives the pâté eye appeal and protects the filling from drying during baking.

Pâté dough is a pie dough.

YIELD: 2 LB (900 G)

Variation 1

All-purpose flour	1 lb, 2 oz	500 g
Butter	3½ oz	100 g
Lard	3½ oz	100 g
Salt	⅓ oz	10 g
Water	3¾ oz	130 ml
Egg yolk	1⅔ oz	50 g

Variation 2

All-purpose flour	1 lb, 2 oz	500 g
Lard	5⅓ oz	150 g
Salt	⅓ oz	10 g
Water	5 oz	150 ml
Eggs (2)	3¼ oz	90 g

Variation 3

All-purpose flour	1 lb, 2 oz	500 g
Margarine 200 g (for puff pastry)	7 oz	
Salt	⅓ oz	10 g
Water	3¾ oz	130 ml
Egg	5⅓ oz	150 g
Malt, powdered (for browning)	½ oz	15 g

Method
- Rub flour and fat together until fine.
- Shape mixture into a circle on a pastry board. Make a hole in the center.
- Place the rest of the ingredients in the hole.
- Shape into a rectangle. Cover and refrigerate for 1 to 2 hours.

Preparing Pâtés
The preparation of pâtés can be divided into the following major steps:

- Prepare forcemeat.
- Prepare dough.
- Get aspic ready.
- *Roll out pâté dough:* Roll out the dough about ⅛ inch (3 to 4 mm) thick. Mark the size of the pâté mold on the dough, adding about ¾ inch (1 to 2 cm) on all sides. Make sure there is enough dough for the top and decorations.
- *Line the pâté mold with dough:* Grease the mold, or line it with parchment. Dust the dough lightly with flour, and carefully place in the mold. Press gently against the mold walls. If desired, line the mold completely with unsalted fatback, cooked ham slices, raw cured ham, smoked salmon or the like. Let the lining hang over the mold edge.
- *Fill with forcemeat:* Place one-quarter of the forcemeat on the bottom about ¾ inch (2 cm) deep. Depending on the recipe, place marinated garnishes atop the forcemeat and then add the rest of the forcemeat. Distribute the garnishes evenly, and fill the mold about three-quarters full.
- *Top with dough lid:* Fold the fatback or other lining toward the center. Brush the dough edges with egg white or water. Place the dough lid on top, and pinch edges closed. Flute with the back of a fork or a pie fluter.
- *Cut hole in the crust:* The steam that forms during baking must escape, so a hole must be cut into the crust; it is referred to as a *chimney*.
- *Decorate the pâté:* Cut decorations of any shape from the leftover dough. Brush with egg or water, and arrange on the lid in a decorative fashion. Let the pâté rest for an hour; brush with egg yolk thinned with milk (egg wash).
- *Bake the pâté in the oven:* As a rule, pâtés start baking at higher temperatures, about 425°F (220°C), for 10 to 15 minutes, and then baking continues at a lower temperature, of 355°F (180°C), with an open vent. The degree of doneness can be determined with a needle, or check if the juices run clear. However, it is best to test doneness with a meat thermometer. Meat farce should have an internal temperature of 130°F (55°C), fish and shellfish, 110° to 115°F (42° to 45°C).
- *Fill the pâté with aspic* and chill. Remove the pâté from the mold. Clean the mold, and line it with clear plastic film. Return the pâté to the mold. Pour lukewarm aspic into the pâté through its chimney, and chill thoroughly.
- *Unmold the pâté:* Remove the chilled pâté from the mold, take off plastic film, and cut into portions.

Terrines
The main ingredient of a terrine is the farce. Unlike pâtés, terrines are cooked and served without a wrapper. Even the basic cooking method is different. Terrines are not baked; they are poached, either in a water bath in the oven or in a combi steamer.

The variety and number of ingredients for terrines are even greater than they are for pâtés. Types include:

Meat terrines–FLEISCHTERRINEN–*terrines de viande* (e.g., house terrine–HAUSTERRINE–*terrine de maison*; veal sweetbread terrine–KALBSMILKENTERRINE–*terrine de ris de veau*; liver terrine–LEBERTERRINE–*terrine de foie*)

Game terrines–WILDTERRINEN–*terrines de gibier* (e.g., hare terrine–HASENTERRINE–*terrine de lièvre*; wild boar terrine–WILDSCHWEINTERRINE–*terrine de marcassin*; venison terrine–REHTERRINE–*terrine de chevreul*)

Poultry terrines–GEFLÜGELTERRINEN–*terrines de vollaille* (e.g., pheasant terrine with red peppercorns–FASANENTERRINE–*terrine de faisan*; guinea hen terrine–PERLHUHNTERRINE–*terrine de pintade*; duck terrine–ENTENTERRINE–*terrine de canard*)

Vegetable terrines–GEMÜSETERRINEN–*terrines de légumes* (e.g., vegetable terrine–GEMÜSETERRINE–*terrine de légumes*; broccoli terrine–

BROCCOLITERRINE–*terrine de brocoli;* mushroom terrine–CHAMPIGNONTER-RINE–*terrine de champignons*)

Fish terrines–FISCHTERRINEN–*terrines de poisson* (e.g., trout terrine–FORELLENTERRINE–*terrine de truite;* eel terrine–AALTERRINE–*terrine d'anguille;* salmon terrine–LACHSTERRINE–*terrine de saumon*)

Method

The preparation of farces is discussed in detail in section 7.5.3.

Classic terrines all are lined with fatback, which should be very thinly sliced. They may also be lined with boiled ham, raw ham, or vegetables. The molds should first be lined with clear plastic wrap.

As a rule, the farce is poached in a long, narrow terrine mold. Oval oven-proof dishes or individual cocottes or round single-portion dishes are also suitable.

The basic cooking method for terrines is *poaching* in a hot water bath in the oven or without the water bath in a combi unit.

Terrines are allowed to cool in the mold, weighted down; this creates a firmer, juicier terrine.

Finishing and Service of Terrines

Remove the plastic wrap and the fat from the surface. Serve the terrine in the mold. Offer guests ⅓-inch (1-cm) slices, or form egg shapes by scooping with two spoons.

Alternately, unmold the terrine, and remove the fat from all sides. Clean the mold, line it with aspic, and return the terrine to the mold. Add more aspic around the sides, cover the top, and chill well. Unmold the terrine, and slice.

Galantines

A galantine is made by encasing farce with meat or a skin.

Classic galantines, which are also called *ballotines,* use a boned piece of meat and replace the bone with forcemeat. It is important that stuffed ballotines retain the natural shape of the animal or the animal part. To bone an animal without tearing the meat or poultry requires skill and time.

Today most galantines are rolled and shaped like a large sausage. This method is easier, because cutting the meat facilitates removing the bones.

The preparation of forcemeats is discussed in detail in section 7.5.3.

Galantines are neither roasted nor baked. They are poached in a suitable stock.

Galantines are grouped in the following manner:

Fish galantines–FISCHGALANTINEN–*galantines de poisson* (e.g., pike galantine–HECHTGALANTINE–*galantine de brochet;* pike-perch galantine–ZANDERGALANTINE–*galantine de sandre*)

Poultry galantines–GEFLÜGELGALAN-TINEN–*galantines de vollaille* (e.g., chicken galantine–HÜHNERGALANTINE–*galantine de poulet;* duck galantine–ENTENGALANTINE–*galantine de canard*)

Ballotines–BALLOTINEN–*ballotines* (e.g., goose ballotine–GÄNSEBALLOTINE–*ballotine d'oie;* lamb ballotine–LAMMBALLOTINE–*ballotine d'agneau*)

These dishes are also grouped with the galantines:

Cold stuffed breast of veal–GEFÜLLTE KALBSBRUST–*poitrine de veau farcie*

Stuffed pig's foot–GEFÜLLTER SCHWEINS-FUSS/ZAMPONI–*pied de porc farci*)

7.19.4 Mousses–MOUSSEN–*mousses*

To make a mousse, puréed meats, poultry, fish, or shellfish are enriched with whipped cream, gelatin, and depending on the recipe, with velouté. This airy mixture is generally placed in an aspic-lined small casserole or metal form and is unmolded after it has been thoroughly chilled. See Table 7-110 for typical mousse ingredient combinations.

Mousselines are small ovals that have been scooped with two spoons from a chilled mousse. They are placed on bread slices, apple slices, or cucumber rounds and, if desired, glazed with a cold mayonnaise-aspic sauce.

Table 7-110. Mousse Ingredients

Primary Ingredient	Velouté	Aspic	Cream	Spirits
Ham 8½ oz (250 g)	Béchamel 3 oz (80 ml)	Meat aspic 3½ oz (100 g)	Whipped cream 3½ oz (100 g)	Madeira 1 oz (25 g)
Beef tongue 8½ oz (250 g)	Béchamel 3 oz (80 ml)	Meat aspic 3½ oz (100 g)	Whipped cream 3½ oz (100 g)	Port wine 1 oz (25 g)
Poultry meat 8½ oz (250 g)	Poultry velouté 1⅔ oz (50 ml)	Poultry aspic 3½ oz (100 g)	Whipped cream 3½ oz (100 g)	Cognac 1 oz (25 g)
Chicken livers 8½ oz (250 g)	—	Poultry aspic 3½ oz (100 g)	Whipped cream 3½ oz (100 g)	Armagnac 1 oz (30 g)
Game meat 8½ oz (250 g)	Béchamel 1⅔ oz (50 ml)	Game aspic 3½ oz (100 g)	Whipped cream 3½ oz (100 g)	Cognac and sherry ½ oz (15 g) each
Fish 8½ oz (250 g)	Fish velouté 1⅔ oz (50 ml)	Fish aspic 3½ oz (100 g)	Whipped cream 3½ oz (100 g)	Pernod ⅔ oz (20 g)

Types of mousse include:

Ham mousse – SCHINKENMOUSSE – *mousse de jambon*

Tongue mousse – ZUNGENMOUSSE – *mousse de langue*

Chicken mousse – GEFLÜGELMOUSSE – *mousse de volaille*

Chicken-liver mousse – GEFLÜGEL-LEBERMOUSSE – *mousse de foie de volaille*

Game mousse – WILDMOUSSE – *mousse de gibier*

Fish mousse – FISCHMOUSSE – *mousse de poisson* (e.g., smoked salmon mousse – RÄUCHERFORELLEMOUSSE – *mousse de truite fumée*)

Vegetable mousse – GEMÜSEMOUSSE – *mousse de légumes* (e.g., asparagus mousse – SPARGELMOUSSE – *mousse de asperges*)

Tomato mousse – TOMATENMOUSSE – *mousse de tomates*

Method

The main ingredient of a mousse is always fully cooked, either sautéed, roasted, or poached.

Depending on its consistency, the main ingredient is ground in a meat grinder (e.g., ham), puréed in a blender with cream sauce (e.g., fish), or strained through a fine-mesh wire sieve (e.g., tomatoes).

The main ingredient can be mixed with a lukewarm velouté, but both ingredients must be at the same temperature. When the whipped cream and the gelatin is added, the ingredients should all be cold, at the same temperature.

The mixture should be filled into molds (if desired, coated with aspic), before the mixture begins to set. The molds can be topped with aspic. They are then chilled.

7.19.5 Aspics – ASPIKS – *aspics*

Molded aspics are added to the appetizer plate, served as a cold first course, or used to add eye appeal to cold buffets. They are produced in various sizes and shapes (Table 7-111 lists some examples). Although the number of ingredients that can be used to make aspics is almost unlimited, it would be a mistake to treat them as a vehicle for using up leftovers.

Table 7-111. Aspic Mold Shapes

Mold	Filling Example
Long rectangle	Ham roll
Kidney shape	Ribs
Small timbale	Poached egg
Large timbale	Lobster medallions
Cake form	Cold cuts

Varieties of Aspic

Like pâtés, terrines, and mousses, molded aspics also must offer a tasty combination of gelatin, garnish, and filling.

- *Fish aspic:* for shrimp aspic
- *Meat aspic:* for veal sweetbread aspic
- *Chicken aspic:* for chicken aspic
- *Game aspic:* for pheasant aspic

Eye-catching Garnishes

The presentation of aspics depends a great deal on the garnish. For the interior of the aspic, only taste is important, as the garnishes are generally invisible. But the garnish must still harmonize with the flavor and the filling of the aspic.

Fillings

Suitable fillings are:

- meat and cold cuts
- poultry
- game
- fish, shellfish, and crustaceans
- vegetables

Examples of Aspics

Aspic with cold cuts – ASPIK VON WURSTWAREN – *aspic de charcuterie*

Calf sweetbreads in aspic – KALB-SMILKENASPIK – *aspic de ris de veau*

Paupiettes of sole in aspic – SEEZUNG-ENRÖLLCHEN-ASPIK – *aspic de paupiettes de sole*

Preparation of Aspic

Paupiettes of Sole in Aspic – SEEZUNGENRÖLLCHEN-ASPIK – *aspic de paupiettes de sole*

Mise en place
- Prepare a mousseline farce for fish (raw).
- Trim fillet of sole, spread with the mousseline farce, and roll up.
- Poach the rolls in fish fumet and let cool.
- Prepare a fish aspic.
- Coat the inside of timbale molds with aspic.
- Cut the garnishes.

Method
- Drain the fish rolls well, and cut into even ¼-inch (5-mm) slices.
- Decorate the aspic-coated timbale forms, and line neatly with the sole slices. Cover with fish aspic.
- Use the trimmed sole pieces to make a fish mousse, and add to the prepared timbales.
- Let gel, and add aspic to fill the mold.
- Chill very well, unmold, garnish and serve.

7.19.6 Cold Fish Dishes – KALTE FISCHGERICHTE – *poissons froids*

Poaching is the basic cooking method used to prepare cold fish dishes. Two methods are possible:

- poaching in fish stock (fillets)
- poaching in court bouillon (whole fish)

Poaching Large Fillets and Fish Rolls

Suitable are fillets of sea trout, salmon, turbot, and sole.

Mise en place
- Prepare a flavorful fish stock.
- Butter a fish kettle insert, add fish fillets skin side down, and secure tightly with plastic wrap. This ensures that the fish will keep its shape. For fish rolls, roll the fish in plastic wrap. Do the same for fish fillets that are planned for rosettes. Puncture the wrapped fish several times with a metal skewer to allow the poaching liquid to penetrate.

Method

- Bring the fish stock to a simmer, and cover the fish fillets completely.
- Dissolve 4 gelatin leaves per 1 qt, 2 oz (1 L) and add to the stock.
- Poach at 175°F (80°C) for about 10 to 15 minutes. The internal temperature should reach 115° F (45°C).
- Let cool in stock, but not in the kettle.
- Remove the plastic wrap, and rewrap tightly in plastic until needed.

Cutting Styles

The fillets can be but are rarely presented whole. Usually the poached fillets are cut into slices, medallions, or cutlets.

Poaching Brook or Rainbow Trout

Mise en place

- Prepare a flavorful court bouillon, and strain.
- With needle and thread, tie the freshly killed and cleaned trout together from behind the gills to the tail to form a ring.
- Cover the tied trout with plastic wrap, and store on ice in the refrigerator for 8 hours.

Method

- Pour boiling court bouillon over the trout, and poach without heat for 10 minutes.
- Let the trout cool in the court bouillon.
- Place the cold trout on a rack, and drain.
- Carefully remove the string, garnish, and cover with aspic.

Presentation of Cold Fish Dishes

Cold fish dishes are served:

- on plates, on glass platters (small fish or portions), or in square bowls (*raviers*)
- on large display platters (glass, stainless steel, or silver) for buffets (whole fish or several portioned pieces)

When cold fish is served on plates, no base is required. The fish is often served with sauce and garnish directly on the plate or sometimes arranged on lettuce leaves.

Larger whole fish are frequently served atop a pool of aspic.

Suitable garnishes are discussed in detail in section 7.19.9.

The following sauces can be served with cold fish dishes:

- Mayonaise with dill, tarragon, chervil, parsley and chives, or puréed anchovy fillets
- Instead of mayonnaise, cottage cheese (smoothly puréed in a blender) or sour cream with lemon juice can be mixed with the aforementioned herbs.

Cold Fish Dishes

Smoked salmon rosettes – LACHSROSETTEN – *rosettes de saumon*

Stuffed small turbot – GEFÜLLTER JUNGER STEINBUTT – *turbotin farci*

7.19.7 Cold Crustacean Dishes – KALTE KRUSTENTIERGERICHTE – *mets de crustacés froids*

Crustaceans are a fixture in the appetizer repertoire and belong on the classic cold buffet. Poaching in court bouillon is the only suitable cooking method.

Excellent for cold dishes are, for example:

- spiny lobster, presented whole, with medaillons
- lobster: presented whole, with medaillons and peeled claws; split in half; as cocktails; in salads
- giant shrimp: whole; as cocktails; in salads

Trimmings and leg meat can be used to advantage with garnishes. They can also be incorporated into terrines and mousses, cocktails, or salads.

Mise en place

When crustaceans are immersed in hot water they react and curl the tail inwards. The curling can be prevented if the crustacean is tied to a small wooden plank, this keeps the tail straight. The tying must be done carefully at the very last minute just before immersion in the boiling liquid. Choose a wide strip of cheesecloth, not a string, for the process.

Court Bouillon for Poaching Crustaceans

YIELD: 5 QT, 10 OZ (5 L)		
Water	5 qt, 10 oz	5.0 L
Leeks	5⅓ oz	150 g
Onion	7 oz	250 g
Carrots	7 oz	250 g
Parsley stems	1 oz	25 g
Salt	2⅔ oz	75 g
Bay leaf	1	1
Peppercorns	⅓ oz	10 g
Caraway seeds	⅟₁₀ oz	3 g
White wine	5 oz	150 ml

Method

- Bring the water to a boil.
- Add cubed vegetables (*matignon*), herbs, and spices and simmer for 10 minutes.
- Add white wine, and bring to a boil.
- Plunge the crustaceans head first quickly into the boiling court bouillon. They should be completely covered with bouillon.
- Bring briefly to a boil, then poach at about 165°F (75°C), for 5 to 7 minutes per pound.
- Crustaceans turn red when they are boiled, because the dark pigments covering the red shell are destroyed by heat.
- Allow the crustaceans to cool in the court bouillon. Drain, and keep in a pan with a perforated insert until needed.

Presentation of Spiny Lobster

- Remove the cooked spiny lobster from the small wooden plank. With a twisting motion, separate the tail from the body.
- Clean body (carcass) with paper towels, polish with a kitchen towel, and cover lightly with aspic.
- Cut the spiny lobster tail with scissors on both sides on the inside, and remove the tail meat.
- Remove the intestine and cut the meat into even slices (medallions).

The intestine can also be removed from the slices.

- Purée any spiny lobster trimmings, and mix with whipped butter.
- Pipe a small rosette of lobster purée on each medallion, and garnish with a dot of black truffle. Cover lightly with aspic.
- Arrange the spiny lobster carcass on a mirror of aspic.
- Pipe lobster purée or lobster butter evenly onto the tail shell.
- Arrange some of the medallions on top. Arrange the rest of the medallions in an attractive fashion on the platter.
- Surround with suitable garnishes.
- Serve with a complementary sauce.

Presentation of Lobster

- Remove the lobster from the court bouillon. Remove the claws.
- Break open the claws, and remove the meat carefully. Open the pincers, and remove the meat from them.
- Split the lobster in half, by placing the tip of the knife in the center of the body near the tail end and pushing the knife down hard, first at the tail end and then all the way to the head. Remove the meat.
- **Or** place the lobster on its back, and with scissors, cut both sides along the whole length of the body. Lift the lower shell off, and remove the meat in one piece.
- Trim the lobster meat neatly.
- Remove inedible parts. Use the liver and coral for purée or mousse.
- Cut the whole lobster tail into medallions, and present on top of the body, using the same method described for spiny lobster.
- **Or** line the halved lobster carcass with lettuce leaves, and fill with a Russian salad or cubed apples mixed with a smooth cottage-cheese mayonnaise.
- Cut the lobster meat into even slices and arrange on top of the salad.
- Serve with a complementary sauce.

7.19.8 Cold Meat Dishes—KALTE FLEISCHGERICHTE—*mets de viande froide*

Cold meat dishes are almost always main entrees. The meat is cooked in one piece and sliced or carved afterward.

Often the whole piece is presented on a large platter and garnished as a showpiece (*pièce de résistance*). The showpiece was once glazed with a cold opaque aspic sauce (*sauce chaud-froid*), a practice that is no longer recommended, as it interferes with clean carving.

Basic cooking methods for cold meat dishes are poaching, simmering, roasting, butter-roasting, and braising.

For cold meat dishes, accurate temperature regulation is essential. Helpful are meat thermometers and internal temperature recorders.

Rare meat must be cooked to a more done degree if it is to be covered with aspic. The aspic draws meat juices to the surface, which could make a rare-cooked meat look unpleasantly bloody.

Before the meats are cut, they should be chilled to the core. Cool the meat on a rack, covered with parchment paper, in the refrigerator.

Excellent for cold meat dishes are:

- Veal: short loin, rack, filet, sirloin, bottom round, top round, eye of round
- Beef: filet, rib roast, loin, sirloin, tongue, brisket
- Pork: loin, filet, boneless loin, boneless fresh ham, ham, shoulder butt, pigs' feet
- Lamb: loin, leg
- Game: loin, rack, leg
- Game birds: pheasant, wild duck
- Poultry: roaster, broiler, turkey (breast, leg), guinea hen, duck

Side Dishes

Side dishes can be placed as a garnish directly on the platter or can be served separately. A buffet of several cold meat dishes should also include an assortment of complementary salads and sauces.

Cold Veal Dishes

Roasted or butter-roasted veal should not be dry. It should be prepared slightly underdone. It is sliced when cold and should be light pink in color.

Garnishes

- Stewed vegetables, Greek style
- Stuffed artichoke bottoms
- Vegetable salads
- Marinated mushrooms
- Fruits, only for decorative purposes

Cold Veal Dishes
Rack of veal with mushrooms—POELIERTES KALBSKAREE MIT PILZEN—*carré de veau poêlé aux champignons*

Cold Beef Dishes

The two preferred basic cooking methods are:

- roasting in the oven or low-temperature cooking: rib roast or loin
- simmering: brisket, tongue

Side Dishes

- Vegetables such as carrots, turnips, knob celery, cucumbers, zucchini, and the like can be cut into barrel shapes (turned) or into small sticks.
- Miniature corn on the cob, pearl onions, peppers, button mushrooms, chanterelles, and porcini can be cooked separately or mixed and marinated.

Cold Beef Dishes
Roast beef with spring vegetables—ROASTBEEF MIT FRÜHLINGSGEMÜSE—*roastbeef printanière*

Boiled beef with mixed pickles—SIEDFLEISCH MIT ESSIGGEMÜSE—*bœuf bouilli aux légumes de vinaigre*

Cold Pork Dishes

The two basic preaparation methods are

- roasting in the oven: pork loin
- poaching: ham, smoked spare ribs

Side Dishes

- Glazed and marinated vegetables, or vegetables cooked in a vinaigrette
- Stewed or poached apples, pears, or prunes
- Preserved mustard fruits
- Tomatoes stuffed with corn kernels

Cold Pork Dishes

Ham with asparagus tips—SCHINKEN MIT SPARGELSPITZEN—*jambon de porc aux pointes d'asperges*

Smoked pork loin with fruits—GERÄUCHERTES SCHWEINSKARRE MIT FRÜCHTEN—*carrée de porc fumé aux fruits*

Cold Lamb Dishes

Loin, rack, and leg of lamb should be well trimmed. All sinew and fat should be removed. Roast the lamb in the oven until medium rare; it should be pink.

Side Dishes

- Tomatoes stuffed with mushrooms
- Green bean salad or mixed bean salad, marinated celery
- Artichoke bottoms with vegetables cooked in vinegar (bell peppers, cauliflower)

Cold Game Dishes

Rack and legs of hare and venison are roasted until slightly rare. Roasts of young wild boar must be fully cooked. Wild game birds are best butter-roasted because the meat stays juicier than if they were dry roasted.

Side Dishes

- Artichoke bottoms with knob celery salad
- Tomatoes stuffed with mushrooms
- Knob celery slices with prunes
- Apples with grapes or Waldorf salad
- Pears with chestnut purée

- Pineapple with kumquats
- Puff-pastry tartlets with game purée and fruits

Cold Poultry Dishes

Whole chicken or parts of larger birds are best poached or butter-roasted.

It is better to glaze only poultry portions with an opaque aspic sauce (chaud-froid), not whole birds.

Side Dishes

- Puff-pastry tartlets or boats with vegetable salad or fruits
- Poached apple halves with currant jelly
- Pear halves poached in red wine
- Apple slices with chestnut purée

Cold Poultry Dishes

Bresse hen with tropical fruits—BRESSE-MASTHUHN MIT EXOTISCHEN FRÜCHTEN—*poularde de Bresse exotique*

Tom turkey breast with poached dried fruits—BRUST VON JUNGEM TRUTHAHN MIT DÖRRFRÜCHTEN—*suprême de dindonneau aux fruits secs*

7.19.9 Garnishes

Every cold dish needs a complementary garnish. The preparation of attractive garnishes requires neat and accurate work.

The garnishes should:

- fit the dish in size and amount
- harmonize in color and taste
- be edible; nonedible decorations should be omitted

Examples of Garnishes

Vegetables

- Fill artichoke bottoms with finely cut mushroom salad and garnish with strips of horns of plenty.

- Fill artichoke bottoms with mixed bean salad (dried green beans, black beans, and speckled borlotto beans).
- Sprinkle large mushroom caps with tiny pickled red and white onions and diced red bell pepper.
- Cut cucumbers into ¾- to 1¼-inch (2- to 4-cm) pieces, scoop out, and fill with a mixture of smooth cottage cheese and apples; garnish with a red cocktail cherry.
- Fill tomatoes with yellow corn, and garnish with black olives.
- Fill tomato boats with tuna mousse.
- Fill fennel boats with cream cheese, and sprinkle with chopped cornichons.

Fruit

- Poach seeded apple rings in white wine and saffron, and top with chopped dried fruits.
- Poach apple halves in white wine, and fill with cranberry sauce.
- Poach halved and seeded pears in white wine, and fill with chopped preserved mustard fruit.
- Poach halved pears in red wine, and cut into fan shapes.
- Garnish melon wedges with melon balls.
- Pipe smooth pistachio cottage cheese onto orange slices, and garnish with a cocktail cherry.
- Poach peaches, quarter, and fill with glazed chestnuts.
- Fill peach halves with smooth cottage cheese and chopped mustard fruits

Miscellaneous

Fill puff-pastry (tartlets or *barquettes*) with:

- poached chicken breast, diced very small and mixed with curry mayonnaise
- game purée with glazed chestnuts
- crayfish mousse with crayfish tails
- vegetable salad

7.20 Sweet Dishes

Sweets are commonly referred to as dessert. This term has become so common that even professionals in communication with guests use the term *desserts* instead of *sweet dishes* (*entremets*).

Sweet dishes have always been very popular. They add the crowning touch to a delicious meal. Sweet dishes, however, have a disadvantage. They are very high in calories. Their sugar and fat content should

be reduced whenever possible.

Served for *dessert* are cheeses, fruits, small pastries, and layer cakes (no such distinction is made in the United States; all are considered desserts).

The categories of sweet dishes are:

Warm desserts – WARME SÜSSPEISEN – entremets chauds

Cold desserts – KALTE SÜSSPEISEN – entremets froids

Frozen desserts – GEFRORENE SÜSSPEISEN – entremets glacés

Pastries and cakes – KLEINGEBÄCK UND TORTEN – friandises et gâteaux

Sweet dishes can be made from fruits, batters, dough, custards, and ice creams or combinations thereof.

The bases for most sweet dishes are:

• dough and batter
• custards and creams
• sauces and glazes

7.20.1 Doughs

Preparing Doughs

• Carefully follow recipe directions
• Accurately measure and weight all ingredients
• Set up all ingredients and utensils before the start of preparation (mise en place)
• Always sift the flour to be sure it is airy and free of lumps
• Never add all the liquid at once
• Sift baking powder with the flour
• Always follow sanitary practices
• Work on surfaces used only for desserts
• Avoid contact with hands as much as possible
• Pay attention to prescribed temperatures for fat and water in the recipes
• Mix ingredients gently
• Rest periods for doughs must be timed correctly
• Store doughs at all times in plastic to prevent drying and crusts from forming

Doughs are grouped in the following manner:

Puff Pastry – BLÄTTERTEIGE – *feuilletages*
German puff pastry – DEUTSCHER BLÄTTERTEIG – *feuilletage allemande*

Quick (Dutch) puff pastry – HOLLÄNDISCHER ODER BLITZ-BLÄTTERTEIG – *feuilletage rapide*

Mock puff pastry – HALBBLÄTTERTEIG – *feuilletage maigre*

Pie Doughs – GESALZENE MÜRBETEIGE
Pie dough – GERIEBENER TEIG – *pâte brisé*

Pie dough for pâté – PASTETENTEIG – *pâte à pâté*

Sweet Pastry Doughs – SÜSSE BUTTERTEIGE
Sugar dough – ZUCKERTEIG – *pâte sucrée*

Sandy cookie dough – SABLÉTEIG – *pâte sablée*

Linzer dough – LINZERTEIG – *pâte de Linz*

Yeast Doughs – HEFETEIGE – *pâtés levées*
Savarin yeast dough – SAVARINTEIG – *pâte à savarin*

Baba yeast dough – BABATEIG – *pâte à baba*

Doughnut yeast dough – BERLINERTEIG – *pâte de Berlin*

Brioche yeast dough – BRIOCHETEIG – *pâte à brioches*

Braided (challah) yeast dough – ZOPFTEIG – *pâte à tresses*

Kugelhopf yeast dough – TEIG FÜR HEFEGUGELHOPF – *pâte à kugelhopf*

Danish yeast dough – TOURIERTERTEIG – *pâte levée tourée*

Choux Paste – GEBRÜHTE TEIGE – *pâte à choux*
Choux paste dough – BRANDTEIG – *pâte à choux*

Specialty Doughs – SPEZIALTEIGE
Strudel dough – STRUDELTEIG – *pâte à stroudel*

Batters – ANGERÜHRTE TEIGE
Pancake batter – PFANNKUCHENTEIG – *pâte à crêpes*

Deep-fry batter – BACKTEIG – *pâte à frire*

Choux paste and batters are of loose consistency, unlike other doughs; however, they are still considered doughs.

Puff Pastry – BLÄTTERTEIGE – *feuilletages*

The Expansion of Puff Pastry

Steam develops from moisture in the dough of double-turned pastry (puff pastry/ danish dough). The enclosed fat layers trap the steam. To ensure a perfect puff pastry, the dough layer should not tear. A steam pillow develops between the dough layers, which forces the dough to expand and become light. The separation of fatty layers creates the flaky consistency.

Composition
Flour: Puff pastry is made only with refined flour. Flour with a high gluten content is best. The development of gluten in flours with low gluten content can be encouraged with the addition of acid.

Fat: Butter, puff-pastry margarine, and commercially available puff pastry fats may be used. Tastiest is butter, but working with puff-pastry margarine is easier.

Salt: ⅔ oz (20 g) of salt dissolved in water is added to about 2 lb, 3 oz (1 kg) of flour.

Malt: Malt is added to dough made with high gluten flour to make the puff pastry more tender.

Method
Combine the flour, fat, and the salt dissolved in water. Knead well into a firm but elastic dough. As a basic rule, about 5⅓ ounces (150 g) of fat is used for every 2 pounds, 3 ounces (1 kg) of flour. This dough should rest for about 30 minutes before touring.

The dough is folded as follows:

1. Roll out the rested dough into a rectangle about ¾ inch (1.5 cm) thick. Place the fat in the center of the dough, fold the dough edges over the fat, and push together well.

2. Roll the dough with the encased fat into a rectangle about ¾ inch (1.5 cm) thick. Fold the sides evenly toward the center. The dough edges should touch. Fold the dough over once more, so that the center fold is now a side seam. This folding process is called a *double turn*.

3. Puff pastry requires four double turns. After two turns have been completed, the dough should rest in the refrigerator. Dough for puff-pastry shells is given an additional turn.

The different puff pastry types are classified as follows:

German puff pastry—DEUTSCHER BLÄTTERTEIG—*feuilletage allemande* (dough outside, fat inside)

French puff pastry—FRANZÖSISCHER BLÄTTERTEIG (fat outside, dough inside)

Quick (Dutch) puff pastry—HOLLÄNDISCHER ODER BLITZ-BLÄTTER-TEIG—*feuilletage rapide* (fat added to dough in cubes)

Mock puff pastry—HALBBLÄTTERTEIG—*feuilletage maigre* (half the amount of fat)

Process
It is important that the dough for German puff pastry be well kneaded, so that it can be easily stretched by hand.

The hardness of the fat has to be similar to the dough. If the fat is too soft, it will be incorporated into the dough. If the fat is too hard, it will be squeezed out through the layers during the touring process. Very hard fat is difficult to handle.

The number of turns depends on the amount of fat:

Little fat—fewer turns

Lots of fat—more turns

For 2 lb, 3 oz (1 kg) of flour:

1 lb, 2 oz (500 g)	margarine	3 double turns
1 lb, 5 oz to 1 lb, 8½ oz (600 to 700 g)	margarine	4 double turns
1 lb, 12 oz to 2 lb, 3 oz (800 g to 1 kg)	margarine	4 to 5 double turns

When rolling out the dough for each double turn, always roll it out evenly, about ⅔ inch thick (1.5 cm), and wipe off the dusting flour before folding the dough.

Work the corners well when rolling out the dough, and fold exactly at the edge.

The dough must rest for 30 to 45 minutes.

The dough is baked at 410° to 430°F (210° to 220°C) with steam.

Pointers
- Cutters and knives for shaping the dough must be very sharp.
- Dough scraps must be placed on top of each other and should not be kneaded.
- Sheet pans should not be greased, only rinsed with water.
- Puff-pastry baking starts at high temperature and finishes at lower temperatures.
- Puff-pastry shells are baked with steam.
- Puff-pastry dough that should not rise too high can be pricked several times with a roller or the tines of a fork. This type of pastry can be made with puff pastry trimmings or mock puff pastry dough.
- Puff pastry dough can be frozen but should be defrosted in the refrigerator.

German Puff Pastry—DEUTSCHER BLÄTTERTEIG—*feuilletage allemande*

YIELD: 2 LB, 3 OZ (1 KG)		
Bread flour, sifted	1 lb, 2 oz	500 g
Butter, not hard	2⅔ oz	75 g
Salt	⅓ oz	12 g
Water	7 oz	250 ml
Margarine for puff pastry	12 oz	350 g

Method
- Rub the flour and butter together until crumbly (fine).
- Dissolve the salt into the water, add to the dough, and knead until elastic.
- Let the dough rest for 30 minutes.
- Fold in the kneaded puff pastry margarine, and immediately give the dough two double turns. After a 30-minute rest, repeat the process with two more double turns.
- After the dough has been refrigerated for another 30 minutes, it is ready to be used as needed.

Quick (Dutch) Puff Pastry—HOLLÄNDISCHER ODER BLITZ-BLÄTTERTEIG—*feuilletage rapide*

YIELD: 2 LB, 3 OZ (1 KG)		
Margarine for puff pastry	14 oz	400 g
Bread flour, sifted	1 lb, 2 oz	500 g
Salt	⅓ oz	12 g
Water	7 oz	250 ml

Method
- Cut the chilled puff pastry margarine into ¾-inch (2-cm) cubes.
- Mix the flour, margarine, and salt dissolved in water, and work quickly into a dough.
- The margarine cubes should stay mostly intact.
- Give the dough 4 double turns, with a brief rest in the refrigerator between turns.
- After dough has been refrigerated for another 30 minutes, it is ready to be used as needed.

Mock Puff Pastry—HALBBLÄTTERTEIG—*feuilletage maigre*

YIELD: 2 LB, 3 OZ (1 KG)		
Bread flour, sifted	1 lb, 2 oz	500 g
Butter, not hard	2⅔ oz	75 g
Salt	⅓ oz	12 g
Water	7 oz	250 ml
Margarine for puff pastry	5⅓ oz	150 g

Method
Same as German puff pastry, with only three double turns.

Pie Doughs—GESALZENE MÜRBETEIGE

Composition
Flour: All-purpose flour; some specialty recipes use whole-wheat

Fat: Butter, margarine, shortening, and lard are suitable

Eggs: Whole eggs, egg yolks, egg whites

Troubleshooting
Problem: Tough dough: The dough was kneaded too much, or the liquid came directly in touch with the flour.

Remedy: Work in finely chopped fat

Short Pastry/Pie Dough – GERIEBEN-ER TEIG – *pâte brisé*

YIELD: 2 LB, 3 OZ (1 KG)		
All-purpose flour, sifted	1 lb, 2 oz	500 g
Butter, not hard	8½ oz	250 g
Salt	⅓ oz	12 g
Water	7 oz	250 ml

Method
- Add small nuggets of cold butter (or lard) to the flour.
- Dissolve the salt in the water, and work rapidly into a smooth dough.
- Knead very gently to prevent the dough from becoming tough.
- Refrigerate the dough for about 1 hour.

Pie Dough for Pâte – PASTETENTEIG – *pâté à pâté*

YIELD: 2 LB, 3 OZ (1 KG)		
All-purpose flour, sifted	1 lb, 2 oz	500 g
Lard	7 oz	200 g
Eggs	3½ oz	100 g
Salt	½ oz	15 g
Water	5⅓ oz	150 ml

Method
- Rub the flour and lard together.
- Add the eggs and salt dissolved in water.
- Knead into a smooth dough, and chill.
- The dough should rest for several hours before being worked.

Sweet Pastry Doughs – SÜSSE BUTTERTEIGE

Sweet pastry doughs are classified in three groups, which are differentiated by their different ratios of butter to sugar, as shown in Table 7-112.

Composition
Flour: All-purpose flour

Fat: Butter or margarine

Sugar: Fine sugar, fine raw sugar, confectioners' sugar (coarse granulated sugar does not dissolve fully and could caramelize during baking)

Eggs: About 40 percent of the amount of sugar; whole eggs, egg yolks, or egg whites

Table 7-112. Types of Sweet Pastry Doughs

Sweet Pastry Dough	Butter	Sugar	Flour
Cookie dough	2.5 parts	2.5 parts	5 parts
Pie dough	3 parts	2 parts	5 parts
Sugar dough	2 parts	3 parts	5 parts

Leavening: Baking powder, baking soda

Other ingredients: Ground nuts, candied fruits, cocoa, vanilla, lemon zest

Note: Ground nuts absorb moisture, and so the amount of flour should be reduced: for every 3 parts nuts, reduce flour by 1 part.

Pointers
- To leaven the dough, baking powder or baking soda is used, which is necessary for dough with less butter. The leavening agent should never come directly in contact with the fat, or it may give a soapy taste to the dough. Baking powder releases carbon dioxide at temperatures of 115° to 140°F (45° to 65°C).
- Add flour only after the butter and eggs have been well blended.
- Mix for a short time, only until all ingredients are well blended.
- Chill before using.

Troubleshooting
Crumbly dough: The fat is too soft (liquid fat merges with the flour particles, and the flour loses its ability to bind), or the dough does not have enough liquid. Crumbly dough is difficult to work with. Careful incorporation of egg white may solve the problem.

Sugar Dough – ZUCKERTEIG – *pâte sucrée*

YIELD: 2 LB, 3 OZ (1 KG)		
Eggs	3½ oz	100 g
Sugar	8⅓ oz	240 g
Vanilla bean	½	½
Butter	5⅔ oz	160 g
All-purpose flour	14 oz	400 g
Baking powder	¼ tsp	5 g
Lemon zest	½	½

Method
- Beat the eggs and sugar until foamy.
- Scrape out the vanilla marrow. Add it and the butter, and beat well.
- Add the flour, baking powder, and lemon zest.
- Knead carefully into a smooth dough.

Uses
- For fruit tartlets such as raspberry or strawberry
- As the bottom layer for fruit tarts and layer cakes
- In confections

Sandy Cookie Dough – SABLÉTEIG – *pâte sablée*

YIELD: 2 LB, 3 OZ (1 KG)		
All-purpose flour	2 lb, 3 oz	500 g
Butter	11⅓ oz	320 g
Confectioners' sugar	5⅔ oz	160 g
Egg whites	2 oz	60 g
Vanilla bean	1	1

Method
- Rub the flour and butter together.
- Beat the confectioners' sugar, egg whites, and the vanilla bean marrow until foamy.
- Gently work into a dough with the flour/butter mixture.

Uses
- Fruit tartlets
- Confections

Yeast Doughs – HEFETEIGE – *pâtes levées*

Whereas sponge cakes and other batters become light through the incorporation of air via whipping egg yolks and egg whites, yeast doughs are leavened through the fermentation of yeast.

Composition
Milk: Strengthens the gluten, gives the crust color, acts as a preservative and improves freshness

Flour: Refined or whole-wheat flour; flour high in gluten will give better volume

Fat: Butter, margarine, oil, and other fats

Malt: Malt, like sugar, nourishes the yeast and also improves color

Yeast: Fresh or frozen yeast cakes, or dry yeast

Eggs: Whole eggs or egg yolks, which add flavor to the dough

Sugar: Regular or fine sugar

Other ingredients: Lemon zest, raisins, currants, rum, and salt

Method
Direct Mixing Method
All ingredients are worked together into a dough.

This method does not produce as much flavor or fermentation acids, so more yeast must be used.

Indirect Mixing Method
A third of the flour is combined with tepid liquid, yeast, and malt or sugar to produce a sponge.

A fermentation time of 8 to 10 hours is ideal. The rest of the ingredients are then worked into the dough.

This method requires less yeast and develops much better flavor.

Pointers
- All ingredients should be at room temperature, the ideal condition for yeast.
- Let the dough rise twice, punching it down in between. The leavening power will be increased, and the texture will be more even.

Brioche Yeast Dough – BRIOCHETEIG – *pâte à brioches*

YIELD: 2 LB, 3 OZ (1 KG)		
Milk, warm	2 oz	60 ml
Yeast cake	1⅓ oz	40 g
Sugar	1 oz	30 g
Malt	1 tsp	5 g
Eggs	7	200 g
Butter, melted	5⅔ oz	160 g
All-purpose flour	1 lb, 2 oz	500 g

Method
- Combine the milk with the yeast, sugar, and malt.
- Add eggs, butter, and salt.
- Add the flour, and knead quickly into a smooth dough.
- Place in the proofing cabinet.
- Use as needed.

Uses
- Kugelhopf
- Savarins
- Babas
- Raised doughnuts
- Brioche
- Braids/challah

Choux Paste – GEBRÜHTE TEIGE – *pâte à choux*

Puff paste is a batter dough, in which the cooking process is begun on top of the stove before oven baking. It is started on top of the stove to bind the starch and denature the gluten.

Batters made with milk will have a stronger color.

Soft dough with more eggs will rise more.

The surface will be smooth if the dough is baked without stem. This is desirable for éclairs that will be glazed or choux paste swans.

Composition
Liquid: Milk or water

Fat: Butter or margarine

Flour: All-purpose flour

Eggs: Whole eggs or egg yolks

Other ingredients: Salt, sugar, lemon zest

Choux Paste Dough – BRANDTEIG – *pâte à choux*

YIELD: 2 LB, 3 OZ (1 KG)		
Milk, warm	13½ oz	400 ml
Butter	5⅓ oz	150 g
Sugar	¾ oz	20 g
Salt	1 tsp	5 g
All-purpose flour	7 oz	200 g
Eggs	12 oz	350 g

Method
- Combine the milk, butter, sugar, and salt. Bring to a boil.
- Add the flour all at once, stirring vigorously over the heat with a wooden spoon for about 10 minutes, until the mixture is smooth and no longer clings to the sides of the pan.
- Remove from the heat, and incorporate the eggs into the hot batter.

Uses
- Cream puffs
- Eclairs
- Profiteroles (small cream puffs)
- Saint-Honoré cake (choux paste border atop a pie pastry base, garnished with small cream puffs)

7.20.2 Sponge Cake Batters – BISKUITMASSEN – *appareils à biscuit*

Sponge cake batters can be divided into the following groups:

Warm Sponge Cake Batters – WARME BISKUITMASSEN
Génoise – GENUESER BISKUIT – *génoise*

Chocolate génoise – SCHOKOLADEN-BISKUIT – *génoise au chocolat*

Cold Sponge Cake Batters – KALTE BISKUITMASSEN
Sponge cake roll – ROULADENBISKUIT – *biscuit à rouler*

Lady fingers – LÖFFELBISKUIT – *pélerines*

Commercial sponge cake mix – BISKUIT MIT AUFSCHLAGMITTEL – *biscuit rapide*

Meringues – SCHNEEMASSEN – *meringues*
French meringue – SCHNEEMASSE – *meringue française*

Swiss meringue – WARME SCHNEEMASSE – *meringue suisse*

Japanese meringue – JAPONAISE-MASSE – *appareil à japonais/pâte à succès/ progrès*

Meringue cookie batter – HÜPPENMASSE – *appareil à cornets*

Composition
Eggs: Whole eggs or egg yolks and egg whites or egg whites only

Sugar: Super-fine sugar or confectioners' sugar

Flour: One-third of the all-purpose flour can be replaced with wheat, corn, or potato starch, which produces a finer and shorter texture for the sponge cake

Fat: Butter or margarine to improve quality; melted butter, not too warm, is folded gently into the batter at the end

Leavening agents: Baking powder sifted with flour; very light mixtures do not require baking powder

Other ingredients: Ground nuts, cocoa powder, grated chocolate, all mixed with the flour before being added to the batter

Method for Warm Sponge Cake Batter

- Warm the eggs and sugar and stir them together until the sugar has been dissolved and the volume has increased. This also increases the binding capacity of the egg yolks.
- Beat the batter at medium speed until foamy, firm, and cold.
- Sift the flour, and fold in gently.
- Melted butter, if used, is very carefully folded in at the end.

Method for Cold Sponge Cake Batter

- Beat the egg yolks and sugar until foamy.
- Whip the egg whites with a little sugar, ⅓ ounce (10 g) per egg white. Scrupulously clean, grease-free bowls and utensils are essential.
- Combine the two batters by folding a little beaten egg white into the egg yolk batter, folding in the flour, and then folding in the rest of the egg white.

Pointers

- Prepared batters must be baked immediately, or the incorporated air bubbles will burst, and the sponge will not rise well.
- Baking temperature: 375° to 410°F (190° to 210°C)

Sponge Cake with Volume Enhancers

These commercial products come with recipes from the manufacturer, which should be followed accurately. The batter can stand for about 1 hour without losing volume.

The baking temperatures are higher for these products, about 410° to 430°F (210° to 220°C). They are always baked without steam.

Sponge Cake – GENUESER BISKUIT – *génoise*

YIELD: 2 LAYERS		
Eggs	1 lb, 2 oz	500 g
Sugar	10½ oz	300 g
Lemon	1	1
Cake flour, sifted	7 oz	200 g
Cornstarch	3½ oz	100 g
Butter, melted	3½ oz	100 g

Method

- Combine the eggs and sugar in a mixing bowl, and whip in water bath until the sugar has dissolved. The temperature should be no more than 120°F (50°C).
- Beat the batter at medium speed, until foamy, firm, and cold.
- Add the zest of one lemon.
- Sift the flour and cornstarch together, and fold in gently.
- Fold in the melted butter very carefully.
- Bake at 375°F (190°C) with an open vent and no steam.

Jelly Roll – ROULADENBISKUIT – *biscuit à rouler*

YIELD: 2 ROLLS		
Egg yolks	8½ oz	250 g
Sugar, super-fine	5⅓ oz	150 g
Egg whites	8½ oz	250 g
Sugar, super-fine	3½ oz	100 g
Cake flour, sifted	7 oz	200 g
Butter, melted	3 ½ oz	100 g

Method

- Beat the egg yolks and sugar until foamy.
- Beat the egg whites first with 1⅔ ounces (50 g) of the sugar to soft peaks, then beat in the rest of the sugar.
- Combine both batters, and carefully fold in the sifted flour.

- Fold the melted butter into the batter gently.
- Spread the sponge batter on parchment paper and bake at 395°F (200°C). Sprinkle with a little sugar, and turn upside down on clean parchment paper.
- Remove the baking paper when cold, layer with jam, and carefully roll up. Press together firmly, and dust with confectioners' sugar.

Meringues – SCHEEMASSEN – *meringues*

Like sponge cake batters, meringue can be prepared warm or cold.

All bowls and utensils must be scrupulously clean and absolutely free of grease or fat. The egg whites must not contain even a trace of egg yolk.

Composition

Egg white: Fresh egg white or reconstituted egg white powder

Sugar: Super-fine sugar or confectioners' sugar

French Meringue Batter – KALTE SCHNEEMASSE – *meringue française*

Egg whites	10½ oz	300 g
Sugar	1 lb, 2 oz	500 g
Cornstarch	1 oz	30 g

Method

- Beat one-third of the sugar with the egg whites.
- Add another third slowly, while beating constantly.
- Fold the last third into the stiff meringue batter.
- For every 2 pounds, 3 ounces (1 L) of egg whites, 3½ oz (100 g) of cornstarch can be added to prevent the meringues from taking on color.

Swiss Meringue – WARME SCHNEEMASSE – *meringue suisse*

Egg white	7 oz	200 g
Confectioners sugar	14 oz	400 g

Method

- Beat the egg whites and confectioners' sugar in a hot water bath until the sugar is dissolved. The temperature should be no more than 120°F (50°C).

- Start baking at 300°F (150°C), lower the temperature to 230°F (110°C), and bake with the vent open until dry.

Japanese Meringue – JAPONAIS-MASSE – *appareil à japonais/pâte à succès/progrès*

YIELD: 6 LAYERS		
Egg white	8½ oz	250 g
Sugar, super-fine	1 lb, 2 oz	500 g
Ground hazelnuts	7⅓ oz	220 g
Cake flour, sifted	2 oz	60 g
Butter, melted	1 oz	25 g

Method
- Beat the egg whites and sugar to soft peaks.
- Mix the hazelnuts with the flour, and fold gently into beaten egg whites.
- Fold in the tepid melted butter.
- Bake at 320°F (160°C).

7.20.3 Creams – CREMEN – *crèmes*

Creams are used to fill pastries, or they can de served on their own, in stemmed bowls and glasses as desserts. The thickness of the cream depends on its use.

Using heavy cream or whipped cream increases the quality of the finished cream.

The name of the cream is based on its ingredients.

Creams are perishable and cannot be stored long. During the preparation of creams the following sanitary measures must be followed:

- The cream should be heated to at least 185°F (85°C) and then chilled immediately.
- Produce only small quantities.
- Store below 42°F (5°C).
- Pasteurized eggs should be used for creams that are not fully heated.

Creams can be grouped into the following categories:

Vanilla Creams – VANILLECREMEN – *crèmes à la vanille*
Vanilla cream – VANILLECREME – *crème à la vanille*

Pastry cream – FÜLLCREME – *crème pâtissière*

Vanilla mousseline cream – DIPLO-MATENCREME – *crème mousseline*

Bavarian cream – BAYERISCHE CREME – *crème bavaroise*

Crème brûllée – GEBRANNTE CREME – *crème brûllée*

Buttercreams – BUTTERCREMEN – *crèmes au beurre*
Buttercreams – BUTTERCREMEN – *crème au beurre*

Various Creams – VERSCHIEDENE CREMEN – *crèmes diverses*
Lemon cream – ZITRONENCREME – *crème au citron*

Orange cream – ORANGENCREME – *crème à l'orange*

Cottage-cheese cream – QUARKCREME – *crème de séré*

Yogurt cream – JOGHURTCREME – *crème de yogourt*

Vanilla Cream – VANILLECREME – *crème à la vanille*

YIELD: 1 QT, 2 OZ (ABOUT 1 L)		
Milk	1 qt, 2 oz	1 L
Sugar	5⅓ oz	150 g
Egg yolk	3 oz	80 g
Vanilla cream powder	2 oz	60 g

Method
- Combine 1 pint, 14 ounces (900 ml) of the milk and the sugar, and bring to a boil.
- Mix the egg yolks, vanilla powder, and 3½ oz (100 ml) milk.
- Stir into the hot milk with a wire whisk.
- Bring to a boil. Chill immediately in ice water.

Bavarian Cream – BAYERISCHE CREME – *crème bavaroise*

YIELD: 10 SERVINGS		
Gelatin leaves	⅓ oz	12 g
Milk	13½ oz	400 ml
Vanilla bean	½	½
Egg yolk	3 oz	80 g
Sugar	3 oz	80 g
Heavy cream, 36 percent	13½ oz	400 ml

Method
- Soak the gelatin leaves in cold water.
- Bring the milk and vanilla bean to a boil.
- Cream the egg yolks and sugar until foamy. Beat in the hot milk.
- Heat carefully to 185°F (85°C).
- Squeeze the gelatin leaves, add to the egg/milk mixture, and strain through a fine-mesh sieve.
- Place in ice water, and when the cream begins to thicken, gently fold in whipped heavy cream.
- Use immediately.

Buttercream – BUTTERCREMEN – *crème au beurre*

YIELD: 2 LB, 3 OZ (1 KG)		
Sugar	10½ oz	300 g
Eggs	10½ oz	300 g
Butter, sweet	1 lb, 2 oz	500 g
Confectioners' sugar	7 oz	200 g

Method
- Heat the sugar and eggs in a hot water bath, stirring constantly.
- Beat with a mixer until foamy.
- Beat the butter and confectioners' sugar until light and creamy.
- Add the egg mixture to the butter mixture.
- Flavor as desired.

7.20.4 Sauces – SAUCEN – *sauces*

Fruit sauces are prepared from fresh berries or from poached fruits.

Berry sauces are puréed in a blender, strained, and thickened with powdered sugar. (Berry sauces lose color and flavor when cooked.) The sauce can also be thickened with corn syrup.

Poached-fruit sauces: Poach apricots, peaches, or other fruit in hot syrup, cool, and purée. Flavor with Kirsch or as desired.

Cream sauces are made from the same ingredients as creams. They can also be made with cream recipes that are thinned with extra milk or cream.

Sauces are grouped in the following manner:

Berry Sauces

Raspberry sauce—HIMBEERSAUCE—*sauce Melba*

Strawberry sauce—ERDBEERSAUCE—*sauce aux fraises*

Currant sauce—JOHANNISBEERSAUCE—*sauce aux groseiles*

Poached-Fruit Sauces

Apricot sauce—APRIKOSENSAUCE—*sauce aux abricots*

Peach sauce—PFIRSICHSAUCE—*sauce aux pêches*

Cream Sauces

Vanilla sauce—VANILLESAUCE—*sauce à la vanille*

Chocolate sauce—SCHOKOLADENSAUCE—*sauce aux chocolat*

Wine Sauces

Red-wine sauce—ROTWEINSAUCE—*sauce bichof*

Sabayon—WEINSCHAUMSAUCE—*sabayon*

Raspberry Sauce—HIMBEERSAUCE—*sauce Melba*

YIELD: 1 QT, 2 OZ (1 L)		
Fresh raspberries	2 lb	900 g
Confectioners' sugar	8½ oz	250 g
Lemon	1	1

Method

- Purée the raspberries with the sugar, and strain.
- Flavor with the juice from the lemon.

Apricot Sauce—APRIKOSENSAUCE—*sauce aux abricots*

YIELD: 1 QT, 2 OZ (1 L)		
Apricots	1 lb, 10 oz	750 g
Water	8½ oz	250 g
Sugar	7 oz	200 g
Lemon	1	1

Method

- Blanch the apricots, peel, and seed.
- Cook water, sugar, and juice from the lemon to the syrup stage.

- Add the apricots, and purée in the blender.
- Strain the sauce, and flavor with brandy or Cognac.

Vanilla Sauce—VANILLESAUCE—*sauce à la vanille*

YIELD: 1 QT, 2 OZ (1 L)		
Milk	1 qt, 2 oz	1 L
Vanilla bean	1	1
Sugar	5⅓ oz	150 g
Egg yolks	8½ oz	250 g

Method

- Combine 1 pint, 14 ounces (900 ml) of the milk with the split and scraped vanilla bean and the sugar, and bring to a boil.
- Mix the egg yolks with 3½ ounces (100 ml) milk.
- Stir into the hot milk with a wire whip.
- Bring barely to a boil. Chill immediately in ice water.

Sabayon—WEINSCHAUMSAUCE—*sabayon*

YIELD: 10 SERVINGS		
White wine	13½ oz	400 ml
Sugar	8½ oz	250
Lemon juice	1 oz	30 ml
Egg yolk	8⅓ oz	240 g
Curaçao	2¾ oz	80 ml

Method

- Combine all ingredients except the Curaçao.
- Beat in a hot water bath until thick and foamy.
- Add the Curaçao. Fill balloon glasses with the sabayon.

Notes

Sabayon, also known as *zabaglione* (Italian), can be made with various sweet wines, such as Marsala, port, or sweet sherry. The proportions should be 75 percent sweet wine and 25 percent white wine.

7.20.5 Glazes—GLASUREN—*glaces*

Glazes finish the appearance of pastries and desserts. Pastries are usually first brushed with apricot glaze, which prevents the moisture from the glaze from seeping into the pastry.

Glazes are also used to garnish sweets and cakes and for decorative script.

Fondant is made with 10 parts sugar, 1 part corn syrup, and 3 parts water, and can be bought commercially. Heat fondant slowly to about 105°F (40°C). It can be thinned with syrup and flavored as desired.

Sugar glaze is 3 parts confectioners' sugar dissolved in 1 part hot water. It is used for carrot cake and confections.

Decorating glaze is 5 parts confectioners' sugar dissolved in one part hot water and beaten until foamy. Cover with plastic to prevent crusting. It is used for decorating and script.

Chocolate glaze is coating chocolate (*couverture*) dissolved in a little water and Kirsch, which is then heated slowly to about 105°F (40°C).

Compound coating chocolate is a commercial coating chocolate in which the cocoa butter content has been replaced with other fats. It is simple to use, as it does not need tempering. It is available in different colors and flavors. It is used to coat cakes and cake slices.

Apricot glaze is apricot jam that has been boiled with a little sugar and strained. It is used hot.

Sugar syrup: (28° to 30° Beaumé): Boil sugar and water in a 3:2 ratio, and skim. Let cool, and store. It is used to thin fondant, to prepare fruit glazes, or to soak sponge cake, for example.

7.20.6 Warm Desserts—WARME SÜSSPEISEN—*entremets chauds*

Warm desserts are divided into the following groups:

Soufflés—AUFLÄUFE—*soufflé*

Vanilla soufflé—VANILLAAUFLAUF—*soufflé à la vanille*

Cottage-cheese soufflé—QUARKAUFLAUF—*soufflé au séré*

Fruit soufflé—FRÜCHTEAUFLAUF—*soufflé aux fruits*

Molded Puddings—GESTÜRZTE PUD-DINGS—*poudings démoules*
Soufflé pudding—AUFLAUFPUDDING—*pouding saxon*

Hot baked almond pudding—FRANK-FURTER PUDDING—*pouding Francfort*

Diplomat pudding—PUDDING DIPLO-MATEN ART—*pouding diplomate*

English Puddings—ENGLISCHE PUD-DINGS—*poudings anglais*
Rice pudding—REISPUDDING—*pouding de riz anglaise*

Semolina pudding—GRIESSPUDDING—*pouding de semoule anglaise*

Bread pudding—BROT UND BUTTER PUDDING—*pouding de pain et de beurre*

Sweet Yeast Dough Desserts—HEFETEIGSÜSSPEISEN—*entremets à la pâte levée*
Savarin with fruits—SAVARIN MIT FRÜCHTEN—*savarin aux fruits*

Savarin with sabayon—SAVARIN MIT WEINSCHAUMSAUCE—*savarin au sabayon*

Rum baba—BABA MIT RUM—*baba au rhum*

Sweet Omelets—OMELETTEN—*omelettes*
Omelet Stephanie—OMELETTE STEPH-ANIE—*omelette Stéphanie*

Surprise omelet—ÜBERRASCHUNGS-OMELETTE—*omelette surprise*

Pancakes—PFANNKUCHEN—*crêpes*

Apple pancakes—PFANNKUCHEN MIT ÄPFELN—*crêpes normande*

Pancakes, Paris style—PFANNKUCHEN PARISER ART—*crêpes parisienne*

Fritters—GEBACKENE KRAPFEN—*beignets*
Apple fritters—APFELKÜCHLEIN—*beignets de pommes*

Pineapple fritters—ANANASKÜCHLEIN—*beignets d'ananas*

Puffed fritters—BRANDTEIGKRAPFEN—*beignets soufflés*

Turnovers—TEIGKRAPFEN—*rissoles*
Jam turnovers—KRAPFEN MIT KON-FITÜRE—*rissoles à la confiture*

Cottage-cheese turnovers—QUARK-KRAPFEN—*rissoles au séré*

Fruit turnovers—FRÜCHTEKRAPFEN—*rissoles aux fruits*

Warm Fruit Sesserts—WARME FRÜCHTESÜSSPEISEN—*entremets chauds aux fruits*
Hot apple charlotte—APFELCHARLOTTE—*charlotte aux pommes*

Apple dumplings—APFEL IM SCHLA-FROCK—*pomme en chemise*

Baked apples—ÄPFEL HAUSFRAUENART—*pommes bonne femme*

Apple strudel—APFELSTRUDEL—*stroudel aux pommes*

Puff-pastry pear strip—BIRNENJALOU-SIEN—*jalousie de poire*

Fruit au gratin—FRÜCHTEGRATIN—*gratin de fruits*

Soufflés—AUFLÄUFE—*soufflés*

All soufflés are served in the soufflé dishes in which they were baked. They must be served at once, or they will collapse.

The ingredient combinations of soufflés are rather simple. However, their preparation is somewhat labor intensive and precise.

Vanilla Soufflé—VANILLAAUFLAUF—*soufflé à la vanille*

YIELD: 10 SERVINGS		
Butter for mold	⅓ oz	10 g
Butter	3 oz	80 g
All-purpose flour	3½ oz	100 g
Vanilla bean	1	1
Salt	¼ tsp	1 g
Milk	13½ oz	400 ml
Egg yolks	4 oz	120 g
Egg whites	7 oz	200 g
Sugar	3½ oz	100 g
Confectioners' sugar	⅓ oz	10 g

Mise en place
• Butter a soufflé dish, and dust with flour; tap out excess flour.
• Do not touch the prepared inside surface, or the soufflé will not rise properly.
• Melt the butter in a pan, add the flour, and make a *roux*. Cool slightly.
• Separate the egg yolks and egg whites.

Method
• Split the vanilla bean, remove the marrow, and add with the salt to milk. Bring to a boil.
• Strain the milk. Add to the *roux*, stirring with a whisk.
• Cook, working vigorously with a wooden spoon, until the batter does not stick to the side of the pan. Remove from heat, cool slightly, and beat in one egg yolk after the other.
• Beat the egg whites and sugar together until stiff.
• Fold a little beaten egg white into the batter (to temper).
• Fold the rest of the beaten egg whites carefully into the batter.
• Fill a soufflé dish three-quarters full.
• Preheat well in a water bath on top of the stove.
• Set on a rack, and bake at 395°F (200°C). The heat must stay constant; soufflés do not tolerate heat variations.
• Check doneness with a needle. The needle should come out clean.
• Dust the baked soufflé with confectioners' sugar, and serve at once.

Notes
Bake the preheated batter (water bath) as follows:

• large soufflé dish: 20 minutes
• portion dish: 8 minutes

Variations of Vanilla Soufflé
Mocha soufflé—MOKKA AUFLAUF—*soufflé au mokka*: Same preparation as the vanilla soufflé, but ⅓ oz (10 g) of instant coffee is added to the hot milk.

Chocolate soufflé—SCHOKOLADENAU-FLAUF—*soufflé au chocolat*: Same preparation as the vanilla soufflé, but 1 oz (25 g) cocoa powder without sugar is mixed into the egg yolk batter.

Other examples include:

- Apple soufflé
- Soufflé Rothchild
- Grand Marnier soufflé
- Cottage-cheese soufflé

Molded Puddings – GESTÜRZTE PUDDINGS – *poudings démoulés*

All warm puddings are unmolded and turned upside down.

They are prepared like soufflés but contain more flour and egg yolk.

After the pudding has been cooked, it should rest a few minutes before it is turned out. The mold will separate from the pudding more easily.

Examples
- Soufflé pudding
- Hot baked almond pudding
- Diplomat pudding
- Rice soufflé pudding
- Cottage-cheese soufflé pudding

English Puddings – ENGLISCHE PUDDINGS – *poudings anglais*

English puddings are baked and served in special forms. These puddings tolerate temperature changes and can be held warm. It is important to add the sugar after the semolina or rice is cooked, or the starch grains may not become soft.

Examples
- Bread pudding
- Semolina pudding
- Rice pudding

Sweet Yeast Dough Desserts – HEFETEIGSÜSSSPEISEN – *entremets à la pâte levée*

These desserts are made with sweet yeast dough.

Savarins
Portion-size savarins are easier to soak and to fill and look prettier when served. However, large savarins are decorative on a buffet, though difficult to serve.

Savarins absorb hot liquid more evenly if baked a day ahead. Fill the form with a pastry bag no more than ¾ full. Let rise well before baking to make sure they are light and airy.

Savarins are brushed with apricot glaze and filled neatly.

Babas
Babas are prepared with savarin dough into which soaked raisins or currants have been mixed. The dough should be firmer (less liquid) than savarin dough and is placed in a timbale (ring).

Babas are also soaked in hot syrup and glazed with apricot.

Raised Jelly Doughnuts – BERLINER
Each doughnut should have a light-colored ring all around the center after frying. The dough should be light and completely risen before it is deep-fried.

These doughnuts are generally filled with seedless raspberry jam, which is injected with a specialty tube after frying.

Steamed Dumplings
This dessert is difficult to bake. A brioche dough is best, and a baking pan with a high rim is required; the pan must also be able to be covered. (A braising pan works well for larger quantities.) When setting the dumplings in the pan, enough space must be allotted to allow them to expand.

Sweetened cream is poured onto the dumplings after they have baked for 10 minutes. Baking continues until all the cream has been absorbed by the dumplings.

Serve with a vanilla sauce.

Sweet Omelets – OMELETTEN – *omelettes*

Omelet Stephanie
The omelet batter is baked in a frying pan in the oven. One-half is covered with jam or marinated fruits. The omelet is folded, slid onto a warmed plate, and served at once.

Puffed Omelet
The omelet mixture is piped onto a buttered plate, dusted with confectioners' sugar, baked in a medium-hot oven, dusted again with confectioners' sugar, and served at once.

Surprise Omelet
The surprise omelet is filled with sugar-marinated fruits (so they won't freeze) and ice cream. The whole omelet is covered and decorated with soufflé batter, dusted with powdered sugar, and baked briefly in a very hot oven. It is dusted again with confectioners' sugar, and served at once.

Pancakes/Crêpes

Preparation
- Prepare batter, and make very thin pancakes (crêpes).
- Prepare fillings, such as stewed apples with raisins or other stewed fruit.
- Fill, and brush with apricot glaze or dust with confectioners' sugar, then glaze in oven.

Examples
- Apple pancakes
- Pancakes, Paris style
- Crêpes Suzette

Fritters – GEBACKENE KRAPFEN – *beignets*

Fritters are divided into two groups, those made with batter and those made with choux paste. Fruit fritters are often partially fried in oil and then deep-fried crisp on demand, placed on paper to drain, turned in cinnamon sugar, and served with a vanilla sauce.

Fruits for fritters should be marinated and drizzled with lemon juice to increase their flavor and protect their color. Choux-paste fritters are deep-fried at lower temperatures to allow them to expand properly.

These desserts should be deep-fried in a fryer used for desserts only.

Examples
- Apple fritters – APFELKÜCHLEIN – *beignets de pommes*
- Pineapple fritters – ANANASKÜCHLEIN – *beignets d'ananas*
- Puffed fritters – BRANDTEIGKRAPFEN – *beignets soufflés*

Turnovers – TEIGKRAPFEN – *rissoles*

Today, turnovers are generally baked. During the preparation process, attention should be given to tightly sealing the edges to prevent the turnovers from popping open and spilling their filling.

Examples

Fruit turnovers – FRÜCHTEKRAPFEN – *rissoles aux fruits*

Jam turnovers – KRAPFEN MIT KONFITÜRE – *rissoles à la confiture*

Cottage-cheese turnovers – QUARK-KRAPFEN – *rissoles au séré*

Warm Fruit Desserts – WARME FRÜCHTESÜSSPEISEN – *entremets chauds aux fruits*

This group of fruit desserts is very popular with today's guests.

Examples
• Baked apples, Basel style
• Hot apple charlotte
• Apple dumplings
• Baked apples
• Apple strudel
• Puff-pastry pear jalousie
• Gratinated fruit

7.20.7 Cold Desserts – KALTE SÜSSPEISEN – *entremets froids*

Cold desserts are divided into the following groups:

Custards – GESTÜRZTE CREMEN – *crèmes renversées*
Custard cream caramel – KARAMEL-KÖPFCHEN – *crème renversée*

Classic blanc-mange – MANDELCREME – *blanc-manger*

Bavarian Creams – BAYERISCHE CREMEN – *crèmes bavaroises*
Charlotte russe – CHARLOTTE RUSSISCHE ART – *charlotte russe*

Cold charlotte flavored with Kirsch – CHARLOTTE KÖNIGLICHE ART – *charlotte royale*

Puff Paste Desserts – BRANDTEIG-SÜSSPEISEN – *entremets à la pâte à choux*
Cream puffs with whipped cream – WINDBEUTEL MIT CREME – *choux à la crème*

Eclairs with Kirsch-flavored pastry cream – BLITZKRAPFEN MIT KIRSCH – *éclairs au Kirsch*

Profiteroles with chocolate – KLEINE WINDBEUTEL MIT SCHOKOLADE – *profiteroles au chocolate*

Whipped Cream Desserts – RAHM-SÜSSPEISEN – *entremets à la crème*

Meringues with whipped cream – MERINGUES – *meringues Chantilly*

Vacherin with strawberries – VACHERIN MIT ERDBEEREN – *vacherin aux fraises*

Chestnuts with whipped cream – KASTANIEN MIT SCHLAGRAHM – *vermicelles Chantilly*

Cold Puddings – KALTE PUDDINGS – *poudings froids*
Cold rice dessert – REIS KAISERINART – *riz impératrice*

Cold semolina pudding – GRIESS VICTORIA – *semoule Victoria*

Cold semolina pudding with strawberries/strawberry flummery – FLAMMERI MIT ERDBEEREN – *flamri aux fraises*

Cold Fruit Desserts – KALTE FRÜCHTESÜSSPEISEN – *entremets froids aux fruits*
Poached pears in port wine – PORTWEINBIRNEN – *poires au porto*

Strawberries Romanoff – ERDBEEREN ROMANOW – *fraises Romanov*

Fresh fruit salad – FRUCHTSALAD – *macédoine de fruits*

Fresh figs in crème de cassis – FRISCHE FEIGEN IN CASSIS LIKÖR – *figues à la crème de cassis*

Mousses – SCHAUMCREMEN – *mousses*
Chocolate mousse – SCHOKOLADEN-SCHAUMCREME – *mousse au chocolat*

Orange mousse – ORANGENSCHAUMCREME – *mousse à l'orange*

Desserts with Cottage Cheese and Yogurt – SÜSSPEISEN MIT QUARK UND JOGHURT – *entremets au séré au yogourt*
Yogurt cake with pears – JOGHURT-SCHNITTE MIT BIRNEN – *tranche au yogourt et aux poires*

Light apple-lemon cottage cheese – LEICHTER APFEL-ZITRONEN-QUARK – *mousseline de séré aux pommes et au citron*

Fruit Tarts and Tartlets – FRÜCHTETORTEN UND FRÜCHTETÖRTCHEN – *tartes et tartelettes aux fruits*
Strawberry tart – ERDBEERTORTE – *tarte aux fraises*

Apple tart – APFELTORTE – *tarte aux pommes*

Fruit tartlets – FRUCHTTÖRTCHEN – *tartelettes aux fruits*

Custards – GESTÜRZTE CREMEN – *crèmes renversées*

Custards thicken when poached in a water bath. The exception is classic blanc-mange, in which ground almonds are the binding agent. Binding agents are eggs or egg yolks, which with milk, sugar, and vanilla are the basic custard mixture. The mixture is placed into small custard cups and poached in a water bath. The temperature should not rise above 177°F (80°C), otherwise the custard will show air holes.

These custards can also be poached in a commercial steamer. After the custard has been chilled, it is placed on a serving plate. Invert the cup and rap sharply but briefly and remove the cup carefully.

Examples
• Vanilla custard
• Custard with meringue cookies
• Custard cream caramel
• Classic blanc-mange

Bavarian Creams – BAYERISCHE CREMEN – *crèmes bavaroises*

Bavarian creams are heated to just below simmering and are thickened with gelatin. They are made light and airy with the addition of whipped cream, which is folded in just before the cream gels.

It is important to recognize the right time to add the whipped cream. If the mixture is too warm, the whipped cream will melt; if it is too cold, the mixture will gel too fast and cannot be molded well.

Place the Bavarian cream into molds, and chill in the refrigerator. Dip the mold briefly into hot water, and unmold.

Bavarian creams are a part of the classic dessert repertoire; however, the portion size should be adjusted downward to fit the eating habits of today.

The recommended amount of gelatin should be strictly adhered to: even one extra leaf can turn a light airy delight into a gummy mess.

Examples
- Bavarian cream
- Charlotte royale
- Charlotte russe
- Peach cream cake
- Cold charlotte flavored with Kirsch

Choux-paste Desserts – BRANDTEIGSÜSSPEISEN – *entremets à la pâte à choux*

Cream puffs become soft very quickly after they have been filled with cream, so fill them just before service. Cream puffs combined with fresh fruits of the season add a new twist to a classic favorite.

Choux paste must be cooked completely on top of the stove to ensure that the gluten coagulates and the starch particles stick together, or the pastry will collapse when removed from the oven.

Also important is the slow incorporation of each individual egg into the hot batter. The dough might otherwise flake and will not hold together.

Eclairs are prepared with more egg for a lighter product. Choux paste used for garnishes and decorations should be produced with fewer eggs, and a firmer dough.

Examples
- Eclairs with Kirsch-flavored pastry cream

- Eclairs with mocha cream
- Eclairs with chocolate
- Profiteroles with red currant sauce
- Profiteroles with chocolate
- Saint-Honoré cake (garnished with small cream puffs)
- Cream puff swans with pastry cream
- Cream puffs with whipped cream

Whipped-cream Desserts – RAHMSÜSSPEISEN – *entremets à la crème*

Whipped cream desserts have always been popular and are still popular today. To take into account nutritional concerns, the heavy cream can be replaced with lower-fat creams (25 percent creams can still be whipped well) without creating preparation problems. However, lower-fat cream must be thoroughly chilled to whip well.

Desserts prepared with lower-fat creams by law must be identified as such on the menu.

Whipped-cream desserts lose eye appeal rapidly. They must be prepared to order or for immediate use only.

Examples
- Baba with whipped cream
- Almond lace cookies with whipped cream
- Chestnuts with whipped cream
- Meringues with whipped cream
- Vacherin with strawberries

Cold Puddings – KALTE PUDDINGS – *poudings froids*

Cold puddings are thickened with gelatin and are made airy with whipped cream.

It is important to add the sugar after the semolina and rice are cooked, or they may not become soft.

Puddings in large molds are not easily served; it is advisable to prepare them in individual portions for more attractive service. The amount of gelatin can be reduced in such cases. It was once customary to coat pudding molds with a white-wine jelly

(aspic); this is now rarely done.

Dip the mold briefly in hot water, unmold, and garnish with suitable fruits and whipped cream. Serve with fruit sauce.

Examples
- Apricot rice pudding
- Cold semolina pudding with strawberries
- Cold semolina pudding
- Cold rice dessert

Cold Fruit Desserts – KALTE FRÜCHTESÜSSPEISEN – *entremets froids aux fruits*

The most popular of cold fruit desserts is fruit salad, which should only be prepared from fresh fruit. Pointers to observe are:

- Start with acid-containing juicy fruits, such as oranges or pineapples. Lightly sugar the cut fruit immediately. The juicy fruits contain enough acids to protect apples, pears, and bananas from oxidizing.
- The various fruits should be balanced to make a pleasing mixture.
- Use only unblemished and ripe fruits.

Examples
- Birchermuesli
- Stewed prunes
- Strawberries Romanoff
- Fresh figs in crème de cassis
- Fresh fruit salad
- Peach compote
- Poached pears in port wine

Mousses – SCHAUMCREMEN – *mousses*

Mousses are popular. They should be light and airy, and because they are high in calories, they should be served in small portions. Since they are often served tableside (scooped with two small spoons), it is easy to respond to the wishes of the guest.

Examples
- Apple mousse
- Dark chocolate mousse
- Strawberry mousse
- Orange mousse
- White chocolate mousse

Fruit Tarts and Tartlets – FRÜCHTETORTEN UND FRÜCHTETÖRTCHEN – *tartes et tartelettes aux fruits*

This group comprises many desserts that are not only after-dinner treats, but are very popular with coffee in mid-afternoon, in the European tradition.

They are easy to prepare in advance and can be kept without loss of quality for quite some time. This is especially true if they are covered with a juice-flavored clear pectin glaze.

Examples
- Apple jalousie
- Open-face apple tart
- Apple cake
- Glazed apple tart
- Apricot cake
- Pear cake
- Strawberry tart
- Strawberry tart with meringue
- Fruit tartlets
- Yogurt layer cake slices
- Prune plum cake

7.20.8 Frozen Desserts – GEFRORENE SÜSSPEISEN – *entremets glacés*

Frozen desserts are categorized as:

- ice creams
- ice-cream desserts

Frozen desserts are further grouped as follows:

Basic Ice Creams – EINFACHE EIS-SORTEN – *glaces simples*
Ice Creams – CREMEGLACEN – *glaces*
Vanilla ice cream – VANILLAGLACE – *glace à vanille*

Chocolate ice cream – SCHOKOLADEN-GLACE – *glace au chocolat*

Mocha ice cream – MOKKAGLACE – *glace au moka*

Fruit Ice Creams – FRUCHTGLACEN – *glace aux fruits*
Strawberry ice cream – ERDBEERGLACE – *glace aux fraises*

Raspberry ice cream – HIMBEERGLACE – *glace aux framboises*

Apricot ice cream – APRIKOSENGLACE – *glace aux apricots*

Sherbets – EISPUNCH – *sorbets*
Lemon sherbet – ZITRONENSORBET – *sorbet au citron*

Orange sherbet – ORANGENSORBET – *sorbet à l'orange*

Apple sherbet – APFELSORBET – *sorbet à la pomme*

Ice-cream Desserts – LEICHTE EIS-SORTEN – *glaces légères*
Ice-cream Creations – PHANTASIEEIS – *glaces fantaisie*
Ice cream charlotte – EIS-CHARLOTTE – *charlotte glacée*

Iced mandarins – EISMANDARINEN – *mandarines givrées*

Ice cream meringues – EISMERINGUEN – *meringues glacées*

Parfaits – RAHMGEFRORENES – *parfait glacé*
Parfait with Grand Marnier – RAHM-GEFRORENES MIT GRAND MARNIER – *parfait glacé Grand Marnier*

Frozen Mousses – SCHAUM-GEFRORENES – *mousses glacées*
Frozen raspberry mousse – HIMBEEREN-SCHAUMGEFRORENES – *mousse glacées aux framboises*

Frozen black currant mousse – CAS-SIS-SCHAUMGEFRORENES – *mousse glacée au cassis*

Miscellaneous Ice-cream Creations
Ice-cream bombe – EISBOMBEN – *bombes glacées*

Ice-cream cake – EISBISKUITS – *biscuits glacés*

Ice Creams – EINFACHE EISSORTEN – *glaces simples*

Ice-cream production must be extremely sanitary. Close attention must be paid to the following points:

- The ice-cream mixture must be cooked to just below simmer, and chilled *immediately*.
- Uncooked ice-cream mixtures are placed into sanitized containers and covered to ripen.
- The ice-cream freezer is sanitized after each use.
- Ice-cream mixtures are never to be touched with bare hands.
- Portioning tools can be bacteria carriers and must be constantly rinsed under running water and sanitized.

Ice Creams
- Milk is a freezing component and contributes fat.
- Egg yolks are thickeners and contribute fat.
- Sugar sweetens. The amount of sugar must be great enough to prevent crystals from forming. Too much sugar prevents freezing.
- Vanilla flavor improves all ice-cream varieties.
- Heavy cream improves flavor and makes ice creams taste richer.

Fruit Ice Creams
- Fruit purées and juices are the flavor components.
- Sugar syrup is the sweetener and adds volume.
- Lemon juice intensifies the fruit flavor.
- Commercial products or egg whites thicken and bind fruit ice creams.
- Cream improves the texture and mellows the fruit flavor.

Sherbets
- Fruit juice, fruit purée, wine, or liqueur can be used to flavor.
- Sherbets should be light and softer than regular ice creams.
- Italian meringue is used as the thickener.
- Sherbets can be piped into champagne flutes with a pastry bag.

Light Ice Creams – LEICHTE EIS-SORTEN – *glacés légers*

These ice creams are so light and airy that they can be frozen without beating, and are poured immediately into molds.

Pointers
- Too much sugar or alcohol prevents proper freezing.
- Chill the mold well before filling with ice cream.

- Unmolded ice creams can be decorated with whipped cream (the sugar in the cream stops it from freezing).
- Parfaits and soufflés should not be hard-frozen when served.

Parfaits – RAHMGEFRORENES – *parfait glacé*

The basis is an egg/sugar mixture, flavored with liqueur and mixed with whipped cream.

Frozen Mousses – SCHAUMGE-FRORENES – *mousses glacés*

The basis is an Italian meringue mixture, flavored with fruit purées and whipped cream. From these basic mixtures, the following ice cream specialties are prepared:

- Cassata
- Frozen soufflés
- Ice cream with sponge cake layers
- Ice cream bombes
- Ice cream cakes

7.20.9 Professional Terms

Almond paste
Finely ground mixture of almonds, sugar, and lemon rind

Ascorbic acid
Added to dough to stabilize gluten

Blind baking
Puff pastry tartlets or shells are baked unfilled

Burned dough
Sweet short dough that is too crumbly usually due to insufficient water content

Chocolate glaze
A coating chocolate that contains vegetable fats instead of cocoa butter

Couverture/Coating
A commercially prepared coating chocolate that contains a minimum of 32 percent cocoa butter

Dextroglucose
Used to prevent crystal formation in sugar confections

Active dry yeast
Tiny dehydrated yeast granules

Folding
Carefully mixing ingredients such as flour, melted butter, or beaten egg whites into a dough

Gelatin
Animal-based product to bind dessert creams

Glazing
Tarts or baked desserts are brushed with a glaze

Gluten
Proteins in flour that cannot dissolve in water and therefore build structure in doughs

Hard flour
Flour with a high gluten content

Modified food starch
A thermally altered starch that can bind in cold water

Needle test
Testing puddings and baked goods for doneness

Parchment paper
Liners for baking pans and sheets

Pores
Small and large air holes in baked goods

Potassium carbonate
Used as a leavening agent in combination with acid, only used in doughs containing honey

Rising times
The time yeast dough has to rest between formation and baking

7.21 Desserts

Desserts are cheeses, fruits, small pastries, and layer cakes.

Small Pastries – KLEINGEBÄCK – *friandises*

Small pastries are offered with coffee after an elegant menu. Three to six varieties are usually served, one piece for each guest, nicely arranged on a platter and placed on each table. The variety depends on the season. During the Christmas holiday season, for example, the usual chocolate truffles and confections are supplemented with cinnamon stars and almond cookies. During the summer months, small fruit tarts with fruit creams make a lovely dessert.

Examples
- Shortbread pretzels – BRETZELN – *bricelets*
- Butter macaroons – BUTTERMAKRO-NEN – *macarons au beurre*
- Cat tongues – KATZENZUNGEN – *langues de chat*
- Almond butter cookies – MAILÄN-DERLI – *petits milanais*
- Sandy cookies – SABLÉS – *sablés*
- Madeleines – SCHMELZBRÖTCHEN – *madeleines*

Cakes

Cakes are recommended for dessert. Here are some basic rules that should be remembered:

- For all cake recipes, soft butter should be used. This increases the cake volume, making it light and airy.
- Eggs should be at room temperature.
- If the cake mixture curdles, some flour should be added immediately.
- If a crack is desired, the partially baked product must be cut down the center with a dough scraper dipped in oil.
- Fruit cakes stay moist longer if the fruits have been marinated for about 2 hours.
- To prevent fruits from sinking to the bottom, they should be lightly floured before they are folded into the dough.

Cakes can be kept for some time. They also freeze successfully.

Examples

Fruit cake – CAKE MIT CANDIERTEN FRÜCHTEN – *cake aux fruits confits*

Almond or hazelnut cake – MANDEL- ODER HASELNUSSCAKE – *cake aux amandes ou aux avelines*

Chocolate sponge cake – SCHOKO- LADENCAKE – *cake au chocolat*

Lemon cake – ZITRONENCAKE – *cake au citron*

Layer Cakes – TORTEN – *gâteaux*

The production of layer cakes is very varied. Some are very labor intensive. It makes sense to produce some of the components and ingredients in quantity and keep them on hand.

Sponge cake layers and other components can be frozen to be quickly available when needed.

Layer cakes such as carrot cake, Sacher torte, and the like can be kept for some time without losing quality.

Many layer cakes can be prepared as sheet cakes. Sheet cakes can be easily cut into individual portions and look attractive on a dessert tray or cart or on a dessert buffet. Most layer cakes are more easily cut if the knife has been dipped in hot water.

Examples

Carrot cake – AARGAUER RÜBLITORTE – *tarte aux carottes argovienne*

Pineapple upside-down cake – ANANASTORTE – *gâteau à l'ananas*

Strawberry cream layer cake – ERD- BEERRAHMTORTE – *tarte aux fraises Chantilly*

Cherry layer cake – KIRSCHTORTE – *tarte au kirsch*

Linzertorte – LINZER TORTE – *tarte de Linz*

Sachertorte – SACHERTORTE – *gâteau Sacher*

Black Forest cake – SCHWARZWÄLDER TORTE – *tarte Fôret-Noire*

Bibliography

Baur, Eva Gesine and Beat Wüthrich. *Der Reichtum der Einfachen Küche: Schweiz*. München: Deutscher Taschenbuch Verlag GmBH & Co. KG, 1997.

Bennion, Marion and Osee Huges. *Introductory Foods*. Sixth edition. New York: Macmillan Publishing Co., Inc., 1975.

Birle, Herbert. *Die Sprache der Küche*. Weil der Stadt: Hädecke Verlag.

Birchfield, John. *Design & Layout of Foodservice Facilities*. New York: Van Nostrand Reinhold, 1988.

Bittman, Mark. *Fish: The Complete Guide to Buying and Cooking*. New York: Macmillan Publishing Company, 1994.

Bjornskov, Elizabeth. *The Complete Book of American Fish and Shellfish Cookery*. New York: Alfred A. Knopf, Inc., 1984.

Boxer, Arabella and Philippa Back. *The Herb Book*. London: Octopus Books Limited, 1980.

Bremness, Leslie. *Herbs*. New York: Dorling Kindersley Inc., 1994.

Bridge, Fred and Jean F. Tibbetts. *The Well-Tooled Kitchen*. New York: William Morrow and Company, Inc., 1991.

Chalmers, Irena. *The Great Food Almanac*. San Francisco: Collins Publishers, 1994.

Dittmer, Paul R. and Gerald G. Griffin. *Principles of Food, Beverage, and Labor Cost Controls*. Fifth edition. New York: Van Nostrand Reinhold, 1994.

Drummond, Karen Eich. *Nutrition for the Foodservice Professional*. Second edition. New York: Van Nostrand Reinhold, 1994.

Escoffier, Auguste. *Ma Cuisine*. New York: Crown Publishers, Inc., 1984.

Friberg, Bo. *The Professional Pastry Chef*. Third edition. New York: Van Nostrand Reinhold, 1996.

Culinary Institute of America. *The New Professional Chef*. Sixth edition. New York: Van Nostrand Reinhold, 1996.

Gööck, Roland. *Das neue grosse Kochbuch*. Gütersloh: Bertelsmann Verlag, 1963.

Gorys, Erhard. *Das neue Küchenlexicon*. München: Deutscher Taschenbuch Verlag, GmBH & Co. KG, 1994.

Griegson, Jane. *The World Atlas of Food*. London: Mitchell Beazley Publishers Limited, 1969.

Grigson, Sophie. *Gourmet Ingredients*. New York: Van Nostrand Reinhold, 1991.

Hamilton, Eva May Nunnelley and Eleanor Noss Whitney. *Nutrition Concepts and Controversies*. Second edition. St. Paul: West Publishing Company, 1982.

Heatters, Maida. *Book of Great Chocolate Desserts*. New York: Alfred A. Knopf, Inc., 1980.

Herbst, Sharon Tyler. *Food Lover's Companion*. Hauppauge, N.Y.: Barrons, 1990.

Hodges, Carol A. *Culinary Nutrition for Food Professionals*. Second edition. New York: Van Nostrand Reinhold, 1994.

Howe, Robin. *The International Wine and Food Society's Guide to Soups*. New York: Crown Publishers, Inc., 1971.

Lichine, Alexis. *New Encyclopedia of Wines and Spirits*. Fifth edition. New York: Alfred A. Knopf, Inc., 1987.

McClane, A. J. *Field Guide to Freshwater Fishes of North America*. New York: Henry Holt and Company, 1978.

National Institute for the Foodservice Industries. *Applied Foodservice Sanitation*. Third edition. Chicago: Wm. C. Brown Publishers and NIFI, 1985.

Meyers, Perla. *The Peasant Kitchen*. New York: Random House, 1978.

Margen, Sheldon and the editors of The University of California at Berkeley Wellness Letter. *The Wellness Encyclopedia of Food and Nutrition*. New York: Rebus, 1992.

Murdich, Jack. *Buying Produce*. New York: Hearst Books, 1986.

Olney, Richard. *The Good Cook: Fish*. New York: Time-Life Books, Inc., 1980.

Pennington, Jean A. T. and Helen Nichols Church. *Food Values of Portions Commonly Used*. Fourteenth edition. New York: Harper & Row, Publishers, Inc., 1985.

Peterson, James. *Fish & Shellfish*. New York: William Morrow and Company, Inc., 1996.

Peterson, James. *Sauces: Classical and Contemporary Sauce Making*. New York: John Wiley & Sons, 1998.

Pijpers, Dick, Jack G. Constant and Kees Jansen. *The Complete Book of Fruit*. New York: W. H. Smith Publisher, Inc., 1986.

Reed, Lewis. *Specs*. Second edition. New York: Van Nostrand Reinhold, 1992.

Riely, Elizabeth. *The Chef's Companion*. New York: Van Nostrand Reinhold, 1986.

Rubash, Joyce. *Master Dictionary of Food & Wine*. New York: Van Nostrand Reinhold, 1991.

Sheraton, Mimi. *The German Cookbook*. New York: Random House, 1965.

Schneider, Elizabeth. *Uncommon Fruits and Vegetables: A Commonsense Guide*. New York: Harper & Row, Publishers, Inc., 1986.

Szathmáry, Louis. *The Chef's Secret Cook Book*. Chicago: Quadrangle Books, 1971.

Trager, James. *The Foodbook*. New York: Grossman Publishers, 1970.

Tsuji, Shizuo. *Practical Japanese Cooking*. Tokyo: Kodansha International, 1986.

About the Authors

Philip Pauli, born in 1957, is the publisher and author of, and holds the copyrights for, *Lehrbuch der Küche*. He was graduated from commercial college in Neuenburg, Switzerland, and hotel school in Lausanne, Switzerland. In 1982, after the untimely death of his father, he completed the new edition of *Lehrbuch der Küche*, which was in the process of revision. That tenth edition, published in 1984, was followed in 1985 by the *Unterrichts- und Prüfungsfragen* (a teachers' guide). These were followed in 1986 by the second French edition and the second English edition and, a year later, by the first Italian edition. Philip Pauli is the trustee and a partner of PRT, Pauli + Reichsteiner Treuhand AG, in Wintherthur, Switzerland, where he is responsible for the hotel and restaurant department.

Walter Schudel, born in 1942, is an executive chef with a Swiss state diploma. After completing his cook's apprenticeship, he worked in several first-class kitchens. He also served as the chef of the culinary information center in Zürich. From 1966 to 1976, he became well known as a culinary Olympian and appeared on television.

As the production chef in several large kitchens, he acquired knowledge of large-quantity production techniques. From 1976 to 1988, he was a member of the Swiss commission for culinary training in the hospitality industry and thus had a strong impact on the concepts and materials used to teach professional cooks.

In addition to serving as an examiner for apprentice and master cooks in Switzerland, he uses his professional expertixe as a judge in international culinary competitions. Walter Schudel is a cooking teacher and department chair at the Schaffhausen trade college in Switzerland and is president of the Swiss cooking teachers' association.

Peter Blattner, born in 1947, has been involved in *Lehrbuch der Küche* since 1977. Prior to that, he obtained a degree in business and was responsible for the development and marketing of several trade magazines. He oversaw production of the ninth and tenth editions, as well as all translations. In 1986 he began production of the eleventh edition. In 1990 he became a partner in the publishing/marketing firm "creaplan" and was asked by the book's author to produce an entirely new eleventh edition and marketing plan.

Peter Blattner and the staff at "creaplan" are especially interested in introducing *Lehrbuch der Küche* to those outside the professional culinary world. They believe this book can serve as a basic text for all lay and hobby cooks, introducing them to the fascinating world of the culinary arts.

Index